NO IVORY TOWER

NO IVORY TOWER

McCarthyism and the Universities

Ellen W. Schrecker

New York   Oxford
OXFORD UNIVERSITY PRESS
1986

Oxford University Press

Oxford   New York   Toronto
Delhi   Bombay   Calcutta   Madras   Karachi
Petaling Jaya   Singapore   Hong Kong   Tokyo
Nairobi   Dar es Salaam   Cape Town
Melbourne   Auckland

and associated companies in
Beirut   Berlin   Ibadan   Nicosia

Published by Oxford University Press, Inc.,
200 Madison Avenue, New York, New York 10016

Oxford is the registered trademark of Oxford University Press

Library of Congress Cataloging-in-Publication Data

Schrecker, Ellen W.
No ivory tower.

Bibliography: p.
Includes index.
1. Academic freedom—United States—History—
20th century.   2. College teachers—United States—
Political activity—History—20th century.   3. Anti-
communist movements—United States—History.
4. Subversive activities—United States—History—
20th century.   5. Communism—United States—1917–
I. Title.
LC72.2.S37   1986   378'.121   86–8417
ISBN 0–19–503557–7

9 8 7 6 5 4 3 2 1

Printed in the United States of America

To Marvin

Acknowledgments

Any book the scope of this is in many respects a collective endeavor. I owe a special debt to the men and women I interviewed. Not only did they tell me their own stories, lend me their personal papers, and give me valuable leads, but they also allowed me to feel that what I was doing mattered. I could not have written this book without their encouragement and cooperation. I cannot thank each of them by name, but I hope that this book will repay them in some small way for their assistance.

Many other people helped as well, either by sharing their own research with me, lending materials, or else by steering me to otherwise unknown sources. Alfred F. Young unhesitatingly shipped the contents of several of his own invaluable files of documents about academic freedom. Martin Sherwin and Victor Navasky graciously loaned me the tapes and transcripts of interviews that they had done. Sigmund Diamond, Martin Peretz, Charles Weiner, Michael Frisch, and the late H. H. Wilson helped in other ways. My main debt here is to the late Fred Zimring. Fred's devotion to his and my research and his skill and persistence in ferreting out vital source materials quite literally enabled me to write this book. His untimely death has deprived me of a selfless colleague and a beloved friend.

Tom Hickerson of the Cornell University Archives, Mary Jo Pugh of the Michigan Historical Collections at the Bentley Historical Library at the University of Michigan, James Dallett at the University of Pennsylvania Archives, Spencer Weart and Joan Warnow at the American Institute of Physics, Center for the History of Physics, and Nancy Bressler at the Seeley G. Mudd Library of Princeton University greatly facilitated my work. I assume that I don't even know how much I owe Jordan Kurland of the American Association of University Professors for his patient support in my quest for access to the Association's files.

From the first, friends and colleagues have been willing to listen to monologues, read drafts, and help me clarify and focus my ideas and my prose. At various stages of this project Barton Bernstein, Alan Lawson, Paul Mattingly, Barbara Shortt, Lawrence Veysey, Jon Weiner, Tony and Mary Alice Wolf, and Sheldon Wolin offered invaluable advice. Here, I am particularly indebted to Mark Naison and Joanne Kenen. Sheldon Meyer, my editor at Oxford, has been a gentle, but persistent, mentor. I am grateful, above all, for his encouragement and good judgment.

A research fellowship at the Bunting Institute of Radcliffe College in 1977–78 while this book was still the somewhat inchoate project of a fledgling Americanist gave me the psychological, as well as the financial, support that I needed at that early stage. I also received assistance from the Louis M. Rabinowitz Foundation and the Mark deWolfe Howe Fund of the Harvard Law School.

My husband, Marvin Gettleman, has been my closest colleague ever since he answered my author's query in the *New York Review of Books* and offered to share his research with me. Without neglecting his own work, he read, critiqued, and improved the entire manuscript and lovingly performed all the domestic and editorial services that earlier generations of academics used to receive from their "non-working" wives. More than that, his own example, his prodigious energy and belief that scholarship could make a difference, sustained and inspired me. My children are only the most recent victims of McCarthyism. They had to put up with a grouchy and distracted mother whose work must have seemed like an incomprehensible obsession. I don't ask them to forgive me; I only hope that their future work will be as satisfying.

New York   E. W. S.
April 1986

Contents

NO IVORY TOWER

INTRODUCTION

McCarthyism: The Anatomy of an Inquisition

By February 3, 1960, Joseph R. McCarthy had been dead for nearly three years, and the movement that had received his name was presumably over. But not for Chandler Davis. On that day, Davis, a former instructor of mathematics from the University of Michigan, ended a six-year struggle against McCarthyism, said good-bye to his family, and surrendered to a federal marshal in Grand Rapids to begin serving a six-month prison term. Davis's crime had occurred on May 10, 1954, when he refused to tell the House Un-American Activities Committee (HUAC) whether or not he had ever been a Communist. Davis challenged the committee, insisting that its questions about his politics infringed upon his freedom of speech and, as he put it, overstepped "the bounds placed on Congress by the First Amendment." He knew that he would probably lose his job and be convicted for contempt of Congress, but he hoped that the Supreme Court would eventually exonerate him. Instead, on June 8, 1959, the Court in effect ruled against him in the similar case of Lloyd Barenblatt, another former college teacher who had also defied HUAC on First Amendment grounds. The 5 to 4 decision affirmed that the committee did not violate its witnesses' constitutional rights by asking them about their relationship with the Communist Party (CP). That ruling sent both Barenblatt and Davis, whose case was determined by Barenblatt's, to Danbury Federal Penitentiary.[1]

These two academics went to prison because, as Justice John Marshall Harlan stated for the majority in the *Barenblatt* decision, the Supreme Court "has consistently refused to view the Communist Party as an ordinary political party" and has let the government behave in ways that "in a different context would certainly have raised constitutional issues of the gravest character." Thus, even as late as 1959, almost five years after the Senate censured Joseph McCarthy, the Supreme Court could still cite the Cold War as an excuse for depriving American Communists and suspected Communists, like Davis and Barenblatt, of their constitutional rights. In this, of course, the Court was only echoing the anti-Communist consensus that swept the country in the late 1940s and 1950s, a consensus that viewed the American Communist Party as one of the gravest threats to its security the United States had ever faced.[2]

In retrospect, it now appears that this assessment was wrong. Whatever perils the Cold War might have brought on the international level, the danger that a few thousand American Communists, acting on secret instructions from Moscow, were about to take over the United States was not one of them. And yet, so pervasive was the image of the Party as a lethal foreign conspiracy and so useful was that image as a way to cope with the uncertainties of the new atomic age that few American leaders could or would accept a more realistic assessment. The onset of the Cold War had shocked and confused them. Suddenly, the Soviet Union, which only a few years before had been America's ally against Nazi Germany, was now its enemy. And Stalin, whose armies had installed Communist regimes throughout Eastern Europe, seemed to be as dangerous as Hitler. President Truman responded by talking tough and pouring aid into Western Europe. But the situation only seemed to worsen. The Communist coup in Czechoslovakia in the spring of 1948 touched off a frightening war scare, intensified a few months later by the Berlin blockade. Then, the following year came the news that the Soviets had detonated an atomic bomb. A few months later, China "fell" to the Communists.[3]

To give the American Communist Party any credit for these revolutionary changes was ridiculous. Even during its supposed heyday in the 1930s the CP had been neither numerous nor popular. Yet the logic of politics demanded that the Truman administration, which had committed itself to combatting the spread of Communism abroad, confront it at home as well. The Republican party, its own anti-Communist credentials never in doubt, was ready to pounce on any indication of laxity. Accordingly, both Democrats and Republicans threw themselves into the domestic Cold War against the American CP. Local Communists suddenly became potential Soviet agents, who, if they were not about to take over the government, could nonetheless subvert it in more subtle ways or, at least, send vital secrets back to Moscow. Each politician had his own assessment of the extent of this conspiracy and his own formula for fighting it. But almost everybody agreed that the danger was immense. If nothing else, the nation's security demanded that there be no reds in the government.[4]

Truman was already under considerable pressure from the Republican-controlled 80th Congress when, on March 22, 1947, he issued Executive Order 9835 establishing a new loyalty-security program for federal employees. Since the security measures already in place had largely eliminated most Communists and other dissidents from sensitive positions, the new program was superfluous, except as a political gesture. Its real function was to protect the Democratic administration from the Republican party. It failed. It did, however, succeed in establishing anti-Communism as the nation's official ideology, and, several years before Senator Joseph McCarthy entered the scene, it laid the foundations for the movement we now call McCarthyism. Until then anti-Communism had been a haphazard crusade, the province of right-wing ideologues and embittered former reds. The CP was unpopular, of course, but opposition to it had not yet become central to the nation's politics. When in 1947 Truman promulgated Executive Order 9835 and created a loyalty-security system, he legitimized, as only a President could, the project of eradicating Communism from American life.[5]

No other event, no political trial or congressional hearing, was to shape the internal Cold War as decisively as the Truman administration's loyalty-security program. It authorized the economic sanctions that were crucial to the success of McCarthyism. Communists and suspected Communists could now be fired from their jobs. Other institutions followed and they, too, began to examine their employees' politics. Within a few years, this process had spread far beyond the Potomac; political tests were being used to screen individuals for almost everything from jobs and passports to insurance policies and fishing licenses. In addition, because the federal government's loyalty-security program borrowed so many of its procedures and ideas from traditional right-wing anti-Communism, it was administered in a disturbingly reactionary manner. Other employers copied this aspect of the program as well.

Executive Order 9835 not only barred Communists, fascists, and other totalitarians from the federal payroll, it also excluded anybody guilty of "sympathetic association" with such undesirables or their organizations. Every federal employee had to be checked out, usually by the FBI or a similar investigatory organization. People with "derogatory information" in their files then had to clear themselves. Despite the existence of some individual safeguards, abuses flourished. "Sympathetic association" was hardly a precise tool for separating the pinks from the reds. Nor was the list of potentially subversive organizations that the Executive Order authorized the Attorney General to compile any more meticulous. It included the Communist Party, of course, but it also cited many already defunct left-wing groups in which both Communists and non-Communists had been active in the 1930s and 1940s. In addition, because the FBI, which handled most of the investigative work, insisted that it would not be effective if it had to reveal the identity of its informers, anonymous accusations could cost people their jobs. The program had its critics; Truman himself deplored its injustices. But, once in place, its flaws were not corrected. And in fact, as political pressures increased, first the Truman and then the Eisenhower administration were to revise the loyalty program to make it easier to discharge undesirable employees.[6]

As the 1948 election approached, the Truman administration took other steps to prove its devotion to the anti-Communist cause. The third-party campaign of former Vice President Henry Wallace, who had broken with the administration over its hard-line policy toward the Soviet Union, gave the Democrats a perfect opportunity to distance themselves from the left. Since the Communist Party supported Wallace, it was easy for Truman and his allies to accuse Wallace of being its tool. Such attacks not only diverted attention from Truman's own alleged softness on Communism, but, by so thoroughly identifying Wallace's rather mild critique of the Cold War with the hated CP, they also eliminated all effective domestic opposition to American foreign policy. This was probably not what the liberals who led the assault on Wallace intended. They did not think that they were McCarthyites, but because their red-baiting narrowed American politics by excommunicating its left, they inadvertently fostered the furor to come.[7]

Perhaps the most obvious indication of the Truman administration's conversion to a tough anti-Communist position was its decision in the summer of 1948 to prosecute the top leaders of the American Communist Party under the Smith Act, an infrequently used 1940 statute that made it illegal to "teach and advocate the overthrow and destruction of the Government of the United States by force and violence." Putting the Party's top brass on trial served several functions. It crippled the CP, first by forcing it to divert its energies to self-defense, and then by jailing its leaders. Even more important, the Smith Act trial gave the government a way to publicize the menace of Communism. The prosecution put the Party's ideology on trial and sought to show that Communist theory, as contained in the writings of Marx, Engels, Lenin, and Stalin, committed the CP to force and violence. Instead of arguing that the Truman administration had no right to prosecute them because the Smith Act violated their First Amendment right of free speech, Party General Secretary Eugene Dennis and the other Communist leaders accepted the battle on the government's terms and tried to refute the prosecution quote for quote. They lost; the ex-Communists and undercover agents who were the government's main witnesses had little trouble convincing the jury that Dennis and his colleagues were violent revolutionaries. A few years later, the Supreme Court upheld that verdict by a 5 to 2 margin, thus giving the Constitution's blessing to the government's purge of American Communists.[8]

By the summer of 1951, when the Supreme Court rendered its decision in the *Dennis* case, the McCarthyist furor was at its height. It had grown slowly since the late forties, the product of an interaction between the insecurities of the Cold War and the Republican party's essentially partisan attempt to exploit those insecurities. The international crises of the late forties had been deeply unsettling. By the time the Soviet Union got its bomb and the United States "lost" China, it seemed as if Communism was unstoppable. Of course, China had never been an American possession, nor was the secret of nuclear fission an American monopoly. But from the perspective of an edgy public, worried about America's apparently slipping primacy in a dangerous world, each of these crises seemed increasingly more frightening and more difficult to understand.

The Communist invasion of South Korea in June 1950 confirmed everyone's worst fears.

The Republican right offered an explanation. America had been betrayed by a worldwide Communist conspiracy. Stalin's agents had penetrated the Democratic administration and subverted the nation's foreign policy; Soviet sympathizers elsewhere had filched the secret of the bomb. Since there *had* been Russian spies, the slight core of truth in this scenario made it all the more attractive to the GOP. This was especially the case after Truman's surprise victory in the 1948 presidential election revealed that the Democrats were relatively invulnerable with regard to traditional domestic issues. Accordingly, the Republican party, looking for a way to recoup its electoral fortunes, began to attack the Truman administration as "soft" on Communism. By claiming that the Democrats had condoned Soviet subversion, the conservatives in the GOP could mount an assault on the New Deal, which they could not do on social or economic grounds. Moreover, since Truman had already enlisted the government in the anti-Communist crusade, he was in a poor position to rebuff the Republicans' claim that they were simply trying to help him clean house.[9]

Most of this housecleaning took place at congressional hearings. Legislative investigations gave the conservatives a perfect arena for their campaign against the New Deal and its supposed sympathy for Communist subversion. To begin with, as congressmen constitutionally immune from lawsuits, they could make accusations without having to worry about being sued for libel. In addition, since legislative investigations were not judicial proceedings, these politicians could use witnesses whose testimony did not have to stand up in court. Best of all, committee hearings created headlines. American politics had never offered a more dramatic spectacle than the confrontation between the investigators and their witnesses, especially when those witnesses pulled microfilms out of pumpkins and talked of false names, clandestine meetings, secret passwords, and the arcane workings of a shadowy underworld peopled by Soviet agents and urbane upper-class spies. Once the rise of Richard Nixon showed how a smart politician could parlay his berth on an investigating committee into the Vice Presidency, congressmen clamored for such positions. In 1952, 185 of the 221 Republicans in Congress applied for seats on the House Un-American Activities Committee, an unpopular assignment only a few years before.[10]

Nixon, of course, had come to prominence because of his involvement with the Hiss case. His tenacity in trying to prove that Alger Hiss was a Soviet spy not only made Nixon's career, but also justified the use of congressional investigating committees as a way of uncovering Communist espionage. HUAC's investigators had made the case. According to the committee's star witness, the self-confessed former Soviet agent Whittaker Chambers, Hiss, a distinguished product of Harvard Law School and an eminent public servant, had been such a devoted Communist during the 1930s that he was willing to give Chambers secret information for Moscow. Whether Hiss actually handed over government documents to Chambers is ultimately less important than the political consequences of the case. Hiss's conviction for perjury legitimized HUAC's activities. In addition, it so thoroughly bolstered the right-wing contention that the New Deal was infested with Soviet spies that by the time Hiss was convicted for perjury in January 1950, it was no longer politically possible to ignore allegations of Communist subversion, no matter how ridiculous or unfounded. Five and a half weeks later, Senator Joseph McCarthy began to flaunt his ever-changing lists of alleged Communists in the American government.[11]

In charging that the Truman administration was harboring some 57—later 205, 81, 10, or 116—Communist agents within the State Department, the junior senator from Wisconsin was only doing, albeit more flamboyantly, what many other reactionary politicians had done before. Even his charges were old-hat; they had been circulating for years within the network of professional anti-Communists who proffered their expertise to individuals and institutions eager to eliminate subversives. McCarthy's first round of attacks, like those on the eminent Johns Hopkins University China expert Owen Lattimore, were related to the GOP's contention that the Truman administration had betrayed China to Mao Zedong. As a result, McCarthy received the tacit support of the more respectable leaders of the Republican party, who welcomed the damage that their disreputable colleague was inflicting on the incumbent Democrats. The outbreak of the Korean war in June, 1950, gave McCarthy's charges added saliency; the electoral defeat of some of his main critics in the fall only increased his clout. Within a few years, McCarthy's erratic campaign against the Army ended his political career. Because he was so uniquely pathological, it is easy to forget how much McCarthy resembled the other right-wing politicians who also used the issue of Communism as a way to further their own fortunes and those of their party. After all, what made McCarthy a McCarthyite was not his bluster but his anti-Communist mission, one which, in one way or another, almost every American political leader claimed to support.[12]

McCarthy never found any subversives. Most of the men and women he denounced were perfectly loyal, though politically unpopular, American citizens. So, too, were most of the witnesses who appeared before the other anti-Communist investigators of the period. These people were not, however, selected at random. Almost all of them had once been in or near the Communist Party. Except for a handful of people like Owen Lattimore, there were few "innocent liberals." This was crucial. McCarthyism succeeded because the people it targeted were already political outcasts. They were Communists or ex-Communists. And, by the late forties and early fifties, the Truman administration, the Supreme Court, and most private citizens believed or claimed to believe that Communism was so alien to the American way of life that its adherents did not deserve to be protected by the Constitution. Many decent people deplored the excesses of McCarthyism; they just did not think that punishing Communists was excessive. Those who did, though they fought valiantly for the rights of individuals, did so in vain. Moreover, once the political establishment legitimated the denial of civil rights to members of the Communist Party, it was relatively easy for the more reactionary practitioners of anti-Communism to extend that denial to yet other types of political undesirables by claiming that those people also served the Party's cause.

McCarthyism was amazingly effective. It produced one of the most severe episodes of political repression the United States ever experienced. It was a peculiarly American style of repression—nonviolent and consensual. Only two people were killed; only a few hundred went to jail. Its mildness may well have contributed to its efficacy. So, too, did its structure. Here, it helps to view McCarthyism as a process rather than a movement. It took place in two stages. First, the objectionable groups and individuals were identified—during a committee hearing, for example, or an FBI investigation; then, they were punished, usually by being fired. The bifurcated nature of this process diffused responsibility and made it easier for each participant to dissociate his or her action from the larger whole. Rarely did any single institution handle both stages of McCarthyism. In most cases, it was a government agency which identified the culprits and a private employer which fired them.

We know the most about the first stage of McCarthyism, for it received the most attention at the time. Yet the second stage is just as important. For without the almost automatic imposition of sanctions on the people who had been identified as politically undesirable, the whole anti-Communist crusade would have crumbled. In a sense, it was this second stage that legitimated the first. Had HUAC's targets been able to survive their encounters with the committee without losing their jobs, the committee would have lost its mandate. This did not happen. On the contrary, private employers often rushed to impose sanctions on these men and women, sometimes without waiting for the official machinery to run its course. The fate of the Hollywood Ten is illustrative here. When these radical screen-writers and directors refused to cooperate with HUAC in October, 1947, it was not clear which side had won, the witnesses or the committee. The movie studios' decision to fire the Ten before either the judiciary or public opinion had delivered a verdict may well have influenced that outcome as significantly as the Supreme Court's later refusal to review their conviction for contempt. Other employers followed the studios' example. By the time the investigative furor that characterized the first stage of McCarthyism abated in the late fifties, thousands of people had lost their jobs. And thousands more, whether realistically or not, feared similar reprisals and curtailed their political activities.[13]

Every segment of society was involved. From General Motors, General Electric, and CBS to the *New York Times,* the New York City Board of Education, and the United Auto Workers, there were few, very few, public or private employers who did not fire the men and women who had been identified during a first-stage investigation. The academic community went along as well and dismissed those of its members McCarthy, HUAC, and the FBI had nominated for such treatment. There were quite a good number of these people, for the nation's faculties housed hundreds of men and women whom official and unofficial red-hunters were to single out as undesirable. Exact figures are hard to come by, but it may well be that almost 20 percent of the witnesses called before congressional and state investigating committees were college teachers or graduate students. Most of those academic witnesses who did not clear themselves with the committees lost their jobs.[14]

Chandler Davis, the young mathematician who went to prison for defying HUAC, was no exception. A few months after he appeared before the committee, the University of Michigan fired him. He was not, however, dismissed without a hearing. Although Davis lacked tenure, the Michigan administration was sufficiently concerned about academic freedom to draw up formal charges against him and convene a faculty committee to hear his case. Actually, Michigan's authorities were so punctilious that Davis received three separate hearings before he was finally dismissed. His experiences were not unique. Unfriendly witnesses at other schools had similar trials. While these elaborate proceedings did not, in the end, protect many people, they did produce thousands of pages of testimony. An ironic legacy, these records contain what well may be the most comprehensive, cogently argued, and carefully thought-out defense of McCarthyism available. They also show how the academy, an institution ostensibly dedicated to intellectual freedom, collaborated in curtailing that freedom.[15]

At no point did the college teachers, administrators, and trustees who cooperated with McCarthyism by evicting unfriendly witnesses and other suspected Communists from their faculties admit that they were repressing dissent. On the contrary, in their public statements and in the documentary record that they produced, they often claimed that they were standing up to McCarthyism and defending free speech and academic freedom. It is important, therefore, to go beyond the rhetoric of the period and examine what these people were doing rather than what they were saying. They said that they were opposing Senator McCarthy and the more rabid red-baiters of the period. Yet, when given an opportunity to transform that opposition into something more concrete than words, almost all of these essentially liberal academics faltered. Either they participated in and condoned the dismissals or else, when they opposed them, did so in such a limited fashion that they must have known they would not succeed.

It is important to identify the players here. Since there are only a handful of instances in which an academic institution itself instigated these dismissals, it is clear that the nation's colleges and universities would not have purged their left-wing faculty members during the McCarthy era without pressure from outside. It is also clear that not every group within the academic community had equal responsibility for those purges. Trustees, for example, were both more powerful and more sensitive to outside pressures than professors and, thus, more directly responsible for what happened. Yet in a sense, because of the limited nature of their contact with the academic community, trustees were really outsiders. Though legally in control, they rarely involved themselves on a day-to-day basis with individual cases or with the development of policy for the academic community as a whole. For that reason, this study will focus on the next two echelons of the academic world and will explore the response of administrators and faculty members to the anti-Communist furor of the 1940s and 1950s. These were the men and women who had made a full-time, life-time commitment to the academy. Though they lacked the formal authority of the trustees they nonetheless exercised considerable power and could have, had they wanted to, prevented much of what happened. That they did not is the most interesting aspect of the academy's response to McCarthyism and is, thus, the focus of this book.

It does not purport to be exhaustive. In order to explain how the academic community administered the economic sanctions that constituted the second stage of McCarthyism, I have had to limit the scope of this study. It does not cover every case or every way in which the anti-Communist furor touched the nation's campuses. Rather, it discusses those cases that had the most impact on the academic community as a whole and it deals with them not as individual examples of injustice (though that they were) but as stages in the evolution of the academy's institutional response to the political pressures of the period. McCarthyism, like any other political movement, had its own history. College teachers who appeared before HUAC in 1954 did not behave in the same way or receive the same treatment from their employers as those who were subpoenaed in 1948. Important changes had taken place. This book analyzes those changes and shows how the academic community came to adapt itself to the suppression of dissent.

I

"An Excellent Advertisement for the Institution": The Development of Academic Freedom, 1886–1918

On February 15, 1953, twenty-five presidents of America's most prestigious universities met in New York City and attempted to define academic freedom. As members of the Association of American Universities (AAU), these men ordinarily gathered once a year to deal with more mundane matters, like inter-library loans and graduate school admissions. But McCarthyism, then at its peak, had altered the agenda. After sending a congratulatory letter to Dwight Eisenhower, their former colleague, who had just been inaugurated as President of the United States (he had been president of Columbia University some years before), the group got down to work. Though the AAU's decision to release a policy statement on academic freedom was unprecedented, it was not sudden. The organization had been toying with the wording of a report on Communism and the universities for several years. But by the beginning of 1953, with several congressional committees about to start looking for subversives on American campuses, there could be no further delay.[1]

The minutes of the meeting reveal that the presidents dealt mainly with the practical problems of Communist professors and congressional investigations. But they also recognized the need for a general statement on the nature of academic freedom, something that would, as one president put it, "induce feelings of confidence and respect in the minds of thoughtful people." But the more these men discussed the matter, the more elusive it became. Each president, it seemed, had his own definition. One claimed that academic freedom "was broader and more inclusive than civil rights." Another insisted that it should "offer no more freedom than the Constitution." And a third considered it only "a special shield under which a professor could speak within his field." Significantly, the final product of these deliberations, issued at the end of March, was not a definition of academic freedom but a response to the issues raised by congressional investigations and Communist Party members. It mentioned academic freedom only in passing, and then only in quotation marks, as the necessary—but undefined—prerequisite for what the AAU called intellectual "free enterprise."[2]

A few weeks after the AAU meeting, another group of academics, this one at Wesleyan University in Middletown, Connecticut, debated the same issues with the same inconclusive result. By then, the House Un-American Activities Committee had already begun to question college teachers, and a few young Wesleyan professors called a special meeting of the junior faculty so that its members could discuss the problems the hearings had raised without being constrained by the presence of their senior colleagues. Like college teachers elsewhere, they were puzzled by what was happening and worried about the academic community's response. The minutes of that meeting, rendered anonymous to prevent repercussions if they became public, differ little from those of the AAU. Both groups spent most of their time discussing congressional investigators and Communist professors, though, it is true, some of the Wesleyan teachers were both more hostile to the former and more tolerant of the latter than any of the presidents had been. But the Wesleyan participants were just as vague about the nature of academic freedom.

"We are not sure what academic freedom is," one of the Wesleyan speakers pointed out, adding, however, that he was "reasonably certain that academic freedom is a matter of relative value." For one man, "it may vary depending on [the] department involved." For another, it was "basic to [the] concept of American democracy." But defining that concept proved impossible. "We know what academic freedom is in specific cases," a fourth professor remarked, "the difficulty is in formulating a general definition." His colleagues gave him little help. "Any generalized discussion of academic freedom will fail," was the advice one of them proffered. The comment of yet another speaker summed up the group's predicament. "If we don't know what academic freedom is, who does?" No doubt he was being sarcastic, but, given the almost identical confusion of twenty-four of the nation's leading university presidents, it is possible that in early 1953, at the height of the McCarthy era, there was no agreed-upon definition of academic freedom.[3]

1953 was not the first time that American college teachers and administrators had agonized over the meaning of academic freedom. Ever since the modern university took its present form at the end of the nineteenth century, the concept of academic freedom has been periodically debated and redefined. Rarely were these reappraisals stimulated by what was happening on campus; the academy usually revised its notion of academic freedom in response to external demands for the removal of individual dissenters. These pressures threatened the university's independence. And, in order to keep outsiders from intervening in such sensitive matters as the hiring and firing of teachers, faculty members and administrators scrambled to show their critics that they could handle their political problems on their own. They did this by claiming that all personnel decisions within the academy were technical ones, determined by the intellectual demands of each discipline, and thus beyond the competence of anyone who lacked a Ph.D. The concept of academic freedom became a useful way to describe in ostensibly professional terms the permissible limits of political dissent. It created an intellectually defensible zone of political autonomy for the professoriat, which, as we shall see, was sufficiently circumscribed so as to exclude as unscholarly whatever political behavior the leading members of the academic community feared might trigger outside intervention.[4]

The creation of that zone of political autonomy was a continuous process. From the late nineteenth century on, the definition of academic freedom underwent a series of changes, many of which reflected the relative insecurity of the academic profession as well as the cultural climate of the day. It was never easy for extreme left-wingers to teach. Even during the most tolerant of times, the most notorious heads have fallen. But these belonged to outspoken, energetic activists who were so controversial and conspicuous that they could be barred from the academy under a fairly broad definition of academic freedom. During periods of crisis, however, outside pressures for purging the universities of their supposedly disloyal elements increased; ideas and activities once tolerated came under attack. Professors and administrators responded by revising the normally vague definition of academic freedom to exclude in a surprisingly explicit way the types of behavior the rest of the community did not like. As a result, were we to plot the violations of academic freedom on a graph, instead of a smooth line we would have a series of peaks, each corresponding to some larger social or political crisis, with the biggest one in the 1950s.

The first such peak, and the one which precipitated the invention of academic freedom as a collective safeguard for the professoriat, occurred at the end of the nineteenth century. This was a period of real social unrest; it was also the period when, not coincidentally, American higher education took its present form and the first generation of college teachers with Ph.D.s were beginning to make their careers within the nation's universities. The concept of academic freedom was, thus, a reflection in part of the concern that these newly self-conscious academics felt about their professional status as well as a concrete response to a series of politically charged confrontations between individual faculty members, on the one hand, and trustees and administrators, on the other. It was also an important element in defining the mission of the new research-oriented American university as one committed to investigation instead of reform.[5]

This had not always been the case. Among the first generation of professionally trained academic economists were a handful of men who were essentially social reformers and who hoped to contribute their expertise to the solution of the nation's social ills. In an earlier day, no doubt, these men would have become ministers. They had, it seemed, an almost religious sense of vocation. They sympathized with labor unions, urged government regulation, even ownership, of basic industries, and in general hoped to move their field away from the uncritical acceptance of classical *laissez-faire* doctrines and infuse it with ethical concerns. At the same time, however, they were ambitious men who had chosen to make their careers within an academic world whose leaders were already seeking to establish a separation between inquiry and reform. Thus, when these early social scientists found that their advocacy of social change got them in trouble with university authorities, they were forced to compromise. Since some of them were among the leaders of their field, the compromises that they made set a pattern that was to dominate the academic profession from then on.[6]

In many ways, the first of these academic freedom cases was the most typical: it was secret. Its protagonist, Henry Carter Adams, was a young, German-trained economist who held two half-time jobs, one at Cornell, the other at Michigan. Although he was qualified and eager for tenure, the presidents of both schools held back because of his supposedly unsuitable politics. When Adams gave a major lecture at Cornell denouncing the behavior of the nation's industrialists during the crisis that followed the anarchist bombing at Haymarket in 1886, the Board of Trustees quietly decided not to reappoint him. Realizing that making a public issue out of his case would endanger his remaining chances at Michigan, Adams refused even to comment on the incident. Instead, he wrote to Michigan's president disavowing his earlier radicalism and admitting that his Cornell speech had been "unwise." He got tenure and spent the rest of his career advising the government and investigating such neutral subjects as the public debt. Economists, he was to argue, should eschew the role of reformers and concentrate instead on using their expertise to solve technical problems.[7]

Another economist who also had to moderate his political views in order to save his job was Richard T. Ely. One of the most prolific and widely known academics of the late nineteenth century, Ely, who taught at Johns Hopkins and the University of Wisconsin, had almost single-handedly founded the American Economic Association (AEA) as a way to modernize the profession as well as to convert it into a force for social reform. Because of his outspokenness and his attachment to the Christian left, his colleagues in the AEA felt that he was an embarrassment to the field and ultimately eased him out of his post as secretary of the organization. Then, in 1894, a member of the University of Wisconsin's Board of Regents attacked Ely's writings and charged that Ely supported strikes and boycotts and had actually entertained a union organizer in his home. Such charges could not be ignored. The Regents convened a special committee and summoned Ely to justify himself before it.[8]

Faced with the prospect of unemployment, Ely caved in. Instead of turning his trial into a defense of academic freedom by denying that the Regents had any right to investigate his writings and extracurricular activities, Ely chose to prove that the Regents' specific charges were false and to demonstrate the conservatism of his thought. No doubt Ely's stature in his field and that of his many former students, as well as the personal support of Wisconsin's president and the Regents' own dislike of Ely's accuser, may have helped. Not only did the Regents reinstate Ely, but they did so with a grandiose statement affirming their commitment to academic freedom. Ely had won, but only by accepting the Regents' authority to censor his political views and, more significantly, by accepting a restricted notion of appropriate academic behavior. Were the charges against him true, Ely explained, they would "unquestionably unfit me to occupy a responsible position as an instructor of youth in a great university." And, careful to avoid further trouble, Ely published little after his trial. He stopped writing for a popular audience and developed an appropriately scholarly niche for himself in the relatively obscure field of land economics.[9]

The fate of Ely's own student, Edward W. Bemis, at the University of Chicago further reinforced the lesson of Ely's trial: that political controversy was not conducive to an academic career. Like many late nineteenth-century reformers, Bemis advocated the public ownership of railroads and utilities. His outspokenness on the issue earned him the hostility of the University administration, not to mention the conservative businessmen who had just established the University. And in 1895, a year after Chicago's president had specifically warned Bemis to "exercise great care in public utterance about questions that are agitating the minds of the people," he was fired. Although the University administration hoped to keep the matter quiet, Bemis decided to make a public issue of his dismissal. The response of the president and of Bemis's immediate superiors was significant. They attacked his competence, not his politics. They issued a public statement claiming that "the 'freedom of teaching' has never been involved in the case" and explaining that Bemis's agitation "has compelled us to advertise both his incompetency as a University Extension lecturer, and also the opinion of those most closely associated with him that he is not qualified to fill a University position." Though Bemis was no more radical than Ely, since he was both scrappier and less eminent, his decision to publicize his dismissal cost him his academic career. Bemis had trouble getting another teaching job and eventually had to make a life for himself outside the university.[10]

By 1895 it was clear that the academic profession was not going to accept the advocacy of controversial social or political reforms as legitimate scholarship. Academic victims of political repression could, it seems, retain their jobs if they kept quiet and gave up their political activities. Only if the victim was so eminent and the offense against him such a blatant affront to the autonomy and prestige of the rest of the profession could he afford to have his case become public and still remain employable. This is what happened in the last and most notorious of the turn-of-the-century academic freedom cases, that of E. A. Ross at Stanford.

A student of Ely's, Ross was such a respected economist that he was chosen to replace his mentor as secretary of the American Economic Association. Like Ely, he, too, was concerned with the important social issues of the day and, since he was a gifted public speaker, he frequently lectured outside the University. He probably would not have gotten into trouble anywhere else, but Stanford was under the control of an imperious one-woman Board of Trustees, the widow of Leland Stanford. She had already forced President David Starr Jordan to fire a young sociologist whose religion was too pessimistic and whose politics too pro-Bryan. Ross supported Bryan and free silver as well, but Jordan managed to shield him from Mrs. Stanford's wrath—for a while. Two well-publicized speeches Ross gave in May 1900, one denouncing the railroads, and the other Chinese immigration, were too much for Jane Stanford. Jordan, who apparently felt that the University's very existence was at stake, caved in and forced Ross to resign.[11]

The case became a sensation. The dignified and respected chairman of the History Department protested, and he, too, was fired. Six other faculty members quit in sympathy. The controversy spread beyond Palo Alto. The American Economic Association set up a special investigating committee; there was even talk of a nationwide boycott of Stanford. These measures had little practical effect. Institutional loyalty and the economic facts of life induced the majority of the Stanford faculty to sign a public manifesto in support of their president, and the shortage of good academic jobs made it easy for the University to replace the dissidents. Ross was fortunate in being able to find a temporary position at the University of Nebraska, one of the few institutions willing to hire such a controversial figure, but he had to wait five years before his mentor, Ely, felt it safe to bring him to Wisconsin.[12]

The next decade and a half was a fairly tranquil period on the nation's campuses. The social and political turmoil of the 1890s had died down, and in the sunnier climate of the Progressive era, professorial politicking did not seem so threatening. It is also possible that the nation's college professors had themselves learned the lessons of the Ely, Bemis, and Ross cases and were avoiding controversy. The handful of academic freedom cases that occurred—at Duke, at Columbia, at Lafayette College—were generated by local circumstances and individual frictions; as such, they constituted the ordinary background noise of academic life, the kinds of conflicts that were endemic to the heterogeneous nature of American higher education. Accordingly, despite an important academic freedom case in 1913, the small but distinguished group of academic leaders who founded the American Association of University Professors (AAUP) in 1915 were not particularly worried about protecting colleagues from politically inspired dismissals. "Such cases," the organization's first president, John Dewey, explained, "are too rare even to suggest the formation of an association like this." The AAUP's mission was the typically Progressive one of "developing professional standards."[13]

But, though the urgency was gone, the memories of the late nineteenth-century academic freedom cases could not have been far from the minds of the Association's founders. To begin with, many of them had been personally involved with those cases. Arthur O. Lovejoy, the AAUP's first secretary, had left Stanford over the Ross case; E. R. A. Seligman, the first chairman of the organization's crucial Committee A on Academic Freedom and Tenure, had organized the abortive American Economic Association investigation; and the rest of Committee A included, among others, a member of that AEA panel, another Stanford émigré, and Richard T. Ely. In addition, the AAUP's stated concern with the special vulnerability of social scientists was an obvious reflection of what had been, until then, the main threat to the professoriat's position.

The organization's founding document, the 1915 Report of Seligman's committee, reveals how deeply enmeshed the notion of academic freedom was with the overall status, security, and prestige of the academic profession. The function of academic freedom, as the AAUP's early leaders defined it, was, thus, in part to protect that status and, in particular, to ensure that outsiders did not meddle with a scholar's teaching and research. It was, the Report emphasized, "in any case, unsuitable to the dignity of a great profession that the initial responsibility for the maintenance of its professional standards should not be in the hands of its own members." The AAUP's task was, thus, to define those standards and to do so in a way that would ensure widespread acceptance by professors and laymen alike.[14]

Accordingly, Seligman's Report offered a set of norms for college teachers which, if followed, would entitle them to the protection of academic freedom. They must behave in an appropriately scholarly way; their conclusions "must be the fruits of competent and patient and sincere inquiry, and they should be set forth with dignity, courtesy, and temperateness of language." Above all, professors should be careful about dealing with controversial matters and should take pains to give all sides of an issue in order, so Committee A insisted, to avoid "taking unfair advantage of the student's immaturity by indoctrinating him with the teacher's own opinions before the student has an opportunity fairly to examine other opinions upon the matters in question." This proscription—which most academics still accept—was, of course, a codification of the results of the Ely, Ross, and Bemis cases. By focussing on a problem which had long since been settled, this version of academic freedom was, in many respects, obsolete. As a result, when new issues challenged the academic profession, the custodians of academic freedom had to scramble to come up with new rules.[15]

Just as important as Committee A's guidelines for faculty behavior were the specific procedures it set forth for dealing with cases in which academic freedom issues arose. The crucial element, of course, was to ensure faculty participation in all personnel decisions. The Report also recommended tenure after ten years and the provision of adequate notice before dismissal. In cases where an institution wants to remove a professor with tenure, the Report demanded that it formulate the grounds for that removal and provide the professor with a fair trial before a committee of his peers. As the events of the McCarthy period were to prove, such procedural safeguards could not protect a professor against unsympathetic colleagues or an administration that was determined to remove him. Nonetheless, these procedures were not totally worthless and did, in a few cases, provide enough of a buffer to save the endangered instructor's job.[16]

In any event, at the time of their promulgation, these guidelines were largely of symbolic importance, for the academic profession was too fragmented, too economically insecure, and thus too worried about its public standing to let the AAUP do more than issue statements. The new organization recognized its weakness. In its annual report on academic freedom in the spring of 1918, Committee A admitted that two and a half years of experience had shown pretty clearly that "we can rarely expect to obtain the actual redress of an individual grievance, and we do not believe that we should intervene merely to secure the professional rehabilitation of one unjustly dismissed." Instead, it hoped that by accumulating reports on actual cases, it might eventually create general principles upon which the force of professional opinion would prevail. Given the universities' growing concern with public relations, this was not completely unrealistic. In fact, however, the AAUP's preoccupation with developing principles instead of helping individuals simply reinforced the standard practice. For, despite the existence of the AAUP, academics who lost their jobs for political reasons could only rarely get them back or, in many cases, find new ones.[17]

Such was the outcome of one of the earliest and most important cases the new organization investigated, that of Scott Nearing at the University of Pennsylvania. Unlike Adams, Ely, et al., Nearing was a genuine radical, a socialist whose outspoken opposition to industrial abuses did little to endear him to Penn's conservative alumni and trustees. At the same time he was an extremely effective teacher, and his chairman in the Economics Department of the Wharton School of Business, where he had been teaching for nine years, considered him "a man of extraordinary ability, of superlative popularity, and . . . the greatest moral force for good in the University." Nevertheless, despite his superiors' unanimous recommendation that Nearing be reappointed, the Board of Trustees overrode that advice. On July 14, 1915, Nearing was abruptly notified that he would not be rehired for the following fall. Nearing's sudden dismissal, as well as the trustees' unexplained refusal to abide by the faculty's recommendation, infuriated Nearing's colleagues. They issued statements, signed petitions, and even raised money to pay him a semester's salary. Though they did not share Nearing's political views, they fought his dismissal because, as the chairman of the English Department was reputed to have said of the trustees, "Gentlemen do not do such things!"[18]

Since Nearing knew full well the value of the mimeograph machine, his firing got enormous publicity. Within two weeks the AAUP had entered the case and appointed an investigating committee headed by

Arthur O. Lovejoy. At first, Penn's trustees ignored the furor and refused to say why they had fired Nearing. Then, on October 11, the board released a statement which claimed that Nearing's

> efforts—although doubtless perfectly sincere—were so constantly misunderstood by the public and by many parents of students that, much to the regret of the trustees, they felt unable to give him the promotion to a professorship which would otherwise have obtained.

This admission, that public opinion rather than academic considerations had caused Nearing's removal, as well as the lack of any peer review or judicial procedure, led the AAUP to condemn that dismissal as "an infringement of academic freedom."[19]

The publicity surrounding the case had its effect. In December 1915 the University of Pennsylvania's Board of Trustees issued new guidelines for faculty tenure and for the judicial review of dismissals. Not, of course, that Penn's contrition did much good for Nearing. He received messages of support from all over the country, but only one job offer. That was from the University of Toledo, a municipal school with a strong labor contingent on the Board of Trustees. He taught there for two years, until he was fired for opposing the First World War.[20]

In many ways what happened to academic freedom during the First World War was similar to what would happen to it after the Second. Both times, the entire nation was aroused against an external enemy whose alleged agents seemed both particularly menacing and readily identifiable. Both times the academic community sought to purge itself of such dangerous souls. Though the ranks of academe held few, if any, German or Soviet agents, they did contain professors who for one reason or another were controversial enough to find themselves excluded from the protection of academic freedom in accordance with what the community, under the stress of hot and cold war, had redefined as the limits of that freedom. In a 1917 commencement address, Columbia University's president, Nicholas Murray Butler, described those new limits:

> What had been tolerated before becomes intolerable now. What had been wrongheadedness was now sedition. What had been folly was now treason. . . . There is and will be no place in Columbia University . . . for any person who opposes or counsels opposition to the effective enforcement of the laws of the United States or who acts, speaks, or writes treason.[21]

Sentiments like Butler's were common among his administrative colleagues, and it was not long before the young AAUP found itself besieged by casualties of the wartime hysteria. One historian lists over twenty such dismissals and admits that, given the academic penchant for secrecy, this is probably only the tip of the iceberg. The AAUP's response was suitably academic: it set up a special committee, again under Lovejoy, to report on the crisis. In order to protect the autonomy of the academic profession, the AAUP had to reassure the public that professors could be counted upon to police themselves. It sought, therefore, to ensure that it would not be caught defending any teachers whom the outside world would consider unpatriotic. This meant, of course, a new definition of academic freedom, one which added loyalty to the roster of professional qualifications for academic employment.[22]

Lovejoy's report, "Academic Freedom in Wartime," reflects the underlying insecurities of the academic profession as well as the frenzy of wartime America, for it imposed restrictions on the professoriat's freedom of speech that go far beyond existing laws. Essentially, it refused to protect professors who indulged in any type of anti-war activity, whether that activity was legal or not. Thus, draft resisters and people who counselled draft resistance were beyond the pale of academic freedom, but so, too, were people who merely discouraged "others from rendering voluntary assistance to the efforts of the government." In other words, the AAUP would not defend teachers who were fired for refusing to let fund-raisers for the Red Cross interrupt their classes. In addition, Lovejoy's report went along with the prevailing phobias, by imposing special restrictions on professors of German or Austrian descent who, in order to avoid all ground for suspicion, must "refrain from public discussion of the war; and in their private intercourse with neighbors, colleagues and students . . . avoid all hostile or offensive expressions concerning the United States or its government."[23]

That Scott Nearing, a radical pacifist and vociferous opponent of the war, should lose his teaching job eleven days after America entered the fighting is not surprising. But not all of the other wartime casualties were as deeply committed to anti-war activities as Nearing was. The more notorious academic freedom cases tended to involve people who were already unpopular with their colleagues and administrations and whose less than enthusiastic attitude toward the war provided an excuse for firing them.

William A. Schaper, the apparently prickly chairman of the University of Minnesota's Political Science Department, had already antagonized some of the state's leading businessmen by calling for stricter regulation of public utilities and railroads. Schaper had initially opposed the war, but he had tempered his opposition once the United States became involved. Nevertheless, in September 1917 an anonymous informant charged him with disloyalty. The Board of Regents investigated. It gave Schaper fifteen minutes' notice before it questioned him in secret about his attitude toward the conflict. Then, two hours after what had apparently been a highly acrimonious session, the Board fired him, stating, "his attitude of mind . . . and his expressed unwillingness to aid the United States in the present war, render him unfit and unable rightly to discharge the duties of his position." His colleagues, most of whom shared the Regents' patriotic fervor and few of whom liked Schaper, did not protest. The AAUP investigated but never issued a report.[24]

At Columbia, Nicholas Murray Butler hoped that his patriotic remarks to the class of 1917 would reach faculty ears as well. The address was, he explained, "the University's last and only warning to any among us who are not with whole heart and mind and strength committed to fight with us to make the world safe for democracy." President Butler proved to be a man of his word; four months later he convinced the Board of Trustees to fire two men, James McKeen Cattell and Henry Wadsworth Longfellow Dana, whose commitment to the fight for democracy was insufficiently wholehearted. Dana's lack of tenure and his support for Scott Nearing's anti-war People's Council for Peace and Democracy were clearly fatal. But Cattell was neither so junior nor so radical. In fact, however, his tenure had been shaky for years. An eminent psychologist, Cattell was also a serious critic of the way universities were run. He decried the power of trustees and administrators and advocated greater faculty control, while, at the same time, castigating the code of "gentlemanliness" that kept professors from demanding the necessary reforms. Butler and the Board of Trustees, on the verge of firing him several times before, had been prevented from doing so only by the intervention of his colleagues. But Cattell took his fellow professors on as well, and after he had tangled publicly with E. R. A. Seligman, the most powerful and respected member of the Columbia faculty, that support began to wear thin.[25]

In August 1917 Cattell sent a petition to several congressmen, urging them to support a law which would exempt unwilling draftees from having to fight in Europe. Already sensitive to charges that the highly publicized activities of its more radical students and teachers made Columbia a haven for sedition, the University's establishment, trustees and professors alike, decided to act. The faculty's quasi-official Committee of Nine, which included both Seligman and philosopher John Dewey, recommended (over Dewey's objections, it must be noted) that both Cattell and Dana be dismissed. On October 1, the trustees did just that. Even though most of the faculty felt that the two men's behavior had been improper, there was some opposition to their dismissal. Dewey quit the Council of Nine and, in the most publicized response to the firings, the historian Charles Beard, who had long been unhappy with the trustees' intervention in faculty matters, resigned from the University. The AAUP investigated Cattell's case, not Dana's; instead of producing a special report on it, the organization merely appended to Lovejoy's larger report the observation that "an important university" had fired "a distinguished man of science."[26]

The academic world of Schaper and Cattell, Ely and Nearing, was to change considerably over the next few decades. Especially in the years following the Second World War, the American system of higher education was to expand in size and to become a more democratic and less genteel place. Yet its treatment of political dissidents changed little. The same pattern of pressures and responses that set the early precedents determined the later cases as well. There were some differences to be sure, especially in procedural matters. There was more faculty participation, for example. This was largely the result of the academic profession's success in establishing the principle of tenure. Though its possession did not invariably protect controversial professors from being fired, by the 1940s and 1950s it did usually ensure that they got some kind of a faculty hearing.[27]

Procedures apart, however, there were fewer differences than we might assume. Institutional loyalty was the overriding concern. In almost every situation, faculty members and administrators responded to outside pressures for the dismissal of dissenting faculty members in accord with what they believed would best protect or enhance their school's reputation. The rhetoric of academic freedom obscures those concerns, as, in many instances, it was designed to. After all, even the famous academic freedom statement that the University of Wisconsin released after the Regents reinstated Richard T. Ely in 1894 was planned in part as a piece of institutional promotion—as, in the words of the man who suggested it, "an excellent advertisement for the institution." Stripped of its rhetoric, academic freedom thus turns out to be an essentially corporate protection. And, as we trace its development during the Cold War, we should not be surprised to find that it was invoked more often to defend the well-being of an institution than the political rights of an individual.[28]

II

"In the Camp of the People": Academic Communists in the 1930s and 1940s

The teachers who lost their jobs in the early academic freedom cases were individual dissenters. A few may have belonged to the Socialist party or to one or another of the ephemeral groups that sprang up in opposition to the First World War. But it was their specific political activities that caused their expulsion from the academy, not their party affiliations. With the growth of the Communist Party during the 1930s, however, the type of political activity that was to provoke reprisal changed. For the first time, an organized left-wing movement existed on the nation's campuses. As a result, the academic establishment began to redefine academic freedom so as to exclude people for their associations as well as for their activities. In other words, by the 1940s, men and women who belonged to the Communist Party were no longer welcome in American universities.

That proscription, in part, reflected the special prominence of the Communist Party during the 1930s and early 1940s. On the nation's campuses as in so many other areas of American life during this period, the Communist Party dominated left-wing political activity. There were various other radical and socialist groups around, but they were all much smaller and less visible than the CP. Moreover, many of these organizations, like the Lovestoneites and Trotskyists, were tiny sects whose leaders had been expelled from the Party. Their members' very identity as political activists was bound up in their struggle with the CP, and they tended to devote most of their time and energy to that struggle. In later years, the cultural preeminence of those New York intellectuals who passed through these fringe groups in the 1930s has tended to overshadow the political importance of the academic Communists. But during its period of greatest influence, for the fifteen years from the Depression to the Cold War, the Communist Party was the largest and most effective left-wing organization on the nation's campuses.

We know surprisingly little about the CP's activities within the academic community. Most of the recent scholarship on the Party has dealt with its leaders or its impact on trade unionists, screenwriters, and blacks. The vast and ever-growing literature by and about the New York intellectuals does, it is true, discuss the Communist Party, but usually in such an overwrought fashion as to convey little useful information. In any event, few of these intellectuals were then academics. Thus, despite the general consensus that there was a significant Communist presence among college students and teachers in the 1930s and 1940s, there is only one—dated and incomplete—work on the subject, Robert Iversen's 1959 study *The Communists and the Schools,* and it offers little insight into what academic Communists actually did. Such information is necessary, however, for we cannot understand what happened to these people during the McCarthy period without knowing what they did during the 1930s and 1940s. Nor, and perhaps more important, can we hazard any judgments about the fairness of the treatment they received until we know something about the activities that supposedly produced it.[1]

Here we venture onto treacherous ground. Despite the passage of time, almost half a century to be precise, discussions of American Communism still touch raw political nerves. The controversies refuse to die. Yet, as the historical evidence mounts, the judgmental tone of an earlier era sounds out-of-date. The American Communist Party, for all the emotion it once aroused, can now be studied; it is no longer necessary—if it ever was—to condemn or exonerate it. At its peak it was a dynamic and often effective movement for social change, yet it was also—and at the same time—a doctrinaire, secretive, and undemocratic political sect. Its main flaw, of course, was its uncritical relationship with the Soviet Union, a relationship that required its members to conform their political activities to the dictates of Stalin's foreign policy rather than the exigencies of American life. There were other problems as well. As an ostensibly revolutionary organization, the CP enforced a type of disciplined and conspiratorial behavior that may well have stunted the development of a viable socialist tradition in America. And yet in spite, or perhaps even because, of these serious defects, the Party did make important contributions. It helped build the CIO, and it helped bring the problems of American blacks onto the political agenda. The record is mixed. To view it in any other way is to distort the past.[2]

Unearthing that past presents problems, for the Party was a secret organization. Its members did not advertise their affiliation at the time; even today many of them remain reluctant to reveal that part of their lives. Their reticence is understandable, though regrettable, especially for academics. And it creates real problems for anybody trying to study the Communist Party on the rank and file level. Every scholar who deals with the movement reports the same difficulties. Ironically, contemporary historians need the same kinds of confessions the congressional investigators of the 1950s did, including, if at all possible, the naming of other people's names. Though the documents of the period and the published testimony of the friendly witnesses of the fifties tell us something about what the CP did on campus during the thirties and forties, a more balanced and complete picture can come only from the first-hand accounts of former members. (I specify *former* members here, because, as far as I can tell, just about every professor who was in the Party in the thirties and forties had left by the end of the fifties.) Luckily, many previously reluctant academics have recently decided to discuss their past membership in the CP. I have personally interviewed or corresponded with about seventy of them. Neither Communists nor anti-Communists, they have few regrets about their affiliation with the Party and, despite the wide range of their present views, are willing to share their reminiscences out of the conviction that the time has come to set the story right. As a result, though some academics who probably belonged to the Party still will not admit it and a few others have requested anonymity, enough of these people have been willing to talk openly and at length about their political pasts to make it possible to construct a preliminary account of the scope and nature of Communist Party activity within the academic world.[3]

*   *   *

At the time of the Communist Party's formation, in the years of chaos and repression following the First World War, it seemed unlikely that it would ever be attractive to academics. Composed primarily of the left wing of the old Socialist party, its foreign-language sections in particular, the new American CP identified with the Bolsheviks, readied itself for the leadership of the revolution which it assumed was just around the corner, and immediately—and characteristically—split into two factions. Then, in the face of severe persecution, both groups went underground, only to merge and surface again in 1922 as the Workers Party, a self-consciously proletarian group energized and dominated by the Soviet Union.[4]

   This type of a party was not a comfortable place for middle-class intellectuals or academics; yet, so powerful was the appeal of the Russian Revolution that even in those early days there were a few scholars and writers who gravitated toward Communism. Greenwich Village radicals like John Reed and the former Columbia University philosophy instructor Max Eastman embraced the Russian Revolution and served as the literary vanguard of Communism, writing articles, editing magazines, and publicly celebrating the Soviet triumph. Yet the relationship of intellectuals like Eastman with the Communist Party was a tenuous one at best. Attracted by the dynamism of the Russian Revolution, they were quickly repelled by the squabbling and rigidity that plagued the young movement both in America and in Russia after Lenin's death. As a result, during the 1920s, many otherwise sympathetic radicals never joined up or else, if they did, soon left or were forced out.[5]

   Scott Nearing was a typical case. He quit the Socialist Party in the early twenties over its opposition to the Soviet Union. But, though he felt that the Communists "were the only group actively trying to cope with the situation in the United States," their in-fighting made him hesitate for years. "It looked as though if I were to join the party then I would have to give up my serious work in social science and devote myself to taking sides in factional squabbles." Nevertheless, he finally gave in and, in 1927, joined the Party. He then spent the next few years doing under Party auspices just what he had always been doing—speaking, writing, organizing, and teaching. His celebrity status attracted a wide range of students to his classes at the New York Workers School, including, among others, a young dropout from Columbia named Whittaker Chambers. But Nearing's affiliation with the Party lasted only three years; he left when it refused to let him publish a book he had spent years working on. His definition of imperialism did not coincide with Lenin's.[6]

Yet it was not merely the Party's sectarianism, nor even its barely disguised hostility toward bourgeois intellectuals, that kept it from recruiting successfully among academics before the Depression. The objective conditions were, in a word, unfavorable. The 1920s were, on campus as in the outside world, conservative years. So low was the level of political activity during this period that there were only a handful of academic freedom cases, and most of them dealt with matters of religion, not politics. Left-wing professors, if there were any, kept a low profile, and student radicalism was all but nonexistent. Fraternities and football dominated college life; politics were as peripheral to most Jazz Age undergraduates as their courses. Even so, it is important to examine the tiny undergraduate left of the 1920s, not because of its influence, but because it provided a group of future Communist academics with their first taste of left-wing politics.[7]

Most of these people belonged to their colleges' Liberal or Social Problems Clubs, the renamed remnants of the lively Socialist Clubs that had flourished before the First World War. In the 1920s, however, these groups were pretty pallid. The philosopher and future Communist William Parry recalls that, while he was in Columbia's Social Problems Club in the mid-twenties, it "didn't have a definite political affiliation [and] didn't follow a particular party line." It was mainly a discussion group which rarely did anything more daring than sponsor outside speakers. Even so, the times were so conservative that bringing a Socialist or Communist to the campus could cause an uproar. Harvard's Liberal Club, for example, whose members included such future academic radicals as Horace Bancroft Davis, Granville Hicks, and Corliss Lamont, created a furor in 1924 when Lamont tried to invite Nearing, Eugene V. Debs, and William Z. Foster to address the student union. The dean, Lamont recalled, told him that such speakers "were not appropriate for our speaking program." Nor was Harvard exceptional. The president of Clark University personally turned out the lights in the middle of a lecture in order to stop Nearing from speaking.[8]

Though there were a few ephemeral protests against such repression—

usually from the editors of student newspapers, which were themselves subject to censorship—the only issue that caused any real student unrest was compulsory ROTC. In part this was because of the compulsory nature of the program, but it was also because anti-militarism, even in the twenties, was the main concern of campus activists. Students knew that they would be on the front lines of the next war. In addition, they shared the growing national suspicion that America's participation in the First World War had been a mistake. Most of the future academic Communists among the students of the twenties and thirties subscribed to the pacifism of the period. But they were not alone. And, by the early thirties, the international tensions that accompanied the Depression and the rise of Hitler lent a real sense of urgency to the anti-war fervor that was sweeping the nation's campuses. In a 1933 poll at Columbia University, 31 percent of the undergraduates declared themselves absolute pacifists and another 52 percent maintained that they would not fight unless the United States itself was invaded. At the same time, thousands of students all over the country signed the Oxford Pledge, a pacifist import from Great Britain that stated, "We pledge not to support the United States government in any war it may conduct."[9]

By this time, there was a left-wing student movement in place which was able to channel these pacifist sentiments into an organized struggle. This movement was to radicalize an entire generation of academics, not only because it introduced its members, the future academic Communists among them, to political activity, but also because it created a climate within the academic community that encouraged faculty leftists to organize as well. The student protest of the thirties was brand new; never before had students organized themselves on such a large scale, nor with such militance. By the middle of the decade, there were anti-war demonstrations on almost every campus—from the Ivy League, the Seven Sisters, and the Big Ten to teachers colleges, church schools, and even a few black colleges in the South. Only the Catholic schools remained untouched. There were Communists involved from the first. They were active in and often dominated the main student organizations of the period—the National Student League and the American Student Union. And, as the decade wore on, more and more students and teachers were to follow these early activists into the Party.[10]

Though peace supplied the issue, hard times provided the impetus for this new student, and in some cases faculty, radicalism. But not right away. It was to take a few years for the Depression to make itself felt on campus and several more years for that effect to translate itself into any significant political activity among either students or teachers. Obviously, there was no one-to-one correlation between the academic calm of the twenties and the prosperity and sense of affluence that pervaded the American middle class. Nor did the Depression, in and of itself, drive large numbers of students into the Communist Party. It did, however, deprive them of their previous security of knowing that their college degrees would guarantee them a spot in the upper echelons of American society. With 25 percent of the work force jobless, one-third of the class of 1933, it was estimated, graduated into unemployment and another third into underemployment. The future professors among them were, as one of them noted, "highly motivated, ambitious children of the lower middle class for whom going to the university and launching academic careers was (among other things) a convenient channel toward a higher status and security and position." The set-back to their expectations delivered by the Depression was, for many of these people, profoundly radicalizing. "My own view of my future came to a halt," explained a scientist who graduated from Brooklyn College in 1934. At a time when so many people were unemployed, he was lucky to get a job fetching books in the New York Public Library. A few months later, he joined the Communist Party.[11]

If for undergraduates the Depression seemed to curtail their own prospects for social mobility, for faculty members and graduate students it brought more immediate deprivations. Unlike undergraduate enrollment, which began to decline in about 1932, graduate enrollments actually increased in the early thirties. Twenty-six percent more Ph.D.s were awarded in 1935 than in 1931. After all, staying in school was one way an intellectually talented student could avoid outright unemployment after graduation. Not that the prospects for these young academics were very promising. The economies that the Depression forced on the nation's colleges and universities, especially on the public ones, hit their faculties hard. A special survey by the AAUP found that 84 percent of the schools it studied cut professors' salaries, usually by about 15 percent. The brunt of these and other cut-backs fell upon junior faculty members, many of whom were being unceremoniously pushed off the academic ladder. These people were often let go after a year or two to be replaced by other similarly lowly and poorly paid members of the academic proletariat. Many schools created new positions below the regular faculty ranks—tutors, fellows, and instructors, positions which paid miserably and offered no security. By the mid-thirties, 80 percent of the teaching at Brooklyn College was done by people with these off-the-ladder appointments, some of which paid as little as $600 a year. But even these unsatisfactory jobs were hard to find. Harry Marks, a historian who got his Ph.D. from Harvard in 1937, recalls writing more than fifty letters for jobs and getting only one offer, a one-year appointment at a salary so low that he literally couldn't afford to take it. Since like almost everybody who went to college during the Depression he had gotten a teacher's certificate, he taught high school instead.[12]

A further factor which compounded the employment problems of young academics and helped radicalize a significant group of them was anti-Semitism. In recent years, Jews have been disproportionately represented both in academic life and on the left. Though few Jews had risen into the professoriat by the 1930s, significant numbers of them were poised for entry and for the break-through they were to achieve right after the Second World War. They were mostly the second-generation sons (few women in this group) of small businessmen, skilled workers, or professionals, successful students whose social background and intellectual predilections made academic careers seem a particularly congenial route into the professional class. They tended to enter the more highly intellectualized branches of the sciences and social sciences—physics, biochemistry, psychology, sociology, and economics—and avoid those areas like the humanities where more subjective, and presumably more anti-Semitic, criteria might prevail. And they tended to come from and go to school in the urban centers where their immigrant parents had settled, New York City in particular.[13]

Since the twenties, when large numbers of smart first- and second-generation East European Jews seemingly threatened to inundate the nation's top colleges, most of those schools followed the lead of Harvard and imposed quotas on the number of Jews they would admit. As a result, during the late twenties and thirties, a good many very bright, very energetic future academics got their BAs at places like the City College of New York and Brooklyn College instead of Harvard and Columbia. And, though they could get Ph.D.s from the first-rate schools, they could rarely teach there. Jews in tenured positions in elite universities were such a rarity that Lionel Trilling's appointment as the Columbia English Department's first Jew was viewed as a break-through. Like baseball's Jackie Robinson, the Ivy League's first Jewish professors had to be superstars. Lesser lights were lucky if they could scrounge up part-time teaching jobs at their own alma maters. "I would have practically no chance of getting anything outside of New York," a Brooklyn College biologist recalled. "I was Jewish, which I felt at that time represented an obstacle." Even within the presumably hospitable New York City municipal colleges, there was considerable anti-Semitism. Certain practices, like the city colleges' stated desire to avoid the "urban provincialism" that would result from hiring their own graduates, were particularly blatant. With the advent of the Depression, what the AAUP called the "difficulties of employment of professors of certain racial groups" seemed to be increasing. Whether or not the Depression actually heightened the discrimination against Jews in higher education, there is no question that many of them felt it did.[14]

Of course, academic anti-Semitism was not the only reason so many Jewish professors ended up in the Party. In the 1930s, large numbers of middle-class Jews in every profession joined the Party. They came to it, the future academics among them, from a working-class Jewish community which had a strong socialist and trade-union tradition; and, though they had risen into the professions, the Party was not as alien to them as it was to their gentile colleagues. Even so, few of these Jewish academics would have become Communists had not the rise of the Nazis shocked them into political awareness. They felt, far more strongly than non-Jews, the need to respond, and, attracted by what they perceived as the Soviet Union's leadership in opposing Hitler, did so by joining the Party. As a result, although the first generation of Communist professors had few Jews in it, by the late thirties and early forties, at least half if not more of the Party members in the academic community were Jewish.[15]

Even before there was a well-organized radical movement on campus, it was clear that the Depression had made both students and teachers increasingly open to the left. In a 1932 straw poll the students and faculty at Columbia gave a surprisingly large vote to Norman Thomas, the Socialist Party's candidate. Similarly, there was a hefty sprinkling of academics among the fifty-three artists and intellectuals who signed a public manifesto in support of the Communist Party's presidential candidates for that year. The eminence of the signers, who included Edmund Wilson, Sidney Hook, and Granville Hicks, as well as the radicalism of their statement that "as responsible intellectual workers, we have aligned ourselves with the frankly revolutionary Communist Party, the party of the workers," showed clearly that there was a new mood among the nation's intellectuals and that, for some of them, Communism was a plausible response to the problems of Depression America.[16]

At the same time, the CP was itself becoming more open to such bourgeois types as academics. Though the Popular Front would not officially begin until 1935, the Party was slowly moving away from the rigidly revolutionary stance of the so-called Third Period Communism of the late twenties and early thirties and becoming more hospitable to middle-class intellectuals. It never, of course, went out of its way to recruit them, the way it did blacks or blue-collar workers; its leaders and middle-level cadres were often skeptical about the presence of these academic types within a working-class, revolutionary party. But, nonetheless, from the late thirties until the late forties, the CP exercised a continuing attraction for the most radical members of the academic profession. Communism's initial appeal to some of these people was its claim to offer an ideology, an intellectual system that above all seemed to explain the social chaos that they saw around them. It is important to recognize that academics, as intellectuals, have a stronger need than most people to make sense out of their lives. For them, therefore, the intellectual side of Communism, its attempt to provide a systematic analysis of the very obvious failure of capitalism during the Depression, was one of its main attractions. It was also, later, a source of disillusionment, for the quality of the CP's Marxism was often pretty poor. It tended to reflect Party strategy and substituted political cheerleading for independent critical thought.[17]

We must distinguish between generations here. Academics who either as students or teachers became radicalized and gravitated into the Party during the early thirties, before there was a significant left-wing organizational presence on campus, did so slowly, and usually after a preliminary conversion to what they considered was Marxism. Not all converts to Marxism joined the CP, of course; some remained intellectual sympathizers only, others joined one or another of the competing sects and parties. Commitments varied. But of this earlier group, which became radicalized during the early years of the Depression, most were to retain a life-long identification with the left. Their years in the CP were but an episode—albeit a crucial one—in their continuing involvement with Marxist thought and left-wing politics.

Barrows Dunham's experience was typical. A Princeton graduate and second-generation academic who was to inherit the chairmanship of the Philosophy Department at Temple University from his father, Dunham was not himself affected by the Depression. But the obvious inability of conventional thinkers to explain "Why do things like this happen?" encouraged him to seek the answers elsewhere. Sometime in 1935, he recalls, he sent for a book about Marxism that had been advertised in the *New Republic* and was leafing through it when he reached

> by a kind of fatality . . . a passage in Engels' *Anti-Duhring*—his book attacking a German philosopher named Duhring—in which he said words to the effect that the economic bankruptcy of the bourgeoisie occurs regularly every ten years, and its intellectual bankruptcy has become permanent. And I remember as I read that passage a feeling of slipping. I was sliding in the direction that this passage pointed to. It was a sensation that I seemed to feel within my body, and as I slid I kept asking myself, "Do I want to go in this direction?" And I said to myself, "Yes, I do want to go in this direction." And that's the first Marxist book that I read.

He read many more, of course, and soon, like many other young intellectuals of the 1930s, came to consider himself a Marxist. But he did not officially join the Communist Party until 1938.

Lawrence Arguimbau, an electrical engineer who was later to teach at MIT, had a similarly bookish conversion to socialism:

> I suppose it goes back to the period of 1933 or 1934 when I had been reading generalized history in order to get some understanding of the nature of the difficulties that were facing us, the depression, and I was struggling in my own mind to find out what was the cause of it, as a theoretical matter, historically, and also practically, because of the reaction on my friends and myself of the depression. So I began to be forced more or less into a position that was parallel to that of, let us say, the whole socialist movement.

But, like Dunham, he did not become an official Communist until a few years later.[18]

William Parry was another philosopher of Dunham's generation who became a Communist several years after he had become a socialist. Parry had been radicalized earlier than Dunham. Through his reading as a high school student and his later activities as a member of Columbia's Social Problems Club in the mid-twenties, Parry had come to consider himself a socialist—"you might say a Norman Thomas socialist." It was a lukewarm commitment, and during his graduate days at Harvard he all but abandoned politics. Things changed in 1932, not, however, because of the Depression but because Parry spent a year in Central Europe. There, he lost his detachment, for he found it impossible to avoid political involvement when fascist rioting shut down the University of Vienna, where he was studying. His response was intellectual, nonetheless:

> I decided that I really had to come to grips with it and I carefully studied Lenin's writings, especially his *State and Revolution*. And, I studied Laski to represent Left wing socialism, which to me would be the real alternatives at that stage . . . I decided that Lenin was right and he had as it were refuted Laski's advances as far as I was concerned. And so I felt that I believed in the Communist position . . . I decided on this basis not so much on a personal basis, just intellectually I thought the Communist position was right.

And when Parry returned to the United States, he joined the Communist Party.[19]

Robert Gorham Davis's odyssey was similar, though more convoluted. Like Parry, he began to swing toward the left during the 1920's, when, he insists, "any young person who did much reading in this period became critical of the government and society." The Sacco-Vanzetti case radicalized him further. He graduated from Harvard in 1929 and got his master's degree there before he took his first teaching job at Rensselaer Polytechnic Institute in 1930. By then "I was already a leftist, a theoretical socialist at least." The literary critic Granville Hicks was also teaching at RPI at the time, and the two men became close friends. "Granville was already writing for left periodicals and I began writing and in 1932 or 33 set myself up as a proletarian critic." At that point, "I declared myself an official Marxist." But that declaration did not automatically lead into the Communist Party.

> I moved back and forth during those years because I was often extremely critical of the Communist Party. I read the Trotskyist and Lovestoneite literature and I was very early associated with the people who edited *Partisan Review*. . . . Between 34 and 37 I had some very strong criticisms of the Party, being influenced by Trotskyists and other ideas, but in 1937, with my eyes fairly open, I decided that the moment had come that you have to commit yourself.[20]

Later on, the lag that this first—and largely, it must be noted, non-Jewish—generation of academic reds experienced between their initial conversion to Marxism and their later adherence to the Party was to disappear. There was, thanks to Hitler, a greater sense of urgency. And there was also, by the late thirties, at least, the critical mass of radical students and teachers that made it easier for a politically concerned academic to transform his theoretical attachment to the left into an organizational one. Even so, the process whereby many of these people read themselves into the Party remained the same. The future scientist from Brooklyn

College who became a Communist while working in the New York Public Library explained that he did so after he started to read in order to understand what was going on around him. Marxism seemed to make sense; it also "afforded a vision of a brighter future for all mankind."

And, once in the Party, he continued to read—mainly history, he recalls. Clement Markert was another scientist whose intellectual curiosity propelled him into the Party. He grew up in Pueblo, Colorado. His father, a steelworker, lost his job in the middle of the Depression "when they closed the steel mill down." Markert, in high school at the time, "was just intellectually very aggressive about trying to understand the world . . . and, after some reading and studying and paying attention," he came "to take a very hostile attitude against the capitalist system. . . . I began to consider myself a communist." He went to the University of Colorado and there, "completely on my own, without having read any Communist literature or having ever met a Communist, I then proceeded to organize . . . a group of students similarly minded, and we formed a Communist group there." But it was not until a few years later that Markert, who had by then considered himself a Communist for years, officially established contact with the Party and actually joined up.[21]

Markert's independence was unusual—few members of his generation of left-wing professors had quite as solitary a conversion. But he was not the only future academic who, in the late 1930s and early 1940s, entered college already a Communist. Most of the others, however, had grown upon the left. Some were "red diaper babies," men and women whose parents belonged to the CP and for whom joining the Party was simply a family tradition. For the future biologist Leon Wofsy, it was the family business as well. His father was a district organizer for the Party during the 1930s and 1940s, and Wofsy "never dreamed of going into anything else." When he got to CCNY in 1938, he plunged into political work and was soon head of the Marxist Cultural Society and the City College unit of the Young Communist League (YCL), the Party's official youth group. Others of his contemporaries among the Communist students at City College also came from Party families or, if not from radical homes, at least from radical neighborhoods, places where, the musicologist Norman Cazden remembers, "even hiking clubs were *left-wing* hiking clubs." A teenager growing up in one of these political ghettoes could hardly avoid daily exposure to parties, sects, and splinter groups. And though the revolution may not have been around the corner, in certain parts of Brownsville, Brooklyn, for example, a political rally always was. In such an environment, joining the CP was just another adolescent ritual, one that often seemed to give entrée into the most attractive social cliques. At New York City's Stuyvesant High School in the early forties, every member of the school's honor society was reputed to belong to the YCL.[22]

Peer pressure, family background, intellectual curiosity—all helped push a generation of left-wing students and teachers into the CP. But the Party's single most effective recruiter, by far, was Adolf Hitler. The spread of fascism and the subsequent failure of the Western democracies to stand up against it convinced a lot of worried, but hardly revolutionary, men and women to take the drastic step of joining the Communist Party. Of course, by the late 1930s, the Party no longer seemed to be the radical sect it had formerly been. The Soviet Union's desperate search for collective security against the Nazi threat spurred the international Communist movement to adopt the Popular Front and enlist any allies it could find into the struggle against fascism. As a result, the American party, which had already begun to slough off some of its hard-line sectarianism, accelerated the process, and, in certain areas, embraced a kind of warm-hearted "progressivism" that was not far to the left of the New Deal. "Communism," the CP's new slogan declared, "is twentieth-century Americanism." This new line, it must be noted, created serious contradictions within the CP. For, despite its apparent moderation, the Party still retained its central commitment to Stalin's Russia and attacked Trotskyists and other critics of the Soviet regime with all its old sectarian fervor. In addition, it retained its traditional authoritarian structure and expected its new recruits to follow its albeit less revolutionary line with the same unquestioning devotion older Communists did.[23]

It is hard to tell whether the academics who embraced the CP during the Popular Front period would have done so had its line been more intransigent. Few of them were revolutionaries, nor were they even particularly interested in the Soviet Union. They joined the Party, almost all of them, because they thought it was the best way to fight fascism. A sense of urgency surrounded that decision. They were confused and worried; and, as with the Depression, the Communist Party seemed to have most of the answers with regard to Nazi Germany. This was important for people who were just coming to political awareness in the late thirties. The future philosopher of science David Hawkins recalled that he was "pretty unworldly" until he "became concerned about what appeared to be the imminent drive toward war in Nazi Germany." He soon came to feel that "this drive toward war could be stopped by a collective security policy and when I looked around to find people who strongly supported that policy, at least in California, the Communist Party seemed to be the principal group that was taking that position." For Jews, as we have seen, Nazism was a particular threat. "I am a Jew," one mathematician told an investigating committee in the 1950s,

> I feel deeply as a Jew, and I felt very deeply as a Jew then. When I joined the Party, as I recollect, I had a very strong feeling about Munich. I think that was the sort of thing that turned me into the Party. Here was Nazism growing up. It seemed as though the democracies had not been able to stem the tide. Munich looked like a collapse, as perhaps it was. That was the thing that brought me in.[24]

Then there was Spain, the issue that stirred as much political emotion on the campuses of the thirties as Vietnam did in the sixties. The Spanish Civil War, Barrows Dunham recalled "showed you . . . the facts of international life, and showed you where you had to stand." When General Francisco Franco led a military revolt against the legally elected Popular Front government in the summer of 1936, all the left-wing rhetoric about the need to stop fascism turned into reality. Hitler and Mussolini rushed planes, men, and munitions to Franco; the Western democracies did nothing. President Roosevelt, concerned about an isolationist backlash, declared America neutral and refused to send arms to either side. Only Russia came to the aid of the desperately beleaguered Spanish Republic. It shipped a few boatloads of supplies and mobilized its worldwide network of Party members and fellow travelers. As a result, the Communist Party essentially got the American franchise for aid to the Spanish Loyalists.[25]

Of course, most of the men and women who sympathized with and worked for the Republican cause did not become Communists, but many did. Especially in academic circles, where the Spanish Civil War enflamed an entire generation of left-wing students and teachers, the Party's support for the Spanish Republic turned out to be an effective recruiting device. To begin with, everybody who wanted to help the Loyalists had to work with the Communist Party, for its international connections gave it an edge in making the clandestine arrangements necessary for getting American volunteers and medical supplies to Spain. In addition, the Soviet support for the Spanish Republic seemed to legitimize the Party's claim to be the leading anti-fascist organization in the world. For politically involved activists, it was a claim that many could not resist. Some, like the California teacher who later confessed that the Spanish Civil War "was the hook that caught me," joined on the spur of the moment. Others, like Barrows Dunham and Robert Gorham Davis, who already agreed with much of the Party's agenda, responded to the Spanish crisis by transforming their ideological affinity into a concrete commitment.[26]

Davis's affiliation is of interest in that he was no political innocent and had long been critical of both Russia and the American CP. In 1937, however, he shed his ambivalence:

> The moment had come that you had to commit yourself in the light of the increasing power of the Nazis and the situation in Spain and it seemed to me that, on the whole, with all of my reservations about the Soviet Union and the Party, it was the only body of any considerable influence that was standing effectively against the Nazis.

He soon left the CP, for once the Soviet Union defected from the anti-fascist cause, Davis, who had disliked the Party's rigidity and its adulation of Stalin, could remain a Communist no longer. Nonetheless, the fact that someone as sophisticated and critical as Robert Gorham Davis could submerge his doubts and accept the discipline of the Communist Party—

even if for only two years—makes it easier to understand why so many otherwise intelligent men and women shut their eyes to the Party's defects and its apologia for Stalinist Russia. A lot of rationalizing went on. Once people believed that international Communism was, as the sociologist Sigmund Diamond put it, "a political force which stood for justice," few of them "investigated in the most meticulous of fashions the philosophical principles of Marxism-Leninism and knew all that was happening in the Soviet Union or even in the Communist Party of the United States."[27]

Such ignorance was largely deliberate. Convinced that the CP, despite its problems, was the most effective political organization around, many academic Communists simply avoided informing themselves about those problems, and stifled their doubts about the Moscow purge trials. Since American reporting from the Soviet Union during the early phases of the Revolution had been notoriously unreliable, these Party members dismissed news about the purges as the usual hostile propaganda of the capitalist press—"a tissue of lies spawned by the class enemy and the agents of Japanese imperialism and the agents of fascism and so on." Now, they know they were wrong. Like the critic Saul Maloff, they regard their apologies for Stalin as a "rather shameful" part of their lives:

> All of the information was there. The Trotskyite critique had been mounted then and it had matured. The Dewey Committee had been over there. An enormous amount of information was available. It's a question of what you want to look at and what you want to see and what interpretation you choose to put upon whatever.

Not every ex-Communist is equally contrite. Some were more tough-minded. Like the former CCNY chemistry instructor Sidney Eisenberger, they were proud of their loyalty, proud that "we defended the Soviet Union right up to the end." Russia's defeat of Hitler in World War II vindicated them, so they felt. Later on, even Eisenberger discovered things that he "couldn't swallow"; like just about every other academic Communist, he, too, quit the Party.[28]

Whatever the reasons that impelled them into the Party and however they rationalized their membership, the academic Communists of the 1930s and early 1940s could not have known that joining the Party— though never a trivial decision—was the momentous step that McCarthyism later made it. American campuses seethed with politics during the late thirties. Every day there would be some kind of rally or speaker at Saither Gate at the University of California at Berkeley or on the steps of Low Library at Columbia. Though most students and teachers were, as always, not very involved, their more politically oriented contemporaries found it hard to avoid coming into contact with the Party. In an atmosphere like Berkeley's, where even rather apolitical people took out subscriptions to the Communist Party's paper, it was considered "quite respectable," the philosopher Stanley Moore recalled, to join the CP. So much so that, as another former Berkeley student explained, "A question one had constantly to answer, to others and especially to oneself, was whether one should join the Communist Party and if not why not." People hovered on the fringes, going to the same meetings, working in the same organizations. Official membership seemed unimportant, at least at Berkeley.

> One began to hear that it did not really matter whether one joined the Communist Party or not. If one was seriously against Hitler, if one was for peace, labor, and racial equality, one would find oneself in the long run in the camp of the people. The contradictions of capitalism would take care of the rest.

Berkeley's may have been a particularly fluid situation. The physicist Philip Morrison recalls that while he was in the Party there, his unit would welcome to its discussion meetings "many people who were not Communist. It would be very hard to say which members were Communists." But, elsewhere as well, many people recalled that for them belonging to the Party was rather casual, "a matter of attitude basically, feeling you are a member of a group and working in the group." The formal apparatus was secondary. "We thought of ourselves as comrades, as Marxists, as Communists," was the way one former graduate student described the ambience at Columbia. Like Clement Markert at Colorado, if one felt oneself a Communist, one was.[29]

Actually joining the Party, like getting the wedding ring, legitimized the relationship. (Later on, of course, the difference between having been a capital "C" Communist or a lower-case one was the difference between losing a job and losing a security clearance.) It was a simple ceremony. As one former member explained, "In 1938, on every campus in America, it was easier to join the Party than it was to join a posh sorority, and at Wisconsin, well, the best and the brightest were in the CP." Another man recalled, "It looked so easy and seemed so unimportant at the time." The Party found its academic recruits in certain self-selected circles—the people who participated in Marxist study groups at CCNY and Harvard or became active in the teachers' union at Brooklyn College or even took their meals at a particular cooperative house at the University of Chicago. The Party was only one piece, though an important one, in a larger network of causes, concerns, and, above all, people. The men and women the Party tried to recruit worked on the same committees, shared the same interests and, often, even the same friends as people who were already in the Party. Melvin Rader, a University of Washington philosopher, recalls that his work for the Spanish Loyalists resulted in repeated invitations to join the CP. He never did. Other people were signed up by their friends. William Ted Martin's roommate brought him into the Party. "I was—happened to have an apartment with a person who was a member and whom I respected," the MIT mathematician explained; "I don't know if he actually invited me, but we talked these things over and I came in as a result of that."[30]

Some academic Communists took the first step themselves. David Hawkins was a graduate student at Berkeley when he joined the CP. "I resolved to do this, and I went and looked up the local campus branch of the Communist Party. This wasn't difficult to do in those days. Then I went to a meeting at which I signed up." The physicist Frank Oppenheimer (Robert's brother) clipped a form out of a Communist Party newspaper and sent it in. Another man described how, when he became interested in the Party, he sought out people he assumed had connections with it:

> I was in San Francisco. There was a girl I knew slightly. I asked her if she knew any way I could make contact with the Communist Party. I didn't think of going to their headquarters for some reason or other. She said she might know someone in San Francisco who might know someone in Los Angeles who might get in touch with me.
>
> I returned to Los Angeles. Some time later I received a telephone call to come to a certain address at a certain time. I met a man who introduced himself to me as Sidney Freeman. . . . He asked me why I wanted to get into the Communist Party. I told him on account of Spain, and he handed me a membership card and I signed it.[31]

Most of these people belonged to units connected with their colleges or universities. This was especially true during the late thirties and early forties, when there were enough Party members on the more politically active campuses to make up a separate unit. The membership of these groups fluctuated, for, like most other American Communists, academics usually joined the Party only to leave it within a few years. In addition, academics, especially the younger ones who constituted most of the membership, were a mobile group and circulated from one campus to another to take up jobs or fellowships or, as was particularly the case with the Popular Front generation, to join the armed forces or do some kind of military-related work during the Second World War. As a result, there was a rapid turnover within the membership of the academic units. MIT's Lawrence Arguimbau belonged to five or six different groups during the ten years he was in the Party.[32]

Significantly, though some of Arguimbau's units contained Harvard, as well as MIT, professors and some even had non-academic members, they never included students. Academic Communism was surprisingly hierarchical in nature. Except in those places where there were so few Communists as to make separate student and faculty units impractical, the Party rigidly segregated its professorial members from its undergraduate ones. Graduate students were in between. Often, at large schools like Berkeley or Columbia, they had their own units. There was, for example, a unit at Harvard which consisted of some seven or eight teaching assistants, tutors, and instructors who considered themselves "a kind of elite group of scholars and intelligent men." When in the late thirties the Party grew, Harvard's "rather rigidly exclusive" group broke up into at least two units: one was composed primarily of people who were studying with F. O. Matthiessen in American Studies and the other, apparently more eclectic, group seemed to contain scientists from MIT as well as Harvard men. Later, when Party membership declined, these units apparently recombined. At CCNY, whose approximately forty-man unit was probably the largest academic branch in the nation, there was apparently some kind of a distinction between junior and senior people. In addition, the unit included low-level administrators as well as faculty members. The Brooklyn College unit had separate sections for its day and its evening teachers. Sometimes, as was apparently the case at Cornell, students had their own groups, and faculty members met with people from the outside community. The students suspected that there might be some professors in the Party but they never knew for sure.[33]

There were a number of reasons why, as one ex-Communist, the pharmacologist Mark Nickerson, put it, "there has always been a distinct reluctance on the part of the Communist Party to have faculty members associating with students." In the first place, fraternization would breed inequality:

> There is a pressure relationship there. Students, particularly if they have any academic contact with the faculty member, are very apt to be reluctant to express themselves freely, and to contradict the faculty member when they do not agree with his point of view and so on.

It would be, Nickerson said, "an improper relationship." Even worse, it would be a dangerous one. Security was the paramount consideration here. It had long been standard practice within the Party to preserve the anonymity of those of its members whose affiliation, if it were known, might jeopardize their political work or professional careers. This was especially the case with academics. "Our chief interest in not revealing our association," an MIT mathematician explained,

> was an understandable one, to try to keep our jobs. . . . We knew that it was unpopular to be a member of the Communist Party and I think most of us felt that if it became public knowledge, our scientific careers which were far more important to us would be in jeopardy.

Graduate students feared expulsion. Professors feared for their jobs. The risks involved in collaborating politically with undergraduates were simply unacceptable, especially given the other problems such an association would create.[34]

Besides isolating themselves from student activists, Communist teachers protected their identities in other ways and were often willing to put up with some of the more ridiculous aspects of the Party's apparatus of secrecy. The CP was, after all, a supposedly revolutionary organization and its academic members, some of them at least, were, as one recalls, "willing, *if necessary*, to support the violent overthrow of capitalism." They therefore accommodated themselves to the clandestine behavior that belonging to such an organization required. They took Party names, for example. Professors who wrote for left-wing magazines, like the Party's literary journal *New Masses*, sometimes used pseudonyms. Barrows Dunham published as "Joel Bradford," Robert Gorham Davis was "Obed Brooks," and Howard Selsam, a Brooklyn College philosopher, called himself "Paul Salter." Other professors, however, wrote openly for the left-wing press and even the pseudonymous authors did not always guard their identity very closely. Robert Gorham Davis listed his "Obed Brooks" articles on his résumé. On the other hand, the members of those Party units which put out shop papers at schools such as CCNY, Wisconsin, and Brooklyn College did not bother with pseudonyms. They wrote, edited, and distributed the papers completely anonymously.[35]

This policy of secrecy was not without its problems. It fed the suspicions of those who were later to attack the CP as a clandestine, conspiratorial organization. That Party members usually concealed their affiliation for the perfectly understandable purpose of self-protection did not make that concealment any more acceptable to their academic colleagues. In retrospect, it would probably have been wiser for Communist professors to have been more open, especially during the Popular Front period. But, understandably, not every policy the Party followed was wise, and its insistence on secrecy came from a long history of repression and concealment. When in the 1950s the ex-Communist professors looked back on their years in the CP, many of them were willing to admit as Lawrence Arguimbau did that concealing their membership "may have been a mistake." Some even had misgivings at the time. Mark Nickerson was quite explicit:

> I have more regrets, I think, about not having been able, at least I thought, to continue a scientific career, and to be openly and above-board, an in and out member of the Communist Party when I was a member. That bothered me a great deal.

It bothered other people as well. One man, a former Communist from Philadelphia, recalls, "the fact that we considered it necessary to be secretive, that's a very uncomfortable thing." And, for the historian Richard Schlatter, "concealing an important part of my life from some of my best friends" was one of his main regrets about the Party. "Secret political groups, about which some of one's best friends are kept in the dark, exact a heavy human cost."[36]

Though it was, in many ways, ultimately self-defeating, the Party's attempt to keep the identity of its academic members secret did succeed. Friends and colleagues knew that some of these people sympathized with the Party, but never knew that they were actually in it. The physicist and future president of Cornell, Dale Corson, shared an office with Philip Morrison at Berkeley during the late thirties. Corson knew that his fellow physicist was a left-winger, but had no idea that he was in the CP at the time. Daniel Aaron had a similar experience. His office mate was the historian, and future Librarian of Congress, Daniel Boorstin, and though they participated in a Marxist study group together it was not until Boorstin testified before HUAC in 1953 that Aaron learned of his affiliation. Wendell Furry's colleagues in the Physics Department at Harvard were even more surprised to find out that he had been in the Party. They knew Furry supported left-wing causes, but they felt he was far too ethereal for anything as down-to-earth as joining the Communist Party. Even at CCNY, home of the largest and most aggressive academic unit in the country, Communist teachers were able to conceal their affiliation. When the New York State legislature's Rapp-Coudert Committee identified them in public, the doughty anti-Communist who headed the History Department confessed, "It's news to me" that eight of his teachers belonged to the Party. It was news to the Communist students as well. Leon Wofsy recalls his own surprise at learning which professors had been in the CP.[37]

Not every academic Communist kept his membership a secret. Many of them were so active in public that there was never any question about their affiliation. They could always be counted on to speak at campus rallies or serve as the official faculty advisers for left-wing student organizations. Morris U. Schappes, an English tutor at City College and the acknowledged leader of the CCNY Party unit, was, as he recalls, "the most conspicuous, the most vociferous, the most open," Communist on campus. He helped organize CCNY's Anti-Fascist Association and its teachers union; he sold Party literature to his colleagues; he organized demonstrations and spoke at them—this despite a pronounced stutter. In addition, he was one of the few academics to have a Party career outside the university, serving first as the Educational Director for the Party's section on the lower West Side of Manhattan and later in a similar capacity for the entire state. Schappes was so absorbed in politics at this time that, as one apparently true story goes, he once noticed a sign on a wagon advertising "Free Firewood" and wanted to know who "Firewood" was. Howard Selsam was similarly active at Brooklyn College. Probably the most well-known academic Communist during this period was Granville Hicks who, as a regular contributor to the *New Masses*, was the Party's main literary guru. Perhaps because he left academic life and became a freelance writer after he lost his job at Rensselaer Polytechnic Institute, Hicks had no hesitations about publicizing his own involvement with the CP or his final break with it in 1939. On the whole, the more politically active a Communist professor was, the more likely it was that he or she would be publicly identified with the Party.[38]

Though many of these academics, whether known to be Communists or not, were ambivalent about the Party's insistence on secrecy, they were almost unanimous in refusing to use their classrooms for purposes of indoctrination. Openly recruiting students was considered beyond the pale and Communist teachers generally tried not to let their political views affect their teaching. This was as much the case in genteel Cambridge, where, Robert Gorham Davis explained, "we had a lurking feeling that it wasn't quite good sportsmanship to try to influence young people—at least to make use of our position in the classroom to do this," as it was at the more proletarian CCNY, where the faculty unit actually rebuked one of its members who had boasted about how he had managed to insinuate Marxist terminology into his lectures. In part, these people refrained from bringing their politics into class out of the understandable desire to avoid the kind of trouble that would probably ensue if the administration caught them trying to convert their students. Security was an important consideration, as the following testimony from a friendly witness reveals.

> If a teacher is going to be promulgating in his class the Communist Party line day after day, in most cases it would become a little too obvious that he was teaching the Communist Party line and not teaching his subject, which would be the same as exposing himself and branding him.[39]

Professionalism as well as prudence encouraged these people to separate their politics from their teaching. They were, after all, highly trained scholars who, despite their radicalism, shared their colleagues' commitment to the standards of their calling, in particular its concern with objectivity and fairness. They believed that it was unprofessional to use the classroom for other than educational purposes. "I have never," declared the former CCNY history professor Philip Foner, "made any effort whatsoever to impose my point of view on my students. There has always been full freedom of discussion in my classes." Howard Selsam also maintained that he had always tried to be "extremely fair and objective." Other professors actually prided themselves on presenting their material in such a neutral fashion that their students could not tell what their politics were. Robert Gorham Davis claimed that during the height of his involvement with the Party "a politically conscious student came up to me at the end of the year and said he had been trying to figure out just what my position was." And the testimony of other students, both at the time and later, reveals that even the most well-known radicals were "very businesslike" and "effective."[40]

Precisely because these teachers were so politically active, their classes were scrutinized far more carefully than those of other faculty members. The chairman of CCNY's English Department actually sat in on Schappes's classes; his students were no less vigilant. One of them, a science major, recalls how he "suffered through" a poetry course with Schappes in which he "carefully listened to the teacher to see whether he would propagandize us. I remember no such effort." Columbia also seemed to have been sensitive about its left-wing faculty members and apparently even monitored their classes on occasion, in large part to ward off complaints from outside the University. Thus, when the Sociology Department received "one or two complaints" about the political activities of Bernhard Stern that "gave a little worry to the authorities," the chairman "looked into the matter at that time and found . . . there was nothing to justify the suggestion that he was using his classes for propaganda purposes." A similar investigation of the Columbia anthropologist Gene Weltfish returned a similar verdict.[41]

*   *   *

Perhaps the most telling evidence for the fairness and lack of bias on the part of these allegedly Communist teachers was that produced during the McCarthy period, when more than a hundred people were dismissed or threatened with dismissal for political reasons. Had the college and university administrators who sought these dismissals possessed any information that the teachers they were trying to oust had proselytized in class, they certainly would have produced it. But they had none. The most damaging evidence about undue influence on students that any administration could dredge up came from New York University where, it was alleged, the left-wing student leaders enrolled in Professor Edwin Berry Burgum's literature courses. Elsewhere the academic authorities did not even charge teachers with having misused their classrooms. Thus, despite all the Cold War rhetoric about Communist teachers indoctrinating their students, there is no evidence that they did. If anything, the opposite seems to have been the case. In the early thirties, before there were any organized units on the campus, students actually recruited teachers into the Party. This is what happened to Howard Selsam at Brooklyn College and to Bella Dodd at Hunter. Significantly, those faculty members who seem to have been most influential among the radical students of the late thirties were not Communists, but men like Robert Oppenheimer at Berkeley, Franz Boas at Columbia, and F. O. Matthiessen at Harvard whose impact on their students came from their brilliance and charisma as teachers, not their political views.[42]

Even though Communist professors generally refrained from outright proselytizing in class, this does not mean that their political beliefs did not influence their academic work. Naturally, scientists—and probably close to half of the academic Communists were scientists—had no problem keeping their politics separate from their scholarship. People in other fields, however, sometimes taught their courses from what they considered to be a Marxist perspective. Some, like the Brooklyn philosopher Howard Selsam, even taught Marxism. Taught, not indoctrinated. The distinction is important, for whatever the intellectual quality of the Marxism these teachers purveyed, they all struggled to present it in an unbiased way. Many went out of their way to let their students know that they were Marxists, if not Communists. Though Daniel Boorstin kept his office mate in the dark about his political affiliation, he invited at least one of his undergraduate tutees in for tea and, as that former Harvard student recalls, "told me that he thought I ought to know he was a member of the Communist Party and that I should be alert for any bias that might result." Herbert Phillips, a philosopher at the University of Washington, routinely told his classes that he was a Marxist and warned them to take that fact into account in assessing his lectures. When Barrows Dunham dealt with the *Communist Manifesto* in his social ethics course, a former student recalls, "he didn't conceal that he thought it was applicable and useful and wise."[43]

Understandably, student leftists gravitated into these professors' classes—sometimes because they wanted to learn about Marxism, sometimes because they thought, incorrectly it usually turned out, that their radicalism would earn them good grades, and often because these professors were considered the most exciting teachers on campus. Most of these teachers, for all their own personal radicalism, limited their contacts with left-wing students to the classroom. Some, however, did not and, though they seemed to be scrupulous about avoiding favoritism in their classes, did establish extracurricular political ties with the student left. Faculty activists like Morris Schappes, for example, had "a good deal of personal contact" with their student counterparts, but in an informal, not an organized way. Professors would help student groups with money and advice (not always appreciated); students would provide the "body count" for picket lines and demonstrations. Sometimes Communist professors served as political mentors for left-wing undergraduates. This was especially the case in the early thirties when there were few Communists on campus—students or teachers. At Columbia, as a former Communist student recalls, two young economists, Addison T. Cutler and Donald Henderson

> were the voluntary and unofficial faculty advisors to the still small communist set on the campus. . . . They did influence young men, including me; to some of us they were the major faculty personalities of the era, and the bull sessions we had with them off the campus, amid beer-drinking and the singing of revolutionary anthems, had probably greater impact than anything said in the classrooms.

Sometimes these contacts were more scholarly. In 1936, the classicist A. D. Winspear, then a visiting professor at Swarthmore, started a Marxist study group for his undergraduate followers. Were such activities indoctrination? Perhaps, but they were also the same kind of off-campus socializing that like-minded students and teachers had always indulged in.[44]

Most Communist professors, of course, had no political contact with their students. They had other things to do. If nothing else, belonging to the Party took a lot of time. There were meetings, study groups, fund-raisers, and demonstrations—in short all the kinds of day-to-day organizational work that any community or political group, from the PTA to the peace movement, expects of its members. One former CCNY professor recalls that, during the height of his involvement with the CP, he went to twenty-seven meetings in one week. Naturally, few people could sustain such a level of commitment for long. The most active students ran the risk of flunking out of school; their professors discovered that Party work was interfering with their research, if not necessarily with their teaching. "The activity of the Communist Party unit," another former CCNY professor concluded, "certainly did not permit the members of that unit to devote themselves adequately to their work as scholars. . . . I was robbed of time that I could otherwise have devoted to research."[45]

Different units had different expectations. It is clear that the one at CCNY was particularly militant. People who belonged to the graduate student unit at Columbia during the late thirties, for example, recall that the Party was rather solicitous of their studies and did not make heavy demands on their time. Individuals differed as well. What for one person may have been a normal level of activity might have been a considerable burden for another. People like Morris Schappes probably gave as much time and energy to Party work as a full-time cadre would. Others were part-time members at best; one MIT teacher told HUAC that he had missed as many meetings of his unit as he had attended. Most academic Communists were probably somewhere in between; they joined the Party in response to a specific problem or set of problems and remained active only as long as those problems seemed important to them or as long as the Party seemed to be dealing effectively with them. When they left the CP, which they all ultimately did, the reason for many was not any specific disagreement with the Party but simply that they could no longer spare the time.[46]

It is hard to tell in what ways academic Communists differed from the rest of the CP rank and file. What we know about ordinary Party members elsewhere suggests that, at least in certain areas, the academic units had a lot of autonomy—more autonomy, in fact, than the Party was reputed to offer. There were a number of reasons for this. In the first place the CP had never been eager to recruit professors. It wanted workers; its leaders and field organizers spent much more time and energy trying to develop Party units within blue-collar communities than they did on campus. In addition, the academic units needed little help. Their members already possessed many of the essentially middle-class skills that good Communists required. They knew how to write leaflets, run meetings, and analyze current events. Above all, they could be counted on to take care of their own educations and run their own study groups. They did not need to have someone from the Party bureaucracy come in to give them the latest line. As intellectuals, they were able to develop it on their own. The CP's resources were not inexhaustible, and because the academic Communists did not *need* much direction, they did not get it. "We made our own decisions," a former Harvard Communist admitted. "I cannot recall of any directive coming down." Granville Hicks agreed. "We all felt free, within fairly large limits, to disagree with party functionaries."[47]

Nonetheless, there were limits. Party functionaries did keep tabs on the academic units, probably more vigilantly in New York than elsewhere. And in every unit there was the realization that ultimately its members would have to accept Party decisions on major political matters, if not always on the more routine aspects of their daily personal and professional lives. That most academic Communists may well have agreed with most of those decisions does not negate the fact that these men and women, in the name of Party discipline, were able to accommodate themselves to highly undemocratic decision-making procedures. Moreover, the situation changed over time. By the late forties and fifties, when the Party itself was becoming more rigid and doctrinaire, it put its dwindling academic units on a shorter leash. But even then, many academics recall, there was little discipline. Courtney Cazden, who was active in Urbana, Illinois, in the early Cold War years, claims that she could "never remember any situation in which we were told what to do, what to think, given a line and told to carry it out." Here, as with so many other aspects of Party life, the amount of direction from the central bureaucracy varied over time and from one campus to another.[48]

The kinds of activities each unit indulged in varied as well. Some, like CCNY's, were more action-oriented than others. Not surprisingly, most academic units spent a lot of time reading and discussing Marxist texts. During the late thirties, Harvard's undergraduate Communists used to collect in the basement of one of the University's buildings to read Lenin's *State and Revolution* together. The faculty Communists were equally intellectual. One member recalls Party meetings as "more or less in the nature of a college bull session." Another, the biologist Marcus Singer, characterized the unit as "an intellectual group which liked to argue and discuss" and talk about "what you might call heavy stuff." Meetings were like seminars:

> We read individual books. We would take chapters for example in Karl Marx' book or in Engels' works for example, and I remember clearly, since I was very interested in it, the *Dialectics of Nature* which had a scientific application. We would take a chapter or two chapters. Each one would have a turn and he would lead the discussion within the group and there would be argument and debate and so on on the application and nature of the substance of these chapters.

The graduate student branch at Columbia also functioned as a seminar at times. Its members worked at "trying to explain their own work from a Marxist point of view." Graduate students at the University of Iowa actually presented papers at Party meetings. Even the CCNY Communists, who belonged to what was probably the most disciplined and militant academic unit in the country, wrestled with the problems involved in integrating Marxism into their own particular disciplines and did so on what appears to have been a highly theoretical level.[49]

Though nobody joined the Party in order to read and talk, few are the academic ex-Communists who did not describe the intellectual side of Party life as lively, if not, as one man recalled, "the best part of it all." There was always a lot of talk. Philip Morrison remembered discussions about "everything under the sun." Robert Rutman, a biologist who joined the CP at Berkeley after the war, recalls that within meetings of the Communist Party group there may have been discussions ranging from political topics to topics of the most recent novel, the most recent discovery in science, the general problems of philosophy, the need for encouraging community endeavor of some kind; the scope and range is, as far as I would know, greater in the Communist Party. Its interests are wider.

For many academics, otherwise disenchanted with the Party, the magic of those discussions, with their intensity, breadth, and sheer intellectuality, still lingers. "I once attended an all-night bull session which included, beside myself, a physical chemist, a physicist, and an astronomer," an ex-Communist chemist from CCNY reminisced:

> I sat silently enthralled at the spectacle of extremely bright minds playing with ideas. The subject? What is the relationship between measurements and truth? . . . I have never witnessed such a brilliance of intellect, thirst for knowledge, and quickness of understanding in a group of people before or after this period of my life. I have mourned the loss.

Other academic ex-Communists assimilated the intellectual ferment of their years in the CP directly into their own teaching and research. Marxism was important here, but even more so was the sense of commitment that the Party gave its members, the feeling that, as the historian Richard Schlatter put it, "the academy is lifeless and pedantic unless it remains in touch with the great moral issues of the outside world." Schlatter credits his experience in the CP with having forced him "to uncover his own assumptions" and "look at them critically."[50]

Being a Communist had its more prosaic aspects as well. Party members were expected to sell Party literature and push Party causes in the wider community. "You might be asked," Robert Rutman recalled, "to undertake to sell tickets to a rally. That would be in the nature of an assignment. You did your best on it. It wasn't an order to sell tickets, but the necessity of building that event was stressed." This type of Party work created conflicts for a lot of academics who feared that someone might recognize them as they peddled leaflets from door to door or tried to collect signatures on Communist Party nominating petitions. Some people liked this type of work. There were a number of City College activists who prided themselves on their militance and their willingness to sell subscriptions to the *Daily Worker* in Harlem. Barrows Dunham was also willing to sell the *Worker* but, because his students came from all over Philadelphia, the other members of his Party unit were reluctant to let him expose himself in that way. Like Dunham, some academics enjoyed the contacts with ordinary people that the more routine Party tasks offered; others did not. Given batches of pamphlets to distribute and tickets to sell, more than one academic simply paid for the materials himself rather than try to push them on his friends or acquaintances. A California professor describes what happened:

We were supposed to get rid of copies of such things as transcripts of the Moscow trials. We would be assigned two or three copies and told to go out and sell those and bring back the money. In some cases people would be afraid to do that sort of thing, so they would merely bring back the money and dispose of the literature somewhere else.

Sigmund Diamond recalls that the people in his unit at Johns Hopkins dealt with the problem by "distributing literature at night," in other words leaving the tell-tale pamphlets on people's doorsteps.[51]

A lot of fund-raising went on. There were dues, of course. Assessed at a percentage of each person's salary, they were not heavy. As a graduate student at Berkeley in the 1930s, Philip Morrison paid twenty-five cents a month; as a faculty member in Philadelphia ten years later, Robert Rutman gave ten dollars a month. Other people paid no regular dues but, like the members of Bernhard Stern's tiny group of Communist intellectuals, made "token contributions." There were numerous special levies as well, some for the Party itself and its perennially debt-ridden newspaper, others for the many outside causes that CP people backed. For Marcus Singer, among others, these constant solicitations got to be "irksome." People even began to tire of what one former Columbia graduate student remembers as an endless round of fund-raising parties. There were always tickets to sell, benefits to attend. During the late thirties, most of them were for Spain. Harvard students and teachers bought an ambulance for the Loyalists from the proceeds of their fund-raising concerts, lectures, and dance recitals. In New York, a mass meeting where the Hunter College activist and later Party functionary Bella Dodd spoke produced over $12,000. Elsewhere, there were clothing drives, white elephant sales, and cocktail parties. Frank Oppenheimer even gave a flute concert for the Spanish Republic.[52]

Like people in other units, academics were supposed to supply manpower for demonstrations. "We were always in a picket line," one former CCNY instructor recollected. There were left-wing unions to support, German battleships to protest, and May Day parades to march in, suitably attired, as many New York teachers were, in their academic caps and gowns. In California, people joined picket lines for striking farm workers or for Harry Bridges's longshoremen's union; in New York, they helped Mike Quill's Transport Workers' Union; and in Chicago, they supported the strikers at Republic Steel. Because of the risk of exposure, not to mention arrest, faculty members were sometimes more reluctant to participate in such demonstrations than students were. Here again, there were differences. The CCNY unit apparently expected more of this type of activity. And there were always a few individual academics who gravitated toward such visible political work. The economist Horace Bancroft Davis got picked up by the police while distributing leaflets at a small Massachusetts town near the college where he taught in the middle thirties.[53]

Davis was also quite active as a speaker at meetings and demonstrations. This was an area in which the professional skills of college teachers were extremely useful to the CP. Davis recalls that he became something of a fixture at anti-war rallies around Boston during the Nazi-Soviet Pact period because he "was looked on as someone who would present the Communist Party's point of view." Granville Hicks, who was an even more public Communist when he was teaching at Harvard in the late thirties, often spoke two or three times a week. And Brooklyn College professor Frederick Ewen recalls that he "spoke all the time" to student groups, temple sisterhoods, any organization that would give him an audience.[54]

Academic Communists were also in demand as teachers. Members of the Harvard unit got requests to lead study groups for rank and file people in the neighboring industrial towns of Revere and Chelsea. The future Nobel laureate Lawrence Klein taught economics to a small group in Chicago. Besides these informal sessions, academics also taught regular courses at the various Party and labor schools that sprang up in the thirties and forties. George Mayberry, a part-time instructor in the Harvard English Department, offered "a very innocuous course on modern American literature" at the Boston Central Labor School; so, too, did Robert Gorham Davis. Another member of their unit, the philosopher William Parry, actually became the school's director after he lost his job at Harvard. Though these schools had been founded originally to give Party members a basic grounding in Marxism-Leninism, many of them later developed a broader constituency and began to offer courses on everything from dialectical materialism to guitar playing. By the late 1940s, New York's Jefferson School of Social Science, an offshoot of the earlier School for Democracy which was founded to provide employment for the New York City municipal college teachers who lost their jobs after the Rapp-Coudert investigations in 1941, had almost five thousand students.[55]

The Party also made use of its academic members' literary talents. They wrote leaflets, articles for the *Daily Worker* and *New Masses*, and, in the schools where the units were large enough to make such an activity feasible, shop papers. These papers, like the CCNY *Teacher-Worker* and the Brooklyn College *Staff*, came out monthly during the late thirties and were put into the mail boxes of every staff member at the school. They covered local college issues as well as national and international ones, thus providing an unusual mélange of information about fascist atrocities in Spain and complaints about tenure practices and the lack of water fountains on campus. They also, of course, urged their readers to join the Communist Party. Because they were anonymously written and often contained personal attacks on administrators and other professors, these shop papers did not always endear the faculty Communists to their colleagues; in fact, long after they had ceased publication, the supposed scurrilousness of the *Staff* and *Teacher-Worker* was invoked by anti-

Communist polemicists as evidence that Party members were unfit to teach. Certainly, as some of these papers' editors and contributors were later to admit, they were somewhat lacking in gentility as well as embarrassingly uncritical about the Soviet Union, but they were, nonetheless, the authentic voice of a politically significant segment of the academic community. They were also, apparently, fun to read.[56]

A somewhat more sedate and longer-lived publishing venture was the journal *Science & Society*. Established in 1936 by a group of Cambridge and New York-based academics, it was intended, one of its founders claimed, as a "forum where Marxists and non-Marxists of good will could argue the case for and against, footnotes in hand, over the entire range of scholarship, from science and philosophy to history and linguistics." Many of its editors—among whom were William Parry, Howard Selsam, Margaret Schlauch, Edwin Berry Burgum, Bernhard Stern, and Dirk Struik—were certainly in or near the Party, but they prided themselves on keeping their magazine "wholly free from guidance or dictation from any quarter." And, for the most part, they do seem to have kept the CP at a distance. When, in the 1950s, some of the Party's functionaries approached *Science & Society* with the suggestion that it deal sympathetically with Lysenko's genetic theories, they were flatly rejected. How independent the magazine actually was is hard to tell; it presented itself as the main American vehicle for serious Marxist scholarship at a time when most academic Marxists belonged to the CP. Assessing the quality of their scholarship is also difficult, especially without a major review of the work of Communist and near-Communist scholars in dozens of fields and a systematic comparison of that work with the mainstream scholarship in those fields. Until that basic research on the left intellectual universe (and not merely its literary coteries) is done, any judgment about the value of Marxist scholarship of the thirties and forties is of necessity preliminary. My own sense is that the men and women who published in *Science & Society* were seriously engaged in offering a critical perspective on their various disciplines. They did not always succeed. When they dealt with Russia, for example, their blinders were obvious. Yet, much of their work, though occasionally doctrinaire and flawed in other respects, was quite solid and pointed in some of the directions later scholars would find fruitful.[57]

Academic Communists, though the most formidably organized activists on each campus, had no monopoly over the progressive causes of the 1930s and 1940s. As a result they often found themselves working with, and often for, non-Communist groups and individuals. The organizations they supported—the "front groups," as they were later called—differed from the Party in that they usually focussed on a single issue like peace, civil liberties, or aid to the Spanish Republic. To what extent these groups were, as they were alleged to be, dominated by the CP is unclear. Certainly, Communists were active in them, often in important leadership or staff positions. The Party encouraged such activities. "Everyone," Stanley Moore explained, "was supposed to participate in some larger outside group." But most of the Communist academics who joined such groups probably did so because they were concerned about the issues that the organization claimed to address, not because Stalin told them to. Once they joined an outside group, it is true, Party members often organized themselves into what was called a fraction, meeting separately so that they could coordinate their work and obtain influence within the organization. Such behavior could and often did become manipulative, especially when the Party people tried to get the organization to take positions on issues that were often unrelated to the group's original mission. The existence of such fractions was no secret, though their membership usually was. Even so, until the Nazi-Soviet Pact destroyed the Popular Front, the non-Communists in these organizations were usually willing to overlook the CP's shenanigans in order to have their group benefit from the efforts of so many effective and dedicated political activists.[58]

For academic Communists, the most important organization of this type was the Teachers Union. Almost everybody belonged. One former CCNY Party member recalled that it was "mandatory" for every member of his unit. Even without the pressure, however, most of them would have joined, for the Teachers Union gave these left-wing intellectuals an organizational link with the working class—a group which, like most 1930s' radicals, they tended to romanticize. Organizing a union was thus an important symbolic act which would, in the words of the Harvard Teachers Union's statement of purpose, "reduce the segregation of teachers from the rest of the workers who constitute the great mass of the community." Of course, the union addressed real economic grievances as well. And, where it did so, it had considerable success.[59]

A teachers' union affiliated with the AF of L had been in existence since the First World War, when a group of socialist teachers founded the American Federation of Teachers in order to combat the harassment that their anti-war politics subjected them to. Throughout the twenties, which was not a fertile period for the labor movement in general, the fledgling union remained tiny and riven by internal battles between its Communist members and its socialist ones. Academics, as individuals, had been active from the start. Scott Nearing was the national president for a short time during the 1920s; and professors, with their presumably greater prestige, were to preside over the AFT for most of the thirties. But although there seems to have been a local at the University of Wisconsin as early as 1930 it was not until the middle of the decade that college teachers began to unionize seriously.[60]

We know the most about what happened in New York City where, during the early thirties, low pay, the lack of job security, and the indifference of senior faculty members impelled the lowest ranking teachers at the municipal colleges to form their own organizations. These groups—the Hunter College Instructors Association, the Instructional Staff Association at CCNY, and the Association of Tutors, Fellows, and Instructors at Brooklyn College—were not very effective in raising salaries or getting tenure for their members. The CCNY organization was, as one of its former members recalls, "even less than a company union"; its leaders were "a pussyfooting bunch who were apparently determined to prevent the ISA from doing anything which the administration would frown on." By the mid-thirties, however, the labor movement had begun to grow and the more militant members of these instructors' groups—many, but by no means all, Communists or Communists-to-be—decided to affiliate with organized labor. In 1935 they founded a separate college teachers' local, Local 537, within the New York AFT. By 1939 it had over 400 members (one former president claimed 1000) and chapters at Hunter, Queens, CCNY, Brooklyn, Sarah Lawrence, Adelphi, and NYU. There were AFT locals outside New York as well. Wisconsin's Local 223 had 127 members in 1937; the Cambridge Teachers Union, founded in 1935 by F. O. Matthiessen, had about 150. There were active chapters at the University of Washington, Berkeley, Cornell, Smith and, presumably, many other schools as well.[61]

Though a few academic notables like Matthiessen at Harvard and Oppenheimer at Berkeley were active in the union, most of its members were junior people, the underpaid, insecure tutors, fellows, and instructors who did most of the teaching at schools like CCNY and Brooklyn College. At Wisconsin, for example, 89 members of the 127-person local were below the rank of assistant professor; 56 of them were teaching assistants. Understandably, therefore, union locals concentrated on traditional bread-and-butter issues: better pay, better working conditions, and more regular terms of employment. They had some success. To begin with, their grievances were real and affected large numbers of non-union teachers. In addition, they were extremely well organized. Because they could mobilize outsiders as well as academics, and even, when necessary, mount a full-scale political campaign, these union locals actually forced their institutions to implement some much-needed reforms. At many places these reforms came about in response to union-orchestrated protests against the firing or non-reappointment of teacher activists. Thus, for example, when in the spring of 1936 the chairman of CCNY's English Department refused to reappoint Morris Schappes, even though he had taught for eight years, the TU organized such a fuss that the Board of Education not only reinstated Schappes but also created a regular tenure system. Similar reforms followed a controversy at Harvard after the Economics Department denied tenure to two union activists, Raymond Walsh and Alan Sweezy.[62]

Schappes, of course, was a Communist, but neither Walsh nor Sweezy were. And it is not entirely clear exactly how much control the Party fractions wielded within the union. There is no question, however, that the CP was heavily involved. Party meetings at schools like CCNY and Brooklyn College were often devoted to union business. "We would discuss the Teachers' Union," a former Brooklyn College communist explained. "There was a part of the agenda set aside for the Teachers' Union. We were to discuss things that were coming up in the union. We would discuss candidates for office in the union." Things were no different at Harvard, where Party meetings also dealt with union matters, though in Cambridge, at least, the CP did not dominate the union quite as fully as it did in New York, where by the late thirties the memberships of both organizations were essentially the same. Nationally, the Party's control over the union was less secure, and throughout the thirties factional fighting was intense. Both sides—Communist and anti-Communist—organized and politicked heavily at state and national conventions and within the labor movement as well. For most of the decade, the CP and its allies were in control. But after the Nazi-Soviet Pact scuttled the Popular Front the Party's influence within the union melted away. The New York college teachers' local was expelled from the national AFT. In Cambridge, a conflict over a token contribution to the anti-war Student Union literally destroyed the Teachers Union by exposing the rift between its anti-fascist liberals and their formerly anti-fascist Communist allies.[63]

That the Nazi-Soviet Pact destroyed the Popular Front is common knowledge; that it did not destroy the Communist Party is not. Recent scholarship has been chipping away at the notion that the Pact produced massive defections. But even among otherwise knowledgeable historians the myth persists that intellectuals left the Party in droves. They did not; certainly, the academics I studied did not. A few people quit, it is true, but as far as I can tell no more than five or six did, and most of them were friends of Granville Hicks, whose highly publicized departure may well account for the myth of the intellectuals' defection. Hicks's was a special case. His open identification with the Party deprived him of the opportunity—available to less well-known Communists—to readjust his position slowly and in private. As he explained in the *New Republic* in October 1939: "If the party had left any room for doubt, I could go along with it . . . . But they made it clear that if I eventually found it impossible to defend the pact, and defend it on their terms, there was nothing for me to do but resign."[64]

A few of Hicks's former Harvard colleagues, Daniel Boorstin, Robert Gorham Davis, and Richard Schlatter, followed him out of the Party as they had followed him in. Their resignations may have been unique, based in large part on their closeness to Hicks and, in Davis's case at least, on a growing disaffection with the Party's rigidity and adulation of Stalin. Later on a few other academics claimed that they, too, left the CP because of their disillusionment with the Pact. But the testimony of these people may be suspect. One, William Canning, was to provide a New York State legislative committee with most of its evidence against his former comrades at CCNY. Though he testified that he had quit the

Party soon after the Pact, other members of his unit recalled seeing him at meetings many months later.[65]

It would be a mistake to assume that simply because most academic Communists did not forsake the Party in 1939 the Nazi-Soviet Pact did not upset them. They were not, however, particularly concerned about the content of the agreement. Although they had joined the Party in order to oppose Hitler, they—and a lot of non-Communists as well—could understand why Stalin felt he had to make a deal. "It was," Lawrence Arguimbau explained, "a matter of expediency." Even people who left the Party at the time were not unsympathetic to the Russian move. "I was not convinced then, and am not now," Richard Schlatter maintained, "that the Nazi-Soviet Pact was wicked. The Western powers had made a pact with Hitler at Munich and were apparently hoping that Germany would attack Russia. Why should the Russians not try to turn the tables?"

What bothered Schlatter and prompted his exodus from the CP was the suddenness of the Pact and the speed and enthusiasm with which the American Communist Party changed its line: "From one day to the next Roosevelt and Churchill were transformed from the saviors of peace and civilization to devilish warmongers." Schlatter was not alone in his dismay. This switch bothered a lot of academics who, unlike Schlatter, stayed in the Party. "It was not very palatable to us," a former Columbia graduate student recalled, "but we accepted it." For Barrows Dunham, the Pact "was extremely puzzling. And . . . I was as puzzled as anybody." Later on, Dunham recognized that the Pact and, in particular, the Party's instantaneous accommodation to it was the first blow to the moral legitimacy that the CP had acquired during the late thirties. But at the time, Dunham swallowed his doubts and continued to work for Party causes.[66]

There were a lot of reasons why Dunham and so many other academics were able to accommodate themselves to the CP's new line. Some apparently agreed with it; they were loyal Communists and were willing to go along with whatever policy the Party adopted. Others were more ambivalent, but were not yet ready to break with an organization to which they were still so committed. For some of these people, the Party's new emphasis on peace struck a responsive chord with their own earlier pacifism. In the aftermath of the Pact, the Party, which had abandoned the anti-war movement in favor of collective security in 1935, returned to the cause of peace. Anti-fascist organizations disappeared and anti-war ones sprang up once again. For a whole generation of radicals, both in the CP and outside of it, who had grown up believing that the First World War was a mistake and had been politically socialized by taking the Oxford Pledge and joining student peace strikes, it was possible to argue against American intervention and even against aid to England. It was possible, but it was not easy. The historian Henry F. May, then a graduate student at Harvard, describes how, despite his "inner turmoil," he could align himself with both Communists and America Firsters in opposing the war:

> In long arguments with my friends and still longer ones with myself, I persuaded myself of the truth of the following specific propositions:
>   That the Soviet-Nazi Pact was a brilliant coup for peace, once one really understood it.
>   That the war was phony and that . . . Goering was in contact with British imperial and conservative elements.
>   That in the long run British imperialism and American capitalism were an even more serious menace to the world than Hitler.
>   As I have said, I was more active in support of these positions than I ever had been in support of the earlier easier ones. Part of the reason was that I needed to be, in order to persuade myself against my better judgment.

That it was possible for a radical, but not a Communist, academic like Henry May to support the CP's position during the Nazi-Soviet Pact period makes it easier to understand why, despite their growing discomfort, most academic Communists stayed in the Party. Less than two years later, Hitler's invasion of the Soviet Union saved them from what one former Communist recalled as

> the—to me—acutely embarrassing experience of telling people that the Soviet Union was justified in invading Finland in 1940, that the war between France and England on the one hand, and Germany on the other, was an "imperialist war," and that it didn't matter who won.[67]

Surprisingly, many more academics left the Party during the war when the United States and Russia were allies and the briefly revived Popular Front was flourishing. Their departure was not a dramatic gesture, nor even a repudiation of Party policy. The CP had become patriotic and was insisting that the main task of any Communist was to win the war. Philip Morrison, who was teaching at the University of Illinois when the war began, described how his unit disbanded:

> After Pearl Harbor we were still meeting with a small group in 1941. It was represented to us that the most important task the members of the Communist Party could have was to assist the war effort and nothing should come ahead of that. . . . There was no intention to have people leave the Communist Party in any way, but they simply said that if you are going to teach people in an accelerated program and do research you should not spend time discussing politics.

In other words, war work was Party work. And when people left the campuses where their units were, whether for military service or, as Morrison did, to join the Manhattan Project and work on the bomb, they simply dropped out of the CP. Many, like Morrison, never returned.[68]

Of course, people were always leaving the Party. Even before the pact there were defections in academe. Some people left involuntarily.

Mark Graubard, a Columbia biologist, weathered several months of Party trials before his expulsion for "Belittling Party Authority." The Russian scholar Rufus Mathewson was expelled from the YCL during his sophomore year at Harvard for "bohemianism" and "tailism," the latter a Party epithet for public rowdiness. Mathewson remained close to the CP, nonetheless, and continued to defend Soviet foreign policy throughout the phony war period. Not every ex-Communist academic shared Mathewson's equanimity about his party experiences. Some were quite bitter. Bernard Grebanier, an English professor at Brooklyn College, felt that he had been recruited into "a band of conspirators" for whom "lying and treachery and so forth was a regular tool in getting people into the Party." When, after three years, Grebanier finally extricated himself, he circulated a twenty-five-page letter denouncing his former colleagues. People at other schools were similarly disillusioned. "Relentless academic ideologues," was the way one former City College Communist described the members of his unit. Robert Gorham Davis was equally critical of the doctrinaire types he encountered in the Party at Harvard. But such bitterness was unusual. Most of the academics who left the CP before the Cold War set in did so for personal, rather than ideological, reasons. Harry Marks's departure in 1937 was typical, though early. But then, Marks had joined the CP in 1933 and had been active during the riskier, pre-Popular Front days. By 1937 he was pretty much burned out. In addition, his wife disliked his Party work and he had a dissertation to write. Though he did not formally break with the CP, he became increasingly less active, and by the time he left Cambridge for a teaching job in New York in 1939 he no longer considered himself a Communist.[69]

Just as it often took academics years to decide to join the CP, it took them just as long to ease themselves out of it. They followed the route Marks pioneered, reducing their level of activity, going to fewer meetings, and, finally, taking advantage of a move to let their membership lapse. The wartime dislocations made this whole process easier. Because Communists who joined the armed forces were supposed to sever their ties with the Party, many of these people had an opportunity to rethink their political commitments. The doubts that the Nazi-Soviet Pact initiated began to surface, exacerbated by the Party's subsequent policy shifts and the rapidity with which its leaders first endorsed and then repudiated Earl Browder's wartime collaboration with capitalism. At the same time, these people's lives were changing. They were growing older, beginning families, becoming settled in their careers. Many simply no longer had the time they once had for Party activities. And many no longer felt it was worth the effort. Not every academic Communist quit the Party during or immediately after the war. Some who had drifted away during the war joined up again in the late forties. Others, especially the younger men who were taking advantage of the GI Bill to go to graduate school, became politicized and either joined or rejoined the Party at that time. Henry Wallace's 1948 presidential campaign was to be their equivalent of the Spanish Civil War. But, as we shall see, they, too, eventually left the Party, usually for the same reasons.[70]

Leaving the Party did not mean leaving the left. Bernhard Stern, the Columbia sociologist, had never been an activist and had joined the Party primarily as a gesture of solidarity. When in 1942 it became clear that the Russians were going to defeat Hitler, he dropped out of the Party. His gesture of solidarity was no longer needed, and he felt that as a scholar he should not be a Communist. He remained a Marxist, however. So, too, did William Parry. While he was in the Army, from 1942 to 1945, Parry maintained what he recalled as a "somewhat informal and occasional" relationship with the CP. When he left the Army he considered rejoining the Party but decided against it for both ideological and personal reasons:

> There had been a shakeup in the leadership of the American Party. I had lost confidence in the American Party and also I was disturbed by some aspects of the Soviet policy . . . they didn't allow the Bulgarian Communists and the other Communists in eastern Europe to establish themselves in more autonomy. . . . Also I felt that the basic problem with the Party in the [United] States was that they looked too much towards Moscow. Instead of figuring out for themselves what to do they wanted to find out what Moscow thought they should do.

In addition, Parry had just gotten married and now had a child. He had family responsibilities and his career to think about: "I felt I had to decide between being an active Communist and being a teacher in an American University and I had chosen the latter and I had to live with it."[71]

Once the Cold War had ended the Party's effectiveness and legitimacy, many academics faced the same dilemma Parry did. Had the Party's mission seemed as important as it had been during the late 1930s, many of its academic members would not have resigned. As they later showed, when they refused to cooperate with the anti-Communist investigations of the 1950s, they were ready to make considerable sacrifices for something they believed in. But the Party was no longer that kind of a cause. "Most of us were more sophisticated, not so anxious," Philip Morrison explained. In addition, "so much of the world had changed. The Communist Party was just not that good an organization. We had been all over the world, people were scattered."

A few of the Berkeley physicists who had remained in the Party during the war describe it as "rather ineffective." By 1945 their unit had disbanded. "There was no point to it and nothing we could do." Similarly, Stanley Moore recalls that "most of" what his tiny Party group at Reed College did in the late forties "was a waste of time." Robert Rutman was similarly disillusioned:

I was primarily concerned with the solution of problems in this country first and foremost, and . . . one of the reasons I came to leave the Communist Party was because I felt that too much attention was directed to analysis of what goes on in the Soviet Union or in Czechoslovakia, and too little attention was directed to what I thought were the real problems here.

Rutman's disappointment was typical. For him, as for so many other academic Communists, the Party no longer seemed to be, if it had ever been, a useful vehicle for political action. Once they sensed the futility of the enterprise, these men and women began to disengage themselves from the CP.[72]

Few of these former Communists cite a specific incident that disillusioned them. Their disaffection was a cumulative process and one that depended on a combination of factors—developments in their own lives as well as in the international situation and in the Party itself. Sometimes these elements came together and precipitated a break. We have seen how Granville Hicks's friends followed him out of the CP after the Nazi-Soviet Pact. Similarly, Barrows Dunham's decision to leave the Party in 1945 was largely the result of his friendship with Samuel Adams Darcy, a leading Philadelphia Communist who was expelled from the CP for opposing Earl Browder's lack of militancy. As the Cold War intensified, the Party became more rigid. More and more of its academic members came to feel that, as one of them recalled, the CP "tended to push me around." Things began to sour. Robert Bellah, then a leader of the Harvard undergraduate unit, describes what happened to him:

> Somewhere in the spring or summer of '49 we began to get a lot of pressure from higher levels of the bureaucracy and inspection of people's views and lots of recrimination over things that had been said, sometimes months earlier. . . . There began to take place an inner Party purge of a very hard line sort.
>
> I remember being visited by a couple of members of what was called the Control Committee of the Boston party. They asked such things as, "Have you ever been hungry?" If your class background wasn't working class, as mine certainly wasn't, that was already suspect.
>
> So, in a period of increasing persecution from without, the party itself was engaged in a real intra-party witch-hunt. So I became, in effect, inactive in the fall of 1949. I don't think I was expelled, but . . .

Besides, more information about Russia had become available. The purges and gulags could not be ignored. It was no longer possible to dismiss Stalin's crimes with the explanation that such measures were needed to protect the Soviet Union.[73]

People had professional reasons for leaving the Party as well. Many academics experienced a conflict between the demands of their calling and those of the Party. Like Columbia sociologist Bernhard Stern, they doubted that scholarship and Communism could mix. Significantly, many of these people discovered that this conflict arose at the time they took their first teaching job. The political activities that they had indulged in as students no longer seemed appropriate for faculty members. David Hawkins dropped out of the Party two years after he began to teach at Berkeley, because, as he put it,

> I felt increasingly, as a member of the university community, as a political, I hoped, professor in philosophy, and as a person who wanted to live in the fuller sense of the word among my colleagues and students, that continued membership in the Communist Party would create a gap, and almost necessarily a duplicity.

At first, Hawkins hoped to resolve the conflict between his politics and his profession by joining a Party unit in San Francisco instead of in Berkeley:

> I believed it was possible to continue being in the Communist Party provided it did not become involved in my professional life. Later on I realized it could not be involved in my life in any way. I withdrew because I wanted to be able to stand for what I stand for and have no reservations or secrets about it.[74]

Most academics experienced the conflict on a less philosophical level. They no longer had time for Party work. Mark Nickerson had been an active Communist as a graduate student at Johns Hopkins in the early forties, but after he moved to the University of Utah in 1944 he began teaching full-time, directing a large research program, and going to medical school. "I didn't have much time left for political activity." As a result Nickerson began to drift away from the Party. "I went to fewer meetings," he recalled. "I think in one case I didn't go around at all for four or five months, and then I went again for a month, for one or two meetings." The Party's displeasure with Nickerson's spotty attendance hastened his final departure. He had no complaints about the Party's policies; it was "its lack of flexibility with respect to the time that an individual puts in political activities" that alienated him. Other people's priorities changed. As their careers became more important to them, they were no longer willing to meet the demands of what had become an increasingly irrelevant political movement. "I was tired of it," one man explained, "fed up with it, and I had to devote more time to my serious scholarly work." The biologist Marcus Singer gradually lost interest in left-wing politics altogether. "As I went along in my career," he recollected,

> I realized that my personal talents do not lie either in the direction of politics or in the direction of economics, that my talents lie particularly within my field, and so I devoted myself more and more to research and to my family which had started then and had grown.[75]

For Singer, as for most academics, leaving the Party was painless. Though some people outside the academy found the break traumatic, academics had no such problems. Since they had never lived in the self-enclosed left-wing world that so many other American Communists in-habited, their lives did not change when their politics did. They had another community to rely on, the academic one, into which they were already fairly well integrated by the time they left the CP. In addition, their separation from the Party was so gradual that few of them could give a specific date on which they stopped being Communists. The pro-cess often lasted for several years. Singer began his political "metamor-phosis" right after the war and did not finally become inactive until 1948. It took Mark Nickerson from 1944 until 1948 or 1949 to leave the Party. None of these people ever formally resigned. Instead, like Clement Markert, who had become disillusioned with the CP during the war, they "just drifted away." For many of these academics, the final break came when they moved to a new place. They simply made no effort to estab-lish contact with the local Communist organization. And the local Com-munists, who apparently knew that some of these people had been in the Party, made no effort to bring them back into the fold. After all, by the late forties, certainly by the early fifties, the Communist Party, which was becoming increasingly sectarian and obsessed with secrecy, was as unen-thusiastic about having college teachers as members as the teachers were about being members.[76]

In a perverse way, however, McCarthyism seemed to have kept some people in the Party longer than they would otherwise have stayed. A his-torian who had joined the CP after the Second World War because of his opposition to the Cold War found himself in a "well-meaning" but "in-effectual" organization about which he had serious reservations. "I would have left the party sooner," he recalls, "except that I wanted to be sure I wasn't doing so out of fear." The economic historian Robert Fogel was equally ambivalent. Though he was a full-time cadre during the fifties, he had begun to question the Party's intellectual validity. He thought about going to graduate school but, because he didn't want to be consid-ered "chicken," stayed on at his job and in the Party until Khrushchev revealed Stalin's crimes in 1956. There was, another former Communist recalls, a certain amount of "pride in not being opportunistic." But one person's opportunism was another's realism. And by the late forties and early fifties there were few, maybe a few dozen, academics still willing to incur the enormous personal and professional risks that remaining in the rigid and ineffectual Communist Party would have entailed. After 1956, of course, there were just about none.[77]

Neither dupes nor conspirators, the academics who passed through the American Communist Party during the 1930s and 1940s were a group of serious men and women who sincerely hoped to create a better world. They opposed Hitler, supported the Spanish Republicans, and struggled, as best they could, to build a movement for social change within the United States. That their opposition to fascism and commitment to social justice should take the form of joining the CP was a reflection of that brief moment in history when, because of the Depression and the rise of

Hitler, the Party could become relevant to American problems without abandoning its fealty to the Soviet Union. Earlier and later generations of left-wing academics did not become Communists and, as we have seen, when the Party lost its effectiveness and political appeal, just about all the academics who belonged to it quit. While they were in it, they did, it is true, follow the Party line; but they did so in large part because it was heading in the same direction they were. They did not let the Party interfere with their academic work and, in fact, consciously strove to keep their political activities separate from their scholarly ones. They participated in study groups, organized trade unions, marched in demonstrations, wrote pamphlets, and raised money, but they did not proselytize in class or try to subvert their universities. On the contrary, they were so anxious about protecting their academic careers that they concealed their membership in the Party. Later on, during the McCarthy period, the clandestine nature of their political affiliation was to cause them problems, but had they been more open about their Party membership they might have lost their jobs. For, as we shall see, even during the 1930s the academic community did not welcome members of the Communist Party.

III

"Conduct Unbecoming":
The Political Repression of
Academic Radicals, 1932–1942

Becoming a Communist, becoming a political radical of any type, was a risky business even during the Popular Front. Though the academy then tolerated more left-wing political activity than it did either earlier or later, it did not welcome it. Nor did radical teachers or students feel completely secure in their double commitment to scholarship and left-wing politics. They knew that were they to reveal themselves as Communists in public they might well be expelled or lose their jobs. There were enough dismissals during the 1930s to give substance to such fears. These firings represented a kind of academic background noise, the "normal" level, if one can use such a term, of political repression that tended to single out the academy's most outspoken and conspicuous radicals—the Scott Nearings whose political activities embarrassed their institutions. Such militants lost their jobs in the thirties, as they always had. Though many of them were or became Communists, it was their outspokenness, not as was later to be the case, their political affiliation that brought about their dismissals.

The career of Horace Bancroft Davis illustrates this. A congenital dissenter, Davis would probably have gotten into trouble even if he hadn't been in the Communist Party. A radical since his undergraduate days at Harvard in the early twenties, Davis joined the Party in 1931 and, since he never camouflaged his political views, drifted from one academic job to another. In 1936 he was dismissed from Bradford Junior College in the second year of a three-year contract. Not only had he been arrested while distributing leaflets in a nearby town, but he had caused a stir by asking the Bradford City Council to let the Communist Party use the City Hall for a public meeting. Neither Davis nor the college administration questioned the political nature of his dismissal and the clear violation of academic freedom that it involved. But instead of protesting, Davis found himself another job, this time as an instructor of economics at Simmons College, where he was to remain for six years. When he was fired in 1941 it was on the pretext, he recalls, that "I was not considered available for committee work and so they couldn't put me on tenure." Since Davis had been presenting the Communist Party's line against the war all over the Boston area, it seemed likely that his dismissal had some connection to his obviously embarrassing political activities. Again, Davis did not protest; he had no tenure. Besides, he had little desire to fight for what had by then become an uncongenial job. He decided, temporarily at least, to work outside the academy.[1]

To what extent Davis's experiences were typical for left-wing academics during the thirties, it is hard to tell. There may have been other, similarly junior and radical teachers whose dismissals never received public attention. The secrecy that shrouds so many academic decisions prevents us from knowing whether Davis's troubles were idiosyncratic or the tip of the proverbial iceberg. My hunch is that they were typical, but not very numerous for the simple reason that until the late thirties there were few radical teachers. Faculties were still apolitical, genteel, and essentially conservative; those men and women who were to embrace Communism later in the decade had either not yet begun to teach or else had not yet become radicalized. Moreover, few, if any, of them had tenure and like Davis may have decided to slip quietly into a new job rather than mount a public protest. Thus, for example, in 1936 when Barrows Dunham learned that the president of the Armstrong Cork Company had asked the president of Franklin and Marshall College to fire him for speaking out on the Spanish Civil War, Dunham decided to resign. He realized that, though the college administration had held firm, it might not do so again. Within a few months he had found himself what was actually a better job at Temple University. A desire to remain politically effective as well as to continue the teaching career that he loved dictated Dunham's pragmatic decision to avoid martyrdom.[2]

A few academics did let their dismissals escalate into protest movements. Most were teachers who were either public figures already or else had become involved with left-wing student activities. Because the restrictive political practices of an earlier day still prevailed on most campuses, the new student left of the early thirties often encountered considerable repression. At CCNY, for example, where a relatively large and militant group of student radicals confronted a particularly panicky and authoritarian administration, protests and demonstrations often resulted in dozens of expulsions and suspensions. There were similar incidents at other schools—Michigan, Berkeley, UCLA, Pittsburgh, and Columbia among them—though on a smaller scale. And it was clear that all faculty members who allied themselves with such activities would run similar risks. Few did, of course, for until the sixties most academics, most Communist academics even, avoided political contact with undergraduates. Prudence aside, they felt that faculty participation in student activities was unprofessional. Nonetheless, on a few campuses in the early thirties, where radical students were often the only political allies a left-wing instructor had, there were teachers who collaborated with the student left.[3]

Oakley Johnson had been teaching English at CCNY's evening session for a year and a half when, in the spring of 1932, he was asked to become the faculty adviser of the Liberal Club. Despite its innocuous name, the Liberal Club, and its day-session twin the Social Problems Club, formed the nucleus of the City College CP. It spawned the Communist-run National Student League and supplied the Communist Party with a whole generation of dedicated cadres. Johnson took his responsibilities as a faculty adviser seriously; he skirmished repeatedly with the administration as it sought to harass the Liberal Club by enforcing picayune regulations about speakers, leaflets, and publicity. Johnson, who had already announced that he would support the Communist Party in the 1932 elections, knew that his involvement with the student left was risky. In July, his chairman warned him about "the possibility that . . . schedules will be reduced or dropped." In September, Johnson learned that "no classes had been scheduled" for him. "It was none of my doing," the chairman supposedly told a student delegation. "The President crossed his name off, and said Johnson would have to go." There were protests, demonstrations, arrests, and suspensions, but Johnson was not reinstated.[4]

One of those arrested was Johnson's counterpart at Columbia, the radical economist Donald Henderson. More an activist than a scholar, Henderson was an intense and energetic organizer who, though himself no longer a student, helped build the National Student League and became its first executive secretary. Not only could he be always counted on to address a student demonstration or sign a protest letter, he even tried to unionize the workers at the Teachers College cafeteria. Henderson's classroom performance, to which he probably devoted little attention, may well have been mediocre. Certainly it did not compensate for the embarrassment his politics produced. At the end of 1932 he was informed by his chairman, the New Deal brain-truster Rexford Guy Tugwell, that he would not be reappointed. The usual student demonstrations and petitions followed, again to no avail. Henderson quit academic life, joined the labor movement, and eventually went on to head one of the left-wing unions (Food, Tobacco, and Agricultural Workers) that the CIO expelled in 1949.[5]

Both Johnson and Henderson were the most politically conspicuous teachers at their respective schools. So, too, was Granville Hicks, but in a different, primarily intellectual, way. He was the literary editor of the *New Masses* and, as such, was considered to be the nation's leading Communist man of letters. Even so, Hicks was no militant and, as an assistant professor of English at Rensselaer Polytechnic Institute, was, the AAUP later noted, "punctilious" about keeping "his economic and political views out of his classroom work." Nonetheless, his notoriety apparently cost him his job. On May 10, 1935, the administration informed him that

he would not be rehired for the following year because of "the immediate necessity for retrenchment." Hicks protested and, although he lacked
tenure, was able to get the AAUP to consider his charge that his politics
rather than the Institute's finances occasioned his dismissal. The AAUP,
in its cautious way, agreed. "It is difficult to avoid the inference that Professor Hicks would have been dealt with otherwise, but for his economic
and social beliefs." Except for a one-year stint that F. O. Matthiessen
arranged for him at Harvard in 1938, Hicks never taught again.[6]

None of these people had tenure, and it is possible that if they had
they might well have survived the attempts to oust them. Morris Schappes
did. Ironically, Schappes found out that he was not being reappointed on
April 23, 1936, the very day that he was to address CCNY's annual student peace strike. Schappes had to go, the chairman of the English Department explained, not because of his politics but because

> your efficiency as a teacher of English has not been sufficiently notable to
> justify me in asking your appointment as a permanent member of the
> staff. . . . I have been told that you are a member of the Communist
> party, but I have not investigated this and do not care. So long as any
> one is a satisfactory teacher of English, I shall accept his social creed with
> complete tolerance.

Of Schappes's efficiency as an organizer there was little question. Within
minutes of receiving his letter of dismissal, he began his campaign for
reinstatement. Schappes's own description of the early stages of that
campaign shows how effectively the Party's most energetic academic unit
could function:

> I brought my notice to Lou Lerman in the Education Office and told him
> to get a leaflet out about this dismissal in time to be distributed at 12:30
> that day, when there was a scheduled meeting of the ISA [Instructional
> Staff Association]; also to tip off the student leaders. So there at 12:30 we
> were distributing the leaflet; at the meeting, the ISA resolved to oppose
> my dismissal. At 3 P.M. the student leaders had a couple of thousand
> students outside [President] Robinson's office.*

The Teachers Union mobilized as well. It published a daily bulletin on
the situation and enlisted the help of other unions. Schappes's own contacts with New York's left-wing unions produced the incongruous spectacle of the sailors' and transport workers' contingents in the May Day
parade carrying signs calling for Schappes's reinstatement. The volume
of protest was hard to ignore. "I can see why a branch of the American
League Against War and Fascism or a branch of the Union for Social
Justice should protest Schappes's dismissal," a frazzled member of the
Board of Higher Education was supposed to have exclaimed, "but what
the hell do Meat Cutters want with academic freedom?"[7]

Other left-wingers had been fired before. What made Schappes dif-

---

* This was the first student sit-in ever.

ferent was that, despite his politics, he had been teaching at City College for eight years. His dismissal violated his de facto tenure and exposed CCNY's semi-feudal employment practices. Since the City College administration fired several other teachers at the same time, Schappes's radicalism was not the only issue, and he and his colleagues were able to mobilize their entire cohort of underpaid, insecure, and exploited instructors. Teachers who had little sympathy for Schappes's politics saw his dismissal as a threat to their own careers and took advantage of the storm that the case generated to press for some long overdue reforms. The justice of their demands, as well as the concerted pressure that the Teachers Union, in particular, brought to bear convinced the Board of Higher Education to rescind the dismissals and got the New York State legislature to establish new and more democratic tenure procedures within the city college system.[8]

The Teachers Union, which took, as it deserved, much of the credit for Schappes's reinstatement, could not, however, overturn the dismissal of its own national president, Jerome Davis. Davis, a hard-core Popular Fronter, had been on the faculty of the Yale Divinity School for twelve years. From the start, Davis's appointment had been controversial. As the holder of a chair in Practical Philanthropy, he was supposed to teach in both the Sociology and the Religion Departments. But whether because of his deficient scholarship or his political activities (and, here, the issue seems cloudy), the Sociology Department, in the words of its chairman, wanted to "have absolutely nothing to do with Davis professionally." The Divinity School was divided, though, the dean reported, most of its members felt

> that Mr. Davis is by temperament and choice a propagandist and that as such he lacks the objectivity, poise and accuracy of the scholar and does not possess the patience and the regard for the judgments of others that characterize the effective teacher.

Even so, Davis's colleagues did not repudiate him and deliberately postponed making a tenure decision by simply renewing his contract every time it came due. Yale's administration, no doubt embarrassed by Davis's trade-union activities and anti-capitalist publications, as well as his outspoken defense of the Soviet Union, finally forced the issue early in 1936 by giving Davis a terminal one-year contract. Even if the Divinity School wanted to tenure him, the provost made it quite clear that the administration would never approve.[9]

Davis's termination quickly became a cause. The Teachers Union galvanized the usual forces. Dozens of New York City professors dressed in caps and gowns trooped up to Yale to protest. "I can remember," one of them recalls, "150–200 members of the College Teachers Union driving up to New Haven in a drenching downpour and picketing the campus under a sea of umbrellas. It didn't help." The case stirred up so much publicity, however, that despite Davis's lack of tenure, the AAUP decided to intervene. Its investigating committee, one of whose members was the future president of Brooklyn College, Harry Gideonse, criticized Yale's shilly-shallying and the "excessive length of time" that the University took to decide Davis's fate. Nonetheless, since the basic decision not to give Davis tenure had been made by the Divinity School faculty, his dismissal "did not," the committee concluded, "violate the principle of academic freedom." Yale settled things by granting Davis an additional year of severance pay, and Davis, after some trouble, found another academic job.[10]

The dismissals or threatened dismissals of such visible, vocal radicals as Johnson, Henderson, Hicks, Schappes, and the two Davises, though often disguised as judgments about scholarly or financial matters, clearly demonstrated that there were limits to the amount of political activity the academic establishment could tolerate, even during the presumably liberal Popular Front. These were the traditional limits that the academy had been imposing upon itself since the late nineteenth century; as far as I can tell, none of these cases had been precipitated by pressures from outside. Yet such pressures certainly existed, and as the level of campus unrest rose during the 1930s, so too did the level of outside concern about it. A lot of this concern was journalistic. The Hearst press, in particular, delighted in exposing reds in the classroom. The American Legion was another source of pressure, as was, in New York City at least, the Catholic Church. State legislators also became involved. Education was one of the traditional areas over which local and state politicians had some power, and doing something about eliminating Communist subversion in their state's colleges and universities was a congenial task for many of the conservative and mostly small-town and rural lawmakers who dominated these legislative bodies. Their efforts invariably took one of two forms: loyalty oaths or investigating committees.[11]

Several states had instituted special oaths for teachers during the red scare that followed World War I. Once the panic subsided, however, this movement to single out educators for political monitoring died down as well, and few states paid any attention to teachers' political beliefs until the Depression. Then, the upsurge of radicalism that the bad times brought to the campus inspired a new wave of legislation. Though only a handful of states required teacher oaths before the thirties, by 1936, twenty-one states and the District of Columbia had imposed them. There was even a move to have Congress pass a resolution calling upon the states to enact such measures. Most of these oaths were quite vague; only the District of Columbia specifically required its teachers to swear that they were not "teaching or advocating communism." The Massachusetts oath, which was imposed on professors at private colleges and universities as well as all categories of public school teachers, was typical. The teachers who took it had to pledge themselves to "support the Constitution of the United States and the Constitution of the Commonwealth of Massachusetts" and to "faithfully discharge the duties" of the job according to the best of their ability. New York's oath, vetoed by the governor in 1934 and signed by him the following year, similarly required college teachers to affirm their support for the Constitution. The historian Carl Becker, in signing it, remarked that as far as he could tell the law meant

> nothing except this: that teachers in New York State are obliged to acknowledge in writing that they are obligated by the obligations imposed upon them by the duties they have assumed, and by the obligations imposed upon all citizens by the Constitution of the United States and the Constitution of the State of New York.

In other words, not much.[12]

But despite the apparent innocuousness of the oaths themselves, the motivation behind them roused the educational establishment. Its members had a professional interest in opposing laws which, in the words of the 1936 Republican presidential candidate, Alf Landon, "make teaching into a suspect profession by making our teachers take a special oath." Opposition to these measures spanned the entire political spectrum. Not only did the Teachers Union and the ACLU lobby against the oath, but in Massachusetts, where opposition to the oath was particularly vocal, Harvard's James Bryant Conant led a delegation of college presidents to the State House to protest. Though unsuccessful in attaining their immediate ends, the efforts of these educators and their allies within the liberal and labor communities probably slowed the momentum of the movement. In 1935, though seven states instituted loyalty oaths, nine rejected them. And in 1937, the Massachusetts legislature actually repealed its oath—to no avail, it turned out, since the governor vetoed the measure.[13]

Loyalty oaths, because they singled out the academic profession for special treatment, were more obnoxious in their implications than in the actual damage they inflicted. This was not the case with loyalty investigations, for they were usually directed against specific targets—individual universities and, in some instances, individual professors. The earliest of these investigations had, however, little bite. They attracted publicity, it is true, but the feckless nature of their charges made it impossible for either the educational or the political establishment to take them seriously. In Wisconsin, for example, where the first full-scale inquiry took place in 1935, it was clear that the investigation was more an attempt to discredit the La Follette progressivism of the University's president than a serious effort to expose subversive influences at Madison. No doubt there were reds on campus, but the investigating committee didn't find any. Instead, its final report excoriated the administration and described how its "permission and connivance" had turned the University into "an ultra-liberal institution and one in which communistic teachers were encouraged, and where avowed communists were welcome and allowed to spread their doctrines upon the campus." Since the committee apparently believed that such eminent scholars as E. A. Ross were "communistic teachers," we can understand why the Wisconsin authorities were able to ignore its findings.[14]

An equally ineffectual inquiry took place in Illinois, where a legislative committee took on the University of Chicago in April 1935, after the drugstore magnate Charles Walgreen announced that his niece, an undergraduate at the University, was being subverted by her teachers. The publicity that accompanied Walgreen's charges stimulated the legislature to look into Chicago's allegedly "subversive Communistic teachings and ideas." Besides questioning Chicago's president, dean, and several professors, the investigating committee also took testimony from Walgreen, his niece, and a professional anti-Communist, a suburban Chicago woman named Elizabeth Dilling, who eagerly identified dozens of people, including Supreme Court Justice Louis Brandeis and Senator William Borah, as Communists. The investigators focussed their attention on three professors whom Walgreen and Dilling claimed were the main culprits: Frederick L. Schuman, Robert Morss Lovett, and Harry Gideonse, the future president of Brooklyn College. Though Schuman and Lovett certainly sympathized with the Popular Front, neither they nor Gideonse were Communists, and they were able to convince the majority of the committee that there was no subversion at Chicago.[15]

Had any of these investigations actually unearthed a Communist teacher, it is possible that they would have had more impact. But perhaps not, for until the end of the decade the educational establishment, the trustees and administrators who ran the nation's colleges and universities, seems to have been relatively immune to outside pressures for a purge. Thus, for example, though it was widely known that there were Communist teachers in the New York City colleges, there was no serious attempt to root them out until after the Nazi-Soviet Pact. Repeated calls for a major investigation had little effect; even a session of the newly formed House Un-American Activities Committee under Martin Dies which heard three Brooklyn College professors denounce their Communist colleagues provoked little response. Ordway Tead, the chairman of New York City's Board of Higher Education, claimed to be unconcerned. "Allegations of Communist activity in our city colleges are not news," he told the *New York Times,*

> nor is the fact of such activity unknown to our board. . . .
> If there are Communists in the faculty of Brooklyn College, that . . . is a matter of their personal and private convictions. The political views of the members of our faculties are naturally diverse and are not a matter which we inquire into in the first instance. Our concern is with the scholarship and personal integrity of our faculties. . . . Indeed, differences of opinion and attitude among faculty members are a wholesome sign of vitality, and as this is reflected in the teaching, it supplies students with a useful cross-section of the divergence of views in the community at large.

Significantly, Tead qualified his statement with the remark that he was "confident that the allegations made before the Dies Committee are, like the famous premature report of Mark Twain's death, 'grossly exaggerated!',", a qualification that left open the possibility of future action if the board were ever to decide that its Communist teachers were a threat.[16]

In Detroit, where the Dies Committee also publicized charges against ten teachers in the city's public schools and colleges, the authorities responded with similar unconcern. The superintendent quipped, "There are 8,000 teachers in our school system and if ten of them are Red and the remainder well read, I would be satisfied." However, when another HUAC witness reiterated the charges a few months later, the school board decided to investigate. Its inquiry, which lasted from November 1938 to February 1939, was a sober, low-key affair. The three-person subcommittee, which handled the investigation, insisted that even "one teacher guilty of teaching any subversive activity is one too many," but it made a crucial distinction between belonging to the Communist Party and indoctrinating students. Nonetheless, it still asked the teachers if they were Communists. Since they all denied it and since their supervisors insisted that they had not tried to indoctrinate their students, the subcommittee cleared them. Whether the investigators would have come to a similar verdict had they found Communists teaching in the city's schools and colleges is hard to tell. The moderation and civil libertarian nature of the subcommittee's rhetoric, in particular its explicit insistence that "membership in the Communist Party is not illegal," indicates that, as of the beginning of 1939 at least, the anti-Communist fervor that would require the ouster of Party members from faculties around the country was not yet universal.[17]

But it was growing. Several sources fed the spring. There was, to begin with, the traditional knee-jerk anti-Communism of the right which, as we saw in Chicago and Wisconsin, tended to label as Communist much of the New Deal as well as everything to its left. As the country began to move to the right in the late thirties, the fringes which these traditional anti-Communists inhabited were no longer as far from the political center as they had once been. That legislators in states like Wisconsin and Illinois had been able to mount official investigations of major universities indicates the apparent legitimacy of the Communist issue and the degree to which many politicians professed to be concerned about it. But it was a concern tempered with skepticism, for the red-hunters had, up until then, failed to turn up a single red. An alliance with a growing strain of left-wing and liberal anti-Communism was, however, to change that. The left-wing anti-Communists, unlike the reactionary ones, knew how to distinguish Communists from other types of radicals. They could, therefore, help anti-Communist investigators increase the accuracy of their charges and so ensure that the pressures for a purge of academic Communists would gain a more sympathetic hearing.[18]

The Nazi-Soviet Pact was crucial here. Liberals, who had grudgingly tolerated the CP as long as it was involved in the common struggle against fascism, broke at once. No longer would they shield their erstwhile allies from right-wing attacks. On the contrary, many liberals even joined those attacks and, in the process, helped transform anti-Communism from a right-wing to a mainstream concern. Of course, many of these liberals had never been in the Popular Front; they had been dubious about and even hostile toward the Communist Party throughout the 1930s. And they were not alone.

It is important to realize that the CP had always had enemies on the left. Individual liberals, Socialists, and ex-Communists of all varieties had been battling the Party on many fronts for years. The ensuing polemics enlivened the alcoves of the City College student cafeteria, pervaded the pages of tiny Marxist magazines, and dominated the annual conventions of the Teachers Union. Ultimately, they were to influence the rhetoric of mainstream American politics as well. Here, we must differentiate among the different elements. The left-wing anti-Communism of the 1930s was no monolith; each group, faction, or individual came to oppose the CP by a different route and contributed a different element to the overall mix.

There was, for example, a group of ex-Communist cadres who were to supply the investigating committees with invaluable testimony about the Party's inner workings. Many of these people, like the followers of Jay Lovestone who left the CP after losing a major battle for its leadership in 1929, still retained an essentially Bolshevik mentality. The Party remained the core of their professional lives, only now they sought to destroy rather than run it. They were soon in great demand as interpreters and guides to the ideological complexities of Marxism-Leninism. By the late 1930s some of them, like the former Teachers Union activist Benjamin Mandel, had become professional witnesses and committee staffers, their personal contacts and reminiscences a highly negotiable commodity within the growing anti-Communist circuit. This group also included former fellow travelers, people who had once been close to, but not in, the CP. J. B. Matthews, HUAC's first staff director, was one, an ex-missionary who had embraced the revolution, if not the Party, and headed the main anti-fascist organization of the 1930s until he ended up on the wrong side in a labor dispute and was read out of the movement. Matthews then went on to become the *éminence grise* of the anti-Communist network, valued for his commitment and vast collection of left-wing letterheads. Later informers and professional ex-Communists were a more opportunistic, less ideological group who were often willing to doctor their testimony to conform to the needs of the investigators they worked for. These people were not and had never been liberals, and so when they switched from Communism to anti-Communism, they seemed unperturbed about the reactionary nature of their new political allies.[19]

Another important group of ex-Communist anti-Communists were the Trotskyists, perhaps the purest revolutionaries as well as the fiercest anti-Stalinists among the CP's left-wing foes. Organizationally, Trotskyism with its tiny competing sects and subsects had almost no effect on American politics. Ideologically, however, because such important New York intellectuals as Sidney Hook, Irving Kristol, Dwight Macdonald, Irving Howe, and the editors of *Partisan Review* passed through that embattled movement, Trotskyism's influence on the evolution of anti-Communist thought was considerable. The highly sophisticated critique of the evils of Stalinism that Trotsky and his American followers developed gained widespread acceptance after the end of the Popular Front. Though many of these Trotskyist intellectuals ultimately abandoned the left, during the 1930s they still considered themselves Marxists and insisted that socialism, in some form or another, was a desirable goal. Communism, or Stalinism as they called it, had simply betrayed that goal.[20]

Equally factionalized, though somewhat less resolute in their opposition to the CP, were the dwindling number of radicals who belonged to the Socialist Party in the 1930s. Some of the SP's older militants were as ferociously anti-Communist as any members of the American Legion; others, including the Party's long-time leader, Norman Thomas, were occasionally willing to make wary alliances with the CP over issues like unemployment relief or the Spanish Civil War. During the Popular Front period, however, the Socialists' strong anti-militarism and their opposition to the New Deal forced them to the left of the CP. From that vantage point, many Socialists were often among the most consistent and insightful critics of American and Russian Communism. They were also, along with a few prescient liberals like John Dewey, among the first to call attention to the Moscow purge trials and to insist that they reflected the essentially undemocratic and dictatorial nature of Communism.[21]

Had the Popular Front alliance between the CP and the anti-fascist liberals continued, the left-wing critique of Communism would never have emerged from the sectarian battlefields of the left. However, once the Nazi-Soviet Pact destroyed the Popular Front, the ideas that the Trotskyists, Socialists, and other opponents of the CP had developed during the factional struggles of the 1930s suddenly entered the mainstream. They were ideas which, after all, offered the only fully coherent, but not reactionary, explanation of the nature of Communism then available. As a result, they formed the ideological underpinning of the growing campaign to eradicate the CP from American political life. These ideas became especially important in the academic community where it was necessary to develop a rationale that would make it possible to get rid of Communist teachers without seeming to violate academic freedom.

Central to this new ideology of anti-Communism was its image of the Communist Party. For if, as was to become the case, simply belonging to the CP was to render someone unfit to teach, it was crucial that the Party be seen as an organization which required of its adherents behavior that was by definition beyond the academic pale. The picture of the Party that was to gain currency at this time, though based to a certain extent upon reality, was in many respects a caricature. Nonetheless, because of the Party's isolation during the Nazi-Soviet Pact period, few "respectable" voices either within the academic community or outside of it questioned the assumptions upon which it was based or challenged its almost universal acceptance. Since this new definition of the Communist Party was to shape the academy's response to the issue, both in the period immediately after the Nazi-Soviet Pact and later, it is important to enumerate its several elements. We shall encounter them in committee reports, faculty resolutions, university bylaws, and official pronouncements, as well as books and articles, for the next twenty years.

Perhaps the most important element in this view of the CP was the notion that the Party was not a regular political party but a conspiracy. Dominated by Moscow, its supposed goal was the overthrow of the American government, presumably in the interests of the Soviet Union. The methods whereby the Party pursued these aims were, it was assumed, particularly alien to academic life. Its members abjured common ethics. They operated in secret and often attacked their opponents in scurrilous and abusive language, an offense made all the worse by its anonymity. In addition, Communists were considered to be intellectual automatons who had to follow the Party line as well as indoctrinate their students with it. That only some of these elements corresponded to reality had no relation to the near unanimity with which the academic establishment was to accept them by the time the Cold War made anti-Communism a national priority.

Harry N. Wright, the acting president of City College, who was soon to preside over the largest single purge of academic Communists in American history, offered the standard description of the CP as succinctly as anyone. The Party, he told a New York State legislative investigating committee in 1941, is

> fundamentally impossible of amalgamation in a democratic society, first on the basis of its underground character, its refusing to work in the open, second on the basis of its outside control, its party line control, and third, on the basis of its having discarded the ethical system by which we all live or try to live.

Belonging to such an organization, in other words, was incompatible with the professional obligations of a college teacher. And as anti-Communist pressures built up both within the academic community and outside of it, sentiment was growing for making membership in the CP, rather than any specific activities, grounds for dismissal of faculty members.[22]

Once the notion of the CP as a conspiracy became universal, it was possible for even previously reluctant liberals to endorse the anti-Communist measures that right-wing politicians and journalists had been urging for years. The academy was not unique. The years 1940 and 1941 saw what amounted to a red scare in many segments of American society. The CIO and several of its affiliates adopted anti-Communist resolutions at their annual conventions. Other unions ousted Communist leaders and, in some cases, Communist-dominated locals as well. The

American Federation of Teachers, for example, expelled four such locals, including the New York City College Teachers Union, Local 537. Congress passed the Smith Act and other anti-Communist legislation. The Justice Department and the Immigration and Naturalization Service began to harass Party leaders. Even the American Civil Liberties Union adopted an anti-Communist resolution and forced the veteran radical Elizabeth Gurley Flynn off its board of directors. That this little red scare should have an academic component should not, therefore, surprise us.[23]

The tolerance for radical speakers and radical political groups that had characterized many campuses during the Popular Front disappeared. Repression against student reds intensified; radical teachers came under attack. The first school to explicitly bar members of the Communist Party from its faculty was the University of California. This proscription was the result of the embarrassing case of Kenneth O. May, a teaching assistant in the Berkeley Mathematics Department and the son of a Berkeley dean. May was an open Communist whose political activities provoked the chairman of his department to seek his ouster on the grounds that May's membership in the Communist Party conflicted with his academic responsibilities. The Regents agreed, and at their meeting of October 11, 1940, adopted the following resolution:

> The Regents believe that the Communist Party, of which Mr. May has announced that he is a member, gives its first loyalty to a foreign political movement and, perhaps, to a foreign government; that by taking advantage of the idealism and inexperience of youth, and by exploiting the distress of underprivileged groups, it breeds suspicion and discord, and thus divides the democratic forces upon which the welfare of our country depends. They believe, therefore, that membership in the Communist Party is incompatible with membership in the faculty of a State University.

John Francis Neylan, William Randolph Hearst's representative on the Regents, who was later to become the main protagonist in the loyalty oath crisis of 1949, voted against the resolution. Although he supported its ban on Communist teachers, he wanted the Regents to coordinate May's dismissal with a broader investigation of the faculty aimed at uncovering other Communists as well.[24]

Neylan well knew that, given the clandestine nature of the CP, such an investigation would be the only way the Regents could effectively enforce their anti-Communist resolution. Once membership rather than overt misbehavior became the official criterion for dismissal in California and, it soon turned out, elsewhere as well, identifying the suspect teachers would require a major investigation. The Regents did not make the effort. Perhaps they feared it would stir up too much opposition. Perhaps they realized that they lacked the resources for it.

This was not the case in New York, where in 1940 the state legislature, rather than the educational authorities, took on the task of exposing Communist teachers. This investigation, under the aegis of a special legislative investigating committee, the so-called Rapp-Coudert Committee, was to identify as Communists dozens of New York City college teachers and to initiate what was, until the height of the McCarthy era in 1953 and 1954, by far the largest purge of politically undesirable professors ever. Its significance is more than quantitative. The Rapp-Coudert Committee and its staff pioneered the techniques that later state and congressional investigating committees would employ. It developed evidence, elaborated arguments, and even trained personnel that its successor committees would appropriate, unchanged.

The investigation began not as a search for subversives, but as a long overdue inquiry into the financial plight of the New York City schools. However, just as the investigation was getting organized in the spring of 1940 under the leadership of an upstate assemblyman, Herbert Rapp, the appointment of the British philosopher Bertrand Russell to the faculty of CCNY created a furor. New York City reactionaries were enraged at the idea that the city's youth might be exposed to the controversial philosopher and his unconventional views of marriage. Religious leaders, both Catholic and Protestant, fulminated against Russell and what the Brooklyn diocese's *Tablet* called his "Hitler-Stalin program of anti-religion." Mayor Fiorello La Guardia and the liberals who controlled the Board of Higher Education backed down and rescinded the invitation to Russell. But by then the uproar had reached Albany, where the legislature, already sympathetic to charges that the city's schools were a hotbed of Communism, decided to give Rapp's committee a new mandate. It was to discover the "extent to which, if any, subversive activities may have been permitted to be carried on in the schools and colleges."[25]

Frederic R. Coudert, the only Republican senator from New York City and one of the sponsors of the recently enacted tenure legislation for the city colleges, chaired the subcommittee which carried out the investigation, his appointment presumably designed to allay liberal fears that the inquiry was just a façade for an upstate legislative crack-down on the city's school budget. Similarly, Coudert's legal staff, which, since the legislators on the subcommittee rarely participated in its work, essentially ran the investigation, was composed of equally respectable attorneys. Its chief counsel, Paul Windels, was a pillar of the Republican party and a former City Corporation Counsel under La Guardia; his main assistant, Philip W. Haberman, Jr., had been on the staff of the earlier Seabury investigation of municipal graft and was actively associated with the Anti-Defamation League. These were no rednecks, but sober and responsible men who realized that the credibility and effectiveness of their enterprise required that they expose genuine Communists and not the Popular Front liberals that the Wisconsin and Illinois committees had mistakenly attacked. That they would look for Communist teachers was never in doubt. Though Windels claimed that he "would have preferred" to study school funding first, the pressures on the committee as well as its members' own predilections ensured that it would devote its energies to exposing Party members in the city's schools.[26]

From the first, the committee's staff knew that it had to win the "respect" of the city's establishment and particularly of the "so-called liberals" who controlled the Board of Higher Education. Accordingly the committee intended, Windels declared, "to refrain scrupulously from presenting gossip, rumor or hearsay and to present only such evidence as would be accepted in a court of law." This meant that it would accept as proof of Party membership only what Robert Morris, one of the committee's assistant counsels (later to become the chief counsel for the McCarran and Jenner committees in the 1950s), called "direct sworn testimony to actual conscious participation in the organized Communist conspiracy." Such testimony was necessary, Morris explained, because

> just as only some one at the scene of an accident or crime is ordinarily competent to testify to such accident or crimes, so only someone who himself was a Communist, who sat behind the closed doors of the Communist councils, is competent to say who else attended those councils.

In other words, the committee planned to rely on informers.[27]

First, of course, it had to find them. The committee had as many allies as the academic Communists had enemies. Acting President Wright of CCNY, for example, sent names of potential informers. There was also the growing network of professional anti-Communists. Benjamin Mandel was especially useful. A former Teachers Union activist, Mandel was to devote his life to the Communist Party, first as a cadre and then, after his expulsion along with Jay Lovestone in 1929, as an adversary, doing research for almost every major anti-Communist investigating committee in America. Mandel's own experiences in the Party, as well as his connections with Teachers Union dissidents, were invaluable for Rapp-Coudert. So, too, were the contacts that the committee's staff made with New York's left-wing anti-Communists—"labor leaders, Social Democrats, Trotskyites, Socialists, and, of course, former Communists." These were the people who, Robert Morris explained, because they had been "feuding day-to-day with the Communists, could identify them most readily and could accurately assess their relative importance within their respective sphere." From the first, the committee's staff found the Teachers Union, in Windels's words, "a very fruitful field of inquiry." It knew that, as the TU's president himself had admitted, "whatever Communists there are in the schools are probably in the Union." In addition, Union dissidents who had been struggling against the Communists for years were eager to supply the committee with leads, though many of them were appalled when the committee took the drastic step of subpoenaing the Union's membership lists.[28]

After spending its first few months collecting names and information, the committee began to subpoena suspected Communists in the fall of 1940. In order to persuade them to testify in public against their colleagues, it devised a two-stage procedure, one which all later anti-Communist investigating committees were to copy. First, it questioned the suspected Communists in a private session and then, if they were willing to name names or else if the committee could produce witnesses willing to name them, it would give them a second, public hearing. The teachers, of course, fought back. Their strategy, which was largely directed by Bella Dodd, the Teachers Union's legislative director, consisted of two parts: a conventional legal defense which challenged every aspect of the committee's procedures and a propaganda campaign which accused the committee of undermining public education and, after it subpoenaed the Union's membership lists, the labor movement as well.[29]

The first people to receive subpoenas, some twenty-three Brooklyn College professors, refused to cooperate with the committee. They invoked all kinds of technicalities, claiming that the committee was operating illegally because it often lacked a quorum and denied its witnesses transcripts of their hearings. Though the courts eventually rejected the teachers' petition, their appeal became moot long before the judiciary handed down its decision, for the Board of Higher Education soon forced the teachers to cooperate with Rapp-Coudert. At first, the Board had been skeptical about the inquiry. Many of its members, so Windels believed, "preferred to shut their eyes and say that as long as they didn't *know* what was going on, nothing was going on." In November 1940 the Board adopted a pro forma resolution urging faculty members to "assist the Committee," but it wasn't until January 21, 1941, after the first informer had testified in public and the City's Corporation Counsel had assured the Board that it had the legal right to force its employees to testify, that it announced it would "take disciplinary action" against any teachers who did not obey their subpoenas and answer the Rapp-Coudert Committee's questions.[30]

That first informer was Bernard Grebanier. An overweight, unkempt, and scholarly assistant professor of English at Brooklyn College, Grebanier had become politicized in the early thirties after the American Legion attacked him for showing pictures of World War I casualties in his classes. He joined the Teachers Union and was soon pressed to join the Party as well. He did so in 1935, largely because he wanted to be on the front lines of the struggle for better working conditions at Brooklyn College. Instead, he found that he had "entered a country as foreign as Abyssinia." Disillusioned after nine months, he did not leave the Party until 1939. The break was painful; the polemics on both sides were nasty. Nonetheless, despite his bitterness about the CP, Grebanier did not want to be an informer. At his private hearing, he was willing to talk about himself, but not about others. It was not until the committee's staff presented him with a list of the other people in his former unit that he gave in. "I hadn't supplied a name that they didn't have." In this, Grebanier was like many friendly witnesses in the 1950s. The revelation that there were other informers and that the investigating committee already had the names they were ostensibly seeking somehow made it easier for these otherwise re-luctant men and women to give the names again. Even so, Grebanier did not want to testify about all his former comrades. Though he named over thirty people in private, he identified only eight or nine of the most ac-tive leaders at his public hearing, December 2, 1940. Moreover, because Grebanier was the only person from Brooklyn College to cooperate with the committee, the Board of Higher Education, which, as we shall see, required two witnesses before it would bring charges against a staff mem-ber, did not dismiss most of the people Grebanier had named.[31]

There were more informers at City College. The committee's most important witness, a young Catholic instructor in the History Department named William Martin Canning, gave fifty-four names at his public hear-ing on March 6 and 7, 1941. Unlike Grebanier, Canning had apparently not broken with the CP before his hearing, but he had never been a par-ticularly zealous Communist. Even so, the other members of the largely Jewish City College unit were, as Morris Schappes explained, "glad to have him because the Communist Party at the time was making an over-ture to the Catholics." It is not completely clear why Canning testified. His Catholicism may have had something to do with it. We do know that later on, at least, the Church played an important institutional role in helping ex-Communists become anti-Communists. In addition, since Can-ning's political convictions were lukewarm to begin with, he was probably less willing than his more committed comrades to resist the pressures that were being put on him by "the important members of the faculty" who, Paul Windels conceded, were helping the committee. Three other City College people also named names, though not as many as Canning.[32]

With the important exception of Morris Schappes, every other sus-pected Communist called before the Rapp-Coudert Committee denied belonging to the Party. Some were sincere. Canning had apparently iden-tified as Party members several men and women who had participated in many of the same activities as the Communists without having actually joined the CP. Most of the witnesses, however, were lying. This seems to have been a collective decision made by the leaders of each academic unit, largely because they felt they had no other alternative. The TU's lawyers whom they consulted explained that they would not be able to take the Fifth Amendment because a provision of the New York City Charter required public employees to cooperate with legislative investi-gations. The one teacher who did assert his constitutional privilege against self-incrimination was fired without a hearing. The admission that they were Communists was equally unpalatable. "The idea that you could hold your job and publicly profess that you were a Communist," Schappes insisted, "was inconceivable." Public opinion would not allow it. Nor, it turned out, would the Board of Higher Education. On March 17, in the midst of the Rapp-Coudert Committee's revelations about the City College Communists, the Board of Higher Education issued a resolution declaring that it would not "retain as members of the collegiate staffs members of any Communist, Fascist or Nazi group."[33]

Honesty, then, would have been suicidal. It was not, however, clear at the time that dishonesty was going to be equally disastrous. All the teachers had apparently denied Party membership at their first private hearing, and, when Schappes and his colleagues decided to continue that strategy in public, they did not know that the committee already had witnesses to corroborate Canning's story. Rather than admit they had perjured themselves initially, they decided that they would try to save their jobs by bluffing. Whether or not there was opposition to this decision is hard to tell. Some people now claim that they opposed it, but the sensitive nature of the issue may well have distorted their recollections. The Party was, after all, a disciplined organization; the teachers who were involved apparently felt that they had to present a united front. Even people like the former CCNY instructor who claimed, "I didn't like the performance of the defense," nonetheless "did what everybody else did even though I wasn't part of any deliberative process." In retrospect, what seems most distressing about the behavior of these teachers was not their lying—which, given the no-win situation in which they felt themselves, may well have seemed to offer the only hope for keeping their jobs—but their willingness to let a small group of Party leaders make a decision that was to affect their own careers and livelihoods.[34]

Perhaps because he knew that he was the most conspicuous Communist on campus, Schappes told the Rapp-Coudert Committee at his public session on March 6 that he had been in the Party. But he then qualified his admission so thoroughly as to make it unbelievable. Not only did he claim that he had left the Party in 1939, but, when asked to identify the other members of the CCNY unit, he named three people, none of whom was still at City College. Two had been killed in Spain and the third was a Party organizer in Massachusetts. Understandably, the Rapp-Coudert Committee did not believe that the country's most active academic unit consisted of one man, and it asked the district attorney to prosecute Schappes for perjury. Schappes's lack of candor and that of the other teachers destroyed whatever vestiges of liberal support they could have called upon and simply reinforced the committee's contention that their behavior was part of "an organized conspiracy." Ordway Tead, the chairman of the Board of Higher Education who only a few years earlier had insisted that Communist teachers were "a wholesome sign of vitality," now viewed them in a different way: "They looked guilty, they looked shifty-eyed, they looked double-talking."[35]

Though ostensibly engaged in fact-finding, the Rapp-Coudert Committee certainly assumed that its efforts would have concrete results. But, for that to happen, the Board of Higher Education would have to act. The legislative committee could only identify Communist teachers; it could not fire them. Despite the Board's apparent cooperation with Rapp-Coudert, the committee retained some doubts about the Board's enthusiasm for the purges. It felt that Tead and his colleagues had been remiss in not having dealt with the problem of Communist teachers earlier and, in its final report, pointedly noted that unless the Board acted more vigorously, "it will be incumbent on the Legislature to create new agencies for the task." In fact, once Canning's testimony made the existence of a large City College unit front-page news, the Board immediately imposed sanctions. It suspended all the teachers named by Canning as soon as they appeared in public in the spring and summer of 1941. It also began to prepare formal charges against them in anticipation of the trials that were required for the dismissal of tenured faculty members. Everybody who did not have tenure was either dismissed out of hand or not reappointed. The Board also fired Schappes without a trial after he was found guilty of perjury and given an eighteen-month to three-and-a-half-year prison sentence.[36]

The Board's hearings differed from those of the Rapp-Coudert Committee in that, because they were quasi-judicial proceedings, the teachers had more legal safeguards. They could bring lawyers, cross-examine witnesses, and produce evidence of their own. Though the Board had gone on record opposing the retention of Communist teachers, the only official grounds it had for dismissing tenured staff members were "incompetent or inefficient service," "neglect of duty," "physical or mental incapacity," and "conduct unbecoming a member of the staff." Accordingly, at each trial the Board sought to show that the teacher's political activities and his or her behavior before the Rapp-Coudert Committee constituted just such "unbecoming" conduct.[37]

Whatever specific charges were brought against each teacher—and they varied somewhat from case to case—it was clear that his or her real offense, the "conduct unbecoming" a teacher, was membership in the Communist Party. As the wording of the actual charges reveals, the Board of Higher Education had come around to the by then prevailing view of the CP as an organization which made its members "unfit to serve on the staff of a public instructional system." The Party "advocates, advises or teaches that the government of the United States should be overthrown by force or unlawful means." It requires of its members "unequivocal obedience to the instructions of the said party." In order to bolster its case against the Party, the Board brought in an expert witness, an ex-Communist named Ruben Gotesky, to discuss the CP's advocacy "of the use of force and violence as a means of overthrowing our government." Gotesky testified at the trial of every single teacher.[38]

Probably the most serious, certainly the most verifiable, charge against the teachers was that they had perjured themselves before the Rapp-Coudert Committee. Belonging to the CP was bad enough; lying about it was even worse, a "violation," so the Board insisted, "of the academic duty" of a faculty member to conduct his "extracurricular affairs openly, with candor and without resorting to deceit or concealment." Whether or not the teachers could have kept their jobs if they had been truthful about their political affiliation is unclear. But there is certainly no question that their dishonesty, both with the Rapp-Coudert Committee and the Board of Higher Education trial committees, doomed them. In one case, that of the labor historian Philip S. Foner, a member of the Board explained, "In recommending the dismissal of Foner, I do so not because the prosecutor proved him to be a Communist, but because in doing this he also showed him to be a liar." Regardless of political affiliation, then, lying was "conduct unbecoming."[39]

So, too, was participation in the publication of the CCNY unit's wildly controversial shop-paper, the *Teacher-Worker*. "Indecent, vicious, and coarse" were only a few of the adjectives Board members used to describe the paper. Its "hardened disregard for all canons of decency and gentility," its "bad taste and flagrant disregard of the most elementary decencies" were, so one of the Board's three-man trial committees explained, "sufficient to shock the sensibilities of a person of ordinary refinement." "Proven participation by any teacher in the issuance of a publication such as the 'Teacher-Worker,'" another trial committee insisted, "is sufficient, we hold, to disqualify him from service in any educational institution."[40]

Significantly, the Board never seriously tried to show that any of these teachers had misused their classrooms. It produced Party literature and testimony from Canning and other friendly witnesses to show that the CP expected its academic members to indoctrinate their students, but it never cited any specific instances of such indoctrination. Evidence to the contrary, testimony from colleagues and other scholars in the field, the Board simply brushed aside. Such testimony was "unworthy of belief" and, in any case, of "little if any importance." Whether they tried to convert their students or not—and at least one Board member was willing to concede that at least one of the defendants was "a non-indoctrinating Communist"—their failure to level with the Board's investigators as well as with Rapp-Coudert's was more than adequate grounds for dismissal.[41]

These in-house trials, which began in June 1941, continued throughout the rest of 1941 and 1942. Ultimately they resulted in the dismissal of twenty people. Eleven others resigned while their cases were pending. Because the Board wanted to be sure that its actions could withstand a legal challenge, it only prosecuted those people whom two witnesses could identify as Party members. Most of them taught at City College; the investigators had been unable to find a second witness from Brooklyn to corroborate Grebanier's testimony. As a result, except for three people whom Canning had named as members of the citywide Party fraction of the Teachers Union, all the tenured Brooklyn College teachers Grebanier had fingered kept their jobs. Of course, they knew that the administration knew who they were. And they also knew that any time a second witness surfaced they, too, would be dismissed. The Rapp-Coudert staff was confident that, with time, one of the Brooklyn people would break. Instead, the investigation ended. With America's entry into the war on the side of the Soviet Union, the elimination of domestic Communists no longer seemed an urgent matter. And it was not until 1952, ten years after the Rapp-Coudert Committee handed in its final report, that the second witness appeared. Ironically, that witness was none other than Bella Dodd, the dynamic Teachers Union leader who had masterminded the Party's opposition to the Rapp-Coudert investigation.[42]

Rapp-Coudert left a rich heritage. When Pat McCarran's Senate Internal Security Subcommittee (SISS) took up where the earlier investigation had left off, the same witnesses were to face many of the same investigators. More important, the procedures were the same. McCarran and most of the other major anti-Communist investigators of the McCarthy period copied the careful staff work that helped Rapp-Coudert uncover Communist teachers. Like Windels and his assistants, these later investigators relied upon informers. They pressured witnesses to name names, and they designed their public sessions to expose the presumably subversive behavior of the people who would not inform. They also counted on the employers of unfriendly witnesses to administer sanctions. And, as we shall see, those employers, academic institutions included, responded in much the same way New York City's Board of Higher Education had—by firing the uncooperative souls, often after a special hearing that emphasized the employee's obligation to reveal his or her political affiliations. If nothing else, Rapp-Coudert had demonstrated that individual Communists had few protections once anti-Communism became a part of the American mainstream.

IV

"A Matter of Ethical Hygiene": The Exclusion of Communists from Academic Life after World War II

Many left-wing students and teachers, their academic careers interrupted by the Second World War, returned to the academy and to a political life that, initially at least, seemed not so different from that of the late 1930s. The anti-Communism of the Nazi-Soviet Pact period had receded for the moment. Traces remained, of course, not only in the occasional coldness of their colleagues to the Rapp-Coudert survivors, but also in the unwillingness of liberals to revive the Popular Front alliances with Communists. Yet that unwillingness did not, at first, translate itself into repression. As a result, for a few years until the Cold War intensified, there was a brief, and now forgotten, efflorescence of political radicalism at many of the nation's colleges and universities. Soon, as we shall see, the political atmosphere changed; left-wing activities—and then individuals—came under attack.

Initially, however, political activity on many campuses, though never reaching the level attained during the Popular Front days, was considerable. Students still joined the Communist Party. One Cornell unit in the late forties contained about two dozen people; one unit at Michigan, where there may have been several, had about fifteen. At Harvard, the small core of student Communists could mobilize almost a hundred sympathizers for rallies, demonstrations, speakers, and petitions. Many of these people—and their counterparts at Yale, Berkeley, Chicago, North Carolina, and elsewhere—were veterans who had been radicalized before the war and were taking advantage of the GI Bill to finish college or get a graduate degree. They established their own organizations: the American Youth for Democracy, the successor to the National Student League and American Student Union; the American Veterans Committee, a left-wing alternative to the American Legion; and, later, the Young Progressives and the Labor Youth League, as well as all kinds of local Marxist study groups. These students threw themselves into a flurry of causes:

civil rights, peace, and, above all, the 1948 presidential campaign of Henry Wallace.[1]

Faculty radicals, as always, kept a lower profile. Many were already in the process of disengaging themselves from the CP and, with the exception of the Wallace campaign, had pretty well given up active politics. Those who were still Communists were often affiliated with Party units in the community instead of, as in the 1930s, specifically academic ones. They rarely participated in campus-based political activities. It would have been too risky; besides, the organizations that would have mounted such activities, like the Teachers Union, had not survived the prewar red scare. When, for example, Horace Bancroft Davis arrived at the University of Kansas City in the spring of 1947, he was no longer in the Party, and the most radical group he joined was the AAUP. He may have been prescient, for within a few years the main political activity of both student and faculty leftists was to defend civil liberties against the growing tide of anti-Communist repression, both on and off the campus.[2]

It would be a mistake to exaggerate the amount of left-wing political activity during this period. Harvard's various radical student organizations may have had almost a hundred members, but the Republican Club had four hundred. Similarly, Sarah Lawrence's supposedly radical student body gave Thomas E. Dewey more than twice as many votes in a 1948 straw poll as his nearest rival, Henry Wallace. The strength of Wallace's showing, however, does indicate that at least for a few years and on a few campuses there was some kind of a left-wing alternative to the political mainstream. How many schools harbored student radicals is hard to tell. Certainly, all the major public and private universities and elite colleges had some kind of a student left, as did most big city institutions. Southern schools, Catholic schools, and the smaller, less prestigious public and private colleges probably did not. But such an assessment is essentially speculative, for the late forties is a largely unstudied period in the history of campus activism.[3]

Whatever the extent of the postwar student movement, there is little question that it encountered considerable opposition. Almost from the start, academic administrators from Wisconsin to Wellesley tried to restrict their campus radicals. The repression, though effective, was not severe; it was directed against activities, not individuals. As a result, unlike in the thirties, only a handful of students got into trouble, in most cases either because they were exceptionally militant or their administrations exceptionally authoritarian. The growing anti-Communism of the rest of the country obviated the need for campus administrators to apply much pressure in order to incapacitate the student left.[4]

The first target on most campuses was the American Youth for Democracy (AYD), a group whose affiliation with the Communist Party was no secret. Some schools, for example, simply refused to recognize the organization. Brooklyn College president Harry Gideonse personally intervened with the Student-Faculty Committee to keep the AYD off his campus. Administrations at other schools, which already had chapters, began to revoke their charters. The promulgation of the Truman administration's loyalty-security program in March 1947 prompted much of this action. Designed to eliminate supposedly subversive employees from the federal payroll, the government's initiative encouraged other sectors of society to weed out their own reds. The AYD was particularly vulnerable; FBI director J. Edgar Hoover had publicly cited the group in front of HUAC, and it was widely assumed that it would soon be placed on the Attorney General's list of subversive organizations. There were other pressures as well.[5]

In Michigan, the state senate's Select Committee to Investigate Communist Activities, the so-called Callahan Committee, essentially forced the state's major universities to rid themselves of their local AYDs. There had been a chapter of the organization at Wayne State University since 1944; its program, the University's president, David Henry, explained to his board in February 1947, "has not been subversive in action or intent." A month later, after two members of the Callahan Committee questioned Henry and threatened to block the University's building appropriations if he didn't oust the AYD, the administration decided to review the status of the organization. Henry consulted with the FBI and was told "that AYD chapters are Communist youth recruiting centers." He decided to ask the local chapter to sever all its ties with the state and national organizations; when the group refused, he banned it. The University of Michigan took similar action, checking first with the Department of Justice and then deciding, as Michigan's president explained to Senator Callahan, "that an American Youth for Democracy chapter was not a desirable campus organization." Not surprisingly, Michigan State also banned its AYD.[6]

Though political pressures elsewhere were not quite as blatant as they were in Michigan, educators around the country still rushed to get the offending organizations off campus. At many schools, the faculty, not the administration, revoked the AYD's charter. At Queens College, a local politician forced the issue by demanding,

> all un-American groups and the professors who tolerate them must go. Queens is a god-fearing community and those that don't see eye to eye with us have no place in our midst. We want our students taught "Queens style" or not at all.

The faculty responded by holding a special meeting and ratifying the abolition of the AYD by a 55 to 42 vote. Temple University and the University of Colorado set up faculty committees (Temple's was called the Committee on Controversial Issues) to see whether any student organizations were concealing their real aims and affiliations. Both committees, of course, decided to ban the AYD; at Colorado, because it didn't meet the University's requirement of "forthright and frank statements of purpose" and was, in any case, "under the influence of the Communist Party."

Many other schools, which had long-standing, though long-ignored, policies against letting student groups affiliate with national organizations, simply enforced the rules to drive the AYD from campus.[7]

Not every academic administration was so heavy-handed. Cornell's, for example, wrestled with the problem for years. Its student radicals were few, but militant. The administration preferred to leave them alone. As Cornell's president, Edmund E. Day, explained to an alumnus concerned about the University's tolerance of the AYD, "We are watching its progress—or rather its lack of progress—with interest . . . . and I am confident that it will never become necessary for us to confer upon its members the dignity of martyrdom." Instead, Cornell used an increasingly common approach: it requested membership lists. In the fall of 1947 the University issued new registration forms for student organizations requiring them to list *all* their members instead of, as before, just their officers. At first, the administration claimed it wanted the lists for routine administrative purposes; then it insisted that it needed them to ensure that "the membership is made up of bona fide students in the University." The left-wing student groups protested. The president of the Marxist Study Group, the future economic historian Robert Fogel, complained that "such lists represent a threat to the security of our members and an abridgement of civil rights." The Young Progressives were equally emphatic. "The existence of such lists, regardless of the good intentions evident in requesting them," the organization's chairman said,

> is a threat to the continuation of political groups on campus. In view of the general atmosphere of fear and anxiety current today, it must be obvious that registration on any permanent records would deter potential members from joining any but social groups.[8]

The experience of the left-wing student groups at Harvard shows how effectively the membership-list requirement operated. The administration had been harassing the Harvard Youth for Democracy, as the AYD chapter was called, for some time. In 1947 the dean of students refused to let the organization put out its magazine, *The New Student,* as an official Harvard publication. Claiming that the format was too polished to be the work of undergraduates, the dean and his assistants called in *The New Student*'s editors and grilled them about their politics and the journal's finances. Deprived of the University's approval, the magazine's editors managed to put out two issues in the winter and spring of 1947–48 before going out of business. Meanwhile, at Radcliffe, Harvard's sister college, the dean refused to recognize an AYD chapter unless it submitted a membership list. Such a list was necessary, the dean explained, in order to keep tabs on students in academic trouble. She would not, of course, make the list public—but if a government investigator were to request it, she would naturally comply. The Radcliffe AYD chose to disband instead. Soon Harvard's deans were demanding lists as well. Though there was some student protest—from *Crimson* editors and student council leaders, as well as Communists—the HYD, the John Reed Club, and the Young Progressives soon disappeared from campus. The Young Progressives had, in fact, submitted a membership list, but they had failed to fulfill another organizational requirement: they couldn't find a faculty sponsor. Even the most sympathetic professors shrank from allowing their names on a list.[9]

In the spring of 1947 an informal survey by the Students for Democratic Action, the student affiliate of the Americans for Democratic Action, revealed that many of the nation's most liberal institutions were using membership lists to control the student left. Even the University of Wisconsin, which during the 1950s may have been the only school in America which still had an authorized chapter of the AYD's successor, the Labor Youth League, called for lists. At a time when prospective employers—private as well as public—were checking out people's political records, the repressive nature of the membership-list requirement was obvious. HUAC itself recognized the efficacy of the method. It recommended that, as the best way to destroy the AYD, "its members on each campus should be made publicly known and registered as such. Parents, fellow-students, and faculty members should be provided with these lists." Though few schools actually followed HUAC's advice and published the lists, few kept them confidential. As a result, the SDA report noted, "students have sometimes experienced difficulty in securing employment."[10]

At no point, of course, did the academic administrators who imposed the membership-list requirement admit that they were trying to rid their campuses of politically embarrassing groups. Rather, they advanced all sorts of essentially paternalistic arguments for their attempts to restrict their students' political activities. Many academics, faculty members and administrators alike, apparently believed, as one professor explained at the time, "We should protect students from the harm it will do them in the future if they have joined a Communist League." In addition, many academics felt that radical students needed special help. Given the obvious problems that belonging to a left-wing organization, even if only to a Marxist study group, entailed, students who persisted in such affiliations, so the accepted wisdom went, had to be either obtuse or crazy. Academic administrators, who knew that their local radicals were not stupid, therefore assumed that the political activities of these students were symptomatic of some deeper mental trouble. When Harvard's dean, McGeorge Bundy, was considering the former head of the John Reed Club for a faculty appointment, he made him see a University psychiatrist. Bundy explained, "I wished to reinforce my own assurance to the Corporation that he was nonetheless a man of strength and balance." The University of Michigan's dean of women also considered the radicals she dealt with

seriously maladjusted late-adolescents . . . . Rather than a group of tightly cohesive, rigidly disciplined Party members, I see a pathetic group of social and emotional misfits, cursed with just enough brains to complicate any problem but not enough to go to the heart of it.

Perhaps these students were emotionally disturbed; perhaps they weren't. What matters is that so many of the men and women who dealt with them thought they were, a belief that—thanks to several influential studies—was widespread among liberals at the time. And it was an assumption that could enable academic administrators to feel that there was something almost therapeutic in the measures they took to force left-wing student groups off their campuses.[11]

It was probably harder, however, to justify the growing practice of barring politically undesirable speakers from the campus. Even so, as the Cold War intensified, academic authorities became increasingly reluctant to let Communist, and later merely controversial, speakers address their students. Speaker bans were hardly new. In the previous red scare of 1939–41, Harvard, Dartmouth, Brooklyn, Cornell, Vassar, New York University, Princeton, Oberlin, Swarthmore, and Smith all barred Party leader Earl Browder from speaking. Moreover, many schools, state universities in particular, had long-standing regulations against letting outsiders discuss partisan political issues on campus. The University of Washington had banned such speakers since 1912 and the University of California since 1934. Other schools had elaborate clearance procedures involving faculty or administrative approval of all outside speakers. The University of Pittsburgh even required that a faculty member be present at such meetings and that minutes be taken.[12]

During the late forties and early fifties, college restrictions against outside speakers intensified. Schools whose outside speaker policies had previously been liberal began to tighten them. In 1948 the Harvard administration had apparently let German Communist Gerhart Eisler speak without objecting. The following year, however, the dean of students tried to get the leaders of the John Reed Club to cancel a return engagement. The students refused. And when Eisler's appearance drew some right-wing flak the dean courageously announced,

> If Harvard students can be corrupted by an Eisler, Harvard College had better shut down as an educational institution. I know of no faster way of producing communists than by making martyrs out of the handful of communists we now have. Forbidding them to speak . . . would be accepting communist practises in the name of Americanism. Whatever may have happened elsewhere, Harvard still believes in freedom and the American way.

Several years later, another Harvard dean also upheld "the American way" by trying to ban another speaker, the controversial, but definitely not Communist, China scholar Owen Lattimore. His appearance, the dean explained, would "bring added unfavorable publicity to the college." Lattimore spoke anyhow, his speech so tame that he didn't even advocate the recognition of Communist China. But by the spring of 1954 Mc-

Carthyism had made such inroads on the academic scene that Lattimore was as undesirable at Harvard as Eisler had been five years before.[13]

Harvard, to its credit, did not apparently prevent anybody from speaking. Many other schools were less solicitous of civil liberties and not only imposed speaker bans, but on occasion used the incidents that sometimes accompanied such bans as opportunities to discipline student radicals. Faculties were often as repressive as administrations. The Faculty Lecture Committee of the University of Michigan routinely refused to let left-wing student or faculty groups bring speakers onto the campus. After an incident in the spring of 1952 in which a group of students defied the ban and had a forbidden speaker address a theoretically "private" dinner in the student union, a group of faculty liberals tried to change the rules. They failed. Though the faculty of the College of Literature, Science and the Arts, the liberal arts college, condemned the speaker policy, the larger University Senate, representing teachers from the University's professional schools as well as its liberal arts division, refused to change the policy. Its members went along with the University's president who supported the restrictive policy of the Lecture Committee because, as he explained, "no university . . . is quite willing today to become a Hyde Park and invite anyone to place his stump and to speak wherever he wishes."[14]

Because of their greater political vulnerability, state colleges tended to impose the most wide-ranging restrictions on outside speakers. Small schools had a lot of trouble. Miner Teachers College in Washingon, D.C., refused a platform to Pearl Buck; Riverside State Teachers College in California banned *Nation* editor Carey McWilliams. The most notorious incident, however, occurred at a major university, Ohio State. There, in 1951, after the American Legion protested a lecture by Harold Rugg, a Columbia Teachers College professor whose moderately Keynesian textbooks had been Legion targets for years, the Board of Trustees voted to have the president personally approve every single outside speaker at the school. The nationwide outcry that arose when Ohio State president Howard Bevis then banned Cecil Hinshaw, a Quaker pacifist, quickly forced the University to drop its by then discredited "gag rule." Even during the height of McCarthyism there were limits to the degree of censorship an academic institution could impose.[15]

Of course, Hinshaw was no Communist. Had he been, his exclusion would have been routinely accepted, for most of the academic community—and the wider liberal community as well—did not consider the imposition of a speaker ban against members of the Communist Party a violation of civil liberties. Administrators at many schools rarely even bothered to justify such actions. "Mr. Eisler," Michigan's president curtly announced, "will not be permitted to speak on the University of Michigan campus at this time under any auspices." Even civil libertarians understood. When the University of Wisconsin also banned Eisler, the ACLU's Roger Baldwin noted that, though deplorable, the move was defensible "as primarily a matter of public relations." Of course, few academics, administrators or faculty members, would admit that such considerations influenced their decisions. Communist speakers were unwelcome, so these men and women usually claimed, not because of their political beliefs, but because they were currently involved in criminal proceedings. This was the excuse used to ban Earl Browder ten years before. When a Cornell faculty committee refused to let the Smith Act defendant and Party leader Eugene Dennis speak, it did so with the following statement:

> A person under indictment for so serious a charge and now standing trial in a judicial procedure, commanding nationwide and worldwide publicity, should not be permitted to substitute the campus of Cornell University for the legally constituted courtroom as a forum to plead his case.

Since virtually all the top leaders of the CP were being prosecuted for one offense or another, this formulation meant that few American students got to hear the Party's point of view. For there were few, very few, American institutions of higher learning that did not prevent at least some Communists from speaking. Cornell banned not only Dennis but his lawyers as well, for they, too, were under indictment for contempt as a result of the Smith Act trials. Brooklyn College barred Henry Winston; the University of North Carolina, John Gates; Michigan State, Carl Winter; and Columbia, Gus Hall, to name a few.[16]

Nor was it only Smith Act defendants who were kept off campus because they were under indictment. Novelist Howard Fast, who was, as he claimed, "so far as writers went—more or less the public face of the Communist Party of the United States," was facing a contempt charge stemming from HUAC's investigation of a group to which he belonged. He probably experienced more academic ostracism than any other speaker of the time. The New York City municipal colleges banned him, as did both Columbia and New York University. Nor did a speaker have to be involved in a criminal action to be unwelcome on many campuses. Anybody publicly tainted by Communism was eligible. Thus, for example, Queens College refused to let any of the eight New York City teachers fired under the state's anti-Communist Feinberg law speak on campus. Similarly, in the spring of 1949, Wayne University vetoed a lecture by Herbert Phillips, a Communist philosopher recently dismissed from the University of Washington. In defending his action, Wayne's president, David Henry, who only two years before had claimed that "the University has no right to differentiate among American citizens on the basis of political belief," explained,

> In other years I have held that even a Communist should be heard in an educational setting should there be an opportunity at the same time for the expression of contrary points of view . . . . It is now clear that the Communist is to be regarded not as an ordinary citizen . . . but as an

enemy of our national welfare . . . . I cannot believe that the university is under any obligation in the name of education, to give him audience.[17]

Other administrations, less politically vulnerable than Wayne University's, adopted the device that President Henry was disavowing. They would let the controversial speakers appear as long as there was someone else on the platform to rebut them. Such a format solved the problem that many administrators were facing. They were uncomfortable about the implications for academic freedom of actually preventing someone from speaking, but they were equally uncomfortable about the implications for public relations of appearing to condone that speaker. When the UCLA administration decided to let Herbert Phillips speak, it did so with the proviso that he share the platform with one of the men who had recommended his dismissal from the University of Washington. As a further precaution, the administration closed the meeting to undergraduates. Similarly, when Harvard's dean of students suggested that the students who had invited Owen Lattimore to Cambridge withdraw their invitation, he insisted that at the very least there should be another speaker on the program. There was.[18]

It is possible that requiring a rebuttal enabled college administrators to bar speakers without actually seeming to. When the University of Minnesota, for example, refused to let Paul Robeson give a concert on campus in 1952, the University's president, J. L. Morrill, insisted that he was not trying to censor the singer. Had Robeson been willing to submit his ideas to "the rigorous test of scholarly discussion," the University would certainly have let him appear. It was Robeson's "one-sided and musically overtoned propaganda from a concert platform" that Morrill claimed he was objecting to, as well as the fact that the proceeds of the concert would go to "a program opposed to every democratic principle we are fighting to preserve." The Minnesota administration was quite consistent. A few months later, it stopped the showing of a film about China, unless an arrangement were made to rebut the film's propaganda.[19]

Of course, by the time the Minnesota administration banned the China movie in late 1952 and certainly by the time Lattimore spoke at Harvard in early 1954, few academic administrators were actually in the position of having to reject student demands for an unpopular speaker. McCarthyism was at its height, and few students were willing to risk the notoriety and supposed damage to their future careers involved in sponsoring a controversial speaker. Early in 1952, for example, the student members of the Yale Political Forum withdrew a speaking invitation they had given to Howard Fast. The following year, Harvard students did the same. Fast had been asked to speak about "Communism and Hollywood" at the Harvard Law School Forum, but the recent congressional investigations into the University made the law students who had invited Fast uneasy. They rescinded their invitation, explaining that "putting on such a program at this time would not only embarrass, but hurt, several people connected with the University." There was opposition—from the faculty. After Arthur Schlesinger, Jr., chided the law students for their fears, the student affiliate of the ADA renewed the invitation—with the proviso that Fast agree to debate with Schlesinger.[20]

＊   ＊   ＊

By the early fifties, as we have seen, the student left was all but extinct on American campuses, its demise the product of external repression and personal prudence. Faculty radicalism, which even during the 1930s had always been much less in evidence than the student variety, simply did not exist in any organized form after the Second World War. Nonetheless, there was considerable pressure to rid the nation's colleges and universities of politically undesirable teachers. The focus here was on individuals, on the supposedly subversive professors whose affiliation with the Communist Party disqualified them from academic life. The issues that Rapp-Coudert had raised in 1940–41 resurfaced. It was clear that, once the Cold War intensified, the academic community as a whole would have to grapple with the problem that the New York City Board of Higher Education had tackled a few years before. As in the earlier episode, the academy confronted the issue only after outside political authorities forced it to. And, as the New York authorities had done before, academics—administrators and professors alike—readily accommodated themselves, both in theory and practice, to the demand that they expel Communists from their faculties. The process took but a few years.

Here, too, the federal government's loyalty-security program acted as a catalyst. It transformed the Communist Party from an unpopular political movement into a threat to national security, and in the process legitimized the practice of weeding out suspected Communists from the payrolls of other American employers. College teachers, it was quickly becoming clear, would not be immune. In the fall of 1947 one of the members of the AAUP's ruling Council asked the group to decide whether

> in view of the present international situation and the presidential directive, do you think the American Association of University Professors should recognize membership in the Communist Party, if proven and admitted, as sufficient grounds for dismissal?

Though no cases had as yet come to the AAUP's attention, the growing national concern with domestic Communism convinced the organization's leaders that they might soon have to take a stand.

With only two dissenters, the Council decided to endorse as the organization's official policy the wording of a report drawn up by Committee A. That report disagreed with the government's guidelines and strongly rejected the notion of guilt by association, insisting that, even in the delicate issue of Communism, "this Association should apply the touchstone of individual culpability." Obviously, the report continued, if a teacher "should advocate the forcible overthrow of the government or should incite others to do so" or if he "should use his classes as a forum for communism" or if his thinking should "be so uncritical as to evidence professional unfitness, these are the charges that should be brought against him." And, if these charges could be sustained at a hearing, such a professor

> should be dismissed because of his acts of disloyalty or because of professional unfitness and not because he is a Communist. *So long as the Communist party in the United States is a legal political party, affiliation with that party in and of itself should not be regarded as a justifiable reason for exclusion from the academic profession* [emphasis mine].[21]

There was one important caveat, probably inserted to ensure that the AAUP would not find itself defending people like the Rapp-Coudert witnesses who had lied about their Party affiliation. This stated that "it is assumed that the teacher has not falsified his political affiliation. Lying and subterfuge with reference to political affiliation are in themselves evidence of unfitness for the academic profession." Since few academic Communists had ever openly identified themselves as such, this disclaimer could, in fact, eliminate most of them from the Association's protection. Even so, for the time, Committee A's 1947 Report was a bold statement and was perceived as such. Moreover, despite growing pressure, both within and outside the organization, the AAUP continued to reaffirm its contention that Communism, "in and of itself," should not be grounds for dismissal. Every AAUP convention during the late forties and fifties officially endorsed the 1947 Report, but the gesture had no effect. The AAUP never enforced it and the rest of the academy, less concerned about civil liberties than the members of Committee A, had concluded that Communists were unfit to teach.[22]

The events that precipitated that conclusion occurred in Seattle, where in 1949, as the direct result of an investigation by the state legislature's Fact-finding Committee on Un-American Activities, the University of Washington fired three tenured professors, two of them simply because they were Communists. The product of the Republican electoral victory of 1946, the Fact-finding Committee, under the chairmanship of Albert Canwell, a first-term representative and former deputy sheriff, set out to find Communists in the state's once active Popular Front. Canwell's first target was a local organization of the elderly, but he made it clear that he was planning to investigate the University as well. "For years and years we members of the Senate have heard it," explained one of Canwell's colleagues on the committee,

> there isn't a student who has attended this university who has not been taught subversive activities . . . . I have reports that show definitely that five professors teach subversive activities at the school and other reports that the number is as high as thirty.

Other legislators put the number at 150. And at the Canwell Committee's first set of hearings, several witnesses identified some of the University's professors as Communists. The Board of Regents welcomed the investigation; it would, the Board hoped, clear up the rumors that had been circulating for years. The Board met with Canwell in April 1948 and promised to cooperate with his investigation, assuring him "that if evidence is presented through the work of the Committee, showing beyond any doubt any faculty member to be engaged in subversive activity, it [the Board] would move immediately for such member's dismissal."[23]

The University's new president, Raymond B. Allen, a former medical school dean from Illinois, planned to cooperate as well. In his inaugural address in May 1947, he reminded his faculty about its "special obligation to deal in a scholarly way with controversial questions" and cautioned them that if they strayed from such objectivity "they will lose their security." He warned the faculty again in December, telling them, so he later claimed, "that if there were any Communists, and I was not assuming that there were any on our faculty, but if there were, I thought that they ought to get off the faculty . . . before they were smoked out." He also met with the steering committee of the University of Washington's chapter of the AAUP and convinced its members, as well as the leaders of the faculty Senate, that the good of the University required that they not only cooperate with Canwell, but refrain from criticizing him as well. Finally, on May 12, after the Regents had already promised Canwell their support, Allen called a special faculty meeting to discuss the coming investigation.[24]

Since no transcripts of that meeting exist, it is unclear how strongly Allen may have urged his listeners to let him know about their past or present connections with the Communist Party. He later claimed that he had warned the faculty not to "expect the administration to defend any faculty member who had been carrying on activities the nature of which was unknown." But this may be a self-serving statement, for, when Allen decided to press charges against some of his faculty members, he was to stress their lack of candor with him. At the time, he may not have felt it was quite as crucial as he later did and he may have been giving out mixed messages. Certainly his attitude at the conferences he held with the faculty members whom Canwell had subpoenaed supports that contention. Although he urged them to "stand up and be counted" and tell Canwell all about their relations with the Communist Party, he did not, for example, ask them to name names. The professors were similarly confused. They could not agree among themselves upon a common course of action. Some talked of refusing to honor their subpoenas. Others were planning to answer questions about themselves, but not about others. Some refused to tell Allen whether they were or had ever been Communists. But some of those people then changed their minds and in later conversations with the president admitted that they had been in the Party and had left.[25]

The Canwell Committee's July 1948 hearings into subversive activities at the University of Washington lasted for a week. Perhaps their most interesting aspect was not their findings, that there had been a few Communists at the University; rather it was their similarity to the Rapp-Coudert hearings and to every other anti-Communist investigation then taking place. The same issues were raised, the same procedures were used, and the same witnesses appeared. Professional ex-Communists and former fellow travelers trooped out to Seattle to tell Canwell and his fellow legislators how the CP was planning to overthrow the American government by force, violence, and subterfuge. Little of the testimony of these supposed experts—Louis Budenz, the former managing editor of the *Daily Worker* who left the Party for the Catholic Church and a full-time career as a professional witness, or J. P. Matthews, the ex-missionary and fellow traveler who left the Popular Front for the anti-Communist crusade—concerned un-American activities at the University of Washington. Matthews, for example, accused Eisenhower, then president of Columbia, of harboring Communists there and identified Arthur Schlesinger, Jr. as a Party member. Less flamboyant witnesses discussed the Seattle left and helped the committee link University people to its activities.[26]

Eleven professors appeared. Two, Joseph Cohen and Melvin Rader, denied that they had ever been in the Party.* One, an English professor, Sophus Keith Winther, talked about his few years in the Party and named names. None of the others did. One man admitted that he had been in the CP for a year, but claimed that he couldn't remember any of his comrades. Four others—Maud Beal, Harold Eby, Garland Ethel, and Melville Jacobs—revealed that they, too, had been Communists, but refused to name names. Three professors, Joseph Butterworth, Herbert Phillips, and Ralph Gundlach, were completely uncooperative. They refused to answer any questions about their political beliefs or associates. As a result, Canwell cited them for contempt. The prosecutor refused to charge Butterworth, but the other two went through years of litigation. Phillips was tried and finally acquitted; Gundlach, tried and convicted, actually spent thirty days in jail.[28]

The Canwell Committee's hearings were, it turned out, only the first stage in the two-part process of eliminating supposed Communists from the University of Washington. Canwell had, he announced, provided the

---

* Rader became involved in an elaborate perjury case because of one of the committee's professional witnesses, George Hewitt, had placed him at a CP-run summer school. In trying to obtain proof that Hewitt had lied, Rader discovered that the Canwell Committee had suppressed exonerating evidence. And when the state of Washington tried to have Hewitt extradited from New York to stand trial for perjury, the entire anti-Communist network rallied behind him and managed to convince the New York authorities that Hewitt was himself the victim of persecution.[27]

service of "exposing the Communists who have been active on the faculty and on the campus." Now the University had to act, and President Allen realized that whatever the University did would have far-reaching implications. "The University is in the national spotlight in this matter," Allen wrote to Budenz, whom he was asking to testify in the forthcoming faculty trial, "because it is the first university that has faced this issue squarely." The issue, of course, was the fitness of Communist Party members to teach, and Allen realized that the outcome of the University's deliberations would set a precedent for the rest of the country. Accordingly, he acted with the utmost circumspection. He knew that political pressures from outside the University, as well as the strong anti-Communist sentiments of the majority of the Regents, would probably require the dismissal of at least some professors. And during the faculty hearings he admitted that were he to try to keep an admitted member of the Communist Party on the faculty, he would not "have a prayer of a chance of getting away with it in a public institution now." At the same time he was conscious of the necessity for trying to accomplish the purge without such a serious breach of academic freedom that it would hurt the University's standing within the wider academic community.[29]

This was a twofold task. First, Allen had to ensure that the University observe all the procedural requirements of academic freedom and take no action until the accused professors received a fair hearing from a committee of their peers. The second task was to redefine academic fitness in such a way as to exclude members of the CP. As Allen saw it, this meant showing that the professional requirements of "competency, honesty, and attention to duty" were not "compatible with the secrecy of the Party's methods and objectives, with the refusal of Communists to hold their party membership openly, with the commitment to dogmas that are held to be superior to scientific examination."[30]

Allen was careful to ensure that the accused professors, all of whom had tenure, were granted the fullest measure of procedural due process. He even had the University cover the expenses of the witnesses who testified for the defense of the men he was trying to dismiss. He consulted with the national headquarters of the AAUP and apparently convinced its general secretary, Ralph Himstead, that the University would be so scrupulous with regard to academic freedom that the AAUP did not have to send observers to the forthcoming hearings as the local chapter had requested. Allen brought the faculty into every stage of the proceedings. Thus, for example, as soon as the Canwell hearings ended, Allen asked a special faculty committee to decide whether or not to press charges against the uncooperative witnesses. Though some members of the committee felt that they should not act as prosecutors, the majority apparently believed that, unless they acted, the Regents would intervene and prevent the faculty from dealing with the matter altogether. Accordingly, the special committee recommended that the University's already established Committee on Tenure and Academic Freedom investigate six

people: Butterworth, Gundlach, Phillips, Eby, Ethel, and Jacobs. The
first three had refused to tell Canwell whether or not they were Communists; the others had refused to name names.[31]

On September 8, 1948, the dean of the college officially filed charges
against the six. Though he tried to make the wording of the charges conform to the grounds for dismissal specified in the University's Administrative Code (i.e. incompetency, neglect of duty, physical or mental incapacity, dishonesty or immorality, and conviction of a felony involving
moral turpitude), the charges really involved one or another of the following issues: past or present membership in the Communist Party, lack
of candor with the administration, and refusal to cooperate with Canwell. The dean charged Butterworth, Gundlach, and Phillips with present
membership and claimed that they had, as had the former members,
displayed "dishonesty and incompetency" because they had "consistently
followed the so-called 'party line,' that is to say, the instructions emanat-
ing from Moscow," and had neglected their duty to the University by
spending their time at political meetings. All of the defendants were
charged with not having voluntarily told the administration about their
Communist ties after Allen's request that they do so at the special faculty meeting of May 12, and, further, of either lying, equivocating, or refusing to tell the president about those ties in their private conferences
with him before the Canwell hearings. Such behavior, the University was
careful to stress, clearly violated the AAUP's proscription against "lying
and subterfuge."[32]

When the hearings began, on October 27, Phillips and Butterworth
revealed that they were still in the Party. The administration, thereupon,
dropped all its other charges against them so that, in the words of the
University's counsel, "there will be before the committee the clear-cut
sole issue, as far as they are concerned, that they are now members of
the Communist Party." This was to be the crux of the University's case.
In direct contradiction to the AAUP, it was to insist that Party membership "in and of itself" was sufficient grounds for dismissal. Accordingly,
Allen focussed the hearings on the nature of the CP in order to show that
it was such an alien organization that the mere fact of membership would
disqualify someone from academic life. Specifically, the University was
trying to prove that the Party was not a regular political party since it
did not "freely and openly" advocate peaceful political change, and instead required "that its members conceal their identity, take on assumed
names, deny membership, and use any means . . . to attain its ends, and
has required undeviating compliance with the mandates of Stalin and
the Soviet government."[33]

As the New York City Board of Higher Education had done during
the Rapp-Coudert hearings, the Washington administration culled the
writings of Marx, Engels, Lenin, and Stalin for passages showing the
Party's proclivities for force and violence. It also produced a group of
professional ex-Communists to testify about the nature of the Party. Al-

len tried—and almost succeeded—to persuade Budenz and Whittaker Chambers to come to Seattle. He did manage to recruit two other experienced witnesses: Joseph Kornfeder and Benjamin Gitlow. Though Kornfeder had left the Party in 1934, he nevertheless insisted that it still subscribed to the goal of forcible overthrow. He also identified a long list of organizations as "Communist fronts," including the Consumers Union which, he said, "passed resolutions on various occasions in conformity with the Communist Party line." Gitlow's testimony was even less up-to-date. He had been expelled from the Party in 1929, but, he maintained, none of its basic principles had changed.[34]

The administration also produced some local ex-Communists. One, Professor Sophus Keith Winther, had already cooperated with Canwell. He told the faculty committee about his year in the University's branch of the Party. His testimony conflicted with the official view of the CP as a rigid conspiratorial sect. He explained that he had ever felt constrained about expressing an opinion that might have conflicted with the official Party line and, when asked how the Party had interfered with his academic work, replied that the worst interference he had ever experienced

> was from March 27 of this year to the end of summer school. I came back with a book two-thirds done, and I did not write one word. . . . My classes were interfered with; my home was continually called up; I had investigators standing at my door . . . . I was driven to a state of nervous insecurity by the Canwell Committee.

The other local witness, Howard Smith, had also testified before Canwell. The five years he had spent in the Party had given him considerable insight into the nature of Communism. As he told the faculty committee:

> Marx was a fellow who hated every kind of law and order, or anything else, and he was very intelligent, and he saw people that had property and he could not have it himself, so he decided to divide—to devise a plan by which he could take this property away from them.[35]

The defense brought in its own expert witnesses: Clayton van Lydegraf, the CP's organizational secretary for the state of Washington; Paul Sweezy, a Marxist economist who had formerly taught at Harvard; and a non-Marxist student of Marxism, University of California philosopher and future chancellor at Berkeley, Edward Strong. All three testified that Communist teachings did not invariably call for the violent overthrow of the existing regime.

Significantly, the administration did *not* try to show that the past or present Communism of the defendants had impaired their scholarship. It well knew, as Allen himself was to acknowledge, "that these gentlemen could defend themselves as scholars in their particular fields, as in fact they were." Nor did the administration give any evidence that revealed biased teaching. On the contrary, colleagues and students vouched for the fairness and objectivity of each defendant, and of the two admitted

Communists in particular. Of course, Butterworth, as a specialist in medieval literature, would have had few opportunities for indoctrination. But even Phillips, a philosopher who did discuss more controversial matters in class, always warned his students that he was a Marxist. The defendants also rebutted the administration's contention that they had given up their intellectual freedom when they joined the Party. Since Eby, Ethel, and Jacobs had all left the CP of their own free will, the administration could not charge that they had surrendered their intellectual autonomy to Stalin. For Phillips and Butterworth the problem was more difficult. Phillips insisted that he was "an independent thinker" and did not agree with everything the Party said, but he admitted to the faculty committee, "I despair of convincing people that my agreement with a certain type of policy or a certain line of interpretation is the result of independent thinking, but I think it is."[36]

The heart of the administration's case, however, was the fact that all six defendants had either lied or refused to answer when first questioned by Allen about their membership in the Communist Party. This was a crucial point, for, as the administration presented it, this type of deception was an inherent characteristic of membership in the Party and was, of course, a type of behavior that the academic world could not condone. There is no question that the Party's long-standing policy of concealment was, at least within the academic context, self-defeating. This had been the case during the Rapp-Coudert investigations in the early forties and was to remain an issue throughout the Cold War years. For many, essentially liberal, academics, the furtive nature of the Communist Party and the fact that its members past and present did not announce themselves in public, but rather, as the University of Washington defendants had, tried to evade such a revelation seemed to confirm the image of Communists as conspirators. But did the academic Communists have a choice? Allen himself admitted that, though he personally would defend any present or former Party member who voluntarily revealed his affiliation, given the political situation, such a person would probably lose his job anyhow. Even so, Allen contended, an academic's professional integrity required such a disclosure.[37]

There was, however, another point of view, one that maintained that not only did a professor not have to reveal his political beliefs to his superiors, but that he had an obligation not to do so. As long as a professor's politics did not interfere with his teaching or research, they were his own business and no university had the right to demand that he account for them. If he broke the law, it was up to the state to punish him. For a university to do so would be to circumscribe the political freedom of its members and permit them fewer civil rights than ordinary citizens. This was a radical position, it is true, but not an unreasonable one. Nevertheless, its defense in the super-charged atmosphere of the early Cold War years was to cause serious problems. The case of psychologist Ralph Gundlach illustrates them all.

Gundlach was a stubborn man, a rebel of sorts with a strong streak of anti-authoritarianism in him. Of all the defendants, he was the only one to have had previous run-ins with the administration. Probably the most well-known and productive scholar of the six, he had seen his promotion from assistant to associate professor held up for years until the chairman of his department wheeled a shopping cart into the president's office full of Gundlach's writings and references to them in the works of other scholars. Once promoted, Gundlach was told to avoid controversial research and work with animals. He didn't. He again got into trouble for distributing questionnaires on labor and anti-Semitism to his classes and letting another one of his questionnaires be used in a local congressional campaign. But Gundlach was no Communist; he was not even, as he told the faculty committee, an "intellectual Marxist." He was simply a political radical whose passion for social justice and activist temperament brought him into just about every Popular Front group in Seattle. Since many people assumed that because of his associations Gundlach had to be a Communist, he felt that it was all but impossible for him to deny that he was one, especially since, as he told Allen, "one of the definitions of a Communist is a person that denies he is a Communist." As a result, when Allen had initially asked him whether or not he was in the Party, he had refused to answer, insisting that "no one could prove that I was, but I could not prove that I was not."[38]

No doubt, Gundlach's past troubles and his refusal to cooperate with the University must have antagonized Allen. Given the extent of Gundlach's participation in left-wing activities—greater, Canwell claimed, than that of all the other faculty witnesses combined—it is not surprising that Allen assumed Gundlach had behaved so defiantly because he was a Communist. Accordingly, the administration set out to prove to the faculty committee that Gundlach was in the Party. It was able to find a few witnesses who claimed that they had seen him at "the kinds of meetings the Communist Party members went to," but the ex-Communists Eby, Ethel, and Jacobs, who certainly would have known if Gundlach was in the Party, denied it. The bulk of the case against Gundlach, therefore, was circumstantial. The University presented evidence of his political activities and declared that they were the same as those of any Party member. At one point, the University's counsel asked Gundlach's opinion on a whole list of issues from the draft and the Smith Act trial to the abolition of the poll tax and anti-lynching legislation, and then introduced a Communist pamphlet which favored all the same positions. Throughout the hearings, Gundlach's behavior contributed little to his defense. He was not defiant, but his insistence on maintaining the intellectual and political integrity of his position that a university should not impose political tests on its faculty apparently confused and annoyed some of his listeners.[39]

The hearings lasted for six weeks; on January 8, 1949, the Tenure Committee presented its recommendations to Allen. It was not unanimous. The majority of the committee agreed that the proceedings had shown that belonging to the Communist Party should disqualify a teacher. Yet because the Administrative Code did not specify Party membership as a ground for dismissal, five members of the committee, though convinced that Communists should be fired, did not feel that they had the power to recommend the dismissal of Phillips and Butterworth. Three of the committee members urged a more lenient interpretation of the Administrative Code and recommended that the two men be fired out of hand. The remaining three argued that the administration's case against the CP was irrelevant since it produced no evidence that Phillips and Butterworth were unfit to teach. "We sit to try Butterworth and Phillips," they explained, "not [William Z.] Foster and [Eugene] Dennis."[40]

The committee was closer to agreement on Gundlach; it voted 7 to 4 to fire him, the majority agreeing with the administration that even if Gundlach was not officially a Communist he was, nonetheless, "a more effective agent for communism than the respondents who admit Communist Party membership." Yet since most of the committee felt unable to fire someone on membership grounds alone, they based their recommendation on Gundlach's evasiveness with Allen, set against the "background of unsatisfactory relations between Gundlach and the University administration," and their "conviction that in a number of respects Gundlach has been equally evasive in his testimony before this committee." Such behavior, especially Gundlach's failure to answer Allen's questions, constituted "neglect of duty," which the committee defined as including, in addition to teaching, "a reasonable measure of cooperation with the University in matters affecting the welfare and reputation of the institution." This notion that a professor had the "duty" to safeguard his university's "reputation" was to become an increasingly important element in the academy's response to the growing pressures of McCarthyism.[41]

The committee unanimously recommended keeping Eby, Ethel, and Jacobs. It did not condone everything the three men had done; in particular, it deplored "Jacobs' untruthfulness" at his first conference with Allen, but it did not feel anything the three men did was serious enough to constitute grounds for dismissal. Significantly, the committee took note of the three professors' refusal to name names before the Canwell Committee, but did not think that the University had to deal with it. "The refusal of a faculty member to testify before a tribunal which possesses the power to punish for contempt is a subject to be dealt with by that or other tribunals duly constituted for that purpose."[42]

A few days later Allen forwarded the faculty committee's report to the Regents along with his own recommendations. He disagreed with the committee's majority and urged the Regents to fire Butterworth and Phillips. Technically, Allen pointed out, the Regents were not bound by the Administrative Code and in any case, he argued, the two men were "incompetent" by virtue of their membership in the Communist Party. Allen's argument was important; the reasons he gave for why Communism disqualified its adherents from the academic profession would soon be embraced by the academic world. Essentially, he argued, as the faculty committee had done, that academics "have special obligations" that "involve questions of intellectual honesty and integrity." Communism, because of its demand for uncritical acceptance of the Party's line, interferes with that quest for the truth "which is the first obligation and duty of the teacher." Because it was impossible for even the most "sincere" individual to belong to the Communist Party and yet retain an open mind, Allen concluded that Butterworth and Phillips were "by reason of their admitted membership in the Communist Party . . . incompetent, intellectually dishonest, and derelict in their duty to find and teach the truth."[43]

Allen agreed with the faculty committee that Gundlach should be dismissed, but he felt that the grounds should be Gundlach's political affiliation, not his ornery behavior. Admitting that it was impossible to prove that Gundlach actually belonged to the Communist Party, Allen pointed out that

> he has at the very least been one of that special group of Party workers who deliberately do not become Party members so that they may better serve the purposes of the Party. Entirely aside from whether he pays dues and carries a card, Gundlach has done more for the Party than any other respondent.

He urged the Regents to dismiss Gundlach for that reason. Allen recommended that Eby and Ethel be kept, but made no comment on the case of Jacobs, because he himself had been the man Jacobs had lied to. The Regents met on January 22, and though some of them reportedly wanted to fire all six professors they finally accepted Allen's recommendations and fired Butterworth, Phillips, and Gundlach. They retained Eby, Ethel, and Jacobs, but put them on probation for two years and made them sign an affidavit that they were no longer in the Communist Party.[44]

As expected, the Regents' decision had nationwide repercussions. At the University of Washington, where Allen's request for cooperation with Canwell had muted most of the opposition, the firings triggered it off. Students held rallies and professors circulated an open letter criticizing the dismissals. But out of a faculty of about 700, only 103 signed it. One professor resigned over the incident (though he may have been planning to quit anyhow); a few outsiders, scheduled to teach summer school, cancelled their plans. The faculty Senate, asked to protest the Regents' refusal to follow the faculty committee's recommendations, tabled the motion. No doubt, the fact that the firings confounded several issues of academic freedom made it difficult for the Washington faculty to respond. People who may well have been upset by the procedural aspects of the case—the Regents' technical incursions against the faculty's autonomy—were, nonetheless, in agreement with its substantive aspects and did not want to do anything that could be interpreted as condoning Communists as teachers. In addition, many professors refrained from acting because they assumed that the AAUP would enter the case and they did not want to do anything that would prejudice its findings.[45]

The three fired professors had no such restraints. All went on speaking tours to campuses across the country. They also tried to find new jobs. Butterworth sent out some 2000 letters. Phillips did the same, applying, he claimed, "to most of the American colleges and universities listed in Lovejoy's Guide." Neither man got even a nibble. Gundlach, who was about to become president of the Western Psychological Association, had considerable stature in his field and feared that the faculty committee's criticism of his professional competence might damage his reputation. Accordingly, he asked the two main professional societies in his field, the American Psychological Association and the Society for the Psychological Study of Social Issues, to evaluate his work. Both organizations produced favorable reports; the APA's noted that many of the charges against him "were not only unsubstantiated, but in some instances far fetched," and it concluded that "his dismissal had nothing to do with his professional competence as a social psychologist." It made no difference. Gundlach had been promised some temporary positions by his colleagues at other schools while he waited for the reinstatement that he apparently expected would take place. None of the temporary jobs came through.[46]

The inability of Butterworth, Phillips, and Gundlach to get academic positions, despite their competence as scholars and teachers, shows how unanimously the academy embraced the policy adopted by the University of Washington. Dozens of academic leaders—as well as American Legion posts, DAR chapters, businessmen's organizations, and affiliates of the AF of L—sent congratulatory notes to President Allen. Though there had been a recent spate of politically motivated dismissals, most were at smaller, less prestigious schools and involved people who had been active in the presidential campaign of Henry Wallace. Few concerned tenured professors or grappled directly with the issue of Communist teachers. The University of Washington's was, thus, the first important academic freedom case of the Cold War—and it was recognized as such. Allen took upon himself the task of explaining what Washington had done and became a national spokesman for the movement to eliminate Communists from academic life. He had a special expertise on the matter, he claimed, because the Washington cases

> provide, perhaps for the first time, a well-documented and fairly considered study of the question of Communism and education—a study in which the full procedures and machinery of a well-established academic organization have been utilized.[47]

Of course, the reason Allen's claims to expertise earned him a national audience was not that the University of Washington's investigation had unearthed new truths, but that it provided a model which the rest of the academy, under growing pressure to do something about Communists, could imitate. Allen was far from alone in his mission. The Washington firings had stimulated a national debate and, for a few months in 1949, the question of the fitness of Communists as teachers received considerable attention in the national media. There were debates over network radio and articles in the *New York Times Magazine* and *Saturday Evening Post* as well as in more specialized journals. In them, Allen and such respected thinkers as Sidney Hook and Arthur O. Lovejoy explained why Communists should not be teachers. Their ideas were not new. They had already been articulated during the Rapp-Coudert controversy and had pretty well become common currency within the academic community. The University of Washington cases simply gave them greater saliency.

From the start, Allen, Hook, and the others presented themselves as the defenders of academic freedom. In an important sense, they were. For by redefining academic freedom to require the exclusion of Communists from the academy and explaining that necessity in professional, rather than political, terms, they were hoping to keep outsiders at bay. If we define academic freedom in institutional instead of ideological terms, as the preservation of the professional autonomy of the academy, then we can understand why so many people believed it was necessary to anticipate outside pressures and get rid of Communist professors before reactionary politicians, who were unable to tell a crypto-Communist from an anti-Communist, took over the task. For Sidney Hook, the brilliant polemicist who more than anyone else was to become identified with this redefinition of academic freedom, this form of self-policing was crucial. As early as 1939 he had warned the academic world to cleanse itself of Communists or risk "playing into the hands of native reaction which would like to wipe out all liberal dissent." Allen was equally concerned about the threat of outside intervention and he urged the academy to purge itself of Communists "lest its function of setting the qualifications of its faculty be taken over by some other agencies to the serious and lasting curtailment of academic freedom."[48]

The task, then, was to show how membership in the Communist Party disqualified someone from academic life. Basically, as Allen, Hook, and the others explained, the academic disqualifications of a Party member rested on two specific characteristics of that Party. The first was the CP's demand for total adherence to the Party line. This meant, so it was assumed, that the academic Communist had not only committed himself to the furtherance of undemocratic goals by illegal means, but that he had also surrendered his intellectual freedom. The second was the seemingly conspiratorial nature of the Communist Party. Though the secrecy which surrounded Party membership was but one aspect of that membership, the academic anti-Communists were to fix upon it and establish it as perhaps the most important disqualification of an academic Communist. More serious charges like indoctrination and espionage (the latter with regard to scientists, in particular) did surface on occasion, but they were usually presented as potential dangers rather than real ones, no actual cases of atomic spies or classroom ideologues having ever been found. And, in fact, most of the evidence used to prove the unfitness of an academic Communist was either theoretical or out-of-date. Only rarely did these commentators examine what Communist professors actually did or thought.

Communism was, of course, perceived as a threat in and of itself. Like the prosecution in the Rapp-Coudert and Smith Act trials and the administration in the University of Washington hearings, the academic anti-Communists tried to portray the CPUSA as an organization dedicated to the overthrow of the American system by force, violence, and subterfuge. They ignored every statement to the contrary, whether it came from Party leaders, outside experts (as in the Washington hearings), or academic Communists themselves, dismissing such disclaimers as propaganda and insisting that only the most damaging statements were true. Thus, for example, Sidney Hook embellished his argument with copious quotations from Lenin to show how Communists must use "any and every sacrifice and even—if need be—resort to all sorts of stratagems, manoeuvres, and illegal methods, to evasions and subterfuges." Arthur O. Lovejoy used similar excerpts from Lenin to prove that adherence to Communism requires "the rejection of the generally accepted code of morals."[49]

Dangerous as it was to the rest of society, Communism was particularly threatening to the academic world; the totalitarian proclivities of its adherents jeopardized the very existence of academic freedom. Lovejoy, who as one of the founders of the AAUP had a special commitment to academic freedom, explained why:

> A member of the Communist Party is . . . engaged in a movement which has already extinguished academic freedom in many countries and would—if it were successful here—result in the abolition of such freedom in American universities.
>
> No one, therefore, who desires to maintain academic freedom in America can consistently favor that movement or give indirect assistance to it by accepting as fit members of the faculties of universities, persons who have voluntarily adhered to an organization one of whose aims is to abolish academic freedom.

In other words, because there was no academic freedom in Russia, American Communists had no right to enjoy it here. Moreover, as Lovejoy pointed out, the academy would be collaborating in "the legitimacy and inevitability of its own suicide" if it let Communists continue to teach. This was a common theme. T. V. Smith, a journalist-philosopher from Syracuse University who participated in several round tables on the issue, put it most succinctly. "They do not have a right to teach in institutions whose ends they disavow and whose means they subvert as best they can." Smith emphasized, as did Hook among others, that, in any case, depriving a teacher of a job was not depriving him of any of his civil rights or punishing him in any legal sense. "The enforcement of the proper professional standards," Hook explained, "is a matter of ethical hygiene not of political heresy or persecution."[50]

This argument rested on the explicit assumption that all Communists followed all of the Party line all the time. This meant not only that academic Communists would commit illegal acts if ordered to do so by the Kremlin, but also that they had surrendered their intelligence to the Party as well. Both Lovejoy and President Allen were vehement on the matter. For Allen, the University of Washington's hearings "proved beyond any shadow of doubt that a member of the Communist party is not a free man—that he is instead a slave to immutable dogma. . . . He has abdicated control over his intellectual life." As proof, Allen referred to Lysenko and described how enforcement of his genetic theory had gutted Soviet science. Allen ignored the fact that at the Washington hearings Herbert Phillips, whom Allen condemned as a "robot," confessed that he thought Lysenkoism was "stupid." Allen stressed this argument more forcefully than some of the other writers did, for, as many people pointed out, one could also charge Catholics or Quaker pacifists with a similar lack of independence. A more nuanced approach admitted that there might be different standards for different disciplines. Though Marxism-Leninism might not necessarily disqualify someone from teaching in the physical sciences, it might, in the words of the ACLU's Roger Baldwin, "in relation to appointments in an economics or government department where professional fitness might be compromised by party membership or even fellow-travelling."[51]

Baldwin, who had learned anti-Communism in the wake of the Party's 1939 flip-flop, assumed as did most Americans that academic Communists automatically followed where Moscow led. In fact, of course, this was not the case. As the eminent mathematician Norbert Weiner, several of whose colleagues in the MIT Mathematics Department had been in the Party, explained privately to Baldwin, "It is not the task of the non-communist to hold all members of the Communist party to a party discipline which is scarcely shared with respect to matters of private thought by a very considerable number of people who have attached themselves to the group." Joseph Butterworth complained publicly that

> because Professor Phillips and I believe in Marxism-Leninism, and because we are members of the Communist Party, we are therefore responsible, by association, for all the words and deeds of the Communist movement since 1848, irrespective of time, place, nationality or context.

If the testimony of its former academic members is to be believed, the Party did not demand absolute obedience from them. It didn't have to. As Herbert Phillips put it, "I am a member of the Communist Party because I hold the ideas I do; I do not hold the ideas I do because I am a member of the Communist Party." Many people expected a Communist to resign from the Party the minute he or she disagreed with one of its policies, but most Communists had a less black-and-white vision of their affiliation. Certainly they had reservations about some aspects of the Party line, but they supported most of it most of the time. And, had the Party demanded absolute conformity in intellectual matters, its academic members would have bolted sooner than they eventually did. But so strong was the need to present the CP as a monolith that even someone as sophisticated as Arthur O. Lovejoy insisted that the only way a Communist professor could prove that he was intellectually independent was to quit the Party and denounce it in public.[52]

Unquestionably, a Communist teacher who indoctrinated his students would have committed the cardinal sin of academic life. But there was no evidence that any of them had, only the assumption, as Sidney Hook put it, that such "professional misconduct" was what a Communist

> has pledged himself to engage in by virtue of his membership in an organization whose professed aim is to indoctrinate for the Communist party in classrooms, enroll students in Communist Youth organizations, rewrite textbooks from the Communist point of view, build cells on campus, capture departments, and inculcate the Communist line that in case of war students should turn their arms against their own government.

To bolster his argument for indoctrination by association, Hook quoted William Z. Foster and other Party notables to show that the CP wanted its academic members to teach the Party line. The most telling quotation he cited was by a pseudonymous "Richard Frank" who, in a 1937 article in *Communist* magazine, had written, "Only when teachers have really mastered Marxism-Leninism will they be able skillfully to inject it into their teaching at the least risk of exposure and at the same time to conduct struggles around the schools in a truly Bolshevik manner." This passage, which had been uncovered by Benjamin Mandel during the Rapp-Coudert hearings, was the main authority cited as evidence for the Party's desire to promote Communism in the classroom. Not only did Hook use it; Lovejoy did too, and so did T. V. Smith, J. B. Matthews, HUAC, and the Senate Internal Security Subcommittee.[53]

There was no other proof, no doubt because there was no indoctrination. As we have seen, Communist teachers, both for professional and prudential reasons, did not try to proselytize in class. None were even charged with doing so. Smith and Hook both insisted that in order to obtain evidence of Party-line teaching, college administrators would have to send spies into the classroom and that, they claimed, would disrupt the educational process far more than firing the teachers.[54]

Since evidence of twisted teaching was hard to come by, the academic anti-Communists cited other, primarily extracurricular, activities of the Communist teachers as reasons for disqualifying them from academic life. Here they had more evidence, though much of it, too, was out-of-date. Communist teachers were disruptive. For T. V. Smith, they "ruin, as a handful of them can and will, our fine professional colleague-ship." Sidney Hook was similarly concerned about the disruptive behavior of Communist professors. Unlike Smith, he gave some concrete examples. In a 1939 article he cited an "Open Letter" signed by some 400 intellectuals which defended Russia as a "bulwark against war and aggression" and attacked him, Norman Thomas, John Dewey, and the other left-wing and liberal leaders of the anti-Communist Committee for Cultural Freedom as "Fascists and allies of Fascists." And in a 1949 article he pointed to the damage done by the shop-papers put out by Party units to the faculties at Brooklyn College and CCNY. He quoted and misquoted excerpts from some of the papers' more scurrilous attacks on individuals and explained that such practices "can destroy the morale of the staff, keep an institution in ferment and make teaching and learning more difficult." True, the anonymously edited shop-papers were, as some of the editors themselves were later to admit, often irresponsible and in bad taste. But they had all ceased publication by 1939, ten years before Hook unearthed them as proof that Communists were unfit to teach.[55]

Perhaps the most widely disseminated charge against Communist academics was that they lied about or concealed their membership in the CP. That this lack of candor should disqualify someone from academic life seems to have been the result of the Rapp-Coudert investigation, when it became clear that it was the only charge to which the Communist teachers were vulnerable. It was true. Communist professors did hold clandestine meetings, take Party names, publish anonymous shop-papers and leaflets, and try, with varying amounts of success, to keep their political affiliation a secret. They did this in part because had they acknowledged that they were Communists, they almost certainly would have been fired. On balance, as many of them now admit, they probably should have been more open, but they did not then know that the main charge against them was to be the secret nature of their political affiliation. Nor did they know that the new Cold War definition of academic freedom was to include as one of the professor's main professional obligations the duty to be candid about his past political activities.[56]

Opposition to this updated version of academic freedom was limited. Despite some dissatisfaction within the rank and file, the AAUP stuck to its insistence that Communism didn't automatically disqualify a teacher. A few academic leaders spoke out. Harold Taylor, the president of Sarah Lawrence College, debated Allen and insisted that a professor should be judged by his actions, not his affiliations. He offered the standard civil libertarian objection to firing Communists: "If we begin excluding Communists, we will end by excluding anyone who says anything provocative, unorthodox, or interesting." Alexander Meiklejohn, the former president of Amherst, took a similar position. He questioned the assumption of Allen and Hook that Communist professors were automa-

tons; since they could quit the Party any time they chose, Meiklejohn
pointed out, their acceptance of its doctrine and policies "is voluntary."
What particularly disturbed him, however, were the undemocratic methods used to deal with supposedly undemocratic enemies, the belief "that
suppression is more effective as an agency of freedom than is freedom
itself."[57]

Civil libertarians like Taylor and Meiklejohn were exceptions; for all
their eloquence, they made few converts. The arguments of Allen and
Hook, on the other hand, were to become something like the gospel—
even among liberals—with regard to the issue of Communist teachers.
This was largely because they expressed a consensus that was already in
place. Had other college presidents confronted an avowed Communist
on their faculties, all but a handful of them would have acted as Allen
had. In January 1948 Cornell's Board of Trustees discussed "whether or
not the University could get rid of one of its full professors if he turned
out to be a Communist." At first, President Day argued that it would
be difficult to fire a tenured professor unless he or she had been engaging
in subversive activities. On reflection, Day changed his mind. As he admitted a few weeks later in a letter to one of the trustees,

> it is a part of the established technique of Communistic activity to resort
> to deceit and treachery. . . . anyone accepting formal membership in the
> Communistic [sic] party presumably subscribes to this way of doing busi-
> ness, and hence creates a presumptive case against his being on the faculty
> of Cornell or any other American institution of higher education.

Day's position was a common one. In September 1948, for example, the
dean of the University of Michigan's College of Literature, Science and
the Arts suggested that the Regents might issue a statement explaining
that because

> the fundamental doctrines of the Communist Party deny to its members
> that freedom to think and speak independently which is the basis of Uni-
> versity policy . . . the University will not appoint to its staff nor con-
> tinue on its staff any person who is a member of the Communist Party.[58]

The Washington firings brought all these heretofore private musings
into the open. University presidents rushed to put themselves on the record. Sounding much like President Allen, Cornell's Day proclaimed:

> A man who belongs to the Communist Party and who follows the party
> line, is thereby disqualified from participating in a free, honest inquiry
> after truth, and from belonging on a university faculty devoted to the
> search for truth.

Stanford's Wallace Sterling made a similar pronouncement:

> I doubt very much that a member of the Communist Party is a free agent.
> If he is not a free agent, then it would seem to follow that he cannot be
> objective. If he cannot be objective, he is by definition precluded from
> being an educator.

Academic freedom was not an issue; the presidents pledged themselves to protect it. "There will be no witch-hunts at Yale," declared President Charles Seymour, "because there will be no witches. We do not intend to hire Communists." James Bryant Conant of Harvard expressed similar views. "As long as I am President of the University, I can assure you there will be no policy of inquiry into the political views of members of the staff and no watching over their activities as citizens." But there was one exception:

> In this period of a cold war, I do not believe the usual rules as to political parties apply to the Communist Party. I am convinced that conspiracy and calculated deceit have been and are the characteristic pattern of behavior of regular Communists all over the world. For these reasons, as far as I am concerned, card-holding members of the Communist Party are out of bounds as members of the teaching profession.[59]

In Conant's case—and there is little reason to believe that other academic leaders were different—his public statements reflected his private sentiments. If anything, he seemed to be more vehemently anti-Communist than the public record revealed. A former colleague recalled "that Conant was one of the first to express to him during World War II the opinion that the United States must inevitably oppose the Soviet Union and Communism as well as the Nazis." Another colleague, the dean of the Harvard Business School, noted that "Conant's opposition to Communism is almost violent in its strength." In a letter to Zechariah Chafee, a law school professor, Conant explained that his hatred of Communism came from

> my experience during the War when I knew something of the espionage of party members . . . and from the clear statement of party doctrine in which it is frankly declared that the ethics of war are the prevailing ones vis-à-vis the bourgeois on one hand and the Party on the other.

A recent incident at the University of Minnesota in which physicist Frank Oppenheimer had first told his superiors that he had not been in the Party and then, two years later, reversed himself in front of HUAC had, Conant continued,

> reinforced my reluctant conviction that we are dealing not with a political party but something more akin to a fanatic religious movement . . . . this kind of deceit is in accord with the indoctrination of party members and the calculated policy of conspiracy.[60]

Conant's views had influence far beyond Harvard, for as a member of the National Education Association's twenty-man Educational Policy Commission he, along with Columbia's president Dwight Eisenhower, helped draw up the NEA's report on the problem of Communist teachers. The report, adopted by a 2995 to 5 vote at the organization's national convention in June 1949, gave the standard analysis of the CP. Party "membership, and the accompanying surrender of intellectual integrity, render an individual unfit to discharge the duties of a teacher in this country." Such statements served several functions. To begin with, they registered the overwhelming consensus of the academic profession, certainly of its most visible members, regarding what by 1949 was considered the paramount domestic issue of the day. They also served as a warning to campus radicals that the academy would no longer protect those of its members who belonged to the Communist Party. And, most important, these statements showed the outside world that the nation's colleges and universities were fully cognizant of the dangers of Communism and fully capable of handling those dangers by themselves.[61]

* * *

While the dangers of Communist teachers were, as we have seen, largely theoretical, the dangers of outsiders interfering with the autonomy of the academic profession on the pretext of eradicating those Communist teachers were all too real. Washington's Canwell was unusual only in that his investigation actually unearthed some Communist professors. His goals and methods were otherwise completely typical. During the early years of the Cold War, driving Communists from their states' colleges and universities was an almost universal pastime among the nation's local politicians. Almost every state either held some kind of an investigation or enacted, or tried to enact, some kind of legislation to eliminate Communist teachers. Many of these investigations were amateurish, and the laws that were produced unworkable or unconstitutional. But such was the temper of the times that a bill which failed in one session would be reintroduced or remodelled and passed in the next. Most of these measures, it is true, affected elementary and secondary schoolteachers more directly than college professors. Yet until congressional investigators began seriously looking at education in the spring of 1953, the main pressures on the nation's colleges and universities came at the state level.[62]

Even Harvard was affected. A bill introduced into the Massachusetts legislature in November 1947 would have made it illegal for any of the state's public or private colleges or universities to hire "Communists and others who advocate the overthrow of government by force, violence or other unlawful or unconstitutional means" and would have punished anybody who employed such a person with a stiff fine and up to a year in jail. Though the bill's sponsor, State Attorney General Clarence Barnes, insisted that his measure was aimed at the Party-run Samuel Adams School and would not affect Harvard, the University opposed it. Conant, along with the presidents of MIT and Wellesley, testified publicly against it. Whether or not this opposition was crucial is unclear—the Barnes bill was so poorly drafted that it might have been abandoned in any case.[63]

The fate of the Broyles bills in Illinois encourages similar speculation. Here, too, opposition from academic leaders—Robert Hutchins of the University of Chicago and Edward J. Sparling of Roosevelt University—may well have helped defeat some anti-Communist legislation. The bills, themselves a haphazard mixture of loyalty oaths and provisions against the public employment of Communists, were the product of two years of labor by the so-called Broyles Commission, a group of lawmakers and laymen set up by the state legislature in 1947 at the urging of the American Legion to investigate subversive activities in Illinois. Like most such state investigating committees, the Broyles Commission focussed on education, and on the University of Chicago in particular. After a group of noisy students demonstrated publicly against its proposed bills, the commission decided to hold public hearings on the University of Chicago. It recruited the usual witnesses, J. B. Matthews and Benjamin Gitlow, and at its hearings, conducted in the spring of 1949, it let these and other experts reel off the supposedly incriminating connections of such Chicago luminaries as Rexford G. Tugwell and Harold Urey. But unlike the Canwell hearings which they resembled, the Broyles hearings fizzled.

To begin with, it may have been hard to take them seriously. Even among the normally unsophisticated state investigators, the Broyles Commission stood out. Its final report, a masterpiece of illiteracy, urged "the passing of nihilitory [*sic*] legislation" and decried the "dissilitory [*sic*] reactions of the unthinking citizens." Even so, other schools had cooperated with similar types of investigations and had given credence to the testimony of Matthews, Gitlow, et al. Chicago did not. Perhaps it was because Broyles found no Communists on the faculty and so it was easy to rebut his allegations. Perhaps it was because the University, having already weathered a similar investigation in 1935, was a uniquely independent and cohesive institution. The defiant attitude of Chancellor Hutchins, his insistence that activities like those of the Broyles Commission were "the greatest menace to the United States since Hitler," indubitably had some impact. If nothing else, Hutchins's stance encouraged the subpoenaed professors to defy the committee, and it may even have influenced Governor Adlai Stevenson to veto the Broyles bills. Had other academic leaders been as outspoken as Hutchins in opposing off-campus investigations, they might have mitigated the damage.[64]

In any case, anti-Communist investigations *à la* Broyles and Canwell were the exception, not the norm. Most states legislated rather than investigated. They established clearance procedures for teachers or else they imposed loyalty oaths. Many states did both. The spring of 1949 was a particularly busy time.

The New York State legislature spent only three weeks on its anti-Communist law. Introduced by the senate majority leader Benjamin Feinberg, the measure sped through both houses without any hearings at all. That was fast even for something as popular as a bill to eliminate Communist teachers. But New York was a special case, for the legislature was simply finishing the job that the Rapp-Coudert Committee had begun. Not only had the earlier investigations ended before the committee had exposed all the suspected Communists in New York City's schools and colleges, but there was the possibility that its achievements might be reversed. In 1948, Francis T. Spaulding, the state's Commissioner of Education, confirmed his predecessor's reinstatement of a former CCNY instructor on the grounds that the evidence which the Board of Higher Education had used to fire him was "insufficient to establish that he was a member of the Communist Party." In any case, Spaulding's predecessor claimed that without an anti-Communist law on the books, "a board of education would be without legal justification in dismissing a teacher because of membership."[65]

The Feinberg law supplied that justification. It directed the Regents to draw up a list of subversive organizations, membership in which would automatically constitute "evidence of disqualification for a position in a public school in the state." It also required school administrators to investigate their employees and certify that they did not belong to any organization on the list. The law was immediately challenged in the courts, and in 1952, in the case of Irving Adler, a mathematician whom anti-Semitism had forced into high school rather than college teaching, the Supreme Court upheld the constitutionality of the Feinberg law. As it turned out, the law was never to affect college teachers; the Board of Higher Education discovered that it could avoid the cumbersome procedures that the law required by invoking a provision of the New York City charter to fire any teacher who took the Fifth Amendment before a congressional investigating committee. At the time of its passage, however, New York's politicians believed that in the Feinberg law they had found the final solution to the problem of Communist teachers.[66]

Politicians elsewhere tried similar remedies. Maryland's legislation was typical—and influential. Several other states actually copied its anti-Communist Ober law word for word; others adopted the procedures it set up. The Ober law's provenance was impeccable. Its father was the Harvard-educated president of the Maryland Bar Association, Frank B. Ober. After a highly publicized speech in August 1948 urging the passage of an anti-Communist law, Ober became the chairman of a special commission of legislators and private citizens to draw up such a law. The commission, most of whose members were either lawyers or businessmen, conducted its work in an atmosphere of sobriety. Ober, though such a fervent anti-Communist that he publicly announced that he would no longer give money to his alma mater until Harvard expelled all its left-wing faculty members, concerned himself with ensuring that the proposed legislation was legally enforceable. His commission held all its sessions in secret, apparently hearing evidence on Communist subversion in Maryland from members of the FBI and military intelligence. It also consulted the records of previous investigations and in its final recommendations cited the findings of, among others, Canwell, HUAC, and Rapp-Coudert.[67]

Public hearings on the measure were perfunctory. Arthur O. Lovejoy of Johns Hopkins testified against it, to no avail. The law itself, which passed both houses of the Maryland legislature with only one dissenting vote, was an amalgam of different types of measures. It made subversive organizations illegal and made their members ineligible for state employment. All such employees and candidates for political office as well had to sign loyalty affidavits. Enforcement was in the hands of a "special assistant attorney general in charge of subversive activities." With regard to higher education, the measure was vague. People at public colleges and universities, like all state employees, had to submit written statements to the effect that they were not trying to overthrow the government by force and violence and did not belong to any organization that did. Private institutions which received state aid had to do their own housecleaning and had to report what steps they had taken to detect and eliminate the subversives on their staffs. All the private colleges complied. The presidents of the smaller schools personally vouched for the loyalty of their teachers. Johns Hopkins, which everybody knew was the real target of these provisions, set up a special faculty committee which decided that the University's normal hiring procedures adequately ensured against the danger of subversives. Its report was submitted to and accepted by the attorney general, whose lenient enforcement of the Ober law mitigated what otherwise could have been an extremely repressive piece of legislation. In New Hampshire, for example, where an identical law went into effect, a more gung ho attorney general investigated eagerly and actually prosecuted several people, including the Marxist economist Paul Sweezy.[68]

Other states followed Maryland's example in passing legislation that required college administrators to police their own ranks. In Pennsylvania, there was the Pechan Act, a loyalty-oath bill sponsored by the small-town dentist who was the state legislative chairman of the American Legion. Because the bill was introduced in January 1951, somewhat later than similar measures elsewhere, it encountered more opposition than they had and did not pass until December. During that time it was modified to include, at the suggestion of Harold Stassen, then president of the University of Pennsylvania, a provision requiring the presidents of all the state-aided colleges and universities to submit an annual report declaring "unequivocally" that they "had no reason to believe any subversive persons are in [their] employ" and describing "what steps, if any, have been or are being taken to terminate the employment" of such subversives. As it turned out, this self-policing was somewhat less pro forma than in Maryland. Wendell S. McRae, an employee of Penn State, refused as a matter of conscience to take an oath or fill out a questionnaire. He was fired, but since he was not a Communist and was willing to prove it in other ways, he was quickly reinstated. Other Pennsylvania schools were later to cite the Pechan Act as a justification for dismissing faculty members who refused to cooperate with an anti-Communist investigation. This, though most of the administrations in question had, it should be noted, already certified that these professors were loyal.[69]

Almost every state, whether or not it investigated its universities or had them investigate themselves, imposed some kind of a loyalty oath on its teachers. Both the Ober and the Pechan laws, for example, contained loyalty oaths in addition to their provisions for academic self-certification. By the late fifties, thirty-two states required loyalty oaths. Their inefficacy in no way interfered with their popularity among state legislators, for they were inexpensive to administer and easy for voters to understand. "Any teacher who doesn't want to take a loyalty oath ought to go back to Russia," was the way one rural Pennsylvania legislator viewed the matter. And the fact that in practice many of the people dismissed for refusing to sign such oaths were civil libertarians or Quakers did not keep state legislators from passing them, and often adding new provisions to old oaths.[70]

Two types of oaths were involved. The first was essentially a pledge of allegiance, calling for loyalty to the state, the nation, and their constitutions. Many states had had such oaths on the books for years. Since 1934, for example, New York academics had been pledging to support the federal and state constitutions. Since 1942, every employee of the University of California had had to take a similar oath. Though there was criticism of these oaths for singling out the academic profession and, as one critic pointed out, "reducing the professor to a second-class citizen," they were in themselves innocuous. Neither Communists nor civil libertarians objected to taking them.[71]

The second type of oath presented more problems. The product of the Cold War, it required its takers to swear that they did not subscribe to certain beliefs or belong to certain organizations. Its sole function was to eliminate Communists. In the spring of 1949, for example, the Regents of the University of California decided to make all University employees subscribe to an amended form of the 1942 oath and swear,

> I am not a member of the Communist Party, or under any oath, or a party to any agreement, or under any commitment that is in conflict with my obligations under this oath.

In Oklahoma all state employees, including the faculty and staff of the state's universities, had to swear that not only were they not in the CP, but not in any group "officially determined by the United States Attorney General or other authorized public agency of the United States to be a communist front or subversive organization." The problem with such measures, their critics explained, was that they imposed political tests for employment. In addition, the tests they imposed were often so vague that, like Georgia's prohibition of "sympathy for the doctrines of communism," they could conceivably invite all manner of abuse. In times of stress, one man's liberalism could be another's "sympathy for communism." Moreover, the growing tendency of state legislators to amend earlier oaths and add prohibitions against new types of activities created the danger that even the most innocuous of such oaths could be amended until it came to exclude a wide range of unpopular behavior. And, of course, such oaths violated the most basic tenets of academic freedom: outsiders rather than professional colleagues established the criteria for employment.[72]

This, then, is the significance of the notorious California loyalty oath. By imposing a special oath upon all the employees of the University and then by dismissing some thirty professors for refusing to sign it, the majority of the Board of Regents had unquestionably interfered with the faculty's right to govern itself. From the start, the prestige of the University of California and the clear-cut nature of the threat to academic freedom and tenure ensured wide publicity. For academics, the California case was a reminder of the underlying fragility of academic freedom; for liberals, a reminder that the imposition of an ostensibly harmless oath might have disastrous consequences. On closer examination, however, it turns out that the controversy was considerably more complex. The actual firing of a group of principled liberals diverted attention from the other issues involved. To the extent that the California loyalty-oath controversy was different from the other academic freedom cases of the later 1940s and early 1950s, it was because the professors in question were neither Communists nor ex-Communists, but men and women of principle fired for their stand on principle. To the extent that it was similar to the other cases, it was because the issue that initially provoked the conflict was that of excluding Communists from the University.

At the time the Regents adopted the oath, March 25, 1949, it seemed like an innocuous solution to several problems then plaguing the University. Senator Jack Tenney, chairman of the California State Un-American Activities Committee, had recently submitted a set of bills to the legislature, including one that would have taken jurisdiction over the loyalty of University employees out of the hands of the Regents. Though Tenney's measure never got out of committee, it was not because California's politicians were not concerned about the problem. On March 17, the legislature passed a resolution commending the University of Washington for its recent dismissal of two Communist professors and, in an unmistakable gesture, sent copies to all the Regents. The gesture was unnecessary; the Regents had been dealing with the repercussions of the Washington case ever since UCLA's provost let Herbert Phillips participate in a debate on campus the previous month. Communists had been explicitly banned from the faculty in the aftermath of the Kenneth O. May case in 1940; Phillips's appearance prompted the Regents to consider the advisability of banning them from the campus altogether. A public flap over the cancellation of a speech at UCLA by the British socialist Harold Laski made the issue even more sensitive. Thus, the adoption of an anti-Communist oath, modelled on the one in the recently adopted Taft-Hartley labor

law, seemed to the Regents, who passed it unanimously, as well as to
President Robert Sproul, who apparently suggested it, a harmless way to
reaffirm the University's opposition to Communism.[73]

So routine did the matter seem that it got no publicity at first. It was
not until the middle of May, two and a half months after the oath was
adopted, that the faculty found out that it was to be appended to all contracts for the coming academic year. Accordingly, much of the initial opposition to the oath focussed on what, to many professors, seemed to be
the underhanded way in which it was sprung upon them at the very end
of the term. Special meetings of the Faculty Senate, June 14 in Berkeley,
a few days later in Los Angeles, featured prepared speeches by the men
who were to lead the opposition to the oath for the next year or so.
These non-signers were among the most respected people on the faculty.
Their unofficial leader, Edward Tolman, was a nationally honored psychologist who had taught at Berkeley for thirty-two years, and many
others were equally eminent; among the younger recusants were some of
the University's more promising scholars, including its future president
David Saxon. None were Communists; a significant number, however,
had fled from fascist Europe. These people tried to warn their colleagues
about the dangers ahead. The German-born medievalist Ernst Kantorowicz was most graphic:

> It is the harmless oath that hooks; it hooks *before* it has undergone those
> changes that will render it, bit by bit, less harmless. Mussolini Italy of
> 1931, Hitler Germany of 1933, are terrifying and warning examples for
> the harmless bit-by-bit procedure in connection with political enforced
> oaths.[74]

An angry faculty responded by urging the Regents to change or
eliminate the oath. Over the summer, however, while faculty representatives negotiated with Regents and administrators, copies of the oath
went out with the 1949–50 contracts. Salary checks came through for
non-signers, but formal letters of appointment did not. By the beginning
of the fall term, only 50 percent of the faculty had signed the oath.
Moreover, several months of controversy began to bring out new issues.
Originally the faculty's opposition centered on the oath itself and the
threat to academic freedom that a political test for employment seemed
to pose. Withholding the letters of appointment to non-signers showed
that the new requirement might violate tenure as well. In addition, it
was becoming clear that some members of the faculty opposed not only
the oath but the policy it was designed to implement, the automatic exclusion of Communists from the faculty. For these people, the imposition
of a ban on Communists by the Regents seemed to be an additional in-
cursion against the faculty's right to choose its own members. As the academic year progressed, the futile negotiations between faculty moderates, administrators, and Regents made it increasingly clear that the
Communist issue had precipitated a power struggle.[75]

The Regents—particularly their strongest member, John Francis Ney-lan—were determined to enforce their anti-Communist measure. They saw the oath, which even Neylan admitted was "not worth the paper it is printed on," as a symbolic means of making the faculty accede to their views. The case of David Fox intensified the conflict. Fox, a teaching assistant in the Berkeley Physics Department, had signed the oath. Not long afterward, in September 1949, he took the Fifth Amendment before HUAC. The Regents fired him in December, with Neylan apparently convinced that the case showed how poorly the faculty was policing itself. Attempts at negotiations between the increasingly factionalized faculty and the equally divided Regents foundered. Finally, Neylan and his allies, who believed that an "irreconcilable minority of the faculty [the non-signers group] had ruthlessly maneuvered the situation," forced the issue on February 24, 1950, when they voted to require the faculty to sign the oath or an "equivalent affirmation" by April 30 or be dismissed at the end of the term.[76]

This action, quickly labelled the "Sign-or-Get-Out Ultimatum," mobilized the University; tenure was now at issue. However, since Neylan hinted that he might compromise if the faculty accepted an anti-Communist resolution, the Faculty Senate decided to submit the matter to its members in a mail ballot. Accordingly, a two-part referendum went out. The first part was an oblique rejection of the oath. It affirmed the individual's willingness to subscribe to the old oath of allegiance, but replaced the Regents' disclaimer with a statement that the signer acknowledges the University's "policies . . . excluding members of the Communist Party from employment." The second part of the referendum was an affirmation of those policies:

> No person whose commitments or obligations to any organization, Communist or other, prejudice impartial scholarship and the free pursuit of truth will be employed by the University. Proved members of the Communist Party, by reason of such commitments to that party, are not acceptable as members of the faculty.

Along with the ballots, opponents and supporters of this anti-Communist resolution included materials in support of their positions. The proponents of the resolution cited Arthur O. Lovejoy's argument that academic freedom required the expulsion of Communist teachers. The opponents quoted the AAUP's position that as long as the Communist Party was legal, membership "in and of itself" should not exclude someone from the academic profession. The results were counted and made known on March 22. The faculty had voted overwhelmingly against the oath: 1154 to 136, with 33 abstentions. It had also voted almost as overwhelmingly in favor of the anti-Communist resolution: 1025 to 268, with 30 abstentions.[77]

Presumably, the controversy was over. In order to preserve what they considered to be the essence of academic freedom—the principle of tenure and their own autonomy vis-à-vis the Regents—most of the faculty members at the University of California endorsed a political limitation on that autonomy. They rejected the civil libertarian stance of the non-signers and the AAUP and opted for a harder line. No doubt, most of them believed that active Communists were intrinsically unfitted for academic life and would have supported an anti-Communist resolution even if they were not under pressure. Joel Hildebrand, the chairman of the Advisory Committee of the Northern Branch of the Academic Senate and an influential moderate who was one of the main faculty negotiators in the early stages of the controversy, had himself written a letter congratulating President Allen right after the Washington dismissals, several months before the loyalty-oath crisis erupted.[78]

Surprisingly, the March referendum, which some of the more militant professors felt was a sell-out, did not assuage the Neylan faction. Neylan, who had apparently been willing to amend, but not eliminate, the oath if the faculty voted for an anti-Communist resolution, was miffed by the faculty's continued opposition to the oath and was determined to resist what he considered a "minority" that "is going by threat and menace to run the University of California." He prevailed. The board split 10 to 10 over rescinding its ultimatum, and the April 30 deadline for signing remained. By this time, the matter had become completely embroiled in California politics. Earl Warren, the governor and a Regent by virtue of his office, had never attended a Regents' meeting until January 1950; he quickly took command of the liberal faction opposed to Neylan and was to stay involved with the controversy until the end. Outsiders entered the struggle. A special committee of alumni, which had formed earlier, decided to intervene and mediate the conflict. Its report, which the Regents adopted with only one dissenting vote at their April meeting, recommended that instead of the oath each employee accept his or her appointment by taking the regular constitutional oath and signing a statement declaring that

> I am not a member of the Communist Party or any other organization which advocates the overthrow of the Government by force or violence, and that I have no commitments in conflict with my responsibilities with respect to impartial scholarship and the free pursuit of truth.

The oath, in other words, remained. Non-signers, however, could get a hearing before the Faculty Senate's Committee on Privilege and Tenure.[79]

Though the oath's opponents considered this compromise "a complete defeat," most moderates believed that it restored to the faculty control over the employment of its members. They also believed that the tenure committees would save the jobs of most non-signers. "Unless such individuals are proved to be members of the Communist Party, a condition we believe cannot be shown in any instance to exist," a moderate leader explained, "they will not be dismissed from the University, in spite of their unwillingness to sign the suggested contract." By this point, most of the faculty was obviously sick of the entire business. Moderates urged the non-signers to give in "to have an end to the turmoil, division, and ill-will under which we have so long suffered." They viewed the non-signers as intransigents who were sacrificing the good of the University out of stubbornness and a mistaken concern for principle. The non-signers were insecure, bitter, and isolated; uncertainty and economic pressure had steadily reduced their numbers. By May 15, the new deadline for signing the contract, there were fewer than eighty non-signers left for the tenure committees to grant hearings to as well as over 150 non-signers in other, non-faculty positions.[80]

The hearings began in May and lasted for four weeks, both the Northern and Southern committees submitting their recommendations to Sproul in the middle of June. The Northern committee, which heard two-thirds of the cases, was composed of men—the University's next president, Clark Kerr, among them—who had both signed the oath and voted for the anti-Communist resolution. Each hearing took from half an hour to three or four, during which time the committee questioned the "members of the faculty at length with regard to their possible membership in the Communist Party or in other subversive organizations." It cleared anybody who had received a security clearance from the federal government; such a person, it felt, had already been investigated and proved to be loyal. It also cleared anyone who made a statement to the committee

> that he was not a member of the Communist Party, did not like Communists, had no thought of overthrowing the government by force and violence, and had no commitments which would interfere with his complete loyalty to the United States.

Finally, the committee cleared anyone whose testimony "left no doubt in the minds of the Committee that he was not a Communist." The Southern committee cleared 26 of the 27 people it questioned; the Northern, 47 of 52.[81]

In the furor that was to follow, many people lost sight of the fact that the tenure committees had recommended the dismissal of six men and women. The Northern Committee's report explained that it did so, even though it had "no evidence of disloyalty" on these people's part, because they did not provide "sufficient evidence" for the committee to clear them. Each one had refused "to discuss with the Committee either the question as to whether or not he has any connection with the Communist Party or his views with respect to this organization." Each maintained "that to discuss the subject with the Committee would be, in effect, to make a statement which the person had refused to make in the contract of employment." The committee was, thus, cooperating with the Regents to a certain extent by explicitly enforcing the policy behind the disclaimer, by making members of the faculty submit to a political screening. The non-signers who cooperated with the committee, albeit reluctantly, were willing to recognize the right of the faculty to impose a political test on itself. The non-signers who refused to cooperate with the committee were unwilling to grant such a right, even to their peers. Among these hold-outs, most of whom were junior people, was the sociologist Nevitt Sanford, who, ironically, it must have seemed, had just finished collaborating with Theodor Adorno on the landmark study *The Authoritarian Personality*.[82]

President Sproul accepted the tenure committees' reports and presented them as his own to the Regents on June 23, 1950. Many Regents were shocked that the committees had been so lenient. Neylan and his allies had apparently accepted the alumni compromise with the understanding that the tenure committees would clear those people, like Quakers, who on technical grounds could not sign. Since the faculty was not going to enforce the oath in the way the Neylan faction had expected, it was possible that the compromise might fail. The Regents postponed a vote on the matter for a month. When they met again, July 21, the rush of patriotism inspired by the outbreak of the Korean war had reduced the ranks of the non-signers to 39. The Regents voted 10 to 9 to reinstate them, but a parliamentary maneuver by Neylan forced the Board to postpone its final vote until August. By then there were only 31 non-signers. All the Regents agreed that they were not Communists. The issue had changed. A member of the Warren group was puzzled.

> Now I learn we aren't discussing Communism. The issue now as I see it, we are talking about a matter of discipline of the professors who refused to sign the oath and employment contract as submitted. There is no longer an impugning of those individuals as Communists. It is now a matter of demanding obedience to the law of the Regents.

By a vote of 12 to 10, the bitterly divided Regents decided to insist upon discipline and fire the thirty-one.[83]

When the school year began, a weary and demoralized faculty once again debated the matter, voting to ask its members to contribute voluntarily to the financial support of the non-signers. But by then the matter was out of the hands of both faculty and Regents. The non-signers went to court to seek reinstatement. Governor Warren, who had led the faction of the Regents opposed to the firings, called a special session of the legislature in September supposedly to meet the crisis engendered by the Korean war and more probably to revive his own political fortunes in the wake of the oath controversy. The solution he offered was a loyalty oath to be taken by all public employees and civil defense workers. Known as the Levering oath, after one of its sponsors, it included not only the usual oath of allegiance to state and federal constitutions, but also a disclaimer, far more reaching than the one imposed by the Regents, that the taker not only did not advocate or belong to any party advocating the "overthrow of the Government of the United States or the State of California by force or violence or other unlawful means," but also had not belonged to such an organization for the past five years and would not join one as long as he or she remained in the public employ. Despite Neylan's reluctance, the Regents voted to accept the Levering oath in place of their own.[84]

The California Supreme Court agreed. In November 1952, in its long-awaited opinion on the loyalty-oath case, *Tolman v. Underhill,* the court decided that the Levering oath superseded that of the Regents and ordered the reinstatement of the non-signers. Though substantively more objectionable than the Regents' oath, the Levering oath did not single out University employees and was thus not as repugnant to the non-signers. Ultimately, about half of them decided to take the oath and return to their former jobs. Though Warren had by then appointed enough new Regents to reverse the Neylan majority, it was to take a few more years of litigation before the reinstated professors got their back pay and the conflict finally ended.[85]

Ironically, it was not until the Regents settled with the non-signers, in the spring of 1956, that the AAUP finally got around to censuring the administration of the University of California for its behavior during the loyalty-oath controversy. The delay, of which more elsewhere, was more unexpected than the censure, for it had been clear from the start that most of the academic community, certainly most of its aware and articulate members, considered the conflict to be a disaster for academic freedom. Academics around the country recognized, as this excerpt from a letter from the Princeton faculty put it,

> that this action of the Regents constitutes a denial of an enlightened policy of tenure and repudiates the principle of the self-determination and responsibility of the faculty.

Professors everywhere signed petitions and sent letters of protest. Prominent academics like Howard Mumford Jones, Robert Merton, Rudolf Carnap, and Robert Penn Warren publicly refused invitations to California. Less prominent ones did too: Chandler Davis, the son of Horace Bancroft Davis and a radical in his own right, turned down a job in the UCLA Mathematics Department in the spring of 1950. Professional associations passed resolutions condemning the firings; several, including the Modern Language Association and the American Psychological Association, even requested their members not to accept positions at the University of California. Some departments had real trouble recruiting. The chairman of the Physics Department, which lost five people as a result of the controversy, claimed, "We cannot now induce a single first class theoretical physicist to accept a position at Berkeley."[86]

Not only did the academic community try to boycott California, but it put itself out to help the non-signers. Faculty members at Chicago, the dean of the Graduate School at Brown, offered to find jobs for the recusants. Since many of the non-signers were eminent scholars, they had little trouble and often ended up at places like the Institute for Advanced Study, Johns Hopkins, Vassar, and Harvard. Even the younger people found jobs. The experience, though difficult at the time, did not seem to have had any long-lasting negative effects on people's careers. And it did seem to give them a sense of pride. "I am sure," Tolman wrote to one of the other non-signers several years later, "we all feel better for having stood to our guns. And I believe it is true that we did have a chastening effect upon other university administrations." Tolman was not alone in his assessment of the influence of his group. In their survey of the impact of loyalty programs, sociologists Marie Jahoda and Stuart W. Cook noted that their academic respondents considered the non-signers "both a symbol of the traditional values of American democracy and academic freedom and a source of strength and high morale."[87]

Such an assessment, though satisfying, lacks credibility. When we consider the one school most affected by the oath controversy and the one where the example of the non-signers should have been a preeminent "source of strength and high morale," we find, in the words of observers, "apathy, fear, insecurity," "suspicion, antagonism, irritability, defensiveness, and aggressiveness." The University of California was demoralized, its faculty polarized and embittered. The non-signers and their supporters came to view the moderate leaders who sought to negotiate a compromise as at best misguided, at worst traitors. Feelings ran particularly high after the March 1950 referendum seemed to show that the majority of the faculty had surrendered the original principle of "no political test." Moderates viewed the non-signers as "stiff-necked malcontents," unconcerned about the overall good of the University, needlessly prolonging the struggle to vindicate their own personal stubbornness. Paranoia flourished. Professors were afraid to discuss the oath over the phone. In the spring of 1950 a group of faculty members, sympathetic to the non-signers, decided to produce a book about the case. Significantly, only one man, a signer, affixed his name to the project; the rest of the authors chose to remain anonymous. "To the shame of our state and of our University," they wrote,

> we felt it necessary to organize for the writing of this book as the French organized their *Resistance* during the years of the Nazis, with radiating lines of responsibility and with no one knowing all the others who were involved.[88]

These teachers were probably overdramatizing. Their fears and those of their colleagues that "the University of California has become a second rate institution within the past year" were largely unfounded. But there were scars. The bitterness and acrimony that divided the California faculty may well have dissuaded other people, both at California and elsewhere, from exposing themselves in the way that the non-signers had. There was, for example, little opposition to the Levering oath, even though it was more objectionable than the original one. Only one member of the University of California faculty, Russell Fraser, an instructor in the English Department at UCLA, refused to take the new oath. The

California Supreme Court upheld his ouster, and he found himself as unemployable as Butterworth, Gundlach, and Phillips. The same thing happened to the seven teachers at San Francisco State College who also refused to sign the Levering oath. Their ostracism from the academic community indicated that that community was accommodating itself to some of the most discreditable aspects of McCarthyism. Not only had it agreed to exclude from its ranks those people, i.e. Communists, whom it had defined as unqualified, but it was becoming willing to sacrifice as well people who, though never accused of being Communists, were unwilling to submit to a political test and prove that they were not.[89]

The University of Washington case had cleared the way. As a result of that case and its aftermath in California and elsewhere, large segments of the academic community—professors and administrators alike—had decided that Communists were no longer fit to teach. Outside elements—the Canwell Committee in Washington, state legislatures elsewhere—certainly forced the issue; many academic decision-makers believed that the measures they took were necessary to forestall more serious pressures from outside. Yet the professors and administrators who participated in these early efforts to drive members of the CP off their faculties were not unwilling accomplices. They believed in what they were doing. They neither questioned the anti-Communist agenda that came out of Washington nor reflected upon the repressive nature of their own ban on Communist teachers. Moreover, once the anti-Communist consensus and the machinery for enforcing it was in place, it was to become all too easy for academic institutions to turn against other types of political undesirables. This is what civil libertarians had warned against at the time the University of Washington fired three tenured professors. And once outside pressures from HUAC and the other congressional investigating committees began to build up, this is exactly what happened.

V

"Drawing the Line": The Academy's Early Response to Congressional Investigations and Right-Wing Attacks

On December 16, 1949, at the height of the oath controversy, the Regents of the University of California held a day-long meeting. They discussed the oath in the morning and then, in a special afternoon session, heard testimony from David Fox, a teaching assistant in physics at Berkeley. The Regents had summoned Fox to explain why he had refused to answer certain questions put to him by the House Un-American Activities Committee the previous September. Fox, who had worked on the Manhattan Project at the Berkeley Radiation Laboratory during the war, had been called before the committee along with several other young and formerly radical physicists as part of HUAC's investigation of what it called "Communist Infiltration of Radiation Laboratory and Atomic-Bomb Project at the University of California, Berkeley." Fox had not cooperated with HUAC. When asked, "Were you a member of the Communist cell at the radiation laboratory?" he invoked the Fifth Amendment: "I refuse to answer that question on the ground that it might tend to incriminate me." He then took the Fifth twenty-five more times, to questions about his own political activities and those of his colleagues. The committee, as was its custom, had a long list of names for Fox to identify, but each time HUAC's counsel asked him if someone "is known to you as a member of the Communist Party," he refused to answer. He did, however, stress that he had been scrupulous about security, adding,

> I have never known of any case of espionage that took place in the laboratory. There was only one case where I suspected there might be espionage, and I reported that to the security officer. If I had known of other cases I would have reported them and would not have approved or condoned it.[1]

Though Fox would not discuss his politics with HUAC, he was considerably more forthcoming with the Regents. He described his participation in the left-wing student movement of the late thirties and his attraction to Communism in the forties, and even admitted that, in the early forties, he had been "for all intents and purposes . . . a member of the party." But, Fox told the Regents, he soon grew disillusioned: "As I began to see more and more of the organization, I felt it was not for me, and once I left it, I was able to think things out very carefully and could see that I disagreed with them." He regretted that his appearance before HUAC had embarrassed the University, but felt that even if he had named names, the school still would have suffered.[2]

The Regents disagreed. Many considered him politically suspect. For them, an ex-Communist who "is still sticking to the people who were communists along with him" had not broken completely with the Party. They also felt that he had not been frank with them and that, in the words of Regent Neylan, his testimony had not "repaired the damage he did to the university." No one, it is true, tried to prove that Fox was still a Communist; he had, after all, signed the loyalty oath. With only one dissenting vote, the Regents resolved to dismiss him from the University on the grounds that "he did not meet the minimum requirements for membership in its teaching departments." Admittedly, Fox, as a teaching assistant, enjoyed far fewer protections than a regular faculty member. And few people on the already embattled campus were willing to protest his dismissal, even though they recognized that he had been fired on dangerously vague grounds. No code, no set of regulations had ever spelled out any "minimum requirements" for an academic position at the University of California. Fox's dismissal, however, seemed to imply that those requirements were political and that they might well come to include a willingness to name names before a congressional investigating committee.[3]

* * *

By the end of 1949, when the Regents fired Fox, or certainly by the time the Korean war broke out six months later, the academic world had largely reached a consensus that self-professed members of the Communist Party were unfit to teach. The result of the University of Washington cases, this consensus had little practical impact, for there were few, if any, admitted Communists on the faculties of America's colleges and universities by late 1949. The problem that was to roil the academic world was not that of so-called "card-carrying" Communists, but of "Fifth Amendment" ones—most of them, like Fox, former Party members who did not want to cooperate with congressional investigating committees or name names. This was not an immediate problem, however. In the late forties and early fifties, only a handful of college teachers were unfriendly witnesses, and they had been called up for reasons unrelated to their academic positions. It was not until late 1952, when it became clear that the main congressional investigating committees were about to look into the alleged Communist subversion of education, that the academy as a whole had to grapple with the issue. Until then, those

schools with uncooperative witnesses on their faculties handled the matter on an ad hoc basis. Even so, they set precedents.

One reason the academic world did not become concerned about
uncooperative witnesses until fairly late in the game was that the problem was brand new. The first academic to invoke the Fifth before an
anti-Communist investigation did so during the Rapp-Coudert hearings
in 1941, and he was dismissed at once. Understandably, other witnesses
in similar circumstances did not follow his example. When a reactivated HUAC resumed the search for Communists after the Second
World War, few uncooperative witnesses, academic or otherwise, took
the Fifth. Instead, they refused to answer the committee's questions on
the grounds that the questions themselves were unconstitutional. These
witnesses and their lawyers assumed that the First Amendment's guarantees against congressional interference with freedom of speech and
association prohibited investigating committees from asking people about
their political beliefs and activities. This was the presumption under
which the Hollywood Ten testified in the fall of 1947. Instead of taking
the Fifth, as later hostile witnesses were to do when asked if they belonged to the Communist Party, they shouted back at their inquisitors
and lectured them about the unconstitutionality of the proceedings. They
never thought they would go to jail. But by the time their case reached
the Supreme Court (which refused to hear it), the Court had ruled that
congressional committees did have the right to ask witnesses about their
politics and to jail them for contempt if they balked.[4]

The judicial decisions that allowed this aspect of McCarthyism to
flourish involved the academic community from the start. One of the
defendants in an important early case was Lyman Bradley, the long-time
treasurer of the Modern Language Association and chairman of New
York University's German Department. Bradley was also the treasurer of
a supposedly Communist-dominated organization, the Joint Anti-Fascist
Refugee Committee, and had, along with Howard Fast and the rest of
the JAFRC's board, voted not to surrender the organization's records to
HUAC. When on April 4, 1946, the committee asked Bradley about the
board's action, he refused to answer. The committee's questions, he insisted, were "not pertinent." Neither he nor the other board members
invoked the Fifth. They were immediately cited for contempt, indicted,
and, in June 1947, convicted. They appealed, and a year later the Supreme Court refused to grant a hearing, thus sustaining two lower court
rulings that HUAC did not violate the First Amendment by asking suspected Communists about their political activities. The JAFRC case,
known as *Barsky v. United States*, was one of the three landmark decisions of the late forties which essentially freed congressional investigators from having to worry unduly about infringing their witnesses' constitutional rights.[5]

Barsky was a serious setback for political freedom. It increased the
power of congressional investigators by allowing them to ask witnesses

about their political beliefs and associations—a sphere of activity that a more civil libertarian Court might have protected with greater care. But the Supreme Court of the early Cold War years was no defender of individual rights. On the contrary, its decisions either avoided the substantive issues of civil liberties that cases like *Barsky* presented or, worse, seemed to endorse the limitations on political freedom that the other branches of government had imposed. At the time, Felix Frankfurter and his colleagues in the Court's majority justified their hands-off policy toward governmental repression by invoking "judicial restraint," a doctrine formulated in large part as a response to an earlier period when a conservative Supreme Court had nullified a great deal of the New Deal's social legislation. The Justices did not like what HUAC was doing, but, as Robert Jackson explained, they felt "it would be an unwarranted act of judicial usurpation to strip Congress of its investigatory power or to assume for the courts the function of supervising congressional committees." In retrospect, it is hard to avoid the conclusion that what the constitutional scholar Robert McCloskey identified as the Court's "pattern of acquiescence" toward "the cold civil war" stemmed as much from prudence as from respect. The Supreme Court shrank from the political consequences of taking an unpopular position on the Communist issue.[6]

Later on, and in a very limited and largely procedural way, the Court did place a few restraints on the committees. It ruled that the questions they asked had to be pertinent to the subject matter of their inquiry and that that inquiry had to be within the scope of the committee's original authorization. But these limitations were limited indeed, for as late as 1959 the Court was still to rule, in the case of the former Vassar instructor Lloyd Barenblatt, that when dealing with the issue of Communist subversion HUAC could still ask someone the so-called $64 question: "Are you now or have you ever been . . . ?"[7]

That left the Fifth. The only way that a witness could refuse to answer a committee's questions and still be protected against a contempt citation and possible jail sentence was to invoke the Fifth Amendment on the basis that answering the questions would tend to incriminate him. This privilege, which derived from a seventeenth-century English provision designed to protect dissenters from being mistreated by the authorities, guaranteed that people did not have to supply an inquisitor with information that could be used against them. In the fifties, when anti-Communist investigators as a rule had access to all the power of the state, the Fifth Amendment did provide witnesses with one small, but crucial, area of protection against that power and, in that sense, redressed at least in part the imbalance between a single individual and the American government. The Supreme Court was to protect the privilege in the face of the anti-Communist furor largely because it was procedural. The Justices, thus, did not have to rule on the substantive issue of whether the type of information requested was protected by the First Amendment; they merely had to ascertain whether it could provide the basis for a criminal prosecution. In practice, this meant that witnesses could apply the Fifth to a broad range of questions, since simply belonging to the CP could expose them to criminal charges. This was especially the case after the Court rendered its *Dennis* decision in 1951 and acquiesced in the Smith Act conviction of the Party's leaders for advocating and teaching subversive doctrines.[8]

As it turned out, government prosecutors never tried to indict rank and file Communists or ex-Communists under the Smith Act. Its provisions were reserved for higher ranking reds. Perjury was the indictment of choice for littler fish, in particular for witnesses who tried to rebut a committee's charges. Even political innocents were vulnerable. Government informers could—and did—lie and, though many of them were later discredited, many of the people they named feared that they might be indicted for perjury if they denied the informer's accusations. That such a fear was no chimera was revealed by the government's attempt to prosecute Johns Hopkins professor Owen Lattimore after he tangled with the Senate's Internal Security Subcommittee in the spring of 1952. The committee questioned Lattimore for an unprecedented eleven days and then pressured the Truman administration to indict him for perjury on the basis of a few trivial inconsistencies in his testimony. Though the indictment was thrown out of court twice, the very fact that a scholar of Lattimore's stature—who had never been involved with the CP—could be subjected to such an ordeal revealed that *anything* a witness said before a committee might open him or her to prosecution. Far better to say nothing at all, and the judiciary agreed. Soon court decisions permitted people to take the Fifth Amendment to any question that might provide even the tiniest link in a chain of possibly incriminating evidence. The high point came in 1955 when the federal judiciary overturned the contempt conviction of Temple University philosopher Barrows Dunham, even though he had taken the Fifth to everything but his name, age, and home address.[9]

In the late forties, however, when Berkeley T. A. David Fox appeared before HUAC, no one knew that the courts were going to enforce the privilege against self-incrimination as vigorously as they ultimately did. Fox did not want to name names and his lawyer advised him to use the Fifth. But it was a gamble, for the issue was still in contention. Fox was, in fact, indicted for contempt. However, by the time his case got to trial, the Supreme Court had decided the question and he was promptly acquitted.[10]

*   *   *

Fox was not alone in his troubles. He was one of a handful of relatively young and unknown physicists who were to tangle with HUAC during the course of that committee's extensive search for spies in the atomic bomb project. Though the committee did not uncover any espionage, it did produce the academic community's first batch of uncooperative witnesses. HUAC had not been trying to show that these men were subversive educators. It had little interest in their teaching or scholarship and had subpoenaed them only because they had worked for the Manhattan Project, a target that the committee's publicity-hungry members were eager to hit. HUAC's concern about the bomb manifested itself early in 1947, when the committee's new Republican chairman, J. Parnell Thomas, announced an ambitious eight-point program that included an investigation of "those groups and movements which are trying to dissipate our atomic knowledge for the benefit of a foreign power." In the years that followed, HUAC held dozens of hearings, but, since its investigations never led to Klaus Fuchs or the Rosenbergs, it did not present much real evidence of atomic espionage. Even so, it managed to construct an elaborate—and elaborately publicized—scenario which purported to show how Communist sympathizers in the Manhattan Project had leaked the secrets of the bomb to the Soviet Union.[11]

These allegations of HUAC's, though never substantiated, were not a complete fabrication. They had been formulated during the war by the military intelligence officers in charge of security at the Manhattan Project and had created problems for the scientists involved as early as 1943. Since these charges were to embellish HUAC's hearings and reports for the next few years and were to crop up yet again in the most important security case of the 1950s—that of J. Robert Oppenheimer—let us examine them in some detail.

From the first, security was an issue at the Manhattan Project. Much of the trouble stemmed from a kind of cultural conflict between the scientists and the military intelligence officers assigned to keep them from the unauthorized disclosure of information. Professionally, intellectually, and politically, the two groups inhabited such different worlds that it would have been surprising had they not come into conflict. The hierarchical, authoritarian practices of the military alienated many scientists; the more iconoclastic among them had real trouble accommodating themselves to what they considered were the unreasonable regulations imposed by the security men. Leo Szilard, the unorthodox Hungarian physicist who had first suggested building a bomb, was so contemptuous of security that he was in constant danger of being tossed off the project he himself had initiated. For other, less eminent, scientists the dangers were considerably greater. "I know only too well that science and military organizations do not always mix," Nobel laureate James Franck warned a younger colleague, "and difficulties are bound to arise if one does not learn the art of only swearing in an empty room."[12]

Unfortunately for some of these people, there were no empty rooms. The military intelligence agents assigned to the project kept them under heavy surveillance. Their phones were tapped; their homes searched; their mail opened. This was particularly true of those scientists who worked on the bomb at places like Berkeley or the University of Chicago, which were more exposed to the outside world than were the insulated communities of Los Alamos or Oak Ridge. Within a few months, most of the people on the project had become accustomed to their retinue of security officers. "Part of the scenery" was the way one Berkeley scientist described them. He recalled:

> A touring car with two individuals unknown to the neighborhood, but with Detective or Private Eye written all over them, maintained a vigil half a block up from my house much of the time in 1943 and 1944. . . . Women, nervous because their husbands were away at the wars, phoned in complaints to the police and were told the police could do nothing. On one occasion an irate husband home on leave forced them to identify themselves.[13]

Since they knew little of the science involved, these agents could not differentiate between sensitive information and common knowledge or, at least, what was common knowledge among scientists. In their eagerness to plug leaks, they clamped down on harmless conversations, while, because of their technical ignorance, overlooking potentially serious disclosures. The project itself was supposed to be a secret; yet it was widely known in the Berkeley community, for example, that scientists there were developing some kind of a big weapon. And any well-informed physicist could have figured out what was going on at the Radiation Laboratory just from knowing who was working there. But the security men were not physicists and, like later critics of American atomic security, did not realize that most of the secrets they were so zealously guarding belonged to Mother Nature, not Uncle Sam. The tightest security in the world would not keep a determined and technologically advanced nation from developing a nuclear weapon, especially after the American government gave away the main secret of the bomb by dropping it and, thus, showing that it could be made. Ironically, though the rigid security that surrounded the Manhattan Project did not keep a real spy like Klaus Fuchs from communicating with the Russians, it did seem to hamper work on the bomb. Some of the security measures that were imposed, though standard military procedures, clashed with the requirements of scientific research. In addition, the security people sometimes forced valuable scientists off the project for reasons that in retrospect seem to have reflected their own prejudices rather than a realistic assessment of project security.[14]

Politically, as well as bureaucratically and intellectually, the security men were at odds with their charges. Military intelligence officers had a long anti-radical tradition, one which, a recent scholar noted, "made left political parties and even civil libertarians seem like the enemy." Colonel John Lansdale, in charge of security for the entire project, believed that Russia, not Germany or Japan, was America's main enemy and that Communists and Communist sympathizers were fanatics who would willingly spy for the Soviet Union. His views were typical.

One of his subordinates at the Berkeley Radiation Laboratory actually rejoiced at the death of Roosevelt.[15]

The scientists, on the other hand, were at the opposite end of the political spectrum. Physicists in particular had a reputation for radicalism. No doubt exaggerated, this reputation may have come in part from the visibility of Robert Oppenheimer in the Berkeley Popular Front. In addition the field itself, the dynamism of theoretical physics in the late 1930s, attracted all kinds of creative and unconventional people, "self-conscious and daring intellectuals," Philip Morrison called them, men and women who questioned authority as readily in politics as they did in science. Finally, there were a good many Jews, some refugees from Hitler, in the physics community who, if not politically active themselves, certainly sympathized with the anti-fascism that pervaded the American left at that time. For many of these scientists only their hatred of fascism and their fear that Germany might get the bomb first stilled their qualms about working on such a terrible weapon. Given the political coloration of such a group and the clear unlikelihood that any of its members would be spying for the Germans or Japanese, it was understandable that the rather reactionary security officers on the Manhattan Project focussed their attention on the politically radical scientists. They assumed—not incorrectly, we must admit—that the main threat to the project's security would come from Communist sympathizers who wanted the results shared with the Soviet Union. Accordingly, the security officers sometimes refused to clear people with left-wing connections for work on the bomb. And they tended to interpret any contact between a scientist on the project, especially one with a past history of radical activities, and a Communist—Russian or domestic—as a possible case of espionage.[16]

This is what happened to Clarence Hiskey, a chemist and former student radical from the University of Wisconsin, who joined the Manhattan Project in September 1942 while it was still at Columbia. Hiskey's radicalism initially kept him from getting a clearance, but his superior, Harold Urey, appreciated the importance of Hiskey's research on the separation of heavy water and managed to get him approved. The project then moved to Chicago and Hiskey with it. But not for long. The military intelligence officers who had been watching him concluded that "Hiskey's attitude was un-American, and his discretion and integrity" questionable; he "was Communistic in his beliefs." As if Hiskey's politics weren't bad enough, he was in contact with a Canadian citizen named Arthur Adams, or Adamson, as he was sometimes called. Adams, at the time Hiskey knew him, was working as a kind of free-lance trade inspector for the Russian government, evaluating material that was purchased in the West to make sure that it was not defective. A mutual interest in the chemistry of plastics brought the two men together and, though their relationship was apparently social, a suspicious security staff could easily see in the contacts between a purchasing agent for the Soviet Union and a left-wing chemist on the Manhattan Project a clear-cut case of atomic espionage. "We were convinced he was a subversive agent," one of the project's security officers explained to HUAC several years later.

> Now the question was what to do with Hiskey. We had trouble with scientists when we tried to move one. Someone, I think it was Colonel Lansdale, found in Hiskey's record that he had a second lieutenancy in college in the ROTC.

Hiskey's draft deferment was cancelled, his reserve commission reactivated, and he was promptly shipped off to the Canadian Northwest. This, though the bomb project was desperate for trained scientists and all the scientists working on it were routinely deferred.[17]

Hiskey, at least, had been a left-wing activist. This was not the case with Martin Kamen, the protagonist in another HUAC atom spy melodrama. The co-discoverer of carbon 14, Kamen was a chemist working at the Berkeley Radiation Laboratory on the separation of uranium isotopes. Like many scientists, he was rather cavalier about the security precautions surrounding the project and did not take them as seriously as the military intelligence people wished. More a personal than a political radical, Kamen was, nonetheless, a member in good standing of what he called Berkeley's "cocktail front" and went to his share of fund-raising parties for such causes as the Joint Anti-Fascist Refugee Committee and Russian War Relief. A gifted violist, Kamen even gave concerts for such causes. This was not unusual; many people were doing that at the time, including Kamen's friend and sometime chamber music partner, the violinist Isaac Stern. It was Stern who coincidentally introduced Kamen to his supposed Russian contact, an official of the Soviet Consulate who was anxious to meet someone from the Berkeley Radiation Laboratory. One of Kamen's co-workers there had published a paper about the use of radioactive phosphorus in the treatment of cancer; the Russian, one of whose colleagues had leukemia, wanted to find out more about that form of therapy. Kamen put him in touch with the author of the paper and thought no more about the matter.

A few weeks later the grateful consul invited Kamen out to dinner. Both Kamen and the Russians were under surveillance. The military intelligence agents who had tailed the chemist and his Soviet hosts to Bernstein's Fish Grotto in San Francisco let the FBI men who had been watching the Russians set up their recording equipment in the booth next to Kamen's while they sat nearby and tried to overhear the conversation. The restaurant was noisy and neither set of agents got more than some "scraps of conversation . . . so sketchy," one of them later admitted, that "you could read a page [of the transcript] and not be able to tell what was being said." Nevertheless, the intelligence men assumed that what Kamen later described as a "pleasant casual conversation" about the use of radiation in therapy and the general state of Soviet-American relations was a serious violation of security, if not an outright case of espionage. Kamen claimed that he had been deliberately misleading the Russians about the nature of the work at the Radiation Lab, but, because of their lack of scientific sophistication, the intelligence men could not tell the difference between a harmless explanation of theoretical physics and the disclosure of sensitive material about the bomb. A few days after his evening at the Fish Grotto, Kamen was dropped from the Manhattan Project.[18]

HUAC's third case of so-called espionage involved David Fox and a group of his colleagues at the Berkeley Radiation Laboratory: David Bohm, Max Friedman, Giovanni Rossi Lomanitz, and Joseph Weinberg. Most were students of Oppenheimer. They were also radicals. Some, like Fox, a "red diaper baby" and student activist at Los Angeles City College in the late thirties, had been left-wingers before they got to the University of California; others were radicalized by the volatile atmosphere of Berkeley. As David Bohm explained: "We were all close to Communists at the time." Ross Lomanitz, by all accounts the political sparkplug of the group, recalled how easily a Berkeley radical could slide into the Party.

> I attended some meetings, because at that time meetings were much more open, free, and easy. There wasn't any great distinction . . . . I was at some discussion meetings where members of the Communist Party spoke. Who was officially a member or what it took to be officially a member, I can't tell you to this day. It just wasn't all that conspiratorial.

One could, as Lomanitz did, go to Communist Party meetings without actually belonging to the Party and subjecting oneself to its discipline. Or one could, as Bohm did for a while in 1942–43, join up officially. Bohm's affiliation, like that of many academic Communists, was short-lived. He soon dropped out because "the meetings were interminable" and "didn't amount to much." His unit discussed local problems and tried to stir up protests on campus. Espionage was never on the agenda. The testimony of R. R. Davis, a former technician at the Radiation Laboratory, corroborates Bohm's recollections. Davis, who claimed that Lomanitz had recruited him into the Party, went to three or four meetings and then quit. The Berkeley CP "seemed to be very disinterested" in what was going on at the Radiation Lab, he told HUAC. "It was all about Negroes in the South and the Catholic Church."[19]

From the viewpoint of the security agents on the Manhattan Project, however, these contacts between project scientists and the local Communist Party seemed more sinister. This was especially the case because during the early forties the CP's local leaders had unusually close ties to the scientists of Berkeley. One of the Party's two full-time officials in Alameda County—the Berkeley-Oakland area—was Kenneth O. May, a former graduate student in mathematics who became the CP's educational director after the Regents fired him from his teaching assistantship at Berkeley. Steve Nelson, May's superior in the Party, recalls him as "an

aggressive young intellectual" who had a lot of connections within the
academic community. So, too, did Nelson. Nelson was something of a
"catch" for the Berkeley Communist Party, for he was a genuine hero
from the Spanish Civil War, the cause into which the Berkeley left had
thrown its collective soul and much of its money. Wounded in action,
Nelson returned to the United States, went out to the West Coast in 1939,
and became the Party's leader in Berkeley. His exploits in Spain gave
him entrée far beyond the Party's usual circles, and his personal warmth
and vigor earned him the respect and admiration of Communists and
non-Communists alike. He was, for example, close to Robert Oppenheimer. Later, during the Cold War, this relationship was to create problems for both men, but during the late thirties and early forties the two
had much in common. Not only did they share political interests—Oppenheimer, though not a member of the Party, was well within its orbit and
had first met Nelson when the two men shared a speakers' platform at
a rally for the Spanish cause—but they also had a personal tie. Several
years earlier, Nelson had befriended Oppenheimer's future wife after her
first husband, a close friend of Nelson's, was killed in Spain. Kitty Oppenheimer renewed her friendship with Nelson and his wife and, until Oppenheimer joined the Manhattan Project, the two families were close.[20]

By the early forties, the left at Berkeley was but the "tail end" of
the effervescent movement it had once been; even so, little clusters of
left-wing intellectuals still continued to get together at each other's
houses. Nelson met occasionally with such groups—to discuss the state of
the world or the future of American foreign policy. These meetings, as
both Nelson and Lomanitz recall, though small and informal, were open
to Party members and outsiders alike. They were not secret. Certainly
the security men on the Manhattan Project must have known that they
were taking place, for Nelson, as well as the Radiation Lab scientists,
was under surveillance. Nelson also saw people from the Soviet Consulate a few times. This was because Russian war relief was a big Party
cause at that time and Nelson needed Russian speakers for some of his
local fund-raising events. There was nothing subversive about any of
these contacts; Russia and America were allies, and the CPUSA had
thrown itself into winning the war. Yet to the military intelligence agents
at the Manhattan Project, trained, after all, to sniff out all possible
breaches of security, such contacts—between the project scientists and
the local Party leader and between the local Party leader and the Russian
consul—were highly suspicious. Later HUAC was to claim that espionage
had been involved, but it never produced much in the way of evidence.[21]

One story involved Joseph Weinberg's dictating of a secret formula
to Nelson in the middle of the night. Government agents claimed that
they had climbed a tree near Nelson's house and watched the whole
transaction. For Nelson, the very notion of transcribing a set of mathematical equations was absurd.

Now, I don't know what the formula looks like. And how I would write it down, I don't know, considering I only had five years of education. And to write some complicated formula down, must have been a damn simple one if they expected me to copy it.

And how they could have seen at night time what formula I was writing down, it's so fantastic, it's hard to believe.

Another, somewhat more likely, occurrence involved the testimony of former Manhattan Project security officers who had climbed to the roof of the apartment building next door to Weinberg's to witness "some type of a meeting" between Nelson and a group of scientists—Weinberg, Fox, Bohm, Friedman, and Lomanitz among them. This was probably one of the innumerable bull sessions Lomanitz and Bohm described. HUAC later played it up, no doubt, because it could provide the basis for a perjury indictment against Weinberg, who had denied knowing Nelson.[22]

As if dallying with Nelson and the Communist Party was not provocative enough, these young physicists further antagonized the military by trying to organize a union at the Radiation Laboratory. The union, the Federation of Architects, Engineers, Chemists, and Technicians (FAECT-CIO), had established locals in some of the industrial laboratories outside of Berkeley, most notably at the Shell Development Corporation in Emeryville. Union activists from Shell apparently encouraged Lomanitz, Fox, and some of the others to start a local in the Lab. There was little need for it; the scientists' salaries were adequate. But "it seemed like a dramatic thing to do," Lomanitz explained, a way to participate more fully in the resurrected wartime Popular Front of the time. It was, he now concedes, "a sort of stupid adolescent drama."[23]

The project's security officers, however, saw this attempt to unionize the Radiation Laboratory in somewhat more ominous terms, especially since FAECT (the union to which, by the way, Julius Rosenberg belonged) reputedly had Communists in its leadership. And the Army responded to the matter in a rather unenlightened way. It drafted Lomanitz, a punitive measure which had the unfortunate result of setting back some of the research at the Lab. Lomanitz, though only a graduate student, had been working on a crucial aspect of the electromagnetic separation of uranium and was about to become a group leader so that he could handle the Laboratory's liaison with Oak Ridge. The Army's sudden decision to revoke his deferment in August 1943 threatened to disrupt the project. Ernest O. Lawrence, the director of the Radiation Laboratory and no friend to the union, was mystified by Lomanitz's call-up but unable to prevent it. Even an urgent telegram from Oppenheimer to the headquarters of the Manhattan Project and an attempt by Lomanitz's own draft board to restore his deferment failed. The Army rushed his induction through so quickly that he was unable to leave instructions for his successor, Edward U. Condon, and much of the work he had done had to be repeated. Moreover, every attempt that Lomanitz made to find a draft-exempt job that would utilize his scientific background—and he found several—fell apart at the last moment. Clearly, the Army was out to punish Lomanitz and set an example for other radicals. Lomanitz recalled that when he tried to find out why he had been drafted, the military officers he talked to questioned him

> for a long time on my interest in unions in general and the Federation of Architects, Engineers, Chemists, and Technicians in particular. I was then told that some unknown person had instigated the charge that I am connected with "communistic organizations."

Later on the other FAECT activists at the Radiation Laboratory left the project and the union disappeared.[24]

Once the war ended, most of these scientists hoped to put their troubles with the Manhattan Project's security officers behind them and return to academic life. Hiskey was in the Army until the summer of 1946. Then he took a position as an associate professor of chemistry at Brooklyn Polytechnic Institute. After Kamen was dismissed from the Radiation Laboratory, he searched unsuccessfully for some kind of job that would enable him to continue his scientific work. He finally ended up working in a shipyard for several months until he got a position as an associate professor of biochemistry at Washington University in St. Louis. Fox came out of the Navy in 1946 and went back to graduate school. Lomanitz also returned to Berkeley, but left in 1947 and went to Cornell to finish up his degree. A year and a half later, he took a job as an associate professor of physics at Fisk University. Bohm stayed in Berkeley until 1947 when he became an assistant professor at Princeton. Weinberg also left California at about this time and took a position at the University of Minnesota. He was joined there by another physicist from the Manhattan Project, Frank Oppenheimer, the younger brother of Robert and a former Communist, who was soon to run into trouble even though he had not had any problems during the war.

None of these people were to have normal academic careers. In the spring of 1946 the Canadian government announced that the defection of Igor Gouzenko, a code clerk in the Soviet Embassy in Ottawa, had revealed the existence of an atomic spy ring. A month later Scotland Yard arrested Alan Nunn May, a British scientist who had worked on the bomb project in Canada during the war. There were indications that May was not the only person connected with the Manhattan Project who had been leaking material to the Russians. At once the FBI, which had by then taken over most American counter-espionage work from the military, apparently set out to track down the traitors. It selected the most probable candidates it could find—the left-wing scientists on the Manhattan Project—and pulled them in for questioning.[25]

Clarence Hiskey, who was just about to be discharged from the Army, was in the process of divorcing his first wife so he could marry his second. The FBI must have thought that exploiting Hiskey's marital troubles might help it get information; it brought both Hiskey and the two women into the federal courthouse on New York's Foley Square. Agents interrogated Hiskey for an entire day, asking him about his contacts with Arthur Adams and behaving in what he later recalled as an intimidating way. Lomanitz, who was still in Berkeley in 1946, was picked up for questioning and driven into San Francisco. There, the proverbial "Mr. Tough Guy" and "Mr. Nice Guy" quizzed him for hours before they returned him to his apartment, with the hint that he'd be seeing them again. Weinberg had a similar session with another pair of agents who asked him again and again if he knew Steve Nelson. Kamen and Frank Oppenheimer were also questioned by the FBI at this time. So, too, was Haakon Chevalier, a left-wing Berkeley professor and former friend of Robert Oppenheimer. During the war, Chevalier had told Oppenheimer that a British scientist who worked at the Shell Development Corporation had asked him to find out if Oppenheimer was interested in sharing scientific information with the Russians. Oppenheimer brushed Chevalier off and then later reported the incident in a garbled form to the Manhattan Project security people. This incident was to be central to Oppenheimer's own security hearing in 1954, but, curiously, it never became an important element in HUAC's search for atomic spies.[26]

By 1947 the FBI must have realized that its interrogations of Kamen, Hiskey, et al. had not uncovered an atom spy ring. The Justice Department had studied the case several times and concluded "that the evidence was insufficient for successful prosecution." But the FBI, eager to alert the nation to the danger of Communist subversion, did not give up. It had its suspects, even if it didn't have its crime. What happened next was to happen over and over again during these early Cold War years. Government investigators, lacking a case that would stand up in court or, as with suspected Communists, lacking the basis for criminal charges, since Party membership was still no crime, apparently turned their information over to Congress. I use the word "apparently" on purpose. Evidence for this kind of collaboration between the FBI and the congressional investigating committees is only just beginning to surface. Scholars, using materials released under the Freedom of Information Act, have discovered that in early 1946 the FBI officially launched an "educational" campaign of providing covert support to HUAC and other anti-Communist groups. Since congressional records are immune from the FOIA and the Bureau usually hid its tracks, it may be impossible to prove FBI complicity in specific cases. Even so, given what we do know about the way the Bureau and the committees operated, it is, I think, reasonable to assume that the FBI let HUAC see its files on Fox, Lomanitz, and the other Manhattan Project radicals. Certainly, the committee's dealings with these unfortunate scientists seem to substantiate such a scenario.[27]

In the years when HUAC was looking for atomic spies, roughly from 1947 to 1950, it was still feeling its way toward its future role in the Cold

War political system. Until the Internal Security Subcommittee of the Senate Judiciary Committee (SISS) was set up in 1951, HUAC was the only full-time investigating committee in town. It was not yet completely respectable, but its hearings were, nonetheless, a politician's dream: the source of seemingly endless publicity. The committee introduced Louis Budenz, Elizabeth Bentley, and Whittaker Chambers to the American public; it staged a front-page confrontation with the Hollywood left. And, in the coup that was to legitimize the committee's heretofore controversial activities, as well as establish the career of one Richard Milhous Nixon, it orchestrated the case against Alger Hiss. The Hiss case confirmed what a lot of right-wing politicians had discovered, that a congressional investigation was the perfect medium for harassing the Truman administration. Ultimately, congressional conservatives of both parties were to use anti-Communist investigations to build up a complete indictment of Truman, Roosevelt, and the New Deal for being "soft" on Communism.[28]

This explains the political motivation behind HUAC's search for atom spies. The committee must have been hoping to make another Hiss out of Hiskey. It knew about Hiskey's dealings with Arthur Adams, about Chevalier's conversation with Oppenheimer, about Kamen's dinner at the Fish Grotto, and about the left-wing activities of the young scientists at the Berkeley Radiation Laboratory. In its hearings and public reports, HUAC used these incidents to highlight what it insisted was the Democratic administration's shocking indifference to the evidence of Communist subversion. "Doubtless the Department of Justice has conclusive evidence to support criminal prosecution of certain named persons," the committee claimed. Yet neither Roosevelt, nor Truman, nor any of their Attorney Generals had done anything to apprehend or punish the culprits, though they knew quite well who they were. Such a "shocking" lack of action, so the committee and its supporters believed, should not be condoned. In addition, the committee and, in particular, its chairman Parnell Thomas seemed to have taken sides in the ongoing battle over the control of atomic energy and to have conducted the investigations into atomic espionage with an eye to discrediting the Manhattan Project scientists whose lobbying had prevented Congress from turning the Atomic Energy Commission over to the military in 1946.[29]

From the start there was a haphazard quality to HUAC's investigations. A member of the committee or its staff would make charges or issue a report and then drop the matter. The committee tried to build up suspense. It would hold secret hearings, leak some testimony, publish some more, and then announce that national security and the lives of "certain persons" would be in danger if the committee were to reveal all it knew. Since HUAC's records are immune from public scrutiny, we may never know why its search for atomic spies seemed so disorganized. The intelligence files it received may have been incomplete. There may also have been internal dissension within the committee. Atomic espionage was Chairman Thomas's obsession, and some of his activities, like his single-handed release of a report calling the highly respected physicist Edward U. Condon, the head of the Commerce Department's Bureau of Standards, "one of the weakest links in our atomic security," apparently provoked criticism within the committee as well as within much of Washington and just about the entire scientific world. In addition, at the time HUAC began its investigations, congressional hearings were not yet the efficient mechanisms for the exposure of political undesirables that they were later to become. Neither the committee nor its witnesses seemed to know exactly what they were doing. Later hearings were clearly designed to force unfriendly witnesses to take the Fifth, but in 1948, when HUAC seriously began to question atomic scientists, it seemed more interested in extracting information from them than in exposing them as Fifth Amendment reds. After all, it was far more newsworthy to uncover a den of atomic spies than a group of ex-Communist academics.[30]

HUAC's first revelations about the Manhattan Project came in the fall of 1947, some eighteen months after the Gouzenko case had brought atomic espionage to the nation's attention. On the final day of the Hollywood Ten hearings the committee's chief investigator, Louis Russell, took the stand to testify about espionage and the atom bomb. He gave a lot of information, most of it about the Oppenheimer-Chevalier incident. But no other witnesses were heard and the matter was dropped. Thomas's release of the "weakest link" report on Condon in March 1948 showed that the committee—or, at least, some of its members—was still looking for atomic spies. In the following months HUAC began secret hearings and started collecting evidence from intelligence sources. It leaked selected tidbits to friendly newsmen, while hinting that national security prevented it from revealing even more explosive material.[31]

Then, in the beginning of September, it issued a press release charging that an unnamed scientist—identical in every respect with Kamen— had divulged "atom secrets" to the Soviets. A few days later, it subpoenaed Kamen for an executive session. It had already questioned Hiskey and was about to hear from one of his former colleagues as well. Though all these people testified in secret, HUAC released selected transcripts from their hearings along with a 20,000-word "Report on Soviet Espionage Activities in Connection with the Atom Bomb." Not only did the report describe the supposed indiscretions of Kamen and Hiskey, but it also devoted a long section to "Scientist X," a mysterious individual who, the committee claimed, had given a Russian agent "a formula of importance in the development of the atom bomb." "Scientist X," it turned out, was Joseph Weinberg. But from HUAC's perspective he was a far more interesting character as "Scientist X" than he was as Joe Weinberg. For Weinberg, as Weinberg, was a disappointing witness. Though the committee heard several former intelligence officers testify they had seen Weinberg meeting secretly with Steve Nelson, the committee could get no first-hand evidence. Nelson took the Fifth, and Weinberg denied everything. He said that he didn't know Nelson, and he refused to take the Fifth. Frustrated, no doubt, by Weinberg's obstinancy, the committee revealed his identity the following year and pressed the Justice Department, as it had done with Alger Hiss, a similarly recalcitrant witness, to indict him for perjury.[32]

Between April and October 1949 the committee held its most extensive set of atom spy hearings. It called up many of the former Berkeley radicals as well as a number of military intelligence agents and professional witnesses. One of the latter was Paul Crouch, a voluble ex-Communist whose enthusiasm outweighed his veracity to such an extent that the Supreme Court had to throw out a major case against the Communist Party because of his perjured testimony. But in 1949 Crouch's reputation was still intact and he testified about both Hiskey and the Berkeley people. Crouch claimed to have met these scientists while he was working for the Party, first in Tennessee, where Hiskey had taught, and then in California. His testimony, as well as that of a few other cooperative witnesses and intelligence agents, apparently convinced the committee that Hiskey had been a spy and that there was a group at Berkeley "that did deliver to the Soviet government every piece of scientific information they had from the Radiation Laboratory."[33]

In January 1950 the arrest of Klaus Fuchs, then the chief theoretical physicist in the British equivalent of Los Alamos and a far more distinguished scientist than any of those HUAC had grilled in public, rendered the committee's investigations moot. Fuchs, a refugee from Nazi Germany and an ardent, but secret, Communist had been passing information to the Russians since he began to work on the bomb in 1942. None of the people the committee questioned had been involved with Fuchs and, though HUAC was to ask a few more witnesses about their experiences with the Berkeley left, it essentially abandoned its hunt for atomic spies, a quest that had produced many headlines, several volumes of testimony, and not a single spy.[34]

*   *   *

Trivial as the outcome of HUAC's investigations was, there was nothing trivial about the consequences of those investigations for the people involved, the former Manhattan Project scientists who had come under the committee's scrutiny. For them, HUAC's attentions were, in some cases, permanently shattering, in others, temporarily annoying. But no one was untouched. As we shall see, most of these people were to lose their jobs as a direct result of appearing before the committee. In addition, Hiskey, Lomanitz, Bohm, and Fox were to be indicted for contempt of Congress and Weinberg for perjury. Moreover, simply appearing before the committee created problems. It was HUAC's practice to deliver its subpoenas only a few days before the hearings were scheduled to take place. As a result prospective witnesses rarely got much time to prepare. Martin

Kamen, vacationing in California, was told on a Thursday to appear in Washington on that Friday or Saturday; he managed to postpone the hearing until the following Tuesday.[35]

For people like Bohm and Lomanitz, who did not want to cooperate with the committee, finding someone to represent them was a serious problem. There were few attorneys who knew anything about the legal issues involved, fewer still who were willing to become associated with unrepentent radicals. Edward U. Condon, who, during this period, acted as a sort of den mother for the younger physicists, referred the two men to Abe Fortas, the lawyer who had helped him during his own brush with Parnell Thomas. Fortas was reluctant to take on such controversial clients as Bohm and Lomanitz. He did talk with them, however, and Lomanitz recalls that he even offered to represent him for free. Lomanitz also recalls that Fortas wanted to know about his political activities and those of his friends. Ultimately, though Fortas was later to represent other academics—most notably Owen Lattimore—before other congressional committees, he refused the case. "We have decided that we don't think we can ever afford to represent anybody that has ever been a Communist," was the explanation he gave to Clifford Durr, the lawyer to whom he recommended the two physicists. Fortas's response was a common one within the legal community during the early Cold War years. Lawyers often found that defending Communists or other politically unpopular clients seriously damaged their practices. As a result, prospective witnesses who did not want to cooperate with a congressional committee often had to approach many lawyers before finding someone willing to take their cases, and they usually ended up relying on the small handful of attorneys whose ties to the Communist Party or commitment to civil liberties overrode their desire for a normal, if not lucrative, practice.[36]

Clifford Durr, who was to represent not only Bohm and Lomanitz but most of the other young physicists as well, was one such lawyer. A former member of the Federal Communications Commission, he was the most important member of the Truman administration to resign in protest against the imposition of the loyalty program in 1947. As a result, he soon became one of the main Washington lawyers to specialize in the cases the program spawned. Both Bohm and Lomanitz remember him as "a sympathetic person" in whom they had great confidence. Since the Supreme Court had invalidated a First Amendment defense the year before by refusing to hear the appeal of NYU's Lyman Bradley and the other *Barsky* defendants, Durr recommended that Bohm and the others take the Fifth. To do so was not without risk, for the Court had not yet ruled—as it was soon to do—that the danger of prosecution under the Smith Act made it legitimate to invoke the privilege against self-incrimination when asked about membership in the Communist Party. For someone who did not want to cooperate with the committee, however, it seemed to offer the best legal protection against jail. True, it did not prevent the committee from bringing contempt charges against Hiskey, Lomanitz, Fox, and Bohm. But by the time their cases reached the trial stage, the Supreme Court's recent decisions had firmed up the Fifth and all four were acquitted.[37]

Not all the former Manhattan Project scientists took the Fifth. Martin Kamen, for example, had nothing to hide and, in fact, tried to force the committe to give him a public instead of a secret hearing. He answered all the committee's questions, no doubt telling the congressmen far more than they wanted to know about security lapses on the Man-Project and the physical structure of carbon 14. Frank Oppenheimer also eschewed the Fifth. He spoke openly about his own involvement with the Communist Party, but refused to discuss that of others. "I do not wish to talk about the political ideas or affiliations of any of my friends," he told the committee. This may well have been because he did not want to bring his brother's name into the hearings. Thus, though he admitted he knew Steven Nelson socially, he steadfastly refused to tell the committee where he had met him.[38]

The position Frank Oppenheimer took, later known as "the diminished Fifth," was the stance that Lillian Hellman had wanted to take in her eloquent statement, "I cannot and will not cut my conscience to fit this season's fashions." Legally it was much riskier than relying on the Fifth. This was because of the "waiver" doctrine. Once a witness talked about himself, as Oppenheimer had, according to the courts he had waived his privilege against self-incrimination and would be in contempt if he refused to answer questions about other people. However, in 1949, when Oppenheimer and the other Manhattan Project people testified, the scope of the Fifth Amendment had not yet been established definitively and it was not clear what kind of behavior would put someone in contempt. The committee did not cite Frank Oppenheimer, though later on, witnesses who took the same position he had were routinely indicted for contempt and people who took the Fifth were left alone.[39]

Legally, therefore, all of the Manhattan Project scientists were to escape unharmed. Professionally, however, they were all to suffer. We know what happened to David Fox. The Regents of the University of California fired him. As a teaching assistant at a university already in a state of crisis, he was in a vulnerable position to begin with. Invoking the Fifth under any circumstances would have cost him his job. Invoking it before a committee investigating subversion that had supposedly taken place on the campus of his very own university positively ensured that he would lose it. There was some protest, mainly among the other teaching assistants; but Fox was too lowly and the University too crisis-ridden for his case to get much attention.[40]

Kamen, on the other hand, was never in that kind of danger. He had cooperated fully with HUAC and apparently had convinced its members that he had not been disloyal in the Fish Grotto. The publicity that accompanied his case was, of course, unwelcome, but his job was not at stake. Before hiring Kamen in 1945, Arthur Holly Compton, the Nobel laureate who headed Washington University in St. Louis, had looked carefully into the Fish Grotto business and had satisfied himself that the charges against Kamen were baseless. Thus, when Kamen's case became public, Compton himself went before Washington University's Board of Trustees and vouched for his subordinate's loyalty. Compton's protection ensured that Kamen would not lose his job. It could not shield him from other harassments.[41]

Kamen could not, for example, get a passport. In 1947, on the eve of a trip to set up a laboratory at the Weizmann Institute in Israel, the State Department turned down his application for a passport. He was told it would not be "in the best interests of the United States" for him to leave the country. Repeated applications were to no avail, and Kamen was forced to turn down invitations to lecture and to do research in France, Argentina, Australia, England, and elsewhere. There was the Fish Grotto incident, of course. In addition, as the State Department's passport chief, Ruth Shipley, explained, "it has been alleged that you were a Communist." Finally, in December 1953, upset because he felt that his passport problems were jeopardizing his career, Kamen sued. He was already involved in litigation. In July 1951, the Washington *Times-Herald*, the Chicago *Tribune*'s Washington paper, had resuscitated the old charges and published a front-page article about the unfortunate chemist. "Atom Experts Who Gave Reds Data Named," was the headline. Kamen sued for libel and, though the case dragged on until May 1955, he eventually won. A few months later the State Department, by then on the defensive as the result of a recent Supreme Court decision in a similar passport case, capitulated and issued a passport to Kamen. He had other troubles as well. In August 1954 the Public Health Service cancelled the third year of a three-year grant it had awarded him. Though he found another source of money for his work, like dozens of other politically tainted scientists he was never allowed to serve on any of the panels that awarded government research grants. Today, Kamen views his exclusion from such panels as a blessing of sorts, but at the time the damage to his reputation, career, and family life that the government's harassment caused him was anything but trivial. And Kamen, a non-Communist and a friendly witness, survived his brush with the inquisition better than most academics. He kept his job.[42]

So did Clarence Hiskey. His congressional appearances—before HUAC in 1948 and 1949 and then, again, before the Senate Internal Security Subcommittee in 1953—were only part of the overall pattern of harassment he was subjected to during those years. The FBI "went in for character assassination," Hiskey recalls, "visiting the Polytechnic, visiting neighbors where I lived and telling them I was a Communist spy." As a result, people "would just avoid you. They didn't come to visit

you, they didn't invite you to visit them, and they were very aloof."
Worse yet were the crank calls

> at all hours of the night and day, with messages to my wife like, "Your
> husband doesn't have long to live," and "We know where you are and
> we're going to get you," and this sort of thing, this kind of crazy intimida-
> tion. Some times you'd pick up the phone and you'd hear heavy breathing
> and nobody would say anything.

The harassment lasted for years. Even after the congressional hearings
ended and Hiskey's indictment was quashed, the case refused to die.
Columnists Howard Rushmore and Bob Considine "were always digging
it up." Rushmore, Hiskey recalls, "was really making quite a living off
me for a while." The case affected his work; grants dried up and with
them the possibility of attracting good graduate students to help with his
research.

His job, however, remained. He had tenure and Harry S. Rogers,
the conservative, but gritty, president of the Brooklyn Polytechnic Institute, had little sympathy for the tactics of the congressional investigators. In a statement he released the day after HUAC's report on Hiskey
came out, Rogers explained that "the charges of a Congressional committee do not constitute a legal indictment against a private citizen" and
may, in fact, "do a grave injustice and irreparable harm. . . . The Administration of the Institute must proceed upon the presumed integrity
of its staff members until such time as that integrity is challenged or dis-
proved by the orderly process of justice." Rogers suspended Hiskey when
he was indicted for contempt and reinstated him when he was acquitted.
Even so, there were problems. Rogers did not dare to promote Hiskey
from an associate to a full professor. To do so, he would have had to
present the matter to the Board of Trustees which, he feared, might fire
the controversial chemist rather than promote him. Since the school's by-
laws specified that only the president could initiate business, as long as
Rogers did not bring Hiskey's name before the Board its members could
not dismiss him. But it was not a comfortable situation, and Hiskey
finally decided that "it was just too rough to stick around Poly." He resigned and became an industrial consultant.[43]

Lomanitz wasn't exactly fired as a result of his appearance before
HUAC. He had been teaching at Fisk for only a semester, and, though
an associate professor, did not yet have tenure. The University's president, Charles S. Johnson, the first black to head this all-black school, was
understandably concerned about the impact on the college of Lomanitz's
refusal to testify and his probable contempt citation. He called the young
physicist into his office and, Lomanitz recollected,

> he told me that he had a contract, approved by the Trustees, in his desk,
> but that he would not issue it to me until "this matter was cleared up."
> He suggested that meanwhile I continue to work without a contract. I
> could not see doing this.

So Lomanitz and his wife packed their belongings, left Nashville, and moved back to Oklahoma, the place from which ten years before a $650 fellowship had lured them to Berkeley.[44]

Things had been going well for David Bohm at Princeton before HUAC subpoenaed him. His contract had been renewed the previous year and, though there was considerable publicity about his case, the University did not seem upset. Its official statement noted his "zealous and effective" work and insisted that "at no time has there been any reason for questioning his loyalty toward the government and democratic institutions of the United States." Then, in December 1950, after his indictment, President Harold W. Dodds apparently called in Bohm and suggested that he cooperate with the committee. "We talked it over," Bohm recalled, "and he sort of kept on intimating that it would be best to testify. . . . I couldn't," Bohm explained, "you know, I couldn't mention names." Dodds then suspended him. Bohm received his salary but was forbidden to teach or even to appear on the campus. Meanwhile, his department had recommended that he be reappointed for a second three-year term. This seems to have been a fairly routine matter; tenure was not at issue. Bohm had been at Princeton for three years and there was, at least from the perspective of the Physics Department, no reason not to keep him for an additional three. Nonetheless, the faculty's Advisory Committee on Appointments and Advancements, the group which reviewed all such reappointments before they reached the president, turned Bohm down. It gave no reason. In an oral history interview that President Dodds granted in 1962, he claims that the decision to let Bohm go was a professional one—"in his own scholarly life, he didn't merit a promotion." But the fact that Bohm was not up for a promotion as well as the tone of Dodds's remarks, his insistence that Bohm "was also a communist" and, thus, not a teacher that Princeton had an obligation to protect, makes it quite clear that the presumably professional criteria that governed the decision not to reappoint Bohm had a large political component.[45]

Like Bohm's, Frank Oppenheimer's career had been thriving. He had been teaching at the University of Minnesota for two and a half years and the Physics Department had just recommended him for tenure. As a former left-winger he had had some problems after the war: he could not get a passport, and the FBI had questioned his neighbors about him. In the summer of 1947, the Washington *Times-Herald* came out with a front-page story claiming that Oppenheimer had been a Communist and had engaged in all sorts of nefarious activities. Called by a reporter in the middle of the night, Oppenheimer foolishly denied the whole story. Even more foolishly, he then had his lawyer write a letter to the University authorities also denying everything. Much of the *Times-Herald*'s story (which may have been planted by the FBI to discredit Robert) was a fabrication, but not all of it. Oppenheimer had been a radical during the late thirties. He had raised money for all sorts of progressive causes—migrant workers, left-wing unions, and, of course, the Spanish Civil War. He joined FAECT and from 1937 to 1941 was a member of the Communist Party, first in Pasadena, where he was a graduate student at Cal Tech, and then in Palo Alto, where he was a teaching assistant at Stanford. But Oppenheimer did not tell his employers this until HUAC subpoenaed him.[46]

Before he left Minnesota for his date with the committee, Oppenheimer made the gesture of sending President Morrill a letter of resignation. But he neither wanted nor expected that it would be accepted, for he was planning to cooperate with HUAC as fully as he could without naming names. It was not a realistic expectation. State universities always feel vulnerable to public opinion. For some reason, Minnesota's administration seemed particularly sensitive, almost hypersensitive, to allegations of radicalism during this period. True, both Frank Oppenheimer *and* "Scientist X," Joseph Weinberg, were on the faculty and the publicity that surrounded their HUAC appearances must have been damaging, especially since it was revealed that Oppenheimer had been less than candid in his original dealings with the press and the University administration. Thus, no sooner had Oppenheimer finished testifying than he received a phone call from the University asking him to resign. He returned to Minnesota and, in his interview with President Morrill, discovered that it was not only his original dissembling that had cost him his job, but also his continued association with the left. Morrill cited one incident in particular, where Oppenheimer had appeared at a public meeting in support of Henry Wallace's presidential campaign along with two fellow-traveling Harvard professors and Paul Robeson.[47]

*   *   *

These cases had little impact on the rest of the academic community. Colleagues of the afflicted physicists were concerned—some of them at least. Faculty liberals at the University of Minnesota tried to organize some kind of a protest on behalf of Oppenheimer and Weinberg. But Oppenheimer, who felt himself tainted by his initial lack of candor, did not press for reinstatement. Instead he left Minnesota and took his family to live on a ranch he had recently bought in Colorado. Weinberg, who had troubles with grand juries as well as with academic administrators, was suspended by Minnesota after being indicted for perjury in May 1951. Ultimately acquitted, he lost his job, nonetheless, and went into private industry. Bohm moved to Brazil. Though clearly fired for political reasons, none of these people had tenure and so did not expect that the AAUP, which, despite disclaimers, essentially defined academic freedom in terms of tenure, would take up their cases. Moreover, the uncertainty of their juridical status, the fact that many of them had prison sentences hanging over them, hardly strengthened their positions. Thus, they did not request faculty hearings or make any serious attempt to bring the machinery of academic freedom into play. Since a university traditionally had no obligation to explain why it let a junior faculty member go, their failure to act was understandable.[48]

Had these scientists been tenured, the formal proceedings that would have accompanied their dismissals might have brought into the open the issues that later Fifth Amendment witnesses were to raise. The verdict, however, would probably have been the same. Though the academic establishment had yet to articulate a rationalization for its policy of dismissing faculty members who refused to cooperate with anti-Communist investigations, the policy was already in place. It had grown out of the earlier proscription against active members of the Communist Party. And it rested on the assumption that a professor who refused to tell a congressional committee whether he or she had been a Communist enhanced the possibility that he or she might be one. The prevailing standard of evidence was somewhat zoological: "If it looked like a duck, waddled like a duck, and quacked like a duck." Thus, when academic institutions began to investigate the uncooperative witnesses on their faculties, they scrutinized their political beliefs and affiliations in order to find a pattern of Communist waddling and quacking. Taking the Fifth Amendment, it was assumed, was part of that pattern.

By the early 1950s, the defiance of a congressional committee was often the only indication that a professor had been or still was sympathetic to the left. Radical politics had all but disappeared from the nation's campuses during the McCarthy years, and professors who publicly opposed American foreign policy or supported allegedly Communist organizations ran enormous risks. This was especially true in the cases of dozens of former Party members who knew that their past, as well as their present, political activities might some day get them in trouble. They also feared that their participation would hurt the groups they worked with. "I have for years," Ross Lomanitz explained,

> confined my political activity to conversations with individuals, and often not a great deal of that—mostly because I didn't want to have anyone or any group smeared with "guilt by association," and partly because of personal fears.

As a result, almost all of the academic ex-Communists (not to mention the academics who had never been Communists) abstained from politics. Those who did not and who remained active in left-wing circles were few in number and heavily beleaguered. They were, of course, targeted by HUAC and the rest of the anti-Communist establishment, but they were also under enormous pressure from the institutions they worked for. The experiences of Philip Morrison illustrate just how little left-wing activity the American academic community was prepared to tolerate.[49]

Morrison was a physicist, a former student of Robert Oppenheimer's, and an alumnus of the Manhattan Project. He had also been in the Communist Party from 1936 to 1942. But, unlike the other physicists that we have been following, Morrison remained both politically involved and academically employed. He was as active on the left as any other academic in America, probably more so than any other ex-Communist academic. Yet he never lost his job and, aside from a relatively uneventful session with the Senate Internal Security Subcommittee, never had any serious hassles with official investigators. Even so, the administration at Cornell University, where he taught, kept a close watch over Morrison's activities and tried to keep him from doing anything that might embarrass the institution. For almost ten years Morrison managed to maintain his political commitments while meeting Cornell's demands. His struggle to do so was never public; both Morrison and the Cornell authorities sought to keep their political negotiations secret. Nonetheless, it was a delicate balancing act and one which required considerable effort. Morrison estimates that he spent three months every two years at it. Still, for an ex-Communist physicist from the Manhattan Project to be an active radical *and* keep his job in the 1950s was quite an achievement, even for someone with tenure.

Morrison's left-wing background was no secret. The security men on the Manhattan Project knew all about it; Morrison had once been shown the hundred-page dossier they had collected on him. Yet, at no time did security considerations interfere with his work on the bomb, no doubt because he did nothing that would have made the security officers suspicious. Moreover, it is possible that, like his mentor Oppenheimer, whom we know had real problems getting clearance, Morrison was so valuable to the project that the top brass may have overridden the security people's misgivings. Morrison worked first at the Metallurgical Laboratory in Chicago, a floor below Hiskey, then at Los Alamos. He assembled the test bomb at Alamagordo and then went out to Tinian to put together those that were dropped on Japan. He was among the first group of American scientists to visit Hiroshima and Nagasaki, an experience that could easily explain the tenacity of his later commitment to peace and nuclear disarmament.[50]

When Morrison left Los Alamos he turned down an offer from Berkeley to take a post at Cornell. It was a calculated decision on his part:

> I knew that my views and general stance were not such that I could survive in a state university and I was skeptical about how I could survive in a university in New York or Boston where there was a lot of public attention. The place to go was a private university in a quiet community where there was a sense of detachment and academic freedom.

Cornell also had a first-rate Physics Department. Morrison's political independence, his stature as an atomic scientist, and his eloquence as a speaker and writer quickly made him a leader of the postwar left. He actively supported Henry Wallace for President and was one of the featured speakers at the Progressive Party's nominating convention in 1948.

Morrison was also one of the few non-Communists to be involved with the organized peace movement of the late forties and fifties. An ardent civil libertarian, he gave his name to "every defense committee that appeared." In retrospect, he claims, "I didn't do a great deal." What made it appear as if he had was that "nobody else did." Academics as well known and as politically outspoken as Morrison could literally be counted on the fingers of one hand. (Significantly, most of the others were also, like Harvard astronomer Harlow Shapley and Cal Tech biochemist Linus Pauling, physical scientists.)[51]

Despite Morrison's prominence on the left, the government did not harass him. He was careful, it is true, and did not expose himself unnecessarily to situations which he knew would cause problems. He did not, for example, apply for a passport until 1960. Nor did he try to get a security clearance from the government, though much of the work he did was in the highly sensitive area of atomic energy. For the sake of his position at Cornell, however, he wanted to be able to claim that he had never actually lost his clearance and that he still had access to classified documents. So, he simply let his wartime security clearance lapse, but, because he had been working on atomic energy before the creation of the Manhattan Project, several of his earlier papers, though clearly classifiable, had never been classified and he kept them in his possession. In addition, during the course of his own research in nuclear physics in the fifties, he continued to make scientific discoveries that were because of their subject matter immediately classified. Thus, technically at least, he could state that his security clearance had never been revoked and that he still had access to top-secret materials.[52]

Though Morrison's caution was able to keep him from any direct confrontations with the federal administration, his notoriety ensured constant attention from the nation's professional anti-Communists, the right-wing journalists and congressional investigators who specialized in exposing Communists and their followers. *Life* magazine ran Morrison's picture in an April 1949 article on America's fifty most eminent "Dupes and Fellow Travelers." In April 1951 HUAC released a "Report on the Communist 'Peace' Offensive," four pages of which were devoted to Morrison's supposed Communist connections. Its rhetoric aside, the quality of HUAC's research left something to be desired. Not only were some of the allegations completely false, but the committee's staff had given Morrison a middle initial he had never had. J. B. Matthews, the dean of professional anti-Communists, told the Senate Internal Security Subcommittee in December 1952 that Morrison had "one of the most incriminating pro-Communist records in the entire academic world." Matthews expounded further upon the matter in a 1953 article in *The American Mercury,* in which he attacked Cornell for keeping Morrison on its staff "despite his publicly expressed gratitude that the Soviet Union, too, has the atomic bomb."[53]

Counterattack, a newsletter founded in 1947 by three former FBI men to supplement the government's efforts "to expose and combat Communist activities" (their words), mainly exposed show business people, but it did devote several articles to Morrison. One, on March 6, 1953, for example, dealt with the question: "CAN COLLEGES AND UNIVERSITIES BE COUNTED ON TO DEAL WITH COMMUNIST INFILTRATION?" It then cited "the case of Cornell Univ and Prof PHILIP MORRISON" and went on to give "a partial listing of the many Communist fronts MORRISON has been associated with in recent years." The allegations continued:

> MORRISON has defended the Communist Party (CP) and its convicted Politburo members, he supported the CP's May Day Parades, and has urged clemency for the ROSENBERGS . . . but has refused to condemn anti-Semitism in Stalin Russia and its satellites.

After a few more such charges, *Counterattack* then asked, "What has Cornell Univ done about MORRISON? Nothing."[54]

Counterattack was wrong. Cornell University had been doing quite a lot about Professor Morrison; none of it, however, in public. The University's archives contain dozens of letters from alumni and others complaining about Morrison and asking the University to act. "For the first time in my life I am ashamed of being a Cornell man," one alumnus wrote. Another decried Cornell's toleration of "that sniveling guttersnipe traitor Philip Morrison, alleged atomic physicist and probable spy." Such sentiments were extreme, but even moderates, like the chairman of the annual fund-raising drive sponsored by the class of 1911, believed that "Cornell alumni generally regret the publicity people like Professor Morrison have caused." The trustees were similarly concerned. This was, from the administration's point of view, the main problem with Morrison. Though his activities were neither dangerous nor illegal, they were embarrassing and exposed the University to unfavorable publicity.[55]

By the time Morrison became Cornell's chief source of embarrassment, he already had tenure and so could not be quietly dropped from the faculty. The dismissal of a tenured professor at a university of Cornell's quality and prestige would require formal charges and a quasi-judicial hearing. Besides, what was the University to charge Morrison with? Chairing a meeting at which Paul Robeson spoke? To try to oust Morrison on any such pretext would, the Cornell administration realized, provoke a faculty rebellion. Either the faculty would have to be brought to agree that behavior like Morrison's constituted grounds for dismissal or else Morrison would have to be persuaded to curtail that behavior. The administration did both.

At some point in the late forties, Cornell's faculty, administration, and trustees had begun to discuss a revision of the University's policy on "The Promotion, Appointment, and Dismissal of Members of the Faculty." There is no evidence that when this process began it had any connection with Morrison's activities. Periodic revisions of tenure rules were not uncommon, and Cornell was not the only school to update its by-laws during the 1940s. NYU, for example, also went through the process of revising its regulations and drawing up a new code of academic freedom. The initial revision produced a straightforward, essentially procedural document, but just before the NYU faculty adopted it, an anti-Communist disclaimer was inserted. The same thing happened at Cornell, but it engendered considerable controversy.[56]

On January 17, 1951, the faculty passed a draft of the revised by-laws and sent them to the Board of Trustees for approval. By that time, of course, it had become clear that Morrison's politics were creating problems for Cornell, and the trustees realized that the process of revising the rules for dismissal gave them an opportunity to make the faculty deal with those problems. Thus, though the proposals which the faculty had adopted were purely procedural, some trustees wanted further revision. Specifically, they demanded that the term "misconduct," which was to be the main ground for dismissal, be explicitly defined. As Acting President T. P. Wright explained:

> The views of the Board members who spoke indicated that what they had in mind was the inclusion of membership in the communist party plus types of action which could be shown to result in serious harm to the University.

Wright recognized that it might be difficult to get the faculty to agree to such changes, but he noted, "I feel that the sense of the meeting in the Board of Trustees was such that the faculty members must face up to this very real problem." Wright subsequently told the Committee on University Policy, the Cornell faculty's official policy-making group, that he wanted the faculty to redefine "misconduct" and make "some statement of policy on the question of Communism," because (and here I quote from the Policy Committee's minutes)

> he wished support in meeting recurrent charges against certain members of the Faculty, and he wished specific guidance on the question regarding injury to the University as ground for disciplinary action.

In other words, he wanted the faculty to help him protect and control Morrison.[57]

The committee was hesitant, some of its members reluctant, so the minutes state, "to do anything which might inflame feelings about certain present members of the Faculty." Clearly, some kind of a compromise was in order. While refusing to go as far as Wright indicated the trustees wanted, i.e. include injury to the University as a ground for dismissal, the Policy Committee did agree to replace the word "misconduct" with the presumably more precise phraseology, "personal misfeasance or non-feasance," and to accept a clearly political interpretation of the term "misconduct" by adopting the following resolution:

It is the sense of the Faculty that any member of the Faculty who, publicly, or in his contacts with students, advocates the overthrow of the government of the United States, by force or violence, or the accomplishment of political change by a means not permitted by the Constitution of the United States or of the State of New York is guilty of misconduct.

Similarly, the committee gave in to the trustees' concern with Cornell's reputation by adopting the dean's suggestion that it ask the faculty to reaffirm "as applicable to the present crisis its legislation of May 8, 1918, as follows:

> The Faculty maintains that each of its members in writing or speaking has the same rights and duties as any other citizen.
> The Faculty believes that each of its members in exercising his right of free speech should realize that in the minds of many citizens he occupies a representative position and that in consequence the reputation of the University lies partly in his hands.
> The Faculty recognizes that each of its members is bound in the present crisis to safeguard the reputation of the University with especial care.[58]

The faculty debated these proposals at a special meeting, May 30, 1951. Dale Corson, a physicist and future president of Cornell, recalls how highly charged the atmosphere of that meeting was. The turnout was so large that the group had to move three times before it found a large enough room. The discussion, though heated, was polished. Many participants had written out their speeches in advance; others rewrote them and inserted the revised versions into the official record afterward. Although the faculty ultimately ratified it, every section of the proposal drew criticism. Even so, the debate, especially that over the two resolutions, had an unreal quality to it. As we have seen, both resolutions had been designed specifically to satisfy the trustees' desire for an expression of anti-Communism, on the one hand, and a redefinition of "misconduct" to include damaging the University's reputation, on the other. Yet such was the nature of the academic profession, its need for at least the appearance of self-government, that at no point during the discussion did either the critics or the proponents of the package talk about its real function. Robert Cushman, one of Cornell's leading experts on civil liberties, was probably most forthcoming when, in response to a colleague's fears that the resolutions were "calculated to satisfy an emotional urge rather than to prevent a demonstrated evil," he admitted

> that there is no immediate and pressing need for the action which we are now considering. Frankly I do not feel that any of this is of very great importance. I do believe, however, that there are some reasons why it is desirable that the Faculty should revise its legislation along the lines proposed, and since I am unable to see any disadvantages in the Committee's proposals, I shall support them.

But Cushman did not elaborate on the "reasons why" the measure was "desirable." He didn't have to. John MacDonald, the law school professor who had drafted the revised by-laws for the Policy Committee, had already done that by reminding his colleagues of their legal status:

> We can do no more than propose, and that only by grace of the Board. The By-Laws are solely the concern, and within the sole jurisdiction of the Board of Trustees. Thus, if it be said, "let us fight," I reply "with what do we fight?"

May 30, 1951, was not the first, nor the last, time that pragmatism outweighed idealism in the academic world.[59]

Many years later Morrison claimed that he couldn't remember if he had been at that faculty meeting. Had he been there, he certainly would have voted against the proposals, but he just couldn't remember. For in the spring of 1951 Morrison's own problems with Cornell were coming to a head. The publication of HUAC's report on the peace movement on April 1, naming him as "an important pillar of the Communists' 'peace' movement," must have precipitated the crisis. On April 5, Acting President Wright called Morrison in. He described the barrage of criticism that the University had been receiving and explained to the physicist how his political activities were hurting Cornell. Wright was particularly upset about Morrison's opposition to the Korean war and his continued association with members of the Communist Party. He cited the AAUP's 1940 statement on academic freedom to bolster his contention that a professor, speaking outside of his field, must dissociate himself explicitly from his university and must try not to injure its reputation. Then the two men exchanged a series of letters in which they agreed to a set of ground rules to cover Morrison's future political activities. I have not seen these letters, but references to them, both in Morrison's later correspondence and in the files of Wright's successor, make it clear that Morrison agreed to the following (and I quote from his version):

> 1) To disassociate myself from Cornell whenever engaged in a controversial discussion . . . 2) To avoid active sponsorship of any student organization in the field of controversy . . . 3) To avoid appearing personally on the platform with Communists or with persons of great notoriety, such as might lead to widespread newspaper publicity.[60]

Morrison tried hard to stick with the agreement. It was not easy, for he was constantly being asked to make speeches, sponsor organizations, and sign petitions. "Since my agreement with Dr. Wright," he observed a few years later, "I have certainly joined very few organizations." But try though he did to keep out of the headlines, he did not relinquish all political activity. He remained active in the peace movement and continued to lend his name to all kinds of legal defense groups. Thus, when J. B. Matthews identified him before the Senate Internal Security Subcommittee on December 29, 1952, as someone who was "currently active in this entire communist-front movement," Cornell's new president, Deane W. Malott, became concerned. He spoke with Morrison on December 30, and the two men agreed that the best way to deflect the publicity that Morrison continued to attract was for him to have an informal hearing in front of a special faculty committee. The committee was not to try charges, but rather, as the dean who organized it explained to Morrison,

> to give you an opportunity to describe your activities and define your position . . . in an endeavor to find the best solution to a difficult problem in which both the university and you have an interest.[61]

The committee met secretly with Morrison in early January 1953. Its members, the dean and five of the more respected senior people on the faculty, questioned Morrison at length about his politics and his life. Morrison recalled the sessions as "a very difficult and taxing process, going far into what many people would regard as private and personal areas of feeling and belief." The committee wanted to know: Was he a Marxist? a Communist? If not, what evidence could he give that he wasn't? Did he believe it necessary to bring about social change by revolution? And, would he be loyal in a war between America and the USSR? These questions, for all their naïveté about the academic left in America, reflected the common assumptions of the time and were, at least in part, designed to get statements by Morrison on record which Cornell could use to fend off attacks on him by trustees, alumni, and other concerned souls.

In its report the committee noted that Morrison had been "straightforward, helpful, and sincere." He was definitely "not subversive," but he did have problems. Though he was "indisputably brilliant" as a scientist, the report pointed out somewhat patronizingly, his "guilt and horror" over Hiroshima

> may easily have left a blind or weakened spot in his capacity to think . . . . His apparently honest motives are not censurable, but his methods and associations have left him open to severe censure.

Many of his troubles were not of his own causing. Even so,

> Only by exercising extreme discretion will he be able to avoid news comment adverse alike to himself and to Cornell—even then, bcause of past activities he will not be left alone entirely.

Morrison was on probation, just at the time when the congressional investigating committees were about to look at educators.[62]

Less than two months later, *Counterattack* published its first set of charges against Morrison. President Malott sent copies to the dean and to some of the members of the faculty committee with the comment, "This evidence of continued activity is disquieting." *Counterattack*'s article had been timed to coincide with the forthcoming set of congressional hearings into Communist subversion in education. Given his notoriety, Morrison expected to be called. He was teaching at MIT at the time, on a semester's leave of absence from Ithaca. Even so, Cornell prepared itself for the hearings. In the beginning of March the Policy Committee voted to set up a special "Subcommittee on Academic Problems Arising from Governmental Investigations," but to keep its existence a secret from the rest of the faculty. Clearly, the Policy Committee expected Morrison to be involved, for one of the people it appointed to the secret committee was Morrison's colleague, the theoretical physicist Hans Bethe.[63]

Predictably, when the Senate Internal Security Subcommittee under Indiana's William Jenner brought its investigation of higher education to Boston, it subpoenaed Morrison. Morrison wanted to placate the authorities in Ithaca and so, instead of choosing an attorney who represented left-wing clients, he selected Arthur Sutherland, a staunchly Republican law school professor who had recently come to Harvard from Cornell. Despite Sutherland's warnings, Morrison had decided that he would take the "diminished Fifth" and talk about himself but not about others. Morrison recognized the legal risks involved but, given his past troubles with Cornell, he knew that invoking the Fifth Amendment would cost him his job. In his preliminary hearing Jenner asked Morrison dozens of questions that he refused to answer (most of them about Robert Oppenheimer), but in the second, public, session, Jenner dropped all the questions about Oppenheimer and Morrison was able to answer every question the committee asked. Morrison had been a good witness, Sutherland wrote his former colleague John MacDonald, the chairman of Cornell's secret subcommittee:

> He answered every question that he was asked, testified simply and courteously, and altogether made a good impression . . . . I see nothing which should suggest to Cornell any reason to make trouble for Philip.[64]

The Jenner Committee had other ideas. Despite Morrison's attempt to be conciliatory, when the committee published its report, "Subversive Influence in the Educational Process," on July 17, 1953, it devoted an entire section to Morrison. It described his political activities and his position within the atomic bomb project. It claimed, on the basis of its "limited access" to his security questionnaire, it had evidence that he had withheld information about his Communist past from the Manhattan Project security staff. Cornell's subcommittee noted the Jenner Committee's charges, but took no action. Perhaps it would have had not one of its own members, Hans Bethe, managed to get from Los Alamos copies of Morrison's original questionnaire and discovered that Jenner had based his charges on what he assumed Morrison's answers would have been to a questionnaire that was issued several years *after* Morrison had left Los Alamos.[65]

Politically, Morrison was cautious, but not quiescent. He turned down more speaking engagements than he accepted, but he did accept

some. His activities, at a time when McCarthyism was at its peak, made
the already jumpy Cornell administration even more so. At the end of
September, reports that Morrison had addressed a rally sponsored by a
group rumored to be on the Attorney General's list so disturbed President Malott that he communicated to Morrison through Bethe his desire
for a full explanation. While Morrison was preparing his response to Malott, *Counterattack* published yet another set of charges against the Cornell physicist. This was too much. On December 3, 1953, Malott wrote
Morrison:

> The continued embarrassment which you have caused Cornell University
> through the years has led me most regretfully to the conclusion that some
> action must be taken to protect the good name of the institution and those
> who are members of it from the continuing concern for its integrity caused
> by your repeated backing and support of allegedly subversive organiza-
> tions . . . .
>   You have appeared from time to time to indicate a willingness to
> be cooperative which promise has repeatedly failed of fulfillment.
>   . . . I am therefore asking you to show cause in writing to me why
> I should not institute proceedings for your dismissal from the University.[66]

For Morrison, Malott's letter came "as a sharp surprise." He had, as
he told Malott in his formal response to the president's ultimatum, con-
scientiously tried to avoid publicity and, except for his Senate hearings,
"indeed have received no attention in the press of general circulation
during the two and one-half years since I discussed the matter with Dr.
Wright." But, Morrison realized, because of all the controversy, "my actions [are] more subject to external restraint than those of others who
might now hold the same views." As he saw it, his trouble with Cornell
stemmed from a lack of mutual understanding about what actions he
should avoid. Accordingly, he was willing to make an agreement "to curtail sharply my associations with organizations whose public standing has
been impaired by the legal actions of the Attorney General." He suggested that he and Malott draw up a list of such organizations. Morrison
would then promise not to join them, speak at their meetings, or let his
name be used by them.[67]

Malott refused the offer. "As an administrative officer I ought not to
keep taboo lists, or to regulate the personal activity of any professor in
Cornell University, or to make agreements of permissible conduct." It
just wasn't "a proper procedure," he explained. "You must be, and I am
sure in the last analysis would wish to be, the sole judge in the matter of
your own actions." Malott realized, "This is more difficult for both of us
than your proposal." Morrison would have to decide for himself what activities to give up, though Malott did offer one suggestion:

> Because so much is at stake . . . I cannot help but hope that you will be
> willing carefully to consider the advisability of withdrawing all association
> from organizations lying outside of your professional field.

Once again, Morrison was on probation. And he even more stringently curtailed his political activities. The journalistic attacks on him ceased as well, though that may just have been a reflection of the general easing of McCarthyism that was noticeable by the end of 1954.[68]

At no time during this period had Morrison's teaching and research been an issue. The Physics Department considered him one of its most valuable members and had been trying for several years to get him promoted to full professor. In 1954, Malott refused to recommend Morrison's promotion to the Board of Trustees. The following year, the chairman of the Physics Department again requested the promotion:

> The time has now long passed when this promotion should have been made . . . . It has now become in the nature of a disgrace to hold up Professor Morrison's promotion any further.

The Department felt so strongly about the matter that, the chairman warned, it would not recommend "any other . . . promotions to the rank of full professor until favorable action is taken in Professor Morrison's case." The physicists forced Malott's hand; on April 21, 1956, he submitted Morrison's promotion to the Board of Trustees. Its action seemed to justify Malott's previous reluctance to submit Morrison's name. Though the board promoted the controversial physicist, several of its members were so upset about recent reports of Morrison's political activities that the board decided to appoint a special committee to investigate—yet again—what the committee's chairman delicately told Morrison were "certain of your activities of concern to the Board."[69]

For two days, on October 3 and 4, the trustees' special five-man subcommittee questioned Morrison. They asked about his political background and interrogated him at length about what kinds of organizations or causes he would join or support. Much of the inquiry consisted of rehashing the old right-wing allegations about the supposedly subversive nature of Morrison's affiliations over the previous ten years. Time and again, a trustee would mention somebody whose name had appeared on a letterhead with Morrison's or whose presence had graced the same platform and then ask, "Do you happen to know whether he is a member of the Communist Party?" Morrison tried, as he had so many times before, to make his questioners understand that to him the defense of someone's civil liberties was so important that it did not matter whose civil liberties they were or who else was helping defend them. But the trustees, though courteous and well-meaning, spoke, as Morrison recognized, "such a different language" that like most of their contemporaries they simply could not understand how somebody might knowingly associate with Communists, especially when both his job and his university's reputation were at stake. But as he had done in all his previous hearings, Morrison was able to convince the trustees that he was perfectly loyal.[70]

Once the hearing was over, Cornell gave Morrison no further trouble. In fact, it is likely that for all its apparent severity it was just a charade, a maneuver designed to reconcile some of the hard-liners on the Board of Trustees to Morrison's promotion. Both Morrison and Dale Corson, then chairman of the Physics Department and later president of Cornell, who accompanied Morrison to the hearing as his adviser, were nonetheless upset about certain aspects of the inquiry: its adversarial nature and its concern with irrelevant personal details. Both men felt that since the trustees asked Morrison to give his testimony under oath, he should have had a legal, rather than a lay, adviser. But these were technicalities. "The fundamental issue," Corson told the trustees,

> is the place where we draw the line in requiring the conformity of a faculty member in areas outside that of his primary professional competence. . . . My feeling is that the line has been drawn rather far on the wrong side.[71]

Of course, in 1956, when Corson made that statement, the lines had been long drawn and the precedents set. Philip Morrison had survived the inquisition, one of the few politically active ex-Communists to remain academically employed in the fifties. His former comrades from Berkeley were not so lucky. Like Morrison, their political activities—their refusal to cooperate with HUAC to be precise—embarrassed the universities where they taught. Lacking tenure, they lost their jobs. Because their confrontation with HUAC stemmed from its search for atomic spies, not subversive educators, the academic establishment did not pay much attention to their fate. Their cases were important, nonetheless. The uniformity of their treatment indicated that a consensus was developing within the academic community. Whether implemented by a faculty committee at Princeton, a college president at Fisk, or the Board of Regents at Berkeley, that consensus seemed to imply that "Fifth Amendment" Communists were as unwelcome on the nation's campuses as "card-carrying" ones. The rationale for that consensus was to come later, at a time when congressional investigators were about to descend on the nation's campuses. But as the cases of Fox, Lomanitz, Bohm, and even Morrison reveal, the policy was already in place. College teachers who tangled publicly with the anti-Communist crusade and thus threatened the "reputation" of their institutions could lose their jobs.

VI

"A Very Fertile Field for Investigation": Congressional Committees, Unfriendly Witnesses, and the Academic Community

On February 8, 1951, a group of federal agents, armed with a subpoena from Senator Pat McCarran's newly formed Internal Security Subcommittee, swooped down on a barn in western Massachusetts and hauled its contents back to Washington. The committee's loot, the files of a private research organization called the Institute of Pacific Relations (IPR), would show, so McCarran and his staff believed, how Communist agents had managed to engineer the loss of China. In a series of hearings, which ran from June 1951 until the following summer, the committee used the purloined files to document its contention that, because of their influence on the State Department, Party members within the IPR had subverted American policy in East Asia. These hearings were to have a profound effect on the nation's foreign policy, depriving the State Department of most of its experienced China hands and preventing it from adopting a realistic or flexible approach to later events in the Far East. They were also to have a profound effect on the academic community.[1]

Many of McCarran's witnesses were professors. In part this was because of the quasi-scholarly nature of the IPR. During the 1930s and 1940s, before the field of East Asian Studies had found an academic home, the IPR sponsored most of the serious research then being done on the Far East. As a result, almost every academic interested in Asia belonged to it or contributed to its publications. There was another reason for the McCarran Committee's concern with college teachers. Two of the leading members of McCarran's staff—its research director, Benjamin Mandel, and its special counsel, Robert Morris—had served with the Rapp-Coudert Committee. Morris, at least, had long been hoping for a sequel to that aborted investigation and, though he never diverted McCarran's hearings from their primary focus on China, he was occasionally able to bring in witnesses from that earlier probe. Some of these people, as Morris and his colleagues on the committee no doubt expected, took the Fifth Amendment. In so doing, they forced the institutions that employed them to confront the issues that their failure to co-operate with the SISS had raised. They forced the rest of the academy to do so as well. For by the time the IPR hearings had ended, in the middle of 1952, it was clear that the academic world, which until then had been relatively immune from congressional investigation, was about to lose that immunity. McCarran had been too successful.[2]

In fact, with the possible exception of HUAC's pursuit of Alger Hiss, the IPR hearings were unquestionably the most important congressional investigations of the entire Cold War. Their achievement was to make a politically powerful case for the right-wing charge that Communist sub-versives within the Truman administration had sold China out to Mao Zedong. McCarran was no innovator here. The charges that his commit-tee aired had been circulating for years within the so-called China Lobby and its affiliated network of reactionary journalists, politicians, and professional anti-Communists. Nor was McCarran the first senator to publicize these charges. That was the achievement of Joseph McCarthy. But McCarthy's allegations, tossed off in the spring of 1950 to accompany his ever-fluctuating lists of Communist agents in the State Department, lacked substance. Though he nominated Johns Hopkins professor Owen Lattimore as America's "top Russian espionage agent," he had neither the resources nor the political clout—nor, perhaps, the desire—to make a per-suasive case that subversion among America's China experts had caused the fall of Chiang Kai-shek. Still, despite the verdict of a special investi-gating committee chaired by Senator Millard Tydings that McCarthy's charges were a "fraud and a hoax," those charges did not die.[3]

The Korean war seemingly validated them, and in the more capable and respectable hands of McCarran and his staff, these charges were to reappear as the basis for a devastating attack on the Truman administra-tion's foreign policy. In many respects, the IPR investigation was similar to HUAC's earlier search for atom spies. By focusing on evidence of sup-posed Communist espionage and subversion within the government, it sought to explain why the United States, though obviously the most pow-erful nation in the world, had somehow lost control of events. Such an oversimplified and conspiratorial view of recent history was politically convenient. It was easy to present in the forum of a congressional hear-ing, and it enabled conservative critics of the Truman administration to focus their attacks on the most vulnerable aspects of administration pol-icy. China was crucial here. The bipartisan consensus that had governed American foreign policy in Europe had never extended to Asia. Thus, once the Communists drove Chiang Kai-shek from the mainland, the Republican leadership in Congress, traditionally fascinated by the Orient and eager for an issue that would embarrass the Truman administration, joined the China Lobby in a search for scapegoats. Though a Democrat, McCarran, the powerful chairman of the Senate Judiciary Committee, was a staunch Catholic cold warrior and a long-time supporter of Chiang. The hearings he conducted were his contribution to the China Lobby's campaign. They turned what was originally a matter of policy into one of subversion and forced the American government and the American public to accept the conspiracy theory of the loss of China and its corollary policy, the continued support of Chiang Kai-shek.[4]

As with HUAC's search for Manhattan Project reds, there was just enough seemingly plausible evidence to give McCarran's investigation some credibility. Back in 1945, for example, the OSS, the wartime intelligence agency, had discovered a group of government employees who were leaking classified materials to the editors of *Amerasia*, a small magazine specializing in East Asian affairs. A grand jury refused to indict most of the *Amerasia* people and the less-than-legal surveillance to which the FBI subjected the others forced the government to drop its prosecution. None of the documents were sensitive to begin with, and John Stewart Service, one of the implicated officials, believed that he had been acting in accord with the traditional State Department practice of cooperating with the press and keeping the public informed. Service was one of the State Department's China experts whose realistic assessments of Chinese politics during and after the war had antagonized Chiang's supporters. He was, thus, vulnerable to the charge that he had helped to sell out China. *Amerasia* increased that vulnerability. He was, of course, no Communist; but some of the other people connected with *Amerasia* may have been, if not actually in the Party, then well within its orbit. Philip Jaffe, the magazine's editor, for example, was a close friend of Earl Browder. As a result, *Amerasia* did not disappear. The China Lobby and ambitious politicians continually sought to reopen the case as a way of exposing the Truman administration's softness toward reds.[5]

Amerasia, though significant in right-wing eyes as an example of how Communist agents had subverted the government, could not provide a full-scale scenario for explaining the loss of China. The Institute for Pacific Relations could. Its membership included most Americans with a serious interest in Asia—businessmen, scholars, and diplomats. And, as the McCarran Committee was to show, just about everybody who had a hand in making America's East Asian policy had some connection, however tenuous, with the IPR. In addition, several of the people connected with the IPR were also connected with the Communist Party. The most important of these was the former secretary of the IPR's American Council, Frederick Vanderbilt Field. Even before the IPR hearings, Field's politics had created problems for the Institute. He had resigned from the IPR's staff in 1940 when it became obvious that his extracurricular activities, like picketing the White House to protest American involvement in World War II, were embarrassing the organization. He remained on the IPR's board, however, despite the repeated attempts of several of its members, including the University of California's president Sproul, to purge him. When McCarran subpoenaed him, Field was in jail, serving a sentence for contempt. As a trustee of the organization which posted bail for the defendants in the Smith Act trial of the Communist Party's top leaders, Field, along with novelist Dashiell Hammett and a third man, had refused to give the names of the bail fund's contributors. Significantly, despite the conspicuous nature of Field's political activities, not even the SISS could produce evidence that he had imposed his politics on the IPR. On the contrary, he had consciously avoided using the organization as a political forum and had, along with Lattimore and some others, sponsored *Amerasia* specifically to create an outlet for the type of political articles that the IPR did not publish.[6]

Because of these connections—between American policy-makers and the IPR and between the IPR and the CP—McCarran and his staff planned to build a case that would show, in McCarran's words, "to what extent the IPR was infiltrated and influenced by agents of the communist world conspiracy" and "to what extent these agents and their dupes worked through the Institute into the United States Government to the point where they exerted an influence on United States far eastern policy." The committee organized its hearings to bring out both issues. It used the IPR files both to document an individual's relationship with the organization and to produce a presumably embarrassing or pro-Communist reference from that individual's past publications or correspondence with the Institute. In this way it was able to establish an IPR connection for most of the nation's China experts and top-ranking diplomats as well as for a lot of people, like Alger Hiss, whose relationship with the IPR, superficial as it may have been, could only make the organization look bad. When it called these people to the stand, the committee questioned them in such a way as to make them seem either duplicitous or duped. Here again, the committee's possession of the IPR files enabled it to ask detailed questions about events that had happened ten or fifteen years before and then introduce into the record some presumably incriminating document that pointed up the inconsistencies in the witness's recollections. In comparison with the wilder accusations of McCarthy or the men from HUAC, McCarran's use of documentary evidence, out of context though much of it was, gave his committee a reputation for reliability and made it easier for moderates to accept its conclusions.[7]

Naturally, the IPR files contained little evidence about the Communist affiliations of its members and employees. For that the committee relied on the by-then standard methods of proof—informers and the Fifth Amendment. It put each suspected subversive through the same routine. And, when confronted with the ritual question, "Are you now or have you ever been?" about a dozen IPR witnesses refused to answer. Such a response, at least in the eyes of the committee and its supporters, was the equivalent of a confession. The unfortunate witness had identified him- or herself as a Fifth Amendment Communist. With that identification in hand, the committee's staff then read into the record those documents from the IPR's files which showed the witness's role in the organization and, if possible, his or her connection to the making of American foreign policy.

The committee had, of course, other ways of identifying IPR people as Communists. Often it supplemented the evidence supplied by a witness's invocation of the Fifth Amendment with the testimony of other, more friendly, witnesses. These people's—often perjured—testimony was especially important for identifying people who, like Owen Lattimore, did not take the Fifth because they had never been Communists. Several categories of informers appeared. There were the professional ex-Communists—Elizabeth Bentley, Harvey Matusow, Whittaker Chambers, Joseph Kornfeder, Herbert Philbrick, and Louis Budenz. Their lack of first-hand knowledge about the IPR did not prevent them from testifying about it or even, as Harvey Matusow was later to confess, inventing evidence about it. Budenz was the committee's most useful witness. He had already identified Lattimore as a Communist during the Tydings Committee's investigation of Senator McCarthy's original charges, and he repeated his apparently spurious charges before McCarran. His former superiors in the Party had called the IPR "the little red schoolhouse for teaching certain people in Washington how to think with the Soviet Union in the Far East." Lattimore had been "specifically mentioned as a member of the Communist cell under instructions" and, as editor of the IPR's journal *Pacific Affairs* during the 1930s, had helped the Party "by more and more bringing in Communist authors." By the time Budenz had finished testifying he had identified forty-three people connected with the IPR as Party members. Few were.[8]

Another type of testimony came from a group of disgruntled diplomats and professors. Their reasons for testifying varied. Most, however, used the hearings as a way of presenting their own views and discrediting those of their former colleagues and associates. The most important of the academics was Karl August Wittfogel, a former German Communist and an eminent China scholar then at the University of Washington. Wittfogel had emigrated to Columbia University in the 1930s along with many of the other scholars from the Institute for Social Research, the famous Frankfurt School. He befriended a group of graduate students in history with whom he discussed Marxism and whom he then obligingly identified as Communists. One, Lawrence Rosinger, was on the staff of the IPR; the others, M. I. Finley and Daniel Thorner, had little or no connection with the Institute. But they all had been named during the Rapp-Coudert investigation. Accordingly, the committee's staff resuscitated Rapp-Coudert's key witness, the former CCNY history instructor William Canning, and had him corroborate Wittfogel's charges. Called before the committee, Rosinger, Finley, and Thorner all took the Fifth.[9]

Wittfogel's main target, however, was Lattimore. The two sinologists had known each other for years, but had fallen out politically and intellectually. Wittfogel never actually called Lattimore a Communist; he merely hinted at it, claiming that he could discern a "consistent pro-Soviet" pattern in Lattimore's political thought. The absence of any trace of Marxism in Lattimore's writing was a ruse, for Wittfogel an obvious sign that Lattimore was one of "those elements of the periphery who are really closely coordinated and integrated into the movement, but who try to promote the advantages of the movement without exposing themselves." By the time Lattimore got his chance to rebut all this testimony against him, early in 1952, he had been under attack for two years. A brilliant, if occasionally abrasive man, Lattimore had never gone to graduate school or college and had abandoned his early career as a businessman in China to become one of America's top China scholars as well as a world renowned expert on Central Asia. He had never worked in the State Department, though he had served as Roosevelt's personal political adviser to Chiang Kai-shek during the war. Politically a liberal and temperamentally a fighter, Lattimore gamely tried to confront the SISS with its own shortcomings—its use of material out of context and its uncritical treatment of such witnesses as Budenz. But the hearings were so biased that, even if Lattimore had been a less combative witness, he still could not have discredited the committee's seemingly plausible and highly documented case against him and the IPR. In its final, unanimous report, the committee declared that Lattimore was a "conscious articulate instrument of the Soviet conspiracy" and recommended that he be indicted for perjury. Such was McCarran's clout as chairman of the Senate Judiciary Committee that he forced a reluctant Justice Department to indict Lattimore not once, but twice. The first indictment, written up by Roy Cohn, was so vague that it was thrown out of court. The second was, too, but not until 1955.[10]

By then, the constant publicity and legal hassles had exacted their toll. Lattimore and his friends and family had spent years on the case. His lawyers, Abe Fortas and Thurman Arnold, contributed for free what one scholar estimates was $2.5 million (in 1950 dollars) worth of legal services. Since he had tenure, Lattimore kept his job, but his reputation and influence within the academic world suffered, especially after Johns Hopkins abolished the Walter Hines Page School of International Affairs and with it Lattimore's position as director. He had to curtail his public speaking engagements. His graduate students and even his former secretaries had trouble getting jobs. And he had trouble getting published. The mainstream press closed its doors to him; though he had reviewed dozens of books for the *New York Times* and *Herald Tribune* before the IPR hearings, he reviewed none thereafter. Other China scholars were affected, for the IPR hearings politicized the entire field. As a result, almost all its practitioners, including some rather conservative ones, had trouble getting passports or security clearances. And those who like Lattimore occasionally wrote for a non-academic audience found their normal outlets gone. Of course, not having appeared before McCarran or taken the Fifth Amendment, these people did not lose their jobs.[11]

Nor, at first, did those who had. Because Lattimore's joust with the committee dominated the press's coverage of the IPR hearings, there was little public furor about McCarran's other academic witnesses. The schools which employed these teachers did not seem seriously concerned about their failure to cooperate with McCarran. At Rutgers, for example, where the now eminent classicist M. I. Finley was an assistant professor of ancient history, the University administration not only took no action, but actually lent Finley money for a lawyer, published a book of his, and invited him to speak on Greek law before a group of trustees, all of this *after* he had taken the Fifth. A few months later, however, when education rather than East Asia was under investigation, the situation of people like Finley became more precarious. By then, the academy could no longer ignore the political pressures that the congressional committees had generated.[12]

* * *

After Robert Morris, the SISS's special counsel, finished the IPR investigation, he resigned from the committee and returned to New York. He was still eager to combat subversion and, when he heard that Bella Dodd, the union leader who had coordinated the Communist teachers' resistance to the Rapp-Coudert Committee, had been expelled from the Communist Party and had returned to the Catholic Church, he persuaded McCarran to launch a new investigation. The SISS would finish the job that Rapp-Coudert had begun. And so, for seven days, in September and October 1952, the McCarran Committee (or, to be more precise, Senator Homer Ferguson of Michigan and the McCarran Committee's staff) questioned over thirty New York City teachers in what was the first congressional investigation ever to focus entirely on Communists in the schools. With a few exceptions like physicist Clarence Hiskey, who was teaching in Brooklyn at the time, most of the SISS's witnesses were graduates of Rapp-Coudert. It was clear that Morris, who seems to have organized this particular set of hearings, was hoping that the testimony of Bella Dodd would force the city colleges to rid themselves of those teachers who, because of the Board of Higher Education's earlier decision not to fire anybody who hadn't been identified as a Party member by two witnesses, had kept their jobs.[13]

These people had been expecting a second round of investigation for years. "We knew we were under a dark cloud," explained Frederick Ewen, a former Brooklyn College English professor, "and we always anticipated that lightning would strike. When I heard Bella Dodd had turned, I knew the ax would fall." Ewen and the other prospective witnesses, most of whom taught at Brooklyn College, Hunter, and Queens, all had tenure. (The non-tenured people who had been fingered during Rapp-Coudert, like M. I. Finley, then an instructor at CCNY, were simply not reappointed.) Yet despite their tenure, the Rapp-Coudert survivors had already suffered professionally as a result of the earlier investigations. Promotions were delayed or withheld; relations with colleagues were often strained, at best.[14]

Brooklyn's president, Harry Gideonse, was especially antagonistic to the Rapp-Coudert teachers on his staff. Himself the target of an anti-Communist investigation at the University of Chicago in 1935, Gideonse was nonetheless a committed anti-Communist who, from the moment he took office in 1939, became embroiled with the radicals on his campus. This may have been deliberate, for he believed that part of his mission to raise the prestige of Brooklyn College involved eradicating its popular image as a nest of Communists. Even so, he threw himself into the task with a ferocity that ultimately drew the criticism of the normally reticent ACLU. He had, Gideonse recalled, "personally welcomed the Rapp-Coudert investigation. Finally somebody was going to be on the job who would have the time and the legal talent and the money to spend in digging this out." The committee, as we have seen, was able to dig out some twenty suspected Party members on the Brooklyn faculty, but only one was an informer. As a result, the Board of Higher Education could purge only the three people who had been identified by witnesses from other campuses. Gideonse knew who the others were, and he did not make things easy for them. Every year, for example, the English Department tried to promote Frederick Ewen, and every year Gideonse refused to do so. Harry Slochower, an assistant professor of German since 1935, had a similar experience. Though his department and all the requisite College committees had recommended his promotion, Gideonse would not approve. Rapp-Coudert had left too many doubts, and Gideonse claimed that he had no evidence that Slochower was not a Communist. Slochower appealed to the Board of Higher Education, and finally, after submitting to a special faculty investigation and signing an anti-Communist affidavit, he received his promotion. But neither his recent promotion nor his tenure could guarantee his job once McCarran took up where Rapp-Coudert left off.[15]

Bella Dodd was the McCarran Committee's star witness. Her testimony was an act of personal contrition, a description of her own disillusionment:

> I, myself, so long as I functioned on the trade union level in the Teachers Union, why, my heavens, I was one of the staunchest of the Communists and would have called your committee a committee to smash the schools.
>
> It wasn't until I entered the Communist Party as a functionary in the Communist Party that I saw that it was a full, true, cynical conspiracy and something which is so thoroughly evil that I would like to spend the rest of my days to tell the teachers who are entrapped in this thing how to get out.

For Dodd, a complicated but enormously gifted woman, the journey from the Communist Party to the witness stand was clearly traumatic. It was atypical as well. To begin with, she did not leave the CP voluntarily, but was expelled on some far-fetched charges that reflected the Party's desire to rid itself of someone who was becoming increasingly critical of its growing rigidity and sectarianism. Her expulsion coincided with a series of personal tragedies, including a disastrous pregnancy in which she had to carry a dead baby to term. The psychological break- down that followed was understandable, as was her return to the Catholic Church and her entry into the self-enclosed world of the anti-Communist network, a world so similar in its sectarianism and ritualistic denuncia- tion of its enemies to that of the Party she had just left. Significantly, her former academic colleagues from the CP and the Teachers Union, who otherwise have little sympathy for informers, recognized the special prob- lems she faced and still speak of her with respect and affection. To some extent, Dodd repaid that esteem by not naming them. She devoted most of her testimony, then and later, to excoriating Party functionaries. Though she described in detail the way the CP had operated within the Teachers Union, she identified only a very few people as former Communists, Rut- gers's Finley among them.[16]

As it turned out, Dodd's testimony was not necessary for the Board of Higher Education to rid the city's faculties of their left-over reds. By taking the Fifth Amendment the teachers actually fired themselves, for they became automatically liable for dismissal under Section 903 of the New York City Charter. Originally designed as a weapon against mu- nicipal graft, this section provided for the summary dismissal of any city employee who "shall refuse to testify or to answer any question regard- ing the property, government, or affairs of the city . . . on the grounds that his answer would tend to incriminate him." That this measure could as easily be invoked against left-wing teachers as against dishonest pols was obvious. And, in fact, Section 903 had been used for this purpose once before. This had happened during the Rapp-Coudert investigations when David Goldway, a teacher at the Townshend Harris High School, had refused to testify by invoking his privilege against self-incrimination and had been summarily dismissed.[17]

The teachers subpoenaed by McCarran knew that their jobs were in danger. On September 22, 1952, two days before the SISS's public hear- ings began, the Board of Higher Education passed a resolution pledging its "full cooperation" and urging all faculty members to "assist the com- mittee" as well. As expected, such a pronouncement had little effect. Of the six academics who took the Fifth before the McCarran Committee on September 24, four—Slochower and Ewen from Brooklyn, Vera Shlakman from Queens, and Bernard Riess from Hunter—taught at the city schools. (The other two, Simon Heimlich and Bernhard Stern, were at Rutgers and Columbia, respectively.) Actually, Ewen was no longer at Brooklyn. He had been teaching in the city system for so long that he was theoreti- cally eligible for retirement. Once he heard that Bella Dodd would tes- tify, he quietly put in for his pension. His retirement went through the day before his hearing. Slochower, Shlakman, and Riess, however, were still on the city payroll. A few days after their hearing, the Corporation Counsel ruled that their refusal to tell the SISS whether or not they be- longed to the Communist Party came within the purview of Section 903.

The next day, October 3, the presidents of their colleges suspended them; on October 6, the Board itself officially terminated their employment. Later hearings before the same congressional committee in October and then again in February and April, 1953, ultimately led to the dismissal of ten other teachers from the municipal colleges. These firings were peremptory, to say the least. No peer review, no faculty committee ever investigated these people's fitness to teach. Under Section 903, as President John J. Theobald of Queens College explained to one of the dismissed teachers, "the Board of Higher Education does not discharge the teacher; rather the teacher by his own act in refusing to testify thereby brings about a termination of his employment."[18]

It was a termination that the thirteen dismissed teachers were determined to contest, for Section 903 had never been reviewed by the courts. The Board of Higher Education, unsure itself of the ultimate legality of its actions, recognized that it might have to use other methods to eliminate the unwanted teachers. Accordingly, it prepared for the possibility of administrative trials for the dismissed teachers and sent a representative to Washington to get evidence from the SISS's files about them. The teachers, for their part, sued at once. Even during the hearings, Harold Cammer, the Teachers Union attorney who represented most of them, tried to build his case by having a member of the Senate committee admit that its investigations did not involve, in the very words of Section 903, "the property, affairs, or government of the city." But Cammer's precautions were of little use. With one important exception, the courts at every level up to and including the Supreme Court, which refused to review the case, rejected the teachers' suit for reinstatement on the grounds that it did not involve a constitutional issue.[19]

That one exception was Harry Slochower. He had separated his case from that of the others, for his testimony had been somewhat different and he wanted to try a different legal strategy. He had never technically belonged to the Party, though he had been a member in all but card during the late 1930s. When the subpoena arrived, Slochower had wavered a bit. His daughter was young, and he knew the consequences of defying the committee. But informing was not for him. So, when Robert Morris asked him the crucial question, he denied current and recent membership and took the Fifth only with regard to the period before 1941. To have answered questions about that earlier period might have exposed him to a perjury indictment on the basis of his Rapp-Coudert testimony. This tactic of Slochower's, to deny current membership while taking the Fifth with regard to an earlier period, was to become a common device among unfriendly witnesses who hoped to keep their jobs by getting a denial of present Party membership into the record without having to inform on others. In Slochower's case, the tactic seemed at first to have failed. The Board of Higher Education fired him anyhow. But the Supreme Court, in a 5 to 4 decision in May 1956, reinstated him. Ruling that Section 903 "operates to discharge every city employee who invokes the Fifth Amendment," the majority made the obvious point that such a provision would reduce the privilege against self-incrimination "to a hollow mockery if its exercise could be taken as equivalent either to a confession of guilt or a conclusive presumption of perjury."[20]

Slochower was reinstated with $40,000 in back pay on January 5, 1957. Within a few days, however, he was suspended again. The Supreme Court had ruled only that his firing for taking the Fifth before the McCarran Committee had been unconstitutional; it had expressly conceded that he could be discharged if he refused to cooperate with a different, and presumably more relevant, type of inquiry. The Board of Higher Education seized the opportunity. It questioned Slochower and scheduled a formal trial against him on the grounds that he had lied about his membership in the Party. President Gideonse claimed that he could produce five witnesses to testify against Slochower at the forthcoming trial. But it never took place. Slochower, by then settled in a new career and convinced that he had already been vindicated by the Supreme Court, resigned rather than go through yet another round of investigations.[21]

Unconstitutional though it turned out to be, in 1952 and 1953, when the pressure from Congress was most intense, Section 903 had enabled the New York City Board of Higher Education to deal with the problem of the Fifth Amendment witnesses on its faculties as if it were a routine bureaucratic matter. Other administrations had more trouble. They felt under considerable pressure to divest themselves of the offending teachers. At the same time, since most of them were also concerned about preserving academic freedom and maintaining faculty morale, they could not simply dismiss a professor for having refused to answer a congressional committee's questions. AAUP regulations and academic tradition required that such a professor receive a hearing before a group of his peers and that his dismissal be justified in professional rather than political terms. Schools would thus have to design policies and procedures that would satisfy most of the academic community's important constituencies. This was more of a collective process than is immediately apparent. Although each institution ultimately dealt with its Fifth Amendment witnesses in its own way, administrators and faculty members who were concerned about the issue acknowledged the need for a common policy. They followed the key cases of the period and consulted with colleagues at other campuses. As a result, in the months that followed the McCarran Committee's New York hearings, the academic community began to develop a set of guidelines and practices for dealing with the problems that uncooperative witnesses had created. As with the common law, the major cases set the precedents. The first important one took place at Rutgers.

As early as August 1951 the Rutgers administration knew that one of its faculty members might be called up before a congressional investigating committee. This was, of course, M. I. Finley, then teaching at the Rutgers Newark campus. Finley had been identified as a Communist during the course of the IPR hearings, first by Karl Wittfogel on August 7 and then by William Canning on the 16th. Both men claimed that Finley, whom they had known as Moses Finklestein in the 1930s, had run a Communist study group while a graduate student at Columbia. Wittfogel added that Finley had also been "the organizer of some academic front organizations." The very day Canning testified, Finley met with a group of Rutgers administrators. In his conversations with them, then and on the following day and in a confidential letter to the dean soon after, Finley denied that he was or ever had been a Communist and refuted in some detail the charges that Wittfogel and Canning had made. His so-called study group was simply a regular Sunday night open house he and his wife held for their circle of graduate student friends; the "academic front organization" he was involved with was the American Committee for Democracy and Intellectual Freedom, a group headed by the anthropologist Franz Boas which fought such incursions against academic freedom and civil liberties as Rapp-Coudert and the Dies Committee. Finley had been its executive secretary from 1938 to 1941. Because of these charges, Finley warned the deans, the McCarran committee might well call him up, and if it did he would probably refuse to testify since he did not want to be an informer. Apparently, these explanations sufficed, for when Finley later informed the administration of his subpoena, Dean Albert Meder told him not to worry.[22]

Finley's appearance before the SISS on March 28, 1952, was in many respects similar to that of Harry Slochower a few months later. Finley told the committee that he was not then a Communist, but invoked the Fifth when asked if he had ever been one. He described his Sunday evening soirées and answered most questions about his activities and acquaintances, but he refused to identify anybody as a Communist. Since Finley's connection with the IPR was non-existent, his testimony got little publicity at the time, and Rutgers apparently ignored it. Finley was, after all, a valuable member of the faculty. Though only an assistant professor, his superiors considered him "an outstanding teacher and scholar," who, as one of the deans explained, was "likely to develop into the University's most distinguished historian." Colleagues in his field rated him just as highly and had never considered him anything but a brilliant and dedicated scholar. They were, one of them noted, "astounded" that he had been called up by a committee.[23]

At first, Rutgers seemed equally unconcerned when another teacher, Simon Heimlich, an associate professor of mathematics in the College of Pharmacy, appeared before the SISS on September 24. Heimlich, subpoenaed on a Monday for the following Wednesday, told his superior about it right away, but the man seemed strangely blasé and the information did not reach the central administration in New Brunswick until after Heimlich had already testified. Why Heimlich was called up is unclear. Most of the people questioned by the SISS had been prominent in radical or front groups like the Teachers Union or else, like Finley, had been identified by at least two witnesses. But Heimlich, though personally outspoken about politics and a leader in the local AAUP, was not a Marxist, and, as far as I can tell, seemed to have no Party ties. Nobody publicly identified him as a Communist, nor did the committee submit any specific evidence about him during his hearing, though this was its usual practice. Moreover, none of the various Rutgers groups which investigated him found any more damaging evidence than his participation in some kind of a scientists' study group in 1946—this, despite repeated requests to both the FBI and the SISS for such information. It is possible, therefore, that some kind of personal, rather than political, connection was responsible for Heimlich's subpoena. "I have good reason to believe that there is somebody in this university that would like to have me removed from my post," he later told a faculty committee. "And I think possibly some such person has comparatively recently turned my name in to the McCarran Committee."[24]

Whatever the reason behind his subpoena, Heimlich, once called, had no intention of cooperating with the committee. He considered it "a threat to our American way of life" and felt that he was doing "a very patriotic thing" by setting "an example to others to stand up and refuse to allow their rights to be trampled on, to refuse to allow the Constitution to be scrapped." Though Heimlich had originally wanted to challenge the SISS on First Amendment grounds and refuse to cooperate with it because it was infringing on his "freedom of conscience, freedom of affiliation," his lawyer, Leonard Boudin, convinced him that taking the Fifth would be an equally principled, though less dangerous, way to assert his opposition. Heimlich's public testimony took less than two minutes, during which time he refused to tell the committee whether he was a Communist, whether he had used an alias, and whether he had recruited for the AYD.[25]

Unlike Finley's, Heimlich's refusal to testify created a furor. Two days later the president of Rutgers, Lewis Webster Jones, called Heimlich in and had him dictate a statement, disclaiming membership in the CP and explaining why he had taken the Fifth:

> I am not a member of the Communist Party and never have been one, nor have I ever used an alias. I am definitely not under any outside discipline or influence which would prejudice me in the unfettered search for truth in research or teaching. Finally, I have never done any recruiting for the American Youth for Democracy.

Jones released Heimlich's statement to the press along with the announcement that he was appointing a special faculty-alumni-trustee committee to advise him on the case. Significantly, Jones said nothing about Finley in that statement and, it seems, had not planned to do anything about him until Finley's name was brought up at a press conference about Heimlich. At that point, a day after Jones had officially announced that Rutgers would investigate Heimlich, the administration reopened Finley's case. Bella Dodd's recent testimony, President Jones later explained, made a reconsideration of Finley's case "inevitable."[26]

Like Cornell, NYU, and some other schools, Rutgers had just revised its by-laws. In December 1950 the Board of Trustees set up a joint Faculty-Trustee-Alumni Committee on Academic Freedom, chaired by the then-Congressman Clifford Case, to consider "appropriate procedure through which academic freedom and freedom of expression for members of the University can be safe-guarded," while at the same time protecting the University "against public misunderstanding arising out of the fact that members of the public sometimes interpret the expression of personal opinion by members of the University as expression of the attitude of the University itself." The issue the committee addressed, in other words, was the same one that bothered the Cornell trustees: how to preserve the University's reputation in the face of growing community pressures to eradicate political non-conformity within its faculty. The recommendations that the committee submitted were unexceptional. In language similar to that of the AAUP's 1940 guidelines, the new by-laws gave the teacher considerable freedom within the classroom as long as he remained within his own field of competence and handled controversial subjects with discretion and "the standards of sound scholarship and competent teaching." Outside of class, the by-laws stressed the teacher's special obligations, his duty to "conduct himself appropriately" and to stress that he was not an official representative of the University. The by-laws also contained the procedures to be followed if "the appropriate administrative officers" felt that a teacher had transgressed the above guidelines "or if, in their opinion, a teacher's utterances had been such as to raise grave doubt concerning his fitness for his position." There was no specifically political reference to the nature of such "utterances," nor did the revised by-laws contain any anti-Communist disclaimer, whether explicit or in the increasingly common form of a provision against faculty members "under any outside discipline."[27]

Of course, Rutgers would not have tolerated any card-carrying Communists on its faculty. President Jones had made that clear in his inaugural address in May 1952, when he exempted from his ritual statement about academic freedom "conspirators who claim its protection in order to destroy freedom." Jones was well within the liberal mainstream. A respected educator, he had previously been the president of both Bennington College and the University of Arkansas, and in 1949 he and Cornell's E. E. Day had been among the few university presidents to denounce a HUAC request for a list of the textbooks used in their institutions' social science courses. Yet Finley and Heimlich put Jones in a difficult position. He was under considerable political pressure, for Rutgers was both a private and a public school, run by its own independent Board of Trustees, but receiving more than half its budget from the state. New Jersey's governor, Alfred E. Driscoll, had already pronounced on the issue: "The professors should have answered the questions—or get out." Communism was too great a threat, Driscoll explained, for employees at a state institution to evade

> their responsibilities to the public that are of even greater importance
> than our private rights and privileges . . . . When a teacher refuses to
> state under oath, in response to a question put to him by a duly constituted representative of the government, whether he is or has been a
> Communist, my confidence in that teacher is destroyed.

The press, especially the Newark *Star-Ledger*, was also urging Rutgers to fire the two men.[28]

The man who, next to Jones, probably had the most influence over the ultimate disposition of the cases was Tracy S. Voorhees, the trustee Jones appointed to head the special advisory committee. Voorhees had already helped Clifford Case revise the University's by-laws. A New York lawyer and former undersecretary of the Army, Voorhees was a prominent establishment figure who, along with such people as Harvard's president James Bryant Conant and Brown's Henry M. Wriston, had just formed the Committee for the Present Danger to lobby for a larger American military commitment to Europe. The question that President Jones asked Voorhees and his committee to settle was procedural: did the behavior of Finley and Heimlich before the McCarran Committee raise "grave doubt" about their fitness to teach? Though it questioned the two teachers and was in touch with the staff of the SISS, the Voorhees Committee did not try to assess the validity of the charges against Finley and Heimlich. "Our committee was not created, and is not equipped, as an investigating committee to probe the lives and records of these men."[29]

As a result, the committee's unanimous report, officially released by President Jones on October 14, ostensibly did not deal with the merits of the case. Rather, it addressed itself to the issue of whether the two men, by taking the Fifth Amendment before the SISS, could have violated the "special obligations" which the newly revised Rutgers by-laws had laid upon them. Without deciding the issue, the committee said,

> The word "utterances" as used in the Statute would appear reasonably to
> include a failure to speak in circumstances in which such appropriate
> conduct requires that the person should speak. In any case, answers which
> contain a refusal to answer are themselves certainly "utterances."

Voorhees's committee also considered the content of the questions that the two men refused to answer, for, the committee believed, refusing to tell a congressional committee "whether they are or have in the past been members of the Communist party" hurts the University. It

> inevitably raises in the mind of the average man a reasonable question
> concerning the witnesses' loyalty to the United States . . . . Such doubt
> as to the loyalty of any of its teachers tends to affect the confidence which
> the public is entitled to feel in a university . . . . In the case of a state

university, such a situation also may tend to impair the confidence of state officials and the legislature in the integrity and value of the university.

The committee suggested that the best way to restore the University's "integrity" would be to appoint a special faculty committee to handle the cases. The committee further recommended that the faculty committee act quickly, a recommendation apparently based on its concern for the future of the University's budget, then about to be submitted to Governor Driscoll, who, the committee well knew, had very little confidence in either Finley's or Heimlich's fitness to teach.[30]

Conscientiousness marked the faculty committee's deliberations from the start. For example, it held a special meeting with Ralph Himstead, general secretary of the AAUP, to ensure that its procedures would be in accord with those recommended by that organization. And, to guarantee the maximum amount of due process, it decided to function "somewhat as a grand jury"; it would determine whether the two men's actions constituted unfitness, but it would let yet another committee decide whether or not to fire them. Thus, rather than investigating the particular circumstances of each case—though it did question both Heimlich and Finley and it did try, without success, to find out from Robert Morris why his committee had subpoenaed Heimlich—it focussed its inquiry on the broader issue of "whether refusal to testify makes a person unfit to teach." Why, the committee wanted to know, would such otherwise reputable scholars and teachers as Finley and Heimlich invoke the privilege against self-incrimination?[31]

Though we now recognize the value of the Fifth Amendment as a guarantee against political repression, at the time even such well-meaning and, presumably, well-informed people as the five professors on the Rutgers Special Faculty Committee knew little about the matter and shared the popular assumption that someone who refused to answer an investigating committee's questions must be hiding something. This was, of course, exactly what the committees wanted people to believe. As Robert Morris explained to an interviewer in December 1952, if a witness refuses to answer questions about his relationship to the CP,

> legally it doesn't necessarily mean he is a Communist, but as a practical matter it shakes public confidence in him . . . . the Subcommittee doesn't ask anybody that question unless it has some evidence that he was involved in communistic activities. Once you begin exploring and the witness invokes his constitutional privilege, then we feel that this, more than anything else, will cause the ordinary American to understand that there must be something very wrong.

Joseph McCarthy was even more positive:

> A witness's refusal to answer whether or not he is a Communist on the ground that his answer would tend to incriminate him is the most positive proof obtainable that the witness is a Communist.[32]

The faculty committee did not, however, want to accept such a conclusion without further investigation. Its members were, after all, trained scholars, accustomed to the practice of critical thought and, unlike the members of the Voorhees Committee, did not automatically espouse the position of the "average man." Instead, they gave themselves a crash course on the Fifth Amendment. They read up on constitutional law and consulted with the experts, including Heimlich's learned lawyer Leonard Boudin, already one of the nation's foremost authorities on the matter. The committee considered other, more pragmatic, issues as well. It recognized both the dangers of affronting public opinion that keeping Heimlich and Finley would entail and the damage to the University's academic reputation that firing them would. But, ultimately, it was the committee's new-found understanding of the reasons why the two men used the Fifth that convinced it to recommend that Rutgers take no action against them.[33]

The committee's report, submitted to President Jones on December 3, was a thoughtful, single-spaced, twelve-and-a-half-page document, replete with notes and legal citations. It discussed each case in detail. Finley's refusal to answer the congressional committee's questions was justified, the report explained, on the "plausible and legally acceptable grounds" that he might otherwise "place himself in a position of being indicted for perjury" should the government use the testimony of witnesses like Wittfogel and Canning as the basis for prosecuting him. (That such a fear was realistic, the indictment of Owen Lattimore two weeks later was to confirm.) Heimlich was also correct, the committee pointed out, when he invoked the Fifth in order to avoid answering questions which, though not directly incriminating, might because of the Smith Act provide "a link in the chain" of possible evidence against him. Moreover, in the light of the Supreme Court's failure to uphold the First Amendment, Heimlich's use of the Fifth to oppose an inquiry into his political beliefs "is also appropriate," for the privilege that he relied upon had originated as a protection against earlier political inquests.

The committee did recognize that an academic "has special obligations and responsibilities," which "require of the teacher a standard of conduct which is over and above that which is simply lawful." But, the committee pointed out, neither man had violated that standard; it could find "no evidence that either Mr. Finley or Mr. Heimlich has ever misused his position as a teacher to propagandize his students." All they had done was rely on their constitutional rights. And, in words similar to those the Supreme Court would use in the *Slochower* decision, the committee chided those

> who because of the teacher's special position would require him to waive his constitutional privileges. The Committee believes that this would be discriminatory and in violation of the spirit and letter of the Constitution.

On the contrary, the committee continued,

it should be recognized that the unique position of the teacher which imposes upon him special obligations and responsibilities renders him likewise particularly vulnerable to criticism and public pressure. The Committee believes that the teacher, far from being denied his constitutional privileges, should, on the contrary, be given their full protection.[34]

Less than ten days after the faculty committee submitted its report, the Board of Trustees met to consider the fate of the two professors. The legal and procedural questions which had been so important to the members of the faculty committee mattered little to the thirty-nine trustees. Communism, not the Constitution, was the issue that concerned them. "What the Committee has done," explained one trustee in a letter to Jones,

> is to treat this whole thing as an abstract situation in which the niceties of the law and the regulations pertaining to the conduct of the teachers of the University are given preeminence. It seems to me that we lost sight of the fact that we are at war with Communism.

It was clear that, for the majority of the trustees, the front lines of that war could as easily be in New Brunswick as in Korea. There was another issue as well. The public image of Rutgers was at stake. With 60 percent of its budget coming from the state, the University "cannot offend public opinion," warned Russell E. Watson, the University's counsel and himself a trustee, adding, "a former Communist should not be on the faculty in the light of the present state of public opinion."[35]

Such views dominated the trustees' deliberations. Communism was dangerous stuff, and it was bad for the University to be involved with it. The businessmen and politicians who served on the board apparently neither understood, nor cared much about, civil liberties or academic freedom. And so, by a unanimous vote, they fired both Finley and Heimlich. They agreed with the faculty committee that the two were legally justified in taking the Fifth, but claimed in their official statement of December 12:

> The question here concerns their special obligations as members of a learned profession, and as representatives of this University . . . .
>   The refusal of a faculty member, on the grounds of possible self incrimination, to answer questions as to his present or past membership in the Communist party, put to him by a properly constituted investigatory body, impairs confidence in his fitness to teach. It is also incompatible with the standards required of him as a member of his profession.

And to make sure that there would be no future misunderstanding of what those "special obligations" were, the board ruled

> that it is cause for the immediate dismissal of any member of the faculty or staff of the University that he refuse, on the ground of the Fifth Amendment to the Constitution of the United States, to answer questions propounded by any duly constituted investigatory body, or in any judicial

proceeding, relating to whether he is, or has been, a member of the Communist Party.[36]

For all its rhetoric, the board had not wanted to fire the two teachers and, even in its resolution doing so, offered them what Tracy S. Voorhees in a private letter to Finley and Heimlich called "a clean and honorable way for you out of this morass." They could go back to the SISS and purge themselves by answering all the questions they had refused the first time. This was not a realistic option. The faculty committee had already considered it and discovered both that the committee was too busy to give its unfriendly witnesses a second chance and that neither Finley nor Heimlich would recant.[37]

The Rutgers faculty received the news with consternation. By overruling the unanimous and considered judgment of a faculty committee—chosen, it must be added, with an eye to making sure that it would not be overly sympathetic to the two professors—the trustees had infringed upon the most coveted prerogative of the academic profession: its right to select its own members. Yet the faculty's response to this clear-cut violation of its collective academic freedom was muted. Instead of protesting, as its more militant members urged at a special faculty meeting on December 18, the faculty decided to poll itself. The results of that poll reveal considerable ambivalence. Five hundred eighty-three of the 690 teachers polled responded, some 84 percent of the full-time faculty. Though the majority of these teachers supported the findings of the Special Faculty Committee, 312 to 261, they were not anxious for a confrontation with the Board of Trustees. The resolution requiring the board to "reconsider its decision" passed by only 30 votes, 299 to 269. That it was the unilateral nature of that decision and not its content that was at issue can be seen in the faculty's 415 to 153 vote to create a committee to reexamine "the entire procedure, *but only the procedure*" [emphasis mine] used in the Finley and Heimlich cases. Significantly, the faculty did not poll itself on the most critical issue involved, the board's policy of automatically firing anybody who invoked the Fifth Amendment. The matter may well have been too controversial, and those professors who were upset about the procedural aspects of that policy may not have wanted to be in the position of seeming to support people who refused to cooperate with a congressional committee. On the by-then less controversial issue of Communism, the Rutgers faculty had fewer reservations. It voted 520 to 52 to endorse the board's policy of excluding members of the Communist Party from the faculty.[38]

Not every school which had an uncooperative witness on its faculty investigated him or her; the academy had not yet reached a consensus here. Two instructors at Columbia University who appeared before the McCarran Committee in the fall of 1952, the sociologist Bernhard Stern and the anthropologist Gene Weltfish, took the Fifth, but Columbia did not take official cognizance of their actions. In part, this may have been because neither of the two held regular faculty appointments. In addition, as we shall see, Columbia's president, Grayson Kirk, was already planning to get rid of Weltfish for other reasons and may have decided not to risk trouble by convening a faculty committee. Finally, Columbia may simply not have formulated a policy for dealing with recalcitrant witnesses. A few months later, when Stern put in a second appearance before a congressional committee, this time during Senator McCarthy's investigation of American libraries abroad, Kirk did request a faculty probe, one which ultimately exonerated Stern. But by then the academic community had pretty well decided that, whatever else a university did, at the very least it had to investigate those members of its faculty who invoked the Fifth Amendment.[39]

This was a consensus that the academy had scrambled to reach. The respite that the congressional committees' previous and rather puzzling indifference to academic radicals had granted ended in 1952. Come the beginning of the new year and the installation of a new Republican-controlled Congress, the nation's campuses could expect to entertain a whole pack of investigators. Though McCarran had concluded his committee's hearings in New York after only eight sessions, he recommended that his successor take up where he had left off. The testimony that his committee had collected made it obvious what schools would be involved. When questioned about the colleges that contained party units, Bella Dodd listed them:

> All of the city colleges here in New York. I mean the four city colleges; Columbia University, Long Island University, New York University, Vassar College, Wellesley, Smith, Harvard, MIT, University of Michigan, Chicago, Northwestern University, University of California, University of Minnesota, Howard University.

HUAC was also planning to look for Communist teachers. Its new chairman, the former FBI agent Harold Velde, made that clear as early as November. "I feel," he explained a few weeks later, "that we should look into the field of education. That has been largely left untouched up till now . . . but I believe that it is a very fertile field for investigation and it should be done." Colleges were going to be HUAC's main target, for, as an unidentified HUAC staff member explained to the FBI, the committee "believes it can obtain more publicity by exposing Communist affiliations of college professors rather than public school teachers." Senator McCarthy, now finally with an investigating committee of his own, also promised that he would be "going into the education system" and would be "exposing Communists and Communist thinkers . . . in your educational institutions," a service that he claimed was one of "trying to promote freedom of thought and expression in college."[40]

The prospect of receiving McCarthy's help in promoting "freedom of thought and expression" forced the academic community to take precautions. The ad hoc measures that a school like Rutgers employed would no longer suffice. Accordingly, faculties and administrations all across the country rushed to create committees and establish procedures for dealing with professors who ran afoul of congressional investigators. They also tried to formulate guidelines that would help the prospective witnesses on their faculties decide what to do as well as help their universities decide what to do about them. This was a collective process. The men and women who developed these guidelines were in touch with colleagues at other campuses. They circulated position papers and kept each other informed about events at their respective schools. Harvard and Yale, for example, pooled their resources and hired a Washington lawyer to observe the investigating committees. Though each institution ultimately dealt with its own faculty members on an individual basis, it did so within the context of a collectively evolved set of practices and policies.[41]

Most schools, certainly most of the major ones, had long had some kind of established procedure for the peer review of the qualifications of a faculty member charged with misconduct of one kind or another. During the early fifties, however, many of these schools revised their procedures or else set up new committees to deal with the problems raised by congressional investigations. We have already encountered Cornell's innovation, its secret faculty "Subcommittee on Academic Problems Arising from Governmental Investigation." New York University, which already had two unfriendly witnesses by the end of 1952, set up a "Special Committee on Faculty Responsibility Toward Governmental Investigative Agencies." MIT, one of whose faculty members, the mathematician Dirk Struik, had been indicted in 1951 under an early twentieth-century sedition law for conspiring to overthrow the Commonwealth of Massachusetts by "force and violence," organized a special "Committee on Responsibility of Faculty Members." Even the University of Miami, which as far as I know had no prospective witnesses on its staff, set up a committee to deal with the problem.[42]

The University of Michigan took particularly elaborate precautions. Its by-laws governing dismissal, though adequate for calmer times, contained, so the administration and the faculty members with whom it consulted believed, an inordinate number of appeals and did not give the president the power to bring charges against a professor. As a result, it was feared, the process might prove so cumbersome that public opinion might force the Regents to act and bypass the faculty altogether. Taking advantage of the annual faculty meeting in the spring of 1953, the Senate Advisory Committee, the Michigan faculty's main policy-making group, suggested that the University set up a joint faculty-administration committee to study the problem and recommend procedures for dealing with unfriendly witnesses. The committee was duly established; its deliberations, stimulated by its recognition "that in times of national stress like these, charges of disloyalty in the faculty may do great harm to the reputation . . . of the University . . . if not promptly investigated and adjudicated," produced the streamlined dismissal procedures that the Michigan authorities had wanted.[43]

Other schools, which did not necessarily alter their by-laws or establish new committees, nonetheless readied existing committees for the task. In many cases these groups, as well as the newly established ones, also tried to formulate policy. For, as the Rutgers imbroglio had revealed, the academic community knew very little about the Fifth Amendment or any of the other problems that the congressional investigations had raised. A clear discussion of those problems, whether or not it established official guidelines for prospective witnesses, would obviously be of use.

One of the earliest of these policy statements came from the University of Pennsylvania. On October 1, 1952, Harold Stassen, the University's president and an ambitious former politician who had just testified against Owen Lattimore and some of the other China experts in the IPR hearings, asked the University Senate to advise him about "the procedure and method which should be followed" should the "incompetence, subversion, or wrongdoing of a member of the faculty" become a problem. The Senate's Committee on Academic Freedom and Responsibilities took up the matter. Its chairman, law school professor Clark Byse, had already been involved, both intellectually and politically, in civil liberties issues and his committee's deliberations reflected the sophistication of its chairman. The committee made some procedural suggestions, full of safeguards for the rights of the faculty member involved. It also stated its opposition to the forthcoming congressional investigations and urged Penn's faculty to consult with other colleges about them. And it tried to grapple with the problem of the Fifth. Recognizing that "a claim of privilege is often misinterpreted by the public and thus is a source of potential embarrassment to the claimant and the institution with which he is associated," the committee urged the prospective witnesses to "carefully consider the implications" of such a claim. At the same time, however, it stated that a refusal to answer questions, whether posed by a government or a University official, did not "by itself, justify suspension or dismissal," though it could require an investigation. The committee refrained from making any further recommendations, except to plead that each case "be judged individually."[44]

A more rational, careful statement would be hard to find. The only problem was that in the case of the only University of Pennsylvania faculty member who took the Fifth in public, these careful procedures were never used. The case, like that of Rutgers's Finley, a spin-off of the IPR hearings, involved Daniel Thorner, an old friend of Finley's and an assistant professor of economics at Penn. Thorner appeared before McCarran on March 19, 1952, and soon after left for India, where he was to spend a year doing research. Instead of submitting his case to a faculty committee, the Penn administration simply refused his department's request to give him tenure; since Thorner was not around to request a hearing, his de facto dismissal received little notice.[45]

Harvard was another school which tried to formulate some guidelines in advance of the investigations. It was one of the schools on Bella Dodd's hit list and, because of its prestige and importance as a symbol of the Eastern establishment, was an obvious target for the publicity-hungry congressmen who sat on the main investigating committees. The men who ran Harvard assumed—correctly, it turned out—that their school would be investigated. One of the people who was most concerned about the University's response to these investigations was William Marbury, a Baltimore lawyer and a member of the seven-man Corporation which ruled Harvard. As Alger Hiss's first lawyer, Marbury had been exposed early to a congressional investigation; in addition, through his social contacts with people at Johns Hopkins, where Owen Lattimore taught, he had come to appreciate how troublesome such investigations could be for a university. The Rutgers case increased his concern about the issue and focussed it specifically on the problem of professors who took the Fifth Amendment. He sought to warn the Harvard administration, and on December 8 sent a confidential memorandum to President Conant expressing his concern about the damage that a professor who took the Fifth might do to the University.[46]

Conant must have been impressed, for he immediately asked the University's counsel, Oscar Shaw of the prestigious Boston law firm Ropes and Gray, to give him an opinion on the matter. Conant's own position on the issue seems to have been rather rigid. As we have seen he was, as one colleague put it, "almost violent" in his opposition to Communism. According to Charles A. Coolidge, the senior member of the Corporation, Conant was equally vehement about Fifth Amendment witnesses and insisted "that the invocation of the Fifth Amendment by a faculty member constituted grounds for dismissal." Yet he did not try to get this position officially adopted. Perhaps this was because, as Harvard's former provost Paul Buck claimed, he did not want to do so without Buck's approval and his implicit assurance that the faculty would accept such a policy. Perhaps, also, he did not do this because he knew he would not be around to enforce it, having just been appointed U.S. High Commissioner to Germany.[47]

Whatever the opinion Shaw delivered on December 12 said (I have not seen it), it apparently did not allay Marbury's concern. On December 29 he wrote a long letter to Zechariah Chafee, the noted civil libertarian and professor at Harvard Law School. In that letter Marbury argued that it "makes no sense whatsoever" for anybody to plead the Fifth Amendment unless actually engaged in some kind of criminal venture. His experience in the Hiss case had convinced him that a witness was in little danger of a perjury prosecution unless the government had some kind of strong corroborating evidence. The real danger, he insisted, was to the University's reputation and that of the academic profession as a whole. Accordingly, he urged Chafee to speak out against "a panicky refusal on the part of the academic community to answer questions."[48]

"I thoroughly agree with you," Chafee replied on January 3, 1953, "that it would be bad for Harvard and the still larger cause of intellectual freedom in this country for members of the Harvard faculty to claim privilege against self-incrimination." And, in order to prevent that from happening, Chafee consulted with his colleague Arthur Sutherland, the former Cornell professor who was to represent Philip Morrison before the SISS and who had just agreed to serve as Harvard's unofficial adviser to the prospective witnesses on its staff. Together the two legal scholars drew up a statement on the matter, which they then released in the form of a letter published in the *Harvard Crimson,* January 8. It purported to be a clarification of the legal issues involved in using the Fifth Amendment. Though Sutherland had apparently drafted the text, it was in complete agreement with the position Marbury had espoused in his letter to Chafee. It said:

> The underlying principle to remember in considering the subject is the duty of the citizen to cooperate in government. He has no option to say, "I do not approve of this Grand Jury or that congressional committee; I dislike its members and its objects; therefore, I will not tell it what I know." He is neither wise nor legally justified in attempting political protest by standing silent when obligated to speak . . . the witness must be subjecting himself to some degree of danger of conviction of a criminal offense . . . the Fifth Amendment grants no privilege to protect one's friends.

According to this interpretation, a professor who invoked the Fifth in order to avoid naming his former political associates would not be legally correct in doing so and could not claim, therefore, that he was exercising his constitutional rights. On the contrary, Chafee and Sutherland seemed to be arguing, he was evading his obligation as a citizen and might well be breaking the law.[49]

The significance of this letter was enormous. As the Rutgers faculty committee had discovered, few citizens, few lawyers even, knew very much about the Fifth Amendment. Its use by uncooperative witnesses before congressional committees was only a few years old and its definitive interpretation was still being worked out in the courts. Though later commentators—including the dean of Harvard Law School, Erwin Griswold—were soon to find that the Chafee-Sutherland statement offered much too narrow an interpretation, its appearance on the eve of the coming investigations was a godsend. Not only did it purport to be the most definitive interpretation of the Fifth yet to appear, but it also bore the name of Zechariah Chafee, probably the most respected civil libertarian in America. Paul Buck, by then the acting president of Harvard, made sure that every member of the faculty received a copy. Later on, when Robert Morris of the SISS paid a courtesy call on the Harvard administration before his committee's hearings in Boston, Buck gave him a copy of the letter and explained its distribution. Morris was pleased, he claimed, that Harvard had been so cooperative.[50]

Other schools found the statement equally useful. Chafee and Sutherland were besieged by requests for copies from colleges and universities around the country. President Jones of Rutgers cited it as a kind of ex post facto justification for the dismissal of Finley and Heimlich. University administrators from Berkeley to MIT emulated Harvard by distributing copies to all their faculty members. Yet, as a guide for academic behavior, the Chafee-Sutherland statement was incomplete. It dealt only with the legal consequences of taking the Fifth and did not touch on the professional ones. If the academic world was to invoke sanctions against those of its members who took the Fifth before a congressional investigating committee, it would be necessary to show how that behavior was professionally, as well as legally, unacceptable.[51]

One of the first academic leaders to address that problem was none other than Rutgers President Jones. Caught between a confused and demoralized faculty and an obdurate Board of Trustees, Jones recognized that he had to present the University's new policy in a way that would explain in an intellectually convincing manner just why a professor's invocation of the Fifth Amendment was, as the trustees had stated, "incompatible with the standards required of him as a member of his profession." Jones's personal position seems to have been that common to many liberals, both in and outside the academy. He disapproved of what the congressional investigators were doing, but he felt that taking the Fifth was self-defeating and simply played into the hands of the committees, allowing them to claim that they were uncovering Communists. In addition, like Marbury, he believed that relying on the privilege against self-incrimination when one had nothing incriminating to hide was "neither honest or courageous." As he told several people in private, Finley and Heimlich should have spoken out, denied that they were Communists, and taken the risk of a perjury charge or contempt citation. *Then* he would have defended the two men, and, so he claimed, would probably even have been able to persuade the trustees to stick with them.[52]

However, in his official statement on the matter, "Academic Freedom and Civil Responsibility," released on January 24 to "the members of the University and to the public," Jones gave no indication that he disapproved of what the committees were doing. On the contrary, he claimed that such investigations were "legitimate and should be frankly met." He recognized that universities were often "out of step with the wider community" and, therefore, perennially under attack. But their "only one truly valid defense against such attacks" was their ability to demonstrate "that their educational methods and their theoretical findings have been arrived at by trained personnel through the use of thoroughly rational procedures." Accordingly, "for members of a university faculty to refuse to give a rational account of their position on vital community matters" seriously damages the university's best defense against the attacks on it and "in fact cuts the ground out from academic freedom itself." As Jones defined it, academic freedom was a "positive freedom," one which "entails the obligation to render an explanation, as clearly and rationally as possible, whenever such an explanation is called for by duly constituted governmental bodies." Because of the critical nature of the Cold War, Jones stressed that the "minimum responsibility" of members of the University was to "state frankly where they stand on matters of such deep public concern, and of such relevance to academic integrity, as membership in the Communist Party." By 1953, of course, Jones was only repeating a truism when he described such membership as "not compatible with the freedom of thought and inquiry on which American teaching and research are based." His contribution to the redefinition of academic freedom was to have shown how relying on the constitutional privilege against self-incrimination violated a professor's obligation to give a rational explanation of his position on "vital community matters." Academic freedom could not, therefore, be invoked to save the jobs of teachers who shirked this brand new professional responsibility.[53]

Jones had been in touch with people at other schools while the Finley and Heimlich case was being decided and had been sending them information about it. He knew, therefore, that like Chafee and Sutherland he would be assailed by requests for copies of his statement, and he took the precaution of having 5000 copies printed. The requests came from all over the academic and political worlds. The president of the University of Washington wanted copies for his Board of Regents; so too did the presidents of the universities of Minnesota, Michigan State, Nevada, Rhode Island, Hofstra College, and Vassar. The letter of Vassar's Sarah Gibson Blandings was typical. "I want to be able to send a copy to each one of my trustees," she explained. "We are in the throes of working out a statement of policy and I think your account will be exceedingly helpful as we struggle through our own problem." Individual trustees from such schools as Harvard, Columbia, and Wheaton College also asked for copies, as did such individuals as Sidney Hook, Alexander Meiklejohn, the counsel to the New York City Board of Higher Education, and Congressman Gordon Scherer of HUAC, who wanted one hundred copies to send out.[54]

This deluge of requests for Jones's statement as well as the similar demand for the Chafee-Sutherland letter show how worried the nation's academic leaders were about the forthcoming investigations and how eagerly they were searching for a common policy. Useful as the two statements were, however, they were hardly definitive. Chafee and Sutherland spoke only for themselves, Jones only for Rutgers. Some more authoritative formulation was needed, a document that could be presented as the academic community's official policy, one that would not only tell prospective witnesses what their institutions expected of them, but also explain the academy's position to the outside world. True, the AAUP's 1947 Report of Committee A still stood. But that statement's opposition to the automatic dismissal of Communists made it controversial, to say the least. Moreover, although the AAUP reaffirmed its commitment to the policy of the 1947 Report at every annual convention, it had never done anything concrete to enforce it. Its failure to take action in the University of Washington case, in particular, made it easy for the rest of the academic world to dismiss the 1947 statement as theoretical and out-of-date.

There was, however, another organization which had some claim to speak for the academic community as a whole. This was the Association of American Universities (AAU), a group whose membership consisted of the presidents of the thirty-seven leading universities in the United States and Canada. Nominally concerned with maintaining the standards of graduate education and with such practical matters as interlibrary loans, the organization responded to the challenge of the Cold War by breaking with its own tradition and making a public statement. By 1950, it had decided to issue a report on "the privileges and responsibilities inherent in academic freedom and tenure." Naturally, drafting such a statement, especially one that would satisfy thirty-seven college presidents, took years. At its annual meeting in October 1951 the group discussed and then rejected the preliminary report that a three-man committee—Sterling of Stanford, Morrill of Minnesota, and Hutchins of Chicago—had drawn up. Replacing Hutchins with Grayson Kirk of Columbia, the presidents instructed the committee to consult with the AAUP and submit a revised draft to the next annual meeting. This draft, discussed for the better part of two days at the October 1952 meeting, was equally unacceptable; it, too, had not been submitted to the AAUP. This was a problem. The AAUP's apparent lethargy discouraged cooperation. In addition, though some of the presidents wanted to work closely with the professors' organization, others, while agreeing that the AAUP should be consulted, did not like its official position. They urged the AAU to issue an independent statement, one which would contain what the official minutes called "a more realistic interpretation of the AAUP formula on academic freedom in the context of contemporary events." Accordingly, a new committee, this one chaired by A. Whitney Griswold of Yale, was appointed to draw up yet another draft, and the group agreed to come together again early the next year.[55]

HUAC was just about to begin its first series of hearings on higher education when the AAU met in New York on February 15, 1953. The twenty-four presidents who showed up recognized that the impending investigations "greatly enhanced the urgency of any document prepared by the Association," and they discussed the revisions to Griswold's admittedly "tactical and political document" with those investigations firmly in mind. They agreed that their statement should be addressed to the American people as a whole and not just to the academic community. They also agreed that it should deal with the problem of Communist teachers and should make, in the words of Brown's Henry M. Wriston, "a clear, compact, and quotable statement on the Communist issue." And, most important, they agreed that it should confront the problem of the Fifth Amendment, "the actual or supposed abuse" of which, the minutes stated, "has done damage to the universities." Speed was crucial; the presidents gave Griswold and Wriston the task of polishing the final draft and publishing it as soon as possible.[56]

The statement, entitled "The Rights and Responsibilities of Universities and Their Faculties," was officially released on March 24 over the signature of all thirty-seven presidents. Much of its eleven pages consisted of the usual rhetoric about academic freedom, couched, however, in language that one assumes the writers thought would appeal to its intended audience. Such a sentence as "Free enterprise is as essential to intellectual as to economic progress" gives an idea of the overall tone of the document. To be fair, not all of it was fluff; the statement did mention a few specific threats to that enterprise, including "special loyalty tests which are applied to . . . faculties but to which others are not subjected." And, in a section entitled "The Present Danger," a title bestowed perhaps by Henry Wriston, the document's co-author and himself a founder and active member of the committee of that name, the AAU described the main threat to academic freedom: world Communism. Teachers who adhered to such a movement—with its commitment to "falsehood and deceit," "revolution," and "thought control"—obviously disqualified themselves from the academic profession. The AAU statement was quite explicit. "Present membership in the Communist Party . . . extinguishes the right to a university position."

The real meat of the statement was its section "Obligations and Responsibilities of University Faculties." Here the AAU dealt with the coming congressional investigations and insisted that "it is clearly the duty of universities and their members to cooperate in official inquiries . . . . When the powers of legislative inquiry are abused, the remedy does not lie in non-cooperation or defiance." Such "ill-advised, though not illegal, public acts or utterances" on the part of a professor "do serious harm to his profession, his university, to education, and to the general welfare." They are also inconsistent with his "obligation to maintain [the university's] reputation," as well as an even more important professional obligation of the college teacher:

> Above all, he owes his colleagues in the university complete candor and perfect integrity, precluding any kind of clandestine or conspiratorial activities. He owes equal candor to the public. If he is called upon to answer for his convictions, it is his duty as a citizen to speak out. It is even more definitely his duty as a professor. Refusal to do so, on whatever legal grounds, cannot fail to reflect upon a profession that claims for itself the

fullest freedom to speak and the maximum protection of that freedom available in our society. In this respect, invocation of the Fifth Amendment places upon a professor a heavy burden of proof of his fitness to hold a teaching position and lays upon his university an obligation to reexamine his qualifications for membership in its society.

This was essentially a restatement of Jones's position, that a professor had an "obligation to render an explanation . . . whenever such an explanation is called for by duly constituted governmental bodies." The AAU, however, had gone beyond Jones in attempting to offer a specifically professional rationale for that obligation: its insistence that because the academic profession had a special need for freedom of speech, its members must, therefore, literally speak up.[57]

As if to underscore its importance, the public-relations officers of all thirty-seven schools simultaneously released the AAU statement to the press. Its reception was all that its framers had hoped for. The committees loved it. The SISS's final report, "Subversive Influence in the Educational Process," quoted it at length. The press reprinted and praised it. Conservative papers picked up on its condemnation of Communist teachers; liberal ones hailed it as a reaffirmation of traditional liberties. In a letter to the other members of the organization, Princeton president Harold W. Dodds, who, as the head of the AAU, coordinated the distribution of the statement, noted that he had received hundreds of newspaper clippings and "the only editorial I have seen which attacked the statement, apart from two or three small local papers on the extreme right, appeared in the New York *Daily Worker.*"[58]

Within the academic community, the statement got a more measured reception. It was, of course, widely distributed. Teachers at the nation's major schools and many of its minor ones as well got copies. The AAU, which had printed 15,000 copies initially, got a grant from the Rockefeller Foundation to produce 35,000 more. Not every academic who received the statement supported it. Even some of its signers had reservations. Grayson Kirk admitted in a private letter that he was "not in full agreement with it." He signed, he said, because "I was sufficiently in accord with the general tenor of the report that I did not wish to hold up its publication because of what some of my colleagues might have regarded as quibbling." Wisconsin's president, E. B. Fred, was even more dissatisfied. The Wisconsin scholars he had consulted believed that the statement's key paragraph, its invocation of the professor's obligation of complete candor, "proceeds from an impossible premise to a doubtful conclusion." They did not think that it was "consistent with our traditional notions of academic freedom for academic authorities to say to their teachers: You answer when asked, or else!" Fred signed the statement with reluctance and with the understanding that his colleagues would consider these objections if they issued a revised version.[59]

Open opposition to the statement was sporadic. The ACLU said nothing at the time. When in 1957 it finally criticized the document it claimed that it had not acted earlier because no school had officially adopted the AAU's pronouncement and so "it seemed unlikely that the principles therein set forth would be applied in judgment on a particular teacher." The real reason for the delay was simply that the ACLU was itself so divided over the issue that it could not release any kind of a statement. The AAUP was similarly silent, though some of its chapters organized meetings to discuss the document and the problems that it raised. At the highly publicized Columbia meeting, for example, the well-known sociologist Robert Lynd attacked the statement as "an offer by the universities to Senator McCarthy to carry on his aims and his work for him." The AAU not only "accepts the principle of, and pledges itself to enforce, a political test for teachers," but also, Lynd explained, "abandoned its teachers who may plead the Fifth Amendment as probably guilty and liable to dismissal." His colleague Robert MacIver, then already at work on a book about academic freedom, agreed, though in somewhat more measured language. At the University of Michigan, where President Harlan Hatcher was hoping to get the University Senate to endorse the AAU statement as the University's official policy, there were similar objections. One professor decried the rigid exclusion of Communists; another noted that the statement, "though fine sounding, is not the courageous statement or defense of basic principles which is needed in these times."[60]

We have, alas, no faculty polls to help us assess the extent of such dissatisfaction. But in the light of the academic profession's later acquiescence in the application of the AAU's principles to specific cases, it is likely that most, but by no means all, faculty members agreed with it. It is important to realize that in the spring of 1953 congressional investigators had only just begun to reach into the nation's campuses, and many academics who later became critical of those investigations and of their institutions' response to them had not yet had any first-hand experience with the problem. When they did, they had second thoughts. The AAU's position was "a little naive, idealistic, and lacking in legal acumen," so a self-confessed conservative professor at the University of Michigan explained. His personal involvement in the case of his colleague Clement Markert convinced him that "the principles of the AAU statement have been distorted and turned against us."[61]

Definitive as that statement sounded, even it was incomplete. It did not specify whether a university should "reexamine [the] qualifications" of teachers who talked about themselves but not about others. Since a few academics had taken such a stance before HUAC as early as 1950, the presidents must have known it was an option that witnesses might take. Their failure to address the issue probably reflected their desire not to dilute the impact of the AAU's position on the Fifth as well as their own considerable uncertainty about the diminished Fifth. After all, to suggest that faculty members answer some but not all of a committee's questions was to recommend behavior that was against the law. More-over, it would have been unrealistic for a quasi-official group like the AAU to make a pronouncement on the issue when the rest of the aca-demic community was still far from a consensus. As debate continued, even those commentators who agreed with the AAU that a professor owed his colleagues "complete candor" about himself disagreed among themselves about whether that obligation entailed equal candor about other people.

Sidney Hook, for example, argued strongly for dismissing teachers who invoked the privilege of self-incrimination, yet was willing to retain those who balked only at naming names. In "The Fifth Amendment—A Moral Issue," published in the *New York Times Magazine* on November 1, 1953, Hook insisted that dismissing Fifth Amendment witnesses was an

> appropriate measure . . . to safeguard the common interest . . . . If an individual who drives a school bus is asked whether he has attempted to peddle dope to school children and refuses to answer on the ground of self-incrimination, would we be justified in asking him to find a job else-where?

Similarly, a professor who refuses to answer questions about membership in the Communist Party—for Hook, the academic equivalent of selling drugs to youngsters—obviously forfeits his right to teach. Hook, however, realized that there may be some people—genuine ex-Communists, former fellow travelers, even innocent liberals—who have "more scruples about testifying against others" or who "wish to express their disapproval of Congressional investigations." But, though he sympathized with their problem, Hook found it "utterly mysterious" why anyone would rely on the Fifth Amendment when he could "protest openly and forthrightly" and could "invoke the First Amendment and leave it to the courts to de-termine whether he is legally justified or not." He dismissed the danger of a perjury indictment *à la* Lattimore as "ridiculous on its face" and called upon prospective witnesses "to take these and other risks and to speak up openly for their convictions."[62]

There were other commentators who felt that the only way for people "to speak up openly for their convictions" was to name names. Some, like Smith College professor Robert Gorham Davis, had already done just that. As one of the few ex-Communist academics to throw himself into the liberal anti-Communist movement, Davis wrote for *Commentary* and *The New Leader* and became active in Sidney Hook's Committee for Cul-tural Freedom. He considered his HUAC testimony to be part of the same campaign. Though he did, it is true, try to distance himself a bit from the more paranoid elements of the committee's world-view, he none-theless, welcomed the "golden opportunity" his hearing offered him to "speak out." As he explained in a letter to the *New York Times*, other ex-Communist professors should do the same:

The more candid their disclosures, the less disadvantageous the naming of names will become in most individual instances. If these disclosures reveal, as I think they will, that the present influence of Communism among educators is slight, the ultimate effect can only be good.[63]

Perhaps the most sophisticated presentation of the case for naming names was that made by a former Harvard radical, Alan F. Westin, who addressed the issue in a June 1953 article in *Commentary* entitled "Do Silent Witnesses Defend Civil Liberties?" Arguing that "the cause of freedom is best served not by silence but by free *speech*," Westin went beyond the AAU's essentially professional rationalization for cooperating with congressional investigators to show how such cooperation is politically as well as academically necessary. Answering all a committee's questions, Westin claimed, gives witnesses an opportunity to confront the committee with their own, presumably liberal, political views, to "strike a meaningful blow on behalf of their profession or institution . . . . to dispel the existing public fear—fanned by silent witnesses—that our country is helpless before a far-flung conspiracy." Though Westin recognized that talking about one's self but not one's associates is an "appealing solution," he opted for "complete responsiveness," i.e. naming names. He gave several reasons. He cited the standard image of the Communist as "an instrument of party policy" and argued that a former Communist cannot be completely sure that his former comrades are no danger to American society. The harmless ex-Communists a witness identifies will be able to exonerate themselves and the dangerous ones will be exposed. The witness's "personal code of honor" must, therefore, give way to considerations of "the national security." In addition, Westin noted that remaining silent, even in a limited way, coincides with the CP's own policy and thus helps the Party "camouflage the activities of Communist Party members." Not only does such a stance further Communism, but it also damages liberalism by allowing the right to lump unpopular groups and causes with Communist ones.[64]

How responsive the academic profession was to such a plea for "complete responsiveness" we will never know. For if a witness turned out to be willing to name names in his initial executive session with a congressional committee, the committee was usually willing to excuse him from testifying in public. Unfortunately, such a practice deprived the cooperative witness of the "golden opportunity" which, Robert Gorham Davis argued, was one of the main political advantages of cooperating. But as far as I can tell, most cooperative witnesses were perfectly willing to forgo the chance to "strike a meaningful blow" for liberalism and instead tell their stories in private. They did not want to defend civil liberties; they just wanted to keep their jobs. The elaborate rationalizations typified by such articles as Westin's were just that—elaborate rationalizations. And, in the end, it is hard to see what effect, if any, these pronouncements—the Chafee-Sutherland letter, the AAU statement, the writings of Jones, Hook, and Westin—had on the academic community. They may well have induced a few prospective witnesses to cooperate with the committees, but not, I presume, because of the brilliance of their arguments. Rather, the quasi-official nature of these statements served notice on the profession as a whole that professors who did not cooperate with congressional investigators would probably lose their jobs. It was a powerful argument.

VII

"Frankly and Freely":
Investigating Committees and Academic
Witnesses in the Spring of 1953

Robert Gorham Davis was HUAC's first witness when, on February 25, 1953, the committee began its long-awaited investigation of subversion in higher education. Though HUAC's chairman Harold Velde had assured a worried college president early in January that his committee's "investigation will be general in character rather than directed at specific institutions," he was not being completely candid. Most of the committee's witnesses during those first few days of hearings had, like Davis, taught or studied at Harvard. Harvard was an obvious target. Its prestige ensured publicity. Moreover, the dozens of people who had passed through the Harvard CP in the 1930s and 1940s guaranteed HUAC a large pool of potential witnesses. The first two days of hearings were the most dramatic. In addition to Davis, two other former Harvard Communists, Granville Hicks and Daniel Boorstin, talked about their Party experiences and named names. The other witnesses were less cooperative. HUAC soon found new targets elsewhere, but over the course of that busy spring the committee continued to call up former Harvard students and teachers. It questioned more than a dozen of them, though not always in public.[1]

Most of these people had long since left both Cambridge and the CP. Many were still vaguely radical, still sympathetic to the ideals that had brought them into the Party, but they were no longer politically active. They were young scholars and young fathers, immersed in the calmer life of career- and nest-building. The committee's subpoenas, though not unexpected in many cases, were an unpleasant intrusion. They deprived these people of the right to remain politically uninvolved and forced them to confront serious moral, political, and personal choices they had no wish to make. They had to choose whether or not to cooperate with HUAC. They knew what the consequences would be. The academy had already made it clear—both in word and deed—that it would not protect those of its members who did not cooperate with congressional investigators. And those investigators made it equally clear what that cooperation would entail.[2]

About half the Harvard witnesses named names. It is easy to condemn these people, to accuse them of weakness or some other character flaw. But most of them were under such enormous pressure that it would be unfair for us to require even in retrospect the kinds of sacrifices that few of us have ever been called upon to make. Some, no doubt, were opportunists and collaborated with the Velde Committee in order to advance their own careers. Others may well have been genuine anti-Communists. Robert Gorham Davis, for example, had never considered taking the Fifth. He was not, however, concerned about his job. Smith College, where he taught, was a liberal place, and Davis, who already had tenure, believes "that if I had refused to testify, they would have supported me." His real concern, and the reason he was willing to cooperate with HUAC, was that he "had strong feelings about the Communist Party." He did not, it is true, think highly of "the very dubious characters" and "publicity seekers" on the committee, but he disliked the Party even more. His own experiences and those of his wife, who had worked in the Communist underground in the 1930s, had convinced him that the CP "was a dogmatic conspiratorial organization totally committed to the defense of the Soviet Union." As a result, he recalls, "I was not prepared myself to defend the Communist Party or oppose the right of congressional committees to investigate the Communist Party."[3]

It was, Davis admits, "humiliating to have to agree to give them names," but, "apart from this business of naming names, there's nothing in this testimony I would now disavow or even want to change significantly except for being bolder about criticizing the committee." Like most friendly witnesses, Davis felt that the committee already had most of the names he could provide. Granville Hicks had given them in a private session the previous summer and had told Davis what he had done. Thus, when the committee's investigator Donald T. Appell visited Davis early in 1953, Davis was willing to identify some of his former associates. "I'm pretty sure that Appell did know their names." Naming them in public, however, turned out to be an unpleasant surprise. Perhaps because he was Velde's first academic witness, Davis had apparently not realized how much publicity that part of his testimony would receive. "The whole emphasis was on the naming of names, and that was, of course, the painful and questionable part of it." Still, Davis did not want to be an uncooperative witness, so he had, he felt, no other choice.[4]

Nor, for that matter, did Richard Schlatter. But unlike Davis, who cooperated with HUAC for largely political reasons, Schlatter did so for personal and professional ones. He had been a mild, essentially cerebral Communist during the late thirties, first at Oxford and then at Harvard. When the Nazi-Soviet Pact ended the Popular Front, Schlatter slipped out of the CP with some negative feelings about its clandestine nature and its tolerance for the evils of Stalinism, but no regrets about the intellectual value of his own experience in the Party. Schlatter's politics had always been subordinate to his academic work, and in the years that followed he increasingly eschewed political activity for the more congenial life of a scholar and teacher. The subpoena which HUAC sent him in the beginning of 1953 could not have been more unwelcome. Schlatter did not want to be an informer, nor did he want to take the Fifth. He was teaching at Rutgers, and Rutgers had not only been the first university in America to fire a faculty member specifically for relying on the privilege against self-incrimination, but also the first to make it an official policy. With a wife and two children to support, unemployment was a disquieting prospect. "But it was not just the question of losing my job—one can always," Schlatter recalled, "find a way to live. But the only way in which I could do anything I felt worth doing was by being a teacher, a scholar, an academic. The thought that all that might come to a sudden end had a dampening effect." And an anxiety-producing one as well. The weeks between his subpoena and his testimony were, he recalls, "the most miserable period I ever had."[5]

Schlatter had another reason for not wanting to take the Fifth. He had, he felt, nothing incriminating to hide. Soon he realized that he had nothing at all to hide. Perhaps for alphabetical reasons, his name was at the end of HUAC's list; and, as the testimony of his former Harvard friends and colleagues was released, it became clear that they had already given HUAC every name Schlatter knew. Naming these people one more time would make little difference. But Schlatter wanted to be sure; before he went down to Washington, he contacted everybody he was planning to name and got their permission for him to name them yet again. Rutgers was delighted. The University had been embarrassed by the dismissals of Finley and Heimlich and did not want to have to fire Schlatter as well. HUAC was less pleased. Schlatter told the committee at his executive hearing what he had done and the committee heard him out, but did not ask him to testify in public.[6]

Schlatter was not the only former Harvard Communist who did not appear in public. His highly qualified testimony could have been of little use to the committee. Furthermore, it was standard practice for HUAC and the other investigating committees to excuse their cooperative witnesses from an open session, especially when those witnesses were ordinary people with nothing newsworthy to confess and no new names to give. The committees also excused people who could prove that they had never been Communists. Displaying a bunch of reluctant informers or innocent liberals contributed little to the committee's luster. Far better, for everyone, to keep such testimony under wraps. The friendly witnesses were especially grateful for anonymity, for, even at the time, cooperating with a committee was not something to be proud of. It was "a traumatic experience," one of these witnesses recalled. A former Harvard Communist then teaching at a state university, he knew that he would lose his job if he did not name names. He had been out of the Party for more than fifteen years and felt that "there seemed to be nothing that was currently of any merit to protect." Nonetheless, he was so "ashamed and embarrassed" by the whole business that he didn't tell anybody about his testimony, not even his mother. Only his wife, his department chairman, and one other colleague, with whom he had conferred before he went down to Washington, knew about it. There was no fuss, no publicity. Even when HUAC released the transcript of his hearing a few months later, it got no attention from the press and did not, he claimed, affect his life.[7]

Unfriendly witnesses had no such luck. Since the committees' avowed function was to expose such political undesirables, they always called up the people who refused to name names. HUAC's Harvard hearings produced about half a dozen of these unfortunate souls, including the only one of its many Harvard-connected witnesses who was still in Cambridge. He was Wendell Furry, an associate professor in the Physics Department. Furry, a soft-spoken Midwesterner, had come to Harvard in 1934 after having taken a postdoctoral fellowship with Oppenheimer at Berkeley. He had joined the Party for the usual reasons during the Popular Front days; it seemed to be the most effective anti-fascist organization around. Like most academic Communists of the 1930s and 1940s, he kept his affiliation a secret, and his colleagues in the Physics Department who knew that he held radical opinions were, nonetheless, surprised that he had actually been a Communist. But somebody must have known about his politics, for Furry was one of the few theoretical physicists to have worked with Oppenheimer who was not cleared for the Manhattan Project, an annoyance that Furry ultimately considered a blessing since it ruled him out as a potential atomic spy. It is also possible that President Conant knew of Furry's politics, for Furry was never promoted to the rank of full professor, even though the Harvard Physics Department had recommended it several times. In addition, Furry had trouble getting a passport in 1950. So when it was clear that the congressional investigations were going to reach Harvard, he expected to be called up.[8]

He was not surprised, therefore, when a federal marshal came to his office in the beginning of January with a subpoena from HUAC. Furry's response, like that of many unfriendly witnesses, was almost automatic, a kind of gut reaction rather than the product of careful thought. He would not cooperate with the committee. "I couldn't see myself doing that. I wouldn't have uttered a name . . . to save my neck." Since he was planning to defy HUAC, he had trouble finding a lawyer to represent him. He talked with several people before he was referred to Joseph Forer, a Washington attorney with a growing reputation for advising unfriendly witnesses. Furry had received a copy of the Chafee-Sutherland statement, so he knew that Harvard would not approve of his forthcoming testimony. He did not discuss it with anybody in the administration, though he did talk with his chairman and some of his colleagues, all of whom, though sympathetic to his predicament, tried to dissuade him from taking the Fifth. But for all his gentleness Furry had a stubborn streak, and not only refused to cooperate with the committee but also issued a press release denying that he was Communist and calling "the Committee's policy of interrogating persons on their private beliefs and associations . . . utterly inconsistent with American traditions of freedom."[9]

Fortunately for Furry, President Conant had just left Harvard to take over the post of U.S. High Commissioner to Germany. What evidence there is (and there isn't much because Harvard is one of the few American universities to keep its archives closed to scholars) indicates that Conant would have taken a hard line and would probably have pressed for Furry's removal. But he was no longer around and during the interregnum before the appointment of his successor, Harvard was run by a committee of trustees and Provost Paul Buck. This meant that, unlike the trustees at other schools who remained distant from what was happening on campus, the Fellows of the Harvard Corporation were involved with their Fifth Amendment case from the start. They were aided in their deliberations by a faculty advisory committee, composed of a few senior professors and the deans of the main professional schools. The faculty group did not produce a report of its own, but rather met regularly with the members of the Corporation and acted as a liaison between the faculty and the Corporation. From the start, everybody agreed that the University would make no blanket rule about those members of its faculty who took the Fifth Amendment, but would, as Provost Buck announced, decide each case "on its merits after full and deliberate consideration of the facts and issues involved." That consideration took a long time, for the Fellows of the Corporation were a judicious lot and were determined not to make a hasty decision. Three of them were lawyers: William Marbury, R. Keith Kane, and the senior member of the Corporation, Charles A. Coolidge. The other two were the banker Thomas W. Lamont and the former president of the American Medical Association, Roger Lee.[10]

Furry appeared before the Corporation several times. He was open and talked at length about his political background. He had to. As Marbury recalls, "We felt definitely that he had an obligation to be candid with us about this subject." It was not a matter of politics, Marbury explained, but of common sense. If someone "refused to answer questions on the grounds that it might incriminate you, we're entitled to know why." Furry feels that the Corporation expected him to do something to restore the good name of Harvard, although Marbury denies it. Accordingly, Furry returned to Washington to file an affidavit with HUAC stating that he was not a Communist and then went back yet again to testify at a second hearing in the middle of April. This time Furry denied that he was a Communist as of March 1, 1951, but took the Fifth about his activities before that date. By this point the Corporation had apparently decided that it would be wrong to dismiss a member of the faculty simply for invoking his constitutional rights. But as it turned out the main problem that Furry presented the Corporation with was not his refusal to cooperate with HUAC but his revelation that during the war he had lied to the FBI about the political affiliations of a fellow scientist. Even though the incident had taken place years before and Furry had volunteered the information about it, there were several members of the Corporation who believed that they could not overlook such duplicity.[11]

Ultimately, the Corporation decided to retain Furry. But, as Marbury recalls, "We didn't find it easy to make up our minds about this thing." The process involved months of intensive discussions between the members of the Corporation and the faculty. Furry's colleagues in the Physics Department lobbied vigorously and effectively on his behalf. They believed in his loyalty and integrity and felt that "the most effective" thing they could do was to present Furry's case as persuasively as possible to the Corporation. They were very restrained about this and consciously decided not to try to organize the faculty in Furry's defense. As the physicist Norman Ramsey, who considered himself "Furry's 'lawyer' " in his dealings with the University authorities, acknowledged, circulating a petition "in the spirit of those times would be counterproductive, you might not have gotten such an impressive array of signatures." Instead, Ramsey and his colleagues talked at length and in private with the members of the faculty advisory committee and the Corporation. It was not easy. As Edward Purcell, a Nobel laureate and former student of Furry's as well as a member of the faculty committee, recalls, the main problem he and the rest of Furry's supporters had was making some of the "hard-liners" on the Corporation understand "why a university is not a bank." Many of them believed that just as a suspected embezzler would be fired from a job as a bank teller, so Furry should be similarly disqualified from teaching. They were, however, open-minded and eventually came to understand why someone like Furry might be morally and even legally justified in relying on the privilege against self-incrimination. As had happened with the faculty committee at Rutgers, the more the Corporation and its faculty advisers learned about the Fifth Amendment, the more they came to appreciate its value. Dean Erwin Griswold of Harvard Law School had originally come onto the faculty advisory committee as a firm supporter of the Chafee-Sutherland position. Within a few months he had changed his mind and was soon to write perhaps the most effective and authoritative defense of the Fifth Amendment produced until then.[12]

Charles Coolidge, the Senior Fellow and a widely respected Boston lawyer, seems to have been the most influential. He was, above all, anxious to preserve the academic reputation of the University and came to recognize what a potentially serious effect firing a tenured professor would have on the morale of the entire teaching staff. This was the argument that Paul Buck stressed in all his conversations with the Corporation and was the subject as well of a long and apparently influential letter that the soon-to-be dean of the faculty, McGeorge Bundy, addressed to the Corporation. Perhaps only at a school with the prestige and independence of Harvard could the trustees have paid so much attention to faculty opinion, and then perhaps only as a result of the very special conditions stemming from Conant's departure, in which, without the usual intermediary of a president, trustees and professors came into unprecedentedly close contact with each other.[13]

As their deliberations continued throughout the spring, it became clear that the members of the Corporation did not want to fire Furry but did not see how they could keep him without seeming to condone what they all considered his very serious offense. The formula that they finally adopted solved that problem by putting Furry on probation. In its official report on the case, issued May 19, the Corporation explained its decision. The only statutory grounds on which it could remove a faculty member were "grave misconduct and neglect of duty." Since Furry's teaching was impartial and "of high quality," the Corporation had to decide whether his other behavior constituted "grave misconduct." Present membership in the Communist Party, "with its usual concomitant of secret domination by the Party," would, the Corporation ruled, definitely be "grave misconduct." But taking the Fifth about one's past membership, though "entirely inconsistent with the candor to be expected of one devoted to the pursuit of truth," was something that the Corporation decided was "misconduct, though not necessarily grave misconduct." Furry's lie to the FBI, however, "fell so far below the standard of moral conduct to be expected of a member of our faculty as to constitute grave misconduct." There were, however, extenuating circumstances. "In view of the fact that this incident occurred nine years ago in a very different climate of political opinion . . . the interests of the University will be best served by some other action than the removal of Dr. Furry at this time." The Corporation put him on a three-year probation instead.[14]

Wendell Furry was not the only uncooperative witness with whom the Corporation had to deal. In March, Senator Jenner brought the SISS to Boston and subpoenaed a handful of Harvard people. Four of them took the Fifth. They were Helen Deane Markham, an assistant professor of anatomy at the Medical School; Leon Kamin, a teaching fellow in the Social Relations Department; and the Lubell twins, Jonathan and David, second-year law students and former radicals from Cornell. Since the Lubells were students and not members of the teaching staff, the Corporation did not have jurisdiction over them. The Law School did, but decided not to press charges against them on the grounds that, though the school "greatly regrets the course of conduct followed by these students," it would tolerate behavior in students that would not be permissible in faculty members. Moreover, there were other kinds of sanctions that could be invoked against the Lubells. They lost their scholarships. And their fellow students deprived them of the positions they had won on the law school newspaper, the Legal Aid Society, and the Law Review.[15]

Markham and Kamin the Corporation handled in the same way it had Furry. It summoned them to a hearing and made them explain why they had invoked the privilege against self-incrimination. Kamin, who had been an active Communist while a Harvard undergraduate in the late 1940s, discussed his political views with the Corporation and explained why, after working full-time for the Party in the year after he graduated, he became disillusioned and quit. He apparently made a good impression on the Corporation which appreciated his honesty and respected, though it regretted, his reluctance to name names before the SISS. Markham also told the Corporation about her political activities and denied that she had ever been in the Party. Compared with Furry's, the cases of Kamin and Markham were easy for the Corporation to handle. Once it decided that neither of them were, in its phrase, "under Communist domination," it was able to rule that their use of the Fifth Amendment before the Jenner Committee was "misconduct," but not the "grave misconduct" that would have required their dismissal. Since neither Kamin nor Markham had tenure, the Corporation did not have to fire them to remove them from the faculty. It simply made sure that their departments did not reappoint them—which was, of course, what happened.[16]

Theoretically, the Corporation's formal announcement on May 19 that it would not dismiss Furry, Kamin, or Markham should have closed their cases. But this was not to happen. A week later Jenner recalled Markham for a second hearing, this time in Washington. Though Jenner insisted that the purpose of the hearing was to examine some new evidence the committee had unearthed about her, the timing of her recall, a week after the Corporation's report came out, made it seem as if the committee was trying to put pressure on Harvard. This was especially the case since the committee had just held a set of hearings in Boston and, as Markham herself observed, "If it had wanted to examine me further, it could have done so then. Why the sudden decision to recall me now?" Her suspicion that Jenner was "trying to punish me and Harvard because neither of us has capitulated" was confirmed by what happened at her hearing, where the committee repeatedly asked her what she had told the Harvard Corporation. She, of course, refused to tell. And she followed up that refusal by releasing a statement to the press blasting the committee. Some members of the Harvard Corporation were annoyed by Markham's statement, for it seemed to imply that the Corporation had approved of her use of the Fifth, but they did nothing.[17]

Jenner continued to press and he escalated matters by producing a witness who claimed Markham was a member of the CP. This was the professional informer Herbert Philbrick, who told the committee on June 17 that a man whom he identified as a Communist had told him that he "knew Helen Deane Markham personally as a CP member." Still, the

University took no action, for as Dean Griswold explained to the Faculty Advisory Committee, Philbrick's statement, based as it was entirely on hearsay, fell "far short of persuasive proof" and did not "warrant the taking of any action by the Harvard Corporation." Then on July 17, Jenner released his committee's final report, "Subversive Influence in the Education Process." The report consisted of a general statement about the problem and a summary of "some controversial cases," Helen Deane Markham's among them. The report cited Philbrick's testimony about her and added to it that of an anonymous informant who claimed that he had paid "Communist dues to her while she acted as treasurer of the Harvard branch of the Communist Party." Jenner alluded to Harvard's apparent lack of cooperation, but denied the charge that his committee was trying to put pressure on the University, insisting that the SISS "does not attempt to tell university or local authorities whom they shall hire as teachers." The committee's function was much more limited, "to present the facts of subversion for the record."[18]

This time Harvard acted. Apprised of the Jenner report in advance, the Corporation decided to suspend Markham and call her for another hearing so that it could examine the new evidence against her. Apparently, the Corporation was not sure that Markham had told the truth when she denied that she was a Communist. Charles Coolidge said as much in a letter to her on August 11:

> Even if we believe your statements to us that you never have been a member of the Party, what bothers us is how we can distinguish your case from a person who is more valuable to the Party if not technically a member.

Neither Markham's testimony nor the affidavits she had collected—including one from a reluctant Leon Kamin denying that there had been a Harvard branch of the CP within the past five years for which she could have collected dues—dispelled the Corporation's doubts. But since it had no substantial proof against her and her contract was to expire in ten months anyhow, the Corporation decided to drop the case. "Philbrick's testimony, the Committee's report and the pattern of her own conduct create in our minds a suspicion" that Markham may well be "under Communist domination," the Corporation announced. "But, as the Committee itself intimates, a case against her has not been proved in the public record . . . . We are not willing to base a finding of grave misconduct . . . on mere suspicion."[19]

At the same time it was dealing with the University's Fifth Amendment professors, the Harvard Corporation was also engaged in the process of choosing a successor to Conant. Ironically, its choice of Nathan Pusey, the president of Lawrence College in Appleton, Wisconsin, was to exacerbate the University's problems with congressional investigators. Appleton was Joseph McCarthy's home town and Pusey, a moderate Republican and former classicist, had been an important member of a group called the Wisconsin Citizens' Committee on McCarthy's Record. As it had been for both Velde and Jenner, Harvard was a tempting target for McCarthy as well. The presence of Pusey simply added a touch of vindictiveness to the Wisconsin senator's attack on the University. Pusey was, McCarthy implied, soft on Communism; Harvard's retention of Furry proved it. To make his point, McCarthy set out to demonstrate just how dangerous the unfortunate physicist was. He subpoenaed Furry as part of his investigation of the Fort Monmouth Signal Corps in the fall of 1953. Furry had never worked at Fort Monmouth, but that made no difference to McCarthy who, after questioning Furry at an executive session in the beginning of November, announced that Harvard was "a smelly mess, and I cannot conceive of anyone sending their children anywhere where they might be open to indoctrination by Communist professors." McCarthy then sent a telegram to Pusey asking him

> what, if any, action the University intends to take in Furry's case and what your attitude generally is toward retaining teachers at Harvard who refused to state whether they are communists on the ground that the truth would incriminate them.

Pusey's response was noncommittal: McCarthy had not released the transcript of Furry's hearing, so Harvard could not take any action on it.[20]

A public confrontation was imminent; Furry and his supporters on the faculty prepared for it by conferring with the administration. In his executive session with McCarthy, Furry had denied engaging in espionage, but continued to rely on the Fifth Amendment when asked about his political activities. McGeorge Bundy, with whom Furry was negotiating, urged him to consider waiving the Fifth if McCarthy asked him whether he had indoctrinated his students. Mark DeWolfe Howe, a Harvard Law School professor who was serving as Furry's unofficial legal adviser, also suggested that Furry give up the Fifth and simply refuse to name names. Such a position, which a few teachers elsewhere had already taken, was legally risky but politically attractive. Thus, when McCarthy showed up in Boston and subpoenaed Furry and—at the last minute—Kamin for a public hearing on January 15, 1954, the physicist answered all the senator's questions about himself and none of those about other people. Kamin did the same. McCarthy, who had clearly been expecting Furry to take the Fifth, was furious:

> This, in the opinion of the Chair, is one of the most aggravated cases of contempt that we have had before us. . . . To me it is inconceivable that a university which has the reputation of being a great university would keep this type of a creature on teaching our children.

Surprisingly, the Harvard authorities, whom Furry and Howe had both expected to be pleased by Furry's waiver of the privilege, were upset. The Corporation had come to terms with keeping a Fifth Amendment witness on the faculty, but the possibility that Furry might be cited, indicted, and even convicted of contempt posed completely new problems. Would the Corporation be willing to retain Furry if he went to jail?[21]

No doubt the fact that it was McCarthy, the most unsavory of the congressional investigators, who brought the charge against Furry made it easier for the Harvard administration to handle the case. It did not, as Furry's supporters feared, suspend him when he was indicted. But it also did nothing to help him fight the indictment. A few other schools—Chicago, Sarah Lawrence, and Williams College, for example—hired lawyers to represent their faculty members before congressional committees, but Harvard did not. Furry's colleagues in the Physics Department took on the burden. Not only did they assess themselves 2 percent of their annual salaries, but they also set up a defense committee to find and pay for an attorney to handle the case. After interviewing a host of reluctant candidates, they found a young civil libertarian willing to do most of the legal work and a more prominent attorney, James St. Clair, to represent Furry in court if the case got that far. It didn't. After several years of litigation, Judge Bailey Aldrich acquitted Kamin on the grounds that McCarthy had overstepped his jurisdiction. The case against Furry, which was the same as that against Kamin, was dropped several months later—ironically, a few days after Furry's three-year probation ended.[22]

On May 27, 1954, one hundred and fifty members of the Harvard faculty gathered under the auspices of the local chapter of the AAUP to present citations to members of the administration and ruling Corporation for having "defended the freedom of institutions of learning" and resisted "attempts on the part of officials of government to dictate University policy in the crucial matter of the determination of the fitness of its teachers." There was a cautionary note as well. The eminent historian Samuel Eliot Morison warned his colleagues "to avoid acts or associations that will bring our university into difficulties." But, on the whole, the atmosphere was festive, full of self-congratulations on all sides, full, too, of the often expressed notion that Harvard had set an example for the rest of the academic world. To some extent, it had. Liberals and even a few radicals hailed the highly publicized retention of Furry, Kamin, and Markham as a great victory for academic freedom. The ACLU, for example, also gave the University a citation and praised its "outstanding solution of three difficult cases involving national security, the integrity of education, and the protection of individual rights."[23]

How influential had Harvard been? Most schools which had Fifth Amendment witnesses on their faculties did, in fact, act in accord with Paul Buck's dictum that "each case will be decided on its merits." But that was such a basic procedure at almost every institution that few indeed were the schools which acted without some kind of an investigation. Nor was Harvard the only one that retained an unfriendly witness after such an inquiry—though it was one of but a few. In every instance, whether the teacher lost his or her job or kept it, the specifics of the case—the political situation within the school itself, its independence from external pressures, and the radicalism and personality of the faculty member involved—determined the final decision far more than any guiding light from Cambridge. Nonetheless, Harvard's example was not ignored.

It certainly influenced the University of Buffalo, a school which solved its Fifth Amendment problem the same way Harvard did. Buffalo, now a part of the New York State university system, in 1953 was a private school whose ruling University Council was run by the same type of financial and professional elites as Harvard's corporation—albeit of a more provincial variety. Buffalo's unfriendly witness was Associate Professor William Parry, a philosopher who had been in the same party unit as Furry while at Harvard in the 1930s. As soon as he was named by Robert Gorham Davis, Parry told Buffalo's chancellor T. R. McConnell that he would probably be called by HUAC and that he would probably refuse to cooperate. McConnell tried to dissuade Parry from doing so and let him know that he might be dismissed if he did. A few days later, McConnell appointed an ad hoc faculty-administration committee "to examine the issues and to advise me concerning what the university's policies on these matters should be." The committee's report, issued on May 8, the very day that Parry received his subpoena, was introduced by McConnell's unconvincing explanation that "the reason for arriving now at a statement of policy for the University of Buffalo is that there is no immediate need to do so." The text of the policy statement was the usual: a declaration that the University of Buffalo "cannot harbor on its faculty any present member of the Communist Party" and the warning

> that members of its faculty if called upon by a legislative committee . . . [should] testify freely and frankly . . . . Refusal to testify will make the person liable to suspension without prejudice until . . . he can demonstrate to the appropriate authorities that he is qualified to continue as a member of the faculty. If he fails so to demonstrate, he will be subject to dismissal.[24]

From the first, Parry decided that he wanted his case "to show that someone could take the Fifth Amendment and stay on. Not only in Harvard but in Buffalo, a city that wasn't notably radical or progressive." This was a political decision, a recognition that to keep his job would be to thwart HUAC's desire to have its opponents fired. Everything he did was directed toward that goal. A few days before his date with the committee, Parry wrote to HUAC offering to testify about himself. "In view of my desire to protect the good name of my university," he explained,

> I am prepared to set aside personal apprehensions, to waive my privilege of not testifying against myself, and to answer freely and frankly any relevant questions about my own activities, provided that your committee agrees not to ask me to name or identify any other person. I will not play the odious role of informer. I will not get innocent people into trouble. If

I did, I would lose all self-respect and forfeit the confidence of my colleagues and students.

Like the playwright Lillian Hellman, whose example he acknowledged, Parry was willing to talk about himself but not others. He knew, of course, that the committee would not accept his "Hellman gambit," but he hoped that his offer to talk "freely and frankly" about himself would not only expose the committee's hypocrisy but also demonstrate his willingness to abide by Buffalo's new policy. He had, however, no desire to be a martyr, and so, at his public hearing on May 19, he took the Fifth. It was the only way he could avoid contempt without having to name names.[25]

As Parry later told Buffalo's Faculty Executive Committee, "I wanted, if you like, to have my cake and eat it too," to defy the committee and still keep his job. That he succeeded stems in large part from his own flexibility and willingness to cooperate. He had other advantages as well. To begin with, there seems to have been little local pressure on the University to oust him. The two newspapers in Buffalo both endorsed the idea that Parry's behavior was the University's problem, not theirs, an idea which the otherwise conservative chancellor endorsed even more vehemently. In addition, there was a strong and vocal group of civil libertarians on the faculty, several of whom served on the committee that heard the case. This made it easier for Parry to do what he knew was politically necessary to keep his job, i.e. cooperate with the University's investigation. He felt that "the majority of the Committee . . . would take a civil liberties attitude and be friendly to me." Accordingly, he recalls, "I answered their questions quite freely—even some of them that I feel they perhaps shouldn't have asked . . . as long as they weren't asking me to name people." What they were asking Parry to do was talk about his past political activities and present political views. They needed to be sure that he was no longer a Communist. Thus, they questioned him at length about his differences with the Party and pressed him to criticize the Soviet Union. Many of these questions revealed the committee's rather naïve preconceptions about Communism, but Parry answered them all and even signed an affidavit to the effect that he had left the Party before he came to Buffalo. He realized that the committee was trying to elicit testimony that would convince the chancellor and trustees not to fire him.[26]

His strategy was successful, but barely. Chancellor McConnell had told the committee that Parry had to be punished; even the liberals on the committee did not want to exonerate him completely. They felt that he should have risked contempt rather than deliberately disobey the University's new policy by taking the Fifth. As a result the committee struggled to find a formula that would satisfy the chancellor's demand for sanctions yet keep Parry on the faculty. Harvard's precedent was useful; the committee's liberals, who suggested it, hoped that Harvard's prestige would make their findings palatable to McConnell and the trustees. Thus, in its final report of June 26, the committee recommended that Parry be put on probation;

> that Mr. Parry's status as a member of the faculty on permanent tenure be revoked; that he be placed on annual appointment as associate professor . . . and that in no instance shall he be restored to permanent tenure within a period of at least three years.[27]

The committee's stated reasons for depriving Parry of tenure—its "grave concern over his refusal to testify freely and frankly before the House Committee on Un-American Activities" and its belief "that the good faith of Dr. Parry's repudiation of Party principles is still on trial"— made little sense and contradicted some of the committee's other findings. But it was the best that Parry's supporters on the committee could get, and though Parry was "shocked at the severity of the judgment," he soon realized that he "couldn't hope for anything better and decided to live with it." The local branch of the ACLU, many of whose members belonged to the Buffalo faculty, issued a statement condemning the University's action as a "serious miscarriage of justice," though recognizing, as well, that "the University of Buffalo showed greater forbearance and deeper respect for typically American procedures than have some other universities in similar circumstances." It recognized, in other words, that for any school to retain a Fifth Amendment witness during the height of the McCarthy period was a victory of sorts. Most colleges and universities with such people on their faculties were firing them.[28]

Perhaps the most egregious of these dismissals occurred at Ohio State University, a school whose previous record showed little regard for either free speech or academic tenure. In 1948, for example, the Board of Trustees imposed a California-like loyalty oath on a seemingly compliant faculty and staff. Then, in 1951, the board responded to American Legion complaints about a speech by a Columbia Teachers College professor whose textbooks the Legion had been attacking for years by requiring that the president approve of all outside speakers in advance. This requirement, the soon-notorious "Ohio State gag rule," provoked so much opposition, especially after President Howard Bevis banned the appearance of a Quaker pacifist, that the board had to rescind it. But the repression continued. In the summer of 1952 Bevis dismissed an instructor in the Fine Arts Department who had refused to cooperate with the state of Ohio's Committee on Un-American Activities. The instructor had taken the Fifth before the committee as a protest against its attack on civil liberties, but had willingly given President Bevis the answers to all the questions the state investigators had asked. Even so, he was fired. Given this record, it was no surprise that Ohio State's administration rushed to rid itself of a tenured associate professor who invoked the Fifth Amendment before HUAC in the spring of 1953.[29]

The professor, a theoretical physicist named Byron Darling, was, in the words of his lawyer, an "unworldly fellow" totally absorbed in his research on the ozone molecule. He had been something of a radical in the late 1930s and 1940s, but had apparently never joined the CP. Called up by HUAC, he testified in secret on March 12 and in public on the 13th, a Friday. The committee was hard on Darling. Because he was a theoretical physicist, though one who had never worked for the Manhattan Project, HUAC resuscitated its earlier interest in atomic espionage and asked him such questions as, "Did you ever communicate to any person known to you to be a member of the Communist Party any information relative to nuclear physics or to atomic energy?" In addition, because he had been in graduate school with Joseph Weinberg, HUAC's former "Scientist X," Darling had to field questions about Weinberg's political connections as well as his own. Darling took the Fifth to all these questions because he wanted to oppose the committee's intrusions into people's political beliefs and protect himself against a perjury indictment. But he was apparently so flustered by HUAC's badgering that when he mentioned some of his colleagues at Ohio State and Congressman Francis Walter asked (as he later explained he always did whenever he heard a name he didn't know) "Were either of those professors members of the Communist Party?" Darling took the Fifth.[30]

No sooner had Darling finished testifying than President Bevis suspended him. Formal charges were preferred on March 24 and the hearing took place April 4, after being postponed for two days so Darling could get a lawyer. The investigating committee was an ad hoc body consisting of Bevis, three faculty members, three vice presidents of the University, and the assistant to the president. Its deliberations were perfunctory; it did not even ask Darling if he had been a Communist. Nonetheless, on April 7, Bevis recommended to the Board of Trustees that the unfortunate physicist be fired. Bevis conceded that Darling was "an outstanding research man in his field" and "a very good teacher," who had conducted himself on campus "with scrupulous propriety" and had given "no indication of bias or leaning toward communist ideology." He further admitted that Darling had signed the University's loyalty oath in 1948, had answered all the committee's questions at his University hearing, and had stated categorically that he was not and never had been a Communist. Nonetheless, for Bevis, and presumably for the Board of Trustees who, on April 20, concurred unanimously in the president's recommendation, Darling's "public refusal to answer pertinent questions" was in itself sufficient grounds for his dismissal. He had, so Bevis explained, violated his "obligation to the University," in particular, his "duty to maintain in the public mind the University's integrity and good repute." The language of Darling's dismissal, with its invocation of "gross insubordination to the University policy" and "lack of candor and moral integrity," was clearly designed to exempt Ohio State from having to comply with its own rule requiring a year's notice for termination except in cases of "immorality or gross insubordination."[31]

Ohio State's treatment of Byron Darling was extreme, not only in the speed with which the administration hustled him off the faculty, but also in the administration's blatant distortion of academic procedures and regulations. But after all, Ohio State was a public university in a politically volatile state, one with its very own Un-American Activities Committee; and Bevis's behavior, though such a flagrant violation of academic freedom that the AAUP was to censure the school, could be understood, if not condoned, as the response of a nervous administrator to what he must have felt was an impossible situation. In fact, however, Ohio State's response to its Fifth Amendment witness differed only in its speed from that of other universities, both public and private. Other schools may have been more deliberate about the matter, but they too dismissed tenured professors who took the Fifth, even those who, like Darling, were willing to cooperate with their institution's investigation.

Temple University was one such school. Similar in many ways to the University of Buffalo, it was a medium-sized, private, urban university which, though independent of state control, did receive part of its operating budget from the state of Pennsylvania. Temple's Fifth Amendment witness, like Buffalo's, was a member of the Philosophy Department, in this case the department's chairman, Professor Barrows Dunham. Dunham had been subpoenaed by HUAC in October 1952 but never brought to Washington. Subpoenaed again in February 1953, he was to be the only academic witness not connected with Harvard to appear at HUAC's first set of hearings into higher education. Temple had known of Dunham's prospective testimony for months, since he had been in touch with the administration from the minute he received his first subpoena. Naturally, the officials at Temple with whom he talked encouraged him to cooperate with the committee, but he didn't. In fact, Dunham was the most uncooperative witness that HUAC had seen to date. He answered only the committee's first few questions about his name, age, and home address and then took the Fifth when the committee asked for his educational background. The stymied investigators immediately recommended that Dunham be cited for contempt, arguing that if other witnesses took the privilege that early in their hearings, HUAC "might as well close up shop."[32]

On his return to Philadelphia, Dunham contacted William W. Tomlinson, the University's vice president and the man who was handling loyalty matters for Temple, and described his hearing. Tomlinson recalls that he told Dunham:

> I think you should have answered, you should have answered frankly. If you're in the clear and if you're in the right, Temple University will fight to the last man for you.

Temple then suspended Dunham. His "lack of cooperation" in refusing to answer HUAC's questions was, explained the University's president, Robert L. Johnson, "inconsistent with your obligations as a teacher and your responsibilities to all members of Temple University, and to the society of which it is a part." Johnson also mentioned the Pennsylvania Loyalty Act, the so-called Pechan Act of 1951, which required all state-aided schools to certify that their faculties were subversive-free. Dunham's refusal to cooperate with HUAC, Johnson wrote, "created a doubt as to your loyalty status."[33]

Temple had set up a special Loyalty Committee in the spring of 1952. Its members, administrators mainly and a few professors, were supposed to deal with whatever problems might arise in implementing the Pennsylvania Loyalty Act. The Dunham case was its first piece of business. It took jurisdiction at once, negotiating with Dunham over the procedures for a hearing and contacting the FBI for what the FBI described as

> any material that would serve as the basis for questioning of DUNHAM at a hearing or as the factual basis on which the University could reach a conclusion regarding the validity of DUNHAM's alleged reasons for refusing to cooperate with the HCUA.

The FBI obliged by sending over a file of material—copies of presumably incriminating letterheads, leaflets, and memorabilia from the many left-wing groups Dunham was associated with—"photostated," the FBI explained, "in such a manner as to conceal any markings that could possibly identify them with the Bureau." Tomlinson, who was chairing the Loyalty Committee, also arranged for its members to receive copies of the recently released AAU statement.[34]

Because President Johnson, like Conant of Harvard, had been called to serve in the Eisenhower administration (he was appointed head of the International Information Agency, the parent body of the Voice of America, just at the time Senator McCarthy was beginning his probe of that organization), Temple was also being run by a small group of trustees, one of whom presided over Dunham's hearing on May 7. It was clear that the FBI materials furnished the basis for the questions asked at that hearing, very specific ones about the organizations listed in Dunham's file. Dunham answered all these questions, explaining to the clearly uninformed trustee who was asking them precisely what each group stood for and why he had joined it. He also revealed that he had been in the Communist Party from 1938 to 1945, and he told his examiners exactly why he left it. He did, however, refuse to answer the one question he was asked about another person.[35]

Neither side was pleased with the hearing. Years later, Dunham recalled his anger at the hypocrisy of these

> people who had known me for 16 years and more years than that, some of them to discuss the question of my loyalty, I felt really soiled by that. That was dirty stuff. They knew damned well better. They didn't have any personal doubts about my loyalty. They were infinitely more loathe-

some than the House Un-American Activities Committee. I still wince
when I think of them; cowards, cowards.

Tomlinson, on the other hand, claimed that the University had no way
of telling "what organization he might or might not belong to, and his
position before the House Un-American Activities Committee confused
and complicated the issue." The trustees discussed the case, but did
nothing. Finally, on July 15, President Johnson, who had returned to
Temple a casualty of McCarthy's attack on the Voice of America, suggested that the University appoint two prominent attorneys as special
counsel "to write an opinion as to the responsibilities of the University
in the case of Dr. Barrows Dunham under the Pennsylvania Loyalty
Act." It was clear that the trustees, fearing that the state legislature
might invoke the Loyalty Act to cut off funding if Temple kept Dunham,
wanted to fire him and were searching for a way to make that action as
palatable as possible. Dunham was, after all, the chairman of his department and one of the most popular and highly regarded teachers on the
faculty.[36]

The special counsels finished their work in the beginning of September, and their recommendation for Dunham's dismissal was ratified by
the full Board of Trustees on September 23, 1953. Because Dunham had
been so cooperative during his hearing before Temple's Loyalty Committee, the University ignored that testimony almost entirely and concentrated on his behavior before HUAC. Though Dunham's contempt
case had only just begun its course through the federal judiciary, Temple's trustees rendered an early verdict of their own. Dunham, so the
University's official statement claimed, "deliberately undertook to misuse
the Constitutional privilege against self-incrimination as a means of evading the duty of giving his testimony" and had, thus, "abused the high
Constitutional privilege he invoked." Not only did the trustees claim that
Dunham's refusal to testify, to them clearly contemptuous, was a sign of
his "intellectual arrogance," but it was also an evasion of his "cardinal
duty" as a member of the academic profession. Here the trustees cited
the AAU statement and actually quoted from its section about the necessity for "complete candor and perfect integrity" on the part of a professor as well as his corresponding obligation to refrain from using the Fifth
Amendment. By basing their decision to fire Dunham on his supposedly
illegal invocation of the Fifth Amendment, the Temple authorities could
insist that his dismissal involved "no issue of academic freedom and no
question concerning the political opinions of Dr. Dunham." Had that
been the case, Temple presumably would have reinstated Dunham when
he was acquitted in 1955. But it did not.[37]

Dunham's behavior before HUAC unquestionably seemed provocative at the time. That was not, however, Dunham's intent. He had wanted
only to avoid informing, and he had taken the Fifth as early as he did in

his hearing only because his lawyer advised him to. He had no idea that his was to become an important test case. It was one of the last to involve the Fifth Amendment; his victory established that the Fifth would give an unfriendly witness almost unlimited protection in front of a congressional committee. But his case also revealed, as did those of Darling and the other Fifth Amendment witnesses fired in the spring of 1953, that to use the privilege during a congressional investigation was to court academic unemployment. Furry and Parry showed that it was possible, but just possible, for a tenured professor to take the Fifth and still keep his job. But most academics who took the Fifth were not so fortunate.[38]

There was, however, another strategy for college teachers who wanted to keep their jobs, yet avoid informing. This was the strategy that Furry and Kamin had used in their public testimony before McCarthy in January 1954. They talked about themselves, but refused to talk about others. They did not cite any constitutional authority for that refusal; they simply said that they would not be informers. Kamin took this stand because he felt he had no other choice. He realized that waiving the Fifth might invite a contempt citation, a protracted legal struggle, and even a prison term. But he also realized that such a strategy had enormous professional advantages. "I had to take a calculated risk of going to jail if I wanted to have an academic career." He hoped—justifiably, it turned out—that the technical arguments his attorneys devised for his refusal to testify would keep him out of prison as well.[39]

Despite its hazards, this strategy appealed to many academics—administrators and prospective witnesses alike. Both the president of Rutgers and the liberal members of Buffalo's Faculty Executive Committee, for example, regretted that their recalcitrant witnesses had not waived the Fifth. The MIT committee set up to explore the issues raised by congressional investigations took a similar position. In a thoughtful memorandum which described the various options open to a subpoenaed professor, it urged him to choose "full disclosure." At the same time, it recognized that such a choice "will almost certainly evoke unfavorable reaction in some segments of the community" and suggested that a professor who could not overcome his "reluctance to inform on other people" take the risk of contempt and "testify completely regarding himself, but refuse to inform on his associates." If such an "individual acted with sincerity and dignity," the committee hoped, he would not be fired and the rest of the faculty would "be willing to contribute to the upkeep of his family while he was in jail."[40]

Frank Oppenheimer was one academic who had already resorted to this strategy during the late 1940s, but it was a practice which soon after fell into disuse when it became clear that the judiciary was willing to uphold a broad interpretation of the Fifth Amendment. In the spring of 1953, however, a few academics began to experiment with the tactic of deliberately waiving the Fifth and answering questions about themselves, but not about others. Before the worst of the witch-hunt had subsided, in 1954, at least ten college teachers were to take this approach.[41]

The first, apparently, was Irving Goldman, an anthropologist at Sarah Lawrence. In some respects Goldman was in a good position to test the limits of a committee's power, for Sarah Lawrence, a small, educationally innovative women's college, was an unusually supportive institution. Its president, Harold Taylor, was a civil libertarian who had spoken out in 1949 against the University of Washington's policy of firing Communists, and the college prided itself on its liberalism and its refusal to impose political tests on its faculty members. When at the end of 1951 the local Westchester County American Legion attacked the school and sent a delegation to Taylor to demand the dismissal of three professors, the Sarah Lawrence Board of Trustees responded by ignoring the Legion's charges and, instead, releasing a statement on academic freedom. The statement, issued January 18, 1952, stressed the faculty's responsibility for encouraging their students' "intellectual independence and maturity" and for dealing "candidly and honestly with controversial questions." Sarah Lawrence would not, the trustees declared, deprive its teachers "of any rights they hold as citizens of this country including the right to belong to any legal political organization of their own choosing." There were limitations, of course. "No person . . . who takes his intellectual orders from an outside authority, whether communist or any other, would be given or could retain the responsibility of membership on the Sarah Lawrence faculty." Though similar in some ways to the kinds of statements other institutions were making, especially in its denunciation of dogmatism, the tone of the trustees' statement with its emphatic assertion of confidence in the integrity of Sarah Lawrence's faculty seemed to imply that the college might defend its teachers against an anti-Communist investigation rather than ask them to cooperate with it.[42]

The test came soon enough. In the middle of March 1953 the Jenner Committee subpoenaed a dozen faculty members. For a school with only seventy full and part-time teachers, that was quite an onslaught. Included in the round-up were the American Legion's three targets: the social philosopher Helen Lynd, the historian Bert Loewenberg, and Joseph Barnes, a journalist and part-time member of the faculty who had already been called up during the IPR hearings. The subpoenaed teachers met together with the chairman of the Board of Trustees, the crusty New York lawyer Harrison Tweed, who, Lynd recalls, warned them, "Now, we want you all to understand that we hope you won't take the Fifth Amendment, but if you do, that's your business. And we never expect you to give the names of any other people." Since most of the prospective witnesses had, like Lynd, never been Communists, Tweed's advice was essentially irrelevant. They could avoid the Fifth and satisfy both the committee and the college without having to name names. Three members of the faculty, however, had been in the Party. One in-

voked the Fifth; one may or may not have cooperated with the committee; and the third, Irving Goldman, followed Tweed's advice and neither
took the Fifth nor named names.[43]

Goldman had joined the Communist Party in 1936 while a graduate
student at Columbia and had left in 1942. He had been an early casualty
of the Truman administration's loyalty program; in 1947 he had lost his
job as a South American specialist in the State Department because he
was a "security risk." He answered all the Jenner Committee's questions
about his career and his own political activities, but when asked to identify the leaders of the Party units at Columbia and Brooklyn College,
where he had taught from 1940 to 1942, he refused. "I cannot as a matter of principle reveal those names," he told the SISS;

> I cannot inform on others to get others into trouble, particularly since I
> have no knowledge that any of these individuals had ever committed any
> offense against the security of the United States . . . . I have come here
> to speak very frankly about myself; I have made no appeal to any legal
> immunities, and I simply cannot allow to rest on my conscience that I
> would get other people into trouble just to save myself some difficulty.

The committee was unsympathetic. "You have been a very cooperative
witness here," Senator Herman Welker explained,

> but yet when you are asked the question as to who the leader of the group
> happened to be, then you hide behind, as I might say, an objection that
> is not valid and has no basis in law and, therefore, I will have to direct
> you to answer those questions, and if not, this committee has no other
> alternative than to seek contempt citation for you, and I assure you again,
> Mr. Goldman, we do not desire to do that.[44]

Goldman did not recant. He knew the legal risks he was taking, but
he also knew that Sarah Lawrence would back him up. Harold Taylor
recalls that the entire school regarded Goldman as something of a hero.
Since the trustees were willing to retain the teacher who had invoked the
Fifth Amendment even though they suspected that he had not leveled
with them about his relationship with the Communist Party, Goldman's
job was never at issue. Had he, in fact, gone to jail, Taylor was planning
to give him a special sabbatical for the purpose. But Goldman did not go
to jail. The SISS did not, though it easily could have, cite him for contempt. In that respect at least the Jenner Committee was, as it had the
reputation for being, more responsible than the other congressional investigators.[45]

The other committees—HUAC and Senator McCarthy's Permanent
Subcommittee on Investigations of the Senate Committee on Governmental Operations—did seek contempt citations against those witnesses
who, like Goldman, talked about themselves but not about others. Though
indicted, none of these people went to jail either. The legal issues that
enabled them to escape punishment differed from case to case. Some
people were able to claim that the committees had overstepped their

original jurisdictions; others, that the questions they refused to answer were not relevant to the legislative purpose of the investigation; still others won their cases on even narrower technical grounds. Though the acquittals of these men and women did give witnesses a bit more protection against the committees, the protections that were granted were all procedural. At no point did the judges who decided these cases—and every defendant waived his or her right to a jury trial—deal with the substantive civil liberties issues involved. As a result, it is hard to avoid the suspicion that those judges may well have been searching for technicalities that would allow them to acquit these people. Otherwise, they would have had to jail men and women whose only crime had been refusing to testify about their former friends and colleagues.[46]

None of this was known in the spring of 1953, however, so Goldman's testimony was for its time quite a daring gesture. Others followed him, but only a few. There was Lawrence B. Arguimbau of MIT. Called for a public hearing before HUAC on April 21, Arguimbau, an associate professor of electrical engineering, apparently followed the MIT faculty committee's advice for someone who was reluctant "to inform on other people." He explained to the committee why he was not going to use the Fifth:

> It doesn't give the public the information that would be useful to them; and in the second place it does leave a misinterpretation on why I have used the fifth amendment . . . . I would like to take the position that I can give all the information that is pertinent without talking about other people and subjecting them to the same difficulties that I have been subjected to. I realize that doesn't give you fully what you would like and I realize it puts me in jeopardy, but I am doing what I can for you and what I feel I morally can do.

Arguimbau was quite open with the committee. He spoke at length about his activities in the CP, which he had joined in 1937 and left in 1950, but he resolutely refused to identify anybody who had been in the Party with him. There was considerable irony here, for in the following two days, three of Arguimbau's colleagues from MIT testified publicly before HUAC and, besides naming Arguimbau, must have named most of the people he had so carefully tried to protect.[47]

One of the people that Arguimbau's colleagues identified as having belonged to their largely academic unit in the early 1940s was a former instructor at the Harvard Medical School, Marcus Singer. In the spring of 1953 Singer was an associate professor of zoology at Cornell. Singer was not the first Cornell professor to face a congressional committee; Philip Morrison was. Morrison had been teaching at MIT during the academic year 1952–53 and, when Jenner came to Boston in the beginning of May, he subpoenaed the controversial physicist. Morrison had decided to waive the Fifth and talk about himself, but not others. For some reason, the committee held back and did not push him to give it any names in public, a lucky break for Morrison, whose position at Cornell was, as we have seen, already shaky. Singer was not so lucky, for HUAC, unlike Jenner, tried to punish its unfriendly witnesses. Singer had talked with members of Cornell's Subcommittee on Governmental Investigations before his hearing. Most of them were, he recalled, "kindly disposed," even though they urged him not to take the Fifth. Not that he was planning to. "A born scrapper," as one of his former students described him, Singer apparently felt that he had nothing to hide and that since he had tenure and had just been promoted to full professor he could afford to take some chances. He also had, in Daniel Pollitt, a good lawyer who enthusiastically supported his desire to test the legitimacy of HUAC's mission.[48]

Singer's public hearing took place in Washington on May 26. He described his experiences in the small Harvard-MIT unit of the Party that met "off and on" during the war years. "It was a group," he explained, "which discussed the Marxian philosophy and attempted to apply what they could from the discussions to the present day." He gave the committee a detailed reading list. But when the committee's counsel asked Singer who had invited him into the unit, he replied,

> Sir, I feel that I am prepared to talk freely about myself, but I honestly feel that in honor and conscience I cannot, I prefer not, I should not talk about my colleagues and associates . . . . these people, they were like myself, they did nothing subversive, and I also feel that should I answer this question on advice of my counsel, that this might tend to incriminate me.

The committee recalled Singer for the next day and again asked him who was in his unit, this time feeding him a long list of names—Furry, Parry, Arguimbau, and Helen Deane Markham among them. Still Singer refused. "I could never, sir, in honor and conscience, trade someone's career for my own, come what may." The committee kept pushing him, trying to force him to concede that because the CP was a conspiracy dedicated to force and violence, he had an obligation to reveal the names of his former comrades. Still Singer resisted. "We did not conspire. We did not do anything subversive . . . . We were intellectuals. We were scholars." And he refused to make the kind of anti-Communist statements that the committee expected its friendly witnesses to make. He would not, for example, agree with the committee that Communists "have no freedom, no academic freedom, in their thinking" or that they were "not worthy to teach our youth today." Eventually the committee gave up in frustration, Congressman Kit Clardy warning Singer:

> You have placed your judgment above that of your Government and your Congress in deciding yourself whether or not the Communist movement is a conspiracy and all those who take any part in it are engaged in that conspiracy; and, so, I must tell you, as one Member, that I think you are in contempt of your Congress and of this committee and I shall do what I can within my power to see that you are cited for that contempt.[49]

Clardy's was no idle threat and, though it took a while, the House of Representatives eventually voted Singer's contempt citation in June 1954. At that point Cornell's president, Deane W. Malott, who had officially ignored Singer until then, called him in and, as Singer recalls, "pressed me to purge myself and threatened me with possible dismissal if I am indicted." Singer of course refused, and when he was indicted in November 1954, Cornell responded by suspending him from teaching. It continued to pay his regular salary and let him continue his research. Singer had a lot of support on campus; a special faculty meeting gave him a unanimous vote of confidence. Malott and his advisers on the faculty and in the administration did not want to dismiss Singer, and they decided that unless someone else lodged a formal complaint against him they would reinstate him automatically as soon as his case was disposed of, except, perhaps, if he went to jail.[50]

No one at Cornell had foreseen that Singer would be away from the classroom for over two and a half years. He was convicted at his first trial in January 1956 and given a three-month suspended sentence and a $100 fine. Even before the sentencing, Malott was willing to overlook a prison term and restore Singer to his old status if he would not appeal his conviction. Singer refused, for his lawyer was confident that he would win on appeal. Malott and his advisers realized that Singer's suspension from teaching was personally demoralizing for him, as well as expensive for the University and onerous for the other members of the Zoology Department who had to cover Singer's classes. Even so, they decided not to reinstate him until his case was settled. They were afraid that a "surprise revelation of additional facts" might come out during the appeal and, though they recognized that "the risk was minimal," they decided that they "ought not to take it." Singer lost his first appeal, but after his lawyer argued and won an almost identical case in the Supreme Court, Singer appealed a second time and on June 28, 1957, was finally acquitted. Cornell reinstated him a few days later.[51]

Eventually vindicated, Singer had, nonetheless, spent over four years in limbo. True, he had considerable support. Colleagues at Cornell and elsewhere helped raise money for his legal expenses and others worked at lining up jobs in the event Cornell fired him. Even so, his situation was difficult. He had trouble with his conservative colleagues in the Zoology Department, who wanted him to drop his appeal and return to the classroom. "The Department had considered me a damn red among other things," he recalls, "and things went from bad to worse on that and other levels." Nor was it easy to live with the uncertainties of his legal battle. Yet for all his worries, Singer has to be considered one of the luckier of the unfriendly academic witnesses; he kept his job.[52]

At least thirty others did not, victims of the unprecedented surge of anti-Communist investigating that dominated the first session of the 83rd Congress. That the academic community was the initial target of this burst of congressional activity was largely fortuitous. Earlier committees had already exposed most of the culprits in such tempting areas as Hollywood and the State Department, leaving the nation's system of higher education as one of the few major havens of presumed subversion still untouched. Thus, in 1953 alone the main congressional investigators called up more than one hundred college teachers. Several dozen more received subpoenas in the following year; the investigations then abated, but individual educators were still being questioned by congressional committees as late as 1959.

Their fates varied, though certain patterns emerge. Most of the professors who cooperated with committees and preserved their universities' reputations by naming names and avoiding publicity had no professional problems. Those professors who cooperated part of the way with the committees and, thus, could convince all but the most irrational anti-Communists that they were no longer in the Party usually managed to keep their jobs. Professors who refused to cooperate with the committees but did cooperate with their colleagues—and this seems to have been the largest group—sometimes kept their jobs, if they had tenure and taught at private colleges or universities, and sometimes lost them, especially if they were at public institutions. Professors who refused to cooperate with both the congressional and the academic investigations were almost always fired. What stands out is the overwhelming consensus within the academic establishment that it had to respond to the congressional hearings. Once HUAC, SISS, or Senator McCarthy questioned a teacher and raised the issue of Communism, the academic community rushed to investigate. Except for a tiny and highly marginal group of civil libertarians, few academics challenged this aspect of the academy's collaboration with the congressional committees. Few seemed to notice that by putting the jobs of unfriendly witnesses in question, America's colleges and universities had given Joseph McCarthy and the members of HUAC a say over selecting their faculties.

VIII

"The Slow Treatment": Academic Committees and Their Unfriendly Witnesses

It was Chandler Davis's third hearing before a faculty panel since he had refused to answer the questions of a HUAC subcommittee on May 10, 1954. He had been trying to make his academic judges understand just why he was refusing to answer their questions. "In the final analysis," the young mathematics instructor explained,

> I reserve the right to follow my own thinking as to what is important to me and how much I care about it, and political liberty is one of the things about which I care a lot more than my job at the University of Michigan.

Davis had invoked the First Amendment before HUAC and had refused to answer any of the committee's questions about his politics on the grounds that such questions "infringe freedom of speech or freedom of assembly." His refusal to answer similar questions put to him by members of the University of Michigan's own investigating committees was, he felt, a necessary concomitant of his earlier refusal to testify before HUAC.[1]

Davis's case is an unusual but important one. His challenge to the legitimacy of both the congressional and the academic investigations exposed their main assumptions and clarified the relation between these two, ostensibly different, types of inquiries. Few other academics were quite so defiant. But, then, few others shared the almost obsessive nature of Davis's devotion to civil liberties. Nor did they share his willingness to risk career and freedom to defend an abstract principle. Davis lost his job, of course; he also went to jail.

In many respects, Davis was the quintessential anti-authoritarian personality. Principled, tenacious, and fiercely independent, he had an almost innate predisposition for political dissent. It may have been hereditary, for Davis came from a long line of rebels and civil disobedients. He had ancestors on both sides of the Revolutionary War, an abolitionist great-grandfather who served as Wendell Phillips's bodyguard, and a grandmother who worked for peace during the First World War and for Sacco and Vanzetti after it. His father, Horace Bancroft Davis, was also a radical and along with his wife had joined the Communist Party during the Depression. Davis himself had been in the Party while a student at Harvard in the forties. He got his Ph.D. in mathematics and came to Michigan in 1950, after turning down an offer from UCLA because of the loyalty oath. Though no longer officially a Communist at the time of his hearing, Davis had never really broken with the Party, and he remained active on its fringes throughout his years in Ann Arbor.[2]

Unlike most of the unfriendly witnesses we have seen, Davis viewed his refusal to cooperate with HUAC more as a political than a moral act. True, he did not want to be an informer. But his primary concerns were constitutional. He wanted to oppose the committee's attack on civil liberties. Because he came before HUAC in the spring of 1954, a year after the congressional committees had launched their main assault on the academic world, he was able to assimilate the experiences of other witnesses and learn from their mistakes. In particular, he realized, as many other academics already had, how ineffective the Fifth Amendment had become, not only as a way to protect one's career and reputation, but also as a vehicle for resisting the investigations. His own father had been called before the Jenner Committee the previous year, but because the elder Davis had also taken the Fifth Amendment, his invocation of the First was completely ignored. His son would not repeat that error.

Davis thus welcomed his subpoena as an opportunity to make an unambiguous political statement. He would refuse to answer the committee's questions on First Amendment grounds alone and would, he hoped, establish the kind of clear-cut case that would force the federal judiciary, if not the rest of the nation, to curb the congressional committees' attacks on freedom of speech. He was not, he explained to HUAC,

> refusing to cooperate with the Government. I am cooperating with the Government to the best of my ability as a citizen in attempting to restrain Government officers who I believe are exceeding the authority of their office.

He knew, of course, that the committee would consider his form of "cooperation" nothing more or less than contempt of Congress. Yet, as he told a faculty committee at Michigan, "I am willing to go to jail in defense of free speech, but I do not expect to have to."[3]

As it turned out, he had miscalculated; he did end up in jail. His case, which he hoped would "restore the reputability of dissent," meandered through the federal courts for eight years. Its final disposition came in 1959 as a result of the Supreme Court's 5 to 4 decision in the case of Lloyd Barenblatt, a former Michigan graduate student who had invoked the First Amendment before HUAC a few weeks after Davis had. In the *Barenblatt* decision, the Court maintained that because of the Cold War, Congress could ask questions about somebody's political affiliations that "in a different context would certainly have raised constitutional issues of the gravest character." But at the time Davis appeared before HUAC, it was not unreasonable for him to hope that the Court might rule in his favor. Certainly, he had no idea that his case would drag on for so long or that he would eventually serve time in Danbury Federal Penitentiary.[4]

Though Davis had never questioned his decision to defy HUAC, he was not, at first, sure what position to take with regard to the University of Michigan investigation that he knew would follow the congressional one. He consulted at length with his friends and colleagues, most of whom urged him to talk about himself. Davis did not discount their arguments. He had been impressed by the testimony of Cornell's Marcus Singer and, at one point, even considered rejoining the Communist Party just so he could give an affirmative answer to the big question. "I was so radical," he explained later, "that to answer 'no' would have been a cop out." Ultimately, he decided that the logic of his position before HUAC required him to take a similar stance before the Michigan authorities as well.[5]

The University had long been prepared for the confrontation. Early in 1953, several weeks before HUAC began its education hearings, the Detroit newspapers carried banner headlines proclaiming that the committee was about to investigate the University. Michigan's president, Harlan Hatcher, acted at once and sent off a telegram to HUAC's chairman, assuring Velde of the University's "willingness to cooperate with [the committee] to the fullest extent." Personally, Hatcher was no fan of the committees; he was aware, as he later told a faculty committee, of their "many abuses that are clear to all of us and are revolting to many of us." Nonetheless he was a cautious man who worried about the University of Michigan's reputation and hoped to limit in advance whatever damage the hearings might cause. He had signed the AAU statement and tried to convince the faculty to adopt it as the school's official policy. Though the Faculty Senate balked at that move, it did amend the University's by-laws to make it easier for the administration to deal with prospective recalcitrants. In addition, the ad hoc committee which drew up the revised by-laws issued a statement dispensing the usual advice. It urged potential witnesses on the faculty "to testify fully and freely when subpoenaed."[6]

For a while it seemed as if Michigan's careful preparations might prove unnecessary. No University of Michigan people were called during the first round of education hearings during the spring of 1953. It was not until November that the long-awaited subpoenas finally reached Ann Arbor. Besides Davis, at least four other professors and a handful of students and former students received them. The hearing—originally scheduled for January 1954 in Lansing, the home base of HUAC member Kit Clardy—was postponed for months, ostensibly because Clardy was sick but actually because the FBI informers who were going to star in it were still testifying at a Smith Act trial in Detroit. This delay enabled everybody involved to consider every alternative and prepare for every contingency. The University administration, for example, took the precaution of ensuring that none of the subpoenaed professors received substantial pay raises or promotions. It persuaded the Executive Committee of the College of Literature, Science and the Arts to turn down the Zoology Department's recommendation of tenure for Assistant Professor Clement Markert. Not all of the subpoenaed teachers were going to be unfriendly witnesses. One man was seriously ill and was eventually excused from testifying. Another, the economist and future Nobel laureate Lawrence Klein, was to cooperate with the committee. The other three, Markert, Davis, and Mark Nickerson, a tenured associate professor in the Pharmacology Department of the Medical School, were planning to defy the committee.[7]

They knew that the University wanted them to cooperate with Clardy at least to some extent. And they all tried, as best they could, to mitigate the professional damage that their testimony would cause. Markert had already been through an academic investigation. He had left the University of Colorado in the middle of his junior year to fight in the Spanish Civil War. When he returned to Boulder at the end of 1938, the American Legion demanded his expulsion. Because he was a straight A student and the highest ranking undergraduate, Markert had the support of the University's administration at his hearing before the Board of Trustees. As a result, even though he tried to shock the trustees, telling them, he recalls, "that I was a militant atheist, that I was a communist, that I didn't adhere to any of their values," the board unanimously voted to keep him. He was more circumspect with the University of Michigan authorities, however, and purposely did not consult anybody in the administration until right before his hearing. He did not want to be in the position of refusing to follow the University's official advice.[8]

Davis and Nickerson, on the other hand, did discuss their prospective testimony with the Michigan authorities, who predictably assured them that they would have no trouble if they answered all of HUAC's questions. Nickerson warned the administration that he would not cooperate with the committee. He was, however, willing to discuss his political past; he told his chairman, several deans, and President Hatcher that he had indeed been a Communist, but was one no longer and hadn't been for as long as he had been at Michigan. Though still a radical, Nickerson had not involved himself with the Ann Arbor left. He had been much too busy in his laboratory, where his work had already earned him a national reputation. According to an outside colleague, Nickerson was "*the* outstanding pharmacologist in his age group in this country." Davis, the youngest, reddest, and least eminent of the three, also warned the administration that he would defy the committee. But, unlike Nickerson, he would not tell the University what he was not going to tell HUAC. Though each of the three professors handled his case in his own way, together they posed a clear challenge to Michigan and the outside world as well: how far would the academic community be willing to tolerate principled dissent?[9]

Because he was planning to make a test case out of his confrontation with the committee, Davis had trouble finding a lawyer and eventually went to Lansing without one. Markert and Nickerson had no such problem. They admired Davis's position, recognizing, as Nickerson put it, that a Fifth Amendment defense, though legal, "clouds the main issue." But they also recognized that taking the First, as Davis was going to do, "would mean a long legal fight," something which, given the other problems they were facing, was hardly an inviting prospect. "I didn't see any way to feed my family while that was going on," Nickerson explained. Thus, like most of the other unfriendly witnesses from academe, they decided to invoke the Fifth Amendment and were able to find a local attorney to accompany them: John Dobson, the son-in-law of Senator McCarthy's nemesis, Joseph Welch. Though inexperienced in representing people before congressional investigations, Dobson helped the two professors as best he could, mainly, Markert recalls, by allowing them to collect their thoughts while pretending to consult with him. The hearing itself occasioned few surprises. Both Markert and Nickerson took the Fifth; Davis took the First. President Hatcher immediately suspended all three.[10]

The University investigation began the next day when the Executive Committee of the College of Literature, Science and the Arts, where Davis and Markert taught, listened to tapes of the two men's testimony. The Executive Committee then questioned each of them separately and discussed their cases with their departments. In the original by-laws governing dismissal, the first stage of an investigation was supposed to be on the college, as opposed to the University, level, but the previous year's reforms had eliminated that early stage, and so the Executive Committee of the CLSA stopped investigating once it realized its inquiries had no official weight. But it had already reached tentative conclusions, and on June 7 it forwarded them to the committee which was to handle the cases.

It recommended the retention of both Markert and Davis. Markert had cooperated fully with the Executive Committee and easily convinced it to recommend his reinstatement. He had valid legal and moral grounds for refusing to answer the questions of the Clardy Committee. Moreover, the Executive Committee added:

> We are convinced that he is not now and has not for some time been a member of the Communist Party or active in its affairs. Nothing in the evidence which the Clardy Committee appeared to have at his hearing contradicts his statements to this effect.

Davis's position, his refusal to discuss his political views and affiliations with the Executive Committee, made its conclusions about him more tentative. It accepted his refusal to cooperate with Clardy because it believed that Davis sincerely felt that he was "within his legal rights as a citizen," whether or not the courts agreed. It regretted Davis's refusal to answer its own questions because that made it difficult for the committee to find out if he was in the Party. But since it had no proof that he was, it concluded, "we must in all justice assume that he is not." As for his lack of cooperation—"We do not see that this unwillingness alone can be considered as an adequate ground for dismissal." And so, a bit reluctantly, the Executive Committee recommended Davis's reinstatement "unless conclusive evidence is found of his unfitness to be a member of our Faculty."[11]

The Executive Committee of the Medical School, where Nickerson taught, also made a preliminary investigation, but, for reasons which we shall return to later, urged his dismissal. Nickerson's willingness to discuss his past and present politics did not, in the eyes of the Medical School's Executive Committee, counterbalance his refusal to do so before the Clardy Committee. That behavior, the Medical School claimed, raised "doubts and suspicions" which have "weakened seriously the confidence of a large number of his colleagues in him." Furthermore, such behavior "is harmful to the Medical School, and may injure the reputation of the University as a whole."[12]

Meanwhile, the University's official investigation was getting under way. Surprisingly, for all of Michigan's elaborate preparations, it turned out that there was some confusion about which committee had jurisdiction over the case. The University Senate's Subcommittee on Intellectual Freedom and Integrity, which Hatcher had assumed would hear the case, refused, claiming that it was supposed to act as an appeal panel. As a result, a new advisory committee of five professors had to be appointed. The committee began by defining its task. Hatcher helped by submitting a memorandum explaining why the three recalcitrants had to be investigated. He cited the AAU statement and quoted at length from that document's discussion of the candor and integrity which a professor supposedly "owes his colleagues in the university." Hatcher also appended a list of questions which he felt the three men had to answer. The Special Advisory Committee elaborated a bit on Hatcher's memo and drew up its own list of substantially identical questions:

1. Do you believe in or advocate the overthrow of our present system of government by force or violence?
2. Are you now a member of the Communist Party or associated with the Communist movement? . . .
3. If the answer to (2) is "no," have you at any time in the past been a member of the Communist Party or associated with the Communist movement? If so—
    (a) Why did you join?
    (b) Indicate the period or periods of such membership or association.
    (c) Why did you cease such membership or association?

      (d) Are you able to prove that you terminated membership or association? How? . . .

  5. If you refuse to answer any of the above, or like or related questions put to you by this University committee, do you consider such a refusal compatible with your responsibilities as a member of the University faculty?

When it handed these questions over to the three men at a preliminary session on May 31, the Special Advisory Committee explained that it had no doubts about "your technical proficiency in your respective fields, or your teaching or research ability." The main issue that the committee would address would be that of each man's "integrity," a category vague enough to include every issue raised by HUAC as well as whatever else the faculty committee itself might decide was relevant.[13]

And what was relevant ultimately turned out to be two things: membership in the Communist Party and willingness to answer questions about that membership. All the faculty committees which examined the three teachers shared the then standard view of the CP as a conspiracy whose members were completely under Party discipline. Such people were so obviously undesirable as teachers that the University investigators felt justified in using extraordinary measures to root them out. They realized that they might be infringing upon their colleagues' civil rights. The Subcommittee on Intellectual Freedom and Integrity, which heard the cases on appeal, acknowledged its "distaste for inquiries into the political beliefs of any member of the faculty," but added, "we cannot ignore the substantial evidence abroad today that the Communist Party is . . . now composed in some significant part of dedicated conspirators." And in order to ensure that the University of Michigan was not harboring such conspirators, this committee and every other faculty group that examined the three teachers asked dozens of politically intrusive questions. Most of these questions were clearly intended to find out if the three men were, as one committee member put it, "actually under the domination of the Party." What did they think of the Soviet Union? Indochina? the Korean war? What about socialism? Would they fight for the United States if it went to war with Russia? These were, of course, exactly the same kinds of questions that university panels in Cambridge, Buffalo, Philadelphia, and elsewhere had been asking their own unfriendly witnesses.[14]

The three Michigan teachers challenged their interrogators' assumptions, in particular the notion that the Communist Party was a conspiracy dedicated to force and violence. All three denied that they, themselves, had ever wanted to overthrow the American government. Even Davis, who refused to answer most questions, answered this one and had answered it before the Clardy Committee as well. Throughout his hearings, Davis kept trying, in his logical way, to get the committee members to question their own assumptions about the nature of the Communist Party:

> If you suspect, for instance, that Communists must be detected because they promote violence, and if you convince yourselves that I do not promote violence, then you must believe, either that I am not a Communist, or that your reason for insistence on detecting Communists was invalid.

Markert and Nickerson, because they admitted that they had once been in the Party, could dispose of the matter in a less abstract way. He knew from his own experience, Markert pointed out, that the notion of the Communist Party as a danger is "absolute nonsense, so far as this country is concerned." Nickerson was more guarded. When asked whether he thought the Party was "a simple political party," he replied:

> I simply can't answer that question. I would say this, that if the present— I have no direct information, no pipeline—if the present Communist Party is as depicted in the newspapers and the Clardy Committee hearings, then I would say it is not a simply political organization.
>
> I am not myself fully convinced that that is the correct picture, because in the past, when I had known some things about it first hand, I found newspaper reports to be often unreliable.

But the three men were arguing against a powerful national orthodoxy, and they were unable to convince their Michigan colleagues that the CP was not a subversive conspiracy and that people like themselves could join the Party without losing their intellectual integrity or their loyalty to the United States. As a result, they were also unable to convince their interrogators that the issue of Communist Party membership was irrelevant to their academic fitness.[15]

This meant that they had to reassure the University that they were not Communists. Their congressional hearing had raised the issue. In the eyes of the administration and the members of the faculty committees, the three men's refusal to answer HUAC's questions about their relationship to the Party created the inference that they were concealing something, an inference that could only have been strengthened by Clardy's assurance to the University of Michigan authorities that his committee never questioned an unfriendly witness in public unless it had solid evidence that he or she had Party ties. Clardy was willing to share that evidence with the University, and on June 2, before it had questioned any of the three professors, the Special Advisory Committee met with HUAC investigator Donald Appell. Appell offered the Michigan panel material from his committee's files, some of it from the public record, some "from sources which they could not disclose, but which was authentic." According to the Special Advisory Committee's report, HUAC's material consisted mostly of allegations that the three men had been Communists and information about the specific charges that had been aired at the May 10th hearing. The faculty committee also interviewed another, unidentified "government investigator" (probably an FBI agent) who, it claimed, corroborated many of the items it had received from Appell. The committee was cautious about its use of this material. "We do not," it insisted, "accept these allegations as proof. That would be unconscionable." But this and later faculty committees used the material from HUAC as the basis for questioning the three professors.[16]

Both Markert and Nickerson were willing to cooperate with the University investigation. They told the Special Advisory Committee why they had joined the Communist Party, what they did when they were in it, and why they left. Despite his admission that he was still a radical, Markert had little trouble convincing his questioners that he had left the CP. HUAC's Appell had already admitted that his committee had no evidence linking Markert to the Party after 1948 and that he personally had a "hunch" that Markert was probably clean. In addition, Markert was so specific about his disenchantment with the CP and his distaste for its dogmatism and obeisance to the Soviet Union that none of his interrogators, President Hatcher included, questioned the sincerity of his break. His departmental colleagues offered further evidence: his complete absorption in his scientific work. As one of them noted, Markert could not have had time for Communism:

> He is over there [the laboratory] night and day working at it, and in fact when I heard of this, I could not see how he could ever have participated in any political activity when as far as I knew he was doing about fourteen hours a day in the Department of Zoology.

The Special Advisory Committee recommended his retention, and Hatcher went along, apparently because he was planning to drop Markert quietly when his contract expired.[17]

Nickerson had more trouble convincing the Michigan authorities that he was no longer a Communist. This was because he refused to repudiate his former beliefs. He had "drifted out" of the Party some time during the late forties. He had not disagreed with its policies; he simply couldn't spare the time. His views had not changed. "I do not," he told the Special Advisory Committee, "have confidence in the ultimate ability of the capitalist system to continue to provide what people in general want from an economic system." Nickerson's radicalism presented problems. How could he prove that he was no longer in the Party? The University's vice president, who was sitting in on the hearing, described the problem:

> I asked a bit ago what evidence there might be of a clean break. There is the fact that you were active, there is the fact that you have used the Fifth Amendment . . . and, the question that we all search for is what have you done which would be inconsistent with your remaining an active Communist?

In many ways the University's desire for evidence of "a clean break" was similar to the congressional committees' demand for names. Both types of requests stemmed from the flawed, but common, assumption that it was not possible for someone to be an ex-Communist without becoming an anti-Communist. To prove that he or she had broken with the Party, the committees required a former member to become an informer. Michigan relied on a somewhat less repugnant standard of evidence. It subjected Nickerson and its other unfriendly witnesses to an ideological test which they could pass only by offering the intellectual equivalent of names—a suitably anti-Communist view of the world.[18]

Nickerson failed. Though both faculty committees which heard him—the first by a 3 to 2 majority, the second unanimously—recommended his retention, President Hatcher agreed with the Special Advisory Committee's minority that Nickerson was still "a Communist in spirit," and he urged the Regents to fire the refractory pathologist. In a special report to the faculty Hatcher explained why he had not found Nickerson's testimony convincing:

> The date which he gave for his final "drifting away"—1948—coincides with the approximate date when the Communist party went "underground" and it became the party line for members to conceal their affiliations.
>
> He has not by words or action indicated any disapproval of the Communist Party or of its actions, or has any action of his been reported which would be inconsistent with continued party membership . . . .
>
> The "frank and candid" disclosures of his past activities which have appeared to impress the committee members are all concerning matters which he knows to be matters of record in government files. He has not disclosed any phase of his activity which was not already a matter of record.[19]

Perhaps Hatcher would have overlooked Nickerson's refusal to recant and his left-wing politics (he had, after all, agreed to retain Markert, who was almost as radical), had he not had the support of Nickerson's superiors in the Medical School who had unanimously recommended dismissal. Here faculty politics intrude. Nickerson and his colleagues had been at odds long before he received his subpoena. Nickerson's unconventional views and outspoken behavior had especially antagonized his chairman, who characterized him as "anti-administration, anti-authority, anti-government, anti-everything" and told the Faculty Advisory Committe that he was

> a troublemaker, an exceedingly difficult person to get along with, and one who has a type of personal arrogance and a lack of candor, and a desire to get ahead, which means tromping on everybody else in the department and elsewhere.

It seems likely that professional jealousy was responsible, at least in part, for this antipathy. Nickerson, though only an associate professor, was an extremely successful scientist. His expanding research was receiving more attention than that of his colleagues in the Pathology Department, and conflicts over laboratory space, outside consulting, and grant money were endemic.[20]

The situation had gotten so bad that even before the HUAC hearing

Nickerson had been looking for another job. His political past made the search difficult. Offered the chairmanship of the Pathology Department at UCLA, he had to turn it down when he discovered that most of the department's research was classified and he could not get the security clearance he would need to work on it. He also had to refuse an even more promising position as the vice president for research at a drug company because the company was a subsidiary of a British firm, and he knew the State Department would never issue him the passport he would need for that job. In any event, it was clear that whatever the outcome of the University hearings, Nickerson would leave Michigan as soon as he could. Hatcher must have known this when he explained that he could not ignore the advice of Nickerson's Medical School colleagues "who may be presumed to know him better than any of the others who have dealt officially with his case."[21]

Ironically, Hatcher had no trouble ignoring the support of his colleagues in the Mathematics Department for Chandler Davis or the preliminary recommendation by the College of Literature, Science and the Arts that he be kept. Of course, the faculty committees that had urged the retention of Markert and Nickerson did not do the same for Davis. He had refused to answer their questions about his political views and activities. This was crucial. In the statement which it handed to the three teachers before their hearing, the Special Advisory Committee warned that "one factor which of necessity will have to be taken into account is the attitude which each of you takes with respect to the work of this committee." In its final report, it stated:

> We believe that a strong, if not absolutely convincing, case exists for disciplinary action or dismissal against a faculty member simply on the basis that he refuses to state fully and frankly to his colleagues and to the University the facts concerning his past or present Communist affiliations and activities, if any.[22]

Markert and Nickerson had cooperated with the Michigan investigation. They were willing to make a practical distinction between an academic inquiry and a congressional one. Markert was quite explicit in this regard.

> I regard the University in an altogether different light than an agency of the government like this congressional Committee. I am quite willing to discuss everything fully with you and I certainly am not willing to do so with the Government.

Markert was not endorsing the University's investigation; he believed that the University probably had no right "to inquire into political affiliation." But he was a pragmatic man and he knew that "one does have to live in a real world, and you have to pay attention to what the realities of the social situation are." In other words, he wanted to keep his job. He had a political, as well as personal, motivation. "I thought it would be far more effective to force the University of Michigan to keep me even after I took the Fifth Amendment," he explained. "If I could win that battle, that would be more politically significant than to be more politically pure." Like William Parry of Buffalo, Markert believed that one of the best ways to resist the inquisition was to survive it.[23]

Davis disagreed. The principle involved, the absolute inviolability of freedom of speech, was too important for him to make the kinds of concessions that the Michigan authorities were demanding. Throughout all of his various University hearings, Davis struggled to make his questioners understand why he was refusing to answer their questions and why that refusal should not disqualify him from the faculty. Essentially, Davis would not answer those of the faculty committees' questions that he considered political for the same reasons he had not answered the Clardy Committee's. To do otherwise would be "abandoning the principle I defended at Lansing." Since his faculty hearings were the direct consequence of his testimony before HUAC, were he to give his colleagues the answers he had refused to give Clardy, "it would be clear that I had been forced to answer by the Clardy Committee." Davis was thus pointing out the connection between the two investigations, a connection that many academics preferred to ignore. Davis did not imply that the hearings were identical. "I do not regard my colleagues as inquisitors, then or now," he explained, "but now we are under the shadow of the inquisition." Accordingly, he would not talk politics with the University panels—or with anyone else at Michigan:

> I feel that forced political disclosure, which is essentially what is involved at the present time, would have very serious, bad effects on the freedom of speech, and specifically academic freedom in this country, and for that reason I choose until I am persuaded otherwise, to reject these questions.[24]

At his third hearing, after Hatcher had recommended that both he and Nickerson be fired, Davis gave an additional reason for refusing to cooperate with the faculty committee: that it had, willingly or not, become a political inquisition. Though Nickerson had answered all the Special Advisory Committee's questions, Hatcher fired him anyhow, because, Davis pointed out, of his "dissatisfaction with the political views that had been expressed by Doctor Nickerson in appearing before the . . . Committee." Such an action, revealing as it did that despite all disclaimers the University was in fact judging the specific political views of its members, strengthened Davis's resolve not to share those views with the committee. His commitment to principle was firm. "I want to avoid both the danger of being fired for my politics and the danger of being reinstated for my politics."[25]

Such statements, one of the committee members later told Davis, "baffled us." Since Davis claimed that he would answer those of the committees' questions that dealt with his "integrity" but would refuse to answer any that dealt with his politics, his hearings often degenerated into tiresome wrangles about the relevance of a particular question to his integrity. All his questioners assumed that Davis's relation to the Communist Party was not merely relevant, but crucial, to his professional integrity, so Davis had no success whatsover in persuading them that it wasn't. And his insistence on maintaining the consistency of his position, even on what seemed to be rather trivial matters, tended to confuse and irritate his judges.[26]

In addition, though he was to be censured for lack of candor, there were times when Davis was too candid and gave the committees information that could only hurt his case. He decided, for example, that questions about whether he had talked politics with students were relevant to his integrity as a teacher, and he proceeded to discuss every political statement that he had ever made in class—all two of them. At another another point in his second hearing, when the committee's chairman reiterated his belief that the Communist Party indulged in illegal activities, Davis disputed his use of the term "illegal," explaining,

> I do not feel that the criterion of legality is always a proper one, because oppressive governments pass oppressive laws and my ancestors defied the oppressive laws of the British Government, for example, and I do not repudiate them for it.

Similarly, in rebutting a charge, brought up by the Clardy Committee, that he had appeared on a platform with Howard Fast and Paul Robeson, he pointed out that the two men had never been in Ann Arbor together during his time there. Then he added,

> I don't mean to imply I would have been ashamed to appear on a program with Howard Fast and Paul Robeson, and as to being willing to appear on a platform with two such excellent Americans, I would be proud.[27]

It was predictable that Davis, with his prickly adherence to a rather rarified principle, his occasional revelation of what seemed to be outrageously radical political views, and, above all, his refusal to cooperate with the investigation, would have antagonized the faculty committees. He antagonized them to such an extent that, in their final reports, both the Special Advisory Committee and the Faculty Senate's Committee on Intellectual Freedom and Integrity based their unanimous recommendations for Davis's dismissal on a highly subjective assessment of his motives. They thought he lied. Despite the virtually unanimous opinion of his colleagues in the Mathematics Department that Davis "is absolutely sincere in taking this position," the members of both faculty committees decided that Davis's avowed adherence to principle was simply a clever trick to avoid having to answer questions about his politics. According to the Special Advisory Committee:

> Mr. Davis's attitude on the issues under consideration shows either that he is guilty of a gross imbalance of judgment or else that he has used a care-

fully contrived tactic to avoid a full and candid disclosure on his part of Communist associations and activities.

And, in its report, the committee cited some of Davis's most combative or infelicitous remarks "as examples of a display of deviousness, artfulness, and indirection hardly to be expected of a University colleague." Davis appealed, but his second hearing was no different from his first. The committee was so suspicious of his motives that one of its members actually asked him, "How do you think a person who wanted artfully and deceitfully to avoid discussion of his Communist Party affiliations could best do so under the guise of principle?" "How do you know I'm not lying?" Davis countered. "Because all my friends on the faculty will tell you I am a person whose word you can trust, and you have no basis for thinking otherwise."[28]

But, of course, the committee did think "otherwise." And, in its carefully argued report, it explained that it would have taken Davis's principles more seriously had not the "pattern of facts" convinced it of Davis's "lack of forthrightness," "evasive tactics," and "deviousness, if not . . . outright dishonesty." And it, too, cited passages from Davis's testimony to bolster its contention that he had lied. Significantly, neither tribunal offered any concrete evidence for such a judgment. There were no witnesses or documents, only inferences. Nonetheless, since his supposed lying so obviously disqualified Davis from academic life, neither committee proposed any other grounds for dismissing him.[29]

Hatcher, however, did. He charged that Davis's refusal to answer the university's questions in and of itself

is inexcusable in a member of our profession who seeks at the same time the protection and continued membership in the University whose policies he disdains and whose responsibilities he ignores.

More important, Hatcher claimed that Davis was trying to conceal what the questions were trying to reveal: namely, "a rather close and continuing involvement in the communist apparatus on the part of Dr. Davis." This was, of course, the implicit assumption behind the faculty committees' recommendations as well. The "pattern of facts" that the Subcommittee on Intellectual Freedom and Integrity had ascertained was one that characterized members of the Communist Party, who would, so the subcommittee and the other Michigan authorities believed, do anything to conceal their membership in the Party. The Cold War logic behind this assumption must have seemed irrefutable. All Communists lie; Davis was probably a Communist; therefore, Davis had lied.[30]

Such inferences would not hold up in a court of law, but the University of Michigan authorities were under no such evidentiary restraints. Once the issue of Communism arose, the normal presumption of innocence did not apply. This was in accord with the AAU's contention that "invocation of the Fifth Amendment places upon a professor *a heavy burden of proof* of his fitness to hold a teaching position [emphasis mine]." Universities did not have to prove that the professors in question were Communists; the professors had to prove that they were not. Not only that, but, as the case of Mark Nickerson illustrates, professors who claimed to have left the Party had to prove that they had done so sincerely. In fact, almost every academic who became publicly enmeshed in an anti-Communist controversy, even if never accused of having been a Party member, had to clear himself by making a political confession. This was what the tenure committees that operated during the California loyalty-oath crisis required of the non-signers who appeared before them. They had no evidence that any of these people were Communists, but, they claimed, they could not clear the men and women who refused to testify about their politics. These people had withheld the information that would have exonerated them. At other schools, where the uncooperative witnesses had been identified as Party members, shifting the burden of proof in this manner enabled faculty committees to recommend their colleagues' dismissal on the technical, and therefore more easily demonstrable, grounds that they had not supplied the committees with the facts necessary for their clearance. The committees were thus spared the necessity of accusing the professors in question of being Communists.[31]

Chandler Davis would have been fired or at least not rehired even if he had cooperated with the Michigan committees. He lacked tenure, taught at a state university, and was facing a possible prison sentence for contempt. But even if his situation had been less tenuous, if he had had tenure and taught at a private school, his refusal to cooperate would still have cost him his job. This is what happened to every other professor who defied a university investigation. We have already encountered a few of these people—Ralph Gundlach at the University of Washington and the handful of non-signers at the University of California who would not talk about their political views. Later on, during the height of the McCarthy era, there were a few more such recusants. Their cases, like Chandler Davis's, reveal how strenuously the academic community demanded that its unfriendly witnesses submit to a political test.

Davis's father, an associate professor of economics at the University of Kansas City, was one of them. Though he had tenure and taught at a private institution, the position of Horace Bancroft Davis was not very secure. He had left the Party in the late forties but was still an avowed Marxist, and his unorthodox politics made him the UKC's most controversial teacher. He had received his promotion only after a battle into which the University's former president cast a tie-breaking vote. His invocation of the Fifth Amendment before the Jenner Committee in June 1953 reopened the controversy. An academic investigation followed. Summoned before a group of trustees in August, Davis refused to answer its questions about his relationship with the CP. Such questions were, Davis claimed, "precisely those which have usually been considered most inquisitorial when asked by Congressional investigating committees." As a matter of principle, he would not answer them. In addition, his counsel, Leonard Boudin, pointed out that to do so might subject him to a contempt indictment from the SISS for having waived his Fifth Amendment privilege. Davis continued his resistance at his final formal hearing before a joint faculty-trustee panel in December. "The whole atmosphere of the hearing," Davis recalled, "was such as to make it appear that I was a prisoner in the dock rather than a faculty member talking to his peers."[32]

The outcome was predictable. In its official report, the University claimed that it did not have to deal with Davis's invocation of the Fifth before the Jenner Committee. His refusal "to tell his associates whether he is a member of an organization, such as the Communist party, which disqualifies him for academic life" sufficed:

> During the course of the hearings Dr. Davis did not avail himself of the opportunity to deny that he is a Communist, or subject to communist influences. No member of this institution may refuse to state his position on a matter of such fundamental importance not only to this academic body but to all of American society. Dr. Davis has, therefore, disqualified himself for further membership in the Faculty of the University of Kansas City.

Though the report did not discuss Davis's presumed Party affiliations, the case the University made at his December hearing focussed heavily on them. The University's counsel spent almost two days documenting the Communist nature of the various groups with which Davis was associated. And, as the faculty members who heard that presentation later admitted to an AAUP investigator, that evidence was highly persuasive.[33]

Similar concerns influenced the outcome of the case of the Marxist literary critic Edwin Berry Burgum. Burgum, an associate professor of English who had been teaching at New York University for twenty-eight years, had survived an earlier run-in with the Rapp-Coudert Committee. He was called up before the McCarran Committee in October 1952 and took the Fifth about fifteen times. The administration, which had known in advance that Burgum would be an unfriendly witness, suspended him within the hour. His academic hearing, which took place before a panel of elected faculty representatives, lasted from February 18 until March 6, 1953. It was an elaborate affair; both Burgum and the University produced expert witnesses. Those on Burgum's side—representatives of the AAUP and the civil libertarians Osmund K. Fraenkel, H. H. Wilson, and Alexander Meikeljohn—tried to explain the legal reasons for taking the Fifth and the professional ones for retaining Communist teachers. Those on the University's side—the noted philosopher Arthur O. Lovejoy, and James Burnham, an ex-Communist and former member of the NYU Philosophy Department—sought to rebut those arguments. They gave the by-then standard opinion that Communists were by definition both dangerous conspirators and intellectual robots.[34]

The University produced two additional witnesses to prove that Burgum was in the Party. Their testimony was somewhat suspect. One witness was the former FBI double agent Herbert Philbrick. Philbrick had never met Burgum, he admitted, but he had heard from another contact in the "red underground" that Burgum was a Party member. In addition, Burgum belonged to the editorial board of the Marxist journal *Science & Society;* Philbrick claimed, "it would be impossible for any person not a trained, disciplined, skilled Communist Party member, to have a position such as that of an editor of an official Communist Party magazine such as *Science & Society.*" To Philbrick's guilt by editorial association, the University's fourth witness, Manning Johnson, added further evidence, some of it hearsay as well as the fact that Burgum as the president of the New York City College Teachers Union had been on the 1938 May Day Committee with him. Johnson's appearance did the NYU administration little credit. He was a professional informer whose zeal for the anti-Communist crusade was greater than his concern for veracity. Even before the NYU hearings he had publicly stated that he would lie under oath "if the interests of my government are at stake . . . . I say I will do it a thousand times." His perjured testimony was soon to cause the Supreme Court to throw out a major case against the Communist Party.[35]

NYU also relied on a file of information donated by HUAC and, throughout the hearings, the University's counsel interrogated Burgum about the allegedly subversive groups he supposedly belonged to. The University also asked Burgum questions that were designed to smoke out his political views: What did he think about the Soviet Constitution? the purge trials of 1937? Burgum refused to answer these kinds of questions. In the first place, as his counsel explained, Burgum would be risking contempt of Congress if he gave NYU the answers that he had refused to give the Senate committee. But it was the content of the questions that Burgum really objected to. Like the two Davises, he insisted that the University had no right to seek information about his political views and activities that was irrelevant to his fitness to teach. "My stand in my case," Burgum later explained, "has been . . . upon the principle that the opinions and associations of a teacher as citizen are of no concern to a university provided only that they are lawful."[36]

The majority of the faculty committee disagreed. Though it did not submit a formal report, it was clear that most of its members felt that Burgum's silence simply corroborated the University's case against him. Like the University of Michigan professors who had judged Chandler Davis, NYU's panelists believed that Burgum had deliberately refused to testify because he wanted to conceal his Communist ties. His testimony, explained the committee's chairman, gives "a summary impression of

legal subterfuge, semantic sparring, and evasion, if not downright lying."
The chairman drew this conclusion, just as the Michigan committees had
done with regard to Chandler Davis, not from any specific evidence, but
from "the pattern of his [Burgum's] conduct." In other words, Burgum's
refusal to say whether or not he was a Communist proved that he was.
The University's elaborate case against him merely intensified that conviction. The faculty committee voted 9 to 3 to dismiss him, and the
Board of Trustees went along.[37]

It is hard to tell whether Burgum's refusal to testify was crucial to
his dismissal. The fervor with which the NYU administration prosecuted
him indicates that, even if Burgum had cooperated with his academic
colleagues, the University might still have found some grounds for dismissing him. No such confusion surrounds the case of Stanley Moore. A
popular and respected professor of philosophy at Reed College, Moore
took the Fifth before HUAC in June 1954 and was fired by the school's
Board of Trustees in August.

Moore had been a Communist. He had joined the CP while a student at Berkeley in the 1930s and remained in the Party during his first
few years at Reed until he realized that much of what he was doing in
the tiny academic unit to which he belonged "was a waste of time."
Marxism was not; Moore had even then begun the life-long interdis-
ciplinary exploration of Marxist theory that was to make him one of
America's most important Marxist scholars. In 1947, the year before he
came to Reed, Moore had been offered a job at Brooklyn College. Unfortunately, one of the letters of recommendation sent on his behalf
apparently described him as "a fanatical Marxist, both in theory and in
practice." The Brooklyn administration, already embroiled with its own
local Marxists, forced the Philosophy Department to rescind the offer.
When Reed made its bid the following year, Moore brought up his
earlier experience with Brooklyn and asked if Reed had, as he put it,
"similar criteria for employment." He was assured, he recalled, "We
don't have anything like that here. We have academic freedom. You
needn't worry about such a question." And Moore didn't. Nor did he
worry about concealing his political views. Reed was a liberal school,
and its faculty and students prided themselves on their independence
of mind and willingness to tolerate, even encourage, controversy. As a
result, Moore's unorthodox views, though quite well known to everybody
at Reed, did not impede his career. Within five years of his arrival,
Moore had gotten tenure and been promoted to full professor. This, despite the fact that both President Ernest B. MacNaughton, who hired
him, and President Duncan Ballantine, who promoted him, had been
explicitly warned by one of the trustees that Moore might be a red. Both
presidents brushed off the warning; Reed was not the sort of place that
would indulge in an academic witch-hunt.[38]

Reed was, however, in a vulnerable position. The social and political
liberalism of its faculty and student body alienated it from the surround-

ing community. Many of the folks in Portland, Oregon, hostile to "the Red College," erroneously believed that the school had been named for the city's most notorious native son, John Reed; tour bus guides would comment on passing the College that "it is inclined to be Communist." Such hostility, similar in many ways to that encountered by Sarah Lawrence, seriously endangered the school's very existence. Reed was poorly endowed and often on the verge of going under. Though it attracted its students and teachers from a national pool, its trustees, upon whom its financial survival depended, were local businessmen and bankers who shared the prejudices and parochialism of their peers.[39]

President MacNaughton, himself a Portland banker, had nonetheless won the respect of the faculty and managed to keep the hostilities more or less under control. Ballantine, his successor, had more trouble. He had come to Reed from MIT in 1952, full of ambitious plans for transforming the school into a West Coast Harvard. But he was young and inexperienced and, even before the Moore case broke, his attempts to strengthen the administration created serious conflicts. He had, for example, insisted on clearing every outside speaker himself and had so antagonized the students that they hanged him in effigy. HUAC's intervention deepened the crisis. At one point, a number of otherwise rational faculty members actually suggested shutting the school down for a year or two until the trouble passed.[40]

Like faculties elsewhere, Reed's acknowledged the imminent threat of a congressional investigation by adopting a statement on academic freedom. It was a strong one, insisting that

> a teacher should be appointed on the basis of his teaching ability and his competence in his professional field, not on the basis of his race, nationality, creed, or religious or political belief or affiliation. Continuation of appointment and the granting of continuing tenure should depend upon a teacher's performance as a teacher . . . . The Faculty of Reed College opposes as contrary to democratic liberties any ban or regulation which would prohibit the employment as a teacher of any person solely because of his views or associations.

On June 2, 1954, the day after the Reed faculty had so firmly declared its opposition to political tests, Stanley Moore appeared before HUAC in Washington, D.C. Two days later, Reed's Board of Trustees met and decided that it would not "examine the conduct of any member of the faculty unless there is substantial evidence of misconduct or unless the good name of the College or the individual requires it." It also promised to review every case on an individual basis and to do so with "the assistance and advice of the President and the Faculty." Apparently, the trustees were planning to follow Harvard's policy of questioning, though not necessarily dismissing, those members of the faculty who had taken the Fifth before a congressional committee.[41]

Moore was not the only Reed professor to defy HUAC that summer.

Lloyd Reynolds, a tenured associate professor of fine arts, and Leonard Marsak, an instructor in the History Department, also took the Fifth at a set of highly publicized hearings in Portland. On June 20, President Ballantine relieved Reynolds of his teaching in the summer session. The faculty, which had not been consulted about the suspension, blew up and by a 39 to 9 vote passed a resolution condemning that action as "a violation of the procedure promised by the President and sanctioned by the Board." Ballantine insisted that his action would not influence the final decision in Reynolds's case and, from then on, both he and the trustees tried scrupulously to ensure faculty participation in every stage of the investigations that followed. The Faculty Council questioned the three men and transmitted its recommendation to the trustees, who then held their own inquiries. Both Reynolds and Marsak cooperated with all these investigations and both men were retained, though Marsak was to be dropped at the end of the following academic year when his contract expired.[42]

Moore, however, was fired. From the first he had decided to make himself into a test case for the academic community and to make his refusal to submit to a political inquisition the sole issue in his dismissal. He believed that his academic credentials were so strong that "it would be difficult to muddy the thing up." He presented his case clearly. On the day after his session with HUAC, he released an "Open Letter to the President, Trustees, Faculty, Students, and Alumni of Reed College," in which he explained not only why he had refused to cooperate with HUAC but also why that behavior should not disqualify him from his academic post. Insisting that firing teachers who took the Fifth was as unjust as it was widespread, he noted:

> There is a quick treatment and a slow. In the quick treatment the teacher is dismissed out of hand, on the ground that failure to cooperate with the committee is misconduct or that pleading the constitutional privilege is an admission of guilt . . . .
>
> In the slow treatment the charges are investigated, that is, the trustees or the administrators conduct a hearing at which, like Congressmen, they question the teacher about his beliefs, associations, and political activities— not to mention those of his friends. I believe that academic officials have no more authority to ask these questions than do Congressmen. It is an abuse of power for an employer to question an employee about his politics. It is a travesty of justice to do so in the atmosphere created by pressure from influential demagogues.[43]

Like Chandler Davis, Moore was challenging the right of an academic institution to impose political tests on its faculty members. He was also challenging the Cold War assumption behind those tests, the notion that Communism disqualified its adherents from academic life. And in his "Open Letter," he pointed out the fallacy of the "official argument . . . that the discipline of the party deprives its members of the intellectual independence essential for teaching and research. If this were true," he explained:

> there would be no need to make a rule about it. Communist Party members would be eliminated in the normal course of faculty selection. And, if it were not true, a Communist's membership has not made him unfit to teach and write . . . . The fact is that some Communist teachers are professionally competent and some aren't. The incompetent get eliminated by their colleagues in the normal course of faculty selection, the competent get eliminated by their employers in the sudden frenzy of political persecution. Behind the falsehood that no Communist is qualified to teach lies the truth that all Communists get fired.[44]

Moore was on sabbatical and living in New York at the time of his hearing before HUAC. He was, therefore, reluctant to return to Portland for what he considered an unnecessary inquisition. But after receiving repeated and ever more minatory "requests" from the president for his return and soliciting the advice of the AAUP's general secretary, Ralph Himstead, Moore decided to go back to Reed. There, he met with the president, the Faculty Council, a subcommittee of the Board of Trustees, and, finally, with the full board itself.[45]

The Faculty Council, true to the faculty's resolution of June 1, did not ask Moore about his politics. Such a question "has not been considered relevant," the Council explained in its formal report to the Board of Trustees. In addition, since the Council believed that political affiliation had never been a criterion for employment at Reed, to ask questions about it now would "change arbitrarily the terms under which indefinite tenure and a contract were granted in the cases before us." Moore's academic performance was, thus, the sole issue into which the Faculty Council inquired. And here, the Council had no trouble amassing evidence about Moore's qualifications. Reed's small size and Moore's unusually rapid advancement ensured that he would be under "an abnormally intensive scrutiny of his record," a scrutiny which, the Council affirmed, "placed him consistently among the outstanding members of the faculty in terms of scholarly preparation, objectivity in the presentation of material and general effectiveness in the classroom." Though one member of the Council felt that Moore's failure to clarify his "true position relative to the party" necessitated further inquiry, the majority recommended that "no charges of misconduct be brought against Dr. Moore and that no disciplinary action of any kind be contemplated."[46]

For Reed's president and trustees, however, Moore's relationship with the CP was *the* issue. They shared the conventional view that membership in the Party disqualified someone from academic life and that such membership was, in the words of the trustees' official report, "beyond the scope of political beliefs and associations and also beyond the scope of academic freedom." As a result, Moore's failure to discuss that membership and so clear himself of the suspicion that he was a Communist was for the president and trustees an act of "misconduct." Moore's case was unusual because he had been so straightforward about refusing to answer political questions that the trustees made that the only grounds for his dismissal. In fact, by the time of his formal hearing before the full Board of Trustees on the charge that he had refused to answer questions at his earlier informal hearing, the issues were so clear that the trustees did not even make a serious attempt to pose the $64 question.[47]

Because of the Faculty Council's earlier refusal to consider anything but Moore's qualifications as a teacher and scholar and its recommendation that he be retained, Moore's dismissal did present the clear-cut academic freedom case that he had hoped to create. In fact, if we view academic freedom in its functional sense, as the faculty's control over its own hiring and promotion, then Reed may well have had the only real academic freedom case of the McCarthy period. For Reed was the only school at which the faculty openly disagreed with the trustees and administration about the basic criteria for employment. At every other school the issue was less clear, for at every other school the faculty was willing to impose some kind of a political test on itself. At schools like Rutgers or the University of Michigan, where administrators and trustees fired teachers whom faculty committees had wanted to retain, the committees had voted to retain those faculty members because they had passed a political test, not because those tests were irrelevant. Reed's may have been the only faculty in the country that refused to adminster those tests.

In restrospect, we can see how these tests violated the civil rights of the individuals concerned. It was unfair, simply as a matter of procedure, to shift the burden of proof to the defendants, yet every institution did it. Even the AAUP agreed, and its definitive report on the academic freedom cases of the McCarthy era stated that "it is the duty of the faculty member to disclose facts concerning himself that are of legitimate concern to the institution." Accordingly, academics who would not let their colleagues and superiors probe their personal beliefs had forfeited the protection of academic freedom; they had not fulfilled their professional duty. Of course, even at the time the more sensitive of the academic investigators knew that they were intruding upon what were normally sacrosanct areas of political belief. But, as is always the case when the rights of individuals are shunted aside, there were other, allegedly more important, issues at stake. Whether the nation's security and the welfare of the institution actually required such sacrifices is irrelevant. Just about everybody in academe believed that they did. And, as a result, no school dared retain on its faculty someone who refused to deny that he was a Communist.[48]

IX

"A Source of Friction": The Quieter Dismissals of Left-Wing Teachers

Academic McCarthyism had a hidden side. Not every teacher dismissed for political reasons during the early Cold War years lost his or her job as the direct result of a public investigation. Some were let go quietly, often in what seems to have been an attempt by the institutions which employed them to rid themselves of potential sources of embarrassment. Evidence for such purges is hard to come by, for many, perhaps most, of these cases—especially those involving junior faculty members—were handled without publicity. In addition, many administrators sought to conceal or deny the political nature of the dismissals, claiming that there were scholarly or bureaucratic reasons for letting the unfortunate teachers go. The teachers themselves assisted in these cover-ups, in the hope that silence might promote future employment. Because of this secrecy, much of the evidence here will be less complete than I, as a historian, feel comfortable with.

This creates a dilemma. To ignore these cases because documentation is inadequate is to produce a lopsided survey. To include them opens this account to justifiable criticism. Yet, one-sided though some of the evidence is, coming as it does from the testimony of the protagonists, the fact that these people lost their jobs is not in question. Moreover, given the conclusive evidence that we do have about a few cases, I feel fairly confident about drawing inferences in others. I cannot, however, draw any conclusions about their number. Since neither the teachers nor the schools where they taught made these dismissals public at the time, there is simply no way to figure out how many there were. Most of those I know about, I know about largely because my research on the more public cases connected me with remnants of an old left-wing network. But the surprising number of incidents that I discovered by accident— the tip from a friend of a friend—convinces me that there is no systematic way to find out exactly how many of these dismissals took place.

One such case occurred at Tulane. The protagonist, Robert Hodes, came to New Orleans in 1949 as a tenured full professor to head the neurophysiology section of the Tulane Medical School's Department of Psychiatry and Neurology. Hodes was a productive scientist who during his years at Tulane published over two dozen papers and received his share of government and private grants. He was also a Communist, which he did not tell the Tulane authorities. But he made no secret of his left-wing views. He often invited colleagues and students to his house for informal discussions. One such gathering, in the spring of 1951, at which a friend collected money for medical supplies for China, was later to be cited by his chairman as a "treasonist meeting." Similarly, his own personal campaign to end discrimination against black scientists in the South did not endear him to the people who ran Tulane, which in the early 1950s was still a segregated institution. When the American Physiological Society met in New Orleans, Hodes encouraged black scientists to attend and tried to find unsegregated facilities for the meeting. Though one of the city's most famous restaurants agreed to let the black physiologists eat there, Tulane's student cafeteria turned them away—an incident Hodes's more conservative colleagues apparently considered an unnecessary embarrassment.[1]

At some point, probably in the spring of 1952, the authorities at Tulane decided that Hodes had to go. Perhaps the FBI or some other official agency told the school that he was a Communist; perhaps the Board of Trustees, then on the verge of a major fund-raising campaign, had become upset about Hodes's left-wing politics; or perhaps the possibility of an imminent loyalty oath galvanized the administration. In any event the decision to dismiss Hodes seems to have been taken before the main congressional investigating committees had begun looking systematically for subversion in academic life. Hodes had tenure, so Tulane could not fire him out of hand. Instead, the administration apparently tried to make his position so uncomfortable that he would quit. The dean intervened in the running of Hodes's laboratory and, without telling Hodes, reappointed two of Hodes's subordinates whom both Hodes and the chairman of his department had previously decided to dismiss. When Hodes discovered what the administration was doing, he went to his chairman, who explained to Hodes that he had become "difficult" and "autocratic" recently; when Hodes denied it, the chairman then, according to Hodes, blurted out, "What's all this stuff about your politics?," and he explained that Hodes's radicalism was causing trouble. He said, Hodes recalled, "that the Dean and the Board of Trustees had gotten wind of the fact that I was a 'red.' "[2]

During the next few weeks, Hodes tried to find out, first from his chairman and then from M. E. Lapham, the dean of the Medical School, exactly what his status was. Lapham, who until then had been entirely friendly, became unavailable; Hodes's chairman advised him to look for another job. When the dean finally talked with Hodes, the day before

Hodes was to leave New Orleans for a summer of research at Woods Hole, Massachusetts, Lapham denied that Hodes's politics were a problem; rather it was his tendency to cause "dissension" within the department. He then asked Hodes to resign. Hodes refused. He would, however, look for another job and would, he told Lapham, let him know if he found one. Whether or not this conversation was a formal notification to Hodes, as the dean insisted, that "his services in the school would terminate" is unclear. Hodes knew that he was unwanted at Tulane, but he did not think that he had actually been fired. A month later, Lapham sent Hodes a rather cryptic letter informing him, "You have been reappointed for the session 1952-53, in accordance with our oral conversation prior to your leaving New Orleans a few weeks ago."[3]

Things got worse in the fall. The administration seemed to be harassing Hodes in dozens of petty ways, preventing him from requisitioning supplies and interfering with the normal running of his lab. He discussed his problems with his chairman who urged him to cool it politically; later on he suggested that Hodes was becoming paranoid and should seek therapy to cure him of his radical ideas. Instead, Hodes sought the advice of the AAUP, whose general secretary advised him to have his status clarified by Dean Lapham. After trying for several weeks, Hodes finally got an appointment with Lapham on December 15. Lapham complained that Hodes was causing so much friction in the department that he was seriously considering terminating his appointment at the end of the first semester. Three days later, the dean formally notified Hodes that he was dismissed as of January 31, 1953. In his letter, Lapham insisted that he had told Hodes back in June that he would have to leave Tulane within the year. Obviously, that was what the dean had *meant* in his interview; but he had not foreseen that Hodes would be stubborn enough to stay where he was clearly unwanted or that he would consult the AAUP.[4]

Hodes appealed, and Tulane, apparently in an attempt to avoid a flagrant abuse of academic procedures, granted him a hearing before a three-man subcommittee from the Board of Trustees. It was an unusual procedure, not only because it occurred after Hodes had been fired, but also because the reason the administration gave for having dismissed Hodes was "the fact that he had become a source of friction." The transcript of the hearing ran to 972 pages and contained testimony from many of Hodes's colleagues and subordinates. Hodes and his supporters tried to show that it was his politics, not his personality that had led to his dismissal; the University tried to show the reverse. Tulane's case was not very strong. Even those of its witnesses who claimed that Hodes was a source of friction admitted, as his chairman did, that Hodes's radicalism "was one of the factors leading to the friction," and that "many persons were being upset by his political activities." Another witness, the chairman of a different department, insisted that he was so distressed by Hodes's political views that he told Lapham that it was impossible for him, "as a loyal American, to voluntarily have further relationship with Dr. Hodes in any area." In fact, there was no witness who did not, in one way or another, allude to Hodes's radicalism as an important, if not the only, source of his problems. Though no one denied that Hodes had conflicts with his subordinates, it was hard to believe that they necessitated his removal. As one of Hodes's colleagues noted, "It seems patent that a full professor should not be dismissed simply on the basis of tension with technicians working under him."[5]

Nonetheless, despite strong circumstantial evidence that the University had cooked up the "friction" charge in order to conceal the political nature of its decision to fire Hodes, the three trustees who conducted the hearing supported the administration and agreed that its "decision to terminate Dr. Hodes's appointment . . . was not made arbitrarily, capriciously, or without justification." In their report, the trustees focused on Hodes's demeanor at the hearing: "The manner in which his statement was presented, his intonations of voice, and his obvious expressions of superiority over and scorn for the other members of the Department with which the difficulties have been most pronounced." Such behavior, the trustees explained, convinced them that the University's charges were true; Hodes's "was a character and personality of such a nature that conflict between him and others was almost inevitable." Hodes, who was obviously under stress, may well have made a bad impression on the panel; even so, it is hard not to believe that, at the height of the McCarthy era, Hodes's admittedly radical politics had more to do with his dismissal than his supposedly abrasive personality. In any event, the abrupt dismissal of a tenured full professor because he was "a source of friction," a charge that the AAUP had never recognized as legitimate grounds for termination, certainly raises questions.[6]

❋ ❋ ❋

Tulane, at least, told Hodes why he was being fired—even if the grounds were questionable. Jefferson Medical College, a private medical school in Philadelphia, did not even bother to do that when, late in 1953, it dismissed three professors and forced a fourth to resign. Though two of the three had—or at least according to AAUP guidelines should have had—tenure, the Jefferson administration never told the men why they were being fired. For that reason, these firings may well have been the single most egregious violation of academic freedom that occurred during the McCarthy period. As the cases of Mark Nickerson and Robert Hodes reveal, medical schools, perhaps because of their professional rather than scholarly orientation, seemed to care less about academic freedom than other types of educational institutions. Jefferson, a medical school which had no affiliation with a larger university, was particularly insensitive to such concerns. In addition, during the 1950s there were allegations that Jefferson discriminated against Jews; several of the people with whom I talked suggested that anti-Semitism may have played a role in the dismissals. All three of the professors involved—William Pearlman, Robert Rutman, and Irvin Wagman—were Jews. There is also some circumstantial evidence that the Jefferson administration was itself aware of these allegations and may have tried to defuse them by bringing a Jewish trustee and a Jewish professor into the decision-making process.[7]

In any event, whether or not anti-Semitism was an issue, anti-Communism certainly was. The men involved were left-wingers, and all had once belonged to the Communist Party. Rutman seems to have been the most politically active. Though he had dropped out of the CP in the beginning of 1951, he continued to work for the same peace and civil rights groups he had been involved with while in the Party. Pearlman, on the other hand, lost interest in politics after the crushing defeat of Henry Wallace and the Progressive Party in 1948 and, believing that he could best serve humanity as a scientist, devoted himself to his biochemical research on the hormones of pregnant women. He remained concerned about peace and social justice, nonetheless, and caused something of a stir at Jefferson when he hired that school's first black lab technician. Even so, neither Pearlman nor the other two men had any serious problems with the administration until the passage of the Pennsylvania Loyalty Act in 1950. Jefferson Medical College complied with the law and sent in the requisite assurance that its faculty was subversive-free. Before the Jefferson administration did so, however, it consulted with the FBI about some "individuals whose nationality and background might indicate subversive activities." In its certification letter to the governor of Pennsylvania, the Jefferson administration did not identify those individuals, nor did it indicate whether the FBI brought their names to Jefferson's attention or the administration itself initiated the investigation. Given their later troubles, it seems plausible to assume that Pearlman, Rutman, and Wagman were among the suspects. And, though cleared by the FBI, they apparently remained under suspicion.[8]

These suspicions came out into the open in the middle of June 1953 when, as the result perhaps of an FBI initiative, the three scientists were suddenly summoned before an ad hoc committee consisting of the dean, the president, the chairman of the Board of Trustees, and Hays Solis Cohen, a lawyer and one of the school's two Jewish trustees. Solis Cohen conducted the inquiry, declaring that the Pennsylvania Loyalty Act made it

> incumbent on us to inquire whether any members of our faculty have been at any time members of the Communist Party or any subversive organization, and if any answer in the affirmative, then on what date they separated themselves, therefrom . . . and then satisfy us that their separation is in fact a truthful separation.

The questions the Jefferson committee posed were the same most other academic investigators were then asking; what was different was that

Jefferson had instituted the inquiry on its own initiative. None of the three men had, as yet, been called before an outside investigation.[9]

They were cooperative witnesses. Both Pearlman and Rutman, for example, told the Jefferson committee that they had once belonged to the CP, and they explained why they had joined and why they had left the Party. That did not suffice. Both Dean George Bennett and Hays Solis Cohen wanted the professors to name names. This was, Bennett and Solis Cohen insisted, a necessary part of the clearance procedure: "We would like to have evidence that you have broken, other than to say that you have, and the best evidence you can possibly give is to become an informant." None of the three complied, even though they were explicitly warned, "Your refusal to tell us will undoubtedly have an effect upon your career at Jefferson."[10]

Though recorded and later transcribed, these June hearings were informal and ostensibly for the purpose of obtaining information. Not so the second round of hearings. These occurred early in August, after the College's solicitor officially informed the professors that the administration was "unable and unwilling to state, unequivocally, that you are not a 'subversive person.'" They could, however, appeal this finding before the College's newly established Loyalty Committee. Besides Solis Cohen and Bennett, the Loyalty Committee was made up of two more trustees and one professor, a Jewish department chairman. Its sessions were formal, with the witnesses giving sworn testimony and the professors represented by lawyers. Once again, Pearlman and Rutman described their experiences in the Communist Party and once again the College's investigators pressed them for names. Once again they refused.[11]

Rutman's lawyer, knowing that such a question would come up, had taken the precaution of contacting the AAUP. General Secretary Ralph Himstead replied by telegram:

> This Association has never been presented with a case of an individual required by a faculty or administration committee to divulge names of associates who might have been members of the same organizations.

Jefferson's demand for names, unprecedented though it was, essentially offered the three scientists an unattractive variant on the more common demand that politically tainted professors prove themselves not Communists. Other institutions required that proof in the form of a confession; Jefferson required names. As a result, Rutman's statement under oath that he was no longer in the Party was not enough. "May I point out," Jefferson's counsel explained,

> that Dr. Rutman has admitted a status as having existed as recently as February or March 1951. A status once having been established, the burden of proof then shifts to the person who claims a change in that status to prove it, and the only proof which has been offered has been from Dr. Rutman's oath.

As congressional investigators did, Jefferson's claimed that only by naming names would Rutman and the others be able to provide them with "objective evidence" that they were no longer in the CP. The College could then call in the people they named and have them corroborate the professors' testimony. In addition, the Loyalty Committee expected the three men to identify those people on the staff of Jefferson who had been in the Party with them. "As a member of our faculty," Solis Cohen explained at Rutman's hearing, "he has an obligation to disclose that fact." It was an obligation that Rutman refused to fulfill. Pearlman was equally reluctant to identify others, though he did assure the Loyalty Committee that "to the best of my knowledge . . . I know of no members of the Communist Party today at Jefferson."[12]

The Jefferson authorities were not convinced. Several documents that I have been permitted to see from the school's archives indicate considerable dissatisfaction among the trustees and members of the Loyalty Committee with the three men's testimony; in particular, with their failure to repudiate the Party with sufficient ardor. The Jefferson authorities adhered to the common notion that all Communists, as one of them put it, "subscribed to the doctrine of revolution by force." These men, therefore, simply couldn't understand why the three professors, who were clearly as well informed about the Party as they were, were not eager to denounce their former associates. There was only one conclusion to be drawn: "I believe that they are subversive to the extent that they still retain the same views of what can be accomplished by the Communistic [*sic*] Party as those they held during their time of membership."[13]

The College did not at first follow up on the hearings; the professors remained in an uncomfortable state of limbo for the next three months until, on November 9, they were called before the dean and again ordered to name names, this time with the warning that if they did not, HUAC would subpoena them. This was no idle threat, for the school had already made arrangements with the committee to call up the professors if they did not comply with the dean's demand for names. They did not, of course, and a few days later, on November 13, they were again summoned to the dean's office, where Bennett introduced them to a member of HUAC's staff who served each of them with a subpoena, dated November 10, ordering them to appear before the committee on the 17th. Pearlman's lawyer apparently convinced HUAC that his client would not be a useful witness; ultimately, Rutman was the only one of the Jefferson people to appear before the committee. He took the diminished Fifth, denying that he was currently in the Party, but reluctantly invoking his privilege for the period before he took the Pennsylvania loyalty oath.[14]

Again, the College did nothing. It filed no charges, convened no committees. But on Monday, November 30, the three professors were again called into Dean Bennett's office and officially dismissed. For what reasons the dean refused to tell. They were to vacate their offices and laboratories at once; by Friday, the locks had been changed. Throughout the months of hearings and investigations, the College had tried to keep the matter quiet and had warned the professors not to seek publicity. Thus, it was ironic that they were to learn from the following day's papers that Jefferson had dismissed them "in the best interest of the institution." Repeated attempts by the professors and their lawyers to find out the specific reason for their dismissal met no success. They had, they learned unofficially, been cleared by the Loyalty Board, but they never received copies of the board's report. Finally, after weeks of negotiations, the College agreed to a financial settlement giving the men the rest of their salaries for the academic year in return for a promise not to initiate legal action against the school. The settlement also contained the following paragraph:

> I can assure you that the decision of the Board of Trustees to terminate your service as a member of Jefferson's faculty was not based upon a finding that you were a subversive person as that term is defined in the Pennsylvania Loyalty Act.

Jefferson's refusal to give any grounds for its highly public dismissal of three faculty members was such a blatant violation of academic freedom that when the AAUP finally dealt with the case, it didn't even bother to send an investigating committee to Philadelphia.[15]

Because Hodes and the Jefferson people had tenure, they could invoke the protection of the AAUP and their institutions had to go through the motions of a formal investigation. Non-tenured teachers had no such rights, either theoretically or in practice. Junior faculty members could be denied tenure or reappointment without any explanation. This was a standard academic procedure and, under normal circumstances, a more or less acceptable one. The assumption behind it was that the teachers had been found wanting for professional, scholarly reasons and would not, therefore, want their colleagues to discuss their inadequacies in public. Naturally, such a practice makes it difficult, if not impossible, to ascertain whether many of the young left-wing academics who lost their jobs during the 1950s were dismissed because of their political or their intellectual failings. Not every radical is a great scholar; there certainly were instances in which people who were let go for academic reasons tried to make a political case of it—even during the McCarthy period. Yet it would be hard to imagine that at a time when senior people were being sacrificed to the prevalent political hysteria, junior ones were not as well. And it is difficult to believe that of all the untenured teachers who publicly defied a congressional investigating committee, the University of Michigan's Clement Markert was the only one worthy of promotion.

We have already encountered a few men and women whose institutions did not reappoint them or denied them tenure after they had taken the Fifth Amendment before one or another congressional committee. There was Helen Deane Markham, for example. Though the Harvard Corporation had decided not to fire her at the time she refused to cooperate with the Jenner Committee, it instructed the dean of the Medical School, where she was teaching, to inform her that, "in view of the Corporation's finding of misconduct on your part . . . when your present appointment expires on June 30, 1954, you will not be reappointed to any of the faculties of the University." Markham's case was typical. As far as I can tell, with only two exceptions (Markert and Bernhard Stern—and Markert may not have been such an exception since Michigan's president was planning to let him go when his contract ran out) every untenured teacher who refused to cooperate with a congressional investigating committee lost his or her job. There were also quite a few young academics who were denied promotions or reappointments who had not appeared in public. These cases are harder to document, but the evidence, at least in some of these cases, does seem persuasive.[16]

Perhaps the most reliable indicator that a junior faculty member was being dropped for political rather than professional reasons was when the decision to do so was made by the central administration rather than by the department. We have already encountered several such cases involving Fifth Amendment witnesses. At Princeton, the Physics Department had recommended the reappointment of David Bohm, only to be overruled by the faculty's Advisory Committee on Appointments and Advancements. At Pennsylvania, it was the acting president of the University who turned down the Economics Department's recommendation of tenure for Daniel Thorner. Thorner's case is of interest, for Penn's administration had not seemed to pay attention to his invocation of the Fifth during the IPR hearings in the spring of 1952. It was not until the following year, when Thorner was in Bombay on a research grant and his department voted him tenure, that the administration took action against him. Thorner thought about returning to Philadelphia to fight for his job, but decided against it. Had he done so, it is possible that he might have prevailed. His colleagues seemed willing to support him, and Penn's new president might have overruled his less secure predecessor's decision. On the other hand, it is possible that an official faculty investigation might have supported the administration's decision.[17]

This was what happened at the University of Colorado, where President Robert Stearns decided to terminate the contract of Morris Judd, a young philosophy instructor. Judd seems to have been something of a sacrificial lamb; his dismissal, the price the administration may have felt compelled to pay for retaining a more senior professor, the philosopher of science David Hawkins. Not only did Hawkins, who appeared before HUAC late in 1950, have tenure, but he had taken the politically astute stand of talking about himself but not about others. He was thus able to win the support of the University's president as well as that of the faculty senate's Committee on Privilege and Tenure, which gave him a hearing. As a result, the Regents voted 4 to 1 to keep him. But because they were worried that there might be other Hawkinses at Colorado, they hired two former FBI agents to check out the political reliability of the entire faculty. When the investigators questioned Judd, he told them that he was not then a Communist, but refused to answer any other questions about his politics. He gave the same answers to President Stearns. Meanwhile, the Philosophy Department, which considered Judd its most promising instructor, unanimously recommended his promotion to assistant professor. Stearns held up the appointment, and on August 10 the Regents voted 4 to 1 to dismiss the young philosopher at the end of the next academic year. There was no announcement, however, and it was not until November that both Judd and his department learned that he would not be reappointed. When the Philosophy Department, which had not been consulted, demanded an explanation, the administration first cited Judd's "pedestrian teaching" and failure to finish his Ph.D. and only later admitted that "his refusal . . . to answer a specific question regarding former political affiliations" was also involved.[18]

Judd appealed and, with the wholehearted support of his department, was able to persuade the Privilege and Tenure Committee to hear his case. President Stearns refused to tell the committee why he had dismissed Judd; he had, he claimed, no obligation to justify a decision not to reappoint a junior faculty member. Though the committee received considerable evidence not only that Judd had been a radical, but that that had been why he had been let go, it voted 4 to 2 to sustain the dismissal. Because Judd did not have tenure, the majority of the faculty committee claimed that he had to shoulder the entire burden of proving that his dismissal was political, which, since most of the evidence was circumstantial or else consisted of rumors and second-hand reports of conversations, he could not. Two members of the committee dissented. They felt that Judd's status should not deprive him of the ordinary guarantees of academic due process and that there was enough evidence that Judd's politics were involved for the University to be compelled to demonstrate that they were not. Judd probably would have been fired even if he had been tenured, for, like Chandler Davis and Stanley Moore, he opposed the University's imposition of a political test on its employees and, except for denying present membership in the Communist Party, refused to talk about his politics. The fact that he lacked tenure simply made it difficult for him and his supporters to show that his dismissal was a political one.[19]

Judd's dismissal was not the only case in which a controversial junior faculty member seemed to have been sacrificed in order to placate the critics of an equally controversial, but tenured, colleague. Such a case occurred at Yale, which in the 1950s harbored a handful of active and outspoken civil libertarians on the faculty of its law school. None of them were or had ever been Communists, but they were willing to defend Communists. As a result, because they belonged to that tiny group of attorneys who would take on such unpopular clients, they became involved in many of the big political cases of the time. No other law school contained so many controversial teachers and, predictably, because of its prestige Yale attracted more than its share of attention from the right-wing press. *Counterattack,* for example, published a five-part series in November and December 1952 entitled, "Who are the Men who Teach Law at Yale?"[20]

By far the most controversial of these men was Thomas I. Emerson. Like Philip Morrison of Cornell, Emerson's political activities were well known and left-wing; and, like Morrison, he was a constant source of embarrassment to his employers. He took a leading role in Henry Wallace's presidential campaign and was even nominated as the Progressive Party's candidate for governor of Connecticut in 1948. (He withdrew when the Democrats put up Chester Bowles.) He was active in the National Lawyers Guild, the left-wing alternative to the American Bar Association, and was its president in 1950 when HUAC denounced it as the "Legal Bulwark of the Communist Party" and tried to get the Attorney General to list it as a subversive organization. Emerson also assisted in some of the Communist Party's second-string Smith Act trials. Because he was at Yale, these activities received considerable attention. The ubiquitous Louis Budenz told HUAC that Emerson was a Communist; the right-wing radio commentator Fulton Lewis, Jr., devoted two whole broadcasts to his record; and *Counterattack* attacked repeatedly. Ironically, it was Emerson's Yale connection that protected him from even more trouble: Senator Robert Taft was on the Board of Trustees and personally interceded with both HUAC and the Jenner Committee to make sure that they did not question Emerson in public.[21]

Even without the publicity a congressional hearing would have generated, Yale's alumni were upset. The papers of Yale's then president, A. Whitney Griswold, contain several files full of complaints from worried alumni, at least one of them threatening the "probable discontinuance of substantial gifts." A letter from Robert Stevens, the future Secretary of the Army and a McCarthy target himself, is typical. "Distressed," as he put it, by the news that Emerson was about to take on the Smith Act case of the Communist leader, Elizabeth Gurley Flynn, Stevens wrote, "This publicity is so bad for Yale that some kind of action really needs to be taken." He could not believe that the University had been consulted about or had condoned Emerson's action, and he suggested that the University discipline him "on the ground that this activity interferes with his responsibilities to Yale." We must, Stevens insisted, "disabuse the public's mind and the mind of Yale Alumni as to Yale's tolerating this sort of thing."[22]

Yale, however, had little choice but to tolerate Emerson's activities. Not only did he have tenure, but he had never been a Communist. Moreover, he was quite conscientious about his obligations to Yale. He had consulted with the dean before he took on the Flynn case, and he sincerely believed that his extracurricular activities in defense of civil liberties were enriching his own teaching and scholarship. Griswold, though clearly unsympathetic to Emerson's activities, never directly intervened or tried to put pressure on him. On the contrary, he worked hard to deflect the criticism that his controversial subordinate aroused. "I have devoted more time to his defense," Griswold wrote to one of Emerson's colleagues in September 1951, "than to all of the other members of the University faculty together—one entire working day just this past week." And, over the years, Griswold even developed a form letter which he dispatched in response to the predictable complaints about Emerson's activities. "Professor Emerson's political views and activities are his own responsibility and in no way reflect the official attitude or policies of Yale University." As Griswold well knew, and tried to explain to the alumni, Emerson's competence, integrity, and tenure made him essentially untouchable.[23]

This was not the case with Vern Countryman, an equally dedicated civil libertarian who, like Emerson, also represented Communist defendants. One of the nation's leading experts on bankruptcy law, Countryman had come to Yale in 1948 from the University of Washington Law School. He apparently had not endeared himself to certain circles in Seattle when, in 1951, he published a critical study of the Canwell Committee and the University of Washington. The word got back to New Haven that, as one Seattle alumnus explained, Countryman

> is strictly "no good." I don't know this of my own knowledge, but my information comes from people out here of the highest authority and in whose judgment I have complete confidence. Vern Countryman may not be a Communist, but if not, it is simply because he thinks it is safer and more effective to work without taking on the risks and responsibility that are involved if he joins up with the Party . . . . he is just as dangerous if he is out of the Party, and possibly more so than if he was a Party member.

Countryman's colleagues had a higher opinion of the man, and, in the middle of the academic year 1953–54, the Permanent Board of the Law School faculty unanimously voted him tenure and a full professorship. The promotion did not go through. Wesley Sturges, the dean of the Law School, was about to retire and President Griswold held up Countryman's promotion, ostensibly until he could consult with Sturges's successor. When he did, in the fall of 1954, Griswold and the new dean, Harry Shulman, decided to withhold tenure and instead simply reappoint Countryman as an associate professor. Here again, we have no direct evidence that Griswold delayed and finally denied Countryman's promotion for political reasons. Even so, there is no question that the decision, contravening as it did the unanimous recommendation of the Law School's senior faculty, was a highly irregular one.[24]

Because the case was leaked to the *New York Times,* the Yale administration had to defend its position in public. It did so on academic grounds. Yale was not, Dean Shulman explained in the University's official statement on the matter, firing Countryman; it was merely postponing its decision to promote him. This was necessary because the Law School's faculty was so tiny and its standards so high that each permanent appointment "must be zealously guarded as one upon which the whole future of the Law School depends." Though the dean believed Countryman "to have much promise," he did not feel "that the evidence of Countryman's objective scholarship warranted a full professorship at this time." Griswold and Shulman had apparently decided that Countryman's book about Canwell and the University of Washington was too journalistic to count as the kind of serious scholarship necessary for tenure. Whether or not that was an ex post facto rationalization, by describing its decision as the result of an assessment of Countryman's scholarship, the Yale administration did manage to defuse some of the outrage which that decision precipitated.[25]

Many of Countryman's colleagues were upset, but, as Emerson recalls, "we didn't really take very vigorous action in protesting." They wrote letters and sent a delegation to Griswold. But only a handful of people wanted to do more; "the rest," according to Emerson, "wouldn't go beyond the written protest stage." In part, this was because of "the general gentility of a faculty group that doesn't like to get involved in controversy." But it was also because Countryman himself did not want to raise a fuss. As he later explained to an investigating committee from the Association of American Law Schools:

> I have serious doubts as to whether your committee can do anything with this case . . . . Frankly, I don't believe that the reason assigned for denying my promotion—the inadequacy of my legal writing is the real reason. Griswold is not qualified to pass judgment on legal scholarship and Shulman was not the sort of man who would pit his judgment on that issue against the unanimous decision of the Permanent Board. This, however, is merely my opinion based on my appraisal of the men who made the decision. There is no objective evidence to prove that my opinion is right. Because there is no such evidence, I have scrupulously refrained from making any charges on this point.

Though he could have stayed on at Yale, Countryman resigned and went into private practice. He later returned to academic life—as a full professor at Harvard.[26]

Perhaps the most egregiously political denial of tenure took place at the University of Michigan. Egregious because there was absolutely no question about the academic quality of the individual involved—the economist and future Nobel laureate, Lawrence Klein—or about his political purity, for he had cooperated with HUAC in 1954. At the time, Michigan's administration seemed satisfied with his performance and did not press any charges against him. Something of a superstar even then, Klein had come to Ann Arbor in 1949 as a research associate with what he considered to be "a deal that I was to skip all the intermediate positions and go right into Full Professorship." The Economics Department had been eager to promote him for some time before it made its formal recommendation early in 1955. His colleagues knew about Klein's previous association with the Communist Party—an apparently minor episode which consisted of going to a few meetings and teaching a few courses about Keynes at the Party-related adult schools in Boston and Chicago—and had, for that reason, refrained from requesting his promotion the previous year while his HUAC subpoena was still pending. But Klein's cooperation with HUAC as well as his rapid evolution away from Marxism gave his colleagues confidence that, in the words of the department chairman, the future chairman of the Board of Economic Advisors, Gardner Ackley, "he had now attained a maturity, balance and judgment which he had earlier so obviously lacked." Even so the department held several long and serious discussions before it decided to recommend Klein's promotion.[27]

Not all of Klein's colleagues supported that decision. The departmental vote on his tenure was 16 to 2. One of the dissenters, a professor of business administration whose political views were so far to the right that, as Ackley noted, "for him such institutions as Social Security are not only 'humbug' but dangerous to the social fabric," took it upon himself to block the promotion. He prevailed upon the administration to solicit letters from outside economists who might support his opposition to Klein. At the same time, the administration had "misgivings" of its own and reluctantly decided to postpone the promotion. The professor who opposed Klein then escalated the campaign by appealing directly to the Regents, not merely to block Klein's promotion but to fire him as well. The administration, for all its timidity, did not support that proposition, though it did take the precaution of checking Klein out with the local FBI agent. Despite the agent's assurance that the young economist was "OK," the case had caused such an uproar among the Regents that the administration could not assure Klein that it would promote him soon. As a result, Klein, who was at Oxford for the year, became concerned about what he considered "a serious deficiency of academic freedom" at Michigan. His career was not in danger, for there was never any question that he would be able to stay at Michigan and probably even get tenure once the political complexion of the Regents changed. Nevertheless, he decided to resign from the University and stay in England.[28]

Of course, Klein's case was an anomaly. Rarely were people who had cooperated with congressional committees given trouble by their universities. But Michigan's administration, still suffering from the aftereffects of the Davis, Markert, and Nickerson cases, must have felt itself so vulnerable that it did not want to risk another confrontation, no matter what the merits of the scholar involved. Klein recalls the period as one of "a lot of emotional stress and strain," but, except for having to use British instead of American data in his research, his career did not suffer. Ironically, when he returned to American academic life in 1957, he went to the University of Pennsylvania, to the very same Economics Department that had been unable to get tenure for Daniel Thorner only a few years before.[29]

For all its weakness, the University of Michigan administration, to its credit, never tried to hide the political nature of the decision to withhold Klein's promotion. Given Klein's stature, it would have been hard for the Michigan authorities to have argued, as Yale's had, that they had refused to promote Klein on scholarly grounds. And, to that extent, their behavior was unusual. Most administrators, when they dismissed or refused to promote politically undesirable professors, concealed the reasons. Sometimes they went to extraordinary lengths to do so. Perhaps the most extreme example of the extent to which an academic administration was willing to go to disguise the fact that it was dismissing a teacher for political reasons occurred at Columbia University. There, the administration implemented an entirely new program for promoting and dismissing members of its off-the-ladder teaching staff in order to rid the University of its most embarrassing faculty member.

She was Gene Weltfish, an anthropologist who had collaborated with Ruth Benedict in writing *The Races of Mankind*. During her seventeen-year tenure as a lecturer at Columbia, Weltfish had aroused more than her share of controversy. She was an ardent feminist and an outspoken radical who was particularly active in the Congress of American Women, an alleged front group, as well as a host of other similarly tainted organizations. Her public appearances during the early Cold War years generated the usual rash of alumni letters. At first, Columbia's administration defended her; it would not discharge her, the University's vice president explained in response to an unhappy alumnus's complaint about a speech she gave in 1949,

> unless there was something outrageous, illegal or immoral in what she said that revealed her as unfit to teach her subject to the students who attend her classes. It is more to the point to inquire whether Miss Weltfish utilizes her classroom opportunities to advocate communism . . . instead of teaching anthropology which she is assigned to teach. On this we have quite conclusive evidence to the contrary.

Columbia's commitment to academic freedom was, in fact, stronger than that of most universities during the McCarthy era. It was willing to hire an ex-Communist like Sigmund Diamond, whom Harvard had ousted because he would not give names to the FBI, and it retained two of the three Fifth Amendment witnesses on its faculty, even though one of them not only lacked tenure but had defied both the McCarran and Mc-

Carthy committees. Weltfish, who had also taken the Fifth before Mc-
Carran, had, however, done something that even Columbia's relatively
liberal administration felt unable to condone.[30]

On June 5, 1952, at a public meeting in New York, Weltfish reportedly charged the United States with using germ warfare in Korea. Her
remarks reached the press, and Grayson Kirk, Columbia's provost and
acting president, called her in for an accounting. Kirk was not satisfied
with her explanation. In an eleven-page memorandum summarizing "the
Weltfish problem," he listed all of her compromising activities and stated
his grounds for believing "that there can be no reasonable doubt concerning Dr. Weltfish's Communist position . . . . it seems to me unimportant as to whether Dr. Weltfish is or is not technically a member of
the Communist Party." There could be only one conclusion: "The connection between Dr. Weltfish and Columbia University must be severed."
The problem was logistical. Should the University fire her immediately
or wait until her contract ran out? Kirk, a conscientious administrator,
opted for the latter; to dismiss Weltfish right away instead of when her
contract expired at the end of June 1953 "might well cause us to be
charged with an arbitrary act taken for political reasons." Furthermore,
it might upset Weltfish's colleagues in the Anthropology Department and
"many other important individuals in the University community." Kirk
was similarly reluctant to follow the University's regular procedure and
submit the question to the faculty committee that dealt with such cases
"because at least three members of this elected committee are individuals who, in my judgment would take the position that the University
should not be concerned with the outside activities of Dr. Weltfish as
long as there is no evidence that these have influenced her teaching and
research."[31]

Kirk's solution was a clever one. Columbia would disguise Weltfish's
dismissal as a bureaucratic reform, the consequence of establishing "a
new University policy . . . namely, to say that any individual on our
teaching staff should not, under any circumstances, remain for more than
a fixed number of years unless that individual has been put on the regular academic ladder." At its regular meeting in November, Columbia's
Board of Trustees quietly voted to limit the number of annual appointments an off-the-ladder faculty member could receive. According to these
new regulations, Weltfish automatically became ineligible for reappointment. The new policy did allow the president to make exceptions for
especially valuable teachers. But when the dean of the School of General
Studies requested such an exemption for Weltfish, Kirk turned it down.
The University did not make this decision public until the end of March
1953, a few days after *Counterattack* appeared with an article entitled
"When will COLUMBIA UNIVERSITY DO SOMETHING ABOUT
'GERM WARFARE GENE'?" Then, in response to a prearranged question from a friendly reporter, the University issued a press release about
its new policy and its applicability to "Germ Warfare Gene."[32]

There is another aspect of the Weltfish case that is of interest. In his memorandum on Weltfish, Kirk included a five-page list of the supposedly subversive organizations she belonged to, everything from the National Council of American-Soviet Friendship to the short-lived End Jim Crow in Baseball Committee of 1945. Kirk documented these affiliations by citing official letterheads and articles in the *Daily Worker*. The source of this information is a mystery. Though Kirk claimed that he "made a substantial inquiry" into Weltfish's activities, it is hard to believe that either Kirk or his subordinates spent years systematically collecting left-wing literature and clipping items from the Party press. There were, however, other organizations which did monitor the activities of people like Gene Weltfish; it seems probable that Kirk had gotten his information from them, most likely from the FBI. Here we tread upon slippery ground. We know that the Bureau was involved in the academy's purge of its political undesirables, but we do not know exactly how. The FBI operated in secret. When it fed information to outsiders, it usually demanded that the source of that information be concealed. Yet, from what the Freedom of Information Act (FOIA) has revealed in other, similar situations, it would not have been unusual for the FBI to have volunteered or Kirk to have requested information about Weltfish's activities. There would be no record of such a request or offer. The FBI would more than likely have sent over a photostated copy of Weltfish's file as what it called a "blind memorandum," a document specifically designed to conceal its origins.[33]

During the 1950s, most liberals, academics included, believed that the FBI was above politics. Congress was the villain—sloppily partisan, hungry for headlines, and as eager to persecute innocent liberals as guilty reds. The FBI, on the other hand, was a competent, professional outfit, which could be trusted to handle the Communist problem in a careful and prudent way. This was untrue. The Bureau's ideology was as ferociously reactionary as that of any red-baiting politico, and its agenda was the same as HUAC's. During the McCarthy years it actively intervened to ensure that the people it considered politically unreliable would lose their jobs. But it did so clandestinely. It insisted that it never let outsiders see information from its files, even as it was regularly leaking dossiers to right-wing congressmen and friendly journalists. These people then publicized the damaging material or passed it along to the employers of suspected subversives without, of course, ever letting on that it had come from the Feds. The academy received its share of such items. In addition to the material on Weltfish, Grayson Kirk's papers contain a letter from the columnist George Sokolsky, one of the Bureau's regular conduits, listing all the compromising affiliations of another Columbia professor, a few days after that professor had appeared before Senator McCarthy. There is, of course, no indication that this material came from the FBI, but in form, content, and method of delivery it bears all the trappings.[34]

The professor in question kept his job. (Columbia was tolerant of most ex-Communists, and the man did have tenure.) Often, however, the subjects of such damaging missives were dismissed, especially if they lacked tenure. The evidence here is spotty; most of it comes from the teachers themselves. Hard data would be preferable, but the FBI purposely left few traces. We do know that in February 1951 the Bureau inaugurated its "Responsibilities Program," which authorized "the dissemination of information to appropriate authorities on a strictly confidential basis concerning Communist or subversive elements in public utilities or public or semi-public organizations." Academic administrators were among those "appropriate authorities." Such information was usually transmitted orally, but occasional documents would get through, "photostated," as one FBI report noted, "in such a manner as to conceal any markings that could possibly identify them with the Bureau." In addition, the FBI would try to compile these files from public sources, like HUAC or the press, as a way of concealing their provenance. University administrators, if they knew, respected the Bureau's desire for secrecy; when they acted upon the information they received, they rarely acknowledged its source. Thus, it becomes doubly difficult to document the FBI's role in purging the academic world of its "Communist or subversive elements." Yet, investigate it we must, for it has become increasingly clear that in one way or another the FBI had a hand in many of the cases with which we are concerned.[35]

The experiences of Norman Cazden are suggestive. Cazden, a musicologist, composer, and pianist, was an assistant professor of music at the University of Illinois. His background and publications made him a strong candidate for tenure. Instead, early in the spring of 1953, he was informed that he would be dismissed at the end of his contract in June. Cazden went to see the president and was shown a typewritten document which, the president claimed, had one day just appeared on his desk. According to the document, an unidentified source "reliably reported that . . . Cazden was a member of the Cambridge, Massachusetts, branch of the Communist Political Association." The document then went on to list some thirteen other associations which, it said, HUAC's files had turned up on Cazden. Since Cazden was in no position to deny the allegations in the unsigned memorandum—most of which were true—he packed up his family and left Urbana at the end of the academic year. He was subpoenaed by HUAC, but not until the following year, when along with a number of former friends and colleagues from the University of Michigan, where he had taught before coming to Illinois, he was called to Washington. He took the Fifth.[36]

What happened to Cazden at Illinois happened to other junior faculty members at other schools—though none of the others received copies of the incriminating dossiers. Instead, they were simply let go without any explanation. Saul Maloff, for example, had been such a successful English teacher at the University of Indiana's Gary Center that he had been slated for a promotion. Instead, the dean called him in and asked him to resign. When Maloff asked why he was being fired, the dean replied, "I am under no obligation to tell you." Nor was the administration any more forthcoming when the AAUP tried to get an explanation. Maloff, who had once been in the CP, suspected that politics were involved, a suspicion that the well-meaning attempt of his own department chairman to get Maloff "to be cooperative" only encouraged. But rather than raise a fuss, which he believed would completely destroy all chances for his academic future, Maloff submitted his resignation and left Gary.[37]

Robert Bedell's experiences were similar. Though he had never been in the CP, he was quite radical and had the kinds of associations that automatically attracted the attention of the FBI. An engineer, he had been teaching at the Cooper Union in New York for two years when, in the spring of 1955, some FBI agents came to his house to question him about his "friends in the international communist conspiracy." Bedell refused to talk with the agents without a lawyer present, and the Bureau did not persist. It did, however, make inquiries about him at Cooper Union, inquiries which might, Bedell's chairman intimated sometime later, affect his career. Bedell's work was "excellent," but his promotion would not go through until he "cleared up" this matter. Bedell had no intention of talking to the FBI; in April of the following year he was told that he would be dropped at the end of the next academic year. The reasons given kept changing. First he was told that Cooper Union had decided that it would no longer grant tenure to people who, like Bedell, did not have doctorates. Then, a few weeks later, his chairman explained that it had been decided "to limit the number of staff people placed in tenure positions." Bedell, who had been assured that he would get tenure once he finished his master's degree, tried to fight what he considered to be a politically motivated dismissal, but to no avail. Even the AAUP refused to help. He did not have tenure.[38]

Had Bedell been more willing to cooperate with the FBI, he might have kept his job. His case was not unique; nor was Cooper Union the only academic institution which seems to have made the giving of information to the Bureau a prerequisite for employment. Harvard also expected its employees to clear themselves with the FBI. In Harvard's case, this was a prophylactic measure; the administration required former radicals to purge themselves before it put their appointments through. Making prospective teachers cooperate with the FBI to the extent of naming names seems to conflict with the University's expressed policy of defending those of its employees who, like Wendell Furry and Leon Kamin, had defied congressional committees rather than become informers. But then, the Harvard authorities would have been happier if the recalcitrant witnesses had been more cooperative, since people who named names usually did not have to do so in public. At a time when McCarthy had singled out Harvard for special attention, the advantages of pre-screening staff members to ensure that they would not embarrass the University as

Furry and Kamin had were obvious. Other schools may have imposed similar requirements; the secrecy that surrounds such policies makes it hard to find out. We know about Harvard's only because Sigmund Diamond, one of its beneficiaries, broke that secrecy in a 1977 article in the *New York Review of Books*.[39]

In a peculiar way, Harvard's policy was more generous than that of other institutions. At least it offered people a chance to clear themselves instead of simply refusing to hire them. This may have been a result of Harvard's inbreeding; it was harder to blacklist potential faculty members if they were already in the University. There were about six of these people—one an assistant professor at the Business School, the others graduate students. All had been radicals of one sort or another; most, in fact, had been Communists. How Harvard identified them is unclear. The administration must have known some of them from their undergraduate careers as political activists; the FBI may have supplied other names.

Harvard's requirements were the same as HUAC's: "full disclosure." Ex-Communists had to produce names, and non-Communists had to prove that they had never been in the Party. The University was not taking any chances, and it seems to have screened anybody whom a committee might call up. Thus, for example, the administration investigated the historian of science Everett Mendelsohn because as a radical undergraduate at Antioch he had been so active in the Wallace campaign and the peace movement that his dossier, like Robert Bedell's, made him appear to be a Party member even though he was not. In the spring of 1954 Harvard's dean McGeorge Bundy called Mendelsohn, then just finishing his first year of graduate school, into his office. Bundy claimed he had information that Mendelsohn was a Communist and he wanted an explanation. Harvard was worried, Bundy explained, about what Mendelsohn might do if he was called before an investigating committee, and he wanted to make sure that Mendelsohn would be able to clear himself before Bundy would approve his appointment as a teaching fellow for the coming year. Mendelsohn recalls that he repeatedly tried to get Bundy to tell him the source of his information:

> I was quite willing to talk with him about what I believed and was quite open, didn't try to hide a thing. I told him what I had and hadn't done as an undergraduate at Antioch College, but still he wouldn't be open and candid with me.

Mendelsohn was upset and told Bundy that he was going to consult a lawyer—which he did. It was an unnecessary precaution, for Bundy accepted Mendelsohn's explanations and did not bother him again.[40]

Things were not quite as simple for those candidates who had been in the CP. They had to deal with the FBI as well as the dean. One of them, the historian Sydney James, had passed through the Party while an undergraduate at Harvard in the late 1940s. Sometime during the fall of 1953 he was approached by the FBI. He put the agents off at first, but his wife, who had just had a baby, persuaded him to cooperate. James was reluctant. He agreed to comment on the "accuracy or inaccuracy" of the FBI's information; he would corroborate the Bureau's facts, but would not volunteer anything on his own. Like many informants, James came to feel that his contributions were unnecessary; the FBI seemed to know more about his activities on the Harvard left than he himself could remember. In addition, cooperating with the FBI was no fun. The Bureau seemed insatiable and the agents with whom he talked "would materialize now and then to pop more questions." Moreover, once James told his former comrades what he had done, they broke with him.[41]

Then, in the spring of 1954, the dean called him in. James had not, he recalls Bundy's telling him, been sufficiently candid with the FBI. Unless he told everything he knew, "no job as teaching fellow; no possibility of academic employment—ever." Whether Bundy couched this as a threat or simply as a piece of realistic advice is immaterial. James got the message. At Bundy's suggestion, James consulted with a number of senior professors, a few sympathetic, most hostile. His original compromise with the FBI deprived him of the support of the civil libertarians on the faculty; his Communist past and refusal to volunteer information on his own displeased the others. Just about all of them recommended that he comply with Bundy's request. With only one exception, James felt, they had "put the welfare of Harvard ahead of mine." Finally, in a state of "emotional paralysis," terrified that he would lose whatever opportunity he had for an academic career, James went back to the FBI. Not until a few months later, when he was doing research for his dissertation in Philadelphia, did James learn from a sympathetic ACLU lawyer that he did not have to give the FBI anything but the kind of information that would stand up in court. A reluctant informer to begin with, once he learned something about his own rights vis-à-vis the Bureau, he began to hold back more. Finally, when the FBI asked him to serve as a prosecution witness at the contempt trial of Chandler Davis, he refused. The agent threatened him with a subpoena, but none materialized. Though James believes that the FBI kept tabs on him until the late 1960s, he never encountered any other trouble.[42]

Sigmund Diamond had a similar experience. He had joined the CP while a student at Johns Hopkins just before the Second World War and had drifted out in the early fifties after he entered graduate school at Harvard. He was a highly successful graduate student, and after a year of postdoctoral research and administrative work, Bundy offered him a combined teaching and administrative position. Because a former member of his Party unit from Baltimore had told him that in about 1953 he had given his name to the FBI, Diamond knew that his past was no secret to the authorities. Yet it was not until April 1954, just as his new Harvard appointment was about to go through, that he received a visit from the Bureau. "I have nothing to say to you, gentlemen," the FBI recorded Diamond as telling the agents who showed up in his office. A few days later, Bundy called Diamond to his office and asked him if he would discuss his past with the "civil authorities." Diamond agreed, but explained that he would not name names. Bundy pressed him and, as he had with Sydney James, suggested that Diamond discuss the matter with other members of the faculty. Diamond's consultations resulted in a compromise: he would tell the FBI about himself, but not about others. He talked with the Bureau twice. His own FBI files describe the encounters:

> The Bureau and other offices will note that DIAMOND'S primary reason for visiting the Boston Office was to provide a partial account of his own activities within the Party over a seven year period without divulging the identity of any Communist Party members. It is apparent that he undertook this device in order to salvage his position at Harvard University which according to his own statement had been denied him after having first been proferred to him. DIAMOND evidently was under the impression that Dean MCGEORGE BUNDY would have recommended renewal of DIAMOND'S Corporation appointment had DIAMOND provided information to the Federal Bureau of Investigation or other Governmental Agencies conducting security investigations.
>
> From information provided the Boston Division by other individuals having Harvard Corporation appointments, it appears that Dean BUNDY is insisting that former Communist Party members, who now have Harvard Corporation appointments shall provide the Federal Bureau of Investigation with a full and complete account of their activities in the Communist Party and shall at the same time identify all individuals known to them as participants in activities of the Communist Party and its related front organizations.[43]

Since Diamond would not name names, Bundy would not appoint him. In later years Bundy has defended his decision on the ground that Diamond's job was an administrative one and thus did not have "all the immunities of academic freedom." But it is clear that the same was required from people with strictly academic positions as well. Bundy was, however, willing to make an exception if the candidate was of such "unusually high quality" that refusing to appoint him would "have an unhappy effect on the morale and temper of" the department that wanted to hire him. This is what happened in the case of sociologist Robert Bellah. Like his former roommate Sydney James, Bellah had been in the Party as a Harvard undergraduate but had become disillusioned and quit sometime in 1949. Five years later, in the summer of 1954, Bundy called him in and threatened to cancel his graduate fellowship if he did not fulfill his obligation of "complete candor." Within a week the FBI showed up. Like Diamond, Bellah was willing to talk about himself but not others. Despite his refusal to name names, Bellah did not lose his fellowship, for it was not under the central administration's jurisdiction.[44]

The following year, Bundy again summoned Bellah to his office. The Social Relations Department wanted to offer the young sociologist an in-

structorship, but, Bundy warned, the Harvard Corporation would not renew it if at any point during his tenure Bellah refused to cooperate with
the civil authorities in any way. Once again, Bundy urged Bellah to name
names, but after questioning him at length—about, in Bundy's words,
"his Communist past and his present beliefs and attitudes"—he became
convinced that Bellah was reliable enough to warrant the risk of an appointment. Bundy also discussed Bellah's problems with Talcott Parsons,
the chairman of the Social Relations Department, and asked him to have
the department reconsider the matter. It did, and unanimously voted to
resubmit Bellah's nomination. Before sending the recommendation to the
Corporation, Bundy took an unusual precaution. Believing, as many people did in those days, that membership in the Communist Party was a
symptom of psychological distress and concerned because Bellah had admitted that he had once been in psychotherapy, Bundy actually had one
of the University's psychiatrists check on Bellah's "current state of mind."
It was, Bellah recalls, a "bizarre" interview, but it apparently convinced
Bundy that, as he explained to President Pusey in his official letter recommending Bellah's appointment,

> Mr. Bellah has the stuff to keep his balance and proportion and give a
> creditable account of himself as instructor, while at the same time doing
> well as a witness if that should come his way. . . . A negative judgment
> here would come very near to a judgment that no ex-Communist need
> apply unless he is prepared to answer all the questions anyone asks him
> about other Communists he has known. I should strongly deprecate such a
> position.[45]

It was the Harvard Corporation that scotched the deal. It approved
Bellah's appointment, but (here I quote from a memorandum written by
Talcott Parsons about the case)

> instructed Dean Bundy to inform him that, if during the term of his ap-
> pointment, Mr. Bellah should be called before any legally authorized in-
> vestigating body and should decline to answer *any* questions put to him
> by members of such a body concerning his Communist past, the Corpora-
> tion "would not look with favor on the renewal of his appointment" after
> the expiration of his term.

Though Parsons and apparently Bundy were willing to press the Corporation to reconsider, Bellah declined this less than perfect offer. He did
not want to be put into a position in which he might end up totally unemployable if he did not name names. Two years later, after the McCarthyist frenzy had abated, he was again put up for an appointment at
Harvard, and this time it went through without a hitch.[46]
    Like so many of the people who became enmeshed in the academic
freedom cases of the McCarthy period, Bellah, Diamond, and Sydney
James suffered for their past, not their present activities; like so many of
the other hidden victims of this period, they were fired or threatened
with dismissal, not because of something that they had done but because

of something that they *might* do. Rather than run the risk of the adverse publicity that these people might create if they were subpoenaed and refused to name names, Harvard and many other schools as well simply got rid of those members of their faculties who might become unfriendly witnesses. Naturally, they also got rid of their few current activists as well. Significantly, the academic authorities who carried out these purges did so as quietly as they could. And when they could not conceal what they were doing, they tried to disguise its political nature.

These deceptions are crucial. At major universities like Columbia, Tulane, Yale, or the University of Colorado, administrators either refused to explain why they were firing controversial faculty members or else claimed that they were doing so for bureaucratic reasons or because the teachers had difficult personalities. That so many respected educators should resort to such furtive behavior—at the same time, we should recall, as they were imposing an obligation of candor upon the rest of the academic community—suggests how seriously the nation's colleges and universities had been compromised by their collaboration with McCarthyism.

X

"A Very Difficult Time of It": The Academic Blacklist in Operation

In the spring of 1954, Helen Deane Markham began to look for a job. Her appointment as an assistant professor of anatomy at the Harvard Medical School was about to expire. It would not have been renewed even had she been willing to cooperate with the Jenner Committee the previous year: Harvard had an eleven-year limit for its non-tenured people, and Markham, as a woman with an academic degree instead of a medical degree, knew her chances for tenure were slight. Her run-in with the Jenner Committee scotched them completely and, as it turned out, made it hard for her to find a new position. She wrote to dozens of colleagues in her field, describing her situation and asking for help. "I feel quite sure," one man wrote her, "that you will have no difficulty in finding the type of thing that you want." Her other correspondents were more pessimistic. "Your situation is truly a difficult one," one of them explained, "made more difficult by what I judge to be a general lack of openings in departments of anatomy." These people were sympathetic, but cautious. They had, they claimed, no openings, but, "even if there were," one man confided, "it is doubtful if I could get you past the watchful and conservative administration we have." Markham persisted, though she soon came to realize, "I may not succeed, in the immediate future, in getting another teaching position."[1]

Markham's difficulties were not exceptional. Almost every academic who lost a job as a result of a congressional investigation had trouble finding a new one. A blacklist was in place, a blacklist at least as comprehensive and far less well known than the one in the entertainment industry. It operated to deny academic employment to almost every teacher who refused to cooperate with an anti-Communist investigation and to an unknown number of other controversial individuals as well. It lasted for years, beginning for some people in the late 1940s and continuing for others throughout the fifties and often into the sixties. Few of the teachers who were identified in public escaped, and even those who did drifted to the margins of academe. For whatever else happened, during the height of McCarthyism, in the middle and late fifties, no academic who was dismissed as the result of a public refusal to cooperate with an investigating committee was able to find a regular teaching position at an academically respectable American college or university.

Documenting the operation of this blacklist is a challenge. Even in ordinary times the process of academic hiring is surrounded by an extraordinary amount of secrecy. During the McCarthy years that secrecy operated to conceal the existence of the blacklist. The people who administered it insisted that it did not exist. The people who suffered from it assumed that it did, but only rarely could they document their suspicions. Moreover, they, too, tried to disguise the nature of their affliction, for outside of the left the stigmata of McCarthyism were a source of shame and hardly conducive to employment. As a result, evidence about the academic blacklist is sketchy. Some comes from the personal testimony of the blacklisted teachers; some from the archives of the schools that blacklisted them. If nothing else, the very fact that most of the people who lost their teaching jobs for political reasons during the McCarthy period could not find new ones does seem to establish a pattern of blacklisting. The few cases for which I have been able to find archival documentation confirm suspicions. These cases probably represent a tiny proportion of such incidents and the schools where they occurred should not, therefore, be viewed as being any more discriminatory than any others—just more willing to let scholars into their archives.

As far as I know, there was no official list, no academic equivalent to the entertainment industry's *Red Channels*, with its elaborate compilations of the compromising affiliations of 151 show business people. The academic community had to make do with other sources of information. There was, for example, the Jenner Committee's July 1953 report, "Subversive Influence in the Educational Process," which listed the roughly fifty professors and former professors who had refused to cooperate with the committee during 1952 and 1953. This was a useful guide and one widely distributed. But it was far from complete; it listed only the uncooperative witnesses that one congressional committee turned up in a year and a half. There was also the series of reports on "Red-ucators" in American schools that Allen Zoll, one of the more disreputable of the professional anti-Communists, put out. Despite Zoll's notoriety (he had been a fascist before World War II) and the inaccuracy of his charges, at least one major university consulted his oeuvre. Actually, the academic community had little need for formal lists, for it had its own traditional methods of ensuring that political undesirables did not get teaching jobs. As the nation's educational leaders liked to point out, these traditional methods were quite effective. No congressional committee had, after all, unearthed any verifiable subversives at the colleges.[2]

Customary hiring practices generally sufficed. At most colleges and universities, the faculty could be counted upon to keep potential troublemakers off campus. The process of winnowing out controversial teachers usually took place at the departmental level, where the chairman and senior professors have always screened candidates before recommending them to the administration. Obviously, it was not in a department's interest to present candidates the higher authorities would reject. Prospective teachers who might create a political problem were simply not considered; they were not treated as serious applicants. One man recalls, for example, his efforts in the early fifties to have the History Department at a major Ivy League university consider hiring M. I. Finley. Even though there was an opening in Finley's field, no one would look at Finley's file. "Why ask for trouble?" was the general response; as a result, Finley's name was not submitted to the executive committee of the department, though he was even then perhaps the outstanding ancient historian of his generation.[3]

Practices differed, depending upon the degree of political independence a particular institution could muster. Public colleges and universities were, understandably, especially reluctant to hire controversial teachers. Schools or departments which had already had trouble seemed particularly vulnerable; they tended to screen out all but the safest candidates. The University of Washington's English Department was one of the more tainted. Of the ten Washington professors called before the state of Washington's Canwell Committee in 1948, six had come from the English Department. As if that wasn't bad enough, controversy continued to surround the department throughout the early fifties. The appointment of the literary critic Malcolm Cowley to a temporary lectureship at the beginning of 1950 drew additional criticism, especially after Cowley, who had been a prominent non-Communist in the Popular Front, appeared as a character witness for Alger Hiss. Things got even stickier when, in 1952, the department tried to give the same temporary position to Kenneth Burke, another literary critic and former Popular Fronter. Though Burke, and the English Department, assured the University's administration that despite his past associations Burke was neither a Communist nor a sympathizer, Washington's new president Henry Schmitz decided to rescind the offer. There was too much concern among "certain influential friends of the University."[4]

The English Department recognized its vulnerability and sought to offset it. As the department's chairman explained to President Schmitz during the height of the Burke controversy, "our department is looked upon as an especial center of 'radical' appointments, a suspicion which I do not think is justified but which nevertheless we are uncomfortably aware of and would like to change." As a result, the department consciously decided not to appoint people whose "past might be unfavorably scrutinized . . . because they *had once had* leftist interests." It filled a recent vacancy by passing over the top four candidates and choosing instead someone who was "entirely safe in these terms." The chairman was not happy with the situation:

The thing I don't like about this is that because of the fear of repercussions we did not attempt to appoint the men that we thought would be strongest. On the other hand, I hope that this decision will help convince any interested parties that we do not appoint people because they are leftist in point of view and that we are making a positive effort to avoid the difficulties which may arise in connection with such appointments.[5]

Despite the English Department's precautions, the University's Regents were worried. They wanted stronger guarantees. President Schmitz responded by setting up a special faculty committee, chaired by the dean, to devise a policy "relative to the appointment of persons whose political backgrounds raise questions as to the appropriateness of University sponsorship." The committee's report, issued in the spring of 1953, stressed the importance of thoroughly investigating the political background of every prospective faculty member. Washington's precautions seem exceptional. Few other schools went quite so far in codifying their procedures for excluding political undesirables. But, then, few other schools were under quite so much pressure. Ultimately, Washington's administrators and trustees went too far. In 1954 President Schmitz cancelled a scheduled series of lectures by J. Robert Oppenheimer after he lost his security clearance, thereby precipitating a nationwide boycott of the school. But at Washington and elsewhere, as long as the blacklist did not get out of control and bar liberals or other innocent but controversial types, most academics seemed willing to administer it.[6]

Perhaps the strongest evidence for the role of faculty members in supervising the blacklist comes from the testimony of the men and women who were affected by it. These people found that the departments to which they wrote for jobs rarely bothered to acknowledge their letters. Even people who had good connections and excellent reputations within their fields got nowhere. Lyman Bradley, an early Cold War casualty, had been the treasurer of the Modern Language Association for twenty years and knew, he recalled, "practically every college teacher in the modern languages." Even so, he discovered, after his defiance of HUAC cost him his tenured position as the chairman of the NYU German Department in 1951, that his network had disintegrated. "While a few colleagues in the field were friendly, they said that they could not buck their administrations. Most colleagues fled and [those] who had been bosom friends vanished." People who lacked Bradley's personal contacts received even less attention. Herbert Phillips recalled that after the University of Washington fired him in 1949 he sent out a three-page inquiry to "most of the American colleges and universities listed in Lovejoy's guide." Only 10 percent of the schools even acknowledged his letter. And of that number, only fifteen expressed any interest. The only offer he got was for a week-long stint at the College of the Pacific's summer institute at Lake Tahoe to defend his political views against Sidney Hook. His colleague Joseph Butterworth had even less luck with a form letter he sent to every member of the Modern Language Association.[7]

Daniel Thorner, the economist denied tenure by the University of Pennsylvania after he took the Fifth before the McCarran Committee, had similar difficulties. In 1957, after several years in India, Thorner tried to get an academic job in the United States. He sent letters to every school that had the library facilities to support someone in his field of Indian economic history. He received one reply. William Pearlman, the most distinguished scientist among the three men fired by the Jefferson Medical College, received but a few more replies to the letter of inquiry that he sent to most of the biochemistry departments in America. None of the replies he received, however, referred to his case, even though it was widely known throughout the field. "We don't have an opening," was the standard response, one that Pearlman knew had little validity for that small and rapidly growing field.[8]

This was the same excuse Helen Deane Markham's correspondents tended to give, though, as we have seen, they did recognize that Markham's troubles with the Jenner Committee and the Harvard Corporation were the real problem. Whole categories of schools were out of bounds. "I suspect," one of her colleagues warned Markham, "that you will find public institutions closed to you and this of course very seriously limits the field." These limitations existed in every discipline. Some of the blacklisted teachers didn't even bother to apply to public colleges and universities. Leonard Marsak, the history instructor and Fifth Amendment witness whose contract Reed College failed to renew, was specifically told that he was unemployable at state universities. Other people figured it out on their own. Few of these men and women had any illusions about any type of school. "One sent letters," a former Queens College professor explained, "but one knew one would not be hired."[9]

Some of these people faced a dilemma. There was the possibility that if they did not discuss their past troubles when they applied for a job, they might be able to find one. Concealing one's past, however, had risks of its own; if an employer found out independently that the teacher had been in political trouble, he could cite that teacher's initial lack of candor as a reason to fire him. Protagonists in highly publicized cases, like the University of Washington's Herbert Phillips, probably couldn't have hidden their past problems even if they had wanted to. But Phillips, who had never concealed his Marxist views from his students, was not about to do so after he lost his job because of them. In the hundreds of job-seeking letters he sent out, he described both his case and his political philosophy. Chandler Davis, who like Phillips had not only been fired but was facing a possible jail sentence for contempt, was similarly frank about his problems. In 1958 he made inquiries to almost 150 mathematics departments. He got a few nibbles. One school actually made him a written offer, but just as he was about to accept it, he told his prospective employers what he assumed they already knew: his case was still in the courts. The job fell through. For a while he did market research for an advertising company, but here he was very careful not to mention his case. He also got a few part-time teaching jobs, a fellowship at the Institute for Advanced Studies in Princeton, and an editorial position with a mathematical journal—all this, it must be noted, during the post-*Sputnik* years of the late fifties when the higher educational system was desperate for mathematicians.[10]

People whose problems were less public had more success in finding jobs, as long as they did not discuss their cases. Once they did, however, the jobs often disappeared. Leonard Marsak recalls "14 academic positions which had first been offered to me, and then denied when I made known my prior 'Reed experience.'" Another man, who as a graduate student at the University of Minnesota had been incorrectly, but publicly, identified as a Communist and had had to clear himself before a special faculty committee, agonized over the issue of telling potential employers about his case. One of his teachers told him not to mention it. He took the advice and got a job. Tom McGrath, a poet who lost his position at Los Angeles State College after a brush with HUAC, was also able to get an academic post by concealing his political past. But when a former colleague revealed it in a belated letter of recommendation McGrath, himself, had solicited, his new employer dismissed him at once.[11]

McGrath's experience illustrates the crucial role of letters of recommendation in the maintenance of the academic blacklist. Since the system of academic hiring depended almost entirely on personal recommendations, it was hard for a politically tainted applicant to avoid having his prospective employer find out about his problems. His former teachers and colleagues would have mentioned his political disqualifications even if the candidate himself did not. Many schools specifically requested such information. "During the past year," one of Helen Deane Markham's colleagues told her, "I have had the privilege of recommending a number of scientists for positions in educational institutions and in industry. Almost invariably I received a letter from the personnel division inquiring as to whether the applicant is in any sense a controversial figure."[12]

Even without being asked, it seems, most professors described the political background of the people they recommended. They were well aware of the impact of such information on the individual's career, but they apparently felt that they had a professional responsibility to alert their colleagues at other institutions to the potential political liabilities an applicant might present. After all, that was why the academic profession relied so heavily on personal recommendations. Gardner Ackley, the chairman of the University of Michigan's Economics Department, was quite candid about the political function of these letters. Two graduate students from his department had been called before the same HUAC session as Davis, Markert, and Nickerson. They had defied the committee, and Michigan wanted to punish them in some way. Ackley argued against expelling them. They had satisfied all the University's academic requirements and, he insisted, unless they had broken some other University rule, there were no legitimate grounds for disqualifying them. Nonetheless, Ackley continued:

> We freely confess that individually we could not, and will not recommend either of these men for teaching or research positions. It has been urged that if we cannot recommend them, we should not grant the degree. But there is a great difference between a private letter of recommendation, giving a personal evaluation, and the formal, legal act of recording course grades and granting degrees. If this were not so, hiring officers would not ask for our letters. . . . In our hiring, in our personal and private associations of every kind, we may consider impressions of character, political beliefs, perhaps even religious views.[13]

The professors who discussed the political background of their former students or colleagues in letters of recommendation certainly knew what the effect of that information would be. Though we can understand why a responsible academic might feel obliged to warn his colleagues, there were times—especially in the late forties, before McCarthyism had become entrenched—when it seemed as if these letters were, if not malicious in intent, at least gratuitously damaging. The letter of recommendation from the acting chairman of the Berkeley Philosophy Department characterizing Stanley Moore as a "fanatical Marxist in theory and practice" sufficed to torpedo a job offer from Brooklyn College in 1947. Saul Maloff recalls that a similarly defamatory letter from his thesis adviser aborted several promising positions in 1949. The Temple University administration's practice of sending copies of the trustee's statement about Barrows Dunham to schools which were considering him was equally devastating and particularly reprehensible, for the statement itself was misleading. In it the trustees claimed that they had fired Dunham because of his unconstitutional use of the Fifth Amendment. To circulate that statement *after* the federal judiciary had upheld Dunham's use of the Fifth, as the Temple administration did, seems like a rather vindictive act.[14]

Sometimes, however, there were legitimate professional reasons for discussing the political activities of a particular candidate. This was especially true for scientists who might require a security clearance for certain jobs. In such cases these revelations were not always fatal. In an otherwise positive letter of recommendation for one of his students, a physicist at the University of Chicago noted "that in his younger days he was a member of a student organization which became suspect, and that due to this he would find difficulty in obtaining official clearance for highly secretive information." Since the job, at a small state-supported technical school, did not involve classified research, the student was hired anyhow.[15]

      ❊   ❊   ❊

Not every appointment was aborted at the departmental level. Even the most notorious of the blacklisted academics occasionally managed to slip through the first screening. Either the people who wanted to hire them didn't know about their political disqualifications or they were willing to make a case for hiring them in spite of these. Not, however, that these people got the jobs their prospective colleagues wanted to give them. In almost every instance, these applicants were to find that the positions which had been offered them at the departmental level disappeared when the appointment reached the administration. Chandler Davis recalls that in 1958 his 150 inquiries turned up "four departments, with openings I would have been most interested in, which tried to get their administrations to tolerate my presence but failed." The Philosophy Department at Louisiana State knew about Barrows Dunham's case, but recommended him for a temporary appointment anyhow. The administration overruled it. "We have been under the eye of anti-communists on account of one or two episodes they considered disloyal," the department chairman told Dunham. "And the consequence is that the administration wants to take no risks of recurrence."[16]

Frank Oppenheimer was another blacklisted academic whose prospective appointments met with administrative vetoes. At the time he lost his job at the University of Minnesota in 1949, his department was on the verge of giving him tenure. Colleagues elsewhere, who considered him an excellent experimental physicist, were eager to find a place for him. "Repeatedly," Oppenheimer recalled, "university appointments were considered and went through department and administrative channels but were finally rejected." The Physics Department at MIT was interested in him; so too were the departments at Chicago, Cornell, and the University of Washington. Physicists at Cornell's Laboratory of Nuclear Studies tried to hire Oppenheimer in the fall of 1949. Cornell's acting president, Cornelius de Kiewiet, met with some members of the Laboratory's staff to try to talk them out of the appointment. Then de Kiewiet presented the matter to a group of deans. Some sympathized with Oppenheimer, but others "wondered if a thorough investigation of all possible applicants had been made and expressed opposition to assuming unnecessary additional burdens in public relations." The appointment did not go through.[17]

Nor, several years later, was Cornell ready to assume the burden of M. I. Finley. The man who taught ancient history at Cornell was due to retire in June 1958. The three-man committee which the History Department had authorized to find a replacement made, it explained, "an exhaustive canvass of American, British, and European scholars under the age of fifty in the field of Ancient History." It came up with a list of candidates but stressed that "the only man on this list of clearly outstanding achievement and promise was Dr. Moses I. Finley." However, because of Finley's past, the department's chairman decided to consult with President Malott about the appointment. Malott indicated his displeasure; taking the Fifth, as Finley had, was "a serious moral and civic error," and he would be "most reluctant" to forward Finley's name to the trustees. The department persisted; it decided to mollify Malott by proposing to give Finley only a one-year visiting professorship so that it wouldn't have to commit Cornell to tenuring him until he had been around for a while. It also wrote to Rutgers to get more information about Finley. Out of deference to the persistence of the History Department, Malott made his own investigation and sent a personal representative to New Brunswick. The representative returned bearing secret and presumably damaging information, on the basis of which Malott again rejected the appointment. As the then-chairman recalls, Malott had just emerged from major battles over Philip Morrison and Marcus Singer and probably did not want another confrontation with the trustees.[18]

This time, the History Department appealed Malott's decision to the faculty's Committee on Academic Freedom and Tenure, a committee created, it should be noted, after the faculty found out about the trustees' secret hearing on Morrison. The committee took its task seriously and mounted a full-scale investigation. Malott was cooperative; he told the committee "emphatically . . . that he does not have and will not have a blacklist of professors who pleaded the Fifth Amendment." Even so, he did have an obligation to assess the qualifications of prospective faculty members who had taken the Fifth. And to convince the faculty committee of the soundness of his assessment, he let its members hear the confidential information which he had gathered at Rutgers. Though they did not feel that Malott's material was persuasive, the faculty committee's members neither supported nor attacked his decision. Their report simply stated that the president had based that decision "on the complex configuration of facts as they were developed in the inquiry." It concluded that because "the President has wide discretion in the matter of appointments to the faculty," Malott's rejection of Finley "did not violate recognized principles of academic freedom and tenure."[19]

Given the political climate of the McCarthy era, it is easy to understand, if not condone, the reluctance of academic administrators to hire people like Frank Oppenheimer and M. I. Finley. Oppenheimer had first denied and then admitted that he had been a Communist; Finley had taken the Fifth. It is, however, somewhat more difficult to understand the reluctance of other administrators, especially those at first-rate, urban universities, to hire people whose only sin was controversiality. The blacklisting of people who had never been Communists and had never defied a government investigation does the academic community little credit. Yet the practice was, it seems, widespread. Sometimes it was a name that was the problem. The sons of the former Communist Party chief, Earl Browder, were mathematicians who had little interest in politics. The oldest, Felix, was particularly brilliant. He had entered MIT at the age of sixteen and graduated two years later. One of his teachers described him as "the best student we had ever had in mathematics at MIT in the 90 years of existence of the institution." He was not a Communist; "he regards the group running Russia as a bunch of dictators, unscrupulous men, and so on, and has said so." Even so, as his teacher explained,

> He's had a terrible time getting a position, and some of the great scientists of our country have tried to help him. The schools and universities of this country have a severe public relations problem. . . . They are rather frightened of his name, and, it's easy to see why they are. They are afraid it will reduce contributions, and so on. So he has had a very difficult time of it.[20]

Simply being controversial could be a problem. The eminent physicist Edward U. Condon found himself almost unemployable after he came under attack by HUAC chairman Parnell Thomas in 1948. Condon had worked on the Manhattan Project during the war and then become the director of the Commerce Department's Bureau of Standards. He had never been a Communist, but he was an outspoken Popular Front liberal who had espoused enough politically suspect causes to give some, albeit far-fetched, plausibility to Thomas's charge that he was the "weak link" in America's atomic security. He wasn't, of course; in retrospect, it seems that Condon was probably a surrogate target, first for Henry Wallace, who had appointed him to the Bureau of Standards, and then for the more progressive remnants of the New Deal within the Truman administration. His innocence, however, did not protect him from the notoriety Thomas's charges created.[21]

Though Condon was known to be on the job market in 1948, when it was assumed that he would lose his government position after Truman lost the presidential election, he did not get a regular academic appointment until 1956. Parnell Thomas's accusations apparently caused Stanford University to withdraw a tentative offer to make Condon dean of the Graduate School. Later, when Condon left the government in 1951, he went not to a university but to the Corning Glass Company, as its director of research. In this, he was only the most eminent of the many politically controversial scientists who found private industry more willing to accept them than the academy. Not that the corporate world was without its problems, for Condon's position required a security clearance. As McCarthyism deepened and the clearance procedure became increasingly tinged with political, rather than security, concerns, Condon had more and more trouble getting cleared. He had been cleared three times in 1948 and again in July 1954 after an exhaustive three-month investigation. Then, in October, two days after his clearance was announced in the press, Vice President Nixon urged the Secretary of the Navy to suspend it yet again. The Eisenhower administration did not want to appear soft in the forthcoming elections. Rather than, as he put it, "continue a potentially indefinite series of reviews and re-reviews," Condon withdrew his application for clearance.[22]

Corning, understandably, felt that its director of research should have a security clearance. Thus, even though none of the work he had been doing was classified, Condon resigned. He continued to work for Corning on a part-time basis as a consultant and began to look for academic jobs. An offer to become chairman of New York University's Physics Department evaporated, amid rumors that the government threatened to withdraw its financial support if the University took Condon on. A similar offer from the University of Pennsylvania, where Condon was a visiting professor in 1955, also never materialized, apparently for the same reason. Finally, in the spring of 1956, Washington University in St. Louis made him chairman of the Physics Department. Once ensconced in a secure academic position, first at Washington and later at the University of Colorado, Condon worked to bring other blacklisted physicists back into academic life. In 1959 he was able to give Frank Oppenheimer a job.[23]

All the men we have been looking at—Oppenheimer, Condon, and Finley—had been in the newspapers. Their problems were well known within academic circles, and any university which took them on might well expect to receive a certain amount of flak. But how can we explain instances of what clearly seems to have been political blacklisting that occurred in the late 1940s and affected people who had not yet received any public attention? The University of Pennsylvania had such a case. In the beginning of 1949, after a considerable search, the History Department decided to fill a vacancy in East Asian history with Lawrence Rosinger, a highly recommended scholar then on the staff of the Institute of Pacific Relations. At the time, before China had been irrevocably "lost," there could have been no way of predicting either that Rosinger was going to figure prominently in the McCarran Committee's IPR hearings or that he would invoke the Fifth Amendment when questioned about his past political activities. All of that was some years in the future and, certainly in 1949, Penn's History Department did not consider Rosinger a political liability. Nor did the dean or the members of the University's Appointment Committee, all of whom went along with the History Department's recommendation. So solid was the support for Rosinger, in fact, that on January 14, 1949, Richard Shryock, the department chairman, wrote to Rosinger offering him an assistant professorship.[24]

Less than two months later, however, Shryock rescinded the offer; much to the History Department's surprise, the University's president, Harold Stassen, refused to approve the appointment. Shryock was baffled; as he explained in a letter to a colleague on leave, "apparently an attack made by a visiting congressman on the Institute of Pacific Relations and on Rosinger specifically as 'pinks' had something to do with the decision." Unfortunately, the University's archives contain no other information that could explain why Penn's president rejected Rosinger. Perhaps Stassen already had a personal animus against the man (he was to

attack him vehemently during the IPR hearings); perhaps he had received some kind of derogatory information about him from an outside
agency.[25]

Here, we come to the most heavily veiled aspect of this already secretive business. To what extent did outsiders—congressional committees,
state and local red squads, professional anti-Communists, or the FBI—
nourish the blacklist by feeding damaging material to academic authorities? We do have some information. Even at the time, a few organizations, like the State of California's Un-American Activities Committee,
publicly boasted of their efforts in the field. The Freedom of Information
Act has given us a few clues, but it has also revealed the FBI's obsession
with covering its own tracks, an indication that the FBI's files may contain few "smoking guns." University archives are similarly puzzling. There
are a few suggestions that academic leaders did seek help from professionals in the area. But there is no way to tell whether or not they received it. The Rutgers archives, for example, contain several pieces of
correspondence complaining about the FBI's unwillingness to forward
information about Finley and Heimlich. We know, however, that the FBI
created paper trails to conceal its leaks, and we have, therefore, no way
of knowing whether the Bureau actually refused the Rutgers request or
whether, as apparently happened in other situations, an agent, during
the course of hand-delivering a letter refusing to cooperate with the University, also handed over the files Rutgers wanted.[26]

Nor do we know the extent of the cooperation between these agencies and the academic world. Were the instances that we know about
common practices or unique events? Given the secrecy with which both
the universities and the outside agencies have concealed their collaboration, it may never be possible to reconstruct the complete picture. The
evidence that I've found suggests that such collaboration was probably
fairly widespread, at least for a few years during the height of the Mc-
Carthy period, but it is hard to tell how routinized it became. We do
know that there were programs in existence that were supposed to supply educational authorities with political information about job applicants on a regular basis. In addition, the FBI, and perhaps other groups
as well, intervened continuously to keep certain people out of academe.
How effective such measures were is another question. I have encountered several people who, as ex-Communists and potential unfriendly
witnesses, were eminent candidates for blacklisting, but who managed
to slip into the academic community and stay there. Though they were
harassed in other ways, their careers were unaffected. The academic
blacklist was not, therefore, completely effective, and the government
and private agencies which presumably helped create it were not omni-
scient. But they did have considerable clout.[27]

We know of at least one case—and it is hard to believe that there
weren't others—of an institution asking the FBI to check out a prospective employee. In the spring of 1953 the University of Michigan's presi-

dent Harlan Hatcher asked Homer Ferguson, Michigan's senior U.S. senator, to have the FBI look into the background of a man the University wanted to hire. Ferguson complied and was able to report that the FBI cleared the candidate completely. Though I could find no other similar cases in Michigan's archives or in those of the other universities I've investigated, the heavily censored FBI files relating to Harvard that Sigmund Diamond has received under the FOIA suggest a pattern of such cooperation. According to the head of the FBI's Boston office, in June 1950 an unidentified Harvard official "asserted that . . . the Harvard University authorities were desirous of cooperating with the Bureau . . . the Bureau's interests and those of the university were identical." Two months later the Boston agent again reported, perhaps about the same Harvard official, perhaps about a different one, "it would appear that contact with him *on applicant and other matters* will be of frequent occurrence [emphasis mine]."[28]

Though the FBI was obsessed with keeping its activities camouflaged, it was willing to go to considerable lengths "in the interest of keeping undesirable characters out of the education field." The case of Bruce Dayton illustrates them all. Dayton was a physicist who, as an undergraduate and graduate student at Berkeley in the late thirties, had hovered around the edges of the Oppenheimer circle of science and Popular Front politics. He knew Morrison, Kamen, Lomanitz, and the other Berkeley scientists who were later to have so much trouble. He went to parties at Oppenheimer's house, worked for the Spanish Loyalists, and was even invited to join the Party by Kenneth O. May. He refused. But his political activities apparently kept him from being cleared for work on the Manhattan Project, both at Berkeley and at Los Alamos, despite a specific invitation from Oppenheimer. Fortunately for Dayton, because he had been neither in the CP nor the Manhattan Project, HUAC did not harass him in its search for atom spies during the late 1940s. In fact, the file the FBI had amassed on him during the war years would have remained dormant had it not been for a friend he made while he was finishing up his Ph.D. at Cornell after the war. The new friend, Alfred Sarant, was an unemployed electrical engineer from New York whose reasons for being in Ithaca were never quite clear to Dayton. Like Dayton, Sarant and his wife were active in the Henry Wallace campaign; the two families soon became close. They even lived together for a few months, while Dayton and Sarant built houses on adjoining lots. Sarant had also been a friend of Julius Rosenberg and, a few days after Rosenberg's arrest, Sarant disappeared—taking Dayton's wife with him.[29]

The FBI moved in immediately. Dayton was questioned intensively. Not only did the Bureau want to know where Sarant and Carol Dayton were, but it tried to connect Dayton himself with the Rosenberg case. It claimed that he had been seen in an apartment in Greenwich Village formerly used by Sarant. Fortunately for Dayton he had been doing research on the Cornell cyclotron at the time he was reputed to be in the

Village, and he had his lab notes to prove it. In addition, his thesis director Dale Corson had his own records of conferences with Dayton. Even so, although Dayton was entirely innocent of whatever it was the FBI thought he might be involved in, the incident was to ruin his career. For the next ten years the Bureau kept Dayton under surveillance on the not unreasonable assumption that his ex-wife might someday contact the two children she had left behind. Worse yet, the FBI visited prospective employers and made it just about impossible for Dayton to work in his field. He was at MIT for a while, on a job he had gotten before his wife left, but it was only a temporary one and, after it ended, FBI intervention kept him from getting another academic position.[30]

In the spring of 1953 a colleague at Syracuse suggested that Dayton replace him while he was on leave. Unbeknownst to Dayton the chairman of the Physics Department contacted the FBI. The Bureau responded by sending an agent to brief the University's vice chancellor about both Dayton *and* the man who had recommended him. Naturally Dayton did not get the job. A few months later the FBI got another request for information about Dayton, this time from Florida State University. Dayton had applied for a job, and although the school wanted him, it was "reluctant to act in view of certain information Dayton furnished along with his application by letter." If Dayton were "an innocent victim of circumstances," the associate dean explained, the school would hire him, but it needed to check out his story. In accord with its socalled Responsibilities Program, the Bureau ordinarily gave information about prospective teachers at state schools to the governors of the states, but Florida's governor was having political problems, so Hoover authorized the local agent to communicate directly with the University's president. Not only was he to discuss Dayton's involvement with Sarant and the Rosenberg case, he was also to describe Dayton's association with left-wing groups in the early forties. Hoover included the usual disclaimer that none of the information was to be attributed to the FBI. The agent saw Florida State president Doak S. Campbell on November 12, 1953. "Of course," he reported, "no recommendation at all was made to Dr. Campbell in this matter; however, he gave the agent the impression that subject would not be employed by Florida State University at any time in the future."[31]

Although he was not aware of just how interested the FBI was in his career, Dayton knew he would have trouble getting a regular academic job in the United States and, as early as 1952, had begun to think about emigrating and finding work abroad. He had an invitation from a friend in India, but, thanks to FBI intervention, was unable to accept it because he could not get a passport. Like many other blacklisted scientists, Dayton eventually found a job in private industry, where Corson was able to get him placed as a senior research physicist at Corning Glass under Condon. But the corporate world was no more hospitable to people the FBI did not approve of than the academic; when Condon left

Corning, Dayton was dismissed. He then landed another industrial job only to have the man who hired him cancel it at the last minute after Dayton had moved his family out to the West Coast. Throughout this period, Dayton kept applying for teaching jobs. More than once, he recalls, jobs would be "all set up and then cancelled at the end by the 'academic vice president.' " When after years of frustration he finally found a teaching job, it was at a local community college in California, a post for which he was, to put it mildly, somewhat overqualified.[32]

In a sense, it was surprising that Dayton was able to get any kind of a job in a publicly supported college in California, for that state had devised what appeared to be the most comprehensive system for keeping politically undesirable applicants out of academic positions. California had long had one of the most aggressive legislative investigating committees in the nation. First under the flamboyant Senator Jack Tenney and then under the somewhat more restrained Hugh Burns, California's Fact-Finding Committee on Un-American Activities sporadically tried to expose campus subversives. In March 1952 the committee called a meeting of all the college and university presidents in southern California and followed it up with a similar meeting in June for the presidents in the northern part of the state. Those meetings produced what Richard E. Combs, the Burns Committee's counsel, called, "a cooperative plan to combat Communist infiltration," essentially a formal system of liaison between the colleges, both public and private, and the committee.[33]

This liaison took place at the highest level. As one of the participants in those meetings reported, "Most of the institutions present indicated that the matter of preventing Communist infiltration was obviously so important that no less person [sic] than the president himself should serve as liaison between the institution and the Committee, and I appointed myself in this capacity." The committee dutifully informed the colleges about the potential subversives on their faculties and kept them up to date on the latest permutations of front organizations. The committee's main service, however, was helping the colleges screen applicants. As Combs explained,

> the committee developed a procedure whereby applicants for positions are referred to us, their names are, and if we do have any documentation concerning their Communist activity over a long period of time, we make that available to the university as a guide to indicate whether or not the individual should be employed.

The committee also helped the larger schools hire full-time security officers to handle some of these chores—men with extensive experience in the anti-Communist field such as former naval intelligence officers and FBI agents.[34]

The system was a huge success. Combs boasted to the Jenner Committee in May 1953 that in the few months since the arrangements had been in place about a hundred people lost their jobs on the faculties of California's public and private colleges and several hundred more did not get hired. (Combs's figures were probably somewhat exaggerated.) Prevention was the core of the California program. It was not always easy to remove people from their jobs, Combs explained: "You run into academic freedom and tenure, front committees organized to protect their rights, Communist recruiters who try to paint them as martyrs, raising of funds, and all that sort of thing." It was very easy, on the other hand, for the committee to check out the names of potential teachers and to forward the "documented facts" to prospective employers. The committee, it must be noted, had a rather broad notion of what constituted a subversive activity. Its 1948 published index of suspect organizations listed twice as many groups as the Attorney General did, including such moderate, even anti-Communist outfits as the ACLU and the Consumers Union. Nonetheless, California's colleges cooperated 100 percent. They had no choice; the committee made it clear that if the colleges hired or did not fire the people that the committee considered dangerous, it would subpoena them and thus force the individuals and the institutions which employed them to confront the unfortunate consequences of a public committee hearing. What this meant was that during the height of the McCarthy era, the California Senate Un-American Activities Committee, and most probably the committee's staff of professional anti-Communists, exercised a veto over every single academic appointment in the state of California.[35]

The academic blacklist had a long life. As the case of Lawrence Rosinger shows, it was already operating in the late forties. Though it did abate a bit by the end of the fifties, the experiences of Leon Wofsy show that there were plenty of schools which even as late as 1964 would not take the kinds of risks that hiring a former radical would entail. True, Wofsy had been quite a radical. A "red diaper baby" like Chandler Davis, he had grown up in a Communist family and, until he left the Party in 1956, had never envisioned any other career for himself than that of a political organizer. During his undergraduate years at CCNY in the late 1930s, he headed both the Young Communist League and the Marxist Cultural Society. In the late forties and fifties, he became a full-time cadre and ran all the CP's youth activities. He left the Party in 1956 and, after finding that his political past blocked his attempt to start a new career as a high school teacher, entered Yale in January 1958 as a thirty-seven-year-old first-year graduate student in chemistry. Despite his late start, he was quite successful and got his degree in three years. He spent two more years as a postdoctoral fellow at the University of California-San Diego in La Jolla and then began to look for a permanent appointment.[36]

His research into immunological systems had, as he put it, "panned out," and so he got a lot of offers. The most attractive was from the University of Buffalo, by then a branch of the State University of New

York. As part of the necessary paperwork involved in getting his appointment through the state bureaucracy, Wofsy had to sign a "Feinberg Certificate," a procedure required of all New York State teachers since 1949. By 1963, the Feinberg Certificate seemed a harmless relic of the bad old days, but Wofsy could not view it as such. Since he had been an open member of the Communist Party, the Feinberg law not only required him to sign a loyalty oath, but also to confer with the president of the University about his political past. Wofsy had reluctantly signed California's loyalty oath when he went to La Jolla in 1961; he was willing to make a similar affirmation for Buffalo. But, as he explained to Buffalo's dean, "it would be violating my personal conscience" to do what the Feinberg law required a former Communist to do:

> to purge myself; to volunteer what "subversive organizations" I was a member of at any time in the past, to prove I had left "in good faith," to promise to accept the judgment of the Board of Regents on what I may or may not join, and what I may or may not say in or out of the university.

Wofsy was, nonetheless, willing to compromise, and in a letter to Buffalo's president he laid out his position. His former membership in the Communist Party was a matter of public record, and he was willing to state that he was no longer a member and that he had never been "treasonous," "seditious," or "subversive." He would even sign the Feinberg Certificate but would do so only with the understanding that he would submit to no other political test. Since the witch-hunt mentality that had produced the Feinberg law was, by the end of 1963, presumably a thing of the past, Wofsy's offer was a reasonable one. He would comply with the letter of the law if the University would agree not to enforce its spirit. The University's president never answered Wofsy's letter.[37]

Once the word about the Buffalo fiasco got out—and here the sixties were different from the fifties in that no one tried to suppress news of the incident—Wofsy received other offers. The best came from the University of Pittsburgh, an associate professorship in a department which housed one of the best people in Wofsy's field. The dean had personally reassured Wofsy that his political background would be no problem; Pittsburgh was a private university with "an established position of respect for academic freedom." Though the dean had made a written offer on April 1, 1964, several months elapsed without any further word. Meanwhile, Berkeley made an overture which Wofsy, though tempted, felt he could not accept in view of his prior commitment to Pittsburgh. That university, however, was having second thoughts. On June 3, the dean wrote Wofsy that the administration would not grant him immediate tenure—"not a good sign, considering the special circumstances surrounding your appointment." When Wofsy pressed for further details, the dean explained that Pennsylvania's Pechan Act required the University to vouch for Wofsy's loyalty. This the Pittsburgh administration was reluctant to do, not because of any doubts about Wofsy's politics but because of Pittsburgh's own vulnerability. The school had already survived a highly publicized loyalty case involving a tenured professor in the History Department, and it did not want to further risk alienating the state legislature, which funded about one-fourth of the school's budget, by taking on yet another controversial teacher.[38]

So Wofsy went to Berkeley, though not without a political skirmish. He had the strong support of the Berkeley administration, as well as that of the University's most eminent scientists, and his backers were able to force the reluctant Regents to approve the appointment. Ironically, Wofsy was soon under fire from Hugh Burns, the head of the California State Senate Un-American Activities Committee, miffed perhaps because the times had changed so much that he could no longer veto such a subversive appointment.[39]

As Wofsy's experiences indicate, the times did change, the academic blacklist did lift—at about the same time, it must be noted, as Hollywood's did. While it lasted, however, that blacklist was a key element in the larger structure of political repression that encumbered the academic community during the McCarthy era. It was, as we have seen, a largely informal procedure; the men and women who administered and complied with the McCarthy era blacklist did so through the regular, often personal, channels of academic communication. This makes the blacklist difficult to document, but it does not diminish its importance. Had most of the college teachers who lost their jobs after defying an anti-Communist investigation been able to find others, the political impact of their dismissals would not have been as great. Moreover, the near-universality of the blacklist indicates that professors and administrators at schools which did not have academic freedom cases themselves nonetheless seemed willing to concur in the verdicts of those cases. Had this been otherwise, had there been any *meaningful* opposition to McCarthyism within the academic community, people like Chandler Davis, M. I. Finley, and Frank Oppenheimer could have found teaching jobs in the U.S. They didn't.

XI

"Not Much Fun":
Coping with the Academic Blacklist

Few of the college teachers who lost their jobs after they refused to cooperate with an anti-Communist investigation had any illusions about
their future in American academic life. Most knew, when they appeared
before HUAC and the other committees, that their careers would suffer.
Though many were seriously affected personally, as well as professionally, few were surprised to find themselves unemployable at mainstream
academic institutions. They coped with their shattered educational
careers as best they could. Some left the academy altogether. Others left
the country. Still others found a variety of expedients to tide them
through the blacklist years until they could resume their interrupted
teaching careers. For the blacklist did end, petering out slowly until,
during the academic boom of the 1960s, almost all of the ostracized
professors who wanted to were able to return to the classroom.

Many never did. Some were simply too old at the time they were
fired to be able to make a fresh start in academic life when the political
ban against them lifted. Herbert Phillips, for example, scraped by in the
years after he was fired from the University of Washington with a variety of odd jobs. He worked for a while on a construction site, later on an
assembly line in a furniture factory. By the time he could have returned
to the academy in the early sixties, he was on Social Security. Phillips's
colleague Joseph Butterworth, whose already severe physical and emotional problems were exacerbated by his dismissal, was unable to get any
kind of paid employment and spent the last years of his life in Seattle
on welfare. The former chairman of the NYU German Department,
Lyman Bradley, was able to remain within the academic orbit. He par-
layed his twenty years as treasurer of the Modern Language Association
into a precarious business of exhibiting books at scholarly conventions,
but he never taught again.[1]

Bradley, Butterworth, and Phillips were early victims. Later ones,
and people like the Rapp-Coudert survivors in New York, were some-

what better prepared for the blacklisting that they knew would follow their refusal to name names. They anticipated the academy's unwillingness to hire political pariahs like themselves, and even before they lost their jobs some of them began training themselves for new careers outside academe. Abraham Keller, an associate professor of French at the University of Washington, had been a Communist while a graduate student at Berkeley from 1938 to 1946. Once his former comrades began appearing before HUAC, Keller assumed that he too would be called. He expected to take the Fifth and lose his job, so he began to plan for a new life as an insurance salesman. Under the guidance of a brother-in-law in the business, he studied life insurance in his spare time and even spent the summer before HUAC subpoenaed him selling policies. He did so well at it that his employer, the Northwest Life Insurance Company, offered him a full-time job. As it turned out, he did not need it, for when HUAC called him up in June 1954, Keller and his attorneys were able to devise a strategy whereby he could talk freely about his own activities but not have to name anybody he could not positively identify as a Party member. HUAC's investigators, who were, it seemed, still on the trail of Communists in the atomic bomb project, wanted Keller to finger his graduate school friend Joseph Weinberg; when Keller claimed that he couldn't do that, the committee lost interest in him. Since Keller had not taken the Fifth, the University of Washington did not fire him. Northwest Life, on the other hand, became upset about the publicity he had received and, a few days after his hearing, revoked his permit to sell life insurance.[2]

Most of the academics who retrained themselves for new careers did not, like Keller, try to enter the business world. Rather, they sought out other professions, but ones in which they would be able to earn a living without having to depend on just one employer. Quite a few became psychotherapists. For men like Ralph Gundlach and Bernard Riess, who were already in the field of psychology, the switch from theory to practice was a logical one. Riess had appeared before the Rapp-Coudert Committee, and he assumed that another round of investigations would cost him his tenured position at Hunter College. Accordingly, several years before he was actually fired, he went into training at the Postgraduate Center for Mental Health. When he did lose his job, after taking the Fifth before the McCarran Committee in the fall of 1952, it took him only a few months to attract enough private patients to support himself. Here his politics were an asset, for many of his first clients were radicals themselves who sought Riess out in large part because they felt they could trust him. Gundlach also became a psychotherapist, but not until he had spent a frustrating year trying to beat the blacklist. Friends and colleagues at other institutions promised to get him temporary teaching jobs, but nothing materialized. He found a few part-time research positions but soon realized that it was "impossible for me to obtain steady professional employment from a college or university, or from a federal or state agency." Just as Riess had done before him, he entered the Postgraduate Center to retrain himself as a lay analyst. Gundlach was eventually able to make a decent living from his private practice, but he never gave up his scholarly interests and he continued to do research and publish in his original field of social psychology until his death in 1978.[3]

Though it may have been easiest for psychologists like Gundlach and Riess to become therapists, the unstructured nature of the profession and its intellectual aspirations made it attractive to people in other disciplines as well. This was especially true for literary critics; their field was just then flirting heavily with psychoanalysis. Harry Slochower, whose popular courses at Brooklyn College sought to reconcile Freud with Marx and the greats of world literature, made the transition easily. Slochower had survived Rapp-Coudert, but barely; in 1947, because he knew how fragile his tenure was, he began to train himself in psychotherapy. He was already seeing patients at the time he was fired for taking the Fifth before the McCarran Committee in 1952, so he simply expanded his practice. He was soon so satisfied with his new career and the opportunities that it offered him that he did not return to academic life, even though the Supreme Court had reinstated him in 1956. NYU's Edwin Berry Burgum was another English professor who became a psychotherapist.[4]

Other literature teachers became writers or went into publishing. Oscar Shaftel had been a stringer for the *New York Times* when he was in college and decided to make a living in journalism after he lost his job at Queens College. A neighbor gave him an entree into the world of trade publications, and Shaftel was able to work as a free-lancer, pseudonymously churning out hundreds of 700-word articles at $25 a piece. "It was the lowest kind of hack writing," he recalls. After two years, Shaftel "simply got fed up to the neck" and found a full-time editorial position on a journal called *American Builder Magazine*. It paid only $6000 a year, but it "was interesting and I felt productive." Shaftel even published his first book while at the journal, a revision of the company's best-selling *House Construction Details*. But in 1957 he was taken out to lunch by the magazine's editors and told that the publisher had found out about "the Queens College business." He had to go, otherwise, he was told, "you might endanger the welfare of a hundred employees." Shaftel then went into public relations work, which paid better, he recalls, but was "slightly disreputable." He quit after six or seven years and supported himself with a half-time job on a heating magazine, part-time editorial work at Schocken Books, and some technical writing. Finally, by the mid-sixties, he was able to work his way back into the academy. A former colleague from Queens, who had just become head of the English Department at the Pratt Institute of Technology, gave him a few night school courses and then managed to get him a regular appointment. Two years later, Shaftel got tenure.[5]

Shaftel was not the only blacklisted professor to take up free-lance writing and editorial work. Saul Maloff had been publishing articles in general magazines for some time before he was forced to give up his academic career, whereupon he decided to become a full-time writer. He had, he claimed, no trouble getting his work published. Later on, he got a job in the publishing industry, working for a man who gave him to understand that whatever happened he "didn't know" anything about Maloff's political past. When the blacklist ebbed, Maloff returned to the academy, but more as a visitor than a native. He taught at Bennington for a few years, then quit to become the literary editor of *Newsweek*. He then went to the City University of New York, only to leave it to write. It was a pattern that he found more invigorating than the placid academic career that he would otherwise have pursued. The poet Tom McGrath was another English professor who turned to free-lancing after an appearance before HUAC cost him his job. For a while McGrath took any kind of work he could find. He was a qualified machinist, but could get no job in that field because most of the companies in the Los Angeles area where he lived did defense work and required a security clearance. Then, for several years, McGrath lived on the fringes of the Hollywood blacklist, writing film scripts under an assumed name, a precarious though moderately well-paying existence, but one which gave him little time for his own writing. Ultimately McGrath returned to the academy.[6]

For scientists, there was the possibility of work in private industry. The chemists and physicists who had lost their jobs after the Rapp-Coudert hearings had already pioneered that route, working first in a private laboratory and later setting up their own company. As the cases of E. U. Condon and Bruce Dayton reveal, however, the corporate world was only minimally more willing to take political risks than the academic. Moreover, many private employers, especially those who did defense contracting, required their employees to get security clearances, something which few of the dismissed academics could or, in some cases, would do. Even so, because of the enormous demand for physical scientists in the mid-fifties—job registers listed two to four times as many openings as there were physicists looking for jobs—most of the blacklisted professors who wanted to were able to make their way into private industry. Even people as tainted as HUAC's supposed atomic spies, Joseph Weinberg and Clarence Hiskey, were able to work in private industry. Weinberg eventually went back into teaching; Hiskey never did. He became an industrial consultant after he left Brooklyn Polytechnic Institute in 1952. He had no trouble finding clients, but recalls that he could not charge as much as other similarly qualified, but politically safer, chemists could. After a few years he decided to set up his own company. It foundered for financial, not political reasons, and Hiskey then took a job with a drug company and eventually ended up working for duPont.[7]

Not every blacklisted scientist could get an industrial job that would take advantage of his or her skills and training. Chandler Davis, for example, found that security clearance problems ruled out every scientifically interesting opening with a major corporation. Ross Lomanitz's experiences were even more frustrating. He never succeeded in finding any kind of a scientific or technical job and, for a while, could barely find any job at all. He lived with his wife in a shack he had built himself on the edge of a swamp outside Oklahoma City and did construction work and other kinds of day labor. But even these menial jobs were precarious, and he was to lose several of them after what appeared to have been FBI visits to his employers. Finally, in the early 1960s, he returned to the academy, but he had been out of touch with his field for ten years and could never restore the scientific momentum he once had.[8]

People who had other sources of income were not as pressed as Davis and Lomanitz. Frank Oppenheimer, for example, decided not to take an industrial job when he was offered one. He had bought a ranch in Colorado several years before the University of Minnesota fired him, and once he realized that he was on the academic blacklist, he decided to move his family to Colorado and become a rancher. He was not a success, but he had enough private income to ensure that he and his family could survive the hard times. Barrows Dunham, who was similarly cushioned against the financial consequences of the blacklist, did not try to begin a new career but continued to write books and lecture to whatever audiences he could find. For many of the other blacklisted professors, however, the most important source of financial aid during this period was their wives. Some of these women already had careers; others went to work when their husbands were dismissed. They rarely found well-paying jobs. Ross Lomanitz's wife was a bookkeeper; Herbert Phillips's did clerical work, boarded babies, and became a dressmaker. The women who had more remunerative positions sometimes themselves had problems because of their husbands' politics, though not every woman was so afflicted.[9]

Ralph Gundlach's wife, the choreographer and dance teacher Bonnie Bird, experienced no political discrimination at all during the blacklist period. Nor did Chandler Davis's wife, the historian Natalie Zemon Davis, who was able to complete her doctorate and land a teaching job at Brown. Though she did not have a regular academic appointment at that time, whatever career problems she faced had more to do with her gender and three small children than with her own or her husband's politics. This was not the case with her mother-in-law, Marian, the wife of Horace Bancroft Davis. She had just been hired to teach at a private girls' school in Kansas City at the time her husband appeared before the Jenner Committee. She was fired at once, without having met a single class. Frederic Ewen's wife, the composer Miriam Gideon, was also fired. She had been teaching nights at both CCNY and Brooklyn College and, since she did not have tenure, she expected that her husband's troubles would cost her her job. She was right. Similarly, the wife of Isidore Pomerance, another Brooklyn College casualty of the Jenner Committee, was called in and told to resign by the Board of Higher Education.[10]

Courtney Cazden, Norman Cazden's wife, also had trouble keeping a job. The Cazdens had moved to Bridgeport, Connecticut, after Norman was fired from the University of Illinois and Courtney, who had an education degree, found a teaching job in a nearby school system. A little over a month after she was hired, however, her husband appeared before HUAC and invoked the Fifth Amendment. The next day, the Superintendant of Schools wrote to warn her that "as soon as the fact becomes generally known . . . that you are scheduled as a teacher here, it will become quite embarrassing to us." He was not firing her, he explained, merely putting her on notice and giving her "an opportunity to express yourself concerning this most unfortunate turn of events." Cazden hired a lawyer and eventually worked out an arrangement that would enable her to keep her job in return for submitting a long autobiographical statement describing her professional and political activities and affirming that she was "a loyal American citizen dedicated to the fundamental democratic traditions of our country."[11]

Their wives were not the only sources of support the blacklisted professors found. In many cases, families, friends, and former students provided help. An ex-student helped one of his former teachers find work in the printing business after he lost his job at Queens College. A politically sympathetic sculptor gave Tom McGrath a job carving wood. The left-wing community mobilized its resources as best it could. The Teachers Union, in which so many of the dismissed New York City academics had been active, was especially helpful. Not only did it provide its members with lawyers for their various hearings and appeals, but it also gave them rent money and tried to help them find jobs. In addition, it sponsored a lecture series which gave the blacklisted professors a small honorarium as well as a forum to replace the classrooms they had lost. The Union was even able to assist one of its members, the former Brooklyn College English teacher Frederic Ewen, to begin a new career. He arranged dramatic readings of literary classics which he would supplement with a learned commentary. One of his productions—using blacklisted actors, of course—actually made it onto Broadway.[12]

Teaching jobs did exist. Though it was all but impossible for the blacklisted professors to get regular academic appointments at a mainstream college or university, they could sometimes find positions in the periphery. They could, for example, get part-time teaching jobs, off-the-ladder appointments, or one-year visiting professorships. Chandler Davis taught nights at the New School for Social Research and at Columbia University's General Studies division. Stanley Moore was a lecturer at Barnard College for five years. And Lee Lorch, a mathematician fired by Fisk University in 1955, spent a year as a visiting professor at Wesleyan in 1958. Norman Cazden, who helped support his family during the blacklist years by giving piano lessons and teaching part-time at the New School, was hired by Vassar as the last-minute replacement for an ailing friend. Even though the man he replaced retired the following year, Cazden was not offered the permanent job that opened up. The year of teaching that he had gotten was, in fact, a rather clandestine affair; he had no contract, no official title, and his salary was paid out of the president's contingency fund. For Cazden and the other black-listed professors, none of the marginal positions that they got during the height of the blacklist in the late 1950s ever turned into regular academic appointments.[13]

To get such a job, a full-time, tenure-track position in an American college, a blacklisted professor would have to go to the South, to the small, poor, denominational Negro colleges that were so desperate for qualified faculty members that they would hire anybody with a Ph.D., including teachers other educational institutions dared not touch. Only a few people exercised this option. The teaching conditions at such schools were depressing; academic standards were low; and professors rarely had the luxury of teaching courses in their own fields. In addition, life in the segregated South was not very attractive to a northern radical. Chandler Davis, for one, felt that it would be hard to raise his children in the South. His father, Horace Bancroft Davis, did, however, teach for several years on the Negro college circuit. He had worked sporadically in Kansas City for two years after his dismissal from the University of Kansas City, first as a milkman and then as a journalist with a photography company, but lost both jobs because of his politics. The dairy claimed that its customers might become upset if they knew that a dangerous radical was delivering their milk, and the photographers, who did public relations work for construction companies, insisted that their employees needed security clearances because they worked on defense installations. In 1956 Davis, an economist, was offered a job as the chairman of the Humanities Department at Benedict College in South Carolina, no other position there being vacant at the time. Political pressures on Benedict's president forced Davis out after two years, but he was able to get a better job, this time in his field, at Shaw College, another black school. Davis's wife also taught at Benedict for a while, as did Forrest Oran Wiggins, a radical black philosopher who had been dismissed, perhaps for political reasons, from the University of Minnesota in 1951, and W. Lou Tandy, an economist who had been fired from Kansas State Teachers College in Emporia because he had signed an open letter to President Truman requesting clemency for the Smith Act defendants.[14]

These schools, though so far outside—and below—the mainstream of American higher education that they could hire politically undesirable professors, did not completely eschew the blacklist. There was the case of Hans Freistadt, for example. Freistadt was a young physicist who had been in the Communist Party while a graduate student at the Uni-

versity of North Carolina. He had become the center of a major controversy when, in 1949, it was discovered that the Atomic Energy Commission had given him a fellowship. During the course of a series of highly
publicized hearings before the Joint Congressional Committee on Atomic
Energy, Republican Senator Bourke Hickenlooper, who was eager to
discredit the AEC and its civilian leaders, latched onto Freistadt as a
symbol of the agency's laxness. Naturally, Freistadt lost his fellowship.
Even so, he was able to get a job at Wilberforce University the following
year. Freistadt knew that his past troubles might be a problem for Wilberforce and he had, he claimed, "taken special pains to inform the
president of my membership and he had already secured approval of my
appointment by the Board of Trustees (or so he told me)." Yet, three
months later, right before the term began, the Wilberforce Board of
Trustees cancelled the appointment. Tolerant as these Negro colleges
were, they were not politically invulnerable, especially when, in the
middle fifties, they became involved in the early stages of the civil rights
movement.[15]

The experiences of Lee Lorch proved that. Lorch had already lost
two academic positions in the North—at CCNY and Penn State—in large
part because of his conspicuous support for civil rights. While at City
College, he had led a tenants' group which was trying to force the Metro-
politan Life Insurance Company to let black families live in its Stuyvesant Town housing project. When CCNY refused to give him tenure
under what seemed to be suspicious circumstances, Lorch went to Penn
State, subletting his Stuyvesant Town apartment to a black family. The
Penn State authorities found out what he had done and, claiming that his
retention of a New York apartment indicated a lukewarm attitude toward his present job, let him go after a year of teaching. The administration at Fisk University must, therefore, have known, when it hired
Lorch to become the chairman of its Mathematics Department, that its
new faculty member would continue his battle against segregation—as,
of course, he did. Not only was he active outside the classroom as the
vice president of the Tennessee NAACP, but he also used his position at
Fisk to help blacks get ahead. Like Hodes in New Orleans, he tried to
bring black mathematicians into the professional mainstream; he also encouraged his students to do graduate work, an unprecedented break with
traditional expectations for students at Negro colleges in the 1950s.[16]

In the aftermath of the Supreme Court's 1954 decision to end segregated education, Lorch tried to enroll his daughter in the local black
elementary school. His one-girl attempt to desegregate the Nashville
public schools resulted in a HUAC subpoena, for, during the 1950s,
Southern segregationists commonly relied upon red-baiting as a way to
discredit civil rights activists. At his hearing before a HUAC subcommittee allegedly investigating subversion in Dayton, Ohio, Lorch questioned the pertinence of the investigation and invoked the First Amend-

ment when asked about some three-year-old allegations that he had been a Communist in 1941. "For the purpose," he explained, "of safeguarding my institution against the barrage of newspaper publicity which might accompany this [hearing]," Lorch denied that he was then a Communist or had ever been one during the time he was at Fisk. These precautions were of little use; Fisk, which had after all fired Lomanitz four years before, after his appearance before HUAC, felt itself too vulnerable to withstand community pressures for Lorch's dismissal. Lorch was not without his defenders, however, for there were some board members who recognized that HUAC was simply carrying out the segregationists' business. They not only publicly protested Lorch's dismissal, but also helped him get another teaching job at another Negro school, Philander Smith, a small Methodist college in Little Rock, Arkansas. Since Lorch was then under indictment for contempt of Congress, the willingness of Philander Smith to take him on was, in fact, a remarkable display of institutional courage.[17]

Lorch's odyssey might have ended in Arkansas had the civil rights struggle not moved to Little Rock as well. This time it was Lorch's wife, Grace, a political activist in her own right, who became involved. During the unrest that accompanied Governor Orval Faubus's attempt to keep three black students out of Little Rock's Central High School in 1956, Grace Lorch defied an angry mob of whites to comfort one of the black teenagers. She was rewarded for her bravery with a subpoena from the Senate Internal Security Subcommittee. Her husband was given to understand that although he wasn't exactly being fired, the president of Philander Smith, who was under considerable pressure at the time, would not be upset if, after Lorch finished his stint as a visiting professor at Wesleyan University the following year, he found a position somewhere else.[18]

He did—in Canada, where by the late 1950s a significant number of blacklisted professors were teaching. As it had been for many of the blacklisted Hollywood writers and directors, emigration enabled these otherwise unemployable academics to continue working in their fields. Canada was the most convenient refuge. Teaching at a Canadian college or university was the closest thing to teaching in the United States. The language and culture were the same and the blacklisted academics did not have to face the kinds of passport problems that plagued their colleagues in other countries. As a result, quite a few of these unemployables went north to teach, some for just a few years, others permanently. Mark Nickerson, for example, went directly from the University of Michigan to the University of Manitoba. Though he took a substantial cut in salary and initially had some trouble getting grants, he continued his research and soon reestablished his scientific reputation. Chandler Davis also went to Canada, though he did not do so until 1962, after he had served his prison term. Byron Darling, the physicist dropped so precipitantly from Ohio State in 1953, ended up in Canada as well, as did Leon Kamin, the Harvard teaching fellow who had defied both the Jenner and McCarthy committees.[19]

For some of the younger academics, like Kamin, Canada was very much a place of exile. Robert Bellah, who went to McGill after he had refused Harvard's offer to name names for the FBI, recalls his stay in Montreal as "about the worst year in my life." Kamin felt the same way at first. He had been a good graduate student and, until his political troubles erupted, had been expecting a good academic job. His adviser had been lining him up for one at the University of Michigan. But after his congressional hearings and his indictment for contempt, the Michigan job evaporated along with all the others he was in contention for. The only solid offer he got was for a one-year position at McGill. When he took it, Kamin recalls, his colleagues at McGill were surprised that such a promising young psychologist would be interested in a temporary job at a place like McGill. Kamin then taught at several other Canadian schools before he returned to the United States in the late 1960s to become the chairman of the Psychology Department at Princeton.[20]

Not every blacklisted professor could get a teaching job in Canada. Horace Bancroft Davis was simply too old; at his age, he needed a full professorship and, since he did not have an established reputation as a scholar, such a position was understandably hard to come by. There were political obstacles as well. In 1954, soon after his dismissal from the University of Illinois, Norman Cazden received an offer to head a new Department of Musicology at the University of Toronto. He had several interviews, met with prospective colleagues and administrators, and was even introduced around as someone who was about to join the faculty. But the official letter of appointment never came—the offer was withdrawn. Sometimes the obstacles were bureaucratic. Almost as soon as he reached Winnipeg, Mark Nickerson busied himself with finding jobs for other blacklisted scientists. In 1956 he managed to obtain a position in his own department for Helen Deane Markham. She was, however, unable to fill it, for the Canadian government had suddenly decided that United States citizens needed passports in order to immigrate to Canada. For a publicly identified Fifth Amendment witness like Markham, whose prospects for getting a passport were slim, this new rule effectively prevented her from taking Nickerson's offer. Markham's troubles were unusual; the Canadian government soon rescinded its passport requirement, and most of the blacklisted academics—certainly most of the scientists and mathematicians—who wanted to did manage to find jobs there.[21]

A lot of people went farther afield. During the height of the McCarthy period, these academic émigrés ended up all over the world, from France and England to India and Israel. Some returned after the McCarthy period ended, others remained abroad to savor in their adopted countries the academic prestige and success that the blacklist had denied them in America. M. I. Finley, for example, went to England in 1954 as a visiting lecturer with a term each at Oxford and Cambridge. He stayed on at Cambridge and eventually earned a knighthood for his scholarship. Since Sir Moses had spent the years between his dismissal from Rutgers and his departure for England unsuccessfully looking for an academic job, it is small wonder that he never returned to the United States.[22]

Most of the other American academics who emigrated, like Finley, did so after first experiencing some time on the blacklist. But there were a few prescient individuals who anticipated the blacklist and went abroad *before* they were called up by a committee or fired from their jobs. They were, or had been, politically active and realized that they would almost certainly be targeted by an anti-Communist investigation if they remained in the United States. Some of these people were already abroad on research fellowships, so they simply transformed a sabbatical into a longer stay. The nuclear physicist Gerald Brown had gone to England in 1950 on what he thought was a Fulbright Fellowship. The fellowship was withheld, and Brown, who had been a Communist while a graduate student at Yale in the late 1940s and had become increasingly alienated and isolated in America, decided to take a job at the University of Birmingham and stay in England. Later, his name came up before HUAC. "Of course," he pointed out,

> nobody in the States would touch me by then, because—even before friends were called up before the Un-American Affairs Committee—I had made no secret whatsoever about my problems so everybody knew about them.

Staying in England was for Brown the only way to remain a physicist. Had he returned to the States he "wouldn't have had a profession." In fact, he couldn't even visit, for the State Department had lifted his passport and had he gone back to America he would have been unable to return to his British job. Not having the passport was a nuisance in other ways, for the British government theoretically required it of all foreign residents and Brown periodically had to convince the Home Office not to expel him.[23]

Daniel Thorner was another academic who converted a year's sabbatical into a permanent stay abroad. Thorner had already appeared before the McCarran Committee when he went to India on a research grant in 1952. He almost lost the grant, and when it became clear that the University of Pennsylvania would not give him tenure, Thorner decided to continue his research in India rather than return to almost certain unemployment in the United States. This was not an easy decision to make. The Thorners had three children and no assured means of support. Penn gave Thorner some money for a second year in India; a colleague helped arrange a grant from UNESCO. "We got Daniel's brother to sell our car," Alice Thorner reminisced, "and we ate that. Then we sold the house we had in Philadelphia and we ate that for a while." Eventually, the Thorners were able to piece together a fairly comfortable life: Daniel teaching part-time at Delhi University and both he and Alice doing research for a variety of Indian organizations. His work on the Indian economy soon earned him an international reputation, and in 1960 the Thorners left India for Paris, where Daniel became a member of the prestigious Sixième Section of the Ecole Pratique des Hautes Etudes.[24]

One of his colleagues in Paris was another American exile, Stuart Schram, a political scientist who had gone to France in 1950 to work on his dissertation and remained there after the State Department revoked his passport. Schram's case was unusual, for he had never been a Communist nor even a political activist and had, in fact, been so politically cautious that he checked with the American Embassy before he went to interview some European Communists for his dissertation. Even so, he got into trouble. Some articles he had written about European politics were critical of American policy and, to make matters worse, were published in a French weekly newspaper that the State Department did not consider completely kosher. By manifesting an unorthodox attitude toward the Cold War in his articles, Schram had, so the State Department claimed, "assisted in the development of various anti-U.S. propaganda campaigns which are Communist controlled and directed." Once he lost his passport, Schram decided to stay in France. He was happy there and assumed that he would have trouble finding work if he returned to the United States. Even after he got his passport back, Schram remained in Europe. Ironically, though he knew Thorner, such was the secrecy that enveloped the academic blacklist that neither man knew the other remained abroad for political reasons.[25]

Another academic who left the United States before she lost her job was Margaret Schlauch, a full professor in the English Department at New York University. Long a fixture of the New York academic left, Schlauch was on a sabbatical in Europe in 1951 when she decided to resign from NYU and move to Poland. Having been implicated during the Rapp-Coudert hearings, Schlauch had good reason to think that she would probably lose her job if a second round of investigations took place. "I am afraid," she wrote in her formal letter of resignation,

> that the economic and political future at home is not auspicious, not even for a Chaucer specialist, if such a person has been and still is a Marxist (no matter how undogmatic) and doesn't intend to deny it; and if she moreover condemns the foreign policy leading to war for the control [of China] through Chiang Kai-shek, and feels an obligation, sooner or later, to engage in active opposition to that policy.

Her choice of an asylum was unusual—few American academics went behind the Iron Curtain—but it may have had something to do with the presence in Warsaw of her sister, a former math teacher at Hunter College who had moved to Poland when her husband Leopold Infeld, one of Einstein's coworkers, was deported from Canada during the early Cold War years. Schlauch, whatever her reasons for being in Poland, had a successful career there and became one of that country's leading linguists. She did not return to the United States.[26]

Robert Hodes did. After losing his job at Tulane in the beginning of 1953, Hodes looked briefly for another position in America and then decided to emigrate. His politics determined his place of exile, for he wanted to go to a socialist country that needed a physiologist. China, so he heard, might be interested in someone in his field; but the negotiations were complicated and, while he was making the arrangements with Peking, he moved his wife Jane and three children to Oxford, where he worked for a year in the laboratory of a politically sympathetic scientist. In 1954 the Hodes family went to Peking. They stayed for five years, during which time, as Jane Hodes recalls, her husband "laid the base for modern neurophysiology in Peking." They returned to America in 1959. McCarthyism was on the wane, and they no longer felt they were really needed in China. They were, after all, Americans; and, politically alienated as they were, they did not want to raise their children in a foreign country. Hodes's brother was on the staff at Mount Sinai Hospital in New York and was instrumental in getting him a research job there.[27]

Joseph Cort was another American scientist who ended up in a Communist country. In his case, however, his decision to settle in Czechoslovakia instead of some more neutral place was motivated largely by professional rather than political concerns. Cort had been in the Party while a medical student at Yale. He received a postdoctoral fellowship and his faculty advisers, who knew of his political activities, suggested that it might be wise for him to take his fellowship abroad. He went to England. Soon after he arrived, the State Department revoked his passport, and his name came up before HUAC—indications, as if he needed them, that he would be unemployable in the United States. He decided to stay in England and was able to get a job at the University of Birmingham. Normally his saga would have ended there and, though passportless like Gerald Brown, he would have been free to pursue his scientific career in peace. He was not to be so fortunate.[28]

Cort was a physician, which meant that he was eligible for the draft. At that time, the Defense Department, as part of what was apparently a carefully orchestrated plan to punish radicals, was systematically drafting left-wing doctors and then court-martialing them or giving them dishonorable discharges. In 1953 Cort received an induction notice but fought it because he knew that, were he to return to America, he would not only suffer at the hands of the military, but also find himself without a career. His resistance brought an indictment for draft evasion, the CIA apparently being particularly eager to press charges. The State Department then urged the British government to deport him. At that point,

Cort's case became a cause célèbre. The press picked it up and the Labour Party brought it onto the floor of Parliament as an example of the government's servility to the United States. The publicity did little good and it was clear that Cort would have to leave England. His British supporters got him visas for Israel and India, but he did not want to go to either country. Israel was, he thought, too dependent on the American government, and India not advanced enough in his field. Instead he decided to go to Prague, because Czech scientists were doing the most sophisticated biochemical research in Eastern Europe. As it turned out, Prague was scientifically better for his career than England would have been. He stayed in Czechoslovakia for twenty-four years. He would have returned to the United States sooner, but Washington had revoked his citizenship. It was not until 1977, after his lawyer Leonard Boudin managed to get his indictment for draft evasion quashed and his citizenship and passport restored, that Cort finally returned to America. He got a job at Mount Sinai, the same place that had welcomed Hodes on his return in 1959.[29]

One of the reasons Cort had for not going to Israel was that he was no Zionist and his wife was not a Jew. Many of the other Jewish scientists on the blacklist did, however, end up in Israel. It was a new nation, ostensibly socialist, which was eager to build up a scientific establishment. In addition, the American émigrés recruited each other. Nathan Rosen, a physicist from North Carolina who had emigrated to Israel in 1952, sometime before his name came up at a congressional hearing, hired David Fox, one of the Fifth Amendment witnesses connected with the Berkeley Radiation Laboratory. Fox then helped recruit his former Berkeley colleague David Bohm and Paul Zilsel, another blacklisted physicist. Fox and Zilsel eventually returned to the United States; but Bohm, who had relinquished his American citizenship so that he could get to Israel from Brazil, where he had gone after Princeton let him go, accepted a position in England and never came back.[30]

Not every blacklisted professor wanted to emigrate. Some felt that it would be too hard for their families or that the task of learning a new language would be insurmountable. Others wanted to stay in America and fight McCarthyism. In addition, some of the academics who wanted to go abroad were unable to; they could not get passports. In 1951, after the passage of the McCarran Act, the State Department began to withhold passports from political dissidents and confiscate those of people who were already abroad. The State Department's blacklist was quite far-reaching and affected people who were otherwise untouched by the McCarthyist furor. As a result, with the exception of those people who assumed that they would not receive passports and did not bother to apply for them, almost every single academic who had political problems during the late forties and fifties could not get a passport. For some of these people, the travel ban prevented them from taking what were often the only jobs they could get in their fields. Bruce Dayton, who could not accept a scientifically attractive offer in Bombay, sued the State Department. By the time the Supreme Court awarded him his passport, in a landmark 1959 decision, the Indian offer was no longer in effect. The government's zeal in keeping the tainted academics from going abroad was quite remarkable. Clarence Hiskey had also tried to go to India. He had several job possibilities there, and the Indian government specifically requested that he be allowed to emigrate. But the State Department not only refused to give him a passport, it even offered to send another scientist to India in Hiskey's place and pay his way there.[31]

Sigmund Diamond was another academic who thought about emigrating. After his refusal to give names to the FBI cost him a job at Harvard, he tried to find another academic position. When a job at Amherst fell through at the administrative level, he decided to go abroad. He had offers from Australia, Israel, and England and was on the verge of moving his family to Cambridge when he got a job in the Sociology Department at Columbia University. Diamond was lucky. The academic blacklist, effective as it was, was not completely foolproof. A few, though only a few, of the men and women who lost their jobs during the McCarthy period were able to land comparable ones—usually because their situations were unusual or the institution was. Columbia's Sociology Department, for example, may have been in a particularly strong position to make a politically sensitive appointment, for it had already fought and won a battle to keep the job of Bernhard Stern, a lecturer in the department who had taken the Fifth before both McCarran and McCarthy. In addition, Diamond's problems were not public, so hiring him may not have been as risky as hiring a more visible recusant.[32]

There were a few schools which took those risks and hired Fifth Amendment witnesses. These decisions seem to have been characterized more by serendipity than by a conscious desire to break the blacklist. Thus, for example, at approximately the same time as the acting president of the University of Pennsylvania was vetoing Daniel Thorner's tenure, a biologist at the University's veterinary school hired Robert Rutman, who had just lost his job at the Jefferson Medical College, to work in his lab. Perhaps because Rutman's salary came from an outside grant, and his job involved only research and no teaching, the University approved the appointment. Within a few years Rutman got a regular position on the faculty, and in 1961 received tenure—not, however, without a fight in which one of his colleagues actually threatened to resign and make a public fuss if Rutman's promotion did not go through.[33]

As Rutman's experiences indicate, it was sometimes possible for blacklisted scientists to return to the academy if they could get research, rather than teaching, appointments. Alex Novikoff, a biologist who was fired from the University of Vermont Medical School after taking a diminished Fifth before the Jenner Committee in 1953, managed to get such a job at the Albert Einstein Medical School. Einstein was a brand new school and, for that reason, may have been in a better position to take political risks. Even so, Novikoff's appointment aroused controversy; in order to placate the trustees, he was made a "Research Professor." Einstein was particularly hospitable to blacklisted scientists. Within a year after Novikoff's appointment set the precedent, the School hired Helen Deane Markham. There may have been other institutions which ignored the blacklist during the 1950s. If they did, however, they kept publicity at a minimum and we know nothing about them.[34]

Eventually the blacklist disappeared, and by the middle sixties most of the blacklisted teachers who wanted to return to the academy did so. But they usually returned without tenure and sometimes had trouble bringing their interrupted careers up to the level they would have reached had they not been evicted from academic life. People in the humanities and social sciences generally returned to the academy later than scientists did. The demand for them was not as great, nor could they ease themselves in with research appointments. In addition, they had trouble finding jobs at the appropriate level. Norman Cazden, for example, had been on the verge of tenure before he was fired. Since he had continued to compose music and publish scholarly articles during his years on the blacklist, he could not come in at other than the senior level. Because Cazden did not want to leave the Boston area, where his wife had been making her own career, he did not return to academic life until 1969, when he became an associate professor of music at the University of Maine.[35]

A few years before Cazden went to Maine, while he was still giving piano lessons in his home in Lexington, Massachusetts, he answered a questionnaire about his experiences that a Rutgers political scientist, Paul Tillett, had sent to some of the blacklisted academics. In addition to eliciting information about these people's political problems, Tillett asked more subjective questions in his attempt to assess the personal and professional damage that had resulted from the respondents' expulsion from the academy. The answers he received are suggestive. Obviously, there is no scientific way to measure pain or worry or to chart the impact of a ten-year hiatus on an academic career. Yet, because Tillett's respondents and the blacklisted professors I interviewed described many of the same problems and anxieties, I do not wish to ignore these issues.

Cazden's response to Tillett contains a straightforward assessment of the professional damage that being blacklisted was causing him. "It hampers my normal professional contacts, standing, performance, and publication." Whereas he had previously been teaching graduate students, he was now dealing with children. As Cazden saw it, his isolation from the academy was "blighting to an unknown degree . . . a particular career and the professional growth that comes only with work." Like many of the unfrocked academics, Cazden continued to keep up with his field and produce scholarly articles. This avenue was, of course, more open to people in the humanities and social sciences than to scientists, who needed their laboratories and their colleagues. Frank Oppenheimer, who was to spend ten years away from the physics that he loved, was particularly depressed about his inability to do science. Observers recall times when he seemed "just really desperate" about it. Dirk Struik, the MIT mathematician who had been suspended from his job for five years while under indictment for subversion, told Tillett that he especially suffered from the loss of "daily contact with my colleagues which in the present period of rapid scientific development has a crippling effect." He missed teaching as well. For Struik, as for many of the other blacklisted academics, losing his students and the stimulation that he used to find in the classroom was one of the most painful consequences of his political troubles. "Teaching was the only outlet of expression I knew," the philosopher Herbert Phillips confessed, "and I felt that I was effective in that vocation."[36]

The blacklisted academics missed other aspects of their academic careers as well. It was hard to adjust to a nine-to-five job when one had spent so many years in the less structured environment of the academy. It was also hard to adjust to the insecurities of life without tenure. Many of the people who went into the business world lived with the knowledge that they could be fired again at any moment. "Will my present employers be subject to pressure," Oscar Shaftel wondered in the early 1960s, "when things get nasty again in the next couple of years?" For people who had carved out independent careers for themselves, the teachers-turned-psychotherapists in particular, there was the insecurity that came from what was essentially a constant hustle for clients. "A man who has had a regular pay check for twenty-eight years finds it difficult to become a professional entrepreneur," was the way one of these former academics described his situation. Similarly, even though he was making twice as much money as a lay analyst than he had made as an English professor at NYU, Edwin Berry Burgum confessed that he was having trouble adjusting to the instability of his income.[37]

Personal lives suffered too. Few were the blacklisted professors who did not talk of the friends and colleagues who had deserted them. The academic community produced its share of cowards, people who crossed the street to avoid having to greet a former colleague or who refused to acknowledge a blacklistee at a scholarly convention. Leonard Marsak, the European historian who lost his job at Reed College after taking the Fifth before HUAC, recalls that his "old friends, fellow students, former colleagues, fled to the hills, in fact behaved like a bunch of frightened rabbits." Similarly, Barrows Dunham noted that, after he was fired, most of his colleagues "at once ended their personal relations" with him. At Brooklyn College the terror was so intense that a former colleague refused to let one of the dismissed teachers acknowledge his assistance in a book that she was writing. For many people, the social ostracism they experienced came as a surprise. As one dismissed scientist put it: "You

find out who your friends are and learn who can afford to be themselves."
It was not a pleasant discovery. Clarence Hiskey recalled that all the
publicity about his supposed atomic espionage

> created a situation in which I lived in a world that was polarized. There
> were those that would say to me, "Hello, Doc, how's the spy business
> today?" and, because they would talk about it, you'd know they were
> friendly. And then there were those that would just avoid you. They
> wouldn't come to visit you; they didn't invite you to visit them. And they
> were very aloof in their behavior.[38]

Since the old China hands and the blacklisted entertainers also tell
similar stories of social ostracism and rejection by their former friends
and fellow workers, it is hard to know whether academics were, as a
profession, less courageous than any other comparable group of middle-
class Americans at the time. My guess would be that they were about the
same. But—and this is important—the blacklisted professors perceived
the members of their own profession as being particularly timid. In their
reminiscences these men and women keep returning to that theme, to the
collective guilt of their colleagues. "I must remark," Oscar Shaftel told
Tillett, "on the loss of nerve of the teaching profession generally, and
the loss of self-respect, not yet regained." Similarly, Bernard Riess noted
that "teaching sometimes seems to have become an intolerable vocation . . . and one which makes people servile and spineless." Mark Nickerson observed a similar phenomenon among his fellow teachers: "Most
were sympathetic, but with very few exceptions they were careful not to
make their position obvious to the administration." Chandler Davis was
equally bitter. His own colleagues in the Mathematics Department were
loyal to him throughout his troubles, but once two faculty committees
had unanimously recommended his dismissal, his supporters in other departments simply disappeared.[39]

It was not just the blacklisted professors who suffered professionally
and socially; their families did as well. Usually the suffering was indirect,
the consequence of the sudden unemployment of the head of the house-
hold. Occasionally, however, the wives and children of the blacklisted
academics had to deal with hostility as well. Things were hardest for the
Lorches, though probably more because of the family's opposition to segregation than because of Lee's academic problems. There were cross-
burnings on their lawn, rocks through their windows, and, once, even
dynamite in their garage. They had to keep changing their unlisted tele-
phone number to avoid crank calls. Friends were few; and in the Lorches'
last year in Little Rock, their fifteen-year-old daughter Alice was beaten
up in school. Mark Nickerson's seven-year-old son was also tormented
because of his father's problems. But these cases were probably exceptional. Many other academics certainly feared that their children would
be harassed in some way, but few actually were. Nobody, for example,

stigmatized Chandler Davis's children when their father went to jail; on the contrary, one of the children's teachers actually told the class that going to jail for one's principles was quite all right. In addition, of course, many of the children of these radical parents were radicals themselves, and though some of the older ones may have themselves suffered for their own political activities, they usually expected and knew how to handle the hostility they encountered.[40]

Just as hard to deal with, and considerably more common among the blacklisted families, was the moving. Some families even had to endure separations as a consequence of the blacklist. Horace B. Davis and his wife were apart for close to a year when he was teaching in South Carolina and she was still working in Missouri. Because Davis's son Chandler regretted the many moves his father's political problems inflicted upon the family when he was growing up, he and his wife Natalie had hoped to spare their own children such uprootings. But in the years before they went to Toronto, the Davises moved at least four times. So, too, did the Lorches; Lee recalls that each move became harder than the last, the final move to Canada being the most traumatic of all.[41]

Moving was particularly difficult for the blacklisted professors who went abroad. Many people simply refused to consider emigrating for just that reason; it would be too hard on their families. No one found it easy. Lawrence Klein recalled how difficult it was to "move a family of three young kids to England. At our age, with our resources at that time, that was not easy." Klein, at least, went to England and did not have to cope with the language problems that plagued some of the other émigrés. Joseph Cort, for example, had a lot of trouble. Because his family spoke Russian at home when he was a child, Cort mastered Czech fairly easily, but his wife never did and thus never really adjusted to living in Prague. The Hodeses had language problems too. Though the children soon became fluent in Chinese, their parents had more trouble. In retrospect, Jane Hodes admits that the move to China "was harder than I allowed myself to think."[42]

There were other, less concrete problems that plagued the wives and families of the blacklisted academics. Oscar Shaftel recalls that his wife had trouble adjusting to his dismissal from Queens College: "It hit her hard. She basically lost her status; she lost her identity as a professor's wife." The strains and insecurities of unemployment, government harassment, and the prospect of emigration tried even the most stalwart of couples. Natalie Davis recalls that though she supported her husband's political struggles throughout the 1950s, she experienced a real emotional crisis when he went to prison. Though she knew it was irrational, she nonetheless felt as if she was being deserted. The Davis marriage survived the experience. But for many of the other blacklisted academics—I know of at least a dozen—their troubles overwhelmed their marriages, Tom McGrath explains:

I would say that the episode *destroyed* a life. But we all have several possible lifelines—maybe it was all to the good. But I would say that it was largely responsible for destroying a marriage and a family because of lack of money to live on, lack of security, the resultant anxieties.[43]

Sometimes it took years before the accumulated tensions of the blacklist culminated in a divorce. Norman and Courtney Cazden did not split up until the late 1960s, more than fifteen years after Norman had been fired from the University of Illinois. "While we were both actively involved in an academic community, as we were through the years in Illinois," Courtney recalled,

we shared a lot. We shared friends, we shared political activities tied to the academic community. . . . There certainly were already stresses in our marriage. . . . But, it was that part of our lives that held us together that was broken by the change in Norman's job situation.

The Cazdens moved to Bridgeport, Connecticut, to be near New York and Norman's family. "It was difficult for me," Courtney explained. Norman was Jewish, she was not, and in the 1950s "it was easier for me to share an interethnic marriage in an academic community where ethnic differences are really minimized." But in Bridgeport, they were "part of the Jewish community," and Courtney "never felt comfortable in it."

When the Cazdens moved to Boston in 1961 so that Courtney could return to graduate school, Norman's lack of an academic job created different problems. His world "was still a very small world," one that revolved around the home where he gave piano lessons, wrote music and articles, and did far more housework and childcare than, in those prefeminist days, most husbands and fathers would do. But as Courtney finished up her doctorate and then got a teaching job at Harvard, her life changed:

I started travelling and getting active and just loved it and so . . . the shared life diminished . . . because I developed a whole new world, found a whole new world, and made paths through a whole new world that he didn't share.

Finally, the disparities between their two situations simply overwhelmed the marriage, and they got a divorce, something that both Cazdens recognize might not have happened had Norman remained a college professor.[44]

All the uncertainties of the McCarthy years—financial, professional, social, marital, and, for those people under indictment, legal as well—took their emotional toll. There were few of the blacklisted academics who did not, at least during the period they were fighting the blacklist, admit to serious anxiety. Things cleared up later for almost everybody, but as Dudley Strauss, a former Queens College English teacher, pointed out, there's no way of conveying those first five years. . . . To be unfrocked at age 42 after an academic lifetime is an absolutely terrifying experience, particularly when there are children, and newspaper publicity, and ugly phone calls.

Leon Kamin made a similar though more low-keyed assessment of his emotional state. "It was not much fun to be 26, with a brand new Ph.D., and no job, and no prospects, and worried about going to jail." Kamin went on to acknowledge that "after the initial adjustment to Canada, there have been no further problems." His observation was shared by most of the blacklisted academics. The first few years were the worst. Ross Lomanitz, who had as hard a time on the blacklist as anyone, recalls how his anxieties shifted over time. At first he was afraid of some kind of a frame-up "akin to what I believe was done to Julius and Ethel Rosenberg." Later, his paranoia receded, and he worried mainly about finding and keeping jobs. Finally, his fears focused on the possibility that he might never be able to do scientific work again.[45]

Being fired, it turned out, did not always produce as much anxiety as the uncertainty that preceded the actual, or possible, dismissal. This meant that many of the people who kept their jobs may have suffered just as much emotionally as the people who lost theirs. One man, retained by Columbia after taking the Fifth before McCarthy in the spring of 1953, nevertheless recalls that the episode caused him and his wife "a very bad year." The situation was especially tense for people who had to face the prospect of both losing their jobs and going to jail. Wendell Furry, whose position at Harvard probably made him the most highly publicized Fifth Amendment academic in America, recalls that he "felt very desperate" at the time. Marcus Singer, the Cornell biologist whose case dragged on for years until he was acquitted and reinstated, describes a similarly desperate state of mind:

> I was very depressed, worried all the time. Then there is the psychological state of the accused—a feeling of guilt even when not guilty with suspicions of oneself. The constant pressure of fighting against the whole array of government powers, the feeling of being alone.[46]

Singer's recollections accord with those of people in other fields as well—entertainers and government employees, for example. Psychologically, it was hard for a middle-class American, no matter what his or her profession or political views, to defy the government and end up on the wrong side of the law. People who had not been connected with the CP seemed to have suffered the most. These innocent liberals were unprepared for their Kafkaesque ordeal and had trouble understanding, let alone accepting, what their own government was doing to them. The China expert John Fairbank, himself falsely accused during the IPR hearings of having been a Communist, described this mental state: "People absorbed the values of their accusers. People who were named began to feel that maybe there was something wrong with them for having made contacts with communists or something like that."[47]

And, of course, there was anger. In a letter to the Cazdens, written some time in the late 1950s, Natalie Davis let out her resentment against the years of anxiety that Chandler's political problems had caused:

> Our only problem is the future. We still do not know where we go. The Constant Uncertainty, the worries about the Case, etc. have lasted too long. This constant absorption with how one is going to live instead of living and acting is a great waste, and takes one's mind off scientific work and humanistic political concerns that go beyond one's own problems. I am quite fed up.

From an outside perspective at the time, it would have seemed as if the Davises were coping with their troubles rather well. Their marriage was not in danger. And during the worst of the blacklist period, Natalie finished her Ph.D. dissertation on sixteenth-century France and raised three children. Other people coped less well.[48]

People differ enormously in their individual temperaments and in the way they react to stress. Some of the blacklisted academics claimed that they were not, emotionally at least, affected. They were radicals and did not expect American society to treat them any differently. "Really, what is there to say," one of them explained:

> I was no innocent. So I lost my job. Nothing came as a surprise. A radical, a leftwinger who is shocked, surprised, dismayed at the materialization of his own understanding is indeed basically disoriented. It certainly wasn't pleasant and it was indecent. . . . It was *physically* impossible for me to do anything but oppose them [HUAC] to the best of my ability. . . . I did *not* suffer, I did not *lose* friends, I did not come down with physical or mental illnesses.

Similarly, the Michigan biologist Clement Markert insisted that he refused to worry about his problems. To let himself get "bugged by it" was to let the other side set the rules, and he felt that politically it was important for him to continue his scientific work and not spend time in his personal political defense. Markert recognized that he was a survivor; after all, he had come through the Spanish Civil War when 450 of the 500 men in his battalion had been killed. He also had a lot of self-confidence:

> One reason why it wasn't so bad for me, and it's clearly a fundamental point, is that if you really are clearly—aw, this sounds awfully self-flattering—exceptionally good at what you are doing it makes it far easier to be peripheral and outside of the mainstream in other respects and get away with it.[49]

But for people who lacked such political clarity or personal strength, the stresses of McCarthyism could be devastating. Many were the people who, according to their own testimony or that of outside observers, were traumatized by the experience. The lawyers who handled the cases of these people often felt that they had to act as psychiatrists as well as attorneys. At least three of the blacklisted academics had serious mental breakdowns, and it is hard to imagine that, whatever the underlying psychological causes were, the difficulties and anxieties connected with the blacklist did not contribute in part. There were three suicides. Though none of the three had been blacklisted, they were all involved, in one way or another, with the political troubles of the time. One was an informer. One was the Harvard literary critic, F. O. Matthiessen, a radical and a homosexual who jumped out of a hotel window in 1950 when the accumulated weight of his own personal and political despair overwhelmed him. "How much the state of the world has to do with my state of mind I do not know," his suicide note explained. "But as a Christian and a socialist believing in international peace, I find myself terribly oppressed by the present tensions." The third suicide was William K. Sherwood, a Stanford biologist who killed himself in June 1957, two days before he was to appear before HUAC. His suicide note leaves little doubt about his motives.

> My life and my livelihood are now threatened by the House Committee. . . . I would love to spend the next few years in laboratories, and I would hate to spend them in jail.[50]

Sherwood's response was extreme. Though there is no systematic way to assess all the psychological damage of the blacklist period, were we to construct a graph, we might find Sherwood at one end of the bell curve, Markert, perhaps, at the other. Some people floundered, most muddled through, and a few managed to escape unscathed. The most traumatic moments were in the beginning, when people were overwhelmed with uncertainties in every area. Eventually, most of them recovered their equilibrium. What Bonnie Bird Gundlach calls their "spiritual India rubber quality" helped them adapt to new lives and new careers. Moreover, quite a few of them felt rather good about what they had done. Most of them had voluntarily sacrificed their careers in order to preserve what they believed was their moral integrity. And, though they knew they might have a hard time as a result, the conviction that they had behaved well, that they had done the right thing, may well have given them a strong psychological boost during an otherwise bleak period. "It is something—perhaps it is a great deal," Barrows Dunham observed:

> to discover that one can stand one's ground against the enemies of culture, and thus help to defeat them. One knows then that one's life has been useful, and that therefore one has not lived in vain. . . . If I can speak without seeming to abandon all modesty, I would want to say that what I did, what I morally had to do, was painful and perilous, but, beyond all that, it was a privilege.[51]

Dunham was not alone. Bernhard Deutch, a physicist who was a graduate student at the University of Pennsylvania in 1954 when he incurred a contempt citation for challenging HUAC on constitutional grounds, spent eight years in legal and professional limbo before the Supreme Court finally ruled 5 to 4 in his favor. As soon as he won his case, he left the country. "I was ashamed of the USA," he recently recalled:

> But the one thing that I am proud of, is that in my personal moment of truth 26 years ago, I refused to exchange my career for those of others. I volunteered to be a test case to eliminate the power of the congressional committees over the Barrows Dunhams and others that have made America great.[52]

Harry Slochower was another blacklisted academic who took pride in his behavior before a congressional committee. "After the stand I took [invoking the Fifth Amendment], I have rarely been happier." Even winning reinstatement from the Supreme Court in a landmark decision was "less gratifying to me than the fact that I was able to take a position in 1952 which seemed to be the only honorable one. For Slochower, as for some of the other blacklisted academics, his forced exodus from the American academy produced professional as well as psychological benefits. By 1952 he had achieved everything that he wanted to as a teacher. His classes were popular, especially among the more intellectual and left-wing students, and he had become a kind of cult figure on the Brooklyn College campus.

> I reached a point where I was God for the students. [Losing my job] gave me a kind of rebirth. For example, if this hadn't happened, I would still be in Brooklyn College, still being adored and deified by the girls and boys. But it wouldn't have helped me grow.

His transition from teacher to therapist liberated Slochower from what he feared might have become an increasingly stultifying way of life. He felt intellectually rejuvenated as well. For years he had been studying literature from a Freudian perspective and, in his new career, he continued that work and also took over the editorship of a psychoanalytic journal devoted to the arts.[53]

Slochower was not alone in crediting his, albeit involuntary, departure from the academy with enabling him to recycle himself intellectually. This happened to people in every field—from economics and literature to physics and philosophy—though, obviously, not every blacklisted professor felt him- or herself so blessed. Even so, there was a positive side to the blacklist. David Bohm, for example, recalls the advantages of the enforced sabbatical Princeton gave him when he was indicted for contempt after taking the Fifth before HUAC. Considered by many the most promising of the group of Oppenheimer's blacklisted students, Bohm had already been doing important work on quantum theory. Being suspended was "a big boon, because I had a lot of time to myself. I did a lot of work and I really was able to do my work much better." In addition, he felt himself "freed from the intellectual pressures to conform to a certain line and my mind was able to work more freely." Emigration was hard. Bohm spent four and a half years in Brazil and two years in Israel before he eventually ended up—happily—in England. "I can't say that I'm worse off as a result of having to leave America. I may be better off." Though we may question the equanimity that, in retrospect, Bohm and so many of the other blacklisted and exiled academics reveal about their experiences, there is no reason to question their final assessment. It would be hard to imagine that Bohm didn't agonize about his decision to renounce his American citizenship so that he could leave Brazil for Israel. But for Bohm as for the others, the hard times passed. And he might not be the only American academic who would rather live in London than Princeton or, as with the Thorners, Paris instead of Philadelphia.[54]

XII

"Without Guidance": The Academic Profession Responds to McCarthyism

As they dig into their memories, the protagonists of the academic freedom battles of the 1940s and 1950s almost uniformly reserve their bitterest condemnation for those of their colleagues who failed to support them, those colleagues whose "speed of flight," in Barrows Dunham's estimation, "was hotter than their love of liberty." Congressional committees, boards of trustees, academic administrators all behaved as they were expected to behave. They were the enemy; and, as the more self-conscious radicals among the dismissed professors noted, what they did was understandable in terms of their desire to protect the status quo. It was the behavior of their fellow academics, especially the self-professed liberals among them, that really rankled. In most cases, it was not so much what these people did that upset the blacklisted professors as it was what they did not do. They did not organize; they did not protest; they did not do anything that reversed the tide of dismissals.[1]

Perhaps nothing that faculty members, individually or as a group, could have done would have worked unless, as the public relations director of a large midwestern university allegedly remarked, whole departments had resigned in protest. Since there were no mass resignations, nor even, with the possible exception of one slightly dubious instance at the University of Washington, individual ones, the efficacy of such a protest must remain a matter of speculation. More to the point, however, is to understand why even limited protests did not take place, why the academic profession did not put up more of a fight against the dismissals of the McCarthy era. To begin with, however, we must assess the accuracy of the protagonists' recollections. Were they, in fact, deserted by their colleagues and abandoned by the rest of the academic profession? Or were their perceptions skewed by a few individual disappointments, no less disappointing for being exceptions, but not really typical of the professoriat as a whole?[2]

The evidence we have suggests that the situation was murky. Some groups and individuals stood by the former professors, while others did not. The failure of those groups and individuals from whom the professors expected help may well account for the bitterness that pervades their recollections. It may also account for the rather common—and I think incorrect—perception that their liberal colleagues deserted them and their conservative ones stood firm. Because the people under attack apparently assumed that their supporters would be liberals, they were both more aware of the conservatives who backed them and more distressed by the liberals who did not. Thus, for example, while deploring the defection of some of Cornell's better-known liberals, Marcus Singer did note that he had more trouble with his own colleagues in the Zoology Department, who were quite conservative. On other campuses as well, it was often the more reactionary members of the faculty who were the most antagonistic to the political dissenters. Usually, however, these right-wing professors had little to do with the disposition of their universities' academic freedom cases; their political extremism barred them from the faculty committees which decided such matters. In a sense, therefore, the displaced academics were right about the liberals' failure to support academic freedom. Their conservative colleagues were probably more antagonistic, but their liberal ones were more powerful. And it was the latter, those moderate and respectable professors who, as the established leaders of the faculty on most campuses, discouraged strenuous opposition to the witch-hunt and so in that way collaborated in its implementation.[3]

The academic community was not unaware of its collective failure of nerve. The Fund for the Republic, an offshoot of the Ford Foundation, was concerned about the apparent erosion of civil liberties on American campuses and gave the sociologists Paul Lazarsfeld and Wagner Thielens, Jr., a quarter of a million dollars to find out how college professors were responding to McCarthyism. The result, an elaborate survey of 2,451 social scientists, done in the spring of 1955, confirms some of the dissidents' perceptions. Many of the respondents, especially those whom Lazarsfeld and Thielens categorized as liberals, confessed that they were scared. Over 25 percent of them revealed that they had indulged in some form of political self-censorship, either in their professional activities or in their private lives. Significantly, the survey exposed a considerable discrepancy between the respondents' unquestionably liberal opinions and their willingness to act upon them. Though 80 percent of the social scientists polled said that they would approve of having Owen Lattimore give a lecture at their school, only 40 percent said they would protest vigorously if the president banned the lecture. Similarly, they would, they claimed, join a support movement to defend a colleague who was unjustly fired for political reasons, but they would not lead such a movement. Moreover, a surprising 28 percent of the respondents felt that were they themselves to face some kind of political charge, they would not receive the support of their colleagues. "One would hope," one professor explained, "but the record nationally is not good and I can't see *this* faculty leading the vanguard." Expectations were low, and Lazarsfeld and Thielens noted that quite a few academics seemed to feel that it would be "beyond the call of duty" for colleagues to come to their aid. "I would expect my close friends to support me," one man admitted, "but if they did not, I would understand." Few of these professors were radicals; for so many of them to take such a negative view of their colleagues' probable response to what would have been a completely unjustified attack on them seems to indicate a lack of steadfastness within the academic profession.[4]

Many of the researchers' questions were hypothetical, and so, as David Riesman noted in a postscript to the study, the answers they received may well have contained more than an element of wishful thinking. "It is striking," Riesman observed,

> how many highly self-conscious men qualified their answers, saying that they hoped they would have the courage of their convictions: not having faced fire, they had the misgivings of green troops. And, in a number of such cases, I gained the sense that the interviewer was simply the rapporteur of an internal dialogue in which the respondent was deeply engaged.

The perspicacity of Riesman's observation comes through when we look at what actually happened. At those schools where dissidents were fired, the internal dialogues he noticed externalized themselves. Not only was the faculty split, but individual professors were themselves torn by ambivalence.[5]

Nowhere perhaps were those contradictions as striking as at the University of Washington, the school which experienced the first major academic freedom case of the Cold War. Many faculty members disapproved of the anti-Communist excesses of the state legislature's Canwell Committee, which investigated the University; yet they refused to take a public stand. To do so would have put them in opposition to the University administration's efforts to placate the committee. The response of George Lundberg, the chairman of the Sociology Department, though perhaps extreme, shows how conflicted even a single professor could be. In June 1948, just as the Canwell Committee was about to begin its investigation, a group of faculty members circulated an open letter critical of the impending probe. Only fifty people signed it; Lundberg was not among them. Instead he sent an open letter to Washington's president Raymond Allen decrying the petition, defending the Canwell Committee, and explaining why he felt Communists should be denied the protection of academic freedom. Allen mimeographed Lundberg's letter and circulated it to the rest of the faculty. In private, however, Lundberg took a different stand. As he explained in a personal letter to a colleague who had criticized his public statement, the Canwell Committee was "an unqualified nuisance, unwise, ineffective, and obscene." Moreover, as a liberal who believed that all points of view should be heard, Lundberg claimed that he was willing to tolerate Communists on the faculty, if—and this was, of course, a significant "if"—it would not create too many other problems.[6]

Lundberg may have been more confused than most of his colleagues, but he was by no means alone. Similar equivocations came out later, after the Regents went along with President Allen's recommendation to overrule the faculty's Tenure Committee and fire two self-professed Communists. The faculty committee itself had been split, several of its members claiming that it was only a technicality which prevented them from voting for the dismissal of the Communists. As a result, at its first meeting after the firing, the faculty senate refrained from censuring the administration and tabled a cautious resolution criticizing the Regents' action on procedural grounds alone. The issue was so sensitive that historian Stull Holt, the man who had sponsored the tabled resolution, refused to sign an open letter protesting the firings. Though he opposed the administration's disregard for academic due process, he feared that by signing the protest letter he might be seen as condoning the behavior of the dismissed professors.[7]

Holt's ambivalence was typical of most of Washington's liberals. Only a tiny handful of civil libertarians considered the case a clear-cut violation of academic freedom; the rest felt that it was far more complicated. On the one hand, they recognized that the Regents had overridden the recommendations of a faculty committee; on the other, they knew that the committee's majority actually agreed with what the Regents had done. In addition, faculty members who were upset about the procedural violations of academic freedom that had taken place eschewed protest lest it seem as if they favored the retention of Communist teachers or condoned Ralph Gundlach's refusal to talk about his politics. Finally, there was the widespread assumption that the task of establishing the legitimacy of the firings was no longer in the hands of anybody in Seattle and that the final judgment on the case would come from Committee A of the American Association of University Professors. Accordingly, many people who might otherwise have spoken out more vigorously did not in the belief that, since the AAUP would intervene, local action was unnecessary. Whatever the reason, the result was that most members of the Washington faculty either took no stand or else waffled and, in so doing, supported by inaction the action of the Regents.[8]

The ambivalence that paralyzed so many of Washington's liberals was endemic. It was to keep academic liberals elsewhere from putting up an effective fight against McCarthyism when it reached their campuses. Some faculties were a bit more resolute than Washington's, but even in the face of the most blatant affronts to their autonomy, they rarely seemed able to do more than make a token gesture. At Rutgers, for example, faculty outrage at the firing of two Fifth Amendment witnesses dissipated so quickly in the face of the president's invocation of the Communist menace that the special faculty meeting convened to censure the trustees decided instead to poll the faculty by mail. Significantly, the only concrete action which the faculty endorsed on its poll was to establish a committee to study the procedures that had led to the dismissals. This was a common solution. At many of the schools which fired people during the McCarthy period, faculties responded by fearlessly resolving to study the problem.[9]

Part of the reason for the failure of the academic profession to speak out against the political dismissals of the McCarthy period was that many of its members supported those dismissals. They shared the general hostility to Communists and Fifth Amendment witnesses and felt that such people did not belong in the academic world. Other professors were less sure but did not want to make a fuss. Propriety was the issue here. Though most of the teachers—certainly most of the tenured ones—at the schools we have been studying knew that they would probably not get into trouble for circulating petitions or organizing meetings, they nonetheless kept their distance. They did not want to put themselves in an adversarial position, either with regard to their colleagues or the administration.

Those who did defy the conventional limits of faculty debate and insisted that the rights of an individual took precedence over the well-being of an institution engendered considerable hostility. When, for example, during the course of a heated discussion about the University of Michigan's treatment of its unfriendly witnesses, the eminent mathematician R. L. Wilder denounced the administration's cooperation with HUAC as "beyond all bounds of morality and decency," many faculty members, though presumably deploring much of what HUAC was doing, were shocked at Wilder's *lèse majesté*. Attacking the president of the University in public did not accord with the "gentlemanliness" expected of a member of the Michigan faculty. Wilder, who later became president of the American Mathematical Society, had sufficient prestige to withstand such collegial disapproval; people with lesser credentials were more vulnerable and more circumspect. So pervasive was this pressure for respectability that even the most committed civil libertarians reined themselves in.[10]

The mathematician Hollis Cooley belonged to the NYU faculty senate committee which handled both the Bradley and the Burgum cases; he disagreed with the committee's majority and voted to retain the two men. He also issued a strong statement defending his position and denouncing the hypocrisy of the administration's stance. In retrospect, however, Cooley feels that he made a political mistake by relying on the salience of his arguments. "I should have raised a bigger fuss." Sarah Lawrence's Helen Lynd felt similar regrets about her own failure to challenge the Jenner Committee in public. Obviously, when people who were as devoted to the rights of individuals as Cooley and Lynd felt that they had pulled their punches, we should not be surprised at the inactivity of men and women who were less committed.[11]

In addition, many academics who were critical of what was going on did not speak up because they felt they could have more influence if they acted in private. Active, open opposition not only violated the gentlemanly norms of the academic community, but, these people believed, was less effective than working on the inside. One of Lazarsfeld's respondents spoke for many others when he explained, "I would not protest publicly, but would within the university. I would not issue a press release, but use the channels through which we go in the university." And, in fact, this was the way many liberal academics responded to the cases that took place on their campuses. They went through channels. Thus, for example, a few months after the president of Ohio State fired Byron Darling for taking the Fifth Amendment, a rump faction of the local ACLU issued a press release condemning the dismissal. A Law School professor there, himself active in the ACLU, was furious, especially with the academics involved. He and his colleagues had been negotiating with the administration behind the scenes and, he explained, for other professors "to take a public position of condemnation would be a serious embarrassment in our efforts to straighten things out in our capacity as faculty members." There was, however, no evidence that such private negotiations worked.[12]

Fear was an issue as well, though primarily at the smaller, weaker colleges, where, as one of Lazarsfeld's respondents noted, "a vigorous protest is not worth much when you can't get an audience, you just get fired." Few schools of this type had Cold War academic freedom cases. At one of those that did, Emporia State Teachers College in Kansas, W. Lou Tandy, the economist who was fired for signing a petition requesting clemency for the Smith Act defendants, recalls that "only *two* out of a faculty of a hundred or so stood up to be counted in supporting my position. The rest were craven, conservative sheep." Yet, even at as sophisticated a place as New York University, there was a surprising amount of timidity. In December 1952 the student paper polled the faculty on the then-pending case of Edwin Berry Burgum. Few professors were willing to express any opinion at all. Only one was willing to let the paper use his name. Another man, informed of that teacher's rashness, told the student journalists, "that fellow won't be here for long."[13]

Such caution, extreme as it seems today, may not have been completely unjustified. There was at least one school at which a teacher apparently lost his job because of his support for a discharged colleague. This happened at Penn State, where an albeit untenured assistant professor of mathematics was suddenly let go after leading the campaign for the reinstatement of Lee Lorch. But this was the only case of this type I've encountered. Though academic administrators elsewhere may have been uncomfortable with the more outspoken critics on their faculties and may even have harassed them to the extent of slowing down promotions or withholding raises, nobody else lost a job for trying to save that of a colleague. Of course, the mere threat of such reprisals may have been deterrence enough.[14]

Perhaps we paint too grim a picture. Certainly there were many academics who, when put to the test, stood up valiantly for their endangered colleagues. Throughout Chandler Davis's ordeal at Michigan, his colleagues in the Mathematics Department wholeheartedly supported his refusal to cooperate with the University's investigation. They spoke up for him at faculty meetings, testified for him at all of his University hearings, and led a determined battle to get him severance pay after his dismissal. Clement Markert's colleagues were equally energetic on his behalf. They formed a committee and solicited letters from leading biologists around the country. Professors elsewhere raised money for their embattled colleagues and sometimes even pledged a percentage of their own salaries to assist the people who had been suspended without pay. Such generosity was, in fact, rather common. It seemed to have been easier for most academics to sign checks than petitions. To do so was a matter of fairness, not left-wing politics. As the group of Cornell professors who organized a fund drive for Marcus Singer explained in their appeal to the faculty:

> Professor Singer, like any American citizen, is entitled to adequate counsel in his defense. Hence a contributor to the fund will not necessarily be expressing his approval of Professor Singer's position.

Yet the fear was so pervasive that even at a school like Harvard some of the contributors to Wendell Furry's legal defense fund requested anonymity, and one donor was so terrified that he asked for his money back.[15]

In any event, fund-raising, though helpful, was hardly the kind of massive protest activity that the academic community needed to mount in order to prevent or rectify the abuses of academic freedom that occurred during the McCarthy period. John Caughey, a UCLA history professor who had refused to sign the California loyalty oath and was thus himself a beneficiary of such collegial generosity, explained to the general secretary of the American Association of University Professors in 1956 that offering financial support to endangered academics "is analogous to coping with the problem of industrial accidents by raising money to cover hospital costs." There was considerable irony in Caughey's remarks, for it was clear that the AAUP, the OSHA of academe, had been delinquent in policing the educational industry during the height of McCarthyism. The organization's stated devotion to the principles of academic freedom remained firm throughout this period. It refused to modify its opposition to the firing of Communist teachers, and it took equally strong stands on loyalty oaths, censorship, and the Fifth Amendment. But it did not censure any school which had violated those principles. And it did not even publish any reports about them. Not until April 1956 did the AAUP belatedly condemn the specific violations of academic freedom that had taken place.[16]

Whether timelier action by the AAUP would have actually prevented any firings, given all the other pressures on university administrations, faculties, and trustees during this period, is hard to tell. Nonetheless, the failure of the AAUP to take any public action at all until the worst of McCarthyism was over certainly did not advance the cause of academic freedom, and it is entirely possible that prompt condemnation of some of the more egregious violations of academic freedom might have deterred some administrations or stimulated more resistance by faculty members at schools where such resistance might have been effective. As the 1950s' favorite political theorist, Alexis de Tocqueville, noted more than a hundred years earlier, when Americans act on public issues they do so through an association. The AAUP was the organization through which the professoriat ordinarily exercised its collective concern for the preservation of academic freedom. Thus, the Association's failure to perform its expected function had a profound and devastating effect on the academic profession's efforts to combat McCarthyism and contributed as much, if not more, to the inability of the nation's college teachers to protect their colleagues as the shortcomings of individual professors and faculties.[17]

Obviously something had gone very wrong. Although, as we shall see, there are many explanations for the AAUP's puzzling inertia, ignorance is not one of them. The organization knew what was going on. Though people involved in academic freedom cases are sometimes reluctant to contact the AAUP for fear that they will be seen as troublemakers and be unable to find another job, this was rarely a problem for the teachers who were dismissed during the McCarthy years. Their cases were front-page news. In many instances, they contacted the AAUP's headquarters in Washington as soon as they suspected that their jobs might be in danger. They wanted what Reed College philosopher Stanley Moore called "preventive (rather than punitive) action"; they expected that the organization would intervene and, if not forestall their dismissals, at least investigate and report upon them.[18]

More often than not the professional staff members from the AAUP's central office in Washington, D.C., responded to these appeals. Sometimes they advised the endangered teachers on specific issues and held out the promise of further intervention. Usually, however, they offered technical advice, explaining AAUP policies and helping administrators and faculty committees organize hearings to accord with the AAUP's guidelines for such inquiries. Thus, for example, the organization's general secretary, Ralph Himstead, spent an entire afternoon with the Rutgers Special Faculty Committee discussing "the procedural aspects of the cases" that the committee was going to hear. This seems to have been the area in which the AAUP was most effective. In a few of the cases that came to his attention, Himstead intervened quite forcefully and was sometimes even able to convince an institution to give its endangered professor a certain amount of procedural due process. This is what happened at Tulane, where it seems likely that a barrage of telegrams from Himstead decrying the irregularities surrounding the dismissal of Robert Hodes persuaded Tulane's president to grant Hodes a formal hearing. Sometimes, of course, such intervention was fruitless. Himstead's eloquent appeals could not prevent the California Regents from imposing the loyalty oath or convince the Michigan Regents to give Chandler Davis and Mark Nickerson a year's severance pay. But the embattled teachers appreciated the support, nonetheless, and of course expected that the organization would follow it up with a formal investigation of their dismissals.[19]

Occasionally, if the protagonist or the local chapter asked for it, Himstead or another representative of the Association would visit the campus where an academic freedom case was in the making. These trips were often for the purpose of mediating disputes. The AAUP has always tried to deal quietly with the cases brought to its attention and negotiate some kind of a settlement rather than mount a public investigation. So Himstead, in accordance with this tradition, intervened in many more cases than he reported on even during the McCarthy period. Of course, when such a politically volatile issue as Communism was involved, these behind-the-scenes negotiations were out of the question. Even so, the AAUP still sent representatives to the troubled campuses, usually to observe or participate in an academic hearing. The main function of these observers, who were either members of the organization's professional staff or, more frequently, individual professors active in the Association, seems to have been to carry the flag and establish the AAUP's presence at these occasions. Sometimes, however, they would participate in the hearings and, as the AAUP's representative at the NYU hearing for Edwin Berry Burgum did, present the AAUP's position on academic freedom. Such activities were normal practices for the organization and were the usual preliminaries to the more formal investigation by Committee A that ordinarily occurred after a dismissal took place. But, as we shall see, these early gestures proved abortive, for some reason Committee A never followed through.[20]

Committee A was not the whole organization, however, and at many schools local AAUP chapters became involved with the cases on their campuses. Whether or not the endangered teachers were themselves active in the chapter, as many of them were, they often sought its support as soon as they knew they were in trouble. The chapters usually responded by bringing the cases to the attention of the national office. In addition, many locals tried to mediate between university authorities and the endangered professors and often were able to ensure that the professors received a fair hearing. Occasionally, AAUP chapters led the fight to save their colleagues' jobs. The Rutgers unit was particularly stalwart; it even sent a representative to the AAUP's annual meeting in

1956 to make sure that Rutgers did not escape censure. The Buffalo chapter was just as energetic—and more successful. A week after philosophy professor William Parry's encounter with HUAC, the Buffalo AAUP took a strong stand and voted a series of resolutions defending Parry's use of the Fifth Amendment and urging his retention. How influential these resolutions were, we may never know. Certainly, it is hard to believe that the AAUP's firm and publicly voiced support for Parry did not make the Buffalo authorities draw back somewhat at the prospect of confronting an angry faculty were they to fire the controversial philosopher.[21]

Sometimes, however, the local AAUP refused to intervene. The chapter at Kansas State Teachers College in Emporia, where W. Lou Tandy was fired for having signed a petition on behalf of the Smith Act defendants, not only gave Tandy no assistance but even decided against taking a position on his case. Similarly, the AAUP chapter at the University of Florida voted 56 to 53 not to support a political scientist who had invoked the Fifth Amendment before HUAC. Though the teacher had been suspended after his congressional hearing, he still had the option of going before a faculty committee and fighting for his job. "Feeling, however, that my cause was hopeless (because of the AAUP vote)," he explained, "I resigned to save myself and my family further distress." Penn State's chapter was so hostile to Lee Lorch that even after Ralph Himstead asked it to help out, it refused. This may have been an exceptional case, for the AAUP's leading representative on the campus seems to have had little sympathy for political dissent and was something of an anti-Semite as well.[22]

There were many reasons why local chapters refrained from action. At smaller, less prestigious public colleges, the administration often dominated the faculty so thoroughly that the AAUP chapter simply could not function. Sometimes the local shrank from trying to assist an untenured teacher. At other schools it was ambivalence about defending Communists or Fifth Amendment witnesses and a desire not to antagonize the administration that kept the chapter from taking a stand. At a few schools, however, the faculty had so much power that the AAUP wasn't needed. This was the case at Harvard, where the chapter was, according to Talcott Parsons, its president during the 1950s, "pretty completely inactive. . . . Though we had a couple of executive committee meetings, I don't think we ever had a chapter meeting." The dormant condition of the chapter did not, however, prevent Parsons from playing a small, though symbolically important, role in the disposition of Harvard's Fifth Amendment cases. Because he was a friend of the University's provost, Paul Buck, Buck used him, Parsons recalled,

> as a kind of sounding board for faculty opinion. He'd call up every now and then and ask what the faculty was feeling and then he could tell people like Marbury [a member of the Corporation] that he'd been in touch with the chairman of the AAUP chapter.[23]

The main reason, however, the local chapters kept their distance from the academic freedom cases on their campuses was that they were supposed to. Hollis Cooley, perhaps the most consistent civil libertarian on the faculty at New York University, was the chairman of its chapter in 1948, when the NYU administration suspended the chairman of the German Department, Lyman Bradley, for his refusal to cooperate with HUAC. Despite his concern, Cooley tried to stay aloof. "As an officer of the AAUP," he explained,

> I have considered that the local chapter should not become involved in the case, in accordance with the constitutional admonition to keep out of disputes between individual faculty members and the administration. The chapter has taken no action whatever in the case, although a few members have thought we should take some stand.

It was the Association's standard policy that once a complaint had been received, jurisdiction over the case would immediately shift to Committee A and the national office. The wisdom of such a policy was obvious: local people were often too close to the individuals involved to preserve the detachment necessary for an impartial investigation. In addition, as was demonstrated at many schools where violations of academic freedom occurred, the members of the AAUP were reluctant to confront their administrations.[24]

Enforcing this policy during the 1950s was not easy. On many campuses, local AAUP activists were upset about what was going on. They wanted to protest or do something that would demonstrate their opposition to the pending dismissals and perhaps forestall them. At Ohio State, where President Howard Bevis announced that he was planning to fire physicist Byron Darling for taking the Fifth Amendment, the local AAUP was particularly hard to control. The chapter had scheduled an emergency meeting on the Darling case, so its president, who wanted to follow AAUP guidelines and keep the group from taking a stand, telegraphed Himstead on the day before the meeting pleading for help. "Efforts to prevent chapter action will be greatly strengthened if you can wire me positive assurance central office or Committee A will make some type of investigation." Himstead responded with a one-sentence telegram: "If Professor Darling is dismissed, his dismissal will be investigated by Association." Even so, it took what the president described as "a very rough and difficult two hour session" to convince the local not to censure the administration.[25]

Though no other chapter required a telegram from Himstead to keep the rank and file under control, it was clear that at many schools local AAUP members refrained from speaking out only because they believed the central office had already entered the case. Otherwise, these people would have given their endangered colleagues much more support than they did. Of course, had there been an active national office, it would have mattered little whether or not local chapters became involved, for the organization's staff would have taken charge—as, by the AAUP's constitution, it was supposed to. But there was something wrong in Washington. In March 1952, Arthur C. Cole, the chairman of the ACLU's Academic Freedom Committee, described his group's difficulties with the AAUP's national office in a letter to Richard Shryock, the organization's president:

> I write to you because the Academic Freedom Committee has become increasingly concerned about the difficulty of communicating with the Washington office of the AAUP. Since June of 1951 several letters have been addressed to Mr. Himstead by Mr. Malin, the executive director of the ACLU, or by Mr. Joughin, the executive officer of the Academic Freedom Committee. No reply to any of these communications has been received. A follow-up telegram has not been answered. A telephone message from the ACLU to Mr. Himstead's secretary yielded a promise of immediate reply but no answer was ever received. The only successful communication which the ACLU has had with Mr. Himstead in the past nine months came about through the fact that our assistant director was in Washington and was able to establish direct telephone contact. A number of persons in whose cases we are interested have indicated to us that they, as individuals, have been equally unsuccessful in communication. In at least one instance the AAUP has been moving actively in a case, but after preliminary exchange of ideas has become inaccessible for further advice.[26]

Himstead, it seemed, was shirking his duties. It had not always been like that. When he first came to the AAUP from Syracuse Law School in the late 1930s, he had done what many of his associates felt was a superlative job in drawing up and putting through the organization's 1940 guidelines on academic freedom and tenure. As a result, the Association's elected officers, all of whom both liked and respected Himstead, considered him indispensable and shrank from challenging his leadership, even when it appeared that he was thwarting the organization's purposes. Himstead's position was crucial, for like most professional organizations, the AAUP depended on the work of its full-time staff. The eminent professors who governed the organization through its ruling Council were dispersed and, though obviously concerned about the state of academic freedom, could not and did not give it the time and attention that the professional staff did. It was up to the General Secretary, therefore, to coordinate the Association's activities: appoint its investigating committees, make the arrangements for their investigations, and sometimes even draft those committees' reports and see that they were submitted to Committee A and published in the *Bulletin*.[27]

By the late 1940s, the AAUP was no longer functioning normally. It published reports on three cases from the early forties in 1946 and 1947, and in 1949 it published a report recommending censure for a small college in Indiana whose president had fired a professor active in the Wallace campaign. But that was to be the last Committee A report to appear in the *Bulletin* for seven years. Whatever else Himstead did during those years—and he could often be quite helpful to people whose jobs were in jeopardy—he seemed unable to follow any case through to its conclusion. This was true even with regard to teachers whose problems were not political. Whatever its cause, this bureaucratic torpor was to prove disastrous when the AAUP had to confront McCarthyism. The trouble began with the University of Washington.[28]

This was the first, and in many ways the most important, academic freedom case of the entire Cold War. The University's dismissal of three tenured professors, two of them simply because they belonged to the Communist Party, forced the entire academic world to confront the most controversial issue of the day. The AAUP was involved from the start. A few weeks before the Canwell Committee began its probe of the Washington faculty, the University's president, Raymond Allen, met specially with three members of the executive committee of the local chapter. He convinced them to support his decision to cooperate with Canwell and to urge the subpoenaed teachers to cooperate as well. Recognizing the seriousness of the situation, the chapter president asked for help from the central office. Himstead complied by sending copies of the AAUP's policy statements to every member of the Canwell Committee and the Board of Regents. Himstead did not want to antagonize anybody in Seattle, and he assured Canwell that the AAUP considered it

> important that these members of the Faculty answer all questions put to them by the Committee courteously, truthfully, and completely. It is important that the attitude of these members of the Faculty toward the Committee be respectful.

Soon after the Canwell hearings, President Allen went to see Himstead in Washington, D.C. He was about to bring charges against six of the professors who had defied the Canwell Committee, but he did not want to be censured by the AAUP, and hoped that by maintaining contact with the organization and scrupulously observing the procedures it recommended he would be able to keep his university off its list.[29]

Allen's campaign to propitiate the AAUP paid off, at least on the local level. So thoroughly had he managed to co-opt the Washington chapter that despite his decision to override the verdict of a faculty hearing and recommend the dismissal of three tenured professors, the local ignored Allen's behavior and instead issued a public statement approving the conduct of the hearings. This did not, of course, forestall an investigation by the national office. The three men who were fired petitioned it to intervene at once. In addition, because the case had received so much publicity, local chapters and individual professors all around the country also asked the AAUP to investigate. Himstead hastened to respond. Within a few days after the firing, he had already begun to organize the investigation and had asked J. M. Maguire, a Harvard Law School professor and a member of Committee A, to serve on the investigating committee.

Maguire had no illusions about the political sensitivity of the task he was to undertake. "Now, whether we like it or not," he warned Himstead, "we are smack up against the trouble in concrete form." Yet he was willing to undertake the investigation, as was at least one other member of Committee A. Had the normal procedures of the AAUP been followed, at that point the members of the investigating committee would have gathered information about the case and then gone out to Seattle to interview the protagonists. For some reason this did not occur. Despite the obvious importance of the case, nobody from Committee A went to the University of Washington.[30]

The investigation continued nonetheless. The AAUP received several copies of the lengthy transcripts of the faculty hearing; over the summer of 1949 a few of the leading members of Committee A plowed through them. Apparently, these gentlemen expected Himstead to write the Washington report himself. It seems they also expected that the report would be highly critical of the University and of President Allen, whose behavior, Committee A chairman William T. Laprade noted, reminded him of "a sheriff who, seeing a mob bent on action, takes the leadership of the lynching party." They recognized, as Edward C. Kirkland, another Committee A stalwart, put it, that because "the case revolves around Communism . . . this report will be read not only by faculties but also by a much wider popular group than usual." He hoped, therefore, that the report would grapple directly with the issues the Washington case had raised and would show the weakness and "doctrinaire" nature of President Allen's contention that Communists were unfit to teach. Though none of these men sympathized with Ralph Gundlach's refusal to cooperate with the University's investigation, they were in agreement that the University would probably have to be censured for the other two firings and for the even more egregious act of putting three ex-Communist teachers on probation. "However larded up with intellectual apparatus," Kirkland observed, "this is political prosecution, pure and simple."[31]

At this point, however, something happened, or rather didn't happen. All discussion of the content of the report, which Himstead and his staff were supposedly drafting, stops. From then on, whenever anyone asked about the status of the case, Himstead would explain that it was still under investigation. He admitted that the case had "given [the] Association a big jolt," but insisted, as he told one of the Washington protagonists, that "progress is being made." In the spring of 1950 Colston Warne, an Amherst professor who was one of Ralph Gundlach's strongest supporters, talked with the leading members of Committee A; they assured him that the report would be out by the summer and that it "would condemn the University of Washington for the discharge of Butterworth and Phillips" and might even "uphold Ralph." Eighteen months later, the report was still unwritten, and Himstead listed the following item on the agenda for the November 1951 meeting of the AAUP Council:

A Request that the Two Members of the Association's Professional Staff, Messrs, Shannon and Himstead, Who Have the Responsibility of Writing the Report on the University of Washington Situation for Committee A, Be Permitted to Disengage Themselves from all Other Work of the Association for Two Weeks to the End that They Might Give their Undivided Time and Energy to this Difficult Job.

In September 1952 Gundlach saw Himstead at his Washington office. Himstead promised the report within three months and explained that it had been delayed "because of the general 'climate' which was adverse to academic freedom and made a strong statement inadvisable, at that time." At the same time Himstead's assistant, George Pope Shannon, was explaining to someone else that the delay in issuing the Washington report "has been due to circumstances entirely beyond the power of the Committee to alter."[32]

Whatever the circumstances were they did not abate, and the delays continued. This, despite the AAUP Council's repeated insistence on the necessity for "getting out such reports" and its specific request in February 1954 that Himstead and Shannon have a draft "in the hands of the other members of Committee A . . . within the next few months." Finally, in the beginning of 1955, after a small-scale revolt brought a new group of leaders to power within the organization, the AAUP Council ordered the organization's president to appoint a subcommittee to prepare a report on Washington as soon as possible. By the middle of April a draft was ready. It had been written by the UCLA historian John Caughey, who, because he was himself a protagonist in the California Loyalty Oath case, wanted to remain anonymous and have the report go out as the product of Committee A. It didn't. First, the chairman of Committee A wanted "to soften" it. Then, the new general secretary of the organization decided to replace Caughey's report with a more general one that would deal with the AAUP's entire backlog of Cold-War-related academic freedom cases. As a result, it was not until the spring of 1956 that the AAUP finally made its belated statement on the University of Washington.[33]

Why the organization delayed so long is unclear. The record here is spotty. We do not know, for example, what Himstead himself thought about the case. It is possible, however, that, despite the desire of the other members of Committee A for conclusive action, Himstead wanted to avoid the controversy that he expected a strong condemnation of the University of Washington would arouse. Even before the Washington case broke, the Communist issue had been creating turmoil within the AAUP. The Report of Committee A for 1947, which endorsed the right of teachers to belong to the Communist Party, had engendered widespread criticism. Individual members and whole chapters, even, complained about the statement. They were not sure that the policy accurately reflected the sentiments of the organization's members and they urged its leaders to poll the membership on the issue. Himstead and the

Council refused. Despite the controversial nature of the 1947 statement, the AAUP's leadership would not modify it. Every year the Council discussed the problem of Communist teachers, and every year it overwhelmingly reaffirmed its original position. Himstead seems to have been in agreement with this policy; he supported it in public whenever he was called upon to do so. But he may have feared that translating it into action would wreck the Association.[34]

And this he would not risk. By 1948 Himstead had established the AAUP as a respected and authoritative organization whose "overall purpose," as he saw it, was "to advance the ideals and standards of the academic profession." Because he apparently believed that political neutrality was crucial to this mission, he desperately sought to keep the AAUP from becoming identified with the political left. "Prudence in the administration of the Association," he explained to a member of the Washington AAUP's executive committee,

> is called for at all times if the Association is to achieve the maximum of influence . . . . The Association is regarded by many, including some of its members, as being one of the several "progressive" and/or "liberal" organizations, of which it is neither.

A strong report censuring the University of Washington for firing its Communist teachers might well be misconstrued. Certainly it would contribute little to the respectable image that Himstead so clearly wanted to maintain, and it might even endanger the organization.[35]

Though Himstead might have feared that censuring the University of Washington would split the AAUP, it is hard to understand his reluctance to release a report on the organization's next major academic freedom case: the California Loyalty Oath. If there was any issue on which the academic community would have rallied behind a strong stand, this was it. The teachers who lost their jobs in August 1950 were liberals, not Communists, and the issues at stake were professional ones: tenure and the faculty's control over its own selection. Everyone involved expected the AAUP to intervene. The non-signers and both the Berkeley and UCLA chapters appealed at once, an appeal that much of the profession supported. The Association responded by sending two investigators—Quincy Wright of Chicago and Rex Arragon of Reed—to California in the spring of 1951. The two men collected documents and talked with Regents, administrators, and "all stripes of faculty." Within a few months, they had drafted a 78-page report. Its length must have bothered Himstead, for early in November he sent copies of the report to two new members of Committee A, inviting them to comment on it and to "indicate specifically the portions of the report which might be eliminated in the interest of reducing its length or might be stated more briefly or more effectively." By the beginning of January 1952 the revised version was ready for publication; in accord with the AAUP's traditional policy of letting the protagonists in each case comment upon the draft report before it appeared in the *Bulletin*, Himstead sent a copy to John Francis Neylan, the Regent behind the oath. At this point the machinery of the AAUP comes to a halt; the California report mysteriously disappears from the record. A few years later one of its authors explained that he had been given to understand by someone on Committee A that it had been withheld because the Washington report was still unfinished "and that it was felt undesirable to publish the California case which arose somewhat later before the Washington case was published."[36]

From time to time, concern about the delayed report surfaced. AAUP activists at the University of California were particularly distressed. A Berkeley professor who had requested a copy of the report in August 1952 complained in October that he had not yet received it: "I do not believe that the Association should defer action for such a long period of time that the value of its inspection and report is lost." The following June, John Caughey, who as a non-signer and president of the UCLA chapter was to become the organization's main internal gadfly on the California case, took up the issue in a letter to Himstead:

> At a time like this, when violations of academic freedom seem to be at a peak, how does it happen that the AAUP does not censure any institution? . . . Isn't the evidence clear and adequate that the University of Washington and the University of California flagrantly violated the rules and practices of tenure?

For the next few years Caughey continued to deplore the AAUP's inaction. He was not alone. In April 1954 the Johns Hopkins economist Fritz Machlup sent an open letter to all members of Committee A, the Council, and the AAUP's staff. Characterizing the "delay in the report on and censure of the University of California administration" as "the most serious of our mistakes and calamities," Machlup called upon the AAUP's leaders to "give their immediate consideration to this issue."[37]

By this time the organization was overwhelmed by McCarthyism. The congressional committees were cruising the country, and dozens of professors had been or were about to be fired. They all appealed to the AAUP—to no avail. Sometimes the Washington office did not answer their letters. Sometimes it promised help but did not deliver. The organization's treatment of W. Lou Tandy, whose firing from Kansas State Teachers College in Emporia was one of the most flagrant violations of academic freedom of the entire McCarthy era, was typical. The AAUP, Tandy noted, "started out excellently and vigorously, but never held any investigation or pursued the matter to the end." Tandy, however, did not have tenure, so it is possible that, given the admittedly limited resources of the national office, Himstead and his staff may have decided to concentrate on helping people forced out of permanent positions. At first, this seemed to be what the organization was doing. In June 1952, for example, it dispatched a three-man delegation to the University of Oklahoma to investigate the case of an ex-Communist zoologist fired by the

Board of Regents because of his past affiliations. Though the man had tenure and thus, presumably, a stronger claim on the organization than a junior person, the AAUP did not follow up on its original intervention. The head of its Oklahoma chapter reported:

> When I talked the matter over with Mr. LaPrade, chairman of Committee A, he indicated that the priority in the consideration of all tenure cases was the so called "Fifth Amendment Cases."[38]

Significantly, this revelation was in response to a complaint from the head of the AAUP chapter at Temple University. Surely, if any "Fifth Amendment Case" deserved priority, it was that of Barrows Dunham. Dunham had tenure. He had cooperated with Temple's investigation. He had even voluntarily taken the Pennsylvania Loyalty Oath. And he had asked the AAUP for help at the very beginning of his ordeal. Here, in the words of the chairman of Temple's chapter, is what happened:

> a. On Monday, March 2, 1953, I called Mr. Himstead at the Washington office and had a useful and helpful conversation with him. Among other things, I asked Mr. Himstead what I should do if Dr. Dunham made an appeal, as I expected he would. Mr. Himstead told me that when an appeal was made I should inform the Washington office, which would then assume responsibility. b. On the next day, Tuesday, March 3, Dr. Dunham sent me a telegram asking for an immediate investigation of his case by the A.A.U.P. On the same day I wrote and mailed to Mr. Himstead a special-delivery letter informing him of the request. Now, three weeks later, the chapter still has not even received an acknowledgment. We here in Philadelphia are thus at this most critical time for American college faculties left without guidance and forced to rely on those at national headquarters who show no intention of doing anything at all.

Two months later, still having received no help from Washington, the new chairman of the Temple unit wrote directly to every member of the AAUP Council asking: "Can you suggest any procedure by which the Washington office can be induced to acknowledge and act upon this request for an investigation?"[39]

Himstead responded at last. He had, he later insisted, delayed intervening in the Temple case because Dunham had not contacted him directly. But finally, on June 2, 1953, three months after the Temple AAUP first asked for help and a few days after its chairman had written to the Council, Himstead sent a telegram to the former chairman of the chapter requesting Dunham's address and phone number. It took three more weeks before Himstead contacted Dunham directly, asking for information about his case and sending him copies of the resolutions adopted at the Association's most recent annual meeting. Dunham complied at once. Though he had already testified before Temple's Loyalty Committee, the University had not yet fired him, and he begged the AAUP to intervene. "The sooner it does so the greater chance there will be of a favorable issue." What, if anything, Himstead did is unclear. He claimed that he had been in touch with the Temple administration about the procedures involved. Once Dunham was dismissed, however, Himstead was unable to organize an investigation. He could not, he told the Temple AAUP, find "competent members of the profession, who understand and concur in views [of] this Association on this issue to accept Temple University assignment. Members of Association's Council best qualified to investigate Temple University situation have declined to serve on committee." Himstead was being less than candid, for he had not made a serious effort to put together such a committee. He sent out a few urgent invitations in the middle of the summer, and then, instead of rescheduling the investigation as the vacationing professors requested, he dropped the matter.[40]

Even when Himstead was able to organize an investigating committee, his inertia sabotaged its work. This is what happened with the Ohio State case. We have already seen how, in order to forestall "precipitate action" by the local chapter, Himstead had had to promise that the AAUP would investigate the dismissal of physicist Byron Darling. By early October 1953, almost six months after Darling was fired, the people in Columbus were becoming concerned and the chapter president asked Himstead for a progress report. Himstead, who had apparently done nothing up until then, went into action. He appointed an investigating committee and began to negotiate with the Ohio State authorities for a visit. These steps placated the Columbus local, but only temporarily. Ralph Fuchs, the University of Indiana Law School professor who had agreed to chair the investigation, came under attack from the American Legion for his activities in the ACLU and decided to drop out of the case. Then, instead of finding a new chairman and continuing with the investigation, Himstead began to stall. He claimed that he had not heard directly from Darling and that, "pursuant procedures of Association, cannot proceed to investigate his dismissal unless he requests investigation or consents to investigation." Darling, whom Himstead finally reached in New York at the end of November, found Himstead's request "somewhat of a disappointment"; he assumed that his dismissal was already under investigation. The head of the Ohio State chapter was even more upset by the delay and by Himstead's belated demand for Darling's okay. "Is this a policy of the central office?" he wanted to know:

> I raise this question since I can not find this procedure set forth in the constitution or by-laws or statement of principles. Is it possible to carry out the wishes of our local chapter for an investigation without getting Professor Darling's consent?[41]

Inexplicably, the delay continued, even though toward the end of March Himstead was able to convince Douglas Maggs, a law professor from the University of North Carolina, to take over the chairmanship of the investigating committee. Maggs could not leave Chapel Hill until

June, and so the investigation was postponed again. Maggs, however, wanted to begin work as soon as he could, so he repeatedly asked the Washington office for the transcripts of Darling's hearing and any other documents it held on the case. Nothing was sent. Then, in the beginning of June, Himstead telegraphed Maggs that he had been unable to make arrangements for a June meeting with the Ohio State administration and would have to postpone the investigation until late August or September. Maggs agreed, though a few weeks later he discovered that the visit might have to be further postponed because many of the key people at Ohio State would still be on vacation. Meanwhile, he continued his futile appeals for documents. On August 13, Himstead telegraphed that "materials in reference Ohio State University at present in use away from office." Almost parenthetically, he added that since the beginning of the week, he had been "immobilized at home with cardiac condition."[42]

Himstead's heart attack brought the already lethargic investigation to a complete halt. On October 7, 1954, Maggs sent the key leaders of the AAUP a detailed account of his frustrations. When his letter provoked nothing more than an acknowledgment from George Pope Shannon, who was manning the office for the still ailing Himstead, he resigned from the investigation. Both Maggs and Robert E. Mathews, an AAUP activist at Ohio State to whom he had sent a copy of his October 7 letter, felt that the AAUP's nineteen-month delay rendered further action "futile." An investigation, Mathews noted,

> would be now a farce; would merely highlight the inadequacy of the A.A.U.P., its inability to meet a crisis . . . . I am disappointed beyond words at the way we have been let down at Ohio State. Dozens of members feel the same; dozens are disgusted. We can't build a strong chapter without a central administration that has the strength and competency to perform the basic functions for which it was created.

No further attempt to send a committee to Columbus was ever made.[43]

Himstead's inactivity is a puzzle. Perhaps he was stalling for political reasons, because he felt that publication of Committee A reports on the sensitive Cold War cases and the censure of schools the caliber of Washington, California, and Ohio State might hurt the AAUP. A letter that he wrote to the newly appointed chairman of Committee A in February 1955 reveals his concern, almost an obsession, with keeping the AAUP from publishing its case reports. He worried that the coming annual meeting might

> wreck the work of the Association on behalf of the principles of academic freedom and tenure, by requiring publication of our case material and also by insisting on a censure in all Fifth Amendment cases. If we should be required to publish all of our case materials relating to academic freedom and tenure, it would end the Association's usefulness to the profession and would probably end the Association. Efforts to prevent this kind of pub-

licity have occupied an enormous amount of my time and energy as General Secretary of the Association. If the Association should get a left-wing or pro-communism tag, this would certainly end the effectiveness of the Association and the Association.

What makes Himstead's behavior so puzzling is that, with regard to general principles at least, he did not take a conservative position. He supported the AAUP's refusal to condemn Communist teachers and on several occasions insisted "that invoking Fifth Amendment is not, in and of itself, justifiable cause for dismissal."[44]

Thus, while political caution no doubt played some kind of a role in Himstead's determined inactivity, there were other factors as well. Certainly, political scruples could not have kept him from acting on every ordinary violation of academic procedure that crossed his desk. Here, I think that Himstead's failure to deal with the University of Washington case may have been crucial, for the fact that Himstead had not published a Washington report may well have kept him from publishing later ones. To have done so would have exposed the embarrassing absence of the one on Washington. As so often happens when an individual or institution tries to cover up for an initial mistake, the operation gets out of hand and the evasions simply compound the original problem. For the AAUP, the problem became a disaster because it occurred in the middle of the most serious attack on academic freedom in American history. We do not know whether Himstead was actually conscious of what was happening; the rationalizations that he gave at the time give no indication. And it is possible that, as the AAUP became more and more delinquent in responding to the crises of the 1950s, Himstead, who seemed to be increasingly preoccupied with fending off his critics, may simply have failed to recognize how much he had contributed to his own discomforture.

The excuse that Himstead and the other members of his staff gave when questioned about the AAUP's failure to respond to the cases before them was that "the unprecedently [sic] large volume of work" had overwhelmed the office. Even before the height of the witch-hunt, Himstead had been complaining about the workload that he was facing and the need for a larger staff to handle it. "It is," he explained in 1950, "a physical impossibility for our small professional staff to keep abreast of all of its correspondence." The office received 100,000 letters a year, some 20,000 of which, he claimed, required his attention or that of his assistant George Pope Shannon. Two more staff members were needed, as well as more space and secretarial help. This should not have been a problem, for the members of the AAUP Council sympathized with Himstead and were perfectly willing to let him hire additional staff. Yet despite his continuing complaints about being short-handed, he did not take on another staff member until February 1952. By then it was clear that the Association needed yet another professional employee, but Himstead never hired one—even though the Council had authorized him to and he had actually interviewed the man his successor eventually hired.[45]

It is possible that Himstead delayed increasing the size of his professional staff because he feared the AAUP could not afford it. Though he continually stressed the need for additional office help, he complained that the organization's finances would not allow for it. Times were hard, he explained, and "it is not improbable that the Association will be confronted with a problem of survival." He may have been exaggerating. In the early 1950s, according to the financial data submitted to the Council, the organization was running with a small surplus. It is possible that that surplus was created by Himstead's economies and that, had Himstead become more active, the AAUP would have gone into the red. Had that occurred, the AAUP could easily have raised its membership dues. In 1950, a poll of the organization revealed that 180 out of the 215 chapters responding favored an increase in dues. Therefore, it seems most likely that Himstead's allegations of impending financial disaster were essentially rationalizations for his own reluctance to hire new employees.[46]

Clearly, then, though the Washington office of the AAUP was understaffed and overworked, that situation was in large part the result of Himstead's inability to get things done, not the cause of it. He seemed unable to delegate authority. And as more and more work piled up in the organization's headquarters, less and less seemed to be getting done. The situation was certainly not improved when Himstead's new assistant, Warren Middleton, was laid up for seven months with a back injury and then Himstead himself had a heart attack in the summer of 1954. Himstead's absence from the office for most of the second half of 1954 brought all work to a halt. The organization's Council even cancelled its regular fall meeting because of Himstead's illness. George Pope Shannon, the second in command, refused to do anything on his own; he was not, he explained to Douglas Maggs in October, "in a position to comment on your letter, or take any action concerning it."[47]

When Ralph Fuchs took over after Himstead's death in 1955, he inherited an office that was, as he put it, "unbelievable." Because Himstead had not been able to keep up with the organization's correspondence, Fuchs recalls, "there were these tremendous piles of material that were around on card tables and other temporary places of storage." Closets were full of unread manuscripts that had been submitted to the *Bulletin*. In addition, though the organization had moved to its present quarters three years before Fuchs arrived, the offices were still unfurnished:

> Rolled up against the walls in a number of the rooms was some carpeting. I asked why that carpeting had never been put in place. The answer was, "Well, Dr. Himstead never took action to put the carpets down."

Since neither politics nor poverty kept Himstead from laying the rugs, it is clear that some kind of psychological factors were involved with his inability to perform the professional tasks of his office. How seriously disturbed Himstead was is hard to tell. At the very least it is clear that by the time the main wave of political dismissals reached the AAUP, its general secretary had ceased to function.[48]

Why was he not replaced? There seem to have been several reasons. Though Himstead was unable to mount much of a defense of academic freedom, he could still muster enough energy and cunning to hang on to his job. Initially, of course, it was not at all clear that he was personally responsible for the AAUP's failure to respond to its Cold War caseload. And many of the organization's leaders swallowed the general secretary's rationalizations. After all, the office was facing an unprecedented amount of work, and its budget was hardly unlimited. Moreover, the AAUP's leaders did not want to contemplate the unpleasantness of having to confront, and possibly fire, someone they liked and respected as much as Himstead. This was especially the case with the men who, like the long-time chairman of Committee A, William Laprade, constituted the organization's old guard. Not only did they support Himstead against his critics, but they seemed unwilling or unable to prod him into taking more vigorous action. Reform, unfortunately, was impossible. As the Johns Hopkins biologist Bentley Glass noted in a letter to Fuchs in January 1953:

> It is clear that the Washington staff is completely unable to keep up with all the pressing things to be done; and yet Ralph Himstead's sensitiveness is such that every proposal to improve matters is taken as an affront.

Himstead had so completely identified himself with the organization that he treated suggestions for change as if they were direct attacks on the AAUP. He complained, for example, that some of the letters he had received from Council members in response to the Temple chapter's criticism of the central office's inaction seemed hostile "to the welfare of the professional staff of this office, and are not conducive to the welfare of the Association."[49]

Not only did Himstead make it unpleasant for the AAUP's leaders to confront him, he made it difficult as well. He cleverly used his responsibility for drawing up the agendas of all the Council meetings and annual conventions to ensure that the AAUP's leaders did not deal with anything that might embarrass him. Here was the AAUP, the only organization in the United States specifically concerned about the preservation of academic freedom, in the midst of perhaps the most serious crisis in the organization's entire history, and what did it discuss? "Selective Service—Its Philosophy and Procedures up to the Present," "The Extension of Social Security Coverage to Colleges and Universities," "Should Graduate School Programs Provide Special Preparation for College Teaching?," "Is Acceleration of the Instructional Programs of Our Colleges and Universities at This Time Necessary and Desirable as Regards the Welfare of the Nation?," "Intercollegiate Athletics—Its Place in Institutions of Higher Education and the Responsibility of the Faculty for the Administration of the Institution's Athletic Program." The meetings were so full of the trivia that Himstead had programmed that the AAUP's leaders never had time to debate the important issues. And when they did, they usually devoted themselves to passing resolutions. Throughout this period, the AAUP adopted some very strong resolutions. It opposed the dismissal of Communist professors. It opposed the censorship of textbooks. It opposed loyalty oaths for teachers. It opposed the abuses of legislative investigating committees. In fact, as far as statements of principle were concerned, it would have been hard to fault the AAUP's defense of academic freedom.[50]

Ultimately, of course, Himstead was unable to keep the Association from dealing with reality. Too many members knew that the Washington office was not doing its job. Bentley Glass, for one, had been trying to get the organization's presidents to crack down on Himstead since 1949. By the time of the annual meeting in the spring of 1952, it was clear that something had to be done. It was. The AAUP decided to study the problem. It reactivated its standing Committee O on Organization and Policies to make "a thorough investigation into the management and functioning of the Association and particularly of the headquarters office." But almost a year later, the committee's members had yet to be appointed. And, at the 1953 annual convention, rank and file members bitterly attacked the national staff's failure to act.[51]

A study was not what the frustrated activists within the AAUP needed. They knew perfectly well what had to be done to reenergize the organization. "My principal objective," explained Douglas Maggs, a member of the AAUP Council since 1953, "has been to bring it about that the AAUP should issue reports on Washington and California." He was not alone. Every year, beginning in 1953, the Council ordered Committee A and the central office to give priority to getting out those two reports. Maggs and his fellow activists within the organization knew how damaging the AAUP's inaction had become. Like John Caughey, whose desperate pleas for censuring the University of California Himstead continually ignored, they worried "that the A.A.U.P. cannot long survive with so great a variance between its stated policy and its line of action." Worse yet, these people believed that the Association's failure to act encouraged university administrations to disregard its principles. "No wonder that other universities emulated the University of California when they found out how tame the professors had become," one of them complained; "no wonder that the practice of test oath requirements and of dismissals in violation of contract rights and tenure rules has spread over the land."[52]

By 1954 there were over a hundred academic casualties of McCarthyism, men and women whose misfortune the AAUP had done little to prevent, and the divisions within the organization that Himstead feared a strong stand on the Washington case would create were appearing anyway. Morale was predictably bad on the campuses most affected.

The Ohio State chapter was in tatters; the one at Temple, which had been split from the beginning, seemed powerless to do anything. There were individual resignations, but the most serious symptom of the growing disaffection with the organization was the movement toward the creation of regional AAUPs. By 1955 there were several of these groups in existence; the one in Chicago was particularly energetic. And it was becoming clear that, unless the central office began to pull itself together, these local groups might try to circumvent it or possibly pull out altogether.[53]

"The Association is now in a crisis in connection with its membership," a long-time activist warned the AAUP's new president, William E. Britton, in January 1955. Himstead's inactivity was at fault:

> the membership . . . has clearly indicated in the last year or two that it is not going to remain satisfied with no or sparse information about Committee A cases until they are finished and done well. . . . The Association is a lot nearer the explosion point than he [Himstead] realizes, and the causes of the incipient explosion must be handled in such a way that it does not take place.

By this point, even the most conservative members of the old guard realized that radical surgery was necessary. William Laprade, who as the long-time chairman of Committee A was, next to Himstead, the person most responsible for the organization's inaction, decided to resign. Britton, despite Himstead's apparent desire to delay such a major change, was able to appoint a replacement. By that point Himstead must have realized what was about to happen. Sick and exhausted, he did not even go to Gatlinsburg, Tennessee, for the annual meeting in March. He sent in his resignation instead. It was not a voluntary act, for the activist professors, who by then had finally gotten control of the organization, were determined to clean house. They were willing to let Himstead save face and remain as the organization's nominal executive, but they had already decided to appoint Ralph Fuchs to succeed him. Unfortunately, Fuchs could not take his new position until September 1955, and so for a few months more the AAUP remained, as it had been for over six years, pathetically inactive. Himstead's lame duck tenure was ended by a second and fatal heart attack in June.[54]

At the Gatlinsburg meeting, the AAUP's Council had also taken another long overdue step and voted to have Committee A prepare the Washington and California reports. Russell Sullivan, the new head of Committee A, felt that his group was already too deluged with current cases to handle the backlog as well and so it was decided that the organization's president would appoint special subcommittees for the task. He failed. He approached several people, but only John Caughey, himself a protagonist in the California case, was willing. Though Caughey's report on the University of Washington was finished within two months, it was not published. Sullivan felt it was too strong, and Fuchs decided that it would be best to issue a general report on the entire backlog of anti-Communist cases. Accordingly, as soon as Fuchs unrolled the carpets in the Washington office, he put together a special committee to draft the long overdue report.[55]

The committee was a high-powered group. Chaired by Johns Hopkins' biologist Bentley Glass, whose proximity to Washington and devotion to civil liberties ensured that he would, as he did, actually work on the report, it contained among its members Douglas Maggs, several other law school professors, and such eminent scholars as the sociologist Talcott Parsons and Robert K. Carr, a Dartmouth political scientist who had written the standard book about HUAC. Fuchs and Glass did most of the work. Because of the heavy workload and everyone's desire to have the report published as soon as possible, the committee skipped the AAUP's usual procedures and, instead of visiting each campus and talking with the people involved, it based its report on the sources available in the public record. Where that record seemed inadequate or confusing, Fuchs and his colleagues postponed a recommendation until a more thorough investigation could take place. Though there was some criticism of the committee's abbreviated procedures—mainly, it must be noted, by people at the schools which were about to be censured—the report itself was what one would have expected from a group of people who had been chosen for their professional stature, judicious temperament, and commitment to academic freedom. Not only did the committee weigh the issues involved in each of the specific cases it studied, but it also dealt with the broader questions raised by those cases: Could teachers be fired for belonging to the Communist Party or taking the Fifth Amendment?[56]

Its conclusions accorded with the position that the AAUP had been espousing since 1947. "Avowed past or present membership in the Communist Party taken by itself" was not sufficient grounds for dismissal. Similarly, "invocation of the Fifth Amendment by a faculty member under official investigation cannot be in itself a sufficient ground for removing him." The committee did not take an absolute position here; it recognized that a professor's use of the Fifth or "other indications of past or present Communist associations or activities" were matters which "his institution cannot ignore." The committee also struggled with the problem presented by people like Chandler Davis and Stanley Moore who were unwilling to tell their colleagues any more about their politics than they told Congress. This issue had, Fuchs admitted, "given us more trouble than any other single one." The committee's final solution was, understandably, something of a compromise. Refusing to testify at a university hearing, the report stated, "is relevant to the question of fitness to teach, but not decisive." A decision in such a case, the committee admitted, would depend upon the teacher's motives and his sincerity. But because it was so difficult to assess something as subjective as sincerity, the committee apparently concluded that the teacher would, in fact, have to answer his colleagues' questions. "It is the duty of a faculty member to disclose facts concerning himself that are of legitimate concern to the institution." In other words, though the AAUP's special committee had explicitly rejected the AAU's demand for "complete candor" before an outside investigation, it supported such a requirement at an internal one. This was, of course, completely in accord with the AAUP's traditional emphasis on maintaining the autonomy of the academic profession. Political tests imposed by the outside world were not legitimate; political tests imposed by the academy were.[57]

Similarly, the body of the report, the section dealing with individual cases, reflected the Association's traditional concern with academic due process. It was clear that the Special Committee's main criteria were procedural; if the trustees and administration of a school at least tried to obey the rules, the committee was loathe to censure. It recognized all sorts of extenuating circumstances—a change of administration or the necessity to comply with a state law was sufficient to keep an otherwise censurable institution off the list. Thus, for example, the committee did not condemn the University of Washington because a new administration there had agreed to new regulations for tenure. It also exonerated the New York City municipal colleges because it claimed that the laws under which the teachers were dismissed were the real culprits. And, in keeping with the AAUP's traditional concern with tenure, it did not censure any schools for letting junior people go.

The schools which it did condemn—Jefferson, Ohio State, Rutgers, Oklahoma, and Temple—were those whose administrators and trustees had behaved most autocratically, ignoring faculty recommendations or flouting due process. It censured California as well. Even though the California Supreme Court had invalidated the Loyalty Oath, the Special Committee felt that Regents' refusal to give the non-signers their back pay and sabbatical leave credit as well as the University's questionable liaison with the state's Un-American Activities Committee merited condemnation. Several other schools were left in limbo. Later investigations put NYU and Michigan on the censured list.[58]

On the whole, the Special Committee's report was unexceptionable. True, its emphasis on the relevance of Communist Party membership to academic fitness seems, in retrospect, to have been an unnecessary concession to the spirit of the age. But this was an understandable lapse given the intensity of Cold War anti-Communism and the widespread misunderstanding of what Communist academics did. Nonetheless, the report did, as Talcott Parsons recalls, "bell the cat" and it did reestablish some, albeit minimal, standards for the academic community to apply in political cases. Had the nation's colleges and universities seriously tried to abide by the AAUP's guidelines and treated the political charges against faculty members according to genuine criteria of academic fitness, most of the political dismissals of the late 1940s and 1950s would not have occurred. The main problem with the Special Committee's report, however, was not its content, but its timing. It came seven years too late. As a result, it was both less influential and less controversial than its authors either hoped or feared.[59]

It encountered some criticism, of course, but nowhere near as much as the AAUP expected. Most of the opposition came from the blacklisted universities, where both faculty members and administrators felt that the organization's delays and its failure to send investigating committees vitiated the whole procedure. Oddly, enough, there was more dissatisfaction later on, when the censured schools were removed from the blacklist without having made restitution to the teachers they had fired. Obviously, none of the institutions which the AAUP condemned welcomed the honor, but they took no action to prevent it. Here, there seems to have been a distinction between administrators, some of whom wanted to avoid censure, and trustees who, because of their greater distance from the academic scene, seemed remarkably unconcerned. At Temple, for example, the administration was worried, as the dean explained to the trustees, that censure would make "it more difficult to secure new faculty members at a period when there is a scarcity of trained faculty personnel." But the trustees ignored these warnings and refused to revise the University's tenure code enough to avoid AAUP action.[60]

As it turned out, censure did not inflict much pain. At some of the schools the AAUP condemned, it had virtually no impact. At Jefferson Medical College the administration simply ignored the AAUP. At Temple, on the other hand, being censured did have an effect, but not a serious one. One trustee claimed that it had not done "any harm" at all. Another, however, insisted that "it has made our faculty members uneasy, and that large foundations look askance at institutions with 'censured' listings." The damage seems to have been more psychological than real. Certainly none of the censured schools enjoyed being in the AAUP's dog house. "Publicity of this kind," Michigan's president Harlan Hatcher explained, "one would like to avoid because of continued vexation from a variety of sources." But, he had no regrets:

> A sound administration judgment, however, cannot be avoided or set aside to escape annoyances that become irksome. We have had no difficulty whatsoever in the recruiting of staff because of the judgment taken against us by the A.A.U.P.

Censure was, thus, an irksome annoyance, a problem for the public relations director, but nothing that interfered with a university's real business.[61]

Even before it became known that the AAUP was immobilized, the threat of censure had little force. When the California Regents were debating the Loyalty Oath, Neylan admitted that firing the non-signers would probably cause the University to be blacklisted, but he appealed to his colleagues not "to bow down to the American Association of University Professors." Harlan Hatcher was similarly undeterred by the prospect of AAUP censure when he recommended the dismissal of Chandler Davis and Mark Nickerson. And, in fact, there is no evidence that the threat of AAUP action kept any academic institution from firing its politically undesirable professors.[62]

Here we must confront the possibility that the organization—even at its most vigorous—had always been ineffective and that Ralph Himstead's fecklessness may have concealed the AAUP's impotence. For even when the threat of censure was most credible, just after the special committee had cleared up the organization's backlog, academic administrators still had no compunctions about ignoring the AAUP. The case of Laurent R. LaVallee at Dickinson College in Pennsylvania is suggestive. LaVallee, an economist who had figured in an earlier academic freedom case at Oregon State in 1949, had taken the Fifth before HUAC in March 1956. Not only did the AAUP fail to prevent LaVallee's dismissal, but it could not even obtain a faculty hearing for him. Local chapter members and national officials tried to intercede, but Dickinson's administrators and trustees viewed the AAUP as an adversary, an organization whose insistence on faculty participation in university decisions posed a direct threat to their own control of the College. Thus, they even refused to let Ralph Fuchs send an observer to LaVallee's hearing before the Board of Trustees and, when Committee A began its investigation, the board's chairman decreed "that while we will be courteous to the committee, we do not recognize that it has any judicial standing in the matter." The censure that quickly followed clearly held no terrors for Dickinson's leaders.[63]

Perhaps the legacy of inaction had, as John Caughey and the other frustrated activists within the organization feared, destroyed the AAUP's effectiveness. Perhaps it had always been a paper tiger. Or perhaps the anti-Communist hysteria of the period was so powerful that no organization, not even one that claimed to protect the status and ideals of the academic profession, could prevent the rest of the academy from collaborating with McCarthyism. Here we confront the old chicken-and-egg conundrum: Was the AAUP's weakness a symptom or a cause of the academic profession's failure to mount any effective defense against McCarthyism? Though the strange pathology of Ralph Himstead adds an element of chance to the situation, had a significant number of American academics seriously tried to oppose the dismissals of their colleagues, it is hard to believe that they would have found Ralph Himstead's personality problems an insurmountable obstacle. And, in fact, given the reluctance of the AAUP's leaders to confront Himstead, it is possible that his procrastination may have provided a convenient cover for their own ambivalence. Like liberals everywhere, they adhered to the ideology of Cold War anti-Communism, with its emphasis on the primacy of national security over individual rights. They were not comfortable with the absolute civil libertarianism of men like Stanley Moore, Chandler Davis, and Ralph Gundlach, and it is possible that, had the

AAUP been functioning during the early fifties, its leaders might not have censured every violation of academic freedom.[64]

Such speculation aside, it is still true that the academic profession failed to defend its members against the anti-Communist purges of the 1940s and 1950s. Perhaps I am being unnecessarily harsh on the academics of the time. Yet the firings now have few defenders; many of the professors who themselves lived through the events of that period now admit that they should have defied McCarthyism more vigorously. Had they done so, it is possible that they might have succeeded. Because there was so little mainstream opposition to McCarthyism, in the academy or anywhere else for that matter, there are only a few instances of successful resistance; but those few, like Robert Hutchins's opposition to the Broyles Committee, are suggestive and indicate that support for the anti-Communist crusade was superficial and that resistance to it entailed far fewer risks than people imagined. By refusing to take those risks, the majority of the nation's college professors must share some of the responsibility for the repression that followed.

CONCLUSION

No Ivory Tower

Restitution came at last. In April 1972, Rutgers invited M. I. Finley to inaugurate its first endowed lecture series. On January 14, 1978, the Reed College Board of Trustees decreed that it had made a mistake in firing Stanley Moore. In July 1981, Temple University's Board of Trustees restored Barrows Dunham to the faculty. In December, CCNY rehabilitated the surviving Rapp-Coudert teachers. In May 1982, New York City's Board of Higher Education reinstated the Fifth Amendment witnesses it had dismissed thirty years before. A year later, the University of Vermont gave Alex B. Novikoff an honorary degree. Slowly, slowly the academic community is making its amends. But many of the blacklisted professors died before they could savor their belated vindication. And only the teachers fired under the Feinberg law and Section 903 of the New York City Charter received any money—and they had been trying to collect for thirty years.[1]

In any event, such reparations, though welcome, cannot repair the damage to careers and personal lives inflicted by McCarthyism. Nor can they redress the injuries that were suffered by the academic community and the rest of the nation. Here, we must look beyond specific cases and campuses and try to assess the impact of academic McCarthyism on American political and intellectual life. This is not an easy task, for one's outrage against the injustices that occurred may inflate estimates of that damage, while, at the same time, evidence for the link between McCarthyism and a specific outcome is tantalizingly elusive. In addition, it is often hard to separate the specifically *academic* effects of McCarthyism from its more general impact. Thus, for example, there is considerable speculation that the devastating effects of the IPR hearings on the field of East Asian Studies made it hard for American policy-makers to get realistic advice about that part of the world. Naturally, greater access to better scholarship would not by itself have prevented the Vietnam war, but there is no doubt that the legacy of McCarthyism in the acad-

338

emy and elsewhere did make it difficult for the government to act wisely in Asia.[2]

In other areas the damage was more subtle. Even at the time, civil libertarians discussed the "chilling effect" of McCarthyism and noted the political reticence that blanketed the nation's colleges and universities. Marxism and its practitioners were marginalized, if not completely banished from the academy. Open criticism of the political status quo disappeared. And college students became a silent generation whose most adventurous spirits sought cultural instead of political outlets for their discontents. Their teachers, as Lazarsfeld and Thielens so devastatingly reveal in *The Academic Mind,* played it equally safe, pruning their syllabi and avoiding controversial topics. Here again, we confront the problem of evidence. Anecdotes abound, but the full extent to which American scholars censored themselves is hard to gauge. There is no sure way to measure the books that were not written, the courses that were not taught, and the research that was never undertaken.[3]

Yet, to look at the academic world's self-censorship is to explore only one aspect of the intellectual fallout of McCarthyism. We must also, and more importantly, examine the scholarship that was done. The fifties were, of course, the heyday of consensus history, modernization theory, structural functionalism, and the new criticism. Mainstream scholars celebrated the status quo, and the end of ideology dominated intellectual discourse. To what extent these developments were a response to the political repression of the day is something that demands further study. The often explicitly anti-Marxist tenor of so much of this oeuvre certainly raises questions about its relationship to the anti-Communist purges that were taking place at exactly the same time. Previous writers have either ignored the connection or else asserted, more as a matter of faith than anything else, that McCarthyism perverted the scholarship of the fifties. Certainly, it is possible that McCarthyism had a malign intellectual as well as political effect, but we cannot accept such a conclusion without evidence. We need further study of the period's main intellectual artifacts as well as serious research into what the nation's college professors thought and taught during the McCarthy years.[4]

By the 1950s the academy had displaced all other institutions as the locus of America's intellectual life. The ideas that shaped the way Americans perceived themselves and their society developed on the nation's campuses. Most of the men and women who articulated those ideas were college teachers. They were not, however, isolated from the political repression that touched their institutions. And, in fact, many of the nation's leading intellectuals were directly involved with one or another aspect of McCarthyism. The American historian and present Librarian of Congress Daniel Boorstin named names for HUAC; Lionel Trilling, perhaps the leading literary critic of the day, chaired a Columbia committee that developed guidelines for congressional witnesses; and Talcott Parsons, whose formal paradigms shaped much of American sociology, participated in the AAUP's special survey of the Cold War academic freedom cases. How these activities affected these men's work, if at all, is certainly worth considering. I raise the question because of its importance, not because I have tried to give definitive answers. This book is but a prelude to such an inquiry.

McCarthyism also affected the institutional life of the nation's colleges and universities. Here, it is hard to escape the conclusion that the failure to protect academic freedom eroded the academy's moral integrity. Professors and administrators ignored the stated ideals of their calling and overrode the civil liberties of their colleagues and employees in the service of such supposedly higher values as institutional loyalty and national security. In retrospect, it is easy to accuse these people of hypocrisy, of mouthing the language of academic freedom to conceal something considerably more squalid. Opportunism and dishonesty existed, of course, but most of the men and women who participated in or condoned the firing of their controversial colleagues did so because they sincerely believed that what they were doing was in the nation's interest. Patriotism, not expedience, sustained the academic community's willingness to collaborate with McCarthyism. The intellectual independence so prized by American academics simply did not extend to the United States government.

The extraordinary facility with which the academic establishment accommodated itself to the demands of the state may well be the most significant aspect of the academy's response to McCarthyism. It was the government, not some fringe group of right-wing fanatics, which initiated the movement to eliminate Communism from American life. It administered the first stage of McCarthyism, acting through the agency of investigating committees and the FBI to identify political undesirables on campus. It let the universities handle the second stage and get rid of the targeted individuals. In another era, perhaps, the academy might not have cooperated so readily, but the 1950s was the period when the nation's colleges and universities were becoming increasingly dependent upon and responsive toward the federal government. The academic community's collaboration with McCarthyism was part of that process. It was, in many respects, just another step in the integration of American higher education into the Cold War political system.

The academy did not fight McCarthyism. It contributed to it. The dismissals, the blacklists, and above all the almost universal acceptance of the legitimacy of what the congressional committees and other official investigators were doing conferred respectability upon the most repressive elements of the anti-Communist crusade. In its collaboration with McCarthyism, the academic community behaved just like every other major institution in American life. Such a discovery is demoralizing, for the nation's colleges and universities have traditionally encouraged higher expectations. Here, if anywhere, there should have been a rational assessment of the nature of American Communism and a refusal to overreact to the demands for its eradication. Here, if anywhere, dissent should have found a sanctuary. Yet it did not. Instead, for almost a decade until the civil rights movement and the Vietnam war inspired a new wave of activism, there was no real challenge to political orthodoxy on the nation's campuses. The academy's enforcement of McCarthyism had silenced an entire generation of radical intellectuals and snuffed out all meaningful opposition to the official version of the Cold War. When, by the late fifties, the hearings and dismissals tapered off, it was not because they encountered resistance but because they were no longer necessary. All was quiet on the academic front.

Bibliographical Essay

Researching this book was an adventure. It forced me to become a journalist, a detective, and a pest, as well as the historian I was trained to be. In part, this is the usual lot of someone who tries to write contemporary history. Though we are fortunate in being able to interview the protagonists, it is often difficult to find other kinds of sources. Yet we must, for valuable as oral history is, people's reminiscences are understandably subjective and often distorted by time. We need to buttress these accounts with contemporary documents, if only to make sure that our informants had the facts straight. In my case, because of the sensitivity of the issue and because I was studying dozens of separate institutions, obtaining the evidence I needed turned out to be a challenge. Ultimately, I was able to locate enough documentation to piece together a reasonably coherent narrative. But I had to consult a veritable hodgepodge of sources. Some were published, some were in college archives, and some were in the personal possession of the people I interviewed. The problems I encountered in finding this material are, in fact, relevant to the subject of this book. Thus, instead of the usual bibliography, I am going to discuss the types of sources I used. For those who need more specific references, I hope the footnotes will suffice.

* * *

The literature on McCarthyism, Communism, and anti-Communism is vast and sometimes disappointing. There is a wealth of partisanship and a paucity of evidence. Contrary to expectations, many of the best studies are the earliest. Because of the importance of the subject during the 1950s, it attracted a lot of sponsored research. Some of it is excellent, in particular the series of books produced under the auspices of a grant from the Rockefeller Foundation and published by Cornell University Press. Among the best of these are Walter Gellhorn, ed., *The States and Subversion* (1952); Gellhorn, *Security, Loyalty, and Science* (1950); Eleanor Bontecou, *The Federal Loyalty-Security Program* (1953); Robert K. Carr, *The House Committee on Un-American Activities* (1952); Lawrence H. Chamberlain, *Loyalty and Legislative Action* (1951); and Vern Countryman, *Un-American Activities in the State of Washington* (1951).

The Ford Foundation's Fund for the Republic, an organization with a strong civil libertarian orientation, also sponsored some publishing ventures. The most ambitious was a series entitled "Communism in American Life." Its products were spotty. Some, like Theodore Draper's two volumes on the early history of the American Communist Party, *The Roots of American Communism* (New York: Viking, 1957) and *American Communism and Soviet Russia* (New York: Viking, 1960), and Daniel Aaron's *Writers on the Left* (New York: Harcourt, Brace and World, 1961), have become classics. The others have more problems—either because of inadequate research or unnecessary partisanship—but they are still of use. For the purposes of this book, the most valuable, by far, is Robert W. Iversen's *The Communists and the Schools* (New York: Harcourt, Brace and Co., 1959). It is the only study which even attempts to cover the subject and, for all its limitations, it remains a useful volume, especially for its detailed treatment of the Teachers Union. The Fund for the Republic also sponsored two major pieces of survey research on McCarthyism, Samuel A. Stouffer's *Communism, Conformity and Civil Liberties* (Garden City, N.Y: Doubleday, 1955) and the useful study by Paul Lazarsfeld and Wagner Thielens, Jr., of what college teachers were thinking, *The Academic Mind* (Glencoe, Ill.: Free Press, 1958). (There was an ironic twist to the Stouffer project. Because the Fund's leaders wanted to allay criticism of the study, they consciously chose the most respectable scholar they could find to direct it. Stouffer was a Republican, a Harvard professor, and a regular consultant for the military. Even so, the project was so controversial that his security clearance was taken away.)* Finally, there are the somewhat unsatisfactory products of another 1950s philanthropic venture, Louis M. Rabinowitz's American Academic Freedom Project: Walter Metzger's *The Development of Academic Freedom in the United States* (New York: Columbia University Press, 1955) and Robert MacIver's *Academic Freedom in Our Time* (New York: Columbia University Press, 1955). MacIver's book is too vague; Metzger's doesn't go beyond the First World War.

A few other near-contemporary books are also helpful. My favorite is Telford Taylor's lucid discussion of legislative investigations, *Grand Inquest* (New York: Simon and Schuster, 1955). Also useful, but quite hard to find because only published in paper, is Frank Donner, *The Un-Americans* (New York: Ballantine, 1961). Other helpful books among the more general surveys from the period include Dan Gillmor, *Fear, the Accuser* (New York: Abelard-Schuman, 1954); John Caughey, *In Clear and Present Danger* (Chicago: University of Chicago Press, 1958); Ralph S. Brown, Jr., *Loyalty and Security* (New Haven: Yale University Press, 1958); and Carl Beck's apparently limited, but surprisingly wide-ranging, *Contempt of Congress* (New Orleans: Hauser Press, 1959), which chronicles every contempt citation HUAC brought. We should note, at least in passing, Richard H. Rovere's *Senator Joe McCarthy* (New York: Harcourt, Brace and Co., 1959), Murray Kempton's *Part of Our Time* (New York: Simon and Schuster, 1955), and Eric Goldman's *The Crucial Decade* (New York: Knopf, 1956)—though dated, they remain a pleasure to read.

Perhaps the most influential contemporary interpretation of McCarthyism

---

* Samuel A. Stouffer to McGeorge Bundy, Dec. 17, 1953; Stouffer to Clifford Case, Dec. 29, 1953; both in Arthur Sutherland Papers, 55–9, Harvard Law School Library.

is the one that appeared in a collection of essays edited by Daniel Bell, *The New American Right* (New York: Criterion, 1955). Arguing that McCarthyism was an essentially populist phenomenon, motivated in large part by the status anxieties of downwardly mobile WASPs and upwardly mobile ethnics, Bell and his colleagues, in particular the brilliant historian Richard Hofstadter, were able to depoliticize McCarthyism and treat it as a by-product of the dislocations of modern life. The sheer force and coherence of their argument, as well as their apparently comforting message that McCarthyism infected the masses, not the elites, allowed this interpretation to dominate intellectual discussion of the subject for years. Methodologically, however, it had serious problems. Hofstadter et al. had described status anxiety as such a widespread phenomenon that it was virtually useless as an analytical tool. After all, the status of almost every American was changing in some way during the 1950s. In addition, the McCarthyism that the Bell book described bore little relation to events.

By the late sixties scholars had begun to take a new look at McCarthyism. Michael Paul Rogin demolished the notion that it was a populist phenomenon in his 1967 study of who actually voted for McCarthy, *McCarthy and the Intellectuals* (Cambridge: MIT Press, 1967). Other historians have added to Rogin's work and have shown that much of what we call McCarthyism was regular partisan politics. Among them are Earl Latham, *The Communist Controversy in Washington* (Cambridge: Harvard University Press, 1966); Alan Harper, *The Politics of Loyalty: The White House and the Communist Issue* (Westport, Conn.: Greenwood Press, 1969); Robert Griffith, *The Politics of Fear* (Lexington: The University Press of Kentucky, 1970); Athan Theoharis, *The Yalta Myths in American Politics* (Columbia: University of Missouri Press, 1970); Richard Freeland, *The Truman Doctrine and the Origins of McCarthyism* (New York: Schocken, 1971); Theoharis and Robert Griffith, eds., *The Specter* (New York: Franklin Watts, 1974); Richard Fried, *Men Against McCarthy* (New York: Columbia University Press, 1976); and Mary S. McAuliffe, *Crisis on the Left: Cold War Politics and American Liberals* (Amherst: University of Massachusetts Press, 1978).

Surprisingly, despite all the scholarship on McCarthyism during the 1970s, there are only two general surveys. David Caute's sprawling *The Great Fear* (New York: Simon and Schuster, 1978) is encyclopedic and useful primarily as a reference tool; the bibliography is particularly helpful. Cedric Belfrage's *The American Inquisition 1945–1960* (Indianapolis: Bobbs Merrill, 1973) is a more partisan account. (Belfrage, an editor of the left-wing *National Guardian*, was himself a victim of the times. He was deported in 1955 after refusing to cooperate with HUAC.) The rest of the literature is largely monographic and of varying quality. Certain topics—not always the most important ones—receive attention, others have been ignored.

The entertainment industry's response to McCarthyism has spawned dozens of books. The most useful are Victor S. Navasky's thoughtful discussion of informers, *Naming Names* (New York: Viking, 1980) and Larry Ceplair's and Steven Englund's plodding, but thorough, *The Inquisition in Hollywood* (New York: Doubleday, 1979). There is also Lillian Hellman's *Scoundrel Time* (Boston: Little, Brown, 1976), as well as a number of other first-person accounts, including Sterling Hayden, *Wanderer* (New York: Knopf, 1963); John Henry Faulk, *Fear on Trial* (New York: Simon and Schuster, 1964);

Alvah Bessie, *Inquisition in Eden* (New York: Macmillan, 1965); Dalton
Trumbo, *The Time of the Toad* (New York: Harper & Row, 1972); and
Lester Cole, *Hollywood Red* (Palo Alto, Ca.: Ramparts Press, 1981). There
were two important studies of the blacklist written while it was in effect. John
Cogley's two-volume *Report on Blacklisting* (New York: Fund for the Republic, 1956) was a Fund for the Republic project; Merle Miller's *The Judges
and the Judged* (Garden City, N.Y.: Doubleday, 1952) was sponsored by the
ACLU. There is also the blacklist itself, *Red Channels: The Report of Communist Influence in Radio and Televison* (New York: American Business Con-
sultants, 1950).

The career of Senator McCarthy has been similarly well documented.
There are, for example, two recent full-scale biographies: Thomas C. Reeves,
The Life and Times of Joe McCarthy (New York: Stein and Day, 1982) and
David Oshinsky, *A Conspiracy So Immense* (New York: Free Press, 1983).
Edwin R. Bayley's *Joe McCarthy and the Press* (Madison: University of Wis-
consin Press, 1981) is a fascinating study of the media. The other investigators
have received less attention. In addition to Robert Carr's study, there is Walter
Goodman's *The Committee* (New York: Farrar, Straus and Giroux, 1968) on
HUAC, but no real scholarship on the Senate Internal Security Subcommittee.
For that committee's doings, the most interesting sources are the memoirs of
its chief counsel, Robert Morris, *No Wonder We Are Losing* (New York:
Bookmailer, 1958) and Ross Y. Koen, *The China Lobby in American Politics*
(New York: Macmillan, 1960, reissue 1974). The Koen book is a story in
itself. It was suppressed and withdrawn from sale at the time it was first published in 1960, apparently because it contained allegations of Kuomintang
involvement in the drug trade. Of course, the best introduction to the congressional committees are the hearings themselves. Eric Bentley's *Thirty Years of
Treason* (New York: Viking, 1971) is a convenient compendium of HUAC's
greatest moments.

There are some other useful studies of specific aspects of the period. The
single most inclusive work on the labor movement is Harvey Levenstein, *Communism, Anticommunism, and the CIO* (Westport, Conn.: Greenwood Press,
1981). Bert Cochran, *Labor and Communism* (Princeton: Princeton University
Press, 1977); Roger Keeran, *The Communist Party and the Auto Workers
Union* (Urbana: University of Illinois Press, 1980); and Len De Caux's memoir *Labor Radical* (Boston: Beacon, 1970) are also of use. Philip Stern, *The
Oppenheimer Case* (New York: Harper & Row, 1969) is the best book on that
subject. Herbert L. Packer, *Ex-Communist Witnesses* (Stanford: Stanford
University Press, 1962) is a thoughtful analysis of four of the most ubiquitous
informers; Harvey Matusow's *False Witness* (New York: Cameron and Kahn,
1955) is only one of a large number of first-person accounts by professional
witnesses. Michal Belknap, *Cold War Political Justice* (Westport, Conn.:
Greenwood Press, 1977) is definitive on the Smith Act trials. Stanley I. Kutler's
The American Inquisition (New York: Hill and Wang, 1982) treats some of
the main Justice Department prosecutions of the period in a strangely superficial way. Since historians have yet to integrate the constitutional history of
McCarthyism into the political, the most useful treatment of that constitutional history is actually a law school casebook: Thomas I. Emerson, David
Haber, and Norman Dorsen, *Political and Civil Rights in the United States,* 3rd
ed. (Boston: Little, Brown, 1967) (later editions carry less material on the

fifties). Other studies of the judicial response to McCarthyism are C. Herman Pritchett, *Civil Liberties and the Vinson Court* (Chicago: University of Chicago Press, 1954) and Robert McCloskey, *The Modern Supreme Court* (Cambridge: Harvard University Press, 1972).

Kutler's book, despite its problems, contains some fascinating material, for Kutler is one of a growing number of scholars who have begun to obtain government documents through the Freedom of Information Act. The most controversial products of that type of research are, of course, Allen Weinstein's account of the Hiss Case, *Perjury* (New York: Knopf, 1978) and Ronald Radosh's and Joyce Milton's similar study of the Rosenbergs, *The Rosenberg File* (New York: Holt, Rinehart & Winston, 1983). (Neither book is completely convincing, in large part because both rely so heavily on censored documents and circumstantial evidence. There may simply be too many gaps in the record for us ever to know what Hiss and the Rosenbergs actually did.) If the Freedom of Information Act has yet to solve the Cold War's most notorious cases, it has, nonetheless, completely changed the way scholars look at the FBI. This new interpretation, which assigns to the Bureau a vastly larger role in formulating and then administering McCarthyism, is in large part the work of Athan Theoharis, his students, and a few other historians. Their painstaking research in FBI files has yielded several invaluable studies, especially Theoharis's own *Spying on Americans* (Philadelphia: Temple University Press, 1981); Theoharis, ed., *Beyond the Hiss Case* (Philadelphia: Temple University Press, 1982); and Kenneth O'Reilly, *Hoover and the Un-Americans* (Philadelphia: Temple University Press, 1983). There is also Frank J. Donner, *The Age of Surveillance* (New York: Knopf, 1980) and David Garrow, *The FBI and Martin Luther King, Jr.* (New York: Norton, 1981). Peter L. Steinberg in *The Great "Red Menace": United States Prosecution of American Communists, 1947–1952* (Westport, Conn.: Greenwood Press, 1984) shows that it is possible to document the importance of Hoover without obtaining access to FBI files.

Concomitant with the efflorescence of scholarship on McCarthyism is that on the Communist Party. Much, but by no means all, comes from former members of the New Left who are casting a scholarly eye on their political predecessors. To date, most of this work has dealt with the thirties and forties. See, for example, Harvey Klehr, *The Heyday of American Communism* (New York: Basic Books, 1984); Maurice Isserman, *Which Side Were You On?* (Middletown, Conn.: Wesleyan University Press, 1982); and Mark Naison's exemplary *Communists in Harlem during the Depression* (Urbana: University of Illinois Press, 1983). The most useful book on the CP in the fifties is actually that of a former member, Joseph Starobin's *American Communism in Crisis* (Cambridge: Harvard University Press, 1972). There are some helpful earlier studies, among them two Fund for the Republic products: David A. Shannon's *The Decline of American Communism* (New York: Harcourt Brace and Co., 1959) and Nathan Glazer's *The Social Basis of American Communism* (New York: Harcourt, Brace & World, 1961), a book whose argument is more persuasive than its evidence; and the only one-volume history of the CP to date, Irving Howe's and Lewis Coser's sprightly polemic *The American Communist Party* (New York: Praeger, 1962; 1st ed. 1957).

Writing about the American CP presents many problems. In the first place, documents are hard to come by. The Party has yet to open its archives (if they exist) to outside scholars. There is also the problem of bias. The Communist Party has been controversial for so long that it seems almost impossible to write about it without taking sides. Though I am no believer in what is usually called "objective" scholarship, I am not sure that the history of the CP is served by judging every action the Party took. In addition, much of the current research seems to be asking the wrong questions. It studies the Party's top leaders instead of middle-level cadres and rank and file, and thus does not look at the most interesting aspect of American Communism: why and how it came to dominate the American left during the 1930s and 1940s. To do that we will have to find out what ordinary Communists did on a day-to-day basis. That information may be harder to find than what line the Party leaders took on a specific issue, but it may well provide more insight into the role of the CP in American political life. Certainly, with regard to my own work on the Party and the academic world, more scholarship about the rank and file would have been invaluable.

That kind of research requires interviews. Because of the Party's secrecy, there really is no other way to find out what its members did. However, because of the repression visited upon them, many ex-Communists do not want to be interviewed or let themselves be identified. Some writers have avoided this problem by rendering their subjects anonymous or using pseudonyms as both Vivian Gornick, *The Romance of American Communism* (New York: Basic Books, 1977) and Paul Lyons, *Philadelphia Communists* (Philadelphia: Temple University Press, 1982) did. Such procedures do not inspire confidence. In my own discussion of Communist academics, I have identified most of them by name either in the text or in the footnotes. I have rendered a few people anonymous at their own request, but they are very few. Most of the men and women I've corresponded with or interviewed for this book have been willing to let their names be used. It was not hard to locate these people. Since many of them had appeared in public before congressional committees, their names were a matter of record and I could, and did, contact many of them directly by mail. Those who did not want to be interviewed never answered my letters; most of the others did. From them and from others, I often got the names of still other people to interview. I also placed author's queries in the *New York Times Book Review* and the *New York Review of Books*. Not all of the people I interviewed had been in the Party and not all of those who had been wanted to discuss that part of their lives. I have, therefore, refrained from identifying anybody as a former Communist who has not done so himself. Fortunately, about fifty of my informants freely admitted that they had been in the CP and talked at length about their activities; as a result I was able to find out quite a bit about what Party members did on campus during the 1930s and 1940s. I was also granted access to tapes and transcripts of interviews that Marvin Gettleman, Martin Sherwin, and Fred R. Zimring held with some of the people I was interested in.

These interviews were not my only source of information about academic Communism. Because I was asking essentially the same questions as the investigating committees of the 1950s, I found much useful material in those comittees' transcripts, both the published congressional ones and the unpublished academic ones. The congressional testimony of both friendly and unfriendly witnesses like Robert Gorham Davis (HUAC, Feb. 27, 1953, 83rd Cong., 1st sess.), Marcus Singer (HUAC, May 26, 1953, 83rd Cong., 1st sess.), Lawrence Arguimbau (HUAC, April 21, 1953, 83rd Cong., 1st sess.), and Isidore Amdur (HUAC, April 22, 1953, 83rd Cong., 1st sess.) was especially valuable. So, too, was some of the testimony that was taken during tenure committee and other academic hearings, in particular that of Philip Morrison (Cornell), Mark Nickerson (University of Michigan), Clement Markert (Michigan), and Robert Rutman (Jefferson Medical College). Another useful source was the unpublished transcript of a conference on Harvard student activism in the 1930s that took place at Hobart and William Smith Colleges in 1975, John Lydenberg, ed., "A Symposium on Political Activism and the Academic Conscience: The Harvard Experience, 1936–1941" (unpublished ms., 1977). Over a dozen former Harvard graduate students and undergraduates took part, among them Henry May, Leo Marx, Carl Schorske, Henry Nash Smith, Rufus Mathewson, and Richard Schlatter. The reminiscences of these people, not all of whom had been Communists, were helpful.

I got a copy of the Hobart transcript the way I got much of the material for this book—one of the people I interviewed lent it to me. Because of the difficulties of obtaining official records (about which, more later), I often had to scrounge for sources. Fortunately, there was so much intra-academic communication that documents about important cases often appeared in several different places. I encountered one of my best sources, a privately printed pamphlet about the Edwin Berry Burgum case at NYU which contained excerpts from the otherwise unavailable official record, in dozens of collections from the NYU library and the ACLU archives to the private papers of at least three different people. Similarly, official reports and documents dealing with the major academic freedom cases turned up in many different files. Cornell's archives contained faculty committee reports from MIT, the University of Miami, and Colorado; Yale's had one from the University of California. The people I interviewed often had the transcripts of their academic hearings as well as correspondence and copies of pamphlets and other ephemera of the time. In addition, Professor Alfred Young of the University of Northern Illinois was extraordinarily generous and lent me several invaluable files of clippings and other materials from his own personal collection.

Unquestionably, the most valuable published source for the academic freedom cases of the McCarthy period are the Committee A reports in the *AAUP Bulletin*. In preparing these reports, the AAUP's investigators usually interviewed the protagonists and read all the pertinent documents. For some of the cases on which I could not get archival materials, these reports were my main source. In addition, there are a few recent monographs, dissertations, and unpublished papers that deal with some of the important cases; I have relied quite heavily on them. The most important are Jane Sanders, *Cold War on the Campus* (Seattle: University of Washington Press, 1979); David P. Gardner, *The California Oath Controversy* (Berkeley and Los Angeles: University of California Press, 1967); Fred R. Zimring, "Academic Freedom and and the Cold War; The Dismissal of Barrows Dunham from Temple University" (Ed.D. diss., Columbia University Teachers College, 1981); Robby Cohen, "Professor William Parry, HUAC, and the University of Buffalo" (unpublished paper, 1976); and Peter H. Hare and Edward H. Madden, "Buffalo in the McCarthy Era" (unpublished paper, n.d., probably 1983).

For what happened at those schools where there was no AAUP investigation and about which there is, as yet, no scholarship, I have had to do my own primary research. Obtaining access to archival materials was not easy. The single most important repository of materials on the academic freedom cases of the period is the AAUP. When I began this study in 1977, I requested access. I was told that AAUP policy, in particular its commitment to maintain the confidentiality of its files, prevented scholars from using them. Many of the people I interviewed—both the AAUP's former officials and its former clients—were surprised that the organization's old files were closed to scholars. Since it was possible to preserve individual privacy and still grant access to archival materials and since there seemed to be such a discrepancy between the AAUP's stated concern for academic freedom and its refusal to open its archives, I continued to petition for access. I finally received it in the beginning of 1984, just in time to include material from those archives in the final draft of the manuscript.

The records of the American Civil Liberties Union at Princeton University, which have been open to scholars for many years, are almost as valuable as those of the AAUP. Many of the endangered professors contacted both organizations. The other important general archive on the subject was collected by the late Rutgers University political scientist, Paul Tillett. It consists of several dozen questionnaires and transcripts of interviews with teachers who had been dismissed during the McCarthy period. These papers are also on deposit at Princeton. I found two oral history collections to be useful as well. Columbia University's venerable Oral History Project had interviews with a variety of academic administrators and others, including a remarkable one with the attorney Clifford Durr. The American Institute of Physics, Center for History of Physics, whose former director, Charles Weiner, was particularly interested in the impact of McCarthyism on the men he interviewed, contains several useful transcripts, particularly those of E. U. Condon and Frank Oppenheimer.

Whether or not an academic institution opens its archives seems almost random, although state schools are usually more forthcoming. Thus, I was able to look at the official records at both the University of Michigan and Rutgers. Some schools seemed not to have any policy with regard to access and seemed to be granting or denying it on an ad hoc basis. This had nothing to do with these schools' records during the McCarthy period. Sarah Lawrence, which apparently did not fire any of its teachers, refused to grant me access. So, too, did Harvard, NYU, and Princeton—although at the last-named the dean of the faculty consulted the records for me and was able to give me some information on that basis. Cornell, Yale, Columbia, and the University of Pennsylvania all let me see some of their records. Through the intercession of Fred Zimring, I was also given material from the archives of Jefferson Medical College and Dickinson College. The haphazard treatment that I received seems to indicate that much of the academic community has not seriously dealt with the issue of its own history. Those colleges and universities which have not opened their archives to scholars may not realize how hypocritical it looks for an institution ostensibly devoted to scholarship to create obstacles to it. Perhaps, when that realization dawns, their policies will change. My own experience with the AAUP encourages me to believe that will be the case.

Then there are FBI files. The Freedom of Information Act is an invaluable tool. Using it, however, is an enormous hassle. To get the full files on the individuals and institutions I was interested in would have been a time-consuming, expensive, and not necessarily successful process. Moreover, it would have been more than likely that the files I would have received would have contained so many deletions that they would not have given much information. Since the FBI's role in the functioning of academic McCarthyism, though important, was somewhat peripheral to my main concerns, I decided not to become involved in a Freedom of Information suit. I was fortunate in being able to look at files that other people's efforts have pried out of the Bureau, in particular some files from the Rosenberg case and some that Sigmund Diamond has received. In addition, many of the people I interviewed shared their own FBI files with me. These limited glimpses into the Bureau's activities make it clear that this is an area where more research needs to be done. In fact, the whole subject of the academy's relations with the government—certainly one of the main themes of this book—needs further research. So, of course, does almost every topic I touched on in this book, for I did not, as I could not, do a definitive study. One must begin somewhere.

Interviews and Other Correspondence with the Author

This list is not complete; several of the men and women I dealt with requested anonymity.

Daniel Aaron, March 27, 1978
Kenneth Bainbridge, June 8, 1978
Morton Baratz, March 30, 1978
Lloyd Barenblatt, December 31, 1977
Robert Bedell, November 29, 1983
Robert Bellah, August 25, 1977
Knight Biggerstaff, October 18, 1979
Eugene Bluestein, May 29, 1978
Max Bluestone, August 4, 1980
Dorothy Borg, April 4, 1977
Leonard Boudin, December 30, 1976
Gerald E. Brown, September 4, 1978
Paul Buck, January 10, 1978
McGeorge Bundy, December 29, 1977
Clark Byse, May 11, 1978
Angus Cameron, December 30, 1976, April 5, 1977
Francis Carpenter, April 6, 1978
Courtney Cazden, May 1, 1981
Norman Cazden, June 9, 1978
Jules Chametzky, April 5, 1978
Robert S. Cohen, October 19, 1977
Hollis Cooley, November 4, 1981
Dale Corson, January 25, 1979
Joseph H. Cort, March 27, 1979
Vern Countryman, December 8, 1976

Chandler Davis, February 21, 1978
Horace Bancroft Davis, July 3, 1979
Natalie Zemon Davis, April 2, 1981
Robert Gorham Davis, February 2, 1982
Bruce Dayton, April 4, 1980
Sigmund Diamond, November 10, 1977, February 1, 1978
Thomas I. Emerson, November 16, 1977
Frederic Ewen, November 7, 1980
John K. Fairbank, March 10, 1977
W. H. Ferry, December 12, 1978
Jacob Fine, July 5, 1977
Robert Fogel, June 2, 1978
Philip Foner, April 9, 1978
Joseph Forer, March 31, 1978
David Fox, August 13, 1981
Ralph Fuchs, October 6, 1978
Wendell Furry, November 4, 1977
Walter Gellhorn, February 16, 1982
Bentley Glass, September 4, 1978
David Goldway, March 11, 1983
Erwin Griswold, December 23, 1977
Harry Grundfest, October 20, 1978
Bonnie Bird (Gundlach), April 15, 1982

Mason Hammond, January 25, 1978
Louis Harap, December 11, 1981
Clarence Hiskey, July 27, 1980
Jane Hodes, April 5, 1980
Donald Horton, February 25, 1982
Ruth Hubbard, June 12, 1978
Everett Hughes, June 16, 1978
H. Stuart Hughes, August 9, 1977
John A. Hutchinson, letter, June 1,
    1978
Sydney James, letter, October 24,
    1977, interview, November 3,
    1977
Louis Joughin, March 30, 1978
Martin Kamen, April 4, 1980
Leon Kamin, October 6, 1977
Martin Kaplan, July 31, 1982
Nikki Keddie, December 29, 1982
Abraham Keller, Spring 1978 (tape-
    recorded reminiscences)
Corliss Lamont, October 18, 1977
Alfred McClung Lee, March 29, 1979
Seymour Martin Lipset, August 26,
    1977
Lee Lorch, July 3–4, 1978
David Lubell, November 8, 1977
Salvatore Luria, March 9, 1981
Helen Lynd, October 20, 1978
Saul Maloff, January 29, 1978
William Marbury, May 25, 1978
Robert H. March, Spring 1978 (tape-
    recorded reminiscences)
Clement Markert, May 30, 1978,
    February 2, 1982
George Markham, February 5, 1983
Harry J. Marks, March 9, 1979
Leonard Marsak, letter, March 28,
    1978
Leo Marx, April 11, 1978
Edward Mason, June 1, 1978
Rufus Mathewson, May 25, 1978
Everett Mendelsohn, November 15,
    1977
Robert Merton, February 5, 1980
Walter Metzger, January 25, 1979
E. E. Moise, April 15, 1978
Stanley Moore, March 3, 1979
Robert Morris, October 29, 1979
Philip Morrison, December 22, 1977

Otto Nathan, February 2, 1978
Steve Nelson, June 17, 1981
Alex B. Novikoff, April 14, 1978
Harvey O'Connor, December 10,
    1977
Talcott Parsons, December 2, 1977,
    May 1, 1978
William Pearlman, July 11, 1978
Stefan Peters, October 29, 1980
Melba Phillips, May 12, 1978
Isidore Pomerance, July 20, 1982
Martin Popper, November 3, 1982
Robert V. Pound, January 26, 1978
Don K. Price, September 21, 1979
Edward Purcell, January 4, 1978
Norman Ramsey, December 15, 1977
David Rein, March 31, 1978
David Riesman, December 19, 1977
Bernard Riess, March 28, 1979,
    September 15, 1982
Paul Rosenkrantz, November 1, 1977
Annette Rubinstein, December 11,
    1981
Robert Rutman, December 26, 1977
Mika Salpeter, October 15, 1979
Morris U. Schappes, March 7, 1983
Boone Schirmer, January 19, 1981
Richard Schlatter, October 21, 1981
Stuart Schram, September 17, 1979
John Anthony Scott, February 5,
    1980
John Stewart Service, August 25,
    1977
Oscar Shaftel, April 13, 1978
Vera Shlakman, March 28, 1979
Harry Slochower, December 29, 1980
Louise Pettibone Smith, July 9, 1978
John Stachel, October 19, 1977
Irving Stein, letter, May 12, 1978
Charlotte Stern, October 30, 1981
Dudley Strauss, July 1, 1982
Dirk Struik, January 6, 1977
Paul Sweezy, July 27, 1982
Richard N. Swift, November 4, 1980
Harold Taylor, June 20, 1978
Alice Thorner, March 16, September
    24, 1979
Wayne Vucinich, April 12, 1980
James Weinstein, April 14, 1978

Forrest Oran Wiggins, letter, May 15, 1978, and tape-recorded reminiscences

Frank Wilkinson, August 11, 19, 1977

H. H. Wilson, April 3, 1977

Leon Wofsy, April 12, 1980

Etta Woodward, October 17, 1979

Charles Wyzanski, January 7, 1978

Howard Zinn, October 24, 1977

Pearl Zipser, May 28, 1977

Other Interviews

Herbert Aptheker, July 5, 1977 (interviewed by Fred R. Zimring in Barrows Dunham/Fred Zimring Oral History Collection, Conwellana-Templana Collection, Paley Library, Temple University, Philadelphia, Pennsylvania)

————, April 1976 (Oral History of the American Left, Tamiment Library, New York University)

Joseph Barnes, 1954 (Columbia University Oral History Project)

David Bohm, June 15, 1979 (interviewed by Martin Sherwin)

Edward U. Condon, April 27, 1968, September 11, 1973 (interviewed by Charles Weiner for the American Institute of Physics, Center for History of Physics)

Seymour Copstein, April 18, 1974 (interviewed by Marvin E. Gettleman)

Charles Coryell (Columbia University Oral History Project)

Harold W. Dodds, February 9, 1962 (Columbia University Oral History Project)

Barrows Dunham (interview with Fred Zimring in Barrows Dunham/Fred Zimring Oral History Collection)

Clifford J. Durr (Columbia University Oral History Project)

Thomas I. Emerson (Columbia University Oral History Project)

Harry Gideonse, February 23, 1961 (Columbia University Oral History Project)

Bernard Grebanier, April 24, 1974 (interviewed by Marvin E. Gettleman)

Lawrence Klein, January 25, 1980 (interview with Fred Zimring in Barrows Dunham/Fred Zimring Oral History Collection)

Irving Kravis, February 4, 1980 (interview with Fred Zimring in Barrows Dunham/Fred Zimring Oral History Collection)

Paul Lazarsfeld (Columbia University Oral History Project)

Owen Lattimore, March 7, 1962 (interviewed by Paul Tillett)

Giovanni Rossi Lomanitz, July 11, 1979 (interviewed by Martin Sherwin)

Robert E. Marshak, September 19, October 4, 1970 (interviewed by Charles Weiner for the American Institute of Physics)

Lloyd Motz, November 16, 1977 (interviewed by Marvin E. Gettleman)

Frank Oppenheimer, February 9, May 21, 1973 (interviewed by Charles Weiner for the American Institute of Physics)

Norman Ramsey, August 5, 1960 (Columbia University Oral History Project)

I. Milton Sacks, March 28, July 10, 1962 (interviewed by Paul Tillett)

Morris U. Schappes, January 31, 1974 (interviewed by Marvin E. Gettleman)

Robert Serber, February 10, 1967 (interviewed by Charles Weiner, for the American Institute of Physics)

Ordway Tead, 1960 (Columbia University Oral History Project)

Charles H. Tuttle, January 13, 1960 (Columbia University Oral History Project)

Manuscript Collections

American Association of University Professors, Washington, D.C.
  Committee A files
American Institute of Physics, Center for History of Physics, New York City
  Donald H. Menzel, manuscript autobiography
Columbia University Archives, Low Library, New York City
  Grayson Kirk Papers
Columbia University, Rare Book and Manuscript Library, Butler Library, New
  York City
  Academic Freedom Committee, records
Cornell University, Department of Manuscripts and University Archives, Ithaca,
  New York
  Knight Biggerstaff Papers
  Edmund Ezra Day Papers
  Cornelius de Kewiet Papers
  Deane W. Malott Papers
  Dean of the Faculty Papers
  Dean of Students Papers
Dickinson College, Special Collections, Boyd Lee Spahr Library, Carlisle,
  Pennsylvania
  La Vallee Case, records
Fund for Open Information and Accountability, Inc., New York City
  Rosenberg Case, FBI files
Harvard Law School, Manuscript Collection, Harvard Law School Library,
  Cambridge, Massachusetts
  Zechariah Chafee Papers
  Mark A. deWolfe Howe Papers
  Arthur E. Sutherland Papers
Harvard University Archives, Pusey Library, Cambridge, Massachusetts
  John K. Fairbank Papers
  Talcott Parsons Papers
Johns Hopkins University Archives, Eisenhower Library, Johns Hopkins Uni-
  versity, Baltimore, Maryland
  History Department Records
Library of Congress, Manuscript Division, Washington, D.C.
  J. Robert Oppenheimer Papers
Michigan Historical Collections, Bentley Historical Library, The University
  of Michigan, Ann Arbor
  Harlan H. Hatcher Papers
  Marvin L. Niehuss Papers
  Alexander G. Ruthven Papers
  Michigan University College of Literature, Science and the Arts Papers
University of Minnesota Archives, University of Minnesota, Minneapolis,
  Minnesota
  AAUP, Minnesota Chapter Papers
  A. O. C. Nier, Papers
  President's Office Papers
New York City, Board of Higher Education Archives, New York City
  "Organization of Special Committee on #903," files

New York University, Office of University Archives, Elmer Holmes Bobst Library, New York University, New York City
    James W. Armsey Papers
    University Senate, minutes
Oklahoma State University, Special Collections, Edmon Low Library, Oklahoma State University, Stillwater
    Miscellaneous documents courtesy of Lloyd Wallisch, librarian
University of Pennsylvania Archives, University of Pennsylvania, Philadelphia
    Thomas C. Cochran papers
    UPA 4 (President's Papers)
    UPB 1.2 (Dean of the Faculty Papers)
Princeton University, Seeley G. Mudd Library, Princeton University, Princeton, New Jersey
    American Civil Liberties Union Papers
    Paul Tillett Papers (I examined these when they were still in the personal possession of Mrs. H. H. Wilson.)
Rutgers University Archives, Rutgers University Library, New Brunswick, New Jersey
    Lewis Webster Jones Papers
Yale University Archives, Manuscripts and Archives Division, Sterling Memorial Library, New Haven, Connecticut
    A. Whitney Griswold Papers
    Charles N. Seymour Papers

Miscellaneous Manuscripts and Private Papers

Robert Bedell, private papers, including FBI file
Gerald E. Brown, private papers
Courtney Cazden, private papers
Norman Cazden, private papers
Jules Chametzky, private papers
Robert S. Cohen, private papers
Chandler Davis, private papers
Sigmund Diamond, FBI files
Sidney Eisenberger, private papers
W. H. Ferry, private papers
Jacob Fine, private papers
Bentley Glass, private papers (AAUP materials)
Jane Hodes, private papers (Robert Hodes)
Everett Hughes, private papers
Martin Kamen, private papers
Lee Lorch, private papers
Clement Markert, private papers, including FBI file
George Markham, private papers (Helen Wendler Deane Markham correspondence)
Robert Merton, private papers
Stanley Moore, private papers
Herbert M. Morais, "Morais transcripts" (Rapp-Coudert) in possession of Mrs. Anne Morais, New York City, photocopies in possession of Marvin E. Gettleman

Philip Morrison, private papers
William Pearlman, private papers
Stefan Peters, private papers (California Loyalty Oath)
Robert Rutman, private papers
Oscar Shaftel, private papers
Harry Slochower, private papers
Charlotte Stern, private papers (Bernhard Stern)
Janet Stevenson, private papers
Dirk Struik, private papers
Paul Sweezy, materials on *Sweezy v. New Hampshire*
Richard N. Swift, private papers
Frank Wilkinson, files of several California-based civil liberties organizations
    from the 1950s. At the time I saw them, in 1977, they were in the
    archives of the National Committee Against Repressive Legislation. They
    have now been transferred to the Wisconsin Historical Society, Madison,
    Wisconsin.
Leon Wofsy, private papers
Etta Woodward, private papers
Alfred F. Young, private papers and files of clippings

Notes

Introduction

1. Chandler Davis, testimony, House Un-American Activities Committee (hereafter cited as HUAC), May 10, 1954, 83rd Cong., 2nd sess., 5350; Chandler Davis, interview with the author, Feb. 21, 1978.
2. Thomas I. Emerson, David Haber, and Norman Dorsen, *Political and Civil Rights in the United States*, 3rd ed. (Boston: Little, Brown, 1967), 1:120.
3. The literature on the Cold War and its origins is vast and still growing. It is also split between revisionists and more traditional historians. Among the more useful studies are Walter LaFeber, *America, Russia, and the Cold War*, 4th ed. (New York: Wiley, 1980); John Gaddis, *The United States and the Origins of the Cold War* (New York: Columbia University Press, 1972); Daniel Yergin, *Shattered Peace* (Boston: Houghton Mifflin, 1977); Vojtech Mastny, *Russia's Road to the Cold War* (New York: Columbia University Press, 1979); Gabriel Kolko, *The Politics of War* (New York: Random House, 1968); and Gabriel and Joyce Kolko, *The Limits of Power* (New York: Harper & Row, 1972).
4. For an intriguing discussion of the relationship between Truman's foreign policy and his domestic anti-Communism, see Richard M. Freeland, *The Truman Doctrine and the Origins of McCarthyism* (New York: Schocken, 1970).
5. H. Stuart Hughes, interview with the author, Aug. 9, 1977; anon., interview with the author, April 12, 1980; Athan Theoharis, *Seeds of Repression* (Chicago: Quadrangle, 1971), 199. Alan D. Harper, *The Politics of Loyalty* (Westport, Conn.: Greenwood Press, 1969), is the best study of the political background of the loyalty-security program.

   Recent scholarship using the Freedom of Information Act and other archival materials is beginning to fashion a slightly revised version of the origins of the Cold War anti-Communist crusade, one that locates much of the impetus for that crusade within the Federal Bureau of Investigation and assigns a crucial role to its director, J. Edgar Hoover. See especially Kenneth O'Reilly, *Hoover and the Un-Americans: The FBI, HUAC, and the Red Menace* (Philadelphia: Temple University Press, 1983) and Peter L. Steinberg, *The Great "Red Menace": United States Prosecution of*

American Communists, 1947–1952 (Westport, Conn.: Greenwood Press, 1984).

6. The best single study of the federal loyalty-security program is Eleanor Bontecou, *The Federal Loyalty-Security Program* (Ithaca: Cornell University Press, 1953). Ralph S. Brown, *Loyalty and Security* (New Haven: Yale University Press, 1958) is a good survey of the broader impact of that program.

7. Mary Sperling McAuliffe, *Crisis on the Left* (Amherst: University of Massachusetts Press, 1978), 33–47; Alonzo Hamby, *Beyond the New Deal* (New York: Columbia University Press, 1973), 121–36, 207–68; Richard J. Walton, *Henry Wallace, Harry Truman and the Cold War* (New York: Viking, 1976), 185–246.

8. Michal R. Belknap, *Cold War Political Justice* (Westport, Conn.: Greenwood Press, 1977) is the definitive work on the Smith Act trials. See also Joseph Starobin, *American Communism in Crisis* (Cambridge: Harvard University Press, 1972), 207; Steinberg, *The Great "Red Menace,"* 157–80; John Gates, *The Story of an American Communist* (New York: Thomas Nelson, 1958), 120–35. For a discussion of the *Dennis* decision, see Emerson, Haber, and Dorsen, *Political and Civil Rights,* 100–120 and Robert McCloskey, *The Modern Supreme Court* (Cambridge: Harvard University Press, 1972), 79–83.

9. Athan Theoharis, *The Yalta Myths* (Columbia: University of Missouri Press, 1970), 7–8, 70–87; H. Bradford Westerfield, *Foreign Policy and Party Politics* (New Haven: Yale University Press, 1955), 203, 306, 325–33; Robert Griffith, *The Politics of Fear* (Lexington: The University Press of Kentucky, 1970), 43–47.

10. Robert E. Cushman, *Civil Liberties in the United States* (Ithaca: Cornell University Press, 1956), 199.

11. The Hiss case has spawned a small library. The most recent additions are Allen Weinstein, *Perjury* (New York: Knopf, 1978); John Chabot Smith, *Alger Hiss* (New York: Holt, Rinehart & Winston, 1976); Edith Tiger, ed., *In Re: Alger Hiss* (New York: Hill and Wang, 1979); and Athan Theoharis, ed., *Beyond the Hiss Case* (Philadelphia: Temple University Press, 1982).

12. The most useful books on the meaning of McCarthy's career are Griffith, *The Politics of Fear,* and Richard M. Fried, *Men Against McCarthy* (New York: Columbia University Press, 1976). The two recent biographies by Thomas Reeves and David Oshinsky add little.

13. There are dozens of books about the impact of McCarthyism on the entertainment industry. The most useful recent account of the Hollywood Ten is Larry Ceplair and Steven Englund, *The Inquisition in Hollywood* (New York: Doubleday, 1980), 254–98.

14. The most ambitious attempt to describe the scope of these McCarthy era dismissals is David Caute, *The Great Fear* (New York: Simon and Schuster, 1978). For some specific cases, see James Aronson, *The Press and the Cold War* (Boston: Beacon, 1970), 132–34; Roger Keeran, *The Communist Party and the Auto Workers Unions* (Bloomington: University of Indiana Press, 1980), 250–89; Ronald W. Schatz, *The Electrical Workers* (Urbana: University of Illinois Press, 1983), 238–40; and Brown, *Loyalty and Security,* 120–59.

15. For a fuller treatment of Chandler Davis's experiences at Michigan, see Chapter VIII.

I: "An Excellent Advertisement for the Institution"

1. Minutes of meeting, Feb. 15, 1953, Association of American Universities, UPA 4, No. 4, in University of Pennsylvania Archives. (Copies of these minutes can also be found in the archives at Columbia and Yale, among other places.)
2. Ibid.; The Association of American Universities, "The Rights and Responsibilities of Universities and their Faculties," March 24, 1953, Princeton, N.J. For a more extended discussion of the AAU statement and its significance, see pp. 187–90 above.
3. "A Quasi-Verbatim summary of the Proceedings of the Special Meeting of the Junior Faculty held March 9, 1953," mimeograph in the private papers of Alfred F. Young.
4. For a somewhat more developed presentation of this argument, that academic freedom played an important role in protecting the collective autonomy of the academic profession, see Ellen Schrecker, "Academic Freedom: The Historical View," in Craig Kaplan and Ellen Schrecker, eds., *Regulating the Intellectuals: Perspectives on Academic Freedom in the 1980s* (New York: Praeger, 1983).

   In their study of how nine major universities filled the vacancies in their liberal arts departments from 1954 to 1956, Theodore Caplow and Reese J. McGee provide considerable evidence for the practice of concealing the non-scholarly aspects of academic personnel decisions. Undesirable characters were excluded for all sorts of reasons; at many schools, not being "socially presentable" or having "the proper personality" was as serious a hindrance to employment as political radicalism. Yet, departments rarely admitted that such factors were important criteria. As an unusually candid informant told Caplow and McGee, if an applicant's "personality were known to be bad, there might be an objection raised, but it would usually be couched as an objection to him as bad scientifically." Caplow and McGee, *The Academic Marketplace* (New York: Basic Books, 1958), 137. See also Christopher Jencks and David Riesman, *The Academic Revolution* (New York: Doubleday, 1968), 202–4.
5. The literature on this first generation of professional academics is vast and growing. It is, of course, but one element of the larger body of scholarship on the development of "professionalism" within an important segment of the American middle class. Though I have done no primary research myself on the growth of the academic profession at the end of the nineteenth and beginning of the twentieth century, the scholarly literature on that subject certainly implies that the drive for professional status and autonomy on the part of these newly professionalized college teachers was an important element in the academic freedom struggles of that time.

   An earlier generation of scholars focussed on a different aspect of the development of academic freedom, claiming that it was, at least in part, a German import which entered the American academy when significant numbers of American college teachers returned from graduate work abroad. Such an explanation ignores the reality of both American and

German university life. The idealized notion of *lehrfreiheit* that has been traditionally invoked, with its stress on the necessary relationship between freedom and the academic enterprise, actually bore little relation to Germany's highly politicized and rigidly classbound university system, but it did give a certain gloss of legitimacy to the *idea* of academic freedom. Ironically, as the concept evolved and acquired its content from the specific cases in which it was invoked, it increasingly came to resemble its German prototype in its subservience to the demands of the state.

The standard discussion of the concept of *lehrfreiheit* is in Walter P. Metzger, *Academic Freedom in the Age of the University* (New York: Columbia University Press paperback ed., 1961), 109–33. An interesting discussion of the concept in its German setting is Frederic Lilge, *The Abuse of Learning* (New York: Macmillan, 1948).

The most useful introduction to the literature on the professionalization of academic life is Laurence Veysey, *The Emergence of the American University* (Chicago: University of Chicago Press, 1965). See also Burton J. Bledstein, *The Culture of Professionalism* (New York: Norton, 1976); Mary O. Furner, *Advocacy and Objectivity* (Lexington: The University Press of Kentucky, 1975); and Thomas Haskell, *The Emergence of Professional Social Science* (Urbana: University of Illinois Press, 1977).

6. Dorothy Ross, "Socialism and American Liberalism: Academic Thought in the 1880's," *Perspectives in American History* 11 (1977–78): 21–24; Robert Crunden, *Ministers of Reform* (New York: Basic Books, 1982), 16–38; Haskell, *Emergence of Professional Social Science*, 104; Furner, *Advocacy and Objectivity*, 50–58.

7. Ibid., 100–106, 127–42; Ross, "Socialism and American Liberalism," 47–48.

8. Furner, *Advocacy and Objectivity*, 69–74, 119; see also Benjamin G. Rader, *The Academic Mind and Reform* (Lexington: The University Press of Kentucky, 1966), 28–129, 138–52; Metzger, *Academic Freedom*, 152.

9. All the scholarly literature on the Ely case deals with the Regents' statement:

> in all lines of academic investigation it is of the utmost importance that the investigator should be absolutely free to follow the indications of the truth wherever they may lead. Whatever may be the limitations which trammel inquiry elsewhere we believe the great University of Wisconsin should ever encourage that continual and fearless sifting and winnowing by which alone the truth can be found.

See Furner, *Advocacy and Objectivity*, 161; Metzger, *Academic Freedom*, 160; and Rader, *The Academic Mind and Reform*, 149.

10. Metzger, *Academic Freedom*, 153–61; Furner, *Advocacy and Objectivity*, 163–98. The statement about Bemis's competence is by Albion W. Small and Nathanial Butler, Oct. 16, 1895, in Clarence J. Karier, *Shaping the American Educational State* (New York: Free Press, 1975), 41.

11. Veysey, *Emergence of the American University*, 397–404.

12. Ibid., 405–7. Furner, *Advocacy and Objectivity*, 229–59, has a perceptive discussion about the collective implications of the Ross case.

13. Metzger, *Academic Freedom*, 194–206.

14. Committee on Academic Freedom and Academic Tenure, "Report," *AAUP Bulletin* 1 (Dec. 1915): 24–25, 40.

15. Ibid., 33–35, 39.

16. Ibid., 34, 40–42.
17. Committee A, "Report," *AAUP Bulletin* 4 (March 1918): 19.
18. "Report of the Committee of Inquiry on the Case of Professor Scott Nearing of the University of Pennsylvania," *AAUP Bulletin* 2 (May 1916); Scott Nearing, *The Making of a Radical* (New York: Harper & Row, 1972), 89.
19. "Report of the Committee of Inquiry," 26–27, 41.
20. Nearing, *Making of a Radical,* chapters 5 and 6.
21. The definitive work on academic freedom during World War I is Carol S. Gruber, *Mars and Minerva: World War I and the Uses of the Higher Learning in America* (Baton Rouge: Louisiana State University Press, 1975). Nicholas Murray Butler's speech, June 6, 1917, is on p. 199.
22. Gruber, *Mars and Minerva,* 174–75.
23. Metzger, *Academic Freedom,* 229–30; Gruber, *Mars and Minerva,* 166–69; "Report," Committee on Academic Freedom in Wartime, *AAUP Bulletin* 4 (Feb.–March 1918): 40–41.
24. Gruber, *Mars and Minerva,* 176–84.
25. Ibid., 187–96.
26. Ibid., 205n; "Report," Committee on Academic Freedom in Wartime, 45.
27. A useful discussion of the development of procedural safeguards for the academic profession is Louis Joughlin, "Academic Due Process," in Joughin, ed., *Academic Freedom and Tenure* (Madison: University of Wisconsin Press, 1969), 264–305.
28. Rader, *The Academic Mind and Reform,* 149.

II: "In the Camp of the People"

1. Robert Iversen, *The Communists and the Schools* (New York: Harcourt, Brace and Co., 1959).
2. See the Bibliographical Essay above for a more extensive discussion of the scholarship on the American Communist Party. Perhaps the most useful assessment of the CP's role in the labor movement is Harvey A. Levenstein's *Communism, Anticommunism, and the CIO* (Westport, Conn.: Greenwood Press, 1981). See also Bert Cochran, *Labor and Communism* (Princeton: Princeton University Press, 1977); Roger Keeran, *The Communist Party and the Auto Workers Union* (Bloomington: Indiana University Press, 1980); and Len De Caux, *Labor Radical* (Boston: Beacon, 1970). For the Party's activities within the black community, the definitive book is Mark Naison's thoughtful and carefully balanced study, *Communists in Harlem during the Depression* (Urbana: University of Illinois Press, 1983).
3. In their afterword to *The Inquisition in Hollywood* (New York: Doubleday, 1980), Larry Ceplair and Steven Englund discuss at some length their own dissatisfaction and frustration with the former Hollywood Communists who still "remain mute and unresponsive to the issues most frequently distorted by their anti-Communist foes: the role of the Communist Party in the progressive political and social activity of the thirties and forties and the question of their relationship to it" (427–29). Roger Keeran noted similar problems in *The Communist Party and the Auto Workers Unions,* 24–25. Paul Lyons resolved the problem by giving all his

informants pseudonyms in *Philadelphia Communists, 1936–1956* (Philadelphia: Temple University Press, 1982).

4. The standard work on early Communist Party history is Theodore Draper,
   The Roots of American Communism (New York: Viking, 1957). See also
   Irving Howe and Lewis Coser, *The American Communist Party* (New
   York: Praeger, 1962; 1st ed., 1957), 41–95, and Nathan Glazer, *The Social
   Basis of American Communism* (New York: Harcourt, Brace and World,
   1961), 30–39.

5. Daniel Aaron, *Writers on the Left* (New York: Harcourt, Brace and
   World, 1961), 137–78 is still the best study of the relationship between
   American intellectuals and the CP. See also John P. Diggins, *Up from
   Communism* (New York: Harper & Row, 1977), 17–51.

6. Scott Nearing, *The Making of a Radical* (New York: Harper & Row,
   1972), 145–54. See also Iversen, *The Communists and the Schools*, 76–78,
   and Whittaker Chambers, *Witness* (New York: Random House, 1952),
   211–13.

7. Paula S. Fass, *The Damned and the Beautiful* (New York: Oxford University Press, 1977), 327–39, describes the political atmosphere on campus
   in the 1920s. A survey of the *Bulletins* of the American Association of
   University Professors published in the 1920s reveals at most four or five
   cases that might possibly involve politics. There are none at all for the
   years 1925 and 1926.

8. Iversen, *The Communists and the Schools*, 121–23; Fass, *The Damned
   and the Beautiful*, 292–300, 337, 486; James Wechsler, *Revolt on Campus*
   (New York: Covici-Friede, 1935), 26–41, 47; Malcolm Willey, *Depres-
   sion, Recovery and Higher Education* (New York: McGraw-Hill, 1937),
   316–18; Eileen Eagan, *Class, Culture, and the Classroom* (Philadelphia:
   Temple University Press, 1981), 38; William Parry, quoted in an unpublished paper by Robby Cohen, "Professor William Parry, HUAC and the
   University of Buffalo" (1976), 4; Granville Hicks, *Where We Came Out*
   (New York: Viking, 1954), 21; Corliss Lamont, *Voice in the Wilderness*
   (Buffalo, N.Y.: Prometheus Books, 1974), 105; *Harvard Crimson*, April
   4, 8, 1924; Horace Bancroft Davis, interview with the author, July 3,
   1979; Corliss Lamont, interview with the author, Nov. 9, 1977. For the
   Clark University incident, see "Report on Clark University," *AAUP Bulletin* 10 (Oct. 1924): 66–77, and Nearing, *The Making of a Radical*, 79–81.
   Similar events occurred at the University of Wisconsin, where until 1921
   even William Z. Foster could speak, but afterward both Nearing and journalist Lincoln Steffens were banned. Marianne Ruth Phelps, "The Response of Higher Education to Student Activism" (Ph.D. diss., George
   Washington University, 1980), 167–68.

9. Wechsler, *Revolt on Campus*, 140–42; Hal Draper, "The Student Move-
   ment of the Thirties: A Political History," in Rita James Simon, ed., *As
   We Saw the Thirties* (Urbana: University of Illinois Press, 1967), 168–69;
   Henry May, "From Berkeley to Harvard," and Carl Schorske, "A New
   Yorker's Map of Cambridge: Ethnic Marginality and Political Ambiva-
   lence," both in John Lydenberg, ed., "Political Activism and the Academic
   Conscience, The Harvard Experience, 1936–41," A Symposium at Hobart
   and William Smith Colleges, 1977, 16, 22. (Hereafter cited as Hobart
   Symposium. This manuscript, the transcript of a symposium held in Dec.

1975, contains recollections of student life and politics of the 1930s from Berkeley, Columbia, and Texas, as well as Harvard. It is invaluable.)

10. Draper, "The Student Movement of the Thirties," 173–75; John Gates, *Story of an American Communist* (New York: Thomas Nelson, 1958), 17–19; Wechsler, *Revolt on Campus*, 171–81; Willey, *Depression, Recovery and Higher Education*, 318–19; Eagan, *Class, Culture, and the Classroom*, 109–52; Phelps, "The Response of Higher Education to Student Activism," 46–48, 109–14, 205, 219–22; Iversen, *The Communists and the Schools*, 124–32.

11. Wechsler, *Revolt on Campus*, 52–55; Willey, *Depression, Recovery and Higher Education*, 42; Arthur A. Ekirch, Jr., *Ideologies and Utopias* (Chicago: Quadrangle, 1969), 30–49; Leo Marx, "The Harvard Retrospect and the Arrested Development of American Radicalism," in Hobart Symposium, 38; William Pearlman, interview with the author, July 11, 1978.

12. Willey, *Depression, Recovery and Higher Education* is a survey commissioned by the AAUP of the state of the academic profession during the Depression. Almost all of it is relevant. See especially 35–51, 229–30, 244–46, 274. See also, Celia Lewis Zitron, *The New York City Teachers Union, 1916–1964* (New York: Humanities Press, 1968), 184; Harry Albaum, testimony, Senate Internal Security Subcommittee of the Senate Judiciary Committee (hereafter cited as SISS), Sept. 25, 1952, 82nd Cong., 2nd sess., 211; Bernard Grebanier, interview with Marvin E. Gettleman, April 24, 1974; Harry Marks, interview with the author, March 9, 1979; Oscar Shaftel, interview with the author, April 13, 1978; anon., interview with the author, March 16, 1979.

13. Everett Carll Ladd, Jr., and Seymour Martin Lipset, *The Divided Academy* (New York: Norton, 1976), 149–54; Stephen Steinberg, *The Academic Melting Pot* (New York: McGraw-Hill, 1974), 79–83, 92, 106, 120–23.

14. Marcia Graham Synnott, *The Half-Opened Door* (Westport, Conn.: Greenwood Press, 1979) is a path-breaking recent study of discrimination in admissions which, unfortunately, covers only Harvard, Yale, and Princeton. See also Harry Albaum, testimony, SISS, 211; Wechsler, *Revolt on Campus*, 359; Richard H. Pells, *Radical Visions and American Dreams* (New York: Harper & Row, 1973), 131; Eagan, *Class, Culture, and the Classroom*, 273n; anon., interview with the author, March 16, 1979; Otto Nathan, interview with the author, Feb. 2, 1978; Lee Lorch, interview with the author, July 3, 1978; Hyman Gold, testimony, SISS, Feb. 10, 1953, 83rd Cong., 1st sess., 441; Willey, *Depression, Recovery, and Higher Education*, 438; Marvin E. Gettleman, "Communists in Higher Education: C.C.N.Y. and Brooklyn College on the Eve of the Rapp-Coudert Investigation, 1935–1939," paper delivered at the Annual Meeting of the Organization of American Historians (1977); Sidney Eisenberger, "Political Memoirs of Sidney Eisenberger" (unpublished ms., 1979), 33.

15. Since the CP was a secret organization, there is no sure way to ascertain such facts as the percentage of Jews within the academic units of the Party. The estimate I've made is based on my own sample of approximately two hundred Communist academics. On the one hand, the sample may be skewed because it contains so many New York City teachers; on the other hand, I may have missed a lot of Jews because many people in the cohort I studied changed their last names in order to escape discrimina-

tion. On the propensity for the left among Jews, see Ladd and Lipset, *The Divided Academy*, 149–67, 194; Paul Buhle, "Jews and American Communism," *Radical History Review* 23 (Dec. 1980): 9–33.

16. Pells, *Radical Visions and American Dreams*, 77; Aaron, *Writers on the Left*, 196–97; James Wechsler, *The Age of Suspicion* (New York: Random House, 1953), 40; Phelps, "The Response of Higher Education to Student Activism," 49; Schorske, "A New Yorker's Map of Cambridge," Hobart Symposium, 13.

17. The most recent and comprehensive study of the CP during the 1930s is Harvey Klehr, *The Heyday of American Communism* (New York: Basic Books, 1984). See also Iversen, *The Communists and the Schools*, 96–97; Pells, *Radical Visions and American Dreams*, 125; Ladd and Lipset, *The Divided Academy*, 37–51.

18. Barrows Dunham, quoted in Fred Richard Zimring, "Academic Freedom and the Cold War: The Dismissal of Barrows Dunham from Temple University, a Case Study" (Ed.D. diss. Columbia University Teachers College, 1981), 98–99; Lawrence Arguimbau, testimony, HUAC, April 21, 1953, 83rd Cong., 1st sess., 4016.

19. Cohen, "Professor William Parry," 4–5.

20. Robert Gorham Davis, interview with the author, Feb. 2, 1982.

21. Pearlman, interview; Clement Markert, interview with the author, May 30, 1978; Markert, testimony, in "Proceedings at a Meeting of the Special Advisory Committee to the President," 7:5, in Box 21, Marvin L. Niehuss Papers, Michigan Historical Collections, Bentley Historical Library, University of Michigan.

22. David Fox, interview with the author, Aug. 13, 1981; Leon Wofsy, interview with the author, April 12, 1980; Norman Cazden, interview with the author, June 9, 1978; Saul Maloff, interview with the author, Jan. 29, 1978; anon., interview with the author, Feb. 1, 1978; Robert Fogel, interview with the author, June 2, 1978.

23. Klehr, *The Heyday of American Communism*, 167–222; Naison, *Communists in Harlem During the Depression*, 169–72; Pells, *Radical Visions and American Dreams*, 326–27; Frank A. Warren, III, *Liberals and Communism* (Bloomington: University of Indiana Press, 1966), 104–21; Draper, "The Student Movement of the Thirties," 175–80; Eagan, *Class, Culture, and the Classroom*, 183–201.

24. Robert Gorham Davis, interview; David Hawkins, testimony, HUAC, Dec. 20, 1950, 81st Cong., 2nd sess., 3425; Isidore Amdur, testimony, in "Ninth Interim Report of the Special Commission on Communism, Subversive Activities and Related Matters within the Commonwealth (Massachusetts)," Jan. 21, 1957, 171; Harry Marks, interview.

25. Zimring, "Academic Freedom," 100–101.

26. Leroy Travers Herndon, Jr., testimony, HUAC, March 27, 1953, 83rd Cong., 1st sess., 501; Robert Gorham Davis, interview.

27. Robert Gorham Davis interview; Sigmund Diamond, interview with the author, Nov. 10, 1977; Horace Bancroft Davis, interview; Rufus Mathewson, comments, Hobart Symposium, 80.

28. Saul Maloff, interview; Sidney Eisenberger, "Political Memoirs," 33; Morris Schappes, interview with the author, March 7, 1983.

29. Dale Corson, interview with the author, Jan. 25, 1979; Schorske, "A New Yorker's Map of Cambridge," Hobart Symposium, 11; Stanley Moore, interview with the author, March 3, 1979; May, "From Berkeley to Harvard," Hobart Symposium, 22; Philip Morrison, testimony before Special Committee of the Board of Trustees of Cornell University, Oct. 3–4, 1956, 38, in private papers of Philip Morrison; Norman Levinson, testimony, HUAC, April 23, 1953, 83rd Cong., 1st sess., 1077, 1081; anon., interview.

30. Vivian Gornick, *The Romance of American Communism* (New York: Basic Books, 1977), 104; Richard Byrd Lewis, testimony, HUAC, March 27, 1953, 83rd Cong., 1st sess., 527; Lewis Balamuth, testimony, SISS, May 12, 1953, 83rd Cong., 1st sess., 951; Harry Albaum, testimony, SISS, 212; George Mayberry, testimony, HUAC, July 1, 1953, 83rd Cong., 1st sess., 1917–18; anon., interview with the author, Sept. 24, 1979; Melvin Rader, *False Witness* (Seattle: University of Washington Press, 1969), 42–43; William Ted Martin, testimony, HUAC, April 22, 1953, 83rd Cong., 1st sess., 1029; Robert Rutman, testimony, "Hearing before the Loyalty Committee of the Jefferson Medical College of Philadelphia, in re Dr. Robert J. Rutman," Aug. 4, 1953, 12–13, typed transcript in private papers of Robert Rutman.

31. David Hawkins, testimony, HUAC, 3419; Frank Oppenheimer, testimony, HUAC, June 14, 1949, 81st Cong., 1st sess., 359; Leroy Herndon, testimony, HUAC, 1053.

32. Arguimbau, testimony, HUAC, 4016–25. Philip Morrison recalls that the Berkeley units he belonged to as a graduate student in the late thirties fluctuated a lot. He estimates that their membership was between 100 and 200 students. Morrison, testimony, Special Committee, Board of Trustees, 17.

33. George Mayberry, testimony, HUAC, 1925; Robert Gorham Davis, testimony, HUAC, Feb. 25, 1953, 83rd Cong., 1st sess., 47; Norman Levinson, testimony, HUAC, 1075; Rufus Mathewson, comments, Hobart Symposium, 79–80; Harry Marks, testimony, HUAC, 1868; Morris Schappes, interview with Marvin E. Gettleman, April 28, 1976; Irving Goldman, testimony, SISS, April 1, 1953, 83rd Cong., 1st sess., 731; Robert Fogel, interview.

34. Mark Nickerson, testimony, in "Proceedings at a Meeting of the Special Advisory Committee to the President," 5–1: 55–57, Box 21, Niehuss Papers, University of Michigan; Isidore Amdur, testimony, HUAC, April 22, 1953, 83rd Cong., 1st sess., 1053; William Pearlman, interview; Robert Gorham Davis, testimony, HUAC, 14. Academics were not the only Communists who kept their political affiliation secret nor, by any means, the most important. Labor leaders were particularly careful to conceal their membership in the Party for fear that they might antagonize potential union members. See Joseph Starobin, *American Communism in Crisis* (Cambridge: Harvard University Press, 1972), 39–42.

35. Sidney Eisenberger, "Political Memoirs," 23; Lewis Balamuth, testimony, SISS, 952; Frank Oppenheimer's Party name was "Frank Folsom," Oppenheimer, testimony, HUAC, 365. See also William Ted Martin, testimony, HUAC, 1024; Isidore Amdur, testimony, in "Ninth Interim Report of the Special Commission," 170; Harry Albaum, testimony, SISS, 214; Leroy

Herndon, testimony, HUAC, 513; Schappes, interview with the author. On pen names, see Zimring, "Academic Freedom," 117–18; Robert Gorham Davis, interview; Iversen, *The Communists and the Schools*, 160.

36. Arguimbau, testimony, HUAC, 4025; Horace Bancroft Davis, interview; Isidore Pomerance, interview with the author, July 20, 1982; Nickerson, testimony, "Proceedings," 5–2: 148; Donald Horton, interview with the author, Feb. 25, 1982; Richard Schlatter, "On Being a Communist at Harvard," *Partisan Review* 44, No. 4 (Dec. 1977): 611–12.

37. Dale Corson, interview; Daniel Aaron, interview with the author, March 27, 1978; Kenneth Bainbridge, interview with the author, June 8, 1978; Iversen, *The Communists and the Schools*, 221; Leon Wofsy, interview; Myron Pleasure to Marvin E. Gettleman, Sept. 6, 1979, in private papers of Marvin E. Gettleman.

38. Morris U. Schappes to Sidney Eisenberger, Feb. 2, 1980, copy in files of Marvin E. Gettleman; Schappes, interview with Gettleman; Iversen, *The Communists and the Schools*, 160–62; Pells, *Radical Visions and American Dreams*, 172.

39. Nickerson, testimony, "Proceedings," 5–1: 55–56; Robert Gorham Davis, testimony, HUAC, 47; Balamuth, testimony, SISS, 964; Gettleman, "Communists in Higher Education," 21; William Ted Martin, testimony, HUAC, 1023; Leroy Herndon, testimony, HUAC, 515.

40. Philip Foner quoted in Gettleman, "Communists in Higher Education," 22; Pomerance, interview; Howard Selsam, reply to questionnaire from Paul Tillett, Tillett Files, Seeley G. Mudd Library, Princeton University; Robert Gorham Davis, testimony, HUAC, 47; Alvin L. Schorr to Marvin E. Gettleman, May 11, 1979; Joseph Ershun, interview with Marvin E. Gettleman; Saul Maloff, interview.

41. Iversen, *The Communists and the Schools*, 153; Daniel Finkel to the author, Oct. 14, 1979; Schappes, interview with the author; Robert MacIver to Harlow Shapley, Oct. 27, 1947, in private papers of Robert Merton; George B. Pegram to Arthur N. Dusenbury, Oct. 26, 1949, File "Gene Weltfish," Grayson Kirk Papers, Columbia University Archives, Low Library.

42. "Academic Freedom & New York University, the case of Professor Edwin Berry Burgum" (N. Y., 1954), 24, 33. (This is a privately printed pamphlet published by the Committee for the Reinstatement of Professor Burgum. I have seen copies of it in many institutional and personal archives and collections of papers.) "Report of the Special Advisory Committee to the President," Box 21, Niehuss Papers, University of Michigan. *Communism and Academic Freedom* (Seattle: University of Washington Press, 1949) is a pamphlet that contains the basic documents about the academic freedom cases at the University of Washington; Iversen, *The Communists and the Schools*, 142; Bella Dodd, *School of Darkness* (New York: Kenedy, 1954), 64. Of course, Oppenheimer, Boas, and Matthiessen were men of the left, at least during 1930s. All three, for example, were active in the Teachers Union. And one could argue that with the exception of Oppenheimer, whose radicalism waned during the Second World War, the work of these men was infused by their political commitments. Boas was largely responsible for discrediting the biological determinism that provided an intellectual underpinning for the racist view of man; Mat-

thiessen worked toward a view of American culture embedded in a social context. George W. Stocking, Jr., *Race, Culture, and Evolution* (New York: Free Press, 1968), chapters 9–11. The following passage by one of Oppenheimer's best friends at Berkeley gives a sense of his impact:

> His students' attitude was one of hero-worship . . . When they learned that Opje was a member of the Teachers Union the young teaching assistants joined the Union too. Many of them were or became left-wingers, by gravitation or contagion.

Haakon Chevalier, *Oppenheimer, The Story of a Friendship* (New York: George Braziller, 1965), 22.

43. Lawrence Arguimbau noted, "In my own field of engineering I have not had any logical reason for talking about political matters and I have not done so." Arguimbau, testimony, HUAC, 4026. See also, "Statement of Committee on Academic Responsibility at MIT" cited in "Ninth Interim Report of the Special Commission," 28; Dr. Rothe, testimony, "Proceedings," 3:19, Box 21, Niehuss Papers, University of Michigan; "Report of the Committee on Conference on Dr. Harry Grundfest," n.d., 6, in Grayson Kirk Papers, Columbia University Archives; Etta Woodward, interview with the author, Oct. 17, 1979; Leo Marx, "The Harvard Retrospect," Hobart Symposium, 33; Jane Sanders, *Cold War on the Campus* (Seattle: University of Washington Press, 1979), 35, 51–52; Vern Countryman, *Un-American Activities in the State of Washington* (Ithaca: Cornell University Press, 1951), 210–13; Barrows Dunham, oral history interview, Oral History of the American Left, Tamiment Library, New York University; Zimring, "Academic Freedom," 112.

44. Joseph Ershun, interview with Marvin E. Gettleman; Eugene Bluestein, interview with the author, May 29, 1979; Ann J. Lane, interview with the author, May 1978; Zimring, "Academic Freedom," 111–12; Schappes, interview with the author; Leon Wofsy, interview with the author; Wechsler, *Age of Suspicion*, 43; Phelps, "The Response of Higher Education to Student Activism," 141. In a December, 1952, letter to an unidentified recipient, Sophie Meyer recalls that in the 1930s Harry Slochower's classes at Brooklyn College were so popular "you could not bribe or browbeat your way into standing room." Letter in the private papers of Marvin E. Gettleman.

45. Sidney Eisenberger, "Political Memoirs," 7; Wofsy, interview; Daniel Boone Schirmer, interview with the author, Jan. 19, 1981; Balamuth, testimony, SISS, 962.

46. Anon., interview; Pearlman, interview; Amdur, testimony, HUAC, 1057–58.

47. For the activities of non-academic Communists, see Lyons, *Philadelphia Communists*, 109–37; Glazer, *The Social Basis of American Communism*, 123; and Naison, *Communists in Harlem During the Depression*, 186–87. On the Party's treatment of its academic units, see Mayberry, testimony, HUAC, 1924; Hicks, *Where We Came Out*, 46; Richard Byrd Lewis, testimony, HUAC, 530.

48. Rufus Mathewson recalls that when he was in the Young Communist League at Harvard, "An emissary came up from the Boston office of the Communist Party to collect our dues and to direct our activities." Com-

ments, Hobart Symposium, 76; Steve Nelson, interview with the author, June 17, 1981; Richard Schlatter, interview with the author, Oct. 21, 1981; Seymour Copstein, interview with Marvin E. Gettleman, April 18, 1974; Robert Bellah, interview with the author, Aug. 25, 1977; Sigmund Diamond, interview with the author, Oct. 11, 1977; Courtney Cazden, interview with the author, May 1, 1981.

49. Rufus Mathewson, interview with the author, May 25, 1978; Mayberry, testimony, HUAC, 1926; Marcus Singer, testimony, HUAC, May 26, 1953, 83rd Cong., 1st sess., 1541–42; anon., interview; Maloff, interview; Lloyd Motz, interview with Marvin E. Gettleman, Nov. 16, 1977.

50. Leonard Marsak to the author, March 28, 1978; Morrison, testimony, Special Committee, Board of Trustees, 12; Rutman, testimony, "Hearing before the Loyalty Committee," 83; Eisenberger, "Political Memoirs," 8; Richard Schlatter, "On Being a Communist at Harvard," 612–13.

51. Rutman, testimony, "Hearing before the Loyalty Committee," 52; Albaum, testimony, SISS, 217; Copstein, interview; Jane Hodes, interview with the author, April 5, 1980; Pearlman, interview; Herndon, testimony, HUAC, 513; Diamond, interview.

52. Morrison, testimony, Special Committee, Board of Trustees, 39; Rutman, testimony, "Hearing before the Loyalty Committee," 24; Amdur, testimony, HUAC, 1057; Thomas B. Drew et al. to Grayson Kirk, June 18, 1953, Grayson Kirk Papers, Columbia University Archives; Singer, testimony, HUAC, 1559; anon., interview; Chevalier, *Oppenheimer*, 24; Schirmer, interview; Mathewson, interview; Dodd, *School of Darkness*, 85, 104; Frank Oppenheimer, transcript of an oral history interview with Charles Weiner, Feb. 9, 1973, 44, in American Institute of Physics, Center for History of Physics.

53. Motz, interview; Pearlman, interview; Balamuth, testimony, SISS, 962; Bernard Riess, interview with the author, March 28, 1979; Hodes, interview; anon., interview; Frank Oppenheimer, interview, American Institute of Physics; Schirmer, interview; Marx, "The Harvard Retrospect," Hobart Symposium, 31; Robert Stange, comments, Hobart Symposium, 72; Horace Bancroft Davis, interview.

54. Horace Bancroft Davis, interview; Granville Hicks, testimony, HUAC, Feb. 25, 1953, 83rd Cong., 1st sess., 148; Frederic Ewen, interview with the author, Nov. 7, 1980.

55. Robert Gorham Davis, testimony, HUAC, 48–49; Lawrence Klein, testimony, HUAC, April 30, 1954, 83rd Cong., 2nd sess., 4992–93, 4995–97; Mayberry, testimony, HUAC, 1918–20; Cohen, "Professor William Parry," 5; Peter H. Hare and Edward H. Madden, "Buffalo in the McCarthy Era: A Case History" (unpublished paper, ca. 1983), 22–23; Iversen, *The Communists and the Schools*, 81; Herbert Aptheker, transcript of oral history interview, April 1976, Oral History of the American Left, Tamiment Library; Copstein, interview.

56. Mayberry, testimony, HUAC, 1918; Robert Gorham Davis, interview; Albaum, testimony, SISS, 218–19; Isidore and Clara Pomerance, interview. For a general discussion of both the *Teacher-Worker* and the *Staff*, see Gettleman, "Communists in Higher Education," 14–20. Some idea of the multiplicity of concerns these shop papers addressed comes across in the contents of a single issue; the CCNY *Teacher and Worker* (the name

was changed in the fall of 1936) of Aug. 1936 carried articles on the Spanish Civil War, the Soviet Constitution, college salaries, and the scarcity of water fountains on campus.

57. Henry F. Mins, "*Science & Society:* The Early Days," *Science & Society* 45, No. 1 (Spring 1981): 86; Thomas B. Drew et al. to Grayson Kirk, Kirk Papers, Columbia University; Starobin, *Communism in Crisis*, 300. Representative articles from the first three volumes of *Science & Society* (1936–39) are Theodore B. Brameld, "American Education and the Class Struggle" (Fall 1936); Margaret Schlauch, "Recent Soviet Studies in Linguistics" (Winter 1937); Granville Hicks, "Literary Opposition to Utilitarianism" (Summer 1937); Herbert Aptheker, "American Negro Slave Revolts" (Summer 1937); Bernhard J. Stern, "Frustration of Technology" (Winter 1937); J. D. Bernal, "Dialectical Materialism and Modern Science" (Winter 1937); and E. Franklin Frazier, "Some Effects of the Depression on the Negro in Northern Cities" (Fall 1938).

58. Stanley Moore, interview; Zitron, *The New York City Teachers Union*, 31; Klehr, *The Heyday of American Communism*, 104–12. Iversen, *The Communists and the Schools*, 148–74, discusses some of these "front groups," but not in much detail. There is also a not particularly useful 1971 Columbia University dissertation on the topic, William Michael Goldsmith's "The Theory and the Practice of the Communist Front," and a widely circulated manuscript about an important "front organization" by Hillman M. Bishop, "The American League Against War and Fascism" (1937) in the Tamiment Library. John P. Roche was supposed to have written a book about these groups for the Fund for the Republic's series on Communism in American Life of which the Iversen book is a part. The book was never written; and, as far as I know, no other scholar has systematically studied these groups.

59. Harvard Teachers Union statement, quoted in Paul Sweezy, "Labor and Political Activities," Sweezy and Leo Huberman, eds., *F. O. Matthiessen (1902–1950): A Collective Portrait* (New York: Henry Schuman, 1950), 62; Barrows Dunham, transcript of oral history interview by Fred Zimring, Oral History of the American Left, Tamiment Library. The most definitive treatment of the Teachers Union to date is Iversen, *The Communists and the Schools*, especially chapters 2 and 4. See also Zitron, *The New York City Teachers Union*. Neither book is satisfactory. Iversen's deals mainly with the New York scene and is suffused with the standard liberal anti-Communism of the 1950s; Zitron's is completely uncritical.

60. Iversen, *The Communists and the Schools*, 21–22, 27; Phelps, "The Response of Higher Education to Student Activism," 184.

61. Eisenberger, "Political Memoirs," 21; Grebanier, interview; Dodd, *School of Darkness*, 65–72. Material on the Teachers Union outside of New York, Cambridge, and Berkeley has been hard to find. I assume that most major campuses probably had chapters, but I have had trouble finding references to them. In addition, some of the information I do have may well be erroneous. Several New York Teachers Union documents put the number of members of Local 537 at one thousand, but that seems inflated. "Get Acquainted with the Teacher Unions," pamphlet, n.d., published by the Teachers Union, in private papers of Oscar Shaftel; Zitron, *The New York City Teachers Union*, 28. For the Harvard Teachers Union, see Harry

Levin, "A View from Within," Hobart Symposium, 5; Henry Nash Smith, "A Texan Perspective," Hobart Symposium, 52–53; for other schools, see Sanders, *Cold War on the Campus,* 7; Robert Gorham Davis, interview.

62. Chevalier, *Oppenheimer,* 19; Sweezy, "Labor and Political Activities," 62–65; Albaum, testimony, SISS, 210–11; Phelps, "The Response of Higher Education to Student Activism," 184–85; Iversen, *The Communists and the Schools,* 152–56; Edward Mason, interview with the author, June 1, 1978; Seymour Martin Lipset and David Riesman, *Education and Politics at Harvard* (New York: McGraw-Hill, 1975), 163–67; Levin, "A View from Within," Hobart Symposium, 4–5.

63. Helen Lynd, interview with the author, Oct. 20, 1978; Albaum, testimony, SISS, 215; Robert Gorham Davis, interview; Iversen, *The Communists and the Schools,* 201–8; Henry Nash Smith, "A Texan Perspective," Hobart Symposium, 52–53.

64. A typical statement from a recent study claims that as a result of the Pact, "Many, *particularly intellectuals,* abandoned the Party [emphasis mine]," Lyons, *Philadelphia Communists,* 138–39. Even people inside the Party at the time claimed that the Pact led to intellectual defections; see Steve Nelson, James R. Barrett, and Rob Ruck, *Steve Nelson—American Radical* (Pittsburgh: University of Pittsburgh Press, 1981), 249. Yet, according to Bernard Grebanier, an extremely embittered ex-Communist from Brooklyn College, no one in the unit there deserted because of the Pact; nor, apparently, did people in the CCNY unit. Because most of the members of these two units were Jewish and, thus, presumably strongly anti-Nazi, the lack of defections from them seems especially significant.

65. Grebanier, interview; Motz, interview; Robert Gorham Davis, interview; Schlatter, interview.

66. Arguimbau, testimony, HUAC, 4027; Hawkins, testimony, HUAC, 3426, 3436; Schlatter, "On Being a Communist at Harvard," 611; anon., interview with the author, March 16, 1979; Dunham, oral history interview, 91–92; Copstein, interview; David Fox, interview with the author, Aug. 13, 1981.

67. May, "From Berkeley to Harvard," Hobart Symposium, 28; Mathewson, comments, Hobart Symposium, 77; Donald Horton, interview; Warren, *Liberals and Communism,* 159–60.

68. Morrison, testimony, Special Committee, Board of Trustees, 34; Woodward, interview; anon., interview with the author, March 16, 1979; Horton, interview; Starobin, *American Communism in Crisis,* 34–35; Kenneth O. May, testimony, HUAC, Dec. 21, 1950, 81st Cong., 2nd sess., 3472.

69. Mark Graubard, testimony, Rapp-Coudert Committee, in private papers of Marvin E. Gettleman; Mathewson, comments, Hobart Symposium, 76–77; Grebanier, interview; Norman LeDoux, interview with Marvin E. Gettleman, June 20, 1974; Robert Gorham Davis, interview; Marks, interview.

70. Albaum, testimony, SISS, 227; Pearlman, interview; Leon Kamin, interview with the author, Oct. 6, 1977; Lloyd Barenblatt, interview with the author, Dec. 31, 1977; Maloff, interview; Arguimbau, testimony, HUAC, 4028.

71. Thomas B. Drew et al. to Grayson Kirk, June 18, 1953, Kirk Papers, Columbia University; Cohen, "Professor William Parry," 7–8.

72. Morrison, testimony, Special Committee, Board of Trustees, 42; Fox, interview; David Bohm, interview with Martin Sherwin, June 15, 1979; Sydney James, interview with the author, Nov. 3, 1977; Moore, interview; Rutman, testimony, "Hearing before the Loyalty Committee," 44–45; Frank Oppenheimer, testimony, HUAC, 367; Nickerson, testimony, "Proceedings," 5–2:155.

73. Zimring, "Academic Freedom," 119–22; Diamond, interview; Bellah, interview; Schlatter, "On Being a Communist at Harvard," 611.

74. Hawkins, testimony, HUAC, 3436–37.

75. Nickerson, testimony, "Proceedings," 5–1:11–12; Lawrence Klein, interview with Fred Zimring, Jan. 25, 1980, 3, Barrows Dunham/Fred Zimring Oral History Collection; Singer, testimony, HUAC, 1540.

76. Vivian Gornick discusses the trauma some people experienced when they left the CP, in *Romance of American Communism*, 107–89. On Singer and Nickerson, see above. Markert, testimony, "Proceedings," 7:31–37, 44–46; Barenblatt, interview; Horace Bancroft Davis, interview.

77. Marsak to the author; Robert Fogel, interview; Maloff, interview.

III: "Conduct Unbecoming"

1. Horace Bancroft Davis, interview with the author, July 3, 1979; Chandler Davis, testimony, in "Proceedings at a Meeting of the Special Advisory Committee to the President," 6:68–69, Box 21, Marvin L. Niehuss Papers, Michigan Historical Collections, Bentley Historical Library, University of Michigan.

2. Fred Richard Zimring, "Academic Freedom and the Cold War: The Dismissal of Barrows Dunham from Temple University: A Case Study," (Ed.D. diss., Columbia University Teachers College, 1981), 101–5.

3. James Wechsler, *Revolt on Campus* (New York: Covici-Friede, 1935), 191, 269–85, 298, is still the most useful single source of information about the left-wing student movement of the 1930s.

4. Oakley C. Johnson, "Campus Battles for Freedom in the Thirties," *Centennial Review* 14, No. 3 (Summer 1970). H. Thompson to H.W.T. [Tyler], Oct. 20; H.W. Tyler to Julius S. Bixler, Nov. 14, 1932; both in "City College–Johnson–Oct. 1932–Nov. 1932," American Association of University Professors (AAUP) Archives.

5. Robert Iversen, *The Communists and the Schools* (New York: Harcourt, Brace and Co., 1959), 199; James Wechsler, *The Age of Suspicion* (New York: Random House, 1953), 43.

6. *AAUP Bulletin* 11, No. 1 (Jan. 1936): 16, 20; Daniel Aaron, *Writers on the Left* (New York: Harcourt, Brace and World, 1961), 262; Richard Pells, *Radical Visions and American Dreams* (New York: Harper & Row, 1974), 172–74.

7. *Teacher-Worker* (City College of New York), April 29, July 1936; Charles F. Horne to Morris Schappes, April 22, 1936, in "City College–Schappes (April 1936–July 1936)," AAUP Archives; Morris Schappes to Sidney Eisenberger, March 8, 1980, in private papers of Marvin E. Gettleman; Morris Schappes, interview with the author, March 7, 1983.

8. Iversen, *The Communists and the Schools*, 153–56; Holland Thompson to H.W. Tyler, May 26, 1936, "City College–Schappes," AAUP Archives;

Celia Lewis Zitron, *The New York City Teachers Union* (New York: Humanities Press, 1968), 183–85.

9. A.G. Keller to Charles Seymour, Jan. 4, 1936; Dean Weigle, "Synopsis of his Memoranda," n.d., both in Box 58, Charles Seymour Papers, Yale University Archives.

10. Sidney Eisenberger, "Political Memoirs of Sidney Eisenberger," (unpublished ms., 1979), 39; Iversen, *The Communists and the Schools*, 166–69; Bella Dodd, *School of Darkness* (New York: Kenedy, 1954), 103; *AAUP Bulletin* 23, No. 5 (May 1937): 256–81; Jerome Davis to Charles Seymour, Aug. 16, 1937, Seymour Papers.

11. Iversen, *The Communists and the Schools*, 184–90; Wechsler, *Revolt on Campus*, 224–36.

12. Claude Bowman, *The College Professor in America* (privately published Ph.D. diss., University of Pennsylvania, 1938), 108–9; Iversen, *The Communists and the Schools*, 178; Malcolm Willey, *Depression, Recovery, and Higher Education* (New York: McGraw-Hill, 1937), 441.

13. "Statement of Committee B," *AAUP Bulletin* 23, No. 1 (Jan. 1937): 27; Willey, *Depression, Recovery, and Higher Education*, 440–50; Bowman, *The College Professor*, 108–10.

14. Iversen, *The Communists and the Schools*, 182–83; Marianne Ruth Phelps, "The Response of Higher Education to Student Activism," (Ph.D. diss., George Washington University, 1980), 225–32.

15. Iversen, *The Communists and the Schools*, 188–90; Jacob Robert Fischel, "Harry Gideonse: The Public Life" (Ph.D. diss., University of Delaware, 1973), 84–90.

16. Lawrence H. Chamberlain, *Loyalty and Legislative Action* (Ithaca: Cornell University Press, 1951), 55–67, 154, 225–28; Edward I. Fenlon, Earl A. Martin, Martin Meyer, testimony, Aug. 23, 1938, HUAC, 75th Cong., 3rd sess.; Ordway Tead, quoted in the *New York Times*, Aug. 24, 1938.

17. Jeffrey Mirel, draft chapter of a dissertation, (University of Michigan, 1983), 67–94.

18. Evidence for the growing conservatism of American politics in the late 1930s can be found in James T. Patterson, *Congressional Conservatism and the New Deal* (Lexington: The University Press of Kentucky, 1967), 288–324.

19. The most useful discussion of these professional informers is Herbert Packer, *Ex-Communist Witnesses* (Stanford: Stanford University Press, 1962). See also Murray Kempton, *Part of Our Time* (New York: Simon and Schuster, 1955), 154–69; Harvey Matusow, *False Witness* (New York: Cameron and Kahn, 1955), 175–77; Victor Navasky, *Naming Names* (New York: Viking, 1980), 6–71; John Diggins, *Up from Communism* (New York: Harper & Row, 1977), 2–3.

20. Pells, *Radical Visions and American Dreams*, 331–62; James Gilbert, *Writers and Partisans* (New York: Wiley, 1968), 166–88; William Barrett, *The Truants* (New York: Anchor Press/Doubleday, 1983), 7–8, 83–92. Irving Howe, *A Margin of Hope* (New York: Harcourt Brace Jovanovich, 1982), 36–89, gives a finely detailed portrayal of life among the Trotskyists in the late thirties and early forties.

21. Frank A. Warren, *An Alternative Vision* (Bloomington: University of Indiana Press, 1974), 146–49; Hal Draper, "The Student Movement of

the Thirties: A Political History," in Rita James Simon, ed., *As We Saw the Thirties*, (Urbana: University of Illinois Press, 1967), 173–80.

22. Harry N. Wright, testimony before Rapp-Coudert Committee, 758, ms. transcript in New York State Library, Albany. One of the earliest and most influential statements of this view of the CP was that of Sidney Hook, "Academic Freedom and 'The Trojan Horse' in American Education," *AAUP Bulletin* 25, No. 5 (Dec. 1939).

23. For the anti-Communist movement within labor, see Harvey A. Levenstein, *Communism, Anticommunism, and the CIO* (Westport, Conn.: Greenwood Press, 1981), 79–152; Roger Keeran, *The Communist Party and the Auto Workers Unions* (Bloomington: University of Indiana Press, 1980), 186–225; Joanne Lisa Kenen, "White Collars and Red-Baiters: Communism and Anti-Communism in the American Newspaper Guild, 1933–1956" (senior thesis, Harvard University, 1980). Iversen, *The Communists and the Schools*, gives a good discussion of the fight within the Teachers Union. For the government's harassment of the CP, see Maurice Isserman, *Which Side Were You On?* (Middletown, Conn.: Wesleyan University Press, 1982), 67–73. And, on the ACLU's expulsion of Elizabeth Gurley Flynn, see Corliss Lamont, ed., *The Trial of Elizabeth Gurley Flynn by the American Civil Liberties Union* (New York: Horizon, 1968) and Lucille Milner, *Education of an American Liberal* (New York: Horizon, 1954), 261–94.

24. David P. Gardner, *The California Oath Controversy* (Berkeley and Los Angeles: University of California Press, 1967), 259, 276n.

25. Chamberlain, *Loyalty and Legislative Action*, 72; Paul Windels, transcript of interview, Columbia Oral History Project, 146; Ordway Tead, transcript of interview, Columbia Oral History Project; Charles H. Tuttle, transcript of interview, Columbia Oral History Project, 53–68; Marvin E. Gettleman, "Rehearsal for McCarthyism: The New York State Rapp-Coudert Committee and Academic Freedom, 1940–41," paper delivered at the annual meeting of the American Historical Association, 1982.

26. Windels, interview, 145–47; Dodd, *School of Darkness*, 119.

27. Windels, interview, 162; Robert Morris, *No Wonder We Are Losing* (New York: Bookmailer, 1958), 7–8.

28. Stephen Leberstein, "The Rapp-Coudert Committee and City College, 1940–42" (unpublished ms., 1981), 13; Morris, *No Wonder We Are Losing*, 11–12; Iversen, *The Communists and the Schools*, 195–96, 201–2, 210, 227; Windels, interview, 148; Chamberlain, *Loyalty and Legislative Action*, 92–93.

29. Dodd, *School of Darkness*, 119–24; Morris Schappes, interview with the author, March 7, 1983; Bernard Riess, interview with the author, March 28, 1979.

30. Chamberlain, *Loyalty and Legislative Action*, 155–61, presents a useful account of the legal by-play that went on during the investigation. See also, Harry Gideonse, transcript of interview, Columbia Oral History Project, 96; Windels, interview, 162.

31. Morris, *No Wonder We Are Losing*, 15–16; Bernard Grebanier, interview with Marvin E. Gettleman, April 24, 1974; Joseph Bressler, interview with Marvin E. Gettleman, April 5, 1980; Harry Slochower, interview with the author, Dec. 29, 1980.

32. Schappes, interview; Windels, interview, 156; Morris, *No Wonder We Are Losing*, 16; Eisenberger, "Political Memoirs," 33; Lloyd Motz, interview with Marvin E. Gettleman, Nov. 16, 1977.

33. Motz, interview; Chamberlain, *Loyalty and Legislative Action*, 163; Slochower, interview; Schappes, interview. David Goldway, a teacher at Townshend Harris High School, took the Fifth Amendment. David Goldway, interview with the author, May 19, 1983.

34. Schappes, interview; Isidore Pomerance, interview with Marvin E. Gettleman, July 5, 1974; Seymour Copstein, interview with Marvin E. Gettleman, April 18, 1974; Harry Slochower, interview with the author, Dec. 29, 1980; anon., interview with Victor Navasky, n.d.; Goldway, interview.

35. Schappes, interview; Windels, interview, 156–69; Tead, interview, 62.

36. Chamberlain, *Loyalty and Legislative Action*, 149; Windels, interview, 159–62.

37. Chamberlain, *Loyalty and Legislative Action*, 153–86 devotes an entire chapter to the Board of Education trials.

38. Board of Higher Education of the City of New York, "In the Matter of the charges preferred against HERBERT M. MORAIS," Amended Charges and Notice, Dec. 18, 1941, Morais Transcripts in the private papers of Marvin E. Gettleman.

39. Amended Charges, Morais Transcripts; Chamberlain, *Loyalty and Legislative Action*, 145.

40. "Report of the Trial Committee, Board of Higher Education, in the matter of the charges preferred against Walter Scott Neff," Aug. 19, 1941; "Report of the Trial Committee, Board of Higher Education, in the matter of the charges preferred against Seymour Copstein," Aug. 18, 1941, both in Morais Transcripts.

41. Copstein, "Report"; Neff, "Report"; Chamberlain, *Loyalty and Legislative Action*, 146.

42. Morris, *No Wonder We Are Losing*, 16; Frederick Ewen, interview with the author, Nov. 7, 1980; Slochower, interview; Thomas Evans Coulton, *A City College in Action* (New York: Harper and Brothers, 1955), 124–25; Fischel, "Harry Gideonse," 197–210.

IV: "A Matter of Ethical Hygiene"

1. John Marquesee, testimony, HUAC, April 7, 1954, 83rd Cong., 2nd sess., 4343; Emmanuel Richardson, testimony, HUAC, April 8, 1954, 83rd Cong., 2nd sess., 4364; David Lubell, interview with the author, Nov. 8, 1977; Francis X. Crowley, testimony, HUAC, June 28, 1954, 83rd Cong., 2nd sess., 5773–4; Saul Maloff, interview with the author, Jan. 29, 1978; anon., interview with the author, Feb. 1, 1978; Leon Kamin, interview with the author, Nov. 6, 1977; Sydney James, interview with the author, Nov. 3, 1977; *Harvard Crimson*, April 1, 1948.

2. Lawrence Arguimbau, testimony, HUAC, April 21, 1953; William Pearlman, interview with the author, July 11, 1978; Horace Bancroft Davis, interview with the author, July 3, 1979.

3. *The Campus* (Sarah Lawrence), Nov. 3, 1948, gives the following figures for its straw poll: Dewey, 136; Wallace, 59; Truman, 54; Norman Thomas, 18. *Harvard Crimson*, April 9, 1948.

4. Jacob Robert Fischel, "Harry Gideonse: The Public Life" (Ph.D. diss., University of Delaware, 1973), 337–39.
5. Fischel, "Harry Gideonse," 311. The single most useful source of information about the repression of left-wing student activities in the 1940s comes from a survey of fifty schools conducted by the Students for Democratic Action, the student affiliate of the ADA, in the spring of 1947, "Civil Liberties on the American Campus," June 17, 1947, in General Correspondence, 1947, Vol. 1, American Civil Liberties Union Archives, Princeton University Library (hereafter cited as SDA, "Civil Liberties"). Marvin L. Niehuss, telegram to Wendell Berge, April 16, 1947, File 6, Box 58, Alexander Ruthven Papers, Michigan Historical Collections, Bentley Historical Library, University of Michigan.
6. David Henry to Board of Education, Feb. 10, 11, March 19, April 8, 1947; Alexander Ruthven to Matthew F. Callahan, May 7, 1947; all in File 6, Box 58, Ruthven Papers. Minutes, Committee on Academic Freedom, April 23, 1947, ACLU, General Correspondence, 1947, Vol. 1.
7. *Harvard Crimson,* May 27, 1949; Yaffa Schlesinger, "The Making of a Law—The Feinberg Law: A Case Study," (Ph.D. diss., New York University, 1975), 150–57; Edward K. Graham to E.E. Day, March 25, 1947, #3/6/8, 5–028, E.E. Day Papers, University Archives, Cornell University Libraries; SDA "Civil Liberties"; Fred Zimring, "Academic Freedom and the Cold War: The Dismissal of Barrows Dunham from Temple University" (Ed. D. diss., Columbia University Teachers College, 1981), 127–29.
8. E.E. Day to Fred F. Bontecou, March 11, 1947, 5–028, #3/6/8, Day Papers. Robert Fogel to F. C. Baldwin, Nov. 3, 1947; Baldwin to Fogel, Nov. 6, 1947; Fogel to Baldwin, Jan. 8, 1948; Rubin Diamond to Baldwin, Jan. 10, 1948; all in Dean of Students Files, #37/1/855, Cornell University Archives.
9. Leon Kamin, interview; Sydney James, interview; *Harvard Crimson,* March 11, 12, 19, April 23, May 13, 1948, Jan. 4, 11, March 1, 1949, April 14, 15, Oct. 5, 1950, Feb. 6, Dec. 4, 1951, Feb. 6, March 3, Oct. 15, Nov. 3, 29, 1952; Zimring, "Academic Freedom," 131.
10. SDA, "Civil Liberties"; Herbert H. Fisher to Lucille Milner, n.d. (ca. Fall 1948), ACLU General Correspondence, 1948, Vol. 1.
11. Paul Lazarsfeld and Wagner Thielens, Jr., *The Academic Mind* (Glencoe, Ill.: Free Press, 1958), 118; McGeorge Bundy to the editor, *New York Review of Books,* July 14, 1977; McGeorge Bundy, interview with the author, Dec. 29, 1977; Deborah Bacon to Harlan Hatcher, May 31, 1952, File 4, Box 58, Ruthven Papers.

   For a typical 1950s discussion of the "psychological" problems of people in the Party, see Morris L. Ernst and David Loth, *Report on the American Communist* (New York: Henry Holt and Company, 1952) and Gabriel Almond, *The Appeals of Communism* (Princeton: Princeton University Press, 1954).
12. Robert Iversen, *The Communists and the Schools* (New York: Harcourt Brace and Co., 1959), 76–78; Fischel, "Harry Gideonse," 184; Maia Turchin, "Academic Epidemic," American Student Union, pamphlet, n.d. (ca. 1940) in private papers of Daniel Boone Schirmer; Jane Sanders, *Cold War on the Campus* (Seattle: University of Washington Press, 1979), 9–10; David P. Gardner, The *California Oath Controversy* (Berkeley and

Los Angeles: University of California Press, 1967), 15; SDA, "Civil Liberties"; ACLU, Committee on Academic Freedom, "What Freedom for American Students?" pamphlet (April 1941).

13. Robert Bellah, interview with the author, Aug. 25, 1977; Leon Kamin, interview; Wilbur Bender, statement in *Harvard Crimson*, March 21, 1949; Robert Watson, quoted in *Harvard Crimson*, Dec. 14, 1953.

14. Fischel, "Harry Gideonse," 337–39. There is a complete file of correspondence on the incident of the unauthorized speaker, Arthur McPhaul, a local official of the Civil Rights Congress, in File 4, Box 58, Ruthven Papers. For the attempt to change the lecture policy, see Burton D. Thoma to Harlan Hatcher, June 3, 1952, File 8, Box 3; and Minutes, University Senate, May 19, 1952, File 3, Box 3; both in Harlan Hatcher Papers, Michigan Historical Collections.

15. Eleanor Bontecou, *The Federal Loyalty-Security Program* (Ithaca: Cornell University Press, 1953), 112; *Harvard Crimson*, Oct. 15, 1951; Iversen, *The Communists and the Schools*, 342; Council Agenda, Nov. 9, 1951, AAUP, in private papers of Bentley Glass.

16. Alexander Ruthven, press release, Dec. 13, 1947, File 5, Box 58, Ruthven Papers; Roger Baldwin, statement, Dec. 18, 1947, ACLU, General Correspondence, 1947, Vol. 1; statement by faculty committee, in clipping from *Cornell Sun*, n.d. (ca. 1948–49), 2001, 3/7/8A, Cornelius de Kewiet Papers, Cornell University Archives; *Harvard Crimson*, May 26, 1949. (In the late 1940s and early 1950s, the editors of the *Harvard Crimson* published an annual survey of academic freedom. These surveys, prepared with the help of the ACLU, provide the single most comprehensive and accessible account of the various academic freedom cases of the period.)

17. Howard Fast, *The Naked God* (New York: Praeger, 1957), 114; *Harvard Crimson*, June 20, 1950; Arthur Cole et al. to Harry N. Wright, June 16, 1950, ACLU General Correspondence, 1950, Vol. 1; David Henry to Board, Feb. 11, 1947, File 6, Box 58, Ruthven Papers.

18. Gardner, *California Oath Controversy*, 14–16; *Harvard Crimson*, Dec. 14, 1953, March 2, 1954.

19. J. L. Morrill, press release, May 27, 1952, cited in Francis Pierce to Louis Joughin, June 1, 1952; Malcolm Willey, statement, Nov. 21, 1952; both in ACLU, General Correspondence, 1952, Vol. 1.

20. *Harvard Crimson*, June 17, 1952, April 8, 14, 15, 1953. So timid had Harvard Law School students become that after David Lubell, himself a law student, took the Fifth Amendment before the SISS, students would get up and leave the table when he sat down in the student cafeteria. A former graduate student from Chicago recalls that he couldn't even get people to sign a petition to put a soft-drink vending machine in their laboratory. David Lubell, interview; Robert March, taped interview, in the author's possession.

21. J. G. Leach, letter, n.d., cited in Appendix 7, Council Letter No. 8, 1950, AAUP, in private papers of Bentley Glass; "Report of Committee A," *AAUP Bulletin* 34, No. 1 (Spring 1948): 126.

22. Ralph Himstead, memorandum, n.d., Appendix 7, Council Letter No. 8, 1950, AAUP, Glass papers, discusses several efforts to change the AAUP's policy on Communist teachers. See also, Himstead to "Dear Colleagues,"

Council Letter No. 1, 1951, Feb. 23, 1951; Himstead to "Dear Colleagues," Council Letter No. 2, 1952, March 12, 1952; Himstead to "Dear Colleagues," Chapter Letter No. 3, 1953, April 24, 1953; all in Glass papers.

23. Sanders, *Cold War on the Campus*, 16; Vern Countryman, *Un-American Activities in the State of Washington* (Ithaca: Cornell University Press, 1951), 73. These two books present detailed accounts of what happened at the University of Washington. They both quote copiously from the relevant documents in the case and I have relied heavily on them.

24. Raymond B. Allen, "The President's Analysis," *Communism and Academic Freedom* (Seattle, 1949), 93. (This document, a specially printed pamphlet, contains most of the main documents in the case as well as Allen's own discussion of it. I have found copies of it in the academic freedom files of most of the college and university archives that I have used; it was very widely distributed.) Countryman, *Un-American Activities*, 222; Sanders, *Cold War on the Campus*, 18–19.

25. Countryman, *Un-American Activities*, 231–35; Sanders, *Cold War on the Campus*, 36; Melvin Rader, *False Witness* (Seattle: University of Washington Press, 1979), 21–22.

26. Countryman, *Un-American Activities*, 78–83; the most useful discussion of Budenz is in Herbert L. Packer, *Ex-Communist Witnesses* (Stanford: Stanford University Press, 1962); the best one of Matthews is in Murray Kempton, *Part of Our Time* (New York: Simon and Schuster, 1955), 151–81.

27. There are detailed accounts of the Rader case in both Rader's book and Countryman's. Countryman recalls that as he was researching his book on the University of Washington, he stumbled across some of the evidence that the Canwell Committee was trying to hide. His work and that of investigative reporter Ed Guthman of the *Seattle Times*, who won a Pulitzer prize for it, ultimately opened up the case. Vern Countryman, interview with the author, Dec. 8, 1976.

28. Countryman, *Un-American Activities*, 86–117, 142–47; Herbert J. Phillips, questionnaire response, Paul Tillett Files, Seeley G. Mudd Library, Princeton University; Ralph Gundlach to "Dear Friends," Nov. 20, 1951, in J. Robert Oppenheimer Papers, Box 36, Library of Congress; Bonnie Bird (Gundlach), interview with the author, April 15, 1982.

29. Sanders, *Cold War on the Campus*, 34; Raymond Allen to Louis Budenz, Sept. 27, 1948, cited in Peter C. Schaehrer, "McCarthyism and Academic Freedom—Three Case Studies" (Ed.D. diss., Columbia University Teachers College, 1974), 72; Countryman, *Un-American Activities*, 223.

30. Raymond Allen, "To the Friends of the University," Oct. 7, 1948, in an undated memorandum, Washington Committee for Academic Freedom, ACLU, General Correspondence, 1949, Vol. 3.

31. Sanders, *Cold War on the Campus*, 42–44.

32. Text of the official charges in Ibid., 181–90.

33. Countryman, *Un-American Activities*, 198; Sanders, *Cold War on the Campus*, 182.

34. Countryman, *Un-American Activities*, 201, 204–5; Schaehrer, "McCarthyism and Academic Freedom," 72.

35. Sanders, *Cold War on the Campus*, 51; Countryman, *Un-American Activities*, 207.

36. Raymond Allen, speech, in *Town Meeting*, 14, No. 4 (March 1, 1949): 11; Countryman, *Un-American Activities*, 210–13.

37. For a discussion of Rapp-Coudert, see Chapter III above. Countryman, *Un-American Activities*, 224–25.

38. Ralph Gundlach, interview with Paul Tillett, June 20, 1962, in Tillett Papers; Bonnie Bird (Gundlach), interview; Countryman, *Un-American Activities*, 231.

39. Sanders, *Cold War on the Campus*, 61–65; Countryman, *Un-American Activities*, 219.

40. Report of the Committee on Tenure and Academic Freedom, Jan. 7, 1949, in *Communism and Academic Freedom*, 22–80.

41. Ibid., 59, 61.

42. Ibid., 80.

43. Raymond Allen, "President's Analysis," in *Communism and Academic Freedom*, 90.

44. Ibid., 101; Countryman, *Un-American Activities*, 275.

45. Sanders, *Cold War on the Campus*, 78–80. Washington Committee for Academic Freedom, undated memorandum; AAUP Chapter Bulletin, University of Washington, Feb. 19; both in ACLU General Correspondence, 1949, Vol. 3.

46. Sanders, *Cold War on the Campus*, 96–97; Phillips, questionnaire response, Tillett Files; Gundlach, interview, Tillett Files; Gundlach to "Dear Friends," Nov. 20, 1951, Oppenheimer Papers; *The Campus* (Sarah Lawrence), April 27, 1949; Bonnie Bird Gundlach, interview.

47. The best description of the minor academic freedom cases of the time is in the special academic freedom supplement of the *Harvard Crimson*, May 25, 1949; see also "Report of Committee A," Feb. 27, 1949, in *AAUP Bulletin* 35, No. 1 (Spring 1949) which deals with the dismissal of an assistant professor at Evansville College because of his work for the Wallace campaign. Allen, "Introduction," *Communism and Academic Freedom*, 11; Sanders, *Cold War on the Campus*, 76–77.

48. Sidney Hook, "Academic Freedom and 'The Trojan Horse' in American Education," *AAUP Bulletin* 25, No. 5 (Dec. 1939): 555; Allen to "Friends," Oct. 7, 1948, in ACLU archives.

    The reference to reactionaries being unable to discriminate between crypto- and anti-Communists comes from the following apocryphal anecdotes. One concerns an innocent by-stander being beaten by a cop at a Communist rally at Union Square. The by-stander protested that he was an anti-Communist; the cop replied, "All you Communists are the same to me." A similar story describes a man who was heckling a picket-line protesting a left-wing meeting. When told that the pickets were anti-Communists, the heckler replied, "I don't care what kind of Communists they are."

49. Sidney Hook, "Heresy, yes—Conspiracy, no," pamphlet published by the American Committee for Cultural Freedom, n.d., 5; Arthur O. Lovejoy, "Communism and Academic Freedom," *American Scholar* 18, No. 3 (Summer 1949): 335. (This issue of the *American Scholar* contains a symposium on the issue of Communist teachers; it will be cited hereafter as *American Scholar*.)

50. Lovejoy, *American Scholar*, 333–34; T. V. Smith, *American Scholar*, 344; Hook, "Heresy, yes," 14.

51. Raymond Allen, *Town Meeting*, 6; Allen, *American Scholar*, 327; Countryman, *Un-American Activities*, 212–13; Roger Baldwin, *Town Meeting*, 8.
52. Lucille Milner, *Education of an American Liberal* (New York: Horizon, 1954), 266–72; Norbert Weiner to Roger Baldwin, May 1, 1949, ACLU, General Correspondence, 1949, Vol. 1; Joseph Butterworth, *American Scholar*, 329; Herbert Phillips, cited in *Harvard Crimson*, March 24, 1950; Lovejoy, *American Scholar*, 337.
53. Hook, "Heresy, yes," 14; Hook, "What Shall We Do About Communist Teachers?" *Saturday Evening Post*, Sept. 10, 1949, 33; Lovejoy, *American Scholar*, 335; Smith, *Town Meeting*, 16. Robert Iversen in *The Communists and the Schools* talks about "the inevitable Frank article," 326, also 71–72, 212, 320, and 379n. See also J. B. Matthews, "Communism in the Colleges," *American Mercury*, May 1953, 115; Frank Tavenner, testimony, HUAC, Feb. 25, 1953, 83rd Cong., 1st sess., 30.
54. Smith, *Town Meeting*, 14; Hook, "What Shall We Do About Communist Teachers?" 165–66.
55. Smith, *Town Meeting*, 10; Hook, "Trojan Horse," 554; Hook, "What Shall We Do About Communist Teachers?" 165.
56. H. B. Davis, interview; Jane S. Hodes, interview with the author, April 3, 1980.
57. Raymond J. McCall to Ralph Himstead, June 20, 1950; Donald P. Irish to Bentley Glass, Jan. 5, 1950; Council Letter 8, 1950, n.d.; all in private papers of Bentley Glass. Ralph Fuchs, interview with the author, Oct. 6, 1978; Harold Taylor, *Town Meeting*, 4; Alexander Meiklejohn, "Should Communists Be Allowed to Teach," *New York Times Magazine*, March 27, 1949, 64, 66.
58. E. E. Day to John L. Collyer, Feb. 5, 1948, #3/6/8, 15–013, Day Papers; Hayward Keniston to James P. Adams, Sept. 22, 1948, File "Literary College," Box 3, Marvin L. Niehuss Papers, Michigan Historical Collections. See also an undated radio talk by John Dickey, the president of Dartmouth College, sometime in 1947, in Albert I. Dickerson to W. H. Ferry, March 21, 1953, in personal papers of W. H. Ferry.
59. E. E. Day in *Ithaca Journal*, May 10, 1949, cited in L. B. Darrah to Day, May 11, 1949, 15–013; Wallace Sterling in *New York Journal American*, April 21, 1949, in 15–014; both in Day Papers. Charles Seymour in *Harvard Crimson*, June 4, 1949; James Bryant Conant in *Harvard Crimson*, June 23, 1949.

   There were similar statements by Lewis W. Jones, the president of the University of Arkansas, who was soon to be the first academic leader to fire somebody for taking the Fifth Amendment, and by James Killian of MIT. Bernard de Voto, "Colleges, the Government, and Freedom," *AAUP Bulletin* 35, No. 3 (Autumn 1949): 474; Killian quoted in "Ninth Interim Report of the Special Commission on Communism, Subversive Activities and Related Matters within the Commonwealth, Commonwealth of Massachusetts," Jan. 21, 1957, 37.
60. For these views of Conant, see the excerpts from his FBI file, quoted in Sigmund Diamond, "The Arrangement: The FBI and Harvard University in the McCarthy Period," in Athan Theoharis, ed., *Beyond the Hiss Case* (Philadelphia: Temple University Press, 1982), 359–60; J. B. Conant to

Zechariah Chafee, June 20, 1949, F-19, Box 34, Zechariah Chafee Papers, Harvard Law School Library.

61. *Harvard Crimson,* June 9, 1949.

62. There is not very much in the way of secondary literature on the various states' anti-Communist activities. The best book on the subject, the collection of essays edited by Walter Gellhorn, *The States and Subversion* (Ithaca, N.Y.: Cornell University Press, 1952), was published before several states had enacted their anti-Communist measures and, though excellent as far as it goes, it is necessarily incomplete. A useful source, or at least a suggestive one, is Thomas I. Emerson, David Haber, and Norman Dorsen, *Political and Civil Rights in the United States,* 3rd ed. (Boston: Little, Brown, 1967), 1:327–50.

63. *Harvard Crimson,* Feb. 6, 9, 1948; Zechariah Chafee, "Revised Memorandum on the Pending Barnes Bills," Dec. 31, 1947, Chafee Papers.

64. E. Houston Harsha, "Illinois: The Broyles Commission," in Gellhorn, *States and Subversion,* 65–66, 99; John Bartlow Martin, *Adlai Stevenson of Illinois* (New York: Doubleday, 1976), 468–71.

65. Schlesinger, "The Making of a Law," 60, 197–215, 223; Iversen, *The Communists and the Schools,* 262–64; Lawrence Chamberlain, *Loyalty and Legislative Action* (Ithaca, N.Y.: Cornell University Press, 1951), 189.

66. Iversen, *The Communists and the Schools,* 266–67; Irving Adler, interview with the author, June 10, 1982. The case is *Adler v. Board of Education,* 342 U.S. 485 (1952).

67. William B. Prendergast, "Maryland: The Ober Anti-Communist Law," in Gellhorn, *States and Subversion,* 140–83.

   Frank Ober's statement that he would stop giving money to Harvard was answered by a carefully written reply by a member of the Harvard Corporation, Grenville Clark. This exchange was given wide publicity and reprinted as a pamphlet by the University. For the complete text, see "Freedom at Harvard," *AAUP Bulletin* 35, No. 2 (Summer 1949): 313–34.

68. For the workings of the Ober law, see Prendergast, "Maryland," 152.

   The New Hampshire prosecution resulted in the only Supreme Court decision of the 1950s that even mentioned academic freedom—ironically, it must be noted, since the defendant, Paul Sweezy, was not a regular academic at the time. A Marxist economist, Sweezy had taught at Harvard during the late thirties and forties and resigned from the Economics Department in 1945 because it was clear to him that he would not receive tenure. Instead of taking another academic job, Sweezy got a grant, did research and writing on his own, and, in 1948, founded *Monthly Review.* His case arose when the New Hampshire Attorney General, Louis C. Wyman, questioned him about a guest lecture that he had given at the University of New Hampshire in 1954. Paul Sweezy, interview with the author, July 27, 1982. For a discussion of the academic freedom aspects of the Sweezy decision, *Sweezy v. New Hampshire,* 354 U.S. 234 (1957), see Leonard Boudin, "Academic Freedom and Constitutional Law," in Craig Kaplan and Ellen Schrecker, eds., *Regulating the Intellectuals* (New York: Praeger, 1983), 184.

69. The most useful discussion of the Pechan Act is in Zimring, "Academic Freedom," 37–91. See also the ACLU's "Report on Civil Liberties, Jan-

uary 1951–June 1953" (Nov. 1953), 61, pamphlet in the private papers of Alfred F. Young.

70. Emerson, Haber, and Dorsen, *Political and Civil Rights,* 327; Zimring, "Academic Freedom and the Cold War," 55.

71. Chamberlain, *Loyalty and Legislative Action,* 54; Gardner, *The California Oath Controversy,* 25; George R. Stewart, *The Year of the Oath* (New York: Doubleday, 1950), 23.

72. Gardner, *The California Oath Controversy,* 26; Emerson, Haber, and Dorsen, *Political and Civil Rights,* 328, 336.

The Oklahoma oath was challenged by a group of nine faculty members at Oklahoma Agricultural and Mechanical College in 1951. Their case was decided by the Supreme Court in *Wieman v. Updegraff,* 344 U.S. 183 (1952). The Court decided that the oath was unconstitutional in that its language was so broad that it deprived the teachers of their procedural rights. (The issue was that of *scienter,* knowingly belonging to a proscribed organization.) See Robert G. McCloskey, *The Modern Supreme Court* (Cambridge: Harvard University Press, 1972), 83–84. On the Oklahoma teachers, Lloyd Wallisch (Librarian, Special Collections, Edmon Low Library, Oklahoma State University) to the author, with enclosures, June 8, 1978.

73. The most useful source for the loyalty-oath controversy is the study by Gardner, *The California Oath Controversy.* Though Gardner's approach seems overly bureaucratic—no surprise from a man who was to become the president of the University of California himself—his extensive citations from contemporary sources and his obvious fairness make his book invaluable.

On the adoption of the oath, see Gardner, *The California Oath Controversy,* 10–26.

74. Ernst H. Kantorowicz, "The Fundamental Issue: Documents and Marginal Notes on the University of California Loyalty Oath," privately published pamphlet (Berkeley, Oct. 8, 1950), in personal collection of Stefan Peters; Gardner, *The California Oath Controversy,* 32–40.

75. Gardner, *The California Oath Controversy,* 49–71.

76. Gardner, *The California Oath Controversy,* 91–94, 115, 246; Edward L. Parsons et al. to the Regents of the University of California, n.d. (received March 25, 1950), ACLU General Correspondence, 1952, Vol. 5.

77. Stewart, *The Year of the Oath,* 148; Gardner, *The California Oath Controversy,* 133–38.

78. Gardner, *The California Oath Controversy,* 38; Sanders, *Cold War on the Campus,* 77.

79. Gardner, *The California Oath Controversy,* 143, 155.

80. John W. Caughey, "A University in Jeopardy," *Harpers* (Nov. 1950): 73; Gardner, *The California Oath Controversy,* 161, 169.

81. Report of the Committee on Privilege and Tenure, Northern Section, June 13, 1950, 5, in private papers of Stefan Peters; Gardner, *The California Oath Controversy,* 174–77.

82. Report of the Committee on Privilege and Tenure, 6; Stefan Peters, interview with the author, Oct. 29, 1980; Nevitt Sanford, "Individual and Social Change in a Community under Pressure: The Oath Controversy,"

Journal of Social Issues 9, No. 3 (1953): 28 (this article, though hardly claiming to be objective, offers Sanford's own reflections on the oath controversy).

83. Gardner, *The California Oath Controversy*, 201.

84. The definitive work on the Levering Oath is Edward Robert Long, "Loyalty Oaths in California, 1947–1952," (Ph.D. diss., University of California-San Diego, 1981); Gardner, *The California Oath Controversy*, 217–26.

85. Stanley Weigel to "Friend," Dec. 10, 1952, in the private papers of Stefan Peters. These contain copies of the extensive correspondence carried on by the non-signers and their lawyer, Stanley Weigel, relating to their attempts to get their back pay.

86. "Academic Freedom and Tenure in the Quest for National Security: Report of a Special Committee of the American Association of University Professors," *AAUP Bulletin* 42, No. 1 (Spring 1956): 100–107; Interim Report of the Committee on Academic Freedom to the Academic Senate, Northern Section, University of California, Feb. 1, 1951, 30, 36. (This pamphlet contains a survey of academic opinion on the oath controversy, as well as a discussion of the oath's effects on the University.) Chandler Davis, interview with the author, Feb. 21, 1978; Robert Merton, interview with the author, Feb. 5, 1980; Robert Serber, interview with C. W. (probably Charles Weiner), Feb. 10, 1967, 72, American Institute of Physics.

87. Group for Academic Freedom, Charles Muscatine to members, Aug. 31, 1950; Brewster Rogerson to Stefan Peters, Oct. 27, 1950; Edward Tolman to Stefan Peters, April 20, 1956; all in Peters papers. Marie Jahoda and Stuart W. Cook, "Security Measures and Freedom of Thought," *Yale Law Journal* 61, No. 3 (March 1952); John W. Caughey, *In Clear and Present Danger* (Chicago: University of Chicago Press, 1958), 151.

88. Sanford, "Individual and Social Change," 38; Gardner, *The California Oath Controversy*, 183, 196; Stewart, *The Year of the Oath*, 11, 73; Peters, interview.

89. Russell Fraser, "Shaping Up," *Canto* (Summer 1978); Long, "Loyalty Oaths in California," 198–236, 324–36. See also the memoir by one of the San Francisco State non-signers, Frank Rowe, *The Enemy Among Us* (Sacramento, Calif.: Cougar Press, 1980).

V: "Drawing the Line"

1. Irving David Fox, testimony, HUAC, Sept. 27, 1949, 81st Cong., 1st sess., 815, 827.

2. David P. Gardner, *The California Oath Controversy* (Berkeley and Los Angeles: University of California Press, 1967), 91; Edward L. Parsons et al. to the Regents of the University of California, n.d. (received March 25, 1950). ACLU, General Correspondence, 1952, Vol. 5, ACLU Archives.

3. Gardner, *The California Oath Controversy*, 92–94; University of California Regents' press release, Jan. 13, 1950, in Parsons et al.

4. David Goldway, a teacher at Townshend Harris High School, was the first person to use the Fifth in this way. See pp. 79, 169 above. Joseph Forer, a Washington attorney, claims that his clients were the first people to use the Fifth: (1) to avoid answering questions about Party membership and (2) before HUAC. Forer, interview with the author, March 31, 1978. The

most useful discussion of the legal problems of the Hollywood Ten is in Larry Ceplair and Steven Englund, *The Inquisition in Hollywood* (New York: Doubleday, 1980), 255–72, 325–60; the most accessible text of their hearings is Eric Bentley, ed., *Thirty Years of Treason* (New York: Viking, 1971); the documentary film *Hollywood on Trial* has footage of the actual hearings.

5. Lyman Bradley, testimony, HUAC, April 4, 1946, 79th Cong., 2nd sess., 8. For discussions of the meaning of the Barsky case (*Barsky v. United States,* 167 F. 2d 241 [D.C. Cir. 1948]), see Thomas I. Emerson, David Haber, and Norman Dorsen, *Political and Civil Rights in the United States,* 3rd ed. (Boston: Little, Brown, 1967), 1:355; Carl Beck, *Contempt of Congress* (New Orleans: Hauser Press, 1959), 25–29; C. Herman Pritchett, *Civil Liberties and the Vinson Court* (Chicago: University of Chicago Press, 1954), 81–86; Telford Taylor, *Grand Inquest* (New York: Simon and Schuster, 1955), 149–52.

6. The Jackson statement comes from *Eisler v. United States* (1949), quoted in Beck, *Contempt of Congress,* 60; Robert G. McCloskey, *The Modern Supreme Court* (Cambridge: Harvard University Press, 1972), 64–85, is a brilliant and utterly convincing discussion of the Supreme Court's failure to withstand the forces of McCarthyism.

7. McCloskey, *The Modern Supreme Court,* 155–56, 185–88, 191–206; Emerson, Haber, and Dorsen, *Political and Civil Rights,* 365–83.

8. There is an extensive literature on the Fifth Amendment. The definitive—at least for laymen—discussion of its origins is Leonard W. Levy, *Origins of the Fifth Amendment* (New York: Oxford University Press, 1968). For an understanding of its use during the 1950s, see Emerson, Haber, and Dorsen, *Political and Civil Rights,* 401–9; Erwin N. Griswold, *The Fifth Amendment Today* (Cambridge: Harvard University Press, 1955); Taylor, *Grand Inquest,* chapter 7; Beck, *Contempt of Congress,* chapters 4 and 5; Daniel H. Pollitt, "The Fifth Amendment Plea before Congressional Committees Investigating Subversion," *University of Pennsylvania Law Review* 106 (1958); Pollitt, "Pleading the Fifth Amendment Before a Congressional Committee: A Study and Explanation," *Notre Dame Lawyer* 32 (1956); O. John Rogge, *The First and the Fifth* (New York: Thomas Nelson, 1960).

9. For evidence about perjured testimony, see Herbert L. Packer, *Ex-Communist Witnesses* (Stanford: Stanford University Press, 1962); Frank Donner, "The Informer," *The Nation,* April 10, 1954; Harvey Matusow, *False Witness* (New York: Cameron and Kahn, 1955); and Melvin Rader, *False Witness* (Seattle: University of Washington Press, 1969). For a recent discussion of the Lattimore case, see Stanley I. Kutler, *The American Inquisition* (New York: Hill and Wang, 1982), 183–214. See also Thurman Arnold, *Fair Fights and Foul* (New York: Harcourt, Brace and World, 1965), 215–26.

10. David Fox, interview with the author.

11. Text of HUAC statement in Beck, *Contempt of Congress,* 42–43.

12. Carol Gruber, "Manhattan Project Maverick: The Case of Leo Szilard," *Prologue* 15 (Summer 1983); James Franck to Martin Kamen, July 30, 1944, in private papers of Martin Kamen.

13. Martin Kamen, "The Life and Times of an Oyster," unpublished ms. in Kamen papers; James Sterling Murray, testimony, HUAC, Aug. 14, 1949,

81st Cong., 1st sess., 878–79; Clarence Hiskey, interview with the author, July 27, 1980.

14. David Bohm, interview with Martin Sherwin, June 15, 1979; Martin Kamen, testimony, HUAC, Sept. 14, 1948, 80th Cong., 2nd sess., 33. Gregg Herken, *The Winning Weapon* (New York: Knopf, 1980) has a good general discussion of the fallacy of the "secret" of the bomb. For more information about the conflicts between security people and scientists, see Martin Sherwin, *A World Destroyed* (New York: Knopf, 1977), 53–63, and Walter Gellhorn, *Security, Loyalty, and Science* (Ithaca, N.Y.: Cornell University Press, 1950), 14, 39–51.

15. Philip M. Stern, *The Oppenheimer Case* (New York: Harper & Row, 1969), 32; Giovanni Rossi Lomanitz, interview with Martin Sherwin, July 11, 1979; Nuel Pharr Davis, *Lawrence and Oppenheimer* (New York: Simon and Schuster, 1968); Joan M. Jensen, "Military Surveillance in Two World Wars: Watching the Workers," paper presented at the Annual Meeting of Organization of American Historians, April 1980, 12–13; David Fox, interview.

16. Dale Corson, interview with the author, Jan. 25, 1979; Philip Morrison, interview with the author, Dec. 22, 1977; Charles Weiner, "A New Site for the Seminar: The Refugees and American Physics in the Thirties," in Bernard Bailyn and Donald Fleming, eds., *The Intellectual Migration* (Cambridge: Harvard University Press, 1969); Bruce Dayton, interview with the author, April 4, 1980; Bruce Dayton, FBI file, document 65-59336-29.

17. Hiskey, interview; Edward Tiers Manning, testimony, HUAC, Oct. 5, 1949, 81st Cong., 1st sess., 881–99; see also, HUAC, "Report on Soviet Espionage Activities in Connection with the Atom Bomb," Sept. 27, 1948. The most accessible text of this report is in the *New York Times,* Sept. 28, 1948.

18. Charles Coryell, transcript of interview, Columbia Oral History Project; Martin Kamen, interview with the author, April 4, 1980; Kamen, testimony, HUAC; Kamen, "Oyster"; Lansdale to Provost Marshal General, July 15, 1944; Harry T. Wensel, testimony, May 4, 1948; all in Kamen papers.

19. Fox, interview; Bohm, interview; Lomanitz, interview; R. R. Davis, testimony, HUAC, April 22, 1949, 1st Cong., 2nd sess., 287.

20. Steve Nelson, interview with the author, June 17, 1981. For the most extensive treatment of Nelson's career, see Steve Nelson, James R. Barrett, and Rob Ruck, *Steve Nelson, American Radical* (Pittsburgh: University of Pittsburgh Press, 1981). Pages 268–70 deal with Nelson's relationship with Oppenheimer in Berkeley. See also Kenneth O. May, testimony, HUAC, Dec. 21, 1950, 81st Cong., 2nd sess., 3485–87; David Hawkins, testimony, HUAC, Dec. 20, 1950, 81st Cong., 2nd sess., 3435.

21. Bohm, interview; Lomanitz, interview; Nelson, interview.

22. Nelson, interview; James Sterling Murray, testimony, HUAC, 799–806; HUAC, "Report on Soviet Espionage," Sept. 27, 1948.

23. Lomanitz, interview; Jensen, "Military Surveillance," 5–6, discusses the extreme hostility military intelligence officials displayed toward labor unions.

24. Lomanitz, interview; Lomanitz, testimony, HUAC, April 26, 1949, 81st Cong., 1st sess., 293; May, testimony, HUAC, 3506; Stern, *Oppenheimer*

Case, 50–52; Edward U. Condon, transcript of an interview with Charles Weiner, American Institute of Physics; Davis, *Lawrence and Oppenheimer*, 191–93, 204.

25. Herken, *The Winning Weapon*, 114–37; Alan Moorehead, *The Traitors* (New York: Harper and Row, 1963), 3–8, 34–40.

26. Hiskey, interview; Kamen, interview; Lomanitz, interview; W. L. Nunn to Roger Baldwin, Oct. 5, 1948, ACLU, General Correspondence, 1948, Vol. 11; Haakon Chevalier, *Oppenheimer: The Story of a Friendship* (New York: George Braziller, 1965), 61–68.

27. Justice Department press release, quoted in the *New York Times*, Sept. 30, 1948. On the behavior of the FBI, the most useful study to date is Kenneth O'Reilly, *Hoover and the Un-Americans* (Philadelphia: Temple University Press, 1983), 76, 91–93, 95–100, 123–29. See also Athan Theoharis, *Spying on Americans* (Philadelphia: Temple University Press, 1978), 133–34, 162–64. Theoharis, ed., *Beyond the Hiss Case* (Philadelphia: Temple University Press, 1982) contains a series of essays dealing with FBI practices and procedures during the Cold War. Theoharis's own piece, "In-House Cover-up: Researching FBI Files," 20–77, explains how the FBI covered its tracks; also useful is his essay "Unanswered Questions: Chambers, Nixon, the FBI, and the Hiss Case," 270–83, and O'Reilly and Theoharis, "The FBI, the Congress, and McCarthyism," 372–75.

28. In addition to the work of O'Reilly and Theoharis cited above, there is an extensive literature on HUAC and a growing one on Hiss. See especially, Walter Goodman, *The Committee* (New York: Farrar, Strauss and Giroux, 1968); Earl Latham, *The Communist Controversy in Washington* (Cambridge: Harvard University Press, 1966); Robert Carr, *The House Committee on Un-American Activities* (Ithaca: Cornell University Press, 1952); and Allen Weinstein, *Perjury* (New York: Knopf, 1978).

29. HUAC, "Report on Soviet Espionage," Sept. 27, 1948; Goodman, *The Committee*, 240–42, 274–76. For the scientists' struggle against military control of atomic energy, see Alice Kimball Smith, *A Peril and a Hope* (Chicago: University of Chicago Press, 1965).

30. *New York Times*, Sept. 25, 1948; Goodman, *The Committee*, 231–39; Richard Nixon to Jacob H. Beuscher, March 15, 1948, ACLU, General Correspondence, 1948, Vol. 11. President Truman was so provoked by Thomas's attack on Condon that he gave a public speech—partly written by Condon—at a special meeting in honor of the physicist organized by the American Association for the Advancement of Science in Sept. 1948. Condon, interview.

31. Stern, *Oppenheimer Case*, 110–11; *New York Times*, Oct. 31, 1947.

32. HUAC, "Report on Soviet Espionage," Sept. 27, 1948; *New York Times*, Sept. 2, 1948; HUAC, "Report on Atomic Espionage," Sept. 29, 1949, 81st Cong., 1st sess.

33. Crouch claimed that he had last seen Hiskey at a party in Berkeley in Aug. 1941, where he, Kenneth May, Steve Nelson, and Hiskey had all talked together in front of a fireplace about FAECT. Crouch, testimony, HUAC, May 24, 1949, 81st Cong., 1st sess., 399–402. For further information about Crouch, see Frank Donner, "The Informer," *The Nation*, April 10, 1954; Victor Navasky, *Naming Names* (New York: Viking, 1980), 14; Dan Gillmor, *Fear, the Accuser* (New York: Abelard-Schuman, 1954),

180; Rep. Burr Harrison, HUAC, Dec. 20, 1950, 81st Cong., 2nd sess., 3422.

34. For Fuchs's career, see Moorehead, *The Traitors,* 50–152; Ronald Radosh and Joyce Milton, *The Rosenberg File* (New York: Holt, Rinehart & Winston, 1983), 8–19.

35. Gillmor, *Fear, the Accuser,* 133; Kamen, "Oyster."

36. Bohm, interview; Condon, interview; Lomanitz, interview; Clifford Durr, transcript of interview, Columbia Oral History Project, 220. For information on the behavior of the legal profession during the McCarthy period, see Jerold S. Auerbach, *Unequal Justice: Lawyers and Social Change in Modern America* (New York: Oxford University Press, 1977), 256–57; Forer, interview; David Rein, interview with the author, March 31, 1978; Vern Countryman and Ted Finman, *The Lawyer in Modern Society* (Boston: Little, Brown, 1966), 586; Albert E. Jenner, Jr., et al., Brief in *Stamler et al. v. Hon. Edwin E. Willis et al.,* 1968, 77–88 (this is a systematic attempt by an attorney in a contempt trial to show how HUAC operates to expose people); Michal R. Belknap, *Cold War Political Justice* (Westport, Conn.: Greenwood Press, 1977), 219–31.

37. Bohm, interview; Lomanitz, interview; Durr, interview; Rogge, *The First and the Fifth,* 187.

38. Kamen, testimony, HUAC, 11–49; Frank Oppenheimer, testimony, HUAC, June 14, 1949, 81st Cong., 1st sess., 355–73; Durr, interview.

39. Lillian Hellman, *Scoundrel Time* (Boston: Little, Brown, 1976), 83–91; Pollitt, "Pleading the Fifth Amendment," 70–73; Pritchett, *Civil Liberties and the Vinson Court,* 87–88; Taylor, *Grand Inquest,* 200–208. The case which established the "waiver" doctrine was *Rogers v. United States,* 1951, but the government had trouble enforcing it. See Emerson, Haber, and Dorsen, *Political and Civil Rights,* 405–7.

40. Fox, interview; Gardner, *The California Oath Controversy,* 93–94, 112.

41. Kamen, interview; Ethan A. M. Shepley, undated affidavit, in Kamen papers.

42. *Chicago Tribune,* July 2, 1951; "What a Passport Means to a Scientist" (unpublished ms., n.d.); "Statement of Dr. Martin D. Kamen, November 12, 1955, re United States Public Health Service Grants." In addition to the above documents, there is much material about his passport problems and his troubles getting grants in Kamen's private papers.

43. Hiskey, interview; Harry S. Rogers, statement, Sept. 29, 1948, quoted in *Polytechnic Reporter,* Dec. 20, 1950.

44. Lomanitz, interview; Lomanitz, questionnaire response, Paul Tillett Files, Seeley G. Mudd Library, Princeton University.

45. Although Princeton's files are not open to researchers, the University's dean Aaron Lemonick reviewed them for me and provided useful information on the disposition of Bohm's reappointment. Lemonick, interview with the author, Oct. 21, 1983. The University's official response to Bohm's hearing was in *The Daily Princetonian,* Dec. 15, 1950. Also, Bohm, interview; Harold W. Dodds, transcript of interview, Feb. 9, 1962, Columbia Oral History Project.

46. Frank Oppenheimer, interview, American Institute of Physics; Durr, interview; Steve Nelson, interview; Stern, *Oppenheimer Case,* 109–10; O'Reilly, *Hoover and the Un-Americans,* 125.

47. Oppenheimer, interview; Oppenheimer to J. W. Buchta, June 13, 1949,

"Oppenheimer, Frank F.," Biographical Files, University of Minnesota Archives. The Minnesota administration seemed peculiarly sensitive to the Communist issue. Gary Paul Henrickson, in his 1981 University of Minnesota Ph.D. diss., "Minnesota in the 'McCarthy' Period: 1946–1954," 28, notes that the University's timidity seemed to be motivated by the "fear of lost funding." Even though Henrickson found "no direct evidence that the Minnesota legislature cut appropriations for the University as punishment for political heresy, there is no lack of evidence that the University administration saw such economic interference—and more direct encroachments on University autonomy—as a threat." As a result, a comparatively large number of academic freedom incidents occurred there. The administration banned a Paul Robeson concert and a film from China; it investigated two graduate students who were named before the Subversive Activities Control Board; and it refused to rehire, for what may have been political reasons, the first black ever hired as a full-time instructor by a major American state university. The man, Forrest O. Wiggins, was a radical and may have been sacrificed as a gesture to certain state legislators. Both the ACLU and the University of Minnesota have large files on the Wiggins case. See ACLU, General Correspondence, 1952, Vol. 3 and General Correspondence, 1953, Vols. 6 and 8; University of Minnesota, "AAUP–1951 Wiggins Case"; Wiggins, questionnaire response, Tillett Files; Wiggins, tape cassette, sent to the author, 1978; Jules Chametzky, interview with the author, May 29, 1978.

48. Oppenheimer, questionnaire response, Tillett Files; Oppenheimer, interview, American Institute of Physics; Bernard Spero to J. W. Buchta, April 29, 1953, Alfred O. C. Nier Papers, University of Minnesota; Joseph Weinberg to Robert Oppenheimer, April 17, 1953, Case File, Box 77. Oppenheimer Papers, Library of Congress; Henrickson, "Minnesota in the 'McCarthy' Period," 40–43.

49. Oppenheimer, questionnaire response, Tillett Files; Lomanitz, questionnaire response, Tillett Files.

50. Morrison, interview; Stern, *Oppenheimer Case,* 47–49; Morrison, testimony before Special Committee of the Board of Trustees of Cornell University, Oct. 3, 4, 1956, 44–46, 50–51, in private papers of Philip Morrison.

51. Morrison, interview; Robert Gilpin, *American Scientists and Nuclear Weapons Policy* (Princeton: Princeton University Press, 1962), 66.

52. Morrison's papers contain a "Secrecy Order" of Nov. 18, 1953, which was sent to him when he filed an application for a patent on a reactor shield.

53. J. B. Matthews, "Communism and the Colleges," *The American Mercury,* May 1953; HUAC, "Report on the Communist 'Peace' Offensive," April 1, 1951, 82nd Cong., 1st sess., 87–90; Morrison, "Guilt by Innuendo: An Analysis," undated critique of HUAC report, Morrison papers.

54. *Counterattack,* March 6, 1953. There is an extensive literature on the role of *Counterattack* in the entertainment industry's blacklist. See Merle Miller, *The Judges and the Judged* (Garden City, N.Y.: Doubleday, 1952); Karen Sue Byers Cailteux, "The Political Blacklist in the Broadcast Industry: The Decade of the 1950's" (Ph.D. diss., Ohio State University, 1972); John Cogley, *Report on Blacklisting* (New York: Fund for the Republic, 1956), Vol. 2.

55. Thomas R. Strahan to William Anderson Kirk, April 1, 1949; and Philip H.

Zipp to E. E. Day, Sept. 29, 1949; both in File 15–014, Day Papers, Cornell University Archives. M. O. Evans to Deane Malott, May 7, 1953, Box 4–009, A3bl; William J. Thorne to Deane Malott, June 6, 1955; both in Malott Papers, Cornell University Archives. These are but a few of the literally dozens of letters that complained about Morrison to the Cornell administration. President Malott's stock reply to these letters was a fairly straightforward, if not overly rigorous, defense of civil liberties:

> Professor Philip Morrison's record has been known to us for some time and he has been thoroughly investigated at my request by a faculty committee. We could find nothing subversive in his record although we are, of course, embarrassed by his speeches and associations in the cause of peace at any price which he espouses. Freedom of speech at Cornell or anywhere for that matter is more important than a dozen Morrisons and we will not be goaded into limiting it by half truths and misrepresentations of the facts, either by the sayings of so-called liberals or the inquisitions of so-called conservatives. I am sure you realize that the complete story cannot be told in a publication such as "Counterattack." Its story is inaccurate in several essentials.

Malott to Dr. Edward J. Welch, June 30, 1953, Box 4–009, A3bl, Malott Papers.

56. Minutes of the Deans' Conference, Jan. 25, 1949; T. P. Wright, memorandum to Neal R. Stamp, Feb. 7, 1951; both in Box 1–059, de Kewiet Papers, Cornell University Archives. Minutes of Meeting of University Senate, March 13, 1947, April 8, 1948, New York University Archives. The text of the amended disclaimer reads:

> Nothing in this Statement of Policy is to be interpreted as giving the protection of tenure to anyone who advocates the overthrow of the government of the United States by force or who follows the dictation of any political party or group which presumes to dictate in matters of science or scientific opinion.

57. T. P. Wright to Dean C. C. Murdock, April 30, 1951, folder 5–057, de Kewiet Papers; Minutes of the Committee on University Policy, April 30, May 7, 1951, Box 3, 11/2/926, Dean of the Faculty Papers, Cornell University Archives.

58. Minutes of the Committee on University Policy, May 7, 1951; text of the resolutions in Minutes of the Meeting of the University Faculty, May 30, 1951, Cornell University Archives.

59. Minutes of the Meeting of the University Faculty, May 30, 1951, 2637c-d, t, Cornell University Archives; Corson, interview.

60. Morrison, testimony, Special Committee, Board of Trustees, 56, 58–60; Morrison to Malott, Dec. 16, 1953, Morrison papers; "Memorandum re Professor X," n.d., Box 20, A3bld, "Morrison," Malott Papers, Cornell University Archives.

61. Morrison, testimony, Special Committee, Board of Trustees, 68, 95; "Memorandum re Professor X" and William H. Farnham to Morrison, Dec. 31, 1952 in Folder "Academic and Tenure Committee #1," Box 3, Dean of the Faculty Papers, Cornell University Archives.

62. Morrison to Malott, Dec. 16, 1953. Morrison does not have a copy of the faculty committee report, nor could I find one in the Cornell Archives. It was, however, summarized and cited at length in "Memorandum re Professor X."

63. Morrison, interview. Minutes of the Committee on University Policy,

March 9, 1953; Farnham to Herrell DeGraff and J. W. MacDonald, March 16, 1953; both in Folder "Academic and Tenure Committee #1," Box 3, Dean of the Faculty Papers, Cornell University Archives.

64. Morrison, interview; Morrison, testimony, SISS, May 7, 1953, 83rd Cong., 1st sess., 900–919; Arthur Sutherland to John MacDonald, May 8, 1953, in Folder "Academic Freedom and Tenure, Committee on (Correspondence, etc. of Governmental Investigations Subcommittee)," Box 3, Dean of the Faculty Papers, Cornell University Archives.

65. MacDonald to "Members of Committee X," Dec. 3, 1953, in Folder "Academic Freedom and Tenure Committee #1," Box 3, Dean of the Faculty Papers, Cornell University Archives.

66. Morrison to Malott, Nov. 25, Dec. 4, 1953; Malott to Morrison, Dec. 3, 1953; all in Morrison papers.

67. Morrison to Malott, Dec. 16, 1953, Morrison papers.

68. Malott to Morrison, Jan. 28, 1954, Morrison papers.

69. Letter from chairman of the Physics Department (Lloyd Smith?), Oct. 27, 1955, cited in "Memorandum re Professor X"; William Littlewood to Morrison, Aug. 10, 1956, Morrison papers.

70. Morrison, testimony, Special Committee, Board of Trustees, 92, 124.

71. Morrison, testimony, Special Committee, Board of Trustees, 118–19; Corson, interview; Corson to Malott, Oct. 8, 1956, Box 20, A3bld, "Morrison," Malott Papers, Cornell University Archives.

VI: "A Very Fertile Field for Investigation"

1. There is some irony about the capture of the IPR files. The organization protested the seizure, but had, in fact, facilitated it by asking the FBI to go over its records in order to clear it from charges that it was Communist-run. The FBI let Don Surine, a former agent on McCarthy's staff, know about the files; Surine told his boss and McCarthy tipped off the SISS. John N. Thomas, *The Institute of Pacific Relations* (Seattle: University of Washington, 1974), 77; Edward C. Carter, testimony, U.S. Senate, Committee on the Judiciary, Subcommittee on Internal Security, "Hearings on the Institute of Pacific Relations," July 25, 1951, 82d Cong., 2d sess., 42–45. (hereafter cited as SISS, *IPR*.)

2. For the most useful discussion of the IPR, see Thomas, *The Institute of Pacific Relations*, passim. Dorothy Borg, interview with the author, April 4, 1977. Robert Morris, *No Wonder We Are Losing* (New York: Bookmailer, 1958) is a useful account of his activities by the special counsel of the McCarran Committee. Robert Morris, interview with the author, Oct. 29, 1979.

3. On the China Lobby, see Ross Y. Koen, *The China Lobby in American Politics* (New York: Macmillan, 1960) and Joseph Keeley, *The China Lobby Man* (New Rochelle, N.Y.: Arlington House, 1969). On McCarthy, see Earl Latham, *The Communist Controversy in Washington* (Cambridge: Harvard University Press, 1966), 219–316; Robert Griffith, *The Politics of Fear* (Lexington: University of Kentucky Press, 1970), 123–30; Richard M. Fried, *Men Against McCarthy* (New York: Columbia University Press, 1976), 124–39; Owen Lattimore, *Ordeal by Slander* (Boston: Little, Brown, 1950), 149–61.

4. Koen, *The China Lobby*, 23, 63–64; Athan Theoharis, *The Yalta Myths* (Columbia: University of Missouri Press, 1970), 20–21, 80–81, 137; Griffith, *Politics of Fear*, 62–63, 75; Ronald J. Caridi, *The Korean War and American Politics* (Philadelphia: The University of Pennsylvania Press, 1968), 6–9; H. Bradford Westerfield, *Foreign Policy and Party Politics* (New Haven: Yale University Press, 1955), 259–60, 343–46, 374–77; Alan D. Harper, *The Politics of Loyalty* (Westport, Conn.: Greenwood, 1969), 130–32.

5. Griffith, *Politics of Fear*, 29–38; Koen, *The China Lobby*, 72, 206–10; John Stewart Service, *The Amerasia Papers* (Berkeley and Los Angeles: University of California Press, 1971).

6. Thomas, *The Institute of Pacific Relations*, 23, 33, 58–61; Frederick Vanderbilt Field, *From Right to Left* (Westport, Conn.: Lawrence Hill, 1983), 125–33, 186–91, 208–56.

7. See, for example, the SISS's treatment of Field, SISS, *IPR*, July 26, 1951, 77–121; Thomas, *The Institute of Pacific Relations*, 79; Morris, *No Wonder We Are Losing*, 118–27. Owen Lattimore, who had to endure an unprecedented thirteen days of such lethal nit-picking, likened his ordeal to that "of a blind man running a gauntlet." Lattimore, SISS, *IPR*, March 1, 1952, 3261.

8. Louis Budenz, testimony, SISS, *IPR*, Aug. 22, 1951, 517, 522, 550, 699; Harvey Matusow, *False Witness* (New York: Cameron and Kahn, 1955), 102–6. On the veracity of these professional anti-Communists, see Herbert Packer, *Ex-Communist Witnesses* (Stanford: Stanford University Press, 1962).

9. Karl A. Wittfogel, testimony, SISS, *IPR*, Aug, 7, 1951, 274–75, 312–13, 321–23; William Canning, testimony, SISS, *IPR*, Aug. 16, 1951, 466–72, 482–85.

10. Wittfogel, testimony, 309, 333; Dorothy Borg, interview; John K. Fairbank to Owen Lattimore, Sept. 25, 1950, in John K. Fairbank, General Correspondence, Box 15, Harvard University Archives, Pusey Library, Harvard University; Thomas, *The Institute of Pacific Relations*, 114, 154–59. Thurman Arnold, *Fair Fights and Foul* (New York: Harcourt, Brace and World, 1965), 215–26, contains an interesting discussion of Lattimore's perjury case.

11. Chairman, History Department (Sidney Painter?) to Owen Lattimore, Feb. 10, 1956, in History Department Records, Johns Hopkins University Archives; Stanley I. Kutler, *The American Inquisition* (New York: Hill and Wang, 1982), 212, 274; Koen, *The China Lobby*, 151; John King Fairbank, *Chinabound* (New York: Harper & Row, 1982), 331–51. Fairbank, the nation's leading China scholar, was denied a visa to Japan after having been named by Budenz. His papers, on deposit at Harvard, contain extensive correspondence about his efforts to reverse that decision. Knight Biggerstaff, a Cornell sinologist, was on the board of the IPR. He was denied a security clearance. Biggerstaff, interview with the author, Oct. 18, 1979. His correspondence about obtaining his clearance is on deposit at Cornell. See also, HSK to Dr. Krout, "Professor Wilbur's Passport," June 30, 1954, Grayson Kirk Papers, Columbia University Archives.

12. Special Faculty Committee of Review, Miscellany, ms. minutes, Nov. 11,

1952, in Lewis Webster Jones Papers, Box 145–1, Rutgers University Archives.

13. Morris, *No Wonder We Are Losing*, 25–30, 136; Morris, interview.

14. Frederick Ewen, interview with the author, Nov. 7, 1980; Bernard Riess, interview with the author, March 28, 1979; Isidore Pomerance, interview with the author, July 20, 1982.

15. Harry Gideonse, transcript of interview, Columbia Oral History Project, 91–97; Gideonse, testimony, SISS, March 11, 1953, 83rd Cong., 1st sess., 561; Jacob Robert Fischel, "Harry Gideonse: The Public Life" (Ph.D. diss., University of Delaware, 1973), 344–54, 409–10; Thomas Evans Coulton, *A City College in Action* (New York: Harper and Brothers, 1955), 113–28; Ewen, interview; "The 'Vanguard' Problem at Brooklyn College," memorandum, April 5, 1951, ACLU, General Correspondence, 1951, Vol. 9, ACLU Archives; Harry Slochower to Mary S. Ingraham, Feb. 5, 1948, in private papers of Harry Slochower.

16. Bella Dodd, testimony, SISS, Sept. 8, 1952, 82nd Cong., 2nd sess., 9; Bella V. Dodd, *School of Darkness* (New York: Kenedy, 1954); Annette Rubinstein, interview with the author, Dec. 11, 1981; Bernard Riess, interview; Morris, *No Wonder We Are Losing*, 136.

17. Joseph B. Cavallaro (chairman, Board of Higher Education), testimony, SISS, June 17, 1953, 83rd Cong., 1st sess., 1135–40; David Goldway, interview with the author, May 19, 1983.

18. Cavallaro, testimony, SISS, 1140; Ewen, interview; John J. Theobald to Oscar Shaftel, Feb. 26, 1953, in private papers of Oscar Shaftel.

19. Arthur Kahn, memorandum, Aug. 4, 1953, Board of Higher Education Archives; Harold Cammer, question in SISS, Oct. 13, 1952, 82nd Cong., 2nd sess., 279; Petition, Vera Shlakman et al., v. the Board of Higher Education of the City of New York, Nov. 18, 1952, in ACLU, General Correspondence, 1952, Vol. 7.

20. Harry Slochower, interview with the author, Dec. 29, 1980; Slochower, testimony, SISS, Sept. 24, 1952, 82nd Cong., 2nd sess., 199–207; *Slochower v. Board of Higher Education of New York*, 350 U.S. 551 (1956).

21. Slochower, interview; Gideonse, Columbia Oral History Project, 97; Fischel, "Harry Gideonse," 412–15.

22. Herbert P. Woodward to Edward W. Fox, Jan. 15, 1958, in 14/17/846, Cornell University Archives; Wittfogel, testimony, SISS, Aug. 7, 1951, 312; Canning, testimony, SISS, *IPR*, Aug. 16, 1951, 482–85; Herbert P. Woodward, confidential memorandum, March 27, 1952, incl. Moses I. Finley to Woodward, Sept. 5, 1951, in Lewis Webster Jones Papers, Box 145–3, Rutgers University Archives; Peter Charles Schaehrer, "McCarthyism and Academic Freedom—Three Case Studies" (Ed.D. diss., Columbia University Teachers College, 1974), 173.

23. M. I. Finley, testimony, SISS, *IPR*, March 28, 1952, 4152–58; Herbert Woodward, "promotion rating blank," March 10, 1950, in Jones Papers, Box 145–3; Edward A. Robinson to Lewis Webster Jones, Nov. 2, 1952, in Jones Papers, Box 145–2.

24. Dean Roy A. Bowers, testimony, Nov. 10, 1952, and Simon Heimlich, testimony, Nov. 7, 10, 1952, in transcript of meeting of Special Faculty Committee of Review; Richard B. Scudder to Sen. H. Alexander Smith, Nov.

12, 1952; Special Faculty Committee of Review-Miscellany, ms. minutes, Nov. 5, 1952, all in Jones Papers, Box 145–1.

25. Heimlich, testimony, Nov. 7, 1952, transcript of meeting of Special Faculty Committee of Review, Jones Papers, Box 145–1; Heimlich, testimony, SISS, Sept. 24, 1952, 82nd Cong., 2nd sess., 187–88.

26. Lewis Webster Jones, statement, Sept. 26, 1952; President's Special Advisory Committee, minutes, n.d.; both in Jones Papers, Box 145–1.

27. Text in "Faculty Newsletter," March, Nov. 1951, Jones Papers, Box 145–1.

28. Jones, statement, Sept. 26, 1952; Alfred E. Driscoll, form letter to ?, n.d.; both in Jones Papers, Box 145–1. Schaehrer, "McCarthyism and Academic Freedom," 195. For Jones's response to the HUAC textbook demand, see Bernard de Voto, "Colleges, the Government, and Freedom," *AAUP Bulletin* 35, No. 3 (Autumn 1949).

29. Report of the Voorhees Committee in Jones, statement, Oct. 14, 1952, Jones Papers, Box 145–1.

30. Ibid.; Schaehrer, "McCarthyism and Academic Freedom," 233–34.

31. Special Faculty Committee of Review-Miscellany, ms. minutes, Jones Papers, Box 145–1.

32. Robert Morris, interview with *U.S. News and World Report,* Dec. 5, 1952, 50–51; Joseph McCarthy to Nathan Pusey, Nov. 9, 1953, quoted in Dan Gillmor, *Fear, the Accuser* (New York: Abelard-Schuman, 1954), 146.

    For an enlightening discussion of the way in which committees forced unfriendly witnesses to use the Fifth, see Frank J. Donner, *The Un-Americans* (New York: Ballantine, 1961), 82–98, and Telford Taylor, *Grand Inquest* (New York: Simon and Schuster, 1955), 184–221.

33. Special Faculty Committee of Review-Miscellany, ms. minutes; Leonard Boudin, testimony, Nov. 7, 1952, in transcript of meeting of Special Faculty Committee of Review; both in Jones Papers, Box 145–1.

34. Report of the Special Faculty Committee of Review, Dec. 3, 1952. This document was widely circulated within the academic community. I have encountered copies of it in many college archives as well as in private collections. Rutgers, of course, has several copies. Jones Papers, Box 145–1.

35. Howard A. Smith to Lewis Webster Jones, Oct. 16, 1952, Jones Papers, Box 145–2; Russell E. Watson, handwritten notes on his testimony, Oct. 31, 1952, in Special Faculty Committee of Review-Miscellany, ms. minutes, Jones Papers, Box 145–1.

36. Rutgers University Board of Trustees, Resolution, Dec. 12, 1952. Like the Special Faculty Committee's report, the trustees' resolution received wide circulation. Just about every college or university archive I consulted had a copy.

37. Tracy S. Voorhees to Simon Heimlich, Dec. 16, 1952; Heimlich, testimony, Nov. 7, 1952; Special Faculty Committee of Review, Miscellany, ms. minutes, meeting with Robert Morris, Nov. 5, 1952; all in Jones Papers, Box 145–1.

38. Karl E. Metzger to "The Faculty and Staff," Jan. 12, 1953, contains the results of the poll and the text. (This poll was so widely known within the academic community that there are copies of it in most archives I've used. The one I have comes from the ACLU, General Correspondence, 1953, Vol. 6.) See also, Emergency Committee of the Rutgers Faculty on the Trustees' Decision, Jan. 19, 1953, in Hubert B. Goodrich et al., "Mate-

rials on Academic Freedom," March 23, 1953 (mimeographed collection of documents prepared for the faculty at Wesleyan University, in the private papers of Robert S. Cohen); Schaehrer, "McCarthyism and Academic Freedom," 206–14.

39. Grayson Kirk, "Memorandum concerning Dr. Gene Weltfish," June 20, 1952, Grayson Kirk Papers, File "Gene Weltfish," Columbia University Archives, Low Library; Bernhard Stern, memorandum, Sept. 29, 1952, in private papers of Charlotte Stern; Thomas B. Drew et al. to Grayson Kirk, June 18, 1953 in Grayson Kirk Papers.

40. Bella Dodd, testimony, SISS, Sept. 8, 1952, 82nd Cong., 2nd sess., 17; Pat McCarran, cited in *Harvard Crimson,* Dec. 1, 1952; Harold Velde, quoted in *Harvard Crimson,* Nov. 26, 1952; Velde, quoted in *U.S. News and World Report,* Jan. 2, 1953; Sen. McCarthy, ibid.; FBI memorandum, Feb. 26, 1953, cited in Fred Richard Zimring, "Academic Freedom and the Cold War: The Dismissal of Barrows Dunham from Temple University: A Case Study," (Ed.D. diss. Columbia University Teachers College, 1981), 177.

41. The evidence of this interuniversity communication is so abundant that it would take dozens of pages simply to document the materials that I found in the various university archives I consulted. Here is a sample from just two schools: Yale and Rutgers.

F. H. Wiggin to Sturgis Warner, March 26, 1953, Box 1, Folder 10; Phillips Ketchum (MIT) to F. H. Wiggin, Feb. 20, 1953, Box 2, Folder 11; Walter G. Muelder (Boston University) to A. Whitney Griswold, Feb. 25, 1953, Box 1, Folder 3; Sturgis Warner, "Memorandum," July 3, 1953, Box 3, Folder 21; all in A. Whitney Griswold Papers, Yale University Archives.

Robert Stearns (University of Colorado) to Lewis Webster Jones, Nov. 10, 1952; Thomas Clark Pollock (NYU) to Jones, Jan. 13, 1953; William W. Tomlinson (Temple) to Jones, Jan. 22, 1953; Jones to Chancellor T. R. McConnell (Buffalo), March 18, 1953, notes that he was "sent 1 set of Heimlich-Finley-Schlatter material." All in Jones Papers, Box 145–2. See also Troy H. Middleton (Louisiana State University) to Jones, Aug. 11, 1953, Jones Papers, Box 145–3. (All these letters are not just requests for Jones's statement, but more detailed requests for advice from institutions facing similar problems.)

42. For Cornell, see Chapter V above. For NYU, Thomas Clark Pollock, "Memorandum to the Faculty," Nov. 20, 1952; Washington Square College, Minutes of faculty meetings, Nov. 18, Dec. 9, 1952, Jan. 13, 1953; "Report of the Special Committee on Faculty Responsibility toward Governmental Investigative Agencies," March 30, 1953; all in private papers of Richard N. Swift. See also "Statement of Committee on Academic Responsibility at MIT," in "Ninth Interim Report of the Special Commission on Communism, Subversive Activities and Related Matters within the Commonwealth," Commonwealth of Massachusetts, 18 Jan. 1957. J. R. Killian, Jr., to Members of the Faculty, April 23, 1953; University of Miami, "Action by the University Council on a Preliminary Report by its Committee on Academic Freedom," May 25, 1953; both in Dean of the Faculty Papers, Box 3, #11/1/895, Cornell University Archives.

43. Minutes, University Senate, May 11, 1953, Harlan Hatcher Papers, Box 8,

Folder 21; "Report of the Joint Committee on Demotion and Dismissal Procedures," Marvin L. Niehuss Papers, Box 21; Alfred A. Connable, "Communism on the Campus," Dec. 3, 1953, Niehuss Papers, Box 2; all in Michigan Historical Collections, Bentley Historical Library, University of Michigan.

44. Alexander H. Frey to William H. DuBarry, March 4, 1953; "Report of the Committee on Academic Privilege and Tenure," Feb. 14, 1953; both in UPA 4, #42, University of Pennsylvania Archives.

45. Daniel Thorner to Thomas C. Cochran, May 24, Sept. 18, Oct. 11, 25, 1953, in Thomas C. Cochran Papers, University of Pennsylvania Archives; Alice Thorner, interview with the author, March 16, 1979, Sept. 24, 1979; Irving Kravis, interview with Fred Zimring, Feb. 4, 1980.

46. William Marbury to James Bryant Conant, Dec. 8, 1952, private papers of William Marbury; Marbury, interview with the author, May 25, 1978. (Harvard does not grant scholars access to its archives, so I was unable to look at the materials relating to its Fifth Amendment witnesses. However, William Marbury had a complete file on those cases and, though he would not show it to me because he did not want to go against the University's policy, he referred to it throughout the interview and did let me see some of the documents that he, himself, had written. As a result, I am inclined to give much more weight to my interview with Mr. Marbury than I ordinarily do to such types of testimony. He was acting, as it were, almost as a research assistant, in that he would respond to my questions by checking the documentation that he had—apparently minutes and transcripts of meetings of the Harvard Corporation, as well as correspondence—before he gave an answer.)

47. Donald Kirk David and Charles A. Coolidge, cited in an FBI report, in Sigmund Diamond, "The Arrangement: The FBI and Harvard University in the McCarthy Period," in Athan Theoharis, ed., *Beyond the Hiss Case* (Philadelphia: Temple University Press, 1982), 359–60; Paul Buck, interview with the author, Jan. 10, 1978; Marbury, interview.

48. William Marbury to Zechariah Chafee, Dec. 29, 1952, in private papers of William Marbury.

49. Zechariah Chafee to William Marbury, Jan. 3, 1953, Marbury papers; Zechariah Chafee and Arthur Sutherland, letter to the editor, *Harvard Crimson,* Jan. 8, 1953; Zechariah Chafee to Curt N. Taylor, April 7, 1954, in Zechariah Chafee Papers, Box 35, File 19, Harvard Law School Archives.

50. Thomas I. Emerson, interview with the author, Nov. 16, 1977; Joseph Forer, interview with the author, March 3, 1978; Paul Buck, interview with the author, Jan. 10, 1978; Robert Morris, interview; Erwin Griswold, interview with the author, Dec. 23, 1977. Griswold served on a Harvard faculty committee that dealt with the University's Fifth Amendment witnesses and began to speak out in public about the Amendment soon after. His rather sympathetic view found expression in Griswold, *The Fifth Amendment Today* (Cambridge: Harvard University Press, 1955).

51. Arthur Sutherland's papers in the Harvard Law School Archives contain over fifty requests for copies of the letter from a wide variety of schools, including Sarah Lawrence, Ohio State, California Institute of Technology, Mount Holyoke, Smith, Brooklyn College, Syracuse, Michigan State, Ober-

lin, Oregon State, NYU, Cornell, University of Colorado, Vassar, and the University of Vermont. See also Grayson Kirk to Zechariah Chafee, Jan. 17, 1953, Wallace S. Moreland (director of Public Relations, Rutgers University) to Chafee, Jan. 16, 1953; Leopold Kohr to Chafee, Sept. 8, 1953; all in Chafee Papers. "Memorandum to Members of the Faculty from Committee on Faculty Responsibilities," Feb. 24, 1953, Dean of the Faculty Papers, Box 3, #11/1/895, Cornell University Archives; draft statement on "Academic Freedom," Executive Committee, Board of Trustees, Feb. 6, 1953, UPA 4 #42, University of Pennsylvania Archives; Hubert B. Goodrich et al., "Materials on Academic Freedom" (Wesleyan); *Harvard Crimson*, Feb. 6, 1953; Report of the Committee on Academic Freedom (Berkeley), March 25, 1953, Griswold Papers, Box 1, Yale University Archives.

52. Lewis Webster Jones to Harold Taylor, Jan. 5, 1953; Jones to Daniel G. Feldberg, Jan. 22, 1953; both in Jones Papers, Box 145–2. Richard Schlatter, interview with the author, Oct. 21, 1981; Norman Ramsey, transcript of oral history interview, Aug. 5, 1960, Columbia Oral History Project, 218.

53. Lewis Webster Jones, "Academic Freedom and Civic Responsibility," Jan. 24, 1953. This statement was also widely circulated, and I found copies in most of the archives I consulted.

54. See the materials cited in n. 41 above. See also Lewis Webster Jones to Gov. Driscoll, Jan. 29, 1953; Sarah Gibson Blandings to Jones, Feb. 23, 1953; Gordon Scherer to Jones, Feb. 26, 1953; all in Jones Papers, Box 145–2. There is an entire file containing these requests in the Jones Papers, "Requests for Copies of Dr. Jones's Statement."

55. J. Wallace Sterling to Harold Stassen, Oct. 14, 1952; Minutes of the Annual Meeting of the AAU, Oct. 28–29, 1952; C. W. de Kewiet to William H. DuBarry, Jan. 29, 1953; all in UPA 4, #44, University of Pennsylvania Archives. Minutes of AAU Meeting, Oct. 23, 24, 1951, Griswold Papers, Box 30, Folder 274. (There are, of course, copies of these mimeographed AAU minutes in the other archives I've seen—Hatcher Papers, Box 3, Folder 22, has a set, for example.) Harold Dodds to James Bryant Conant, Nov. 26, 1952, talks of disillusionment with AAUP, in Griswold Papers, Box 30.

56. Minutes of AAU Meeting, Feb. 15, 1953, UPA 4, #44; handwritten memorandum, n.d. (obviously from Feb. 15 meeting), Griswold Papers, Box 30, File 277. The Griswold Papers contain an entire file, no. 279, of the different drafts and correspondence about them, that Griswold collected while writing the final draft of the AAU statement.

57. Association of American Universities, "The Rights and Responsibilities of Universities and their Faculties," March 24, 1953, Princeton University.

58. Harold W. Dodds to members of the AAU, April 22, 30, 1953, UPA 4, #42; "Subversive Influence in the Educational Process," Report of the Subcommittee to Investigate the Administration of the Internal Security Act and other Internal Security Laws to the Committee on the Judiciary, U.S. Senate, 83rd Congress., 1st sess., July 17, 1953, 27.

59. Minutes of AAU Meeting, Oct. 27, 28, 1953, in Grayson Kirk Papers; Kirk to Robert MacIver, April 24, 1953, in Columbia University Academic Freedom Committee, Box 1, Rare Book and Manuscript Library, Butler Library, Columbia University. Harold Dodds to A. Whitney Griswold,

March 26, 1953; E. B. Fred to Harold Dodds, March 24, 1953, and enclosure, "Suggested Revisions in Second Draft of AAU Statement," March 24, 1953; all in Griswold Papers, Box 30, Folder 279, Yale University Archives.

60. ACLU statement, Sept. 15, 1957, in Niehuss Papers, Box 21. On the ACLU's problems, see Mary Sperling McAuliffe, *Crisis on the Left* (Amherst: University of Massachusetts Press, 1978), 88–107; Robert S. Lynd, "The Report of the Association of American Universities on 'The Rights and Responsibilities of Universities and Their Faculties,'" April 14, 1953, mimeographed ms. in private papers of Robert Merton; Minutes, University Senate, May 11, 1953, Hatcher Papers, Box 8, Michigan Historical Collections.

61. Edward R. Baylor to Theodore Jahn, May 27, 1954, Niehuss Papers, Box 21, Michigan Historical Collections.

62. Sidney Hook, "The Fifth Amendment—A Moral Issue," *New York Times Magazine*, Nov. 1, 1953.

63. Robert Gorham Davis, testimony, HUAC, Feb. 25, 1953, 12, 24; Davis, interview with the author, Feb. 2, 1982; Davis, letter to the editor, *New York Times*, March 25, 1953.

64. Alan P. Westin, "Do Silent Witnesses Defend Civil Liberties?" *Commentary*, June 1953.

VII: "Frankly and Freely"

1. Robert E. Cushman, *Civil Liberties in the United States* (Ithaca: Cornell University Press, 1956); Walter Goodman, *The Committee* (New York: Farrar, Straus and Giroux, 1968), 321–32; Carl Beck, *Contempt of Congress* (New Orleans: Hauser Press, 1959), 99n. Robert Morris, the SISS's chief counsel, recalled that his committee always tried to "observe the amenities" during its education hearings and "tell the administration in advance what was going on" (Robert Morris, interview with the author, Oct. 29, 1979). Harold Velde, telegram to Harlan Hatcher, Jan. 9, 1953, Marvin L. Niehuss Papers, Box 21, Michigan Historical Collections, Bentley Historical Library, University of Michigan.

2. The most readily accessible transcript of the first set of Harvard hearings is in Eric Bentley, ed., *Thirty Years of Treason* (New York: Viking, 1971), 575–625.

    According to the public records and my own research, the following Harvard people were called up by HUAC in the spring of 1953 (there may have been others and there certainly were Harvard-connected people called up by HUAC later on as well): Boorstin, Davis, Hicks, Wendell Furry, Louis Harap, Harry Marks, George Mayberry, William Parry, John Henry Reynolds, Herbert Robbins, Richard Schlatter, Rubby Sherr, and Marcus Singer.

    HUAC also subpoenaed the eminent linguist Roman Jakobson. But he was able to get the subpoena cancelled when it became clear that it had been issued as the result of some wild charges brought against him by a Ukrainian fascist. Jakobson to Arthur Sutherland, May 25, 1953, File 48–4; Arthur Sutherland to Paul Buck, May 27, 1953, File 77–6; both in Arthur Sutherland Papers, Harvard Law School Archives.

3. The definitive book about the moral issues involved in testifying before a congressional committee is, of course, Victor S. Navasky, *Naming Names* (New York: Viking, 1980). Navasky's contention that it was the overall political, cultural, and social atmosphere that made it possible for people to overcome their distaste for informing rings true. The population he studies is a different one, however. Although definitive figures are impossible to ascertain, it seems unlikely that the academic world contributed quite as large a percentage of informers as the entertainment industry. Navasky estimates 30 percent; my own guess, for academics, is 20 to 25 percent. I think that what they did was wrong, and I think that most of them now think that what they did was wrong. But, at a time when most of their colleagues and the leaders in their own profession were insisting on "complete candor," it may be of interest to ask not why so many informed, but why so many did not. See Navasky, 388–427.

Robert Gorham Davis, interview with the author, Feb. 2, 1982.
4. Davis, interview.
5. Richard Schlatter, "On Being a Communist at Harvard," *Partisan Review* 44:4 (Dec. 1977): 612; Schlatter, interview with the author, Oct. 12, 1981.
6. Schlatter, interview.
7. When a group of Chicago professors who had been questioned by the SISS and then released because they had not been Communists called a press conference after their executive session, Jenner was furious. "After receiving all kinds of assurance that their names would be kept secret, the three witnesses . . . issued statements to the press, violating the spirit of the session." Jenner, statement, SISS, June 8, 1953, 83rd Cong. 1st sess., 1075–76.

That Jenner and the other investigators were not anxious to question such people in public, the reminiscences of Wellesley religion professor Louise Pettibone Smith make clear. She was a non-Communist radical who boasted that she "signed everything that came to [her] desk and went to every meeting [she] was asked to go to." Her public testimony, however, would have made the SISS look foolish; when asked in her executive session "what other organizations I belonged to," she recalled.

I listed a nice conservative lot, Winchester Congregational Church, the Ladies Aid Society of Winchester, the National Grange of Winchester Center, the Women's Auxiliary of the Fire Department of Winchester, Connecticut.

Louise Pettibone Smith, interview with the author, July 9, 1978.
Harry Marks, interview with the author, March 9, 1979.
8. Perhaps the most useful descriptions of committee practices are to be found in Frank J. Donner, *The Un-Americans* (New York: Ballantine, 1961); Dan Gillmor, *Fear, the Accuser* (New York: Abelard-Schuman, 1954); Telford Taylor, *Grand Inquest* (New York: Simon and Schuster, 1955); and—perhaps the most valuable, but most difficult to obtain—Albert E. Jenner et al., legal brief in "Jeremiah Stamler, M.D., and Yolanda F. Hall and Milton M. Cohen vs Hon. Edwin E. Willis et al. before Supreme Court," Oct. term 1968, Appendices 4 and 5. This brief in a contempt case tries to show exactly how HUAC conducts its hearings so as to punish its unfriendly witnesses.

Wendell Furry, interview with the author, Nov. 4, 1977; Robert V. Pound, interview with the author, Jan. 26, 1978; Kenneth Bainbridge, interview with the author, June 8, 1978; Edwin C. Kemble, "The Faculty & Mr. Furry," *Harvard Alumni Bulletin*, March 6, 1954; Otto Oldenberg to J. Robert Oppenheimer, March 14, 1950, Oppenheimer Papers, Box 124, Library of Congress.

9. Furry, interview; Norman Ramsey, interview with the author, Dec. 15, 1977; Ramsey, Columbia University Oral History Project, 216–20, 233; Ramsey to Jerrold Zacharias, April 3, 1953, Mark DeWolfe Howe Papers, Harvard Law School Archives; *Harvard Crimson*, Feb. 27, 1953.

10. Mark DeWolfe Howe to James Bryant Conant, Jan. 7, 1953, Howe Papers; Sigmund Diamond, "The Arrangement: The FBI and Harvard University in the McCarthy Period," in Athan G. Theoharis, ed., *Beyond the Hiss Case* (Philadelphia: Temple University Press, 1982), 358–60; Edward Purcell, interview with the author, Jan. 4, 1978; Paul Buck, interview with the author, Jan. 10, 1978; Leon Kamin, interview with the author, Oct. 6, 1977; *Harvard Crimson*, Feb. 18, 1953.

11. William Marbury, interview with the author, May 25, 1978; Furry, interview; Furry, testimony, HUAC, April 16, 1953, 83rd Cong., 1st sess., 247–62.

12. Marbury, interview; Ramsey, interview; Ramsey to Osmund K. Fraenkel, Nov. 7, 1953, Howe Papers; Purcell, interview; Erwin Griswold, interview with the author, Dec. 23, 1977. Griswold's book was *The Fifth Amendment Today* (Cambridge: Harvard University Press, 1955).

13. Marbury, interview; Buck, interview; Charles Wyzanski, interview with the author, Jan. 7, 1978; McGeorge Bundy, interview with the author, Dec. 29, 1977.

14. Marbury, interview; "Statement by the Harvard Corporation in Regard to Associate Professor Wendell H. Furry, Teaching Fellow Leon J. Kamin and Assistant Professor Helen Deane Markham," May 20, 1953. (This statement was printed and issued in the form of a pamphlet. Just about every archive I inspected had a copy, as did the private papers of many of the people I interviewed.) According to Marbury, it was Edward Mason, the dean of the School of Public Administration and a member of the Faculty Advisory Committee, who suggested that Furry be put on probation.

15. David Lubell, interview with the author, Nov. 8, 1977; *Harvard Law School Record*, April 2, 1953, Feb. 18, 1969, Howe Papers; *Harvard Crimson*, April 9, 1953. Arthur Sutherland's papers in the Harvard Law School Archives contain an extensive file of material on the Lubells, including memoranda from Sutherland, himself, n.d.; W. Barton Leach, April 3, 1953; Lon Fuller, April 6, 1953; Erwin Griswold, March 31, 1953; George Gardner, April 6, 1953; Charles Schwartz, April 7, 1953.

16. Leon Kamin, interview; William Marbury, interview. David W. Bailey to Helen W. Deane, March 27, 1953; Charles A. Coolidge to Helen Wendler Deane Markham, April 9, 1953; Helen Wendler Deane to the President and Fellows, Harvard University, n.d.; Helen Wendler Deane to Charles A. Coolidge, May 14, 1953; George Packer Berry to Helen W. Deane, June 15, 1953; all in private papers of George Markham. "Statement by the Harvard Corporation."

17. Helen Wendler Dean Markham, testimony, SISS, May 28, 1953, 83rd Cong., 1st sess., 1008, 1011, 1015; "Statement by Dr. Helen Wendler Deane," May 27, 1953, in Markham papers; Marbury, interview.

18. "Subversive Influence in the Educational Process," Report of the Subcommittee to Investigate the Administration of the Internal Security Act and other Internal Security Laws to the Committee on the Judiciary, U.S. Senate, July 17, 1953, 83rd Cong., 1st sess., 14–16; Arthur Sutherland, memorandum to Erwin Griswold, n.d., Sutherland Papers; Griswold, statement to the Faculty Advisory Committee, June 25, 1953, Howe Papers.

19. Charles A. Coolidge to Helen Wendler Deane Markham, Aug. 11, 1953; Harvard Corporation, statement, Aug. 31, 1953; both in the papers of George Markham. Marbury, interview. Bart J. Bok, affidavit, Aug. 24, 1953; John D. Wild, affidavit, Aug. 25, 1953; Leon J. Kamin, affidavit, Aug. 26, 1953; Mark DeWolfe Howe to Charles A. Coolidge, Aug. 18, 19, 1953; all in Howe Papers.

20. David M. Oshinsky, *A Conspiracy So Immense* (New York: Free Press, 1983), 322–23; *Harvard Alumni Bulletin,* Nov. 28, 1953; *Harvard Crimson,* Oct. 26, Nov. 6, 10, 1953; Gillmor, *Fear, the Accuser,* 146.

21. Furry, interview; Norman Ramsey to McGeorge Bundy, Nov. 13, 1953, Howe Papers; Bundy, interview; Kamin, interview; Pound, interview; Joseph McCarthy, statement, hearings, Permanent Subcommittee on Investigations of the Committee on Government Operations, U.S. Senate, Jan. 15, 1954, 83rd Cong., 1st sess., 45–46.

22. Executive Committee of the Harvard Chapter of the AAUP, draft letter to Nathan Pusey, n.d. (probably Oct. 1954); Edwin C. Kemble to Kingman Brewster, Aug. 18, 1954; Furry Legal Aid Committee, draft report, June 1956; all in Howe Papers. Ms. notes of conference of Arthur Sutherland, Samuel Stouffer, Benjamin Kaplan, and J. M. Maguire, Jan. 27, 1954, in Sutherland Papers; Harold Taylor, interview with the author, June 20, 1978; John Hutchinson to the author, June 1, 1978; Donald Horton, interview with the author, Feb. 25, 1982.

23. *Harvard Crimson,* May 28, 1953, contains the text of the AAUP citations. Patrick Murphy Malin to Paul Buck, May 29, 1953, ACLU, General Correspondence, 1954, Vol. 30; Academic Freedom Committee, minutes, Dec. 8, 1953, ACLU, General Correspondence, 1953, Vol. 3; Louise Pettibone Smith, interview. Typical of the perhaps overly enthusiastic response to the Corporation's action by the academic left is this comment from a letter from Harvard astronomer Harlow Shapley to Helen Deane Markham: "The Corp., by golly, via you, did a good job" (Shapley to Markham, May 19, 1953, Markham papers).

   As time passed, the enthusiasm for Harvard's behavior waned; in its 1956 assessment of the academy's response to McCarthyism, the AAUP took a more nuanced position. It admitted that the outcome of the Harvard cases "embodies, in many respects, the best academic traditions"; but it expressed concern with Harvard's failure to ensure that a faculty committee would judge future cases and with the Corporation's ban on Party membership and its "expressed view that invocation of the Fifth Amendment is misconduct." Bentley Glass et al., "Academic Freedom and Tenure in the Quest for National Security," *AAUP Bulletin* 42, No. 1 (Spring 1956): 95–96.

24. Most of the information that I have about the Parry case at the University of Buffalo comes from two unpublished manuscripts. One, Peter H. Hare and Edward H. Madden, "Buffalo in the McCarthy Era: A Case History," has used the actual tapes and transcripts of the faculty committee which handled the Parry case; the other, Robby Cohen, "Professor William Parry, HUAC, and the University of Buffalo: A Case Study in Repression," 1976, contains much excellent oral history material. Hare and Madden, 3–5; Cohen, 11, 19–23.

25. Cohen, "Professor William Parry," 13–14, 18; Hare and Madden, "Buffalo in the McCarthy Era," 12; William Parry, testimony, HUAC, May 19, 1953, 83rd Cong., 1st sess. The text of Parry's letter is on p. 1529.

26. Cohen, "Professor William Parry," 18–20, 29–33; Hare and Madden, "Buffalo in the McCarthy Era," 6–14.

27. Hare and Madden, "Buffalo in the McCarthy Era," 14–15, Cohen, "Professor William Parry," 34–36.

28. Cohen, "Professor William Parry," 38; American Civil Liberties Union, Niagara Frontier Branch, "Statement on the Parry Case," n.d., ACLU, General Correspondence, 1953, Vol. 7.

29. Robert W. Iversen, *The Communists and the Schools* (New York: Harcourt, Brace and Company, 1959), 248, 342–3; Arthur C. Cole to Howard Bevis, June 9, 1948, ACLU, General Correspondence, 1948, Vol. 1; Robert E. Mathews to Arthur C. Cole, July 16, 1952, ACLU, General Correspondence, 1953, Vol. 6. Lewis C. Branscomb to John Cooper et al., July 10, 1952; Marston G. Hamlin to Ralph Himstead, July 14, 1952; both in "Com A–Ohio State Univ.–Hamlin, M. A.," AAUP Archives.

30. Iversen, *The Communists and the Schools*, 342–43; Joseph Forer, interview with the author, March 31, 1978; Byron Darling, testimony, HUAC, March 13, 1953, 83rd Cong., 1st sess., 133–34, 136, 145–46, 150, June 17, 782. (HUAC had two cooperative witnesses who testified that Darling had been in the CP; it recalled Darling and his wife, as well, for another hearing on June 17. Robert H. Bush, testimony, HUAC, May 25, 1953, cited in Darling, hearing, June 17, 1953, 83rd Cong., 1st sess., 1804–10; Charles Gainor, testimony, May 27, 1953, cited in Darling, hearing, June 17, 1953, 1806–10.)

31. Glass et al., "Academic Freedom in the Quest for National Security," *AAUP Bulletin*, 81–83; James C. Paradise, "Statement by the Cincinnati Chapter of the A.C.L.U.," May 18, 1953, ACLU, General Correspondence, 1953, Vol. 6; "Transcript of Closed Hearing of the Case of Byron Thorwell Darling before President Howard L. Bevis, April 2 and 4, 1953," "Com A–Ohio State Univ.–Darling 1953," AAUP Archives.

32. All of the information that I have on the Barrows Dunham case comes from the invaluable work of Fred Zimring. His research is so thorough and exemplary that I did not try to replicate it. For a more detailed discussion of the Dunham case, therefore, see Fred Richard Zimring, "Academic Freedom and the Cold War: The Dismissal of Barrows Dunham from Temple University: A Case Study" (Ed.D. diss., Columbia University Teachers College, 1981), 159, 162, 188, 192. See also, Barrows Dunham, testimony, HUAC, Feb. 27, 1953, 83rd Cong., 1st sess., 117–19.

33. Zimring, "Academic Freedom," 191–92.

34. FBI memorandum, March 5, 1953, cited in Zimring, "Academic Freedom," 208–9.

35. For an account of Johnson's problems with McCarthy, see Martin Merson, *The Private Diary of a Public Servant* (New York: Macmillan, 1955); Zimring, "Academic Freedom," 237–46.

36. Zimring, "Academic Freedom," 247–48, 271.

37. The text of the Temple trustees' statement of Sept. 23, 1953, is in Zimring, "Academic Freedom," 278–79.

38. For a discussion of the constitutional issues involved in Dunham's case, see Thomas I. Emerson, David Haber, and Norman Dorsen, *Political and Civil Rights in the United States*, 3rd ed. (Boston: Little, Brown, 1967), 1:404; Beck, *Contempt of Congress*, 102. See also Daniel H. Pollitt, "The Fifth Amendment Plea before Congressional Committees Investigating Subversion: Motives and Justifiable Presumptions—A Survey of 120 Witnesses," *University of Pennsylvania Law Review* 106 (1958); and Leonard G. Ratner, "Consequences of Exercising the Privilege against Self-Incrimination," *University of Chicago Law Review* 24 (1957).

39. Kamin, interview.

40. Lewis Webster Jones to Harold Taylor, Jan. 5, 1953, Jones Papers, Box 145–2; Hare and Madden, "Buffalo in the McCarthy Era," 14; Taylor, *Grand Inquest*, 208–9; Committee on Faculty Responsibilities, memorandum to members of the [MIT] faculty, Feb. 24, 1953 (the copy I used was in the Cornell University Archives, 11/1/895).

41. Frank Oppenheimer, testimony, HUAC, June 14, 1949, 81st Cong., 1st sess., 355–73. David Hawkins, a philosopher at the University of Colorado and a former administrator at Los Alamos, also talked about himself, but not about others. David Hawkins, testimony, HUAC, Dec. 20, 1950, 81st Cong., 2nd sess., 3417–52. See also, Daniel Pollitt, "Pleading the Fifth Amendment Before A Congressional Committee: A Study and Explanation," *Notre Dame Lawyer* 32 (1956): 69n.

   As far as I can tell, the following academics talked about themselves, but not others: Lawrence Arguimbau, Bernard Deutch, Wendell Furry, Irving Goldman, David Hawkins, Donald Horton, Leon Kamin, Abraham Keller, Robert Metcalf, Philip Morrison, Frank Oppenheimer, and Marcus Singer.

42. Harold Taylor, interview; Sarah Lawrence College trustees' statement in the *New York Times*, Jan. 23, 1953.

43. Harold Taylor, interview; Esther Raushenbush, transcript of interview, April 12, 1973, Columbia Oral History Project, 453–71; Helen Lynd, interview with the author, Oct. 20, 1978; ms. notes on Sarah Lawrence hearings, n.d., Arthur Sutherland Papers, Harvard Law School Archives.

44. Irving Goldman, testimony, SISS, April 1, 1953, 83rd Cong., 1st sess., 737.

45. Harold Taylor, interview; Esther Raushenbush, interview; Louis Joughin, memorandum to Walter Gellhorn, Sept. 17, 1953, ACLU, General Correspondence, 1953, Vol. 4; Board of Trustees of Sarah Lawrence College to the Students, Faculty, and Alumnae Council, April 21, 1953, in A. Whitney Griswold Papers, Box 4, Folder 24, Yale University Archives.

46. For a discussion of the legal issues involved, see Emerson, Haber, and Dorsen, *Political and Civil Rights*, 405–14.

47. Lawrence Arguimbau, testimony, HUAC, April 21, 1953, 83rd Cong., 1st sess., 4014; Isadore Amdur, testimony, HUAC, April 22, 1953, 83rd Cong., 1st sess., 1048–49; Norman Levinson, testimony, HUAC, April 23, 1953, 83rd Cong., 1st sess., 1075–77; William Ted Martin, testimony, April 22, 1953, 83rd Cong., 1st sess., 1017–18.
48. Philip Morrison, interview with the author, Dec. 22, 1977; Morrison, testimony, SISS, May 7, 1953, 83rd Cong., 1st sess.; Marcus Singer, questionnaire response, Paul Tillett Files, Seeley G. Mudd Library, Princeton University; Mika Salpeter, interview with the author, Oct. 15, 1979.
49. Marcus Singer, testimony, HUAC, May 26, 1953, 83rd Cong., 1st sess., 1539, 1544–45, May 27, 1953, 1552, 1561–63.
50. Singer, questionnaire response, Tillett Files. Cornell University, press release, Nov. 22, 1954; Policy Committee, minutes, Jan. 26, 1955, in 11/1/895; both in Cornell University Archives.
51. Memorandum of conference called by the president, May 19, 1956, 11/1/895, Cornell University Archives.
   Pollitt's other case, *Watkins v. United States*, was a milestone Supreme Court decision in which the Court finally overturned a contempt conviction on the grounds of pertinency. See Emerson, Haber, and Dorsen, *Political and Civil Rights*, 356–72; Beck, *Contempt of Congress*, 135, 161, 169–70.
52. Singer, questionnaire response, Tillett Files.

VIII: "The Slow Treatment"

1. H. Chandler Davis, testimony, Aug. 11, 1954, in "Proceedings, Appeal Hearing before the Senate Subcommittee on Intellectual Freedom and Integrity," 61, in Box 21, Marvin L. Niehuss Papers, Michigan Historical Collections, Bentley Historical Library, University of Michigan (hereafter cited as Appeal); Chandler Davis, testimony, HUAC, May 10, 1954, 83rd Cong., 2nd sess., 5349.
2. H. Chandler Davis, interview with the author, Feb. 21, 1978.
3. Davis, testimony, HUAC, 5366; Davis, testimony, "Proceedings at a Meeting of the Special Advisory Committee to the President," 6:12, in Box 21, Niehuss Papers (hereafter cited as Proceedings).
4. "Behind Bars for the First Amendment," n.d., pamphlet in the private papers of H. Chandler Davis; Davis, interview. For the partial text of the Barenblatt decision, *Barenblatt v. United States*, 360 U.S. 109 S. Ct. 1081, 3 L. Ed. 2d 1115 (1959), and a discussion of its importance, see Thomas I. Emerson, David Haber, and Norman Dorsen, *Political and Civil Rights in the United States*, 3rd ed. (Boston: Little, Brown, 1967), 1:378–79.
5. Davis, interview.
6. Hatcher, telegram to Harold J. Velde, Jan. 9, 1953; Hatcher to the Members of the Council of Ten, Jan. 2, 1953; both in Niehuss Papers, Box 21, File "House Un-American Activities Committee." Hatcher statement, in Proceedings, 7:117. For a more detailed discussion of the revision of Michigan's by-laws, see pp. 181–82 above; see also Report of the Joint Committee on Demotion and Dismissal Procedures, Box 21, Niehuss Papers.
7. Kenneth O'Reilly, *Hoover and the Un-Americans* (Philadelphia: Temple University Press, 1983), 242; Carl Beck, *Contempt of Congress* (New

Orleans: Hauser Press, 1959), 106; Minutes, Executive Committee, May 5, 1954, Box 96, College of Literature, Science and the Arts Papers, Michigan Historical Collections.

8. Clement Markert, interview with the author, May 30, 1978; Davis, interview.

9. Julius H. Comroe, Jr., to Harlan Hatcher, May 21, 1954, "Letters in re Markert, Davis," Box 21, Niehuss Papers.

10. Proceedings, 1:30–32, 2:32, 77–82, 3:6; Markert, interview.

11. Report to Special Advisory Committee to the President, June 7, 1953, Box 21, Niehuss Papers.

12. A. C. Furstenberg to Hatcher, June 11, 1954, "List of Contents," Box 21, Niehuss Papers.

13. Harlan Hatcher, "President's Report to the University Senate on the Procedures and Actions Involving Three Members of the University Faculty," Oct. 5, 1954, 6 (hereafter cited as President's Report); "Report of the Special Advisory Committee to the President," July 5, 1954, 5 (hereafter cited as SAC Report); both in Box 21, Niehuss Papers.

14. President's Report, 2; "Report and Recommendation of the Subcommittee on Intellectual Freedom and Integrity of the Senate Advisory Committee on University Affairs," Aug. 16, 1954, 7–8, Box 21, Niehuss Papers (hereafter cited as Intellectual Freedom Report); Proceedings, 2:31, 5–1:89, 7:69.

15. Proceedings, 6:20, 7:74, 5–1:25.

16. Undated memorandum, "Working Materials," Box 21, Niehuss Papers; SAC Report, 19.

17. Proceedings, 4:9, 8:31–37; SAC, Detroit to Director, FBI, Aug. 6, 1954, in Clement Markert, FBI files.

18. Proceedings, 5–1:57, 89, 5–2:141–42, 159.

19. Hatcher, memorandum, "To the Subcomittee on Intellectual Freedom and Integrity," Aug. 6, 1954, "List of Contents," Box 21, Niehuss Papers; President's Report, 16–17.

20. Proceedings, 1:48–49, 5–1:103.

21. Proceedings, 5–2:121; President's Report, 15.

22. SAC Report, 6, 16.

23. Markert testimony, Proceedings, 7:88–90; Markert, interview.

24. Proceedings, 6:20–21; Appeal, 90.

25. Appeal, 70; Proceedings, 6:23.

26. Appeal, 23; Proceedings, 6:67–70, 96–104.

27. Proceedings, 6:57–59, 67, 101.

28. Appeal, 61–62, 80; SAC Report, 18, 29.

29. Intellectual Freedom Report, 11, 13.

30. President's Report, 10–11.

31. For more information about the AAU statement, see pp. 187–91 above. Report of the Committee on Privilege and Tenure, Northern Section, June 13, 1950, 5–6, in the private papers of Stefan Peters.

32. "The University of Kansas City," *AAUP Bulletin* 43, No. 1A (April 1957): 177–95; "Statement Regarding the Case of Dr. Horace B. Davis," undated mimeographed copy of the University of Kansas City's official report, in ACLU, General Correspondence, 1954, Vol. 7; Horace B. Davis, interview with the author, July 3, 1979.

33. "The University of Kansas City," *AAUP Bulletin;* "Statement Regarding the Case of Dr. Horace B. Davis," ACLU.

34. Edward [sic] Burgum, testimony, SISS, Oct. 13, 1952, 82nd Cong., 2nd sess., 270–77; "Academic Freedom & New York University: The Case of Professor Edwin Berry Burgum" (New York, 1954), 19–24, 38. (This is a privately printed pamphlet published by the Committee for the Reinstatement of Professor Burgum. I have seen several copies, some in private collections, some in academic ones.) See also "New York University," *AAUP Bulletin* 44, No. 1 (Spring 1958): 37–39; Hollis Cooley, "Memorandum on meeting with Carr, Brown, and Smith of Com. A.," Jan. 18, 1957, in "Special Committee, 1955–1958 New York Univ.–Bradley & Burgum," AAUP Archives; Chancellor Henry T. Heald to Burgum, Oct. 13, 1952, in James W. Armsey Papers, Box R63, Folder 19, New York University Archives. (Armsey was in charge of public relations for NYU. Though his papers are open to scholars, the University's official archives are not.)

35. "Academic Freedom & New York University," 24–27; "New York University," *AAUP Bulletin* 45. On Manning Johnson, see Frank Donner, "The Informer," *The Nation,* April 10, 1954, 305, and Emerson, Haber, and Dorsen, *Political and Civil Rights in the United States,* 1:161–62. The case that Johnson fouled up was *Communist Party v. Subversive Activities Control Board* (1956).

36. "New York University," *AAUP Bulletin,* 48–49; "Academic Freedom & New York University," 37.

37. "New York University," *AAUP Bulletin,* 39; "Academic Freedom & New York University," 69–72; Hollis Cooley, interview with the author, Nov. 4, 1981. Cooley, "Memorandum," Jan. 18, 1957; Robert K. Carr to Edwin Burroughs Smith and Ralph Brown, Feb. 19, 1957; Smith to Carr and Brown, April 14, 1957; all in "Special Committee, 1955–1958 New York Univ.–Bradley & Burgum," AAUP Archives.

38. Stanley Moore, interview with the author, March 3, 1979. Moore, "Open Letter to the President, Trustees, Faculty, Students, and Alumni of Reed College," June 3, 1954; "Hearing before the Board of Trustees of Reed College," Aug. 13, 1954, 40–41, both in private papers of Stanley Moore.

39. Joseph A. Barr to E. B. MacNaughton, July 9, 1951, ACLU, General Correspondence, 1951, Vol. 5, ACLU archives; Grover Sales to author, Feb. 25, 1978.

40. Dorothy O. Johansen (Reed College archivist) to the author, May 3, 1978; Stanley Moore, interview; "Reed College," *AAUP Bulletin* 44, No. 1 (Spring 1958): 110. Richard L. Biggs, Joseph F. Bunnett, Barbara West, "Report to the Reed College Board of Trustees concerning Professor Stanley Moore," Jan. 14, 1978, 11, in author's possession; George Pope Shannon, memo to REH [Himstead], July 14, 1954, "Com. A–Reed College Moore 1954," AAUP Archives.

41. "Reed College," *AAUP Bulletin,* 107–8; J. Keith Mann to Robert K. Carr, April 7, 1958, in "Com. A–Reed College Moore 1954," AAUP Archives.

42. "Reed College," *AAUP Bulletin,* 110; Leonard Marsak, letter to the author, Jan. 22, 1984.

43. Stanley Moore, interview; Moore, "Open Letter," 5.

44. Stanley Moore, "Open Letter," 6.

45. "Hearing," 12–13, 24–27. Stanley Moore to Ralph Himstead, June 23, 1954; Himstead, telegram to Moore, June 29, 1954; both in "Com. A– Reed College Moore 1954," AAUP Archives.

46. "Reed College," *AAUP Bulletin*, 114.

47. Trustees' statement, Aug. 7, 1954, in "Hearing," 58.

48. "Academic Freedom and Tenure in the Quest for National Security," *AAUP Bulletin* 42, No. 1 (Spring 1956): 60; "Statement of Committee on Academic Responsibility at MIT," in "Ninth Interim Report of the Special Commission on Communism, Subversive Activities and Related Matters within the Commonwealth," Commonwealth of Mass., Jan. 18, 1957, 29.

IX: "A Source of Friction"

1. Jane Hodes, interview with the author, April 3, 1980; Robert Hodes, testimony, April 13, 1953, in Transcript of Proceedings, "In the Matter of the Hearing Concerning the Termination of Employment of Dr. Robert Hodes at Tulane University," 202, in AAUP Archives (hereafter cited as Hodes transcript).

2. Robert Hodes to Ralph Himstead, Oct. 16, 1951, in "Comm. A Tulane Univ. Hodes 52," AAUP Archives. Margaret Smith, testimony, April 13, 1953, 28–28b; Hodes, testimony, April 13, 1953, 47–48; Robert Heath, testimony, April 13, 1953, 238; all in Hodes transcript.

3. M. E. Lapham, testimony, Feb. 27, 1953, 25–26; Hodes, testimony, April 13, 1953, 52–55; both in Hodes transcript. M. E. Lapham to Robert Hodes, July 18, 1953, in "Comm. A Tulane Univ. Hodes 52," AAUP Archives.

4. Robert Hodes to Ralph Himstead, Oct. 16, 1952; George Pope Shannon to Hodes, Nov. 20, 1952; Hodes to M. E. Lapham, Dec. 7, 1952; Lapham to Hodes, Dec. 9, 18, 1952; all in "Comm. A Tulane Univ. Hodes 52," AAUP Archives.

5. The University's president seemed particularly concerned about observing the proprieties, and he conducted an extensive correspondence with the AAUP's Washington office about the proper procedures for Hodes's hearing. George Pope Shannon to Rufus Harris, Feb. 3, 12, 1953; GPS [Shannon] memorandum to REH [Himstead], Feb. 18, 1953; both in "Comm. A Tulane Univ. Hodes 52." Robert Heath, testimony, Feb. 27, 1953, 40, April 13, 1953, 230; H. S. Mayerson, testimony, Feb. 27, 1953, 83; Frank R. Ervin, testimony, March 19, 1953, 261; all in Hodes transcript, AAUP Archives.

6. George A. Wilson, Joseph McCloskey, Charles L. Eshleman, Report, n.d., in private papers of Jane Hodes.

7. My research on the firings at Jefferson Medical College cleared up one of the small mysteries of my own childhood. I grew up in Philadelphia and, though I knew none of the affected teachers, Hays Solis Cohen, the trustee who handled the case, was my grandfather's law partner. My mother, a shy but tenaciously principled woman, made her stand on the issue by refusing to have anything to do with the man; she would not even talk to him at family parties. Since she was ordinarily a gracious person, her behavior toward Solis Cohen puzzled me for years, until I found out his role in the Jefferson case.

8. J. L. Kauffman to John Fine [Gov. of Pennsylvania], April 8, 1952, in John Fine Papers, photocopy in personal collection of Fred Zimring; Kenneth O'Reilly, *Hoover and the Un-Americans: The FBI, HUAC, and the Red Menace* (Philadelphia: Temple University Press, 1983), 208; William Pearlman, interview with the author, July 11, 1978; Robert Rutman, interview with the author, Dec. 26, 1977.

9. O'Reilly, *Hoover and the Un-Americans*, 208; Clark Byse, "Academic Freedom: Some recent Philadelphia episodes," ACLU, Greater Philadelphia Branch, n.d., 18; WCM [Warren C. Middleton] to REH [Ralph E. Himstead], July 21, 1953, in "Com. A—Jefferson Medical College, Pearlman, Wagman, Rutman 1953," AAUP Archives. Though Pearlman, Rutman, and Wagman were the only members of the Jefferson faculty who were fired, they were not the only teachers under suspicion. The others—there may have been about six—either cleared themselves or, as in one case I have been told about, resigned "voluntarily."

10. Byse, "Academic Freedom," 18; "The Dismissal of Faculty Members from Jefferson Medical College," mimeographed report by the ACLU, Greater Philadelphia Branch, June 11, 1954, in ACLU, General Correspondence, 1955, Vol. 7.

11. Byse, "Academic Freedom," 19; "Hearing before the Loyalty Committee of The Jefferson Medical College of Philadelphia, in re Dr. Robert J. Rutman," Aug. 4, 1953, typed transcript in private papers of Robert Rutman (hereafter cited as Rutman, "Hearing").

12. Rutman, "Hearing," 34, 36–38; Byse, "Academic Freedom," 20; Ralph Himstead, telegram to Edwin P. Rome, July 31, 1953, in "Com. A—Jefferson Medical College, Pearlman, Wagman, Rutman, 1953," AAUP Archives.

13. Anon. to J. Warren Brock, Sept. 25, 1953; Anon. to J. Warren Brock, Oct. 1, 1953. These letters are from a collection of partially expurgated documents released from the Thomas Jefferson University archives to Fred Zimring by Frederic L. Ballard.

14. Rutman, interview; O'Reilly, *Hoover and the Un-Americans*, 208–9; ACLU, "The Dismissal of Faculty Members"; William H. Pearlman to Ralph E. Himstead, Nov. 23, 1953, in "Com. A.—Jefferson Medical College," AAUP Archives.

15. Byse, "Academic Freedom," 22; Receipt and Release, Robert J. Rutman, Ph.D., to The Jefferson Medical College of Philadelphia et al., Jan. 20, 1954, in private papers of Robert Rutman; "Academic Freedom and Tenure in the Quest for National Security," *AAUP Bulletin* 42, No. 1 (Spring 1956); Robert J. Rutman to Himstead, Dec. 7, 1953, in "Com. A—Jefferson Medical College," AAUP Archives.

16. George Packer Berry to Helen W. Deane, June 15, 1953, private papers of George Markham. SAC, Detroit to Director, FBI, Aug. 6, 1954, in Clement Markert's FBI file in the personal possession of Markert, cites a Michigan informant as stating, "MARKERT has one additional year on his contract, and the University proposes to allow his employment to cease at that time."

17. See pp. 147, 182–83 above; Alice Thorner, interview with the author, March 16, 1979; Irving Kravis, transcript of interview, Feb. 4, 1980, Barrows Dunham/Fred Zimring Oral History Collection, Temple University; Daniel Thorner to Thomas Cochran, Sept. 18, 1953, UPT 50. C663,

Thomas C. Cochran Papers, Box 1, General Correspondence, 1953, University of Pennsylvania Archives.

18. Robert MacIver, *Academic Freedom in Our Time* (New York: Columbia University Press, 1955), 295–98. Morris A. Judd to Robert L. Stearns, May 8, 1951; Edward J. Machle, statement, n.d. [probably April, 1952]; Henry W. Ehrmann and Morris E. Garnsey, minority report, May 20, 1952; all in "Com A—Colorado, Univ.—Judd," AAUP Archives.

19. The committee majority which sustained the administration contained no professors in the liberal arts. Its rather strained verdict, that Judd's dismissal did not violate academic freedom, refused to consider the obvious, including the statement of the one dissenter on the Board of Regents that "there has been no representation that the man is not academically fit or that his academic work has been in any way unsatisfactory" and that "if this man is guilty of any act or omission that calls for his discharge, we should have proof of it, not merely a repetition of the accusations of anonymous accusers." Henry W. Ehrmann and Morris E. Garnsey, minority report, and Archibald R. Buchanan et al., majority report, May 19, 1952, both in "Com A—Colorado, Univ.—Judd," AAUP Archives; "University of Colorado Situation: Judd Case," ms. memorandum (for the AAUP's Committee A) in Talcott Parsons, Correspondence and Related Papers, ca. 1930–59, Box 2, Harvard University Archives.

20. Draft of Mr. Wiggin's letter to Sen. Taft, Jan. 8, 1953, Records of President A. Whitney Griswold, Box 137, Folder 1246, Yale University Archives; Vern Countryman, interview with the author, Dec. 8, 1976.

21. Jerold S. Auerbach, *Unequal Justice* (New York: Oxford University Press, 1977), 234–37; Percival R. Bailey, "The Case of the National Lawyers Guild, 1939–1958," in Athan G. Theoharis, ed., *Beyond the Hiss Case* (Philadelphia: Temple University Press, 1982), 146–48, 171–72n. F. H. Wiggin to Sturgis Warner, June 12, 1953, Griswold Papers, Box 2, Folder 11, notes that Emerson was subpoenaed by Jenner. He did not, however, testify in public at that time.

22. F. H. Wiggin to Robert Taft, Jan. 8, 1953; "Bob" [Robert Stevens] to Griswold, Aug. 21, 1951; both in Griswold Papers, Box 137, Folder 1246. Box 137, Folder 1246 is entirely devoted to correspondence about Emerson; Folder 1247 contains correspondence about Fowler Harper, another civil libertarian on the Law School faculty.

23. Thomas I. Emerson, transcript of interview, 2274–76, Columbia University Oral History Project; Emerson, interview with the author, Nov. 16, 1977. Griswold to Ralph Brown, Sept. 25, 1951; Griswold to J. M. Hilbish, Jan. 17, 1951; both in Griswold Papers, Box 137, Folder 1246. .

24. Charles F. Clise to Reuben A. Holden, Dec. 1, 1953, Griswold Papers, Box 2, Folder 14; Wesley A. Sturges to A. Whitney Griswold, Jan. 10, 1955, Griswold Papers, Box 2, Folder 15.

25. "Countryman," memorandum, Nov. 25, 1953, Griswold Papers, Box 2, Folder 14; Harry Shulman to Melvin Gittleman, Jan. 10, 1955, Griswold Papers, Box 2, Folder 15.

26. Emerson, interview; Countryman, interview. Fred Rodell to Harry Shulman, Jan. 3, 1955; Minutes of the Meeting of the Board of Permanent Officers of the Yale Law School, Jan. 13, 1955; both in Griswold Papers, Box 2, Folder 15. Countryman quoted in Association of American Law Schools,

"Report of the Committee on Academic Freedom and Tenure," n.d., ACLU, General Correspondence, 1955, Vol. 7.

27. Lawrence Klein, testimony, HUAC, April 30, 1954, 83rd Cong. 2nd sess., 4991-5001; Lawrence Klein, transcript of interview with Fred Zimring, Jan. 25, 1980, Barrows Dunham/Fred Zimring Oral History Collection, Temple University. Gardner Ackley, "Proposal for the Appointment of Dr. Lawrence R. Klein as Professor of Economics, Beginning with Academic Year 1955–56," Jan. 13, 1955; Gardner Ackley to Dean and Executive Committee, March 18, 1955; both in Marvin L. Niehuss Papers, Box 4, Folder "Lawrence Klein," Michigan Historical Collections, Bentley Historical Library.

28. Gardner Ackley to Dean, March 18, 1955; W. A. Paton to M. L. Niehuss, Aug. 2, 1955; "Lawrence Klein," undated memorandum; Niehuss to Lawrence Klein, Nov. 14, 1955; "Larry" to Gardner Ackley, Dec. 9, 1955; all in Niehuss Papers, Box 5, Folder "Lawrence Klein."

29. Klein, interview with Fred Zimring. The only other case I know of where a friendly witness had trouble with his school occurred at American University. There the unfortunate teacher, an ex-Communist law school professor named Herbert Fuchs, had been sacked, despite his willingness to give names to HUAC, because the University president claimed, "I don't feel a man with that kind of background should be teaching in the University." Clark Byse to American Association of Law Schools Committee on Academic Freedom and Tenure, Oct. 25, 1955, "Committee A General 1955," AAUP Archives.

30. George Pegram to Arthur N. Dusenbury, Oct., 1949, Grayson Kirk Papers, Columbia University Archives, Low Library, File "Gene Weltfish."

31. "Memorandum concerning Dr. Gene Weltfish," n.d., Grayson Kirk Papers, File "Gene Weltfish."

32. Ibid. Louis M. Hacker to Grayson Kirk, Dec. 18, 1952; memorandum, RCH, April 3, 1953; both in Kirk Papers, File "Gene Weltfish." *Counterattack*, March 27, 1953.

33. Using the Freedom of Information Act, scholars have begun to penetrate some of the secrecy around the FBI. Athan Theoharis has been the most tenacious, and his analyses of FBI operating methods and filing procedures are invaluable guides to the way in which J. Edgar Hoover ran his organization. See Athan G. Theoharis, *Spying on Americans: Political Surveillance from Hoover to the Huston Plan* (Philadelphia: Temple University Press, 1978) and Theoharis, ed., *Beyond the Hiss Case*. See also O'Reilly, *Hoover and the Un-Americans*.

34. Frank J. Donner, *The Age of Surveillance* (New York: Knopf, 1980), 110–11, 117–25, 138–47, 177–80; Theoharis, *Spying on Americans*, 133–37, 156–68. O'Reilly, *Hoover and the Un-Americans*, 75–100, 168–93, indicates that the FBI may actually have had a major hand in shaping the liberals' view of the Bureau. George E. Sokolsky to Grayson Kirk, Dec. 1, 1953, in Kirk Papers, "Dr. Harry Grundfest" file.

35. O'Reilly, *Hoover and the Un-Americans*, 207–10. Fred Zimring, "Academic Freedom and the Cold War: The Dismissal of Barrows Dunham from Temple University: A Case Study" (Ed. D. diss., Columbia University Teachers College, 1981), 209, cites an FBI memorandum of March 5, 1953.

36. Undated memorandum, "Norman Cazden," in private papers of Norman Cazden; Norman Cazden, interview with the author, June 9, 1978; Courtney Cazden, interview with the author, May 1, 1981.
37. Saul Maloff, interview with the author, Jan. 29, 1978. Maloff to Ralph Himstead, April 9, 1954, in Indiana Chapter, AAUP, "Committee Report regarding Saul Maloff," n.d.; Herman B. Wells to Himstead, Dec. 30, 1954, in "Com A Indiana Univ. Maloff 54"; both in AAUP Archives.
38. Office Memorandum, SAC, New York to Director FBI, May 10, 1955, in Robert K. Bedell, FBI file. William A. Vopat to Robert Bedell, May 13, 1958; Eugene J. Saletan, memorandum on conversation with Bertram Davis, May 4, 1958; Robert K. Bedell, "Confidential" memorandum, n.d. All in private papers of Robert K. Bedell.
39. Sigmund Diamond, "Veritas at Harvard," *New York Review of Books,* April 28, 1977.
40. Everett Mendelsohn, interview with the author, Nov. 15, 1977; McGeorge Bundy, interview with the author, Dec. 29, 1977.
41. Sydney James to the author, Oct. 24, 1977.
42. Bundy, interview; James to the author.
43. Diamond, "Veritas"; Diamond, interview with the author, Oct. 11, 1977. SAC, Boston, to Director, FBI, April 23, 1954; SAC, Boston to Director, FBI, July 27, 1954; both in Sigmund Diamond's FBI files.
44. Robert Bellah, "To the Editors," *New York Review of Books,* July 14, 1977; McGeorge Bundy to Nathan Pusey, April 27, 1955, in private papers of Robert Bellah; Robert Bellah, interview with the author, Aug. 25, 1977.
45. Talcott Parsons, memorandum to Faculty Advisory Committee on Academic Freedom and Tenure, May 23, 1955, Talcott Parsons Papers, Correspondence and Related Papers, 1930–59, Box 5, Harvard University Archives; Bellah, "To the Editors"; Bundy to Pusey, April 27, 1955; Bundy, "To the Editors," *New York Review of Books,* July 14, 1977; Bundy, interview with the author.
46. Parsons, memorandum, May 23, 1955; Bellah, interview; Bundy to Pusey, April 27, 1955.

X: "A Very Difficult Time of It"

1. Helen Deane Markham to Betty, Nov. 5, 1953; E. B. Astwood to Helen Wendler Deane, March 17, 1954; Louis B. Flexner to Helen Wendler Deane, March 17, 1954; Keith R. Porter to Helen Wendler Deane, March 15, 1954; Helen Wendler Deane to Keith Porter, March 10, 1954; all in private papers of Helen Deane Markham in the possession of George Markham.
2. "Subversive Influence in the Educational Process," Report of the Subcommittee to Investigate the Administration of the Internal Security Act and other Internal Security Laws to the Committee on the Judiciary, U.S. Senate, 83rd Cong., 1st sess., July 17, 1953; Robert W. Iversen, *The Communists and the Schools* (New York: Harcourt, Brace and Co., 1959), 245–47; Jane Sanders, *Cold War on the Campus: Academic Freedom at the University of Washington, 1946–64* (Seattle: University of Washington Press, 1979), 212; memorandum to the members of the Listening Post

(re Dec. 8, 1954, meeting with staff of Joint Committee on Internal Revenue Taxation), in A. Whitney Griswold Papers, Box 2, Folder 18, Yale University Archives.

3. For an overview of academic hiring practices during the height of the blacklist period, 1954–56, see Theodore Caplow and Reece J. McGee, *The Academic Marketplace* (New York: 1958, Anchor Press/Doubleday ed., 1965). For some reason, though Caplow and McGee allude to the political situation of the period, they do not discuss it at length. Anon., interview with the author, Jan. 25, 1979.

4. Sanders, *Cold War on the Campus*, 89–90, 104–12.

5. Robert Heilman to Henry Schmitz, July 18, 1952, cited in Sanders, *Cold War on the Campus*, 108–9.

6. Ibid., 119–21, 126–51.

7. Lyman Bradley and Herbert Phillips questionnaire responses, Paul Tillett Files, Seeley G. Mudd Library, Princeton University. Joseph Butterworth to Ralph M. Park, Oct. 19, 1949, in "Com. A—Univ. of Washington Butterworth, Phillips and Cook," AAUP Archives.

8. Alice Thorner, interview with the author, March 16, 1979; William Pearlman, interview with the author, July 11, 1978.

9. Dwight J. Ingle to Helen W. Deane, March 16, 1954; David Glick to Helen W. Deane, May 10, 1954; both in private papers of Helen Deane Markham. Leonard Marsak, questionnaire response, Tillett Files; Vera Shlakman, interview with the author, March 28, 1979.

10. Phillips, questionnaire response, Tillett Files; Chandler Davis, interview with the author, Feb. 21, 1978; Chandler Davis to W. L. Duren et al., June 30, 1958, in private papers of Chandler Davis; Caplow and McGee, *The Academic Marketplace*, 181–87.

11. Leonard Marsak, questionnaire response, Tillett Files; Jules Chametzky, interview with the author, April 5, 1978; Thomas McGrath, questionnaire response, Tillett Files.

12. Caplow and McGee, *The Academic Marketplace*, 108–9; Dwight J. Ingle to Helen W. Deane, March 16, 1954, Markham papers.

13. Gardner Ackley to Ralph A. Sawyer, Dec. 13, 1954, Marvin L. Niehuss Papers, Box 4, Folder "S", Michigan Historical Collections, Bentley Historical Library, University of Michigan. In an unpublished ms. about the historical profession, Peter Novick of the University of Chicago notes additional evidence for the obligation senior professors felt they had to warn colleagues about the political problems of people they were recommending.

14. "Reed College," *AAUP Bulletin* 44, No. 1 (March 1958): 103; Fred Richard Zimring, "Academic Freedom and the Cold War: The Dismissal of Barrows Dunham from Temple University: A Case Study" (Ed.D. diss., Columbia University Teachers College, 1981), 354–58; Saul Maloff, interview with the author, Jan. 29, 1978.

15. "Academic Freedom and Tenure: Lowell Technological Institute," *AAUP Bulletin* 45, No. 4 (Dec. 1959): 553.

16. Chandler Davis to W. L. Duren, Jr., et al., June 30, 1958, in Davis papers; Peter A. Carmichael to Barrows Dunham, Jan. 18, 1958, in Zimring, "Academic Freedom and the Cold War," 355.

17. Martin Kamen, interview with the author, April 4, 1980; Frank Oppen-

heimer, questionnaire response, Tillett Files; Frank Oppenheimer, interview with Charles Weiner, Feb. 9, 1973, American Institute of Physics, Center for History of Physics; Robert Bacher to J. Robert Oppenheimer, May 23, 1950, J. Robert Oppenheimer Papers, case file, Box 18, Library of Congress; Sanders, *Cold War on the Campus*, 132; Kenneth Bainbridge, interview with the author, June 8, 1978; Minutes of Deans' Conference, Sept. 27, 1949, de Kewiet Papers, Folder 1–059, Cornell University Archives.

18. Knight Biggerstaff, interview with the author, Oct. 1, 1979. F. S. Marcham, ms. note, n.d., also draft letter, unsigned, April 21, 1958, in 14/17/846; Knight Biggerstaff to Theodore Taylor, Jan. 13, 1958; Edward W. Fox to Dean Herbert T. Woodward, Jan. 14, 1958; Subcommittee on the Finley Case, Report, May 30, 1958; all in Dean of the Faculty Papers, Box 3, File "Finley Case," Cornell University Archives.

19. Dale Corson, interview with the author, Jan. 25, 1979. Department of History to University Faculty Committee on Academic Freedom and Tenure, May 23, 1958; Subcommittee on the Finley Case, Report, May 30, 1958; both in Dean of the Faculty Papers, Box 3, File "Finley Case."

20. Norman Levinson, testimony, HUAC, April 23, 1953, 83rd Cong., 1st sess., 1090–95; E. E. Moise, interview with the author, April 15, 1978.

21. Edward U. Condon, transcript of interview with Charles Weiner, Sept. 11, 1973, American Institute of Physics, 48–59.

22. Condon, interview, 85–96.

23. Condon, interview, 97–100; Melba Phillips, interview with the author, May 12, 1978.

24. Richard H. Shryock to Lawrence Rosinger, Jan. 14, 1949, in UPB 1.9H #78, "Rosinger, Lawrence K.," University of Pennsylvania Archives.

25. Richard H. Shryock to Dirk Bodde, March 24, 1949; Shryock to Rosinger, March 8, 1949; both in "Rosinger, Lawrence K.," University of Pennsylvania Archives.

26. Richard B. Scudder to H. Alexander Smith, Nov. 12, 1952, Box 145–1, Lewis Webster Jones Papers, Rutgers University Archives. Kenneth O'Reilly, *Hoover and the Un-Americans* (Philadelphia: Temple University Press, 1983), 126–29, discusses how the FBI tried to conceal what it was doing.

27. Max Bluestone, interview with the author, Aug. 4, 1980; Rufus Mathewson, interview with the author, May 25, 1978; Martin Kaplan, interview with the author, July 31, 1982.

28. Harlan Hatcher to Homer Ferguson, May 28, 1953; Ferguson to Hatcher, June 17, 1953; both in Hatcher Papers, Box 7, Folder 8, Michigan Historical Collections, Bentley Historical Library, University of Michigan. SAC, Boston to Director, FBI, June 19, 1950, FBI 66-2542-3-5-852; SAC, Boston to Director, FBI, Aug. 28, 1950, FBI 66-2542-3-5-893 (these documents are in the FBI files in the personal possession of Sigmund Diamond).

29. W. Bruce Dayton, interview with the author, April 4, 1980. FBI documents 65-59336 (Nov. 10, 1950) and 65-59336-29; C. D. DeLoach to Mr. Mohr, Nov. 14, 1963, FBI 100-335070-32 (these documents are in W. Bruce Dayton's FBI file, which is part of the collection of FBI files

relating to the Rosenberg case in the possession of Marshall Perlin, the attorney for the Rosenberg's sons, Michael and Robert Meeropol, hereafter cited as Dayton FBI Files).

For a detailed discussion of the possible espionage career of Alfred Sarant, see Ronald Radosh and Joyce Milton, *The Rosenberg File* (New York: Holt, Rinehart & Winston, 1983), 110–16. Recently, it appears, Sarant, whom even the FBI probably gave up for lost, had managed to reach the Soviet Union, where until his death in 1978 he worked as an engineer under the name of Filipp Staros. Mark Kuchment, "Beyond the Rosenbergs: A New View from Russia," *Boston Review* (Sept. 1985).

30. Dayton, interview; Corson, interview. Weldon B. Dayton, HQ File #65-59336, Nov. 10, 1950; telegram, July 2, 1952, 65-59336-131; memorandum, June 13, 1952, 65-59336-109; SA Lawrence F. Munley to SAC, Buffalo, June 26, 1952, 65-2007-19; Alexander L. Gucker to SAC, June 18, 1952, 65-1676-112; all in Dayton FBI Files.

31. SAC, memorandum, Aug. 11, 1950; memorandum, Nov. 10, 1950, 65-59336-24; telegram, July 2, 1952, 65-59336-131; Alexander L. Gucker to SAC, June 18, 1952, 65-1676-112; memorandum, Peter G. Roth, Jr., SA, March 11, 1953; Report of conversation with Vice Chancellor Finla [sic] Crawford, March 17, 1953, 65-59336-184; SAC, Mobile to Hoover, Oct. 9, 1953, 65-59336-198; Hoover to SAC, Mobile, Oct. 30, 1953 (document no. unclear); Report of interview with president of FSU, Nov. 17, 1953, 65-59336-v; all in Dayton FBI Files.

32. Dayton, interview. Report of conversation with Dayton, Aug. 20, 1952, 65-59336-151; SAC, Denver to SAC, NY, May 11, 1953, 65-15403-203; Report of conversation with personnel manager at Corning, Dec. 3, 1953, 65-59336-211; all in Dayton FBI Files.

33. Richard E. Combs, testimony, SISS, March 19, 1953, 83rd Cong. 1st sess., 607.

34. Combs, testimony, SISS, 607-8, 610, 616; Sigmund Diamond, "McCarthyism on Campus," *The Nation*, Sept. 19, 1981, 240.

35. Diamond, "McCarthyism on Campus," 240; Combs, testimony, SISS, 607, 609, 611–12, 615; Edward L. Barrett, Jr., *The Tenney Committee* (Ithaca: Cornell University Press, 1951), 17, 137–45, 157.

36. Leon Wofsy, interview with the author, April 12, 1980.

37. Leon Wofsy to Daniel H. Murray, Dec. 20, 1963; Wofsy to Clifford C. Furnas, Dec. 24, 1963; both in private papers of Leon Wofsy.

38. David Halliday to Leon Wofsy, June 3, July 13, 1954, in Wofsy Papers.

39. Wofsy, interview; Leon Wofsy to *San Francisco Chronicle*, June 20, 1965.

XI: "Not Much Fun"

1. Herbert Phillips and Lyman Bradley, questionnaire responses, Tillett Files, Seeley G. Mudd Library, Princeton University; Bonnie Bird (Gundlach), interview with the author, April 15, 1982.

2. Abraham Keller, taped response to letter from the author, n.d., 1978; Keller, testimony, HUAC, June 18, 1954, 83rd Cong., 2nd sess., 6468, 6474, 6478–80.

3. Bernard Riess, interview with the author, March 28, 1979; Ralph Gundlach

to "Dear Friends," Nov. 12, 1950, in J. Robert Oppenheimer Papers, Box 36, Library of Congress; Gundlach, notes on interview, Tillett Files; Bonnie Bird (Gundlach), interview.

4. Harry Slochower, interview with the author, Dec. 29, 1980; Edwin Berry Burgum, questionnaire response, Tillett Files.

5. Oscar Shaftel, interview with the author, April 13, 1978; Shaftel, questionnaire response. Tillett Files.

6. Saul Maloff, interview with the author, Jan. 29, 1978; Tom McGrath, questionnaire response, Tillett Files; McGrath to the author, May 19, 1979. McGrath, by the way, had trouble publishing his own work. It was too controversial.

7. Iven Hurlinger, testimony, SISS, May 13, 1953, 83rd Cong., 1st sess., 967–72, 976–78; Lewis Balamuth, testimony, SISS (printed as an insert in the Hurlinger testimony), May 12, 1953, 83rd Cong., 1st sess., 949–981; Lloyd Motz, interview with Marvin E. Gettleman, Nov. 16, 1977; Clarence Hiskey, interview with the author, July 27, 1980; Irving Stein to the author, May 12, 1978; Joseph W. Weinberg to J. Robert Oppenheimer, April 17, 1953, Oppenheimer Papers, case file, Box 77, Library of Congress; Daniel Kevles, *The Physicists* (New York: Knopf, 1978), 370.

8. Chandler Davis, interview with the author, Feb. 21, 1978; Giovanni Rossi Lomanitz, questionnaire response, Tillett Files; Lomanitz, interview with Martin Sherwin, July 11, 1979; J. J. Reynolds to J. Robert Oppenheimer, Dec. 31, 1953, Oppenheimer Papers, case file, Box 47.

9. Frank Oppenheimer, transcript of interview with Charles Weiner, American Institute of Physicists; Kenneth Bainbridge, interview with the author, June 8, 1978; Barrows Dunham, questionnaire response, Tillett Files; Lomanitz, Tillett Files; Phillips, Tillett Files; Dudley Strauss, interview with the author, July 1, 1982.

10. Bonnie Bird (Gundlach), interview; Natalie Zemon Davis, transcript of an interview, in *Radical History Review* 24 (Fall 1980); Horace Bancroft Davis, interview with the author, July 3, 1979; Frederick Ewen, interview with the author, Nov. 7, 1980; Isidore Pomerance, interview with the author, July 20, 1982.

11. Charles E. Chaffee to Courtney B. Cazden, June 30, 1954; "Autobiographical Statement of Courtney B. Cazden," Aug. 6, 1954; both in private papers of Courtney B. Cazden.

12. Dudley Strauss, interview; McGrath, Tillett Files; Vera Shlakman, interview with the author, March 28, 1979; Ewen, interview.

13. Chandler Davis, interview; Stanley Moore, interview with the author, March 3, 1979; Lee Lorch, interview with the author, July 3–4, 1978; Norman Cazden, interview with the author, June 9, 1978.

14. Chandler Davis, interview; Horace Bancroft Davis, notes of interview with Paul Tillett, July 13, 1962, in Tillett Papers; Forrest Oran Wiggins, questionnaire response. Tillett Files; Wiggins, tape-recorded reminiscences, May 1978, in personal possession of the author; W. Lou Tandy to "Dear Friends," Aug. 17, 1954, in ACLU, General Correspondence, 1954, Vol. 8.

15. Carey McWilliams, *Witch Hunt* (Boston: Little, Brown, 1950), 84–96; Walter Gellhorn, *Security, Loyalty, and Science* (Ithaca: Cornell University Press, 1950), 189–95; statement by Hans Freistadt, n.d., ACLU, General Correspondence, 1952, Vol. 11.

16. Lee Lorch, interview; Lorch, "Discriminatory Practices," *Science* 114, No. 2954 (Aug. 10, 1951).

17. Lorch, interview; L. Howard Bennett to members of the Board of Trustees of Fisk University, April 25, 1955, private papers of Lee Lorch.

18. Lorch, interview; M. LaFayette Harris to Lee Lorch, April 24, 1959, in "Com. A—Fisk Univ. Documents in the Lorch Case," AAUP Archives.

19. Mark Nickerson, questionnaire response, Tillett Files; Chandler Davis, interview.

20. Robert Bellah, interview with the author, Aug. 25, 1977; Leon Kamin, interview with the author, Oct. 6, 1977; Kamin, questionnaire response, Tillett Files.

21. Horace Bancroft Davis, interview; Norman Cazden, interview; Cazden, questionnaire response, Tillett Files; Mark Nickerson to Helen Deane Markham, June 15, 1956, Jan. 14, 1957, in private papers of Helen Deane Markham; Alban Winspear, questionnaire response, Tillett Files; Lee Lorch, interview.

22. M. I. Finley, questionnaire response, Tillett Files.

23. Gerald Brown, interview with the author, Sept. 4, 1978.

24. Alice Thorner, interview with the author, March 16, 1979.

25. Alice Thorner, interview with the author, Sept. 24, 1979; Stuart Schram, interview with the author, Sept. 17, 1979; Agnes Schneider to Stuart Schram, May 28, 1953, in ACLU, General Correspondence, 1953, Vol. 11.

26. Margaret Schlauch, statement in the *New York Times*, Feb. 6, 1951. A chance meeting with a group of young Polish academics sometime in the late 1970s yielded the information about Schlauch's Polish career.

27. Jane Hodes, interview with the author, April 5, 1980.

28. Joseph Cort, interview with the author, March 27, 1979.

29. Cort, interview.

30. Nathan Rosen, questionnaire response, Tillett Files; David Fox, interview with the author, Aug. 13, 1981; David Bohm, interview with Martin Sherwin, June 15, 1979.

31. Oscar Shaftel, Herbert Phillips, Barrows Dunham, questionnaire responses, Tillett Files. On passports, SAC, Denver, to SAC, New York, May 11, 1953, FBI (Dayton file), 65-15403-203. Bruce Dayton, interview with the author, April 4, 1980; Clarence Hiskey, interview with the author, July 27, 1980. Stanley I. Kutler, *The American Inquisition* (New York: Hill and Wang, 1982) devotes an entire chapter to the State Department's passport ban, 89–117.

32. Sigmund Diamond, interview with the author, Nov. 10, 1977.

33. Robert Rutman, interview with the author, Dec. 26, 1977.

34. Alex B. Novikoff, interview with the author, April 14, 1978; George Markham, interview with the author, Feb. 5, 1983.

35. Norman Cazden, interview with the author, June 19, 1978; Lloyd Barenblatt, interview with the author, Dec. 31, 1977.

36. Norman Cazden, Herbert Phillips, questionnaire responses, Tillett Files; Frank Oppenheimer, interview, American Institute of Physics; Clifford Durr, transcript of interview, Columbia University Oral History Project; Martin Kamen, interview with the author, April 4, 1980; Dirk Struik, questionnaire response, Tillett Files.

37. Oscar Shaftel, Harry Steinmetz, Edwin Berry Burgum, questionnaire responses, Tillett Files.

38. Bonnie Bird (Gundlach), interview; Hiskey, interview; Abraham Keller, taped statement to the author, Spring 1978; William Pearlman, interview with the author, July 11, 1978; Norman Cazden, interview; Leonard Marsak to the author, March 28, 1978; Barrows Dunham, questionnaire response, Tillett Files; Melba Phillips, interview with the author, May 12, 1978.

39. Shaftel, Riess, Nickerson, questionnaire responses, Tillett Files; Chandler Davis, interview.

40. Lee Lorch to Eleanor Nelson, July 5, 1959, in "Com A–Fisk Univ., Lorch," AAUP Archives; Lorch, interview; Nickerson, questionnaire response, Tillett Files; Horace Bancroft Davis, interview; Harry Grundfest, interview with the author, Oct. 20, 1978.

41. Horace Bancroft Davis, interview; Chandler Davis, interview; Lee Lorch, interview with the author, July 4, 1978.

42. Shaftel, questionnaire response, Tillett Files; Lawrence Klein, interview with Fred Zimring, Jan. 25, 1980, Barrows Dunham/Fred Zimring Oral History collection, Temple University; Cort, interview; Hodes, interview.

43. Shaftel, questionnaire response, Tillett Files; Natalie Zemon Davis, interview with the author, April 2, 1981; Tom McGrath, questionnaire response, Tillett Files; Bernhard Deutch to the author, June 26, 1978; Leonard Marsak to the author; Cort, interview.

44. Courtney Cazden, interview with the author, May 1, 1981; Norman Cazden, interview.

45. Dudley Strauss, Kamin, Lomanitz, questionnaire responses, Tillett Files.

46. Grundfest, interview; Wendell Furry, interview with the author, Nov. 4, 1977; Marcus Singer, questionnaire response, Tillett Files.

47. Paul Tillett, "The Social Costs of the Loyalty Programs," unpublished ms., 9–15; John Cogley, *Report on Blacklisting* (New York: Fund for the Republic, 1956), 1:102; Robert Vaughan, *Only Victims* (New York: Putnam, 1972), 250–60; Karen Sue Byers Cailteux, "The Political Blacklist in the Broadcast Industry: The Decade of the 1950s" (Ph.D. diss., Ohio State University, 1972), 260–303; John K. Fairbank, interview with the author, March 10, 1977.

48. Natalie [Davis] to Norman and Courtney [Cazden], n.d., in private papers of Courtney Cazden; Natalie Zemon Davis, interview.

49. Irving Stein to the author, May 12, 1978; Clement Markert, interview with the author, May 30, 1978.

50. Here I must respect the privacy of my sources. Political troubles deserve footnotes, personal psychological ones I would like to exempt.

   Just about every lawyer I interviewed discussed the psychological condition of his clients. See also, Clifford Durr, Columbia Oral History Project, 223; Leonard Boudin, interview with the author, Dec. 30, 1976; Joseph Forer, interview with the author, March 31, 1978. On the suicides, I must keep the identity of one of them confidential. For the others, see *Harvard Crimson*, April 10, 1950; Paul M. Sweezy and Leon Huberman, eds., *F. O. Matthiessen (1902–1950): A Collective Portrait* (New York:

Henry Schuman, 1950); Frank J. Donner, *The Un-Americans* (New York: Ballantine, 1961), 175–77.

51. Dunham, Tillett Files.
52. Bernhard Deutch to Fred Zimring, March 20, 1980, in the Barrows Dunham/Fred Zimring Oral History Collection.
53. Harry Slochower, questionnaire response, Tillett Files; Eugene Bluestein, interview with the author, May 29, 1978. Harry Slochower, interview with the author, Dec. 29, 1980.
54. David Pines to the author, June 13, 1979; David Bohm, interview with Martin Sherwin. Among the other academics who have expressed satisfaction with the intellectual results of their enforced career changes are Vera Shlakman, Stanley Moore, Gerald Brown, Oscar Shaftel, and Saul Maloff.

XII: "Without Guidance"

1. Barrows Dunham, questionnaire response, Tillett Files, Seeley G. Mudd Library, Princeton University.
2. Forrest Oran Wiggins to "Max," Feb. 25, 1952, ACLU, General Correspondence, 1958, Vol. 8; Jane Sanders, *Cold War on the Campus* (Seattle: University of Washington Press, 1979), 77–78.
3. Marcus Singer, questionnaire response, Tillett Files; Owen Lattimore, speech at Harvard, May 28, 1975; Eugene Bluestein, interview with the author, May 29, 1978; Paul Lazarsfeld and Wagner Thielens, Jr., *The Academic Mind* (Glencoe, Ill.: Free Press, 1958), 122, 151–52, 443; Richard N. Swift, Hollis Cooley, interview with the author, Nov. 4, 1981.
4. W. H. Ferry, interview with the author, Dec. 12, 1978; Lazarsfeld and Thielens, *The Academic Mind*, 85, 92–93, 232–34. Valuable as this book is and was at the time, as a historian I can only lament the short-sightedness of its authors, who apparently lost the 2451 questionnaires on which it was based. Since the 165 schools at which they conducted interviews included many that had academic freedom cases—Harvard, Cornell, Johns Hopkins, MIT, Yale, Temple, Tulane, Fisk, Berkeley, UCLA, the University of Michigan, Ohio State, Washington, Colorado, Hunter, San Francisco State, and even Emporia State Teachers College in Kansas—the archival tragedy that the missing questionnaires represent is profound.
5. David Riesman, "Some Observations on the Interviewing in the Teacher Apprehension Study," in Lazarsfeld and Thielens, *The Academic Mind*, 283.
6. Sanders, *Cold War on the Campus*, 30–31.
7. Ibid., 79–80, 204.
8. Ibid., 78; Washington Committee for Academic Freedom, memorandum, n.d., ACLU, General Correspondence, 1949, Vol. 3.
9. The faculty of the University of California, like Rutgers's, tried to solve its political problems with a mail ballot. See David P. Gardner, *The California Oath Controversy* (Berkeley and Los Angeles: University of California Press, 1967), 138. For Rutgers, see Peter C. Schaehrer, "McCarthyism and Academic Freedom—Three Case Studies" (Ed. D. diss., Columbia University Teachers College, 1974), 206–9. Among the other schools which established committees were the University of Southern California, NYU, and Temple. Thomas Clark Pollock, Memorandum to the Faculty, Nov. 20,

1952, in private papers of Richard N. Swift; Fred Richard Zimring, "Academic Freedom and the Cold War: The Dismissal of Barrows Dunham from Temple University: A Case Study" (Ed.D. diss., Columbia University Teachers College, 1981), 289, 291.

10. E. E. Moise, interview with the author, April 15, 1978. The Michigan archives contain about thirty-five letters to Hatcher from members of the faculty deploring Wilder's behavior, in "Miscellaneous Correspondence, Letters from faculty. Correspondence with Clardy and Appell," Marvin L. Niehuss Papers, Box 21, Michigan Historical Collections, Bentley Historical Library, University of Michigan; Lazarsfeld and Thielens, *The Academic Mind*, 234–35; Thomas I. Emerson, interview with the author, Nov. 16, 1977; H. H. Wilson, interview with the author, April 3, 1977.

11. "New York University," *AAUP Bulletin* 44, No. 1 (March 1958): 29, 40, 43–48; Hollis Cooley, interview; Helen Lynd, interview with the author, Oct. 20, 1978.

12. Lazarsfeld and Thielens, *The Academic Mind*, 99; Robert E. Matthews to Patrick Murphy Malin, July 8, 1953, ACLU, General Correspondence, 1953, Vol. 5.

13. Lazarsfeld and Thielens, *The Academic Mind*, 251; W. Lou Tandy, questionnaire response, Tillett Files; *Square Bulletin* (NYU), Dec. 5, 1952.

14. Julian Blau to Ralph Himstead, June 16, 1951, in "Com A—Pa. State Coll—Blau, 1950–53," AAUP Archives; Lee Lorch to Louis Joughin, Oct. 8, 1951, ACLU, General Correspondence, 1952, Vol. 6; E. E. Moise, interview.

15. Chandler Davis, interview with the author, Feb. 21, 1978; E. E. Moise, letter to the author, April 3, 1978; Clement Markert, interview with the author, May 30, 1978; G. W. Beadle to Harlan Hatcher, May 17, 1954, in "Letters in re Davis, Markert," Niehuss Papers, Box 21; Irving Stein, questionnaire response, Tillett Files; George P. Adams, Jr., et al., "Singer Expense Fund," in Dean of the Faculty Papers, Box 3, File "Academic Freedom and Tenure Committee #1," Cornell University Archives; Robert V. Pound, interview with the author, Jan. 26, 1978.

16. John Caughey to Ralph Fuchs, May 18, 1956, in "Special Committee Report, Correspondence with Council and others 1955–65," AAUP Archives.

17. Alexis de Tocqueville, *Democracy in America* (New York: Vintage, 1955), 1:198–99.

18. Ralph Fuchs, interview with the author, Oct. 6, 1978; Jose A. Delfin to Ralph Himstead, Feb. 25, 1952, ACLU, General Correspondence, 1952, Vol. 6; John W. Reid to Goodwin Watson, Jan. 19, 1954, ACLU, General Correspondence, 1954, Vol. 8. Stanley Moore to Himstead, June 23, 1954, in "Com A—Reed College Moore 1954"; GPS [Shannon] memorandum to REH [Himstead], Oct. 20, 1952, in "Com A Rutgers University Finley Heimlich 1952–53"; GPS memorandum to REH, Nov. 6, 1952, and WCM [Middleton] memorandum to REH [Himstead], Dec. 9, 1952, in "Com A—New York University—Burgum Case Papers for Committee"; all in AAUP Archives. Among the men and women who contacted the AAUP in Washington during the early stages of their cases were Stanley Moore, Edwin Berry Burgum (NYU), Irving Wagman and William Pearlman (Jefferson), Robert Hodes, Vera Shlakman (Queens), Ross Lomanitz and Lee Lorch (Fisk), David Fox (Berkeley), Mark Nickerson (Michigan),

Saul Maloff (Indiana), and a large contingent of the University of California non-signers. Elsewhere, as we shall see, it was often the local AAUP chapter that alerted the national office to the pending troubles.

19. Hearing before the Board of Trustees of Reed College, Aug. 13, 1954, 18, in private papers of Stanley Moore. Ralph Himstead, telegram to Duncan S. Ballantine, June 29, 1954, in "Com. A—Reed College Moore 1954"; George Pope Shannon to Lee Lorch, Oct. 21, 1954, in "Comm. A—Fisk Univ., Lorch 1954–May 1955"; all in AAUP Archives. Jane Sanders, *Cold War on the Campus*, 43–44, 61; Report of the Special Faculty Committee of Review, Dec. 3, 1952, Lewis Webster Jones Papers, Box 145–1, Rutgers University Archives. W. Lou Tandy, "Statement," Jan. 9, 1953; Tandy to "Dear Friends," Aug. 17, 1954; both in ACLU, General Correspondence, 1954, Vol. 8. Shannon, memorandum to REH, Feb. 18, 1953; Shannon, telegrams to Rufus Harris, Feb. 3, 12, 1952; both in "Comm. A Tulane Univ. Hodes 52," AAUP Archives. Ralph Himstead, telegram to Earl Warren, April 19, 1950, in Council Letter 8, 1950, in private papers of Bentley Glass. George Pope Shannon to Mrs. H. Chandler Davis, Aug. 30, 1954; Shannon to Mark Nickerson, Sept. 2, 1954; both in "Comm. A—Michigan, U. of, Davis, Nickerson 1954," AAUP Archives.

20. Memorandum, n.d., "University of Vermont—Novikoff Case," in Talcott Parsons Papers, Correspondence and Related Papers, 1930–59, Box 2, Harvard University Archives. Lee Lorch to Louis Joughin, Oct. 8, 1951, ACLU, General Correspondence, 1952, Vol. 6. Ralph Himstead, telegram to Edward C. Kirkland, Jan. 2, 1953, in "New York Univ. Burgum"; WCM [Middleton] to REH, Dec. 9, 1953, in "Com A—New York University—Burgum Case Papers for Committee"; Carl H. Fulda to Himstead, March 29, 1951, in "Com A—New York University Bradley Case Papers for Committee"; all in AAUP Archives.

21. Statement made to the Hunter College chapter of the AAUP by its president, n.d., in "Com A—Hunter Coll.—McGill et al. 1955"; AAUP Indiana Chapter, Committee Report regarding Saul Maloff, n.d.; Saul Maloff to Ralph Himstead, May 20, 1954, in "Com A Indiana Univ. Maloff 54"; all in AAUP Archives. Ralph Fuchs, interview; Robby Cohen, "Professor William Parry, HUAC, and the University of Buffalo: A Case Study in Repression" (unpublished ms., 1976), 25–27.

22. W. Lou Tandy, memorandum, "Outcome," n.d., ACLU, General Correspondence, 1954, Vol. 8; John H. Reynolds, questionnaire response, Tillett Files; Norman Cazden, interview with the author, June 9, 1978; Bernard Riess, questionnaire response, Tillett Files; George Rundquist, memorandum to Patrick Malin, April 5, 1950, ACLU, General Correspondence 1952, Vol. 6; Francis J. Tschan to Himstead, March 3, April 15, 1952, in "Com A—Pa. State Coll—Blau, 1950–1953," AAUP Archives.

23. Louis M. O'Quinn to George Soll, Oct. 2, 1950, ACLU, General Correspondence, 1950, Vol. 1; Jose A. Delfin to Ralph Himstead, Feb. 25, 1952, ACLU, General Correspondence, 1952, Vol. 6; Tom McGrath, questionnaire response, Tillett Files; Saul Maloff, interview with the author, Jan. 29, 1978; Marcus Singer, questionnaire response, Tillett Files; Talcott Parsons, interview with the author, May 1, 1978.

24. Hollis Cooley to Ralph Himstead, Dec. 13, 1948, in "Com A—New York University Bradley Case, Papers for Committee," AAUP Archives.

25. Lewis C. Branscomb, telegram to Ralph Himstead, April 15, 1953; Himstead, telegram to Branscomb, April 16, 1953; Branscomb to Himstead, April 17, 1953; all in "Com A–Ohio State Univ.–Darling 1953," AAUP Archives.
26. Koppel S. Pinson to "The General Secretary," June 8, 1955, in "Special Com. 1955–56–Queens College, Straus, Dudley D."; Hollis Cooley to Ralph Himstead, Dec. 13, 1948, in "Com A–New York University Bradley Case, Papers for Committee"; both in AAUP Archives. Zimring, "Academic Freedom," 218–26. Saul Maloff to Ralph Himstead, May 20, 1954; Warren C. Middleton to Henry H. H. Remak, Sept. 9, 1954; Saul Maloff to Ralph Fuchs, April 26, 1956; all in "Com A Indiana Univ. Maloff 54," AAUP Archives. Harry Steinmetz, questionnaire response, Tillett Files; Alfred McClung Lee, interview with the author, March 29, 1979; Arthur C. Cole to Richard H. Shryock, March 24, 1952, ACLU, General Correspondence, 1952, Vol. 4.
27. Ralph Fuchs, interview; Louis Joughlin to editors, *New York Times,* June 9, 1955, ACLU, General Correspondence, 1955, Vol. 6.
28. Zimring, "Academic Freedom," 222–23; "Evansville College," *AAUP Bulletin* 35, No. 1 (Spring 1949). Jordan Kurland, the associate general secretary of the AAUP, has found a fully prepared Committee A report of a non-political firing from 1946 in the organization's files that Himstead simply didn't publish. Jordan Kurland, interview with the author, March 16, 1984; Kurland, letter to the author, June 4, 1984.
29. Sanders, *Cold War on the Campus,* 19, 43–44, 61. R. G. Tyler, telegram to Ralph Himstead, May 3, 1948; Tyler to Himstead, June 4, July 12, 1948; Himstead to Tyler, July 29, 1948; Himstead to Albert Canwell, July 14, 1948; all in "University of Washington, General," AAUP Archives.
30. AAUP Chapter Bulletin, University of Washington, Feb. 1949, ACLU, General Correspondence, 1949, Vol. 3. Herbert J. Phillips to Ralph Himstead, Jan. 19, 1949, in "Com. A–Univ. of Washington Butterworth, Phillips and Cook"; Ralph Gundlach to Himstead, Jan. 25, 1949, in "Com. A–Univ. of Washington–Gundlach." Himstead, telegram to J. M. Maguire, Feb. 2, 1949; Maguire, telegram to Himstead, Feb. 3, 1949; D. R. Scott, telegram to Himstead, April 13, 1949; R. G. Tyler to Himstead, Nov. 9, 1949; Viola P. Barton to Himstead, Feb. 14, 1949; Lloyd B. Williams to Himstead, Feb. 5, 1949; all in "Comm. A–Univ. of Washington–General." All in AAUP Archives.
31. W. T. Laprade to REH [Himstead], Sept. 16, 1949; Edward C. Kirkland to GPS [George P. Shannon], Sept. 28, 1949; Quincy Wright to REH, Oct. 31, 1949; all in AAUP Archives, file unknown.
32. Sanders, *Cold War on the Campus,* 98–99; Himstead to Members of the Council of the AAUP, Nov. 2, 1951, in private papers of Bentley Glass. Colston E. Warne to Himstead, March 10, 1950; Kermit Eby to Himstead, June 7, 1950; Himstead, telegram to Eby, June 30, 1950; Himstead, telegram to W. Stull Holt, March 17, 1950; all in "Comm. A–Univ. of Washington–General." Colston E. Warne to Himstead, Feb. 11, 1952; Gundlach to Himstead, Sept. 15, 1952; both in "Com. A–Univ. of Washington–Gundlach." George Pope Shannon to Wm. H. Fisher, Sept. 29, 1952, in "Com A Washington, Univ. of Butterworth, Phillips, Ethel, Gundlach, Jacobs"; Ralph Gundlach to Ralph Fuchs, Feb. 13, 1956, in "Special Com-

mittee Report Correspondence with Council and others 1955–56." All in AAUP Archives.

33. Ralph Fuchs to Douglas B. Maggs, Sept. 20, 1955; Maggs to Fuchs, Sept. 17, 1955; both in "Special Committee, memoranda and correspondence (to and from) members. 1955–56." Fuchs to Quincy Wright, Oct. 3, 1955; John Caughey, "Remarks to UCLA AAUP Chapter," May 21, 1956, both in "Special Committee Report Correspondence with Council and others 1955–56." Caughey to Ralph Himstead, April 14, 1955; Russell Sullivan to Himstead, May 3, 1955; both in "Special Committee Report 1955–56 University of Washington." Maggs to Himstead, Oct. 7, 1954, in "Com A– Ohio State Univ.–Darling 1953." All in AAUP Archives.

34. Fred Knapman to Bentley Glass, Jan. 5, 1950; Ralph Himstead to Raymond J. McCall, June 30, 1950; Himstead to Council, Feb. 23, 1951; Joseph Cormack to Bentley Glass, March 13, 1951; all in private papers of Bentley Glass. Himstead, "Correspondence with a Chapter Officer," *AAUP Bulletin* 35, No. 3 (Autumn 1949): 551.

35. Ralph Himstead to R. G. Tyler, July 29, 1948, in "Washington, General"; Himstead to Russell Sullivan, Feb. 16, 1955, in "Committee A–General"; both in AAUP Archives.

36. Roland D. Hussey to Ralph Himstead, Sept. 1, 1950; Edward C. Tolman to Himstead, Sept. 19, 1950; Arthur E. Hutson to Himstead, Sept. 19, 1950; Richard H. Shryock to Himstead, Oct. 9, 1950; Ernest Samuels to Himstead, Nov. 4, 1950; Ralph H. Lutz to Himstead, Nov. 27, 1950; James B. McMillan to Himstead, Dec. 11, 1950; Himstead, telegram to Robert B. Brode, March 1, 1951; Quincy Wright to Himstead, March 15, 1951; R. F. Arragon to Himstead, June 29, 1951; Himstead to Bentley Glass, Nov. 7, 1951; Himstead to Ralph Fuchs, Nov. 7, 1951; Himstead to John F. Neylan, Jan. 2, 1952; all in "Com A–California, Univ. of 1949–54." R. F. Arragon and Quincy Wright, "The University of California Loyalty Oath Situation," mimeographed ms., n.d., in "Special Committee, 1955–58 California, University of"; Quincy Wright to Ralph Fuchs, Sept. 28, 1955, in "Special Committee Report Correspondence with Council and others 1955–56." All in AAUP Archives.

37. Robert B. Brode to Ralph Himstead, Oct. 8, 1952; John Caughey to Himstead, June 7, Nov. 3, 1953, March 25, 1954; Fritz Machlup to the President et al., April 1954; all in "Com A–California, Univ. of 1949-54," AAUP Archives.

38. W. Lou Tandy, "Statement," Jan. 9, 1953; Tandy to "Dear Friends," Aug. 17, 1954; both in ACLU, General Correspondence, 1954, Vol. 8. Harry Slochower and Oscar Shaftel, questionnaire responses, Tillett Files; "University of Oklahoma–Blanc Case," in Talcott Parsons Papers, Correspondence and Related Papers, ca. 1930–59, Box 2, Harvard University Archives; Joseph C. Pray to Claude C. Bowman, June 11, 1953, in Zimring, "Academic Freedom," 260.

39. Irwin Griggs to Joseph C. Pray, March 24, 1953; Claude C. Bowman to Members of the Council, May 28, 1953; both in Zimring, "Academic Freedom," 223, 254.

40. Barrows Dunham to Ralph Himstead, June 30, 1953; Himstead to Claude C. Bowman, Oct. 15, 1953; both in Zimring, "Academic Freedom," 267–68, 295. Himstead, telegram to Dunham, June 23, 1953; Bowman and Irwin

Griggs to Members of the Council, July 7, 1953; Himstead, telegrams to Carl Shoup, July 14, 27, 1953; Himstead, telegram to Richard Shryock, July 16, 1953; Himstead, telegram to Lewis Branscomb, July 20, 1953; Himstead, telegram to Fred B. Millett, July 22, 1953; Branscomb to Himstead, July 25, 1953; all in "Com. A–Temple University–Barrows Dunham (1953–1956)," AAUP Archives.

41. Lewis C. Branscomb to Ralph Himstead, Oct. 6, 1953; Himstead, telegram to George W. Martin, Oct. 14, 1953; Himstead, telegram to Ralph Fuchs, Oct. 15, 1953; Himstead, telegram to Frederick Heimberger, Oct. 27, 1953; Branscomb to Himstead, Nov. 27, 1953; Himstead, telegram to Branscomb, Nov. 25, 1953; Darling to Himstead, Nov. 28, 1953; Branscomb to Himstead, Jan. 5, 1954; all in "Com A–Ohio State Univ.–Darling 1953," AAUP Archives.

42. Douglas Maggs to Ralph Himstead, Oct. 7, 1954, in "Com A–Ohio State Univ.–Darling 1953," AAUP Archives.

43. Robert E. Mathews to Douglas Maggs, Oct. 12, 1954; George Pope Shannon to Maggs, Oct. 12, 1954; Maggs to Shannon, Oct. 26, 1954; all in "Com A–Ohio State Univ.–Darling 1953," AAUP Archives.

44. Ralph Himstead to Russell Sullivan, Feb. 16, 1955, in "Committee A General 1955"; Himstead, telegram to Edward C. Kirkland, Jan. 2, 1953, in "Com A–New York University–Burgum Case Papers for Committee"; Himstead, telegram to Rex Arragon, Aug. 3, 1954, in "Com. A–Reed College Moore 1954"; all in AAUP Archives.

45. Council letter, March 12, 1950, in private papers of Bentley Glass; Ralph Fuchs, interview; George Pope Shannon to Robert E. Mathews, Oct. 29, 1954, in "Com A–Ohio State Univ.–Darling 1953," AAUP Archives.

46. Council letter 2, March 16–17, 1951; Council letter 8, Nov. 10–11, 1950, appendix, 15–17; both in private papers of Bentley Glass; Fuchs, interview.

47. George Pope Shannon to Douglas B. Maggs, Oct. 12, 1954, in "Com A–Ohio State Univ.–Darling 1953." Ralph Himstead to Russell Sullivan, Feb. 16, 1955; Harold N. Lee to William E. Britton, Jan. 11, 1955; both in "Committee A General 1955." All in AAUP Archives.

48. Ralph Fuchs, interview.

49. Frederick K. Beutel to Claude Bowman, June 5, 1953; Ralph Himstead to Council, June 11, 1953; both in Zimring, "Academic Freedom," 258, 262. Bentley Glass to Ralph Fuchs, Jan. 17, 1953, in Glass papers; Glass, interview with the author, Sept. 4, 1978; Douglas B. Maggs to Fuchs, Sept. 17, 1955, in "Special Committee, memoranda and correspondence (to and from) members. 1955–56," AAUP Archives; Walter Metzger, interview with the author, Jan. 25, 1979.

50. Council Letter 10, Nov. 2, 1951; Council Letter 2, Agenda for Council Meeting, March 16–17, 1951; Council Letter 8, Agenda for Council Meeting, Nov. 10–11, 1950; all in Glass papers. John Caughey to Ralph Himstead, March 25, 1954; Fritz Machlup to Council, n.d., received April 28, 1954; both in "Com A–California, Univ. of 1949–54," AAUP Archives.

51. Glass to Fuchs, Jan. 17, 1953; Fuchs to Glass, Nov. 4, 1952; both in Glass papers. Eugene H. Wilson to Claude Bowman, June 2, 1953, in Zimring, "Academic Freedom," 256; Alan Whitney, "Professors Prepare for Action," *The Nation*, April 11, 1953.

52. Douglas B. Maggs to Ralph Fuchs, Sept. 17, 1955, "Special Committee, memoranda and correspondence (to and from) members. 1955–56"; John Caughey, "Remarks to UCLA AAUP chapter," May 21, 1956, in "Special Committee Report Correspondence with Council and others 1955–56"; both in AAUP Archives.

53. Abraham Keller, taped response to letter from the author, n.d., 1978. Walter S. Lawton to Ralph Himstead, Dec. 10, 1953; Thomas C. Holyoke to George Pope Shannon, June 17, 1955; both in "Com. A—Temple University—Barrows Dunham (1953–1956)," AAUP Archives. Stuart C. Van Orden to AAUP, April 17, 1956, in "Special Committee Report Correspondence with Council and others 1955–56," AAUP Archives. Ralph Fuchs, interview.

54. Harold N. Lee to William E. Britton, Jan. 8, 1955; Britton to Russell N. Sullivan, Jan. 13, 1955; Harold L. Clapp to Britton, Jan. 11, 1955; Sullivan to Ralph Himstead, March 7, 1955; Britton to Ralph Fuchs, Sept. 9, 1955; all in "Committee A General 1955," AAUP Archives. Fuchs, interview.

55. George Pope Shannon to John W. Caughey, Aug. 29, 1955, in "Comm. A—Univ. of Washington—General." Ralph Fuchs to Douglas B. Maggs, Sept. 20, 1955; Maggs to Fuchs, Sept. 17, 1955; both in "Special Committee, memoranda and correspondence (to and from) members. 1955–56." Fuchs to Quincy Wright, Oct. 3, 1955, in "Special Committee Report Correspondence with Council and others 1955–56"; Russell Sullivan to Ralph Himstead, May 3, 1955, in "Committee A General 1955." Caughey to Fuchs, Sept. 16, 1955; Fuchs to Caughey, Sept. 20, 1955; both in "Special Committee, 1955–58 California, University of." All in AAUP Archives.

56. Bentley Glass and Ralph Fuchs to Members of the Committee on Special Academic Freedom and Tenure Cases, Oct. 12, 1955, in Talcott Parsons, Correspondence and Related Papers, ca. 1930–59, Box 2; Fuchs to William E. Britton, Feb. 21, 1956, in "Special Committee, memoranda and correspondence (to and from) members. 1955–56," AAUP Archives; Fuchs, interview; Glass, interview; "Academic Freedom and Tenure in the Quest for National Security," *AAUP Bulletin* 42, No. 1 (Spring 1956): 49–50 (hereafter cited as "Academic Freedom and Tenure").

57. "Academic Freedom and Tenure," 58, 60; Ralph Fuchs to Rex Arragon, March 2, 1956, in "Special Committee Report Correspondence with Council and others 1955–56," AAUP Archives.

58. "Academic Freedom and Tenure," 63–65, 71, 73–83. "Draft of Report," n.d.; Ralph Fuchs to Committee, Jan. 23, Feb. 21, March 1, 14, 1956; Fuchs memorandum to Committee A, March 28, 1956; all in Talcott Parsons Papers, Correspondence and Related Papers, ca. 1930–59, Box 2, Harvard University Archives.

59. Talcott Parsons, interview.

60. Ralph Fuchs to Douglas B. Maggs, May 2, 1956; John Caughey to Fuchs, April 15, 1956; Carl Wittke to Fuchs, Feb. 16, 1956; all in "Special Committee Report Correspondence with Council and others 1955–56," AAUP Archives. Herbert J. Phillips to Fuchs, Feb. 13, 1956; E. H. Eby to Fuchs, Feb. 6, 1956; both in "Special Committee Report 1955–56 University of Washington," AAUP Archives. R. H. Llewellyn to Fuchs, March 29, 1956, in "Com. A—Temple University—Barrows Dunham (1953–1956)," AAUP

Archives. Kurt H. Wolff to Talcott Parsons, May 21, 1956, in Parsons Papers; Russell A. Smith and Angus Campbell to Robert K. Carr, Jan. 13, 1958, in Niehuss Papers, Box 21, Folder "AAUP"; Zimring, "Academic Freedom," 339.

61. Robert Van Waes to William G. Mather, Oct. 29, 1963; Bernard J. Alpers to William P. Fidler, March 6, 1963; both in "Com. A—Jefferson Medical College, Pearlman, Wagman, Rutman 1953," AAUP Archives. Zimring, "Academic Freedom," 362–63, 366–67; Harlan Hatcher to Tom L. Pope-joy, March 1, 1960, in Niehuss Papers, Box 21, Folder "AAUP."

62. John F. Neylan quoted in Fritz Machlup to Council, n.d., received April 28, 1954, in "Com A—California, Univ. of 1949–54," AAUP Archives; Un-signed [University of Michigan AAUP] to Robert K. Carr, April 19, 1958, in Niehuss Papers, Box 21, Folder "AAUP."

63. Ralph Fuchs to William Edel, April 11, 1956; Bertram H. Davis to Edel, March 8, 1956; Boyd Lee Spahr to Fuchs, April 13, 1956; Boyd Lee Spahr to William Edel, Jan. 21, 1957; Edel to Francis Walter, May 9, 1956; William P. Fidler to Gilbert Malcolm, Jan. 29, 1960; Edel to Ralph Fuchs, Jan. 18, 1957; all in photocopied materials from the Dickinson College Archives, received through the help of Fred Zimring. "Dickinson College," *AAUP Bulletin* 44, No. 1 (March 1958).

64. Ralph Fuchs to Russell Sullivan, Feb. 29, 1956, in "Committee A—General," AAUP Archives.

65. William Marbury, interview with the author, May 25, 1978; McGeorge Bundy, interview with the author, Dec. 29, 1977; Norman Ramsey, inter-view with the author, Dec. 15, 1977; Cooley, interview. Within the enter-tainment industry, which was as terrorized as the academic community, there were only a few cases of resistance. In one, the program's sponsor held firm against blacklisting and insisted that the controversy actually helped business. Karen Sue Byers Cailteux, "The Political Blacklist in the Broadcast Industry: The Decade of the 1950s," (Ph.D. diss., Ohio State University, 1972), 166. David Caute also cites a few instances of successful opposition in the entertainment industry and elsewhere, *The Great Fear* (New York: Simon and Schuster, 1978), 455, 537–38. For the Broyles Commission, see E. Houston Harsha, "Illinois," in Walter Gellhorn, ed., *The States and Subversion* (Ithaca: Cornell University Press, 1952), 96–100, 126, 135. Perhaps the most interesting evidence on the superficiality of anti-Communist sentiment in the United States during this period was unearthed by Harvard sociologist Samuel Stouffer in a study sponsored by the Fund for the Republic in 1954. Stouffer found that despite consid-erable support for firing Communists from their jobs, few people (9 per-cent) were actually worried about Communism. Thirty percent of his sample did not even know who Senator McCarthy was! Stouffer, *Com-munism, Conformity, and Civil Liberties* (Garden City, N.Y.: Doubleday, 1955), 30–44, 59–77, 85–86.

Conclusion

1. *New York Times*, April 2, 1972, Aug. 1, 1981; Richard L. Biggs, Joseph F. Bunnett, Barbara West, "Report to the Reed College Board of Trustees Concerning Professor Stanley Moore," copy in author's possession, Jan. 14,

1978; Marvin E. Gettleman, "Anti-communist Purges on Campuses Recalled," *In These Times,* March 10–16, 1982.

2. O. Edmund Clubb, "McCarthyism and our Asian Policy," *Bulletin of Concerned Asian Scholars* No. 4 (May 1969): 23–26; Richard Kagan, "McCarran's Legacy: The Association for Asian Studies," Ibid., 18–22; Judith Coburn, "Asian Scholars and Government: The Chrysanthemum on the Sword," in Edward Friedman and Mark Selden, eds., *America's Asia: Dissenting Essays on Asian-American Relations* (New York: Pantheon, 1971).

3. Among the stories I was told was one by a professor in Romance languages at a major state university who had to wait almost ten years before he was allowed to teach a course on his specialty, "The Idea of Progress." Another man, an American historian, was told by the famous civil libertarian who was his thesis advisor not to write his dissertation on anything related to civil liberties. The people who were directly affected were even more cautious. The psychologist Leon Kamin recalls that because all his colleagues and teachers knew he had been a Communist, he felt obliged to prove himself as an objective scholar. He worked with rats for years until he felt that his academic reputation was secure enough for him to tackle the work that definitively refuted racist theories about the genetic basis of human intelligence. (Abraham Keller, taped response to letter from the author, n.d., 1978; Howard Zinn, interview with the author, Oct. 24, 1977; Leon Kamin, interview with the author, Oct. 6, 1977.)

   There are literally dozens of contemporaneous journalistic assessments of the political chill. The most famous was William O. Douglas, "The Black Silence of Fear," *New York Times Magazine,* Jan. 13, 1952. See also "The Younger Generation," *Time,* Nov. 5, 1951; Kalman Siegel, survey of seventy-two major colleges, *New York Times,* May 10, 11, 1951.

   For more scholarly assessments, see Kenneth Keniston, *The Uncommitted: Alienated Youth in American Society* (New York: Harcourt, Brace and World, 1965) and Paul Lazarsfeld and Wagner Thielens, Jr., *The Academic Mind* (Glencoe, Ill.: Free Press, 1958), especially pp. 192–236.

4. The seminal work here is, of course, Daniel Bell, *The End of Ideology* (Glencoe, Ill.: Free Press, 1960).

   The New Left historians of the late 1960s made a few tentative examinations of the relationship between Cold War anti-Communism, McCarthyism, and the scholarship of the 1950s. These studies are suggestive but hardly definitive and indicate that much more work will have to be done. The most important are Christopher Lasch, "The Cultural Cold War: A Short History of the Congress for Cultural Freedom," in Barton Bernstein, ed., *Towards a New Past* (New York: Pantheon, 1968) and Jesse Lemisch, *On Active Service in War and Peace: Politics and Ideology in the American Historical Profession* (Toronto: New Hogtown Press, 1975). See also Stephen F. Cohen, *Rethinking the Soviet Experience* (New York: Oxford University Press, 1985), 8–19.

Index